The
HUMAN EVOLUTION
COLORING BOOK
Second Edition

Coloring Concepts books:

The Zoology Coloring Book, by L.M. Elson
The Botany Coloring Book, by P. Young
The Human Brain Coloring Book, by M.C. Diamond, A.B. Scheibel, and L.M. Elson
The Biology Coloring Book, by R.D. Griffin
The Microbiology Coloring Book, by I.E. Alcamo and L.M. Elson
The Biology Illustrated Coloring and Resource Book, by C.L. Elson
The Marine Biology Coloring Book, Second Edition, by T. Niesen
The Physics Coloring Book, by Richard N. Stuart and L.M. Elson

COLORING CONCEPTS INC
Active Learning Through Coloring

Coloring Concepts Inc.
1728 Sycamore Street
Napa, California 94559
1-800-257-1516
www.coloringconcepts.com

The HUMAN EVOLUTION COLORING BOOK

Second Edition

by **Adrienne L. Zihlman**

**Principal Illustrations by
Carla J. Simmons**

COLLINS
REFERENCE

Adrienne Zihlman is Professor of Anthropology at the University of California, Santa Cruz. She has published numerous scientific and popular articles and is an editor of *The Evolving Female: A Life History Perspective*. Her proposal that pygmy chimpanzees are the best living prototype of humans and African apes was featured in the science section of TIME magazine, and she appeared on the cover of DISCOVER in an issue featuring women scientists. Her research on apes and early hominids has taken her to central, eastern, and southern Africa. She is a Science Trustee of the California Academy of Sciences.

This book was produced by Coloring Concepts Inc.
1728 Sycamore St., Napa, CA 94559

Editor: Joan W. Elson
Prepress digital layout: Christopher L. Elson
Line editor: Jennifer Warrington
Digitization: Mark Jones
Film production: Kevin Frye, Frye's Printing
Digital cover production: Mehdi Stephens

The Coloring Concepts name and logo is a registered trademark of Coloring Concepts Inc.

ISBN 0-06-273717-1

20 19 18 17 16 15 14 13 12 11

DEDICATION

This book is dedicated to my teacher
and colleague Sherwood Washburn,
University of California, Berkeley
and to my students at the University
of California at Santa Cruz.

ACKNOWLEDGMENT

I began working on this second edition of the Human Evolution Coloring Book in 1995. Getting to the finish line has been a long journey involving the help of many people.

My constant traveling companion has been Joan Elson, who acted as editor, layout artist, teacher, student, cheerleader, and most important, kept faith in the project despite the inevitable road-blocks, detours, and delays. During our months and years of working together, we bonded over TV dinners and chocolates, with time out for a little bird watching.

Several others went the distance with me, contributing to the writing, editing, research, ideas, and acting as sounding-boards; some of these joined the trip for shorter distances, but without them the journey would not be complete: Debra Bolter, Maggie Dawson, Ted Grand, Jerry Lowenstein, Robin McFarland, Magda Muchlinski, Kim Nichols, and Melissa Remis.

Along the way I was aided enormously by experts in many special fields, generous colleagues who read sections or individual plates, answered my questions, shared their thoughts and comments, and gave me much to think and write about: Robin Abu-Shumays, Stuart Altmann, Jeanne Altmann, Barry Bogin, Dick Byrne, Chris Dean, Dean Falk, Linda Fedigan, Agustin Fuentes, Dorothy Harris, Nina Jablonski, Farish Jenkins, Léo Laporte, Phyllis Lee, Steve Leigh, Don Lenkeit, Roberta Lenkeit, Shannon McFarlan, Marilyn Norconk, Michelle Sauther, Gary Schwartz, Carolyn Martin Shaw, Chris Stringer, Shirley Strum, Bob Sussman, Joanne Tanner, Alis Valencia, and Ann Yoder. Research assistants: Jason Brush, Susannah Staats, and Renee Sharp.

Carla Simmons is the talented artist who provided all the new original artwork, as well as much from the first edition. Chris Elson managed to fit it all together.

Special thanks to those key members of my primate social group who sustained me during the intense last two years: my Editorial Board, TIG, JML, MM, MD, and the Scott Creek Irregulars.

Finally, I give affectionate tribute to four no longer with us, whose love, support, and inspiration were unfailing: Murphy McFarland, Sheila Hough, Carl Zihlman, and Sherwood Washburn.

TABLE OF CONTENTS

Section 4 Primate Diversity and Adaptation

PREFACE TO THE FIRST EDITION

Four years ago, Larry Elson and I were independently asked to be expert witnesses involving evidence of footprints in a court case. We had been graduate students together at University of California at Berkeley (in different departments) but had not seen each other for ten years. Meanwhile, Larry had co-authored the hugely popular *Anatomy Coloring Book*. When we renewed our acquaintance, as witnesses for the defense, he asked me to consider writing a *Human Evolution Coloring Book*. Anatomy, of course, is a natural for this format, but since human evolution includes so much more than anatomy, I wondered for some time how this format might apply.

As I thought about it, I realized that many of the human characteristics I would be writing about are perfectly adapted for this kind of book—namely, color vision, hand-eye coordination, manual dexterity, and a brain especially evolved for tool using!

As a student of Sherwood Washburn in the early 1960s, I learned the importance of short clear verbal presentations and good visual aids in effective teaching—lessons which I have applied to my own teaching of anthropology at the University of California at Santa Cruz during the past fifteen years. A fellow graduate student at Berkeley with whom I have remained friend and co-worker, Ted Grand, has also strongly influenced this book. An original and creative anthropologist/anatomist, Ted has always stressed the value of good illustrations for clearly communicating anatomical concepts. Doug Cramer, a fine and recognized illustrator as well as anthropologist, has shown me through our many collaborations how interrelated the two fields are. Sherwood Washburn, Ted Grand, and Doug Cramer have all, without knowing it, had an important role in shaping this book, though I do not hold any of them responsible for its contents.

Several years of collaborating with Jerold Lowenstein on popular as well as technical articles have further taught me the skills and pleasures of communicating clearly and with humor to a wide audience. Recent joint work with paleontologist colleague Léo Laporte has further brought home to me the rewards of taking a broad view of one's own subject.

Ultimately, I undertook this book with my own students in mind, particularly those in my Anthropology I class, "Introduction to Human Evolution." Having experienced the difficulties of getting across certain tehcnical concepts, like the structure and function of DNA, I could immediately see the didactic value of a coloring book based on these concepts. Many of my students have already benefited from using the *Anatomy Coloring Book*.

Naturally, this book has a point of view, one not always shared by other texts on human evolution. For example, I consider molecules to be facts about evolution as real as fossils and comparative anatomy, and so molecular data are given equal emphasis here with the more familiar evidence. Females, and young, so often invisible in works on the evolution of "man," appear here as equal participants. I have presented much of my own original research on comparative anatomy, fossils and pygmy chimpanzees but have tried to balance my own views with those of others. This is still a very controversial subject, human evolution. Many still deny that there is such a subject.

For me, it has been a long, hard path between those footprints Larry Elson and I examined over four years ago and the 3-million-year-old fossil human footprints on the cover of this book that mark the end of my effort—though only the beginning of the human journey. Each of these 111 plates is a condensate of dozens of scientific articles and book chapters and years of thought. Some of the plates may appear complex, but remember that they have been designed so that you can learn their contents through the coloring process, and they have been tested by both experts and novices to this end.

So prepare to take the human evolutionary journey from molecules to monkeys to modern people. All you need are some coloring implements and the primate brain-hand combination that has made us and our ancestors such successful survivors for the past 60 million years.

Adrienne L. Zihlman

July 1981
Santa Cruz, Ca

PREFACE TO THE SECOND EDITION

In the twenty years since I wrote the first edition of *The Human Evolution Coloring Book*, our knowledge of the topics touched on in the first edition have grown to daunting proportions. What an exciting time this is in the fields of evolution and anthropology! Almost every week journals like *Science* and *Nature* publish important discoveries of new fossils from Africa, Asia, or Europe; or new molecular data throwing light on primate relationships and immigrations. Many of these discoveries are reported in our national and local newspapers and other media. The material bearing on human evolution comes from many directions. Much of it is initially accessible only to specialists and hardly comprehensible to students and the general audience. My goal is to introduce information new and old that bears on human evolution, in a format that can be understood and appreciated by students and nonspecialists.

The warm reception of the first edition by students and teachers and its translation into several languages led me to plan a revision about ten years ago. In 1990, Cabrillo College in Santa Cruz held a round-table discussion on the teaching of introductory courses in physical anthropology. Several colleagues were using the book in their classes and gave me valuable suggestions. Roberta and Don Lenkeit, long-time faculty at Modesto College, California, systematically went through each plate in the first edition, commented on its usefulness, their favorites, and the ones they didn't use at all. The suggested improvements gave me a push toward taking on this major undertaking, to rewrite, expand, and update what we know about human evolution.

The overview of evolution in Section 1 gives historical background to the development of evidence for evolution. Books like Janet Browne's 1996 biography of Charles Darwin helped me take on the impossible task of summarizing Darwin's work into less than 2000 words! The evolution exhibit at the Natural History Museum in London inspired new ways of presenting visual information. The path-breaking research of Rosemary and Peter Grant document evolutionary changes in Darwin's finches on Daphne Major in the Galápagos Islands, updating Darwin's famous deductions about the influence of natural selection in shaping changes in populations over time. During a recent trip to the Galápagos, I felt transported back to 1858, participating in Darwin's thought processes on seeing the unique animals and plants, and their variations from island to island. Nina Jablonski's

research on snub-nosed monkeys in China supports the concept of genetic drift, proposed theoretically more than 60 years ago. These examples of new research confirm the main principles of evolution and natural selection.

The field of molecular evolution changed so much that Section 2 had to be doubled in size. My mentor, Sherwood Washburn, at the University of California Berkeley in the 1960s was ahead of his time in appreciating and teaching how molecular data provided another line of evidence for primate evolution, independent of fossils and comparative morphology. The molecular research of Vincent Sarich and Allan Wilson at Berkeley indicated that humans and African apes had a common ancestor only 5 million years ago (not 25 million, which was accepted then). This conclusion, very controversial at the time, is now the new conventional wisdom! The molecular clock, the brilliant insight of Emil Zuckerkandl and Linus Pauling, is still difficult for students to grasp, so here I devote four plates to this concept, which continues to have a tremendous impact on evolutionary studies. DNA is now such a household acronym that it appears regularly in crossword puzzles, but mitochondrial DNA and minisatellites are not quite so familiar. To convey some of the exciting "new frontiers" in evolution, I include two plates—one on the homeobox, the key to the secrets of development and the connection between genes and morphology; the other on molecular data from extinct species, a real-world view of *Jurassic Park*.

Section 3 on our living relatives has so many dimensions and concepts that it posed a particular challenge. I introduce our primate cousins and the way they live, against the backdrop of the brain and emotions, which are part of our mammalian heritage. Much of my own research has dealt with life history, so this section is considerably expanded to depict variation in life associated with different ages and different sexes. Fortunately, many dedicated field workers have compiled data on differential survival and reproductive outcome of the species they've studied. My own research on Gombe chimpanzee skeletons attempts to bridge the gap between "reading the bones" of fossils and interpreting bone lesions on animals whose life histories have been meticulously recorded by Jane Goodall. Her long-term research on chimpanzees and the studies of other societies make the point that not all chimpanzees are alike, but they are all innovators with their own traditions. I want to convey the continuity between chimpanzees and humans but emphasize that though the gap is narrow, it is also deep, and we're learning more all the time about its dimensions.

Section 4 on the diversity and radiation of the primates is the longest in the book. We know so much more now than we did 20 years ago, thanks to long-term research on primate behavior, fossils, and molecules. The challenge is to convey some of the excitement and findings of dedicated field researchers and inspire young people by their example and by the recognition that there is still so much to learn. Our understanding of Madagascar lemurs is much clearer now, and the little-known tarsier is finding a new place in the primate family tree, slightly closer to the anthropoids than to the prosimians. Thanks also to dedicated field researchers, studies of New World monkeys have blossomed, to reveal the diversity in how they live and the clever ways they get food with remarkable teeth adapted to everything from gouging holes to eating hard seeds. The adaptations of Old World monkeys and apes—orangutans, gorillas, and chimpanzees—also continue to be explored and illuminated. I orient the presentations to anatomy, to give students an "inside" view of the animals' locomotion and feeding patterns, as a basis for their "outside" behavior. This view also aids in the contemplation of the fossil record, where only bones and teeth remain. Unfortunately, the decline of many primate populations and the threat of their very survival is more real than ever. It is tragic to realize how much will be lost to science and world ecology, just when we are achieving some deeper understanding of our primate family.

Section 5 on the hominid fossil record has in some ways changed most dramatically of all. New discoveries are always exciting, and new techniques such as CT scanning promote second and third looks at well-known fossils. Such studies sometimes confirm our previous views of human evolution but more often alter those views substantially. We have learned that fossils alone do not shape our understanding of evolution. Molecular data too have had a profound influence—for instance, in identifying the chimpanzee as our closest relative, in establishing the origin of *Homo sapiens* in Africa about 150,000 years ago, and revealing from fossil DNA that *Homo sapiens* and Neanderthals are separate species that split from a common ancestor about 600,000 years ago. These discoveries have generated huge controversies among anthropologists, especially upsetting those whose previous views have been demonstrated to be inconsistent with the new data! Of course, there are honest disagreements about interpretations and classifications of fossils, such as questions surrounding the origin and species of the genus *Homo* some 2 to 2.5 million years ago. I present what is reasonably established and why professionals disagree. Always I emphasize that the field is in a state of flux and no one can predict what new discoveries and techniques tomorrow may bring.

Section 6 focuses on the human species, from the development of the fertilized cell through individual growth to populations. Humans vary at all levels and through each of the life stages—what George Gaylord Simpson called the fourth dimension in the study of human evolution. Events in individual lives, activity, and population health can be read in bones and teeth, thus extending knowledge of ourselves to historical and prehistoric populations. Human biology has shaped and been shaped by our culture, so that our species has adapted to an astounding variety of different climates and environments, from parasite-ridden tropics to icy breathless altitudes. Wherever we've gone, we've taken our genes, our traditions, and our languages with us.

This book is intended as an introduction to undergraduate students, based on my long teaching experience. Parts will be useful for students and teachers in high school, and parts as a review for graduate students. All of the book is designed to inform interested lay readers. I hope you will have fun exploring the many facets of human evolution. I draw heavily on the specialized work of many colleagues. Some of them may learn from this book what the others are doing. Some plates, like the descriptions of hands or animals, are easy and straightforward to color and understand. Some, involving molecular data and anatomical structures, require more attention, and the information will be more easily grasped when the images are colored. My intention is to convey the excitement of scientific discovery, impart a sense of history, and show that scientists are real people from all over the globe who have devoted years or lifetimes to answering questions about evolution. Naturally, only a sample of this vast sea of information can be offered here, but I hope it will help readers of all ages and backgrounds to understand more about what it means to be a human being.

Adrienne L. Zihlman

November 2000
Santa Cruz, Ca

COLORING INSTRUCTIONS

1. This is a book of illustrations (plates) and related text pages. You color each structure the same color as its name. The structure and its name are linked by identical letters (subscripts: a, b, c, etc.). Later you will be able to relate identically colored names (titles) and structures at a glance.

2. You will need coloring instruments. Colored pencils are best, but colored fine to medium felt-tip pens work as well. Twelve pencils or pens will do, but the more colors you have, the more you will enjoy yourself.

3. The organization of the contents is based on the author's overall perspective of the subject and may follow the order of presentation of a formal course of instruction. To achieve maximum benefit, you should color the plates in order, at least within a group or section.

Once you begin coloring a plate in order of presentation of the titles and reading the matched text, the illustrations will have greater meaning, and relationships of different parts will become clear.

4. As you come to each plate, look over the entire illustration and note the arrangement and order of titles. You may count the number of subscripts to find the number of colors you will need. Then scan the coloring instructions (printed in boldface type) for further guidance. Be sure to color in the order given by the instructions. Most of the time this means starting at the top of the plate with the first title, a, and coloring in alphabetical order. Contemplate a number of color arrangements before starting. In some cases, you may want to color related forms with different shades of the same color; in other cases, contrast is desirable. Where a natural appearance is desirable, the coloring instructions may guide you or you may choose colors based on your own knowledge and observations. One of the most important considerations is to link the structure and its title (printed in large outline or blank letters) with the same color. If the structure to be colored has parts taking several colors,

you might color its title as a mosaic of the same colors. It is recommended that you color the title first and *then* its related structure.

5. Areas to be colored are separated from adjacent areas by heavy outlines. Lighter lines represent background, suggest texture, or define form and should be colored over. If the colors you use are light enough, these texture lines may show through, in which case you may wish to draw darker or heavier over these lines to add a three-dimensional effect. Some boundaries between coloring zones may be represented by a dot or two or dotted lines. These represent a division of names or titles and indicate that an actual structural boundary may not exist or is not clearly visible.

In the event structures are duplicated on a plate, as in left and right parts, branches, or serial (segmented) parts, only one may be labeled with a subscript. Without boundary restrictions or instructions to the contrary, these like structures should all be given the same color.

As a general rule, large areas should be colored with light colors and small areas should be colored with darker colors. Take care with very dark colors: they obscure detail and texture lines or stippling. In some cases, a structure will be identified by two subscripts (for example, a+d). In this case, two light colors are recommended.

The ✿ means to color the title or structure gray. When you see titles with a^1, a^2, etc., this indicates the parts so labeled are sufficiently related to receive *shades* of the same color.

6. In some cases, a plate of illustrations will require more colors that you have in your possession. Forced to use a color twice or thrice on the same plate, you must take care to prevent confusion in identification and review by employing it on well-separated areas.

7. For further guidance on color use, see Getting the Most Out of Color.

The

HUMAN EVOLUTION
COLORING BOOK
Second Edition

SECTION 1
EVIDENCE FOR EVOLUTION

Evolution is the unifying principle explaining the origin and diversity of life on earth. Section 1 introduces the historical, comparative, and adaptive dimensions of evolution. The human species shares with other vertebrates and other primates many aspects of biochemistry, morphology, and embryology. Adaptation and convergence, the patterns by which life has changed through time, are also illustrated in this section.

Understanding evolution has itself evolved during the past 150 years. Charles Darwin (1809–1882) formulated the first comprehensive argument for organic evolution that is the foundation of modern biology. His ideas countered the prevailing belief that species were fixed for all time, were created ideally suited to their environment, and were part of a "Grand Design." Darwin sought scientific explanations based on observable natural processes. He wove together many different lines of evidence and concluded that species do change. In his view, species were not fixed but continually adapted to local conditions, diversified into subspecies, split into separate "daughter" species, or, in the eventual fate of most species, went extinct. The mechanism for this dynamic alteration through time was natural selection. In proposing his theory of natural selection, he had to convince his scientific colleagues of the fundamental validity of species change and to go against the prevailing scientific and religious assumptions of his time.

In 1859, Darwin made his case for these truly revolutionary ideas in his book *On the Origin of Species by Means of Natural Selection: Or the Preservation of Favoured Races in the Struggle for Life,* the culmination of many years of observation, thought, and research. As a young man, Darwin studied geology at Edinburgh and botany at Cambridge University, and went to sea as a naturalist aboard HMS *Beagle* (1-1). Toward the end of the voyage, the *Beagle* called at the Galápagos Archipelago, a group of volcanic islands in the Pacific Ocean 1000 kilometers west of Ecuador. Darwin sensed some force at work in these islands, though he had not yet crystallized his evolutionary concepts. He wrote in his journal: "here both in space and time, we seem to be brought somewhat near to that great fact, that mystery of mysteries, the first appearance of new beings on this earth."

Darwin studied corals, earthworms, orchids, pigeons, barnacles, and human infants; his writings encompassed natural history, geology, zoology, botany, psychology, and anthropology. His insights brought fresh perspectives into the nature of evolutionary processes (1-2). Michael Ghiselin (1969) writes of "the triumph of the Darwinian method." Darwin had a remarkable ability to integrate seemingly unrelated pieces of information into a coherent pattern, for example, connecting natural selection to breeding of domesticated animals. His talent for proposing bold hypotheses led to testing them through observation and experiment.

Embryology and comparative anatomy supported Darwin's ideas about the continuity and relatedness of species. In the first few days or weeks of development, species may resemble one another closely, whereas the adult stages may differ significantly (1-3). The continuity among all vertebrates is illustrated in the head, which houses the senses and central nervous system (1-4). As the organism grows and develops, embryological structures that start the same take on new functions. Structures that become gill arches in fishes may become jaw bones in reptiles or ear bones in humans (1-5).

"Descent with modification" was Darwin's expression for how one species is transformed into others. Mammalian forelimbs all have a similar pattern of bones (1-6), but bats are adapted for flying, moles for digging, dolphins for swimming. Likewise, modification has taken place in teeth and jaws; some mammals feed on animal flesh, some on the bark of trees, others on leaves and fruit (1-7). These variations in ground plans, resulting from natural selection working differentially on descendants of a common ancestor, illustrate Darwin's principle of divergence, what we now call adaptive radiation.

There is another process, called evolutionary convergence, by which unrelated organisms come to resemble each other as a result of similar selection pressures. Ocean dwellers evolved streamlined torpedolike shapes, whether they were fish, reptiles like ichthyosaurs, mammals, or birds (1-8). North American placental mammals and the pouched Australian marsupials show many parallels in body form, locomotion, and diet. All have adapted to similar physical conditions and ways of life (1-9).

Darwin understood that individual variation within a population is somehow passed on from one generation to the next, but he did not know the principles of inheritance. The physical units of heredity (what we call genes today) and the laws of inheritance were being discovered by an Austrian monk, Gregor Mendel, during Darwin's lifetime, but Mendel's findings remained largely unknown to the scientific community until they were rediscovered in 1900 (1-10, 1-11, 1-12). The process of somatic cell division, called mitosis (1-13) and cell division that produces sex cells, called meiosis (1-14), are crucial to the understanding of heredity. Meiosis demonstrates how variation is transmitted and maintained over generations. Meiosis also illustrates the important role of recombination in preserving existing variation and as a source of new variation.

Mendel's observations anticipated the existence of genes that transmit hereditary units from parent to offspring. The rise of genetic knowledge in the 20th century elucidated the connection between genes (genotype) and the outward expression of traits (phenotype) in the individual. Research on fruit flies advanced our understanding about the role of genetic mutation, recombination of genes during sexual reproduction, and sex-linked genes. Genes may spontaneously mutate. Some genes line up on the same chromosome. The process of crossing over shuffles these linked genes and produces new combinations (1-15). During the first decades of the 20th century, geneticists emphasized mutation in the production of new species. The role of mutation overshadowed and even replaced Darwin's concept of natural selection. "Darwinism" seemed to be dead and buried.

Even for many of Darwin's colleagues who were otherwise convinced that organic evolution had indeed occurred, natural selection by itself seemed insufficient to account for the production of new species. The concept of natural selection and its role in the evolutionary process took on new life in the 1930s. A new cadre of mathematically-inclined population geneticists focused on populations and the collective variation in the gene pool. They identified the evolutionary process of "genetic drift." Small genetic changes can accumulate when populations become separated geographically into much smaller breeding groups. The separated populations, with natural selection as a shaping agent and mutation and recombination as sources for new variation, may eventually result in new species. The snub-nosed monkeys serve as a case study to illustrate how genetic drift, the small population effect, or sampling variation, can contribute to speciation (1-16). Environmental fluctuation and increase in human activities during the past 10,000 years contributed to habitat fragmentation. Gene flow of the once widely distributed population was curtailed. Through natural selection and genetic drift, the isolated populations evolved into the four distinct species living today.

It was not a matter of mutation *versus* natural selection in producing new species, but a recognition that both mechanisms work together, in combination with genetic drift, to produce variation in individuals, populations, and species. Several trends in the 1930s, including the rise of population genetics, field studies on natural populations, and new ways of analyzing variation in the fossil record, contributed to the formulation of "the modern evolutionary synthesis."

Natural selection can be observed and measured. The long-term studies of Rosemary and Peter Grant on Galápagos finches (1-17) focus on the reality of evolutionary change within a human lifetime. Darwin had argued, and the scientific community still concurs, that natural selection has no long-term goal. Rather, natural selection acts on the variability available within each new generation, given the prevailing environmental conditions, and as a result alters the features of individuals in the next generation.

Our understanding of species distribution and of changes through time took a giant step forward when the mechanism of plate tectonics was recognized during the 1960s (1-18). Geological processes, like the volcanos and earthquakes Darwin had experienced, help account for the continually moving continents and the consequent distribution of resident plant and animal species. From the formation of the earth's crust and the appearance of early life almost four billion years ago, new species emerged, diverged, flourished, were replaced, and became extinct (1-19). Over eons of geological time, life forms change in rhythm with the changing earth. From the first vertebrates (1-20), the first mammals (1-21), to the first appearance of our own primate relatives (1-22), we recognize that these "products" of evolution have been shaped through the unique combination of natural selection, recombination of genes during sexual reproduction, mutation, genetic drift, and species migrations.

Darwin would have loved it!

1-1
MAPPING THE GLOBE: DARWIN'S VOYAGE

Charles Darwin transformed the way we view ourselves, our world, and the life forms which inhabit our planet. How did this naturalist come to revolutionize biology through his ideas on evolution and natural selection? Darwin's life as a scientist began when he took a position as naturalist and companion to Captain Robert FitzRoy aboard HMS *Beagle*, a ship charting the coastal waters of South America. As the ship circled the globe over a five year period (1831–1836), Darwin, not yet an evolutionist, puzzled over the diversity and distribution of life he observed.

Begin by coloring HMS *Beagle* and its departure from Plymouth, England, (a) and (a^1).

The ship covered great distances, encountered extensive coastlines, and called at innumerable islands and archipelagos. As he voyaged, Darwin came to appreciate "how infinitely small the proportion of dry land is to the water of this vast expanse." At every opportunity, Darwin went ashore, and he spent three of the five years traveling into high mountains, crossing the pampas, and exploring the rain forests. He studied rock formations, collected plants and animals, observed the composition of life in different habitats, and noted the effect of geographical barriers on species distribution. Observations and collections made during these travels laid the foundation for his life's work studying the natural world.

Next, color the voyage to the Cape Verde Islands in the Atlantic Ocean off the coast of West Africa (b) and (b^1). Color the illustration of coral uplift (b^2).

HMS *Beagle* docked 23 days in the Cape Verde Islands and Darwin studied the geology extensively. He had read the newly published *Principles of Geology* (1830) by Charles Lyell, who explained that geological features were products of natural processes such as uplift, erosion, and sedimentation. The Cape Verde Islands were, for Darwin, a textbook case of the processes Lyell had described. Darwin observed that the layers of coral then exposed on the side of the island could have grown only in shallow waters, not above the surface of the water. He concluded that the coral deposits forming a white band in rock far above the present tide level therefore reflected earlier uplift from the sea and changes in the land surfaces due to volcanic activity. Early in his travels, Darwin became convinced of the newly emerging idea in geology that the earth is dynamic and changing, not static and fixed.

Next, color the voyage to Argentina (c) and (c^1). Color the fossil remains of *Megatherium* (c^2).

Exploring the grassy pampas of Argentina, Darwin uncovered fossilized bones of animals now extinct: *Megatherium*, a giant ground sloth; *Glyptodon,* a giant armadillo; and *Toxodon*, a strange animal resembling a hippopotamus. Darwin noticed that some extinct forms seemed to be giant relatives of living inhabitants of South America, whereas others had no living counterparts. Darwin sought to explain why some species suddenly disappeared and became extinct, whereas others were replaced by similar but modified living inhabitants.

Color the voyage around Cape Horn to Concepción, Chile, (d) and (d^1). Color the earthquake and volcanos as well (d^2).

While exploring a forest in southern Chile, Darwin experienced the rocking of an earthquake and the "motion made me giddy." The earthquake had run for 640 kilometers along the coast and was accompanied by the eruption of a line of volcanos, which Darwin had witnessed while aboard the *Beagle*. When HMS *Beagle* stopped at Concepción, the epicenter of the earthquake, Darwin witnessed the havoc and destruction wrought on the town. He estimated that the sea coast had risen significantly above its previous level. These observations graphically demonstrated to him the physical reality of short, violent geological events causing major alterations in what seemed to be a stable earth.

Complete the plate by coloring the voyage to the Galápagos Islands on the equator 1000 kilometers west of Ecuador (e) and (e^1). Color the diverse life forms found on those islands (e^2).

Toward the end of the voyage, the *Beagle* spent five weeks in the Galápagos Archipelago, a group of volcanic islands formed when lava welled up from the earth's interior through a hot spot in the earth's crust. The confluence of warm western surface currents with cold upwelling southern currents accommodated a curious mix of arctic and tropical species. Darwin was astonished at the penguins, fur seals, and sea lions, living side by side with flying fish, cacti, and tropical birds such as flamingos. Giant tortoises, from which the islands take their name, along with lizards and iguanas, thrived, but frogs and native mammals were absent. He wondered how this unusual combination of species ended up on these islands.

Darwin's observations on the diversity of plants and animals and their particular geographical distribution around the globe led him to question the assumption that species were immutable, established by a single act of creation. He reasoned that species, like the earth itself, were constantly changing. Life forms colonized new habitats and had to survive in new conditions. Over generations, they underwent transmutation into new forms. Many became extinct. The idea of evolution slowly began to take shape in Darwin's mind.

DARWIN'S VOYAGE

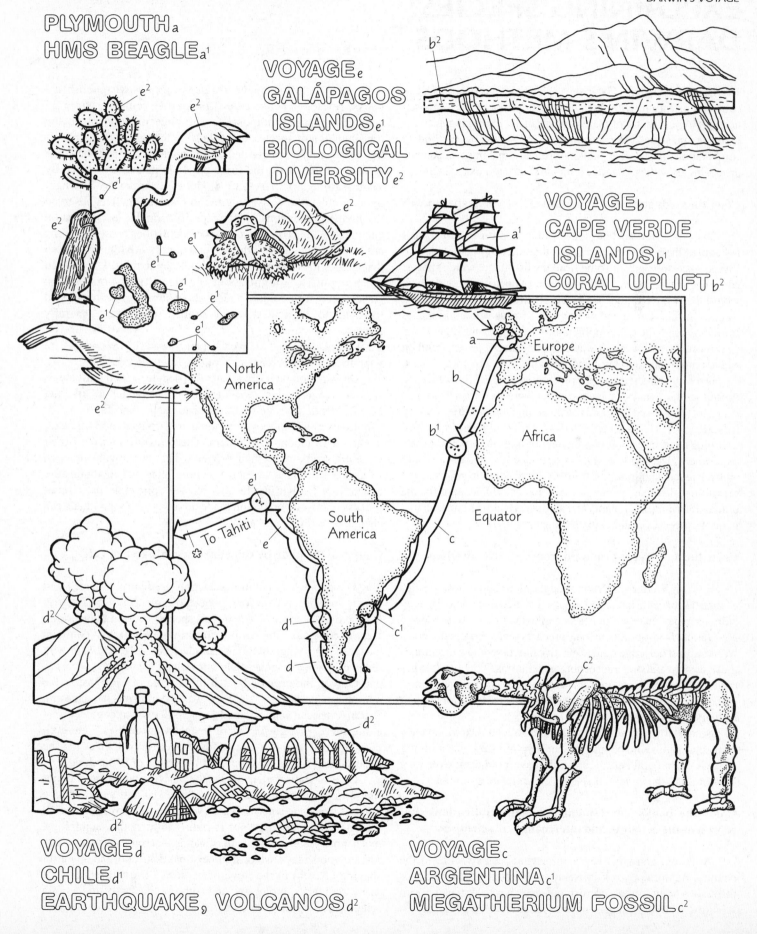

PLYMOUTH_a
HMS BEAGLE_a1

VOYAGE_e
GALÁPAGOS
ISLANDS_e1
BIOLOGICAL
DIVERSITY_e2

VOYAGE_b
CAPE VERDE
ISLANDS_b1
CORAL UPLIFT_b2

North
America

Europe

Africa

South
America

Equator

To Tahiti

VOYAGE_d
CHILE_d1
EARTHQUAKE, VOLCANOS_d2

VOYAGE_c
ARGENTINA_c1
MEGATHERIUM FOSSIL_c2

1-2
EXPLAINING SPECIES: DARWIN'S METHODS

The desolate volcanic Galápagos Islands in the Pacific Ocean confronted Darwin with difficult questions about the supposed unchanging character of plants and animals. In seeking answers to these questions, Darwin applied the scientific method: a combination of observing, thinking critically, making connections, proposing hypotheses, and testing ideas through experiments.

Color the seeds and birds representing Darwin's experiments.

Darwin observed that some Galápagos birds and lizards resembled their counterparts across the water in South America. If their ancestors had all come from the mainland, which species could have made it over 1000 kilometers of open ocean, and which would likely have failed? Birds fly. Shellfish float in their larval stages. Tortoises are good swimmers. Lizards ride on branches from rivers into the sea. Amphibians like frogs, on the other hand, cannot survive long in salt water and are almost never found on islands more than 800 kilometers distant from a mainland.

Darwin wondered how the plants got there. Seeds could have drifted to the islands or been carried there by birds. Darwin's experiments showed that seeds could germinate even after soaking in salt water. He obtained seedlings from the seeds in bird droppings and in the mud on the feet of migratory birds. In one experiment, Darwin kept a dead bird in salt water for a month and retrieved viable seeds from its crop! Darwin rejected the prevailing idea that "centers of creation" could account for the unique distribution of plants and animals. He argued instead that natural processes could explain biogeography.

Color the dog breeds produced from selective breeding.

Back in England, Darwin thought more about how species change. He became interested in selective breeding. Domesticated animals and plants exist in nearly endless varieties. To produce a new variety from an existing one, breeders select those individuals with the most desirable traits. Selective interbreeding concentrates these desired traits in succeeding generations. This process has produced huge St. Bernards for rescue missions in high mountains, collies for herding sheep, and streamlined dachshunds for hunting badgers.

Since "artificial selection" worked so well, Darwin made a connection with wild populations and hypothesized that a similar process of "natural selection" could have produced, over long ages of time, the variety of species observed on earth today.

Color the books, correspondence, and publications that represent the activities and interchanges of scientists.

Although Darwin lived a somewhat reclusive life in the country, he did not work in isolation. He consulted colleagues through a voluminous correspondence, wrote extensively in scientific journals, and presented his research at learned societies.

In the 10 years following the *Beagle* voyage, Darwin published 4 books, revised 1 book, edited 19 journal volumes, wrote 25 scientific papers, composed a 250-page manuscript on the transmutation of species, and filled 7 notebooks with his ideas.

Darwin read widely and systematically. In 1838, he came across "An Essay on the Principle of Population," written by Thomas Robert Malthus in 1798. This essay gave Darwin insight into a problem he was struggling to resolve. Malthus observed that human populations had the capacity to double in a generation and outstrip the food supply. Since populations at any one time are broadly balanced with the food supply, Malthus proposed that checks must be operating to limit populations. Darwin had not previously thought about the stability of populations. Generalizing from Malthus' ideas about humans, Darwin applied the ideas to the natural world. Animals and plants generally produce vast numbers of offspring, of which very few survive. Darwin reasoned that the weakest and "least fit" individuals are winnowed out in a constant "struggle for existence."

Darwin thought more about what decides which individuals will survive and which will perish without progeny. Offspring are not identical to their parents or to each other. In the actual conditions in which they live, some are stronger and fare better in the environment than others. These mature and pass their favorable traits on to their progeny. This winnowing process, which Darwin called "natural selection," goes on generation after generation. Darwin could now clearly appreciate the overall process of how a population made up of varying individuals can change over time.

Complete the plate by coloring Darwin's Tree of Life.

The process of natural selection gradually reshapes and transforms species over long periods of time. New species arise from previous species. Tracing all species back to their origin, Darwin concluded that all life on earth goes back to a common ancestor. All living creatures are related by a Tree of Life with many diverging branches. Darwin viewed the human species as one twig on the primate branch of the Tree of Life, just as the marine iguana of the Galápagos was a twig from the ancestral South American land iguanid branch. Darwin recognized that chimpanzees and gorillas were "man's nearest allies," and even though very few ape or human fossils were known in his day, he deduced that Africa was probably the cradle of humankind.

Over a century after his death, Darwin endures as a major figure in science, his ideas as controversial and as productive today as they were when he was alive. A keen observer and shrewd reasoner, he generally "got it right" without the technology, biochemistry, and genetic understanding that support evolutionary research nowadays. Modest in personal demeanor but an earth-shaking asteroid in the force of his ideas, Darwin remains for many geologists, biologists, and anthropologists the model of a scientist's scientist.

DARWIN'S METHODS

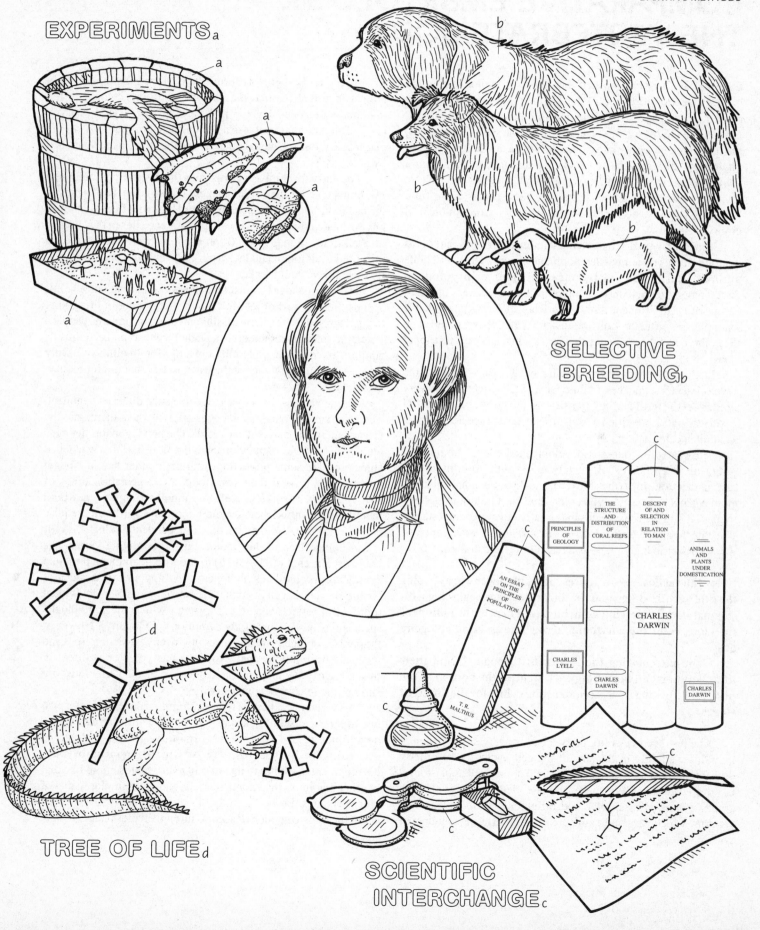

EXPERIMENTS a

SELECTIVE BREEDING b

TREE OF LIFE d

SCIENTIFIC INTERCHANGE c

AN ESSAY ON THE PRINCIPLES OF POPULATION

T. R. MALTHUS

PRINCIPLES OF GEOLOGY

CHARLES LYELL

THE STRUCTURE AND DISTRIBUTION OF CORAL REEFS

CHARLES DARWIN

DESCENT OF AND SELECTION IN RELATION TO MAN

CHARLES DARWIN

ANIMALS AND PLANTS UNDER DOMESTICATION

CHARLES DARWIN

1-3
COMPARATIVE EMBRYOLOGY: THE VERTEBRATE BODY

Even before Darwin proposed the theory of evolution through natural selection, Ernst von Baer claimed that the more closely related any two species are, the more similar their development. His treatise (1828) set the stage for linking the study of ontogeny, the development of the individual through a single life cycle, to phylogeny, the relatedness of species through descent from a common ancestor. When Darwin brought together the diverse lines of evidence to demonstrate that new species arose from previous species, he included the findings from studies on embryos.

Von Baer, who discovered the mammalian egg as part of his detailed studies on animal development, observed that vertebrate animals, during the early stages of their embryological development, seem to have a common design, whereas the adult forms show difference. Arm buds from different species, for example, are virtually indistinguishable when they first form on the embryo, yet they may develop into a wing, an arm, or a flipper (1-6).

In the early stages of growth when vital organs originate, the developmental sequences, or ontogeny, of all vertebrates are very similar. As the fertilized egg transforms into an adult, the general vertebrate plan is modified during growth as each species acquires its adult species pattern.

This plate illustrates six developmental stages (from left to right) of five species of vertebrates—one amphibian (the salamander), one bird (the chicken), and three mammals (the pig, monkey, and human). As you color, note the similarities of body shapes among the five species in the early developmental stages. The late fetal/newborn/adult stages reflect the emergence of species-specific body plans as a result of differential growth.

Color the vertical arrow representing phylogeny gray. Color the title Fertilized Egg and the illustrated eggs beginning with salamander and moving up to human. Then, at the bottom of the plate, color the horizontal arrow representing ontogeny gray.

Continue coloring the forms (b) through (f) and their titles, left to right, beginning each stage at the bottom of the plate and working up. Use contrasting colors for the different stages.

The fertilized eggs (a), or zygotes, are very similar, though they differ slightly in the size of the cell nucleus. The orderly division of the single-celled zygote into a multicelled blastocyst is referred to as cleavage. By the late cleavage stage (b), the embryos look very similar and differ only in their cleavage patterns, which vary due to the presence of differing amounts of yolk in the egg.

As the body segments form (c), all three mammals remain almost identical. Notice the ancestral gill slits, which in the mammals will later develop into parts of the ear and pharynx (1-5). The mammals possess an umbilical cord that leads to the placenta. In contrast, the salamander and the chicken are nourished by yolk.

The early forelimbs begin as buds (d). By the late fetal stage (e), limbs take on their adult shapes. The striking similarities in the late fetal stage between monkey and human reflect their close phylogenetic relationship. The main difference lies in the absence of a tail in the human fetus. (If an ape fetus were substituted for this monkey, it too would lack a tail). The chicken has developed its specialized shell breaker.

The salamander has just hatched into its larval stage (e). It spends the first part of its life in the water, taking in life-giving oxygen through its feathery gill slits and using its limbs as paddles. Later, the salamander undergoes metamorphosis and acquires its adult form with terrestrial limbs and lungs for breathing air. Only then, as an adult, can it leave the water to live, but not reproduce, on dry land.

The newborn of each species receive quite different treatment. The salamander abandons the eggs after she lays them, and the larvae receive no parental care at all. The hen incubates her eggs with body heat while sitting on them in a nest. The newly hatched chicks receive some protection from the mother hen, but begin immediately to find their own food. After gestation times of four (pig), six (monkey), and nine months (human), newborn mammals are nourished by their mother's milk and require extended care before they become independent adults.

A comparison of developmental stages among vertebrates led Ernst Haeckel (1834–1919) to propose his famous principle "ontogeny recapitulates phylogeny." A supporter of the idea of evolution, Haeckel claimed that the development of an individual (ontogeny) reflects the stages through which the individual's species has passed during its evolution (phylogeny). However, the phrase "ontogeny recapitulates phylogeny" oversimplifies and misleads by implying that evolution has goals or is directed. Instead, early developmental sequences of all vertebrates are similar due to common ancestry.

All vertebrate embryos follow a common developmental plan due to having a set of genes that gives the same instructions for development (2-14). As each organism grows, it diverges according to its species way of life. Human embryonic development is similar to that of other vertebrates, more like that of other mammals than nonmammals, and most similar to that of other primates. From the study of ontogeny, we discover clues about the transformation of species through evolutionary change.

THE VERTEBRATE BODY

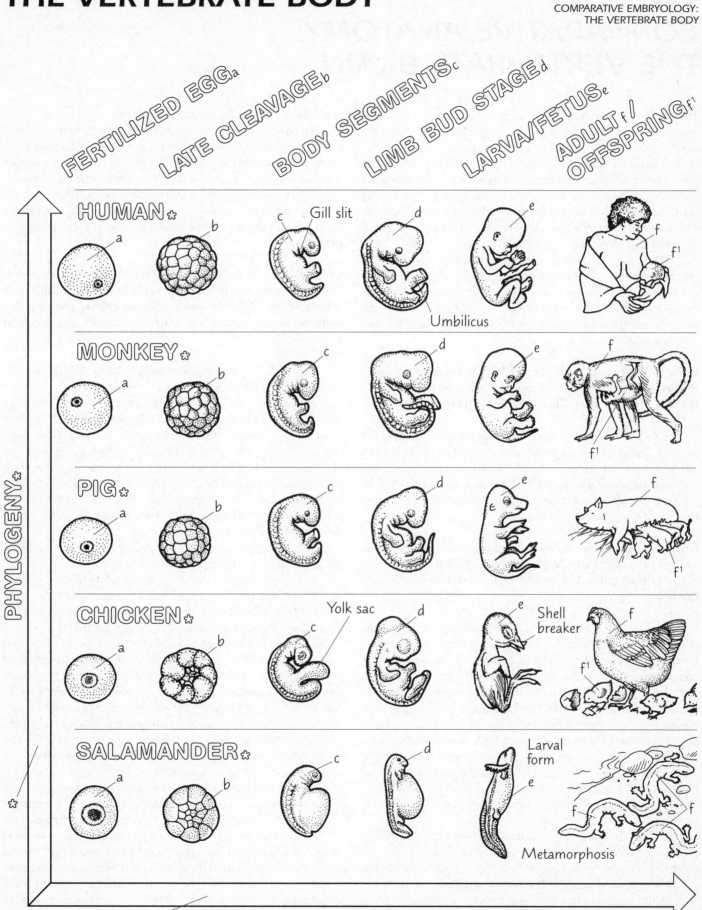

FERTILIZED EGG a
LATE CLEAVAGE b
BODY SEGMENTS c
LIMB BUD STAGE d
LARVA/FETUS e
ADULT f / OFFSPRING f1

PHYLOGENY *

ONTOGENY *

HUMAN *
Gill slit
Umbilicus

MONKEY *

PIG *

CHICKEN *
Yolk sac
Shell breaker

SALAMANDER *
Larval form
Metamorphosis

1-4
COMPARATIVE ANATOMY: THE VERTEBRATE BRAIN

The vertebrate head houses the brain and the sensory modes of smell, sight, and hearing, which receive information from the environment. The brain, along with the spinal cord, forms the central nervous system. Acting as a switchboard, the central nervous system processes information received through the senses and responds by altering the organism's reactions (3-21). During vertebrate evolution, new structures in the brain arose from the elaboration of older structures. Vertebrates first appear in the fossil record as fish some 450 million years ago (mya) (1-20).

The similarities among vertebrates are most pronounced at the earliest stages of life, but during the course of an individual's development, or ontogeny, structures differentiate and take on the characteristics of the species (1-3). Here we examine and compare the basic arrangement of brain structure among four vertebrate species.

Color the titles and the brain swellings of the neural tube in the vertebrate embryo at the top left: forebrain (a), midbrain (b), and hindbrain (c). Choose three contrasting colors.

During development, three swellings appear at the anterior end of a neural tube as the brain takes shape in an embryo. Each swelling develops into a group of specialized structures shared among vertebrates. The major differences in each region reflect the extent to which each species processes and integrates sensory information and generates responses.

Next, color the titles and the related forebrain structures in each of the vertebrates, beginning with the fish and working down to the rabbit. Use shades of the color chosen for the forebrain.

The forebrain includes the olfactory bulb and tract, the optic nerve, and the cerebrum. The olfactory tracts conduct information from the environment, which is brought in through sensory receptors and conveyed to the olfactory bulbs for processing. In fish and reptiles, the olfactory bulbs are relatively large in comparison to total brain size and indicate a heavy reliance on this sense for gathering information. In birds, the olfactory bulbs are small, except in certain scavenger birds that locate their food by smell. In mammals, the olfactory bulbs range from small in some primates (3-15) to extremely large, as in the anteater and aardvark which use their noses to sniff out ants and termites.

The optic nerve transmits information from the eye to the cerebrum.

In fish, the cerebrum is almost exclusively devoted to processing information from the sense of smell. In reptiles, the cerebrum is distinctly larger than in fish and marks the earliest appearance of the neocortex. This "new cortex" or expanded outer wall of the cerebrum becomes larger during the later stages of vertebrate evolution and takes over processing information involving vision, taste, and touch. In fish, the midbrain and hindbrain structures handle these functions.

Among mammals, the expansion of the cerebral neocortex is most marked in humans (3-21). The cerebrum surrounds the midbrain and correlates with the increased capacity for complex learning and memory. A new structure appears in the cerebrum called the corpus callosum. This bundle of nerve fibers connects the two lateral lobes, or cerebral hemispheres, and provides a rapid transfer of information from one side of the cerebrum to the other.

Color the midbrain structures and hindbrain structures, beginning with the fish and proceeding to the rabbit. Use shades of the midbrain and hindbrain colors. The superior colliculi of the rabbit are actually beneath the cerebral hemispheres.

The midbrain includes the optic lobe in fish, birds, and reptiles and the superior colliculus in mammals.

In fish, the optic lobes are small. In reptiles and birds, they are almost always large and conspicuous and attest to their possessors' excellent vision. In mammals, the optic lobes share the same embryonic origin (they are homologous) with the superior colliculi, which appear as two tiny bumps on the back of the midbrain covered by the overhanging cerebral hemispheres. Their small size is due to the relocation of visual processing from the optic to the cerebral occipital lobes during the phylogenetic development of mammals.

The hindbrain includes the cerebellum, the medulla oblongata, and in birds and mammals, the pons.

The cerebellum is the coordinator of voluntary muscle movements and plays a primary role in maintaining balance. In birds, the cerebellum is proportionately largest, where it coordinates intricate movements necessary for flight.

The medulla oblongata is a direct extension of the spinal cord. It coordinates the autonomic, involuntary activities involved with breathing and blood circulation, and integrates sensory impulses from all parts of the body for rapid reflex responses. In fish, the medulla oblongata is the only processing center for touch, temperature, taste, and balance. In other vertebrates, much of the sensory processing functions have been taken over by the neocortex. Yet even in humans, the medulla oblongata retains the capacity to initiate reflex responses.

In birds and mammals, an accessory pons appears and acts as an integration center for increasingly complex neuronal transmissions between the cerebrum, cerebellum, and spinal cord.

The human species has the largest brain relative to body weight of all animals. Among vertebrates, the brain functions to receive information from the external and internal worlds and to respond appropriately. The capacity to gain and process information, to store it as memory, and to recombine it in complex ways reflects the differences among vertebrates. This capacity forms one aspect of what we call "intelligence."

THE VERTEBRATE BRAIN

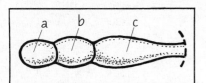

Brain of a vertebrate embryo

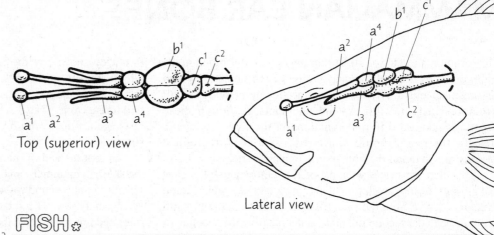

Top (superior) view

Lateral view

FOREBRAIN a
OLFACTORY BULB a¹/**TRACT** a²
OPTIC NERVE a³
CEREBRUM a⁴

FISH ✽

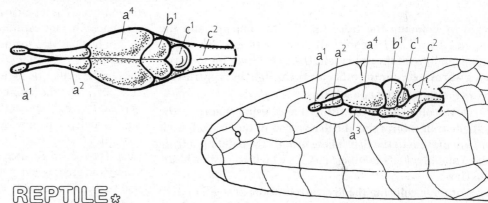

MIDBRAIN b
OPTIC LOBE b¹
SUPERIOR COLLICULUS b²

REPTILE ✽

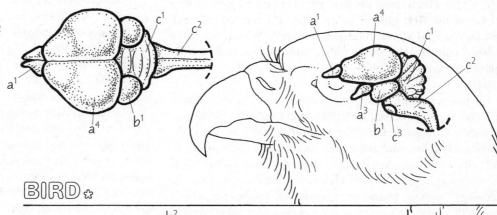

HINDBRAIN c
CEREBELLUM c¹
MEDULLA OBLONGATA c²
PONS c³

BIRD ✽

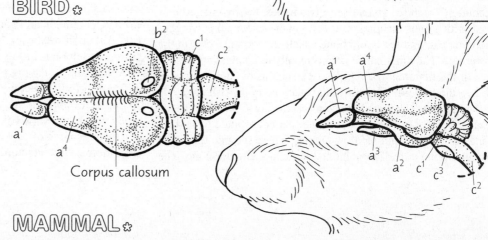

Corpus callosum

MAMMAL ✽

1-5
NEW STRUCTURES FROM OLD: MAMMALIAN EAR BONES

The common ancestry of all vertebrates is well illustrated in the embryonic development and evolution of the human jaw and hearing mechanism. We trace the connection by studying the gill structures in fish, reptiles, and mammals. Although these structures take on different functions in the three vertebrate classes, their embryonic similarities, called homologies, demonstrate in detail the human link to other vertebrates (1-3).

This plate illustrates what happens to embryonic gill arches and gill slits during development in four vertebrate species. Eight structures derive from the first gill arch, three from the first gill slit, four from the second gill arch, and three from the second gill slit

Begin by coloring the titles (a), (b), (c), and (d) and the magnified first and second gill arches and gill slits in the human embryo at the upper left. Use a cool color for one arch and a warm color for the other arch. Use light but contrasting colors for each of the two gill slits.

Next, color the jawed fish (F) and, using shades of the first gill arch color, color the derivatives of the first gill arch that are present in the fish. These include the palatoquadrate (a^1, F) and Meckel's cartilage (a^4, F), which are visible in the side view.

Continue coloring the derivatives of the first gill arch in the reptile (R), mammal (M), and human (H). Then color the titles and derivatives of the first gill slit in each species using shades of the first gill slit color. Color the second gill arch and second gill slit derivatives similarly. When you have finished coloring the whole plate, read the text and identify each structure as it is discussed.

In jawed fish (F), the first gill arch (a), called the mandibular, develops into jaws, consisting of the palatoquadrate above and Meckel's cartilage below. The first gill slit (b), between the mandibular and second gill arches, becomes the spiracle, a tube that pumps water through the gills where gases are exchanged in respiration. (Lungs perform this function in land vertebrates.) The second gill arch (c) gives rise to two bones: the hyomandibular bone which transmits pressure waves in the surrounding water to the inner ear, and the hyoid bone which supports muscles in the lower jaw. The inner ear functions mainly as a balancing organ.

In the mammallike reptiles (R), such as extinct therapsids (1-21), the first gill arch and palatoquadrate of the fish gave rise to the quadrate. The quadrate connects the jaw (mandible) to the skull. The Meckel's cartilage of the fish contributed to several bones of the jaw and skull in reptiles. These include the small articular bone at the jaw joint and the larger angular bone. The front view shows how the first gill slit forms the middle ear cavity, which houses the stapes, a remodeled version of the hyomandibular. The eustachian tube that connects the throat to the middle ear cavity is also derived from the first gill slit. The stapes rests against the eardrum which is derived from the second gill slit.

In reptiles and in mammals (M), the eardrum is sunk into the skull. In mammals, an outer ear, also derived from the second gill slit, funnels sound waves into the middle ear, now containing three ear bones. The quadrate and articular of reptiles have migrated inward to form the incus and malleus respectively, and along with the stapes, transmit sound waves from the eardrum to the inner ear. The reptilian angular bone has become the tympanic ring encircling the eardrum.

In humans (H), the gills are transitory structures appearing about four weeks after conception. The gill slits never open to the outside as they do in fish, but are present as gill pouches. The first gill arch of the fetus becomes the incus, the malleus, and the tympanic ring. Meckel's cartilage derivatives contribute significantly to the lower jaw and face. As in all mammals, the first gill pouch forms the middle ear cavity and the eustachian tube. The second gill arch becomes the stapes and contributes to the styloid process and the hyoid bone which supports the tongue and larynx. The second gill pouch forms the outer ear, eardrum, and ear canal.

The evolutionary process is conservative. It doesn't throw away old structures but finds ways to recycle them for new uses. So, the ancestral pattern is "conserved" in the embryonic stages of descendent species. Through genetic change and natural selection, those persistent embryonic structures are remodeled during the later stages of growth and development and may acquire new functions.

The remodeling during evolution of primitive gill arches and slits permitted mammals to hear a wider range of sounds, especially in the higher frequencies, than their reptilian ancestors could perceive. A keen sense of hearing helped to ensure the survival of mammalian young. Hearing is an integral part of the mammalian adaptation (3-14) and an essential component of primate communication and human language (3-20, 3-22).

Although we are amazed by the marvelous variety of living forms, evolution is in some ways a deeply conservative process, recycling and reshaping old parts into new ones. The changing functions of gill structures demonstrate the continuity of forms throughout vertebrate and mammalian evolution. Later, when we study development, we see that this continuity of outward forms is a manifestation of genetic conservatism too, for similar genes determine the architecture of insects, mice, and humans (2-14).

MAMMALIAN EAR BONES

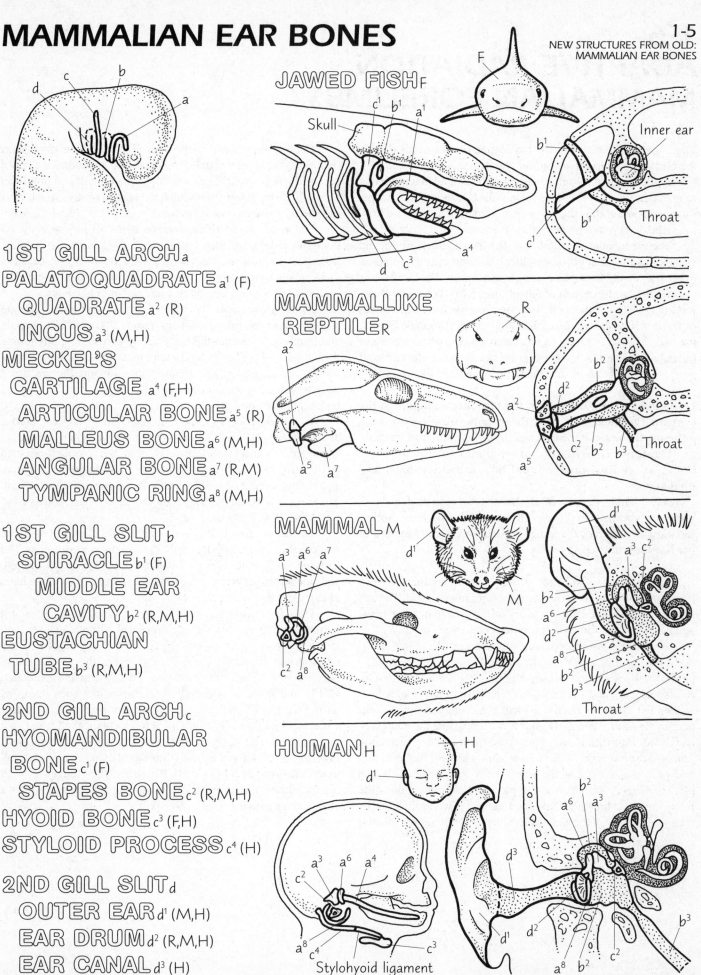

JAWED FISH F

MAMMALLIKE REPTILE R

MAMMAL M

HUMAN H

1ST GILL ARCH a
  PALATOQUADRATE a^1 (F)
    QUADRATE a^2 (R)
    INCUS a^3 (M,H)
  MECKEL'S
    CARTILAGE a^4 (F,H)
    ARTICULAR BONE a^5 (R)
    MALLEUS BONE a^6 (M,H)
    ANGULAR BONE a^7 (R,M)
    TYMPANIC RING a^8 (M,H)

1ST GILL SLIT b
  SPIRACLE b^1 (F)
    MIDDLE EAR
    CAVITY b^2 (R,M,H)
  EUSTACHIAN
    TUBE b^3 (R,M,H)

2ND GILL ARCH c
  HYOMANDIBULAR
    BONE c^1 (F)
    STAPES BONE c^2 (R,M,H)
  HYOID BONE c^3 (F,H)
  STYLOID PROCESS c^4 (H)

2ND GILL SLIT d
  OUTER EAR d^1 (M,H)
  EAR DRUM d^2 (R,M,H)
  EAR CANAL d^3 (H)

1-6
ADAPTIVE RADIATION: MAMMALIAN FORELIMBS

The variety of forelimbs—the bat's wing, the sea lion's flipper, the elephant's supportive column, the human's arm and hand—further illustrates the similar anatomical plan of all mammals due to a shared ancestry. Despite the obvious differences in shape, mammalian forelimbs share a similar arrangement and arise from the same embryonic, homologous structures.

The mammalian forelimb includes the shoulder, elbow, and wrist joints. The scapula or shoulder blade connects the forelimb to the trunk and forms part of the shoulder joint. The humerus or upper arm bone forms part of the shoulder joint above, and elbow joint below. The radius and ulna comprise the lower arm bones or forearm, and contribute to the elbow and wrist joints. Finally, the carpal or wrist bones, the metacarpals, and phalanges form the bat wing, the sea lion flipper, the tree shrew, mole, and wolf paws, the elephant foot, and the human hand and fingers.

Using light colors, begin with the tree shrew scapula in the center of the plate. Next, color the scapula on each of the other animals: the mole, bat, wolf, sea lion, elephant, and human.

Continue coloring the other bones in this manner: humerus, radius, ulna, carpal bones, metacarpals, and phalanges.

After you have colored all the structures in each animal, notice the variation in the overall shape of the forelimb. Notice, too, how the form of the bones contributes to the function of the forelimb in each species.

The tree shrew skeleton closely resembles that of early mammals and represents the ancestral forelimb skeleton. The tree shrew is small bodied, moves easily on the ground or in the trees, and has a flexible forelimb for these functions (3-7).

The mole's forelimb is relatively short and lies close to the body, giving it a somewhat streamlined shape. The shovellike paw comprises almost half the length of the limb. The slender rodlike scapula and the short, peculiarly shaped humerus help anchor the forelimb against the trunk and draw the paws very near to the head. The elbow joint is rotated so that the paws face backward. Powerful muscles attach on the long bony olecranon process; they straighten the elbow joint and help the paws dig and push the soil out to the side. The robust metacarpals and phalanges give strength to the paw and an extra bone (the falciform) adds breadth. Thus, the forelimb is well suited for the mole to dig its way through moist soil as it searches for insects.

The bat's forelimb is adapted for flight. The humerus is short relative to the longer, slender radius; the ulna is reduced and not part of the wrist joint. The metacarpals and phalanges provide a light but strong frame over which the skin is stretched, much as the silk of a kite covers its frame.

The wolf is a swift runner, the better to pursue prey. Its humerus, radius, and ulna are relatively long and make possible a long stride. In marked contrast to those of the bat, the metacarpals are closely packed together for bearing weight. The wolf walks somewhat up on its toes, on bent phalanges.

For its life in the water and on land, the sea lion has a broad scapula, short and robust humerus, radius, and ulna. The scapula and humerus lie within the body cavity and so help streamline the animal (1-8). The relatively long metacarpals and phalanges form a broad paddle. The robust bones support the sea lion's weight on land; this gives the animal mobility when it hauls out on land to mate and give birth.

To support its five ton bulk, the elephant's shoulder, elbow, and wrist joints are stacked one above the other, giving an arrangement like an architectural column; the scapula is oriented downward, so it too is in line with the robust humerus and ulna. The radius is reduced so that the ulna carries most of the weight. The metacarpals and phalanges are short and robust, and a pad of fat and skin cushions the foot.

The human forelimb is long, slender and mobile and, unlike that of other mammals, does not bear weight in locomotion. The ball and socket shoulder joint enables a 360° range of motion, and slender finger bones and a prominent thumb enable the hand to carry out fine manipulations.

The similarity of a bat's wing, an elephant's leg, and a human's arm may not be readily apparent without a closer look at the underlying bony structures. The basic design of the mammalian forelimb (3-7) demonstrates the evolutionary phenomenon of adaptive radiation. Through natural selection (1-17), the form of mammalian forelimbs has been modified during the last 65 million years into many shapes to perform a variety of functions. By adapting to forest, plains, air, water, and underground, mammals have been able to radiate (like the sun's rays) into a diversity of habitats. Studies of comparative anatomy and embryology (1-3) well illustrate the "descent with modification" of Darwin and the branching out of species from a common ancestor.

MAMMALIAN FORELIMBS

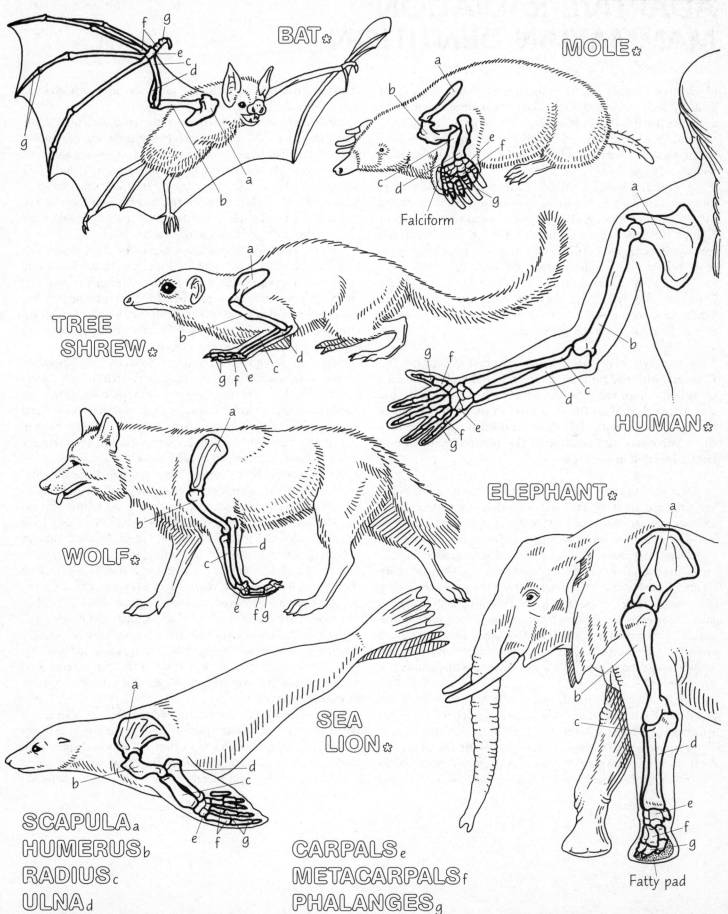

BAT ✱

MOLE ✱

Falciform

TREE
SHREW ✱

HUMAN ✱

WOLF ✱

ELEPHANT ✱

SEA
LION ✱

SCAPULA a
HUMERUS b
RADIUS c
ULNA d

CARPALS e
METACARPALS f
PHALANGES g

Fatty pad

ADAPTIVE RADIATION: MAMMALIAN DENTITION

Mammals eat a wide variety of foods from grasses, leaves, and fruit to insects and animal flesh. The teeth, or dentition, perform a range of functions to obtain and prepare food items for digestion; they cut, peel, slice, pulp, crush, shred, grind, rip, and puncture. Mammals also use their teeth to clean fur or for communicating with facial expressions (3-18).

Mammalian teeth vary in size and shape: they are heterodont (hetero=other, dont=tooth), a contrast with the repetitively similar (homodont, homo=same, dont=tooth) conical-shaped teeth of reptiles. Humans, as other mammals, have two sets of teeth with well-developed roots (6-3). In contrast, reptilian teeth have simple roots, and they are continually replaced during life.

Teeth are only part of the dietary picture. Muscles move the jaw joints, thereby bringing the tooth surfaces together so they can function. Here we examine the dentition and chewing muscles in four different species of mammals.

Color each type of tooth. Color the incisors in all four species. Continue with the canines, premolars, and molars. Finally, using light colors, color the muscles in each of the four species.

After coloring all the structures in each animal, notice the variation in tooth size, shape, and function. Notice how the relative size and position of the muscles contribute to dental function in each species.

Mammalian teeth include: the incisors for biting, peeling, scraping, and gnawing; the canines for ripping and puncturing; and the premolars and molars for grinding, pulping, and shredding.

The jaw joint varies in shape and muscle arrangement, depending on the animal's eating habits. The temporalis muscle, on the top and side of the skull, crosses the jaw joint and attaches on the lower jaw; its main action is fast and powerful jaw closure. The masseter muscle, attached to the zygomatic arch or "cheek bone," crosses the jaw joint and attaches prominently on the lower jaw. Its main action is strength in jaw closure for crushing and chewing; the ptyergoid muscles on the inside of the jaw (not shown) move the jaw from side to side, a motion important in grinding food.

Opossums are omnivorous (omni=all). They eat a varied diet and have all types of teeth: 50 total, 26 in the upper jaw (13 per quadrant), and 24 in the lower jaw. (There are 2 additional incisors in the upper jaw.) The incisors and canines nip the stems and roots of soft food and seize and hold insects; premolars and molars pulp insects, soft-bodied animals, and soft plant foods. Opossum

chewing muscles, temporalis and masseter, are nearly equal in size for this range of action.

Beavers are herbivorous (plant-eating) rodents with 20 teeth. Each quadrant has 5 teeth: 1 large, chisellike incisor, 1 premolar, and 3 molars. The huge incisors, which gnaw trees and branches, are progressively worn down but continue to grow during the animal's life. Beavers have no canine teeth; the absence creates a large space (diastema) between the incisors and molars. The square-shaped premolars and molars crush and grind tough bark, pith, and leaves in preparation for swallowing.

Beavers and other rodents have two types of jaw movement. In one, the masseter muscle pulls the lower jaw (mandible) upward and forward, bringing the incisors edge to edge for pinching, cropping, puncturing, and gnawing. In the second motion, the lower jaw is pulled back, bringing the molar teeth together for grinding. The large masseter muscle facilitates both these motions, and the temporalis muscle has a much smaller role.

Bobcats, along with dogs, otters, badgers, and hyenas, are members of the order Carnivora (flesh-eaters). The bobcat usually has 26 teeth: 12 in the upper jaw and 14 in the lower. (There are 2 additional incisors in the lower jaw.) The small incisors contrast with the well-developed canine teeth, which are used for holding and killing struggling prey. The large premolars and molars have sharp, pointed cusps, which cut and shear like a pair of scissors when they meet. These cutting teeth are called "carnassials" (carni=flesh). The large and powerful temporalis muscle closes the jaw quickly, permitting a secure capture and killing of prey.

Humans, in the order Primates, are omnivorous; they have 32 adult teeth with 2 incisors, 1 canine, 2 premolars, and 3 molars in each quadrant. Incisors break up food into smaller pieces, as in biting an apple. Canines are used much like incisors, which they resemble, and are reduced in size compared to the pronounced canine teeth of many monkeys and apes. Premolars and molars grind and crush food to facilitate swallowing and digestion. The temporalis and masseter muscles are equally developed for repetitive closing of the jaws for biting and grinding. Like other primates, we use our hands in feeding, to bring food to the mouth, rather than bringing our mouths to the food as most mammals do.

Anatomy mirrors adaptation, and the number, shape, and size of teeth reflect mammalian diet, just as the forelimb bones reflect locomotion. Since teeth are the most frequently preserved fossils, their structure is especially important to scientists in identifying species and reconstructing what the animals ate (Sections 4 and 5).

MAMMALIAN DENTITION

TEETH *
INCISOR a   PREMOLAR c
CANINE b   MOLAR d

MUSCLES *
TEMPORALIS e
MASSETER f

OPOSSUM *

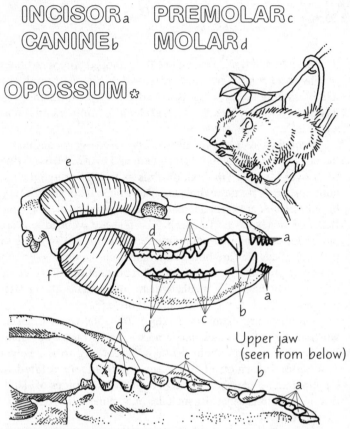

Upper jaw
(seen from below)

BEAVER *

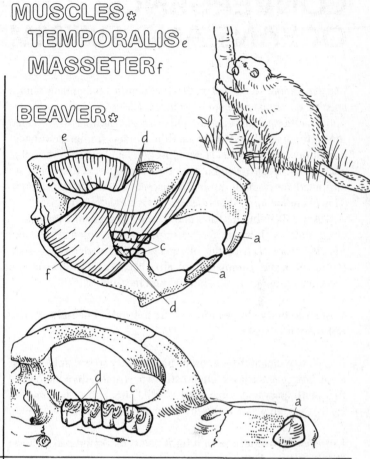

BOBCAT *

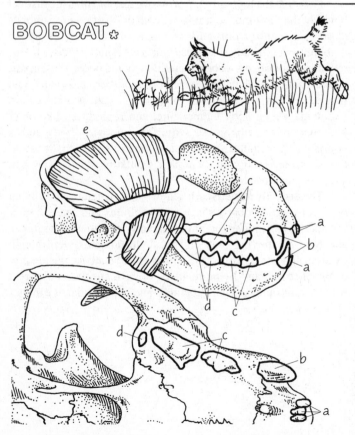

HUMAN *

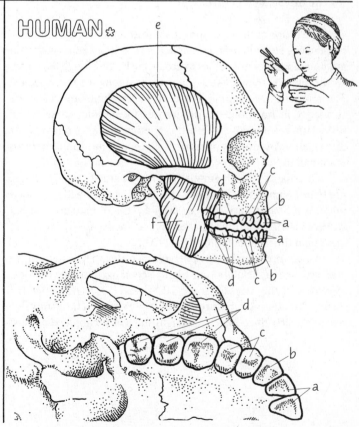

1-8
CONVERGENCE: OCEANS AND SWIMMING

MORPHOLOGIC DIVERSITY

Darwin emphasized that natural selection takes place within specific environmental circumstances. The environment provides opportunities and limitations, and over time, animals are selected through survival and reproduction. Under similar ecological conditions, animal species not closely related come to resemble each other. Such resemblances between unrelated species are attributed, for example, to similar locomotor and feeding behavior. This phenomenon is described as "convergent evolution."

Animals living in water and feeding as predators in oceanic environments illustrate one example of convergent evolution. Species from each of the major classes of vertebrates—fish, reptile, bird, and mammal—look alike because they move, obtain food, and avoid predators in this fluid medium.

Color the body shapes of the four animals. The animals are not drawn to scale.

Notice that all four animals have a body so streamlined that the head appears connected directly to the trunk. All of them have fins or flippers and some kind of tail. This body shape moves easily through water with reduced frontal resistance.

Color each forelimb with a light color, using a darker shade for the internal structure.

The shape of the forelimbs in these animals is very similar— broadened, elongated, and flexible. The forelimbs act as powerful guiding rudders or as paddles to propel the body through the water. Notice that the internal structures differ among the four species. The similarity in external shape of the forelimbs reflects their similarity in function; the differences in the internal structure reflect these animals' different genetics and phylogenies, or divergent evolutionary histories. Compare the limbs here to mammalian forelimbs on (1-6).

The shark, a cartilaginous fish, has no true bone. Cartilage, not bone, supports its forelimb, which is flattened and expanded into a fin. Sharks vary in size. They are major predators with a worldwide distribution. Sharks appear in the fossil record in Devonian times, about 400 mya (1-20).

An ichthyosaur represents the reptiles. This swimming creature, one of the numerous highly specialized marine reptiles, appeared in the Triassic some 200 mya (1-21) and expanded during the Jurassic before becoming extinct. These reptiles reached nearly three meters in length and had streamlined bodies,

legs modified into paddles, and well-developed tails. The bones of the forelimbs were relatively inflexible. Although the ichthyosaur looks like a big fish, the details of its morphology— its deeper structures, teeth, skull, skeleton—firmly identify it as a reptile.

Penguins are adept swimmers. They are largely confined to the oceans of the southern hemisphere and evolved from flying birds over 60 mya. We think of birds as flying through the air, but these birds fly through water. The wings, modified from its bird ancestors, are compact and powerful paddles of fused and flattened bones of the forelimb. The feet are webbed and are placed far back in order not to interfere with the streamlining of the body. Penguins are birds, apparent from the details of their anatomy, physiology, and mode of reproduction. They come ashore to lay their eggs, incubate them, and feed the chicks after they hatch. Their feet provide support on land.

Dolphins are members of the mammalian order Cetacea, which includes the whales and porpoises. This group of mammals invaded the oceans about 40 mya. According to the newer molecular information, they are most closely related to hippopotami, a member of the Artiodactyla, an order of land-dwelling mammals that also includes pigs, camels, deer, antelope, sheep, and goats.

Note that the dolphin's humerus, radius, and ulna are distinct bones in the forelimb, homologous with those of other mammals (1-6) and identify dolphins as mammals. Compared to the dolphin's overall body size, these bones are notably reduced. This reduction contributes to the streamlining of the body. The carpals, metacarpals, and phalanges have been modified to form a broad flipper. Although the dolphin looks like a fish, it breathes air, maintains a high body temperature, and reproduces like other mammals. One fetus grows within the mother's body and is nourished through the placenta (1-9). After its birth in the water, the offspring is fed with its mother's milk, is protected by her, and stays near her for years.

The distantly related shark, ichthyosaur, penguin, and dolphin have converged in body shape and forelimbs and share similar methods of locomotion for moving rapidly through water to forage and feed on moving prey and to avoid danger. Even though external appearance diverges from its close relatives, the identity of the ancestral and living relatives of each species is apparent from details of the deeper structures, and in particular, the modes of reproduction.

OCEANS AND SWIMMING

BODY SHAPE a

FISH FIN b
LIMB
CARTILAGE b¹

Shark

REPTILE
PADDLE c
LIMB BONES c¹

Ichthyosaur

Penguin

BIRD WING d
LIMB BONES d¹

Dolphin

MAMMAL FLIPPER e
LIMB BONES e¹

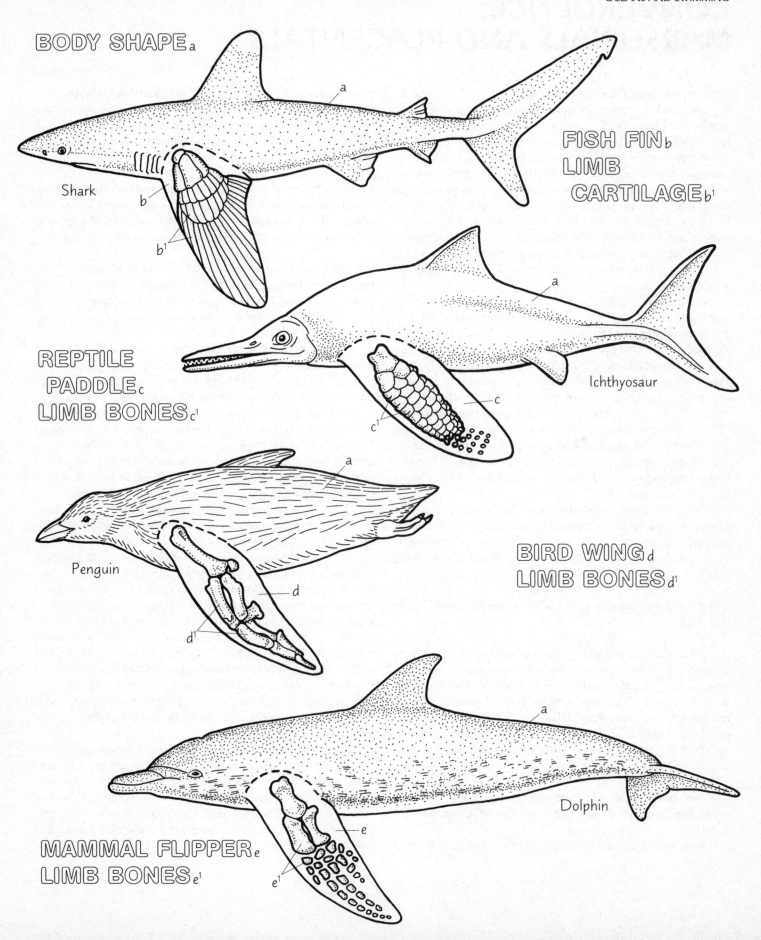

1-9
CONVERGENCE: MARSUPIALS AND PLACENTALS

Marsupials in Australia and placental mammals in North America provide another example of convergent evolution. These two subclasses of mammals have adapted in similar ways to a particular food supply, locomotor skill, or climate. They separated from some common ancestor more than 100 mya, and each lineage continued to evolve independently. Despite this great temporal and geographical separation, marsupials in Australia and placentals in North America have produced varieties of species living in similar habitats with similar ways of life. Their resemblances in overall shape, locomotor mode, and feeding and foraging are superimposed upon different modes of reproduction, the feature that accurately reflects their distinct evolutionary relationships.

Australia, a continent in the southern hemisphere, is the size of North America; 200 mya it was part of Gondwana, the large southern continent that included Africa, Madagascar, New Zealand, Antarctica, and South America (1-18). As Gondwana split up, Australia became isolated and has remained so for over 100 million years. Marsupials entered Australia before this separation and have evolved independently from placental mammals ever since. Marsupials had a similar and successful radiation in South America, which was also an island during this same time period. South America joined to North America as recently as 3 mya, through a land bridge, the Isthmus of Panama. Placental mammals invaded South America and replaced many marsupial species.

Over 200 species of marsupials live in Australia, along with many fewer species of placentals. The marsupials have undergone an adaptive radiation to occupy the diversity of habitats in Australia, just as the placentals have radiated across North America.

Color the placental embryo and adult within the map of North America.

Placental mammals are so called because a placenta connects the growing embryo within the uterus to the mother's circulatory system. The placenta provides the pathway for nourishing the fetus. This allows it to reach a higher level of maturity of body and brain prior to birth. Placental mammals invest more time and energy than marsupials in this early stage of growth. Placentals are much more numerous in North America and on most other continents than are marsupials.

Using a shade of the color you used for (a), color the adult marsupial and joey shown within the map of Australia.

Marsupial young begin life in the uterus but leave to enter the marsupium or pouch while they still qualify as embryos. With immature forelimbs they crawl into the pouch where they remain to complete their development. With their well-developed mouth and ability to suckle, they attach themselves to a teat to obtain milk.

Color each pair of animals, marsupial and placental, as they are discussed before moving on to the next pair. Choose two shades of a color for (b) and (b¹). Choose two shades of a different color for (c) and (c¹). Continue in this manner.

Marsupial mice, like placental mice in North America, are small, agile climbers inhabiting low shrubs. They live in dense ground cover and forage at night for small food items. The two mice exhibit similarities in size and body shape, and each group has numerous species.

Flying phalangers resemble flying squirrels. Both are gliders that eat insects and plants. Both the phalanger and squirrel have skin stretched between forelimbs and hindlimbs to provide greater surface area for gliding from one tree to the next.

Marsupial moles, like common moles in North America, burrow through soft soil to find and eat insects. The streamlined body shape, and the modified forelimbs for digging, facilitate an underground, insect-eating way of life (1-6). Velvety fur expedites smooth movement through the soil. The fur is white to orange in the marsupial mole and gray in the North American mole.

The wombat, like the North American groundhog, uses rodentlike teeth to eat roots and other plants. Both animals excavate burrows.

Rabbit-eared bandicoots resemble rabbits in North America. Both these animals have well-developed hindlimbs, which reflect their hopping form of locomotion, and their long ears emphasize the important role of hearing. The bandicoots have varied diets—some eat insects and plants; rabbits are exclusively vegetarian.

The Tasmanian wolf, a carnivorous marsupial resembling the placental wolf, inhabited mainland Australia as well as Tasmania. Its limb bones were long and adapted for running, and the skull and sharp teeth were adapted for tearing meat. Because it sometimes preyed on sheep and cattle, ranchers started a campaign to exterminate it (about 1900). The last Tasmanian wolf died in the Hobart Zoo in 1936.

Marsupial and placental mammals of Australia and North America illustrate one example of evolutionary convergence, where species not closely related resemble each other because they fill similar niches in each continent. In rain forest habitats of West Africa and South America, for example, or in the deserts of North America and Africa, other convergences in animal and plant life can be found.

MARSUPIALS AND PLACENTALS

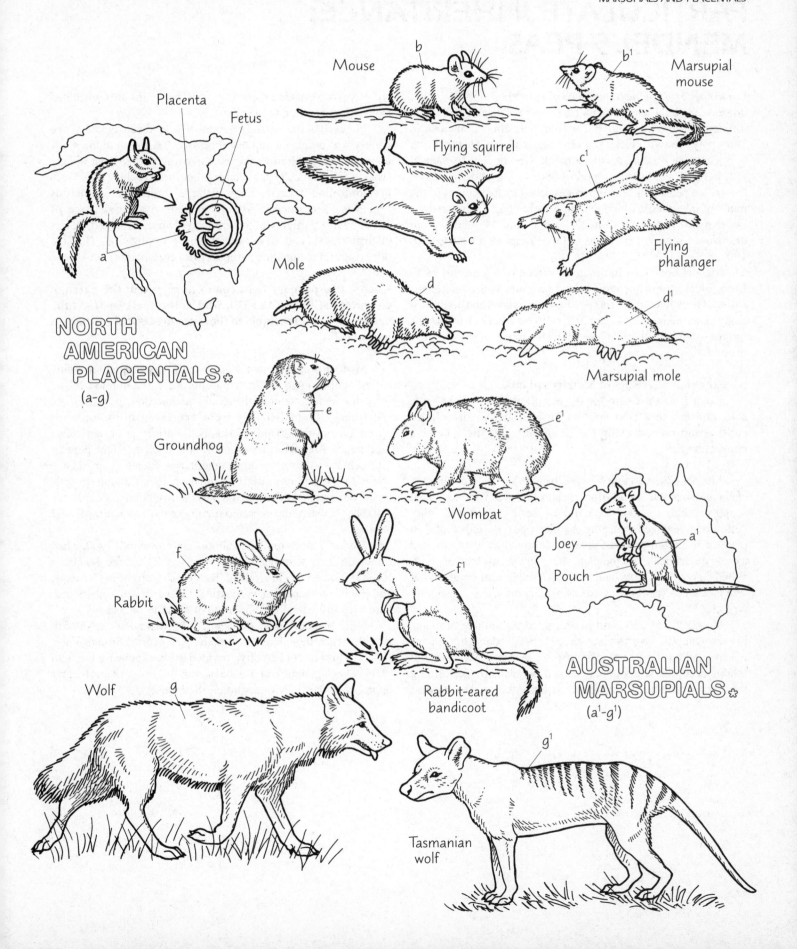

Placenta

Fetus

Mouse

b

b¹

Marsupial mouse

Flying squirrel

c¹

c

Flying phalanger

Mole

d

d¹

NORTH AMERICAN PLACENTALS ✶
(a-g)

a

Marsupial mole

Groundhog

e

e¹

Wombat

Joey

Pouch

a¹

Rabbit

f

f¹

AUSTRALIAN MARSUPIALS ✶
(a¹-g¹)

Wolf

g

Rabbit-eared bandicoot

g¹

Tasmanian wolf

1-10
PARTICULATE INHERITANCE: MENDEL'S PEAS

Darwin recognized the importance of individual variation in the process of natural selection, but could not explain how individual differences were transmitted from one generation to another. In 1866, only a few years after Darwin's publication of *On the Origin of Species*, an obscure Austrian monk, Gregor Johann Mendel (1822–1884), published a report of his breeding experiments on the garden pea plant. This report described many features of the mode of inheritance which Darwin was seeking. Unfortunately, Darwin did not read Mendel's work, and Mendel's great discoveries were not rediscovered by European scientists until 1900.

Mendel botanized in the quiet garden of his monastery in Brno, focusing his attention on the common sweet pea, genus *Pisum.* He meticulously recorded his observations and performed many experiments in order to confirm his results. Even by today's rigorous standards, Mendel's research is a model of the scientific method.

Note the characteristics of Mendel's plants.

Color gray the terms for the pea plant traits: seed shape, seed interior, seed coat, and so forth. Using shades of two contrasting colors, color the dominant and the recessive characteristics.

Mendel observed that his peas had seven easily observable characteristics that came in two, and only two, varieties. Seed shape was either smooth or wrinkled; seed interior was either yellow or green; seed coat, gray or white; ripe pods, either inflated or constricted; unripe pods, green or yellow; flowers positioned axially or terminally on the plant stem; and stems, long or short. When he crossed plants having smooth seeds with those having wrinkled seeds, the results were always smooth seeds, not slightly wrinkled ones.

Mendel noted and carefully recorded the number of plants in each generation with a given trait. He believed that the ratio of plant varieties in a generation of offspring would yield clues about inheritance, and he continually tested his ideas by performing more experiments. From these patient studies, the modest reclusive monk made a great discovery: how traits are transmitted from one generation to the next.

For each of the seven characteristics, he discovered that one variety was dominant and one recessive. Though it didn't show up in the first generation, the recessive trait did reappear in later crosses, in statistically predictable proportions (1-11, 1-12). From his controlled experiments and large samples of numerous breeding experiments, Mendel proposed the existence of fundamental particles of inheritance. These, he noted, act as distinct entities and do not blend during fertilization. Thus the offspring contain distinct particles from each parent.

Choose two primary light colors to represent the parental characteristics (a) and (b), and color the two test tube drawings. Color the liquid in the receiving test tube with both parent colors.

Mendel proposed that factors (or genes, as they are now called) contributed by both parents were maintained in the offspring in discrete units that could be inherited and passed on, regardless of whether they were expressed in the outward appearance of the offspring. This is the principle of particulate inheritance. Mendel's idea of inheritance challenged the popular 19th century notion of blending inheritance. Blending inheritance maintained that traits passed on from the parents through sex cells are blended in the offspring, like mixing two colored liquids in a test tube. No blending occurred for any of the characters Mendel studied.

Mendel's work remained almost unknown until 1900, when three scientists working independently rediscovered Mendel's laws: Hugo de Vries in Holland, Karl Erich Correns in Germany, and Erich von Tschermak in Austria. Modern views of inheritance date back to Mendel's formulation of his laws of heredity.

Since Mendel's time, the science of genetics has exploded in complexity. Although he knew nothing of genes, chromosomes, or DNA, his laws of heredity provided the backbone for the field of classical genetics and a basis for the modern molecular approach to the study of evolution (Section 2).

MENDEL'S PEAS

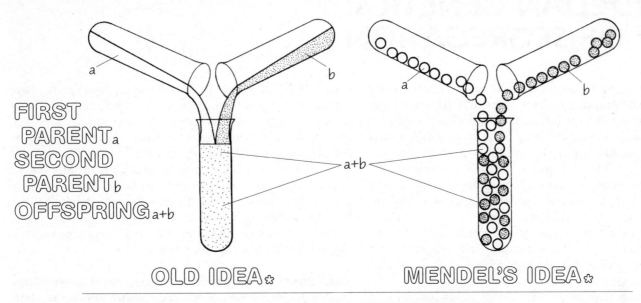

FIRST PARENT a
SECOND PARENT b
OFFSPRING a+b

a+b

OLD IDEA *   MENDEL'S IDEA *

MENDEL'S PEA PLANT CHARACTERISTICS *

DOMINANT c   RECESSIVE d

SEED SHAPE *
SMOOTH c¹   WRINKLED d¹
SEED INTERIOR *
YELLOW c²   GREEN d²
SEED COAT *
GRAY c³   WHITE d³
RIPE PODS *
INFLATED c⁴   CONSTRICTED d⁴
UNRIPE PODS *
GREEN c⁵   YELLOW d⁵
FLOWER *
AXIAL c⁶   TERMINAL d⁶
STEM *
LONG c⁷   SHORT d⁷

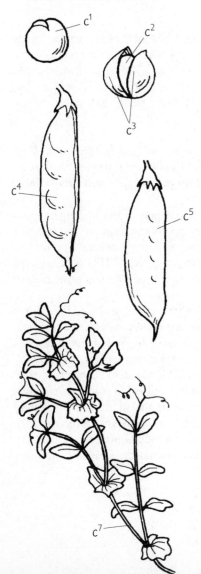

1-11
MENDELIAN GENETICS: LAW OF SEGREGATION

Mendel's Law of Segregation shows how variation is transmitted and reshuffled from one generation to the next. Although a trait may not express itself in each generation, it remains in the genetic makeup of individuals and may be recombined in a later generation. This first law of Mendel explains how the sorting or segregation of "factors" during meiosis (1-14) and their subsequent recombination during fertilization (6-1) can account for the sudden reappearance of recessive traits like wrinkled seeds in the second generation of hybrid offspring.

The discrete inheritable particles that Mendel called "factors" are now called genes. Genes are stretches of DNA molecules that carry the instructions for making proteins (2-4). Genes are arranged on a chromosome like beads on a string.

A gene may have more than one form. Such forms, called alleles, account for the variation in each of Mendel's pea plant characters. Alleles are found in the exact same position on homologous chromosomes and therefore occupy the same gene locus. Alleles differ from one another in a few nucleotide bases. Consequently, each allele codes for a slightly different sequence of amino acids, which results in protein variation (2-5).

Humans and sweet peas, like all organisms that have pairs of chromosomes, have two genes for each trait, one originating from the female parent, the other from the male parent. The genes may be identical with no variation, or a gene locus may have two or more alternate forms (alleles), as in the genes that determine blood type (6-13).

Mendel invented the system of referring to alleles with letters: capital letters stand for the dominant allele and small letters for the recessive allele. For example, R is the allele for smooth seeds, r, the allele for wrinkled seeds.

Follow the fate of the alleles for seed shape through two generations of cross-breeding, just as Mendel did. Start at the top of the plate, coloring the parent pea plants gray. Color the chromosomes (a) and the two alleles of the gene for seed shape (b) and (c). Don't use green or yellow.

A pair of matching or homologous chromosomes carries the alleles for seed shape in each individual.

Each of these parents has a homozygous genotype: the plant on the left for the smooth trait (RR) and the plant on the right for the recessive wrinkled trait (rr).

Color the phenotype of the parent plant seeds two different colors (d) and (e). Color the two genotypes beside the seeds.

Phenotype refers to the outward appearance of an individual, whereas genotype refers to the genetic makeup of an individual.

For example, pea plants with a smooth seed phenotype may have either of two genotypes: RR or Rr. The genotype RR is homozygous; the individual has inherited identical alleles from each parent. This is the case of the parent plant illustrated at the left. A genotype Rr is heterozygous: one of its parents contributed the R allele and the other, the r allele. Since the R allele for smooth is dominant to the r allele for wrinkled seeds, the phenotype of such a plant would be smooth seeds. Two different genotypes can still exhibit the smooth seed phenotype.

The parent plant illustrated at the right has the genotype rr and exhibits the wrinkled phenotype.

Color the arrows to represent the segregation of the seed shape alleles during meiosis. Continue coloring down the plate. Color the gametes, or sex cells, each of which contains one allele for seed shape. Follow the recombination of genes during fertilization. Color the first generation phenotypes and genotypes.

Now it becomes apparent why Mendel observed that, in the first generation, 100% were plants with smooth seeds. Each first generation pea plant contains a recessive allele for wrinkled seeds, but the allele for smooth seeds is completely dominant and prevents the wrinkled allele from being expressed in the phenotype.

Now color the recombination of genes from the first generation plants during fertilization. Complete the plate by coloring the second generation phenotypes and genotypes.

Observe what happens if the first generation of heterozygous genotypes interbreed. Gametes recombine, as the arrows indicate. Random mating produces plants with three different genotypes, one of which is a recessive homozygote, rr. This one genotype causes the wrinkled phenotype to reappear in this generation of offspring.

Mendel harvested over 7000 peas and observed the ratio of three smooth peas to every one wrinkled pea, a phenotypic ratio of 3:1. Through this observation, he deduced that maternally and paternally derived "factors" segregate into separate sex cells.

This segregation of genes that Mendel demonstrated provided Darwin's missing evidence on how variation is maintained over generations. In the formulation of the modern evolutionary synthesis, population geneticist Sewell Wright emphasized the shuffling of genes during sexual reproduction as a source of new genetic combinations and new variation while maintaining existing variation.

LAW OF SEGREGATION

PARENT PLANTS*

HOMOLOGOUS
  CHROMOSOMES_a
SEED SHAPE
  ALLELES: R_br_c

PHENOTYPE*
SMOOTH SEED_d
WRINKLED SEED_e
GENOTYPE*
HOMOZYGOUS R_bR_b
HOMOZYGOUS r_cr_c

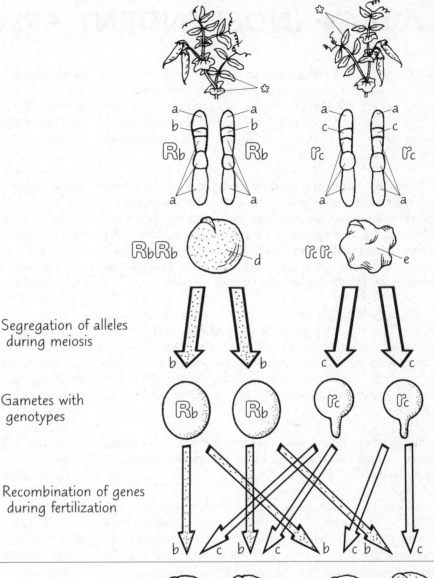

Segregation of alleles
during meiosis

Gametes with
genotypes

Recombination of genes
during fertilization

FIRST GENERATION*
SMOOTH SEED PHENOTYPE_d
HETEROZYGOUS GENOTYPE*

Recombination of genes
during fertilization

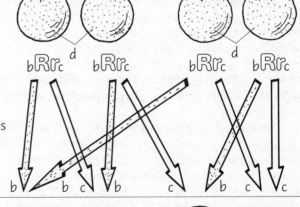

SECOND GENERATION*
PHENOTYPE* 3_d to 1_e
GENOTYPE* 1_b to 2_{bc} to 1_c

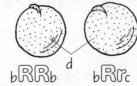
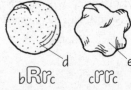

1-12
MENDELIAN GENETICS: LAW OF INDEPENDENT ASSORTMENT

Mendel showed how multiple characteristics, like seed shape and seed coat color are inherited simultaneously. This process is known as Mendel's Law of Independent Assortment. The traits sort independently because they are carried on different chromosomes, though of course, Mendel did not know about chromosomes.

Color the four chromosomes at the top of the plate that belong to one first generation plant. Color the alleles with the (b) and (c) colors from the previous plate, and add two more colors (not green or yellow) for (d) and (e). Color the phenotype and genotype of each first generation heterozygous parent. Use yellow for (y). Then, color the four parent chromosomes at the top left and right of the grid.

We consider four alleles: R=smooth, r=wrinkled, T=yellow, t=green. Now follow the fate of these four alleles when two plants mate. Each first generation parent has a heterozygous genotype for both seed color and seed shape: RrTt. The phenotype is smooth yellow seeds. The alleles segregate during meiosis (1-14) into gametes, or haploid sex cells, with half the full complement of chromosomes.

Color the arrows representing the segregation of alleles during gamete production (meiosis). Color the gamete genotypes which result.

Notice that homologous alleles are segregated from one another in the gametes. R, for example, is never found with r in a gamete. The chromosome carrying R, the allele for smooth seed coat, may pair with either T or t in a gamete. Similarly, the allele t, for green seed coat, may pair with allele R or r.

Each square on the grid represents the union of a gamete from each parent. The genotypes of the offspring are calculated by combining alleles from a gamete at the left of the grid with alleles contributed by a gamete at the right.

Color the offsprings' possible genotypes within the grid. Then color the possible seed coat phenotypes. Use green for (g).

Seed shape is determined by the alleles R and r. Offspring that are homologous RR or heterozygous Rr will all have smooth seeds. Only those offspring containing two alleles for wrinkled seed coat, rr, are phenotypically wrinkled. Seed color is determined by the alleles T and t. Homologous TT or heterozygous Tt offspring will have yellow seed coats. Only homozygous tt offspring will have green seed coats.

In the lower left corner, use your allele colors to color the genotypes for seed shape and seed coat color. Count the number of offspring genotypes RR, Rr, rr, and TT, Tt, and tt. Now determine that they occur in the 1:2:1 genotype ratio. Count and color the phenotype ratios.

As we found in the previous plate, each of the single traits, seed color and seed shape, yielded the phenotype frequency of 3:1. When combining two traits, Mendel found the ratio of 9:3:3:1; that is, of the 16 possibilities, there were 9 smooth, yellow-seeded plants, 3 smooth green-seeded plants, 3 wrinkled, yellow-seeded plants, and 1 wrinkled, green-seeded plant.

The mathematician Mendel saw how the 9:3:3:1 ratio for two characters was related statistically to the 3:1 ratio for an individual characteristic. If two traits are equally mixed during recombination, the two independent probabilities are multiplied. So, if 3/4 will be yellow-seeded, when two traits are combined, we still expect 3/4 yellow ones. Check this for yourself by counting the number of yellow-seeded plants; 12 are yellow. This number is obtained by adding the 9 that are yellow-seeded and also smooth, with the yellow-seeded ones that are also wrinkled, or **9**/16+**3**/16=12/16 or **3**/4. We also expect that 1/4 will be green-seeded. There are 4, or 4/16=**1**/4. This number is obtained by noting that of the 4, 3 of them are also smooth, and 1 is also wrinkled.

Similar reasoning for the smooth and wrinkled phenotypes shows that only 1 of the 16 plants is *both* green-seeded and wrinkled.

Whenever Mendel examined the inheritance of two pea plant traits together, he observed the phenotype ratio of 9:3:3:1. This observation led him to formulate, in 1865, the Law of Independent Assortment.

From his experiments, Mendel discovered that each of the seven pea plant traits is passed on independently. From this we would predict that each of Mendel's characters is located on a different pair of chromosomes. Plant geneticists studying *Pisum* have determined that pea plants have just seven pairs of chromosomes—or fourteen in all. Some people have argued that Mendel was extremely lucky to choose seven features whose gene loci lie on different homologous pairs of chromosomes rather than on the same chromosome (linked genes) (1-15). But, it is also the case that Mendel was a careful and shrewd observer, and fortune favors the prepared mind.

Mendel, like Darwin, made precise observations of inherited traits without knowledge of the actual genetic mechanisms. Now that we know about chromosomes, genes, and DNA, we can appreciate even more the scientific contributions of naturalists like Mendel and Darwin who discerned natural laws without modern technologies.

LAW OF INDEPENDENT ASSORTMENT

HOMOLOGOUS CHROMOSOMESₐ
SEED COAT ALLELES R b r c
SEED COLOR ALLELES T d t e

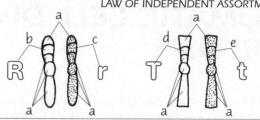

First generation heterozygous parent

$R_b r_c$ $T_d t_e$

Genotype   Phenotype

First generation heterozygous parent

Phenotype   Genotype $R_b r_c$ $T_d t_e$

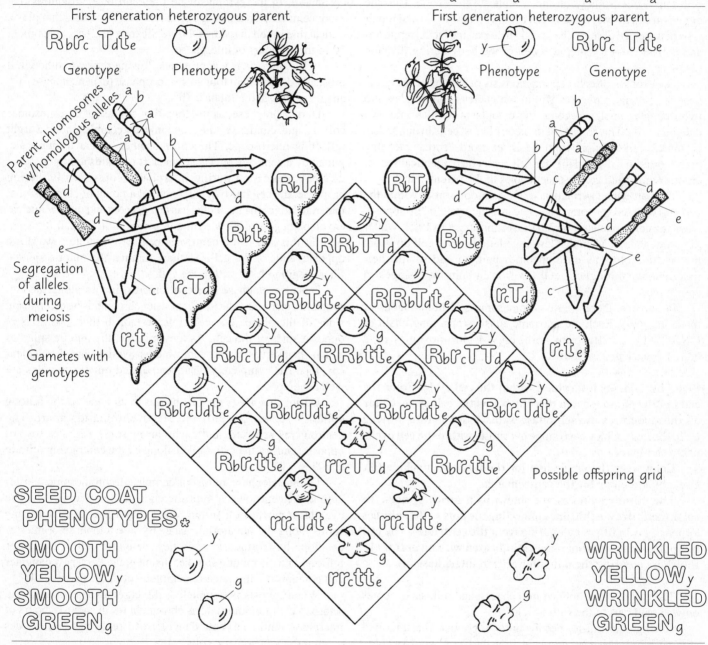

Parent chromosomes w/homologous alleles

Segregation of alleles during meiosis

Gametes with genotypes

$R_b T_d$ $R_b T_d$
$R_b t_e$ $R_b t_e$
$r_c T_d$ $r_c T_d$
$r_c t_e$ $r_c t_e$

$RR_b TT_d$

$RR_b T_d t_e$ $RR_b T_d t_e$

$R_b r_c TT_d$ $RR_b tt_e$ $R_b r_c TT_d$

$R_b r_c T_d t_e$ $R_b r_c T_d t_e$ $R_b r_c T_d t_e$ $R_b r_c T_d t_e$

$R_b r_c tt_e$ $rr_c TT_d$ $R_b r_c tt_e$

$rr_c T_d t_e$ $rr_c T_d t_e$

$rr_c tt_e$

Possible offspring grid

SEED COAT PHENOTYPES *

SMOOTH YELLOWᵧ
SMOOTH GREEₙ

WRINKLED YELLOWᵧ
WRINKLED GREEₙ

GENOTYPE RATIOS h

RR_b $R_b r_c$ rr_c

4 h to 8 h to 4 h

1 h to 2 h to 1 h

TT_d $T_d t_e$ tt_e

4 h to 8 h to 4 h

1 h to 2 h to 1 h

PHENOTYPE RATIOS i

9 i to 3 i to 3 i to 1 i

1-13
SOMATIC CELL DIVISION: MITOSIS

Our bodies are made up of millions of cells and, except for nerve cells and sex cells, they constantly replicate and divide. Thus the organism can grow, replace dead cells with new ones, and repair cells in damaged tissues. The genetic material, the DNA, replicates and is passed on to each new cell of the body during division (2-2).

The process of cell-copying consists of two parts: first, the genetic material replicates within the nucleus and divides into two daughter nuclei; second, the cytoplasm divides into two daughter cells. The process of division of most cells in our bodies is somatic cell division (from the Greek word, "soma" meaning body), or mitosis. The daughter cell nuclei have identical sets of chromosomes and genes, exact copies of the parent cell.

The nature and permanence of the chromosomes within the cell was debated for some time, because they would "disappear" when the cell's nucleus entered the resting stage. In 1903, Walter Sutton explained Mendel's laws in relationship to cell division; that is, homologous chromosomes pair up and retain their individuality throughout cell division in spite of changes in appearance.

In humans, there are 46 chromosomes, 23 homologous or matching pairs. Each chromosome consists of a long chain of DNA (2-1). To illustrate here, only 4 chromosomes or 2 homologous pairs are shown.

Begin by coloring interphase within the cell cycle. Color the cell in interphase located directly below the cell cycle. Color all the structures in each phase as discussed before moving on to the next. Color each stage of mitosis within the cell cycle, using shades of one color.

Color over the single line for the nuclear envelope (d). Use a bright color for the centromeres.

The mitotic spindles are shown as a series of dots. To color them, draw a thin line connecting the dots so the spindles appear as thin fibers emanating from the centrioles. The cell midpoint, or equatorial plane, is indicated with an arrow (j). Finish by coloring the daughter cells in interphase (a).

The cell cycle is divided into phases, and mitosis occupies only a small part of the entire cycle.

During interphase, before mitosis begins, the uncoiled chromosomes appear as chromatin, from the Greek word for color, referring to its affinity with a certain dye. Chromatin lies in a mass in the cell nucleus. The nuclear envelope, a porous membrane, encloses the nucleolus, which is intact, and the chromatin. In the cytoplasm lie the centrioles, structures that produce mitotic spindles, the small tubular structures that play a critical role in cell division. DNA replication (2-2) occupies about 10 of the 18 hours of interphase.

In life, mitosis is a continuous flowing process, although it is usually described in four stages: prophase (b^1), metaphase (b^2), anaphase (b^3), and telophase (b^4).

During prophase, as the long thin strands of chromosomes coil up and condense, they become detectable under a light reflecting microscope. The chromosomes appear in duplicate, joined by a centromere. These sister chromatids are the product of DNA replication during interphase; consequently, during prophase, the cell has twice the normal amount of chromosomal material. Notice the nucleolus has disappeared and that the nuclear envelope begins to disintegrate in preparation for cell division. Also at this stage, the centrioles begin to migrate toward the opposite ends of the cell. As they migrate, the mitotic spindle fibers begin to form within the cell.

During metaphase, the centromeres line up along the cell equatorial plane, and the identical sister chromatids lie on opposite sides of the plane. The centrioles establish their positions at opposite ends of the cell. As they migrate, the mitotic spindles attach themselves to the centromeres. Notice that the nuclear envelope has completely disappeared, and mitotic spindles are well developed.

During anaphase, the cell begins to elongate as the mitotic spindles seemingly pull the sister chromatids apart. The centromeres separate, and each chromosome migrates toward opposite ends of the cell, pulled along by the contracting mitotic spindles.

During telophase, mitosis is completed; chromosomes cluster around the centrioles at opposite ends of the dividing cell. The cytoplasm pinches off in the center, and a new cell membrane forms along the equatorial plane. By late telophase, a nuclear envelope has formed in each new daughter cell; a nucleolus reforms, and the mitotic spindles disintegrate. Each new daughter cell contains the full genetic complement of the parent cell.

When mitosis is completed, the chromosomes uncoil and return to their random state as chromatin for the next 18 hours of interphase until each new daughter cell replicates and divides again into more somatic cells.

MITOSIS

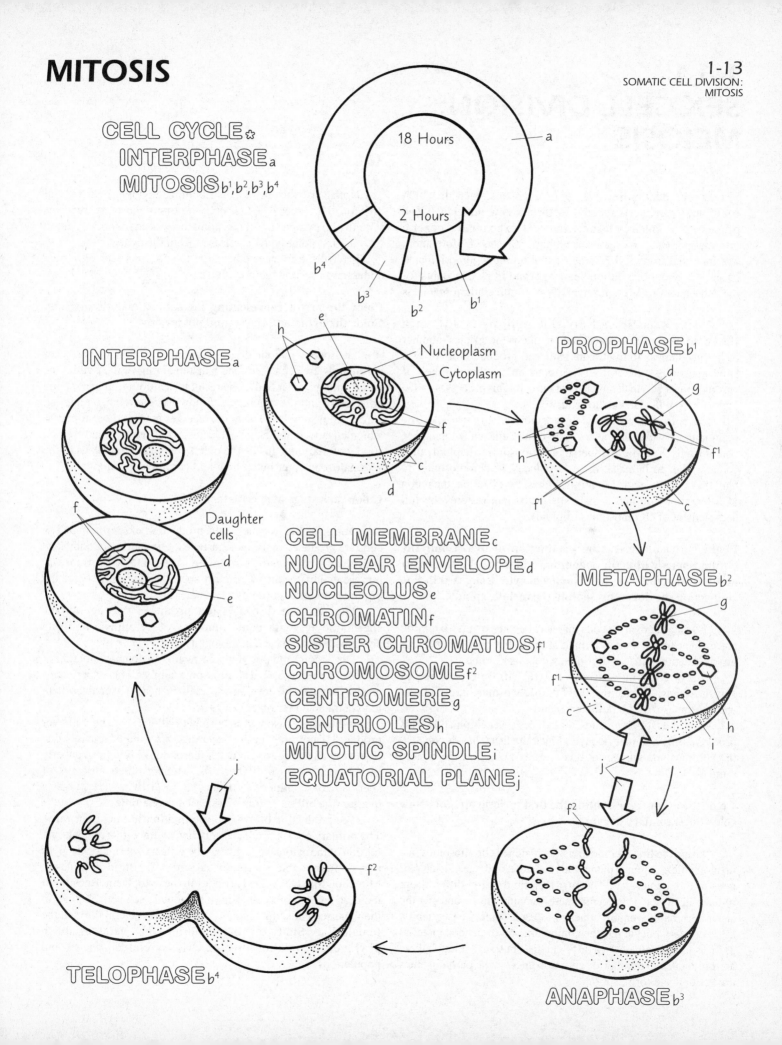

CELL CYCLE ❋
INTERPHASE a
MITOSIS b¹,b²,b³,b⁴

18 Hours

2 Hours

a

b⁴

b³

b²

b¹

INTERPHASE a

h

e

Nucleoplasm
Cytoplasm

f

c

d

PROPHASE b¹

d

g

i

h

f¹

f¹

c

f

d

e

Daughter
cells

CELL MEMBRANE c
NUCLEAR ENVELOPE d
NUCLEOLUS e
CHROMATIN f
SISTER CHROMATIDS f¹
CHROMOSOME f²
CENTROMERE g
CENTRIOLES h
MITOTIC SPINDLE i
EQUATORIAL PLANE j

METAPHASE b²

g

f¹

c

h

i

j

j

f²

f²

TELOPHASE b⁴

ANAPHASE b³

1-14
SEX CELL DIVISION: MEIOSIS

Sexual reproduction involves two organisms, each of which contributes hereditary material to form a new individual. The process is a means of shuffling and exchanging genetic information. The new organism combines two sets of information; one inherited from each parent. Sexual reproduction originated in animals about one billion years ago, and in part accounts for the subsequent increase in diversity of multicellular organisms (1-19).

During somatic cell division, mitosis (1-13), each chromosome duplicates itself and maintains the species' number of chromosomes, 46 in humans. Sex cell production involves a special process of cell division to halve the number of chromosomes within the nucleus of the cell. This process is called meiosis, from the Greek, "to reduce."

Sex cells are produced in specialized organs, like the mammalian ovaries and testes. These sex cells, called gametes, contain only half the number of chromosomes (haploid) of a somatic cell. In humans, meiosis reduces 46 chromosomes to haploid sex cells, with 23 chromosomes. Fertilization, the union of a female ovum and a male spermatozoon, restores the full complement of chromosomes (diploid).

Begin with oogenesis, the production of ova. Color the chromosomes within the oogonium, and then color the arrow and the structures in the primary oocyte. Color a thin line connecting the dots representing the meiotic spindle.

Oogonia are ovarian cells that may become ova. Two million are present in the human female at birth, but only around four hundred actually mature during a woman's lifetime.

The oogonium contains the full diploid number of chromosomes. We follow the fate of two matching pairs of chromosomes (two homologous pairs).

When the DNA replicates, it produces sister chromatids. This process forms a primary oocyte. Since the DNA has duplicated, the chromosome number at this stage is two times the diploid number.

Color the arrow representing the first meiotic division. Now color the secondary oocyte.

During the first meiotic division, matched chromosomes line up along the equatorial plane, then separate, and one of each pair goes to a daughter cell. The first meiotic division differs from mitosis in that: (1) the centromere remains intact; and (2) the sister chromatids remain attached to each other. Consequently, the secondary oocyte has the similar amount of genetic material as in a somatic cell, but in a different distribution. Although there are only half the number of chromosomes, those chromosomes are in duplicate form.

Notice also the unequal distribution of cytoplasm at this cell division. The other daughter cell, the first polar body, receives virtually no cytoplasm. At this point the secondary oocyte, along with its first polar body, is released from the ovary (6-1).

If fertilization takes place after the oocyte's release, it then undergoes a second meiotic division.

Color the arrow representing the second meiotic division. Color the ovum and the second polar body.

The second meiotic division is similar to mitosis. The sister chromatids are separated, one half remaining in the ovum, one half forming a polar body. The result is the formation of a second polar body and the ovum, which now has the requisite haploid chromosome number. The ovum receives most of the cytoplasm, which ensures that the zygote, or fertilized egg, will have a rich supply of nutrients. Inside the ovum, the male pronucleus of the spermatozoan contributes a haploid chromosome number.

Color each stage of spermatogenesis.

During spermatogenesis, the production of sperm, male sex cells are produced in the male testicles. The spermatogonia have a diploid chromosome number. After DNA replication, represented by the arrow, primary spermatocytes have twice the diploid amount of chromosomal material.

The first meiotic division produces two secondary spermatocytes with equal amounts of cytoplasm and one chromosome from each homologous pair.

The second meiotic division results in four spermatids of identical size and haploid chromosome number. These spermatids grow a long tail and develop a specialized head that enables them to penetrate and fertilize the egg.

In humans, a woman is born with all the ova she will ever produce. If not pregnant or lactating, she usually releases one egg every 28 days throughout her reproductive life, from puberty in her teen years until her 40s. Men produce millions of spermatozoa continuously from the onset of puberty. Over a quarter of a billion sperm are released at one time.

The production of ova and sperm differ in important ways. The primary oocyte produces only one ovum with a much larger portion of the cytoplasm, whereas the primary spermatocyte gives rise to four viable spermatozoa with very little cytoplasm. Mitochondrial DNA (2-11) resides in the cytoplasm. Because of the high amount of cytoplasm in the female sex cells, but not in the male sex cells, mitochondrial DNA is passed on through the female line. Study of mitochondrial DNA helps establish phylogenetic relationships of closely related species and populations.

MEIOSIS

CHROMOSOMES a
   SISTER CHROMATIDS a¹
CENTROMERE b
DNA REPLICATION c

CENTRIOLE d
MEIOTIC SPINDLE e
FIRST MEIOTIC DIVISION f
SECOND MEIOTIC DIVISION g

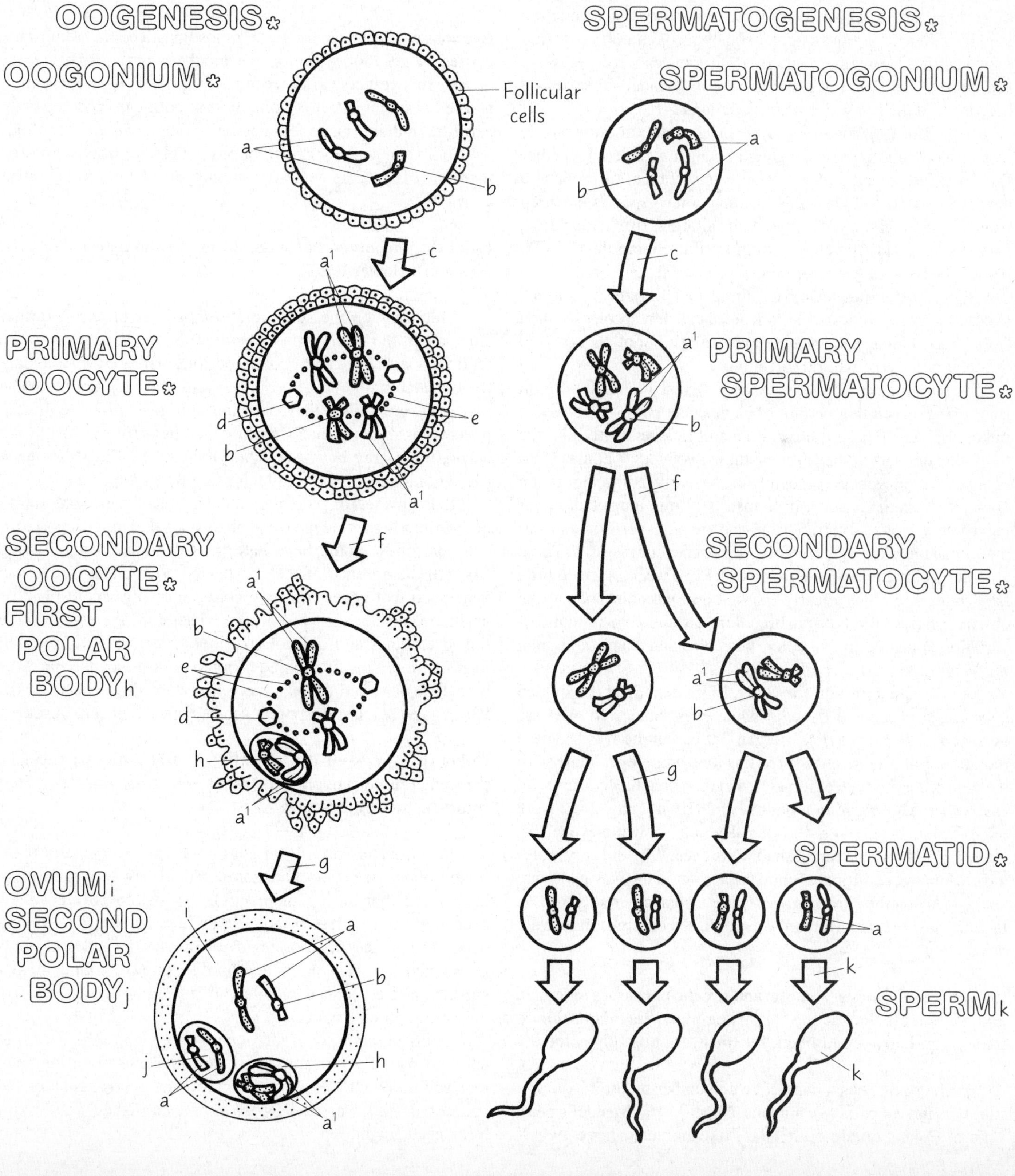

OOGENESIS *

SPERMATOGENESIS *

OOGONIUM *

SPERMATOGONIUM *

Follicular cells

PRIMARY OOCYTE *

PRIMARY SPERMATOCYTE *

SECONDARY OOCYTE *
FIRST POLAR BODY h

SECONDARY SPERMATOCYTE *

SPERMATID *

OVUM i
SECOND POLAR BODY j

SPERM k

1-15
FRUIT FLIES, MUTATIONS, AND LINKED GENES

Variation underlies the formation of new species, Darwin concluded. Individuals with traits that give them some advantage over others, however small, will survive and reproduce in greater numbers. What is the source of the variation? During eight years of work on barnacles (Cirripedia), Darwin observed that variation among individuals arose spontaneously through normal sexual reproduction. He realized inherited differences were necessary for natural selection, but was unaware of Mendel's theories on heredity and the transmission of variation (1-10).

In the late 19th century, another piece of the variation puzzle was added. Hugo DeVries, a Dutch botanist, wondered whether Darwin's idea of natural selection was sufficient to produce a new species. To test Darwin's idea that a new species emerged from the accumulation of many small variations over a long time, DeVries studied the evening primrose. From more than 53,000 plants, 8 new varieties appeared spontaneously and bred true in subsequent generations. DeVries introduced the term "mutation" to describe the new forms. He concluded that new species resulted from large sudden changes that produced new variation, not from the slow process of natural selection.

Elaborating on Mendel's research, British biologist William Bateson observed that certain traits in sweet peas seemed to be linked together. These traits did not sort independently like the traits Mendel had studied. To test these two ideas, Thomas Hunt Morgan began genetic research in the early 20th century on *Drosophila melanogaster*, little insects (4 mm long) that hover persistently around overripe fruit, and are giant performers from the animal kingdom in the ongoing saga of genetic research. These animals produce a new generation every two weeks, take up little lab space, and show clearly marked and variable phenotypic characteristics. By normal breeding, an amazing amount of variation appeared in eye color, wing size and shape, abdomen markings, and bristle arrangement.

A year and a million flies later, Morgan noticed the sudden appearance of a male fly with white eyes. Since red eyes are normal and dominant (R), Morgan felt certain he was seeing a mutation. Initially he cross-bred this lone white-eyed male with the wild red-eyed type of females, and then bred the hybrids with each other. Morgan found that out of 3470 progeny, 2459 were red-eyed females, 1011 red-eyed males, and 782 white-eye males. However, not a single female had white eyes. Why did only males have white eyes? Morgan found the answer in the way genes are "packaged" on the chromosomes, the carriers of heredity (1-13). In 1905, just prior to Morgan's research, sex chromosomes were discovered.

Color the four pairs of somatic and sex chromosomes in female and male fruit flies at the top of the plate. Use light colors. Reserve red, gray, and black for the eyes and body color.

Each species has a characteristic number of chromosomes: fruit flies have 4 pairs (8); humans, 23 pairs (46); Mendel's peas, 7 pairs (14). Female fruit flies, like humans, have two X chromosomes (XX); males have one X and a Y (XY). All eggs have an X. Half the sperm have an X, the other half, a Y.

Color the phenotype and the genotype of the two fruit flies.

Eye color is carried on the sex chromosomes. The X chromosome carries the gene for eye color (R), and the Y chromosome carries no gene for eye color (–). Since females have two X chromosomes, and red is dominant, it is unlikely that both chromosomes will carry the mutant (r), so females rarely have white eyes. Males have only one gene for eye color on a single X chromosome and therefore express the white-eye phenotype whenever the mutant appears.

Color the phenotype and genotype of the wild type and mutant flies on the lower left.

Mutations on the somatic chromosomes provided further clues about the production of new variation. In contrast to the wild flies with gray body color and long wings (BV), a mutant fly appeared with black body color and tiny vestigial remnants of wings (bv). When they bred through generations, only two phenotypes appeared: half were black-vestigial (bv), and half were normal with gray body color and long wings (BV). No black flies with long wings or gray with tiny wings appeared.

If the two sets of genes sorted independently, then one-fourth of the offspring would have had black body and long wings (bV), and one-fourth would have had gray body and vestigial wing (Bv). In the absence of these expected combinations, Morgan concluded that genes for body color and wing length must be positioned on the same chromosome. Therefore, these genes were linked together and did not sort independently during sexual reproduction. This finding led Morgan to map the inheritance of more than one hundred characters. He established four groups of linked genes, each corresponding to one of the four chromosomes.

Color the genes on the somatic chromosomes in meiosis, through crossing over, and in the resulting gametes. Then color the new phenotypes.

In further research, Morgan noted that occasionally these linked genes broke up and combined in new ways. Morgan discovered that during meiosis (1-14), paired chromosomes exchange parts with each other, a process he named "crossing over." The process of "crossing over" unlinks the genes, changes the sequence of base pairs, and produces new combinations of gametes and associated phenotypes, including the bV and Bv that he hadn't observed early on.

Morgan, along with Hermann Muller who used x-rays to damage fruit fly chromosomes and increase mutation rate, received a Nobel Prize for this experimental work. Mutations as sources of new variation were now established as a major influence in evolution.

MUTATIONS AND LINKED GENES

SOMATIC CHROMOSOMES a
SEX CHROMOSOME *
  X b Y c
PHENOTYPE *
  RED EYE d
  WHITE EYE e
GENOTYPE *
  RED EYE d¹
  WHITE EYE e¹

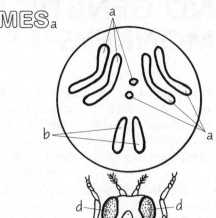
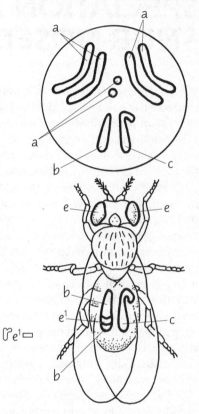

$R_{d¹} R_{d¹}$ $r_{e¹} —$

SOMATIC
  CHROMOSOME
  LINKAGE *
PHENOTYPE *
  GRAY BODY f
  BLACK BODY g
  LONG WING h
  VESTIGIAL WING i
GENOTYPE *
  ALLELES *
    $B_{f¹} b_{g¹}$
    $V_{h¹} v_{i¹}$

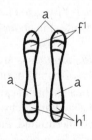

WILD * $B_{f¹} V_{h¹}$

Meiosis   Crossing over   Gametes

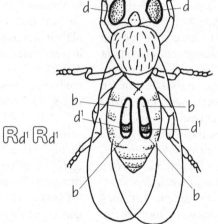

$B_{f¹} V_{h¹} B_{f¹} V_{h¹}$ $b_{g¹} v_{i¹} b_{g¹} v_{i¹}$ $B_{f¹} V_{h¹}$ $B_{f¹} v_{i¹}$

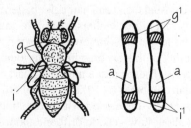

MUTANT * $b_{g¹} v_{i¹}$

NEW PHENOTYPES *

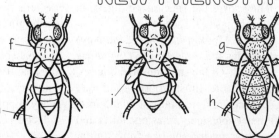

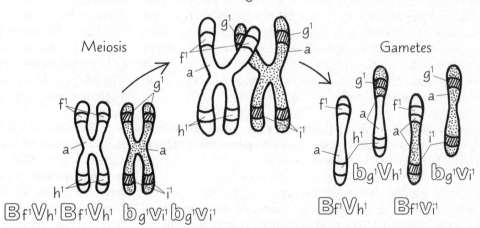

1-16
SPECIATION AND GENETIC DRIFT: SNUB-NOSED MONKEYS

While geneticists argued that mutation accounted for the production of new species, field biologists observed only gradual changes in populations over time. Population geneticist Sewall Wright introduced the concept of genetic drift and added a fourth mechanism of evolutionary change to natural selection, migration (now called gene flow), and mutation.

Genetic drift, also referred to as "the small population effect" or "sampling variation" was so called because of Wright's observations on guinea pigs. When individuals from the same lineage were separated into two groups and inbred, they "drifted apart" in appearance. Wright hypothesized that genetic drift might operate when a small number of individuals become isolated from a larger population. The few individuals reshuffle limited variation, and without gene flow new mutations more easily become fixed. The isolated population eventually "drifts" from the parent population. At the same time, natural selection shapes the small population to survive under new environmental conditions. Thus, working in combination with natural selection and new mutations, genetic drift contributes to speciation.

The snub-nosed monkeys illustrate how genetic drift may account for the highly divergent appearance among four species of *Rhinopithecus*. The research, of primatologist Nina Jablonski and her Chinese and Vietnamese colleagues, on the anatomy, paleontology, and behavioral ecology of these rare and endangered monkeys adds another piece to the evolutionary puzzle.

About one million years ago, the geographic range of *Rhinopithecus* was widespread in eastern Asian forests. As climate became more severe with prolonged cold and dry periods, the habitats of *Rhinopithecus* populations became fragmented, interrupting and reducing gene flow. The surviving, now isolated and less widely distributed populations became concentrated in ancient and remote forests that were most protected from environmental deterioration.

Color each species and its current range. You may wish to color the distinguishing features of each species using natural colors as described in the text.

Four species of *Rhinopithecus* survive in sheltered, relatively secluded areas, in subtropical or temperate montane forests between 1000 and 4500 meters in altitude in China and northern Vietnam. They are similar in aspects of behavior, anatomy, and overall appearance, especially in the distinctive nose shape that gives the genus its name. They share the specialized digestion with other colobine or "leaf monkeys" (3-1, 4-20).

The Vietnamese *R. avunculus*, (Tonkin snub-nosed monkey) is the most tropical and resembles the douc langur (*Pygathrix nemaeus*) of Indochina to the south. Of the snub-nosed monkeys, the Tonkin species is the most gracile, most arboreal, and may most closely resemble the ancestral population. It inhabits subtropical forests at 1000 meters on steep limestone cliffs and consumes a diet of leaves and both unripe and ripe fruit, similar to other colobines. Two isolated groups total only 130 to 350 animals. Adults are black on the back and outer limbs, with creamy white inner limbs, white head, orange throat, and pale blue face.

At the other climatic extreme, *R. bieti* (Yunnan or Biet's snub-nosed monkey) lives under the most severe conditions. It inhabits evergreen forests between 3000 and 4500 meters, the highest altitude of any nonhuman primate. Temperatures in the mountains in Yunnan Province average below freezing several months of the year, and snow accumulates to over a meter. Amazingly, 80% of their diet consists of hanging lichens, supplemented by seasonal leaves, fruits, and seeds. The total population is between 1000 and 1500. The back, head, legs, and tail have gray to black hair; the flanks, chest and front of the neck are white. The *R. bieti* face is gray to white with a pinkish muzzle.

R. brelichi (Guizhou or Brelich's snub-nosed monkey) lives in mixed deciduous and coniferous forests at 1500 to 2200 meters in the Wuling Mountains of Guizhou Province. It survives snow and cold, although average temperatures do not fall below freezing in winter. Their diet changes dramatically through the year with the availability of young leaves and buds, fruits and seeds, barks, and insect larvae. A single population of 800 to 1200 survives. Body hair is brown to gray with golden chest and inner arms. The head is black with a golden brow; the face has white skin with a blue tinge.

R. roxellana (golden or Sichuan snub-nosed monkey) has the widest geographic distribution and largest population (8000–10,000). It lives in separate mountain ranges around the Sichuan Basin, in mixed deciduous and coniferous forests 1200 to 3000 meters high. The proportions of leaves, seeds, flowers, and lichens in the diet fluctuate seasonally. The mantle of bright golden hair around the shoulders gives them their name. The pelage (hair) on the back is brown to black, with white inner thighs and arms, and bluish white skin under the eyes and around the mouth.

These four species of *Rhinopithecus* are isolated today but once were part of a widely distributed and probably single, variable species. With a fragmented habitat preventing gene flow, the small number of individuals within each surviving population interbred and so recombined the limited variation. As a result, the populations "drifted" from each other as they responded to the selection pressures of local conditions. Over time, each population became a little different, and in succeeding generations developed into new species. Unusual facial and hair color patterns became fixed along with new mutations. Jablonski suggests that the bright and distinctive face and body coloration of each species may have enhanced the visibility of the few breeding individuals in adjacent groups in the forests. These unique monkeys, part of the adaptive radiation of Asian colobines (4-19), have been little known until now and are severely threatened with extinction. They supply valuable clues about how genetic drift and natural selection can together produce new species.

SNUB-NOSED MONKEYS

RHINOPITHECUS DISTRIBUTION *

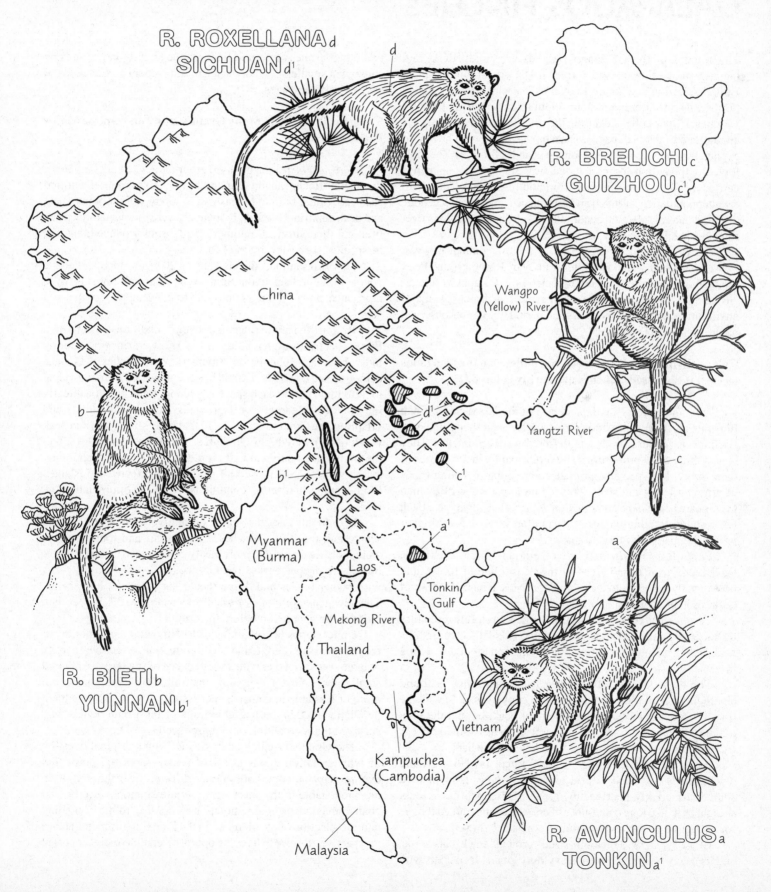

R. ROXELLANA d
SICHUAN d¹

R. BRELICHI c
GUIZHOU c¹

R. BIETI b
YUNNAN b¹

R. AVUNCULUS a
TONKIN a¹

China

Wangpo
(Yellow) River

Yangtzi River

Myanmar
(Burma)

Laos

Tonkin
Gulf

Mekong River

Thailand

Vietnam

Kampuchea
(Cambodia)

Malaysia

1-17
NATURAL SELECTION IN ACTION: GALÁPAGOS FINCHES

The finches of the Galápagos Islands are small, dark, and inconspicuous; they played a role in Darwin's thinking about natural selection and so are known as Darwin's finches. When his friend, orthnithologist John Gould confirmed that the 13 varieties of finch collected during the voyage were distinct species and unique to the Galápagos, Darwin was faced with having to explain how they got to these isolated islands (1-1, 1-2). The most logical explanation, he concluded, was that prevailing winds carried a few ancestral finches from South America. This small founder population survived and reproduced, and through genetic drift and natural selection accumulated sufficient variations over time to establish a variety of new species.

Darwin thought of speciation as a slow, gradual process. However, the remarkable long-term study by Rosemary and Peter Grant and their colleagues documented how Galápagos finches changed significantly over a few generations, in response to major environmental events. Over a 20 year period, the Grants observed natural selection in action!

Color each finch beak, the tool it resembles, and the food items as each is discussed. Finches are darkly colored.

From the largest island, Isabela, 5 of the 10 species of finch illustrate the diversity in body size, beak size and shape, and diet. Each species varies in body length from 7 to 12 centimeters. They have similar body proportions and differ mainly in the shapes of their beaks. The species minimize competition by eating foods of different kinds and sizes. This led biologist Robert Bowman to compare beak shape and function with distinct tool types. Each beak shape is adapted for a particular way of grasping or processing particular food items.

Platyspiza crassirostris, a "vegetarian" finch, eats buds, leaves, and fruit in tall trees in the dense, humid forest, and occasionally descends to the ground for seeds. It has a thick, short beak resembling gripping pliers.

Certhidea olivacea, the "warbler" finch, so closely resembles the unrelated warbler that even Darwin mistook them at first. Its beak is thin, adapted for eating both flying and ground-dwelling insects.

The "woodpecker" finch, *Cactospiza pallidus*, is found chiefly in trees of more humid zones. It converges (1-8) with the true woodpecker in its long and straight beak, but not the long tongue. Instead, this finch is a tool-user: it carries a small twig or cactus spine to dislodge insects from beneath the bark.

Geospiza scandens, the "cactus" finch, is also a ground dweller. It is restricted to arid lowlands, where its main food source, the prickly pear cactus, grows. This finch has a long, straight beak like long chain-nose pliers, and a long, forked tongue for extracting nectar and soft pulp from cactus flowers.

Geospiza fortis, a medium-sized "ground" finch, eats seeds, and its heavy beak resembles heavy-duty pliers. It coexists with two other species of ground finches, one slightly larger and one somewhat smaller. Each of these ground feeders prefers seeds of slightly different sizes.

Color the illustration of the Grant's study on Daphne Major Island.

Geospiza fortis, the medium ground finch, and *G. scandens*, the cactus finch, inhabit Daphne Major. The Grants identified each individual bird and measured its body weight, wing span, and beak depth and breadth. Individuals were followed throughout life, and their survival, number of offspring produced, and the offsprings' survival were tracked.

This information, collected during 20 years, documented the course of natural selection. Some individuals did not survive to reproduce, and so did not contribute to the gene pool of the next generation.

To confirm natural selection, several conditions must be met. First, the traits under study must show variability among individuals in the population. Among *G. fortis* finches, the Grants demonstrated that body size and beak depth varied from individual to individual within each species. Second, traits must be directly inherited from parent to offspring. By measuring parents and offspring, the Grants demonstrated that body size (91%) and beak depth (74%) were highly heritable. Third, the traits must affect the individual's survival and reproduction. During the Grants' study, wide swings in rainfall profoundly affected the island's food supplies and set up conditions for competition among the birds.

In drought years, the supply of relatively soft seeds became scarce and 6 out of 7 finches died! Larger and tougher seeds were more available and more easily cracked and eaten by larger birds with deeper beaks. The Grants showed that the *G. fortis* with bigger bodies and deeper beaks survived at a higher rate. The new generation of *G. fortis* beaks were 4 to 5% bigger than those in the generation before the drought.

Under opposite conditions of El Niño and eight months of record-breaking rainfall and seed production, a relative scarcity of large seeds, together with an abundance of small seeds, favored small finches. Given their particular traits, individual finches are more or less able to compete successfully for food. Subsequent populations retain the heritable traits of those individuals who survived those conditions and reproduced.

The Grant's research addresses Darwin's original question of why variation exists at all. It underscores the point that evolutionary outcomes are neither directed over the long term nor predictable in the short term, but are situation specific and change may occur in any direction, according to the prevailing natural selection of the moment. In the long run, from the species perspective, it's nice to have the option of smaller or bigger beaks!

GALÁPAGOS FINCHES

FINCHES*
VEGETARIAN$_a$
WARBLER$_b$
WOODPECKER$_c$
CACTUS$_d$
GROUND$_e$
TOOLS$_{a^1, b^1, c^1, d^1, e^1}$

DIET*
BUDS, LEAVES
FRUIT$_{a^2}$
INSECTS$_{b^2}$
LARVAE$_{c^2}$
CACTUS$_{d^2}$
SEEDS$_{e^2}$

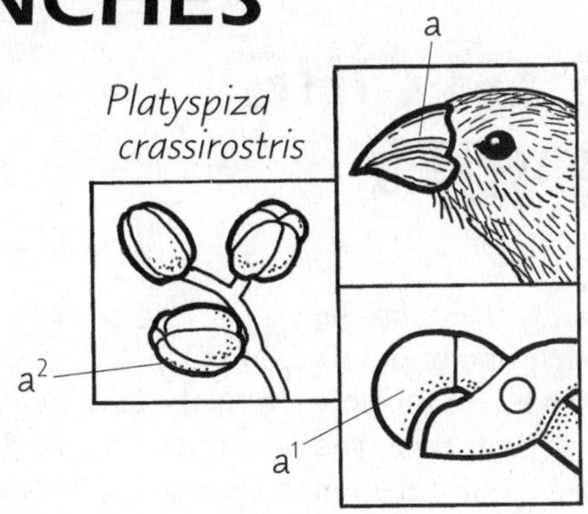

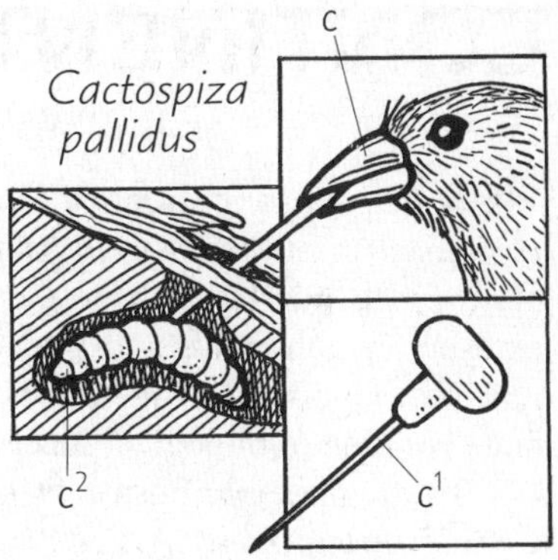

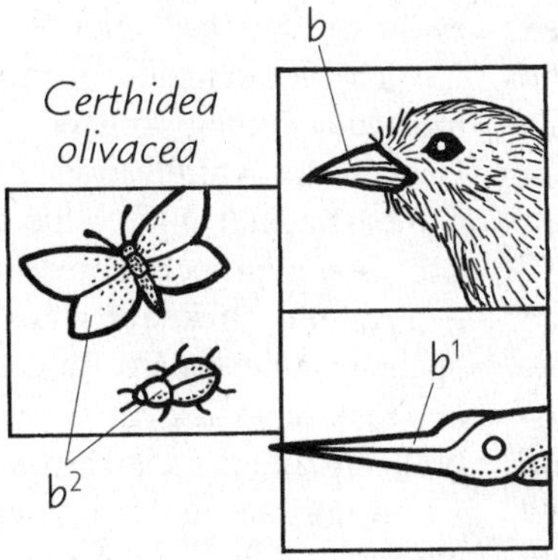

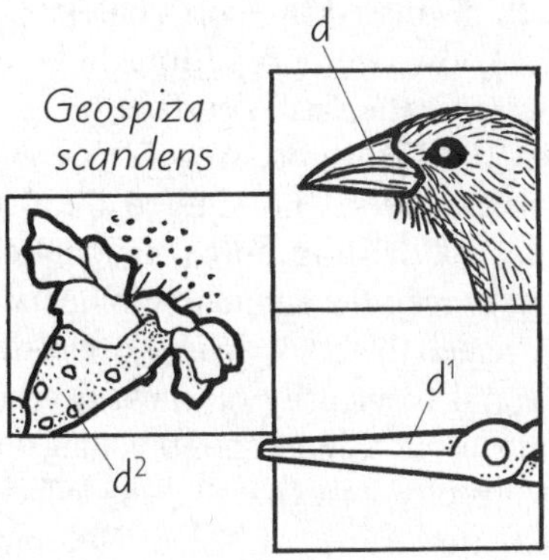

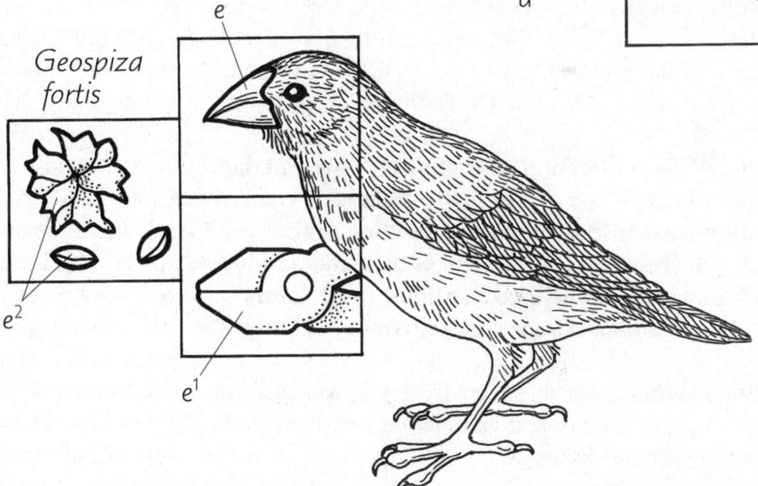

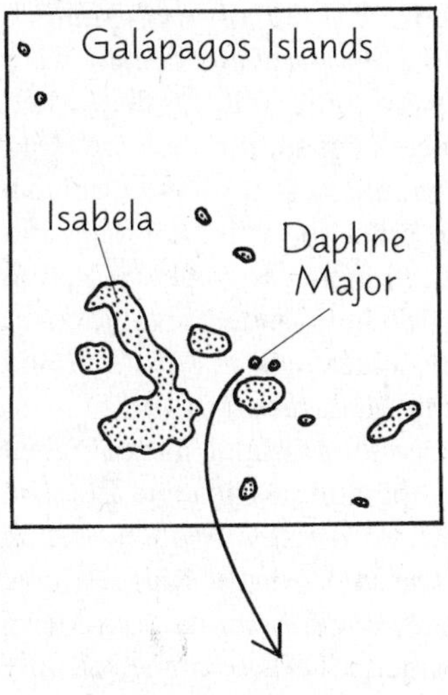

a
Platyspiza
crassirostris
a²
a¹

c
Cactospiza
pallidus
c²
c¹

b
Certhidea
olivacea
b¹
b²

d
Geospiza
scandens
d¹
d²

e
Geospiza
fortis
e²
e¹

Galápagos Islands
Isabela
Daphne
Major

DAPHNE MAJOR STUDY*
DROUGHT$_f$
BEAK, BODY SIZE
INCREASE$_{f^1}$
EL NIÑO$_g$
BEAK, BODY SIZE
DECREASE$_{g^1}$
DEAD FINCHES$_{e^3}$

Drought
El Niño
f
g
Beak, body size
f¹
g¹
e²
e³
Time

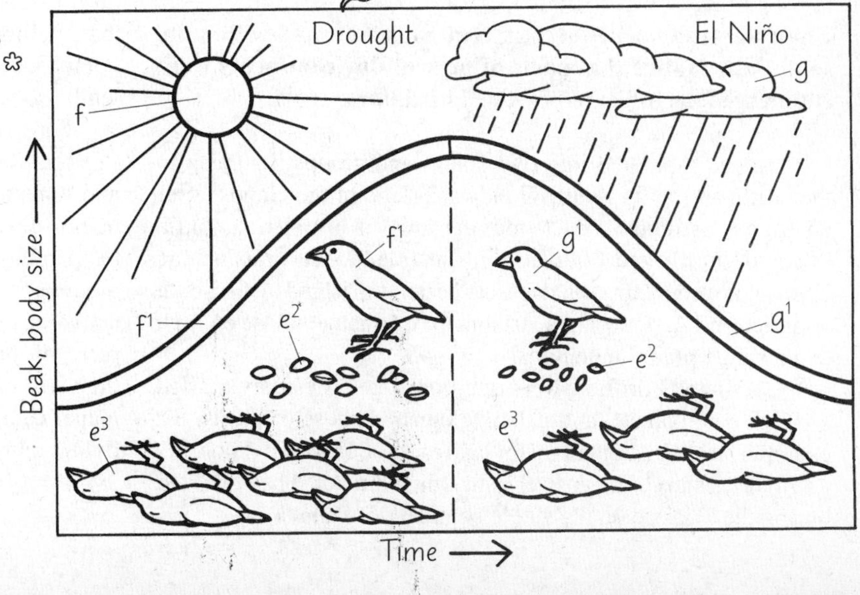

1-18
THE CHANGING GLOBE: CONTINENTAL DRIFT

When Darwin experienced earthquakes and volcanos, he recognized that the earth is a dynamic ever-changing powerhouse. Neither he nor his contemporaries could appreciate how extensively continents and oceans have altered over time, and how profoundly those alterations have affected the distribution and evolution of biological species (1-1).

The remarkable jigsaw fit of the continental margins led German meteorologist Alfred Wegener (1915) to suspect that the continents might have once formed a single giant landmass. This notion was dismissed by most geologists, since no mechanism was then known for propelling huge continents like giant battleships over the earth's surface.

From 1950 onwards, Wegener's conjecture was supported by oceanographers who studied the ocean floor using new techniques of drilling cores, magnetic surveys, and echo-soundings to map the submarine mountains and valleys. These studies revealed that rocks in mid-ocean ridges were of relatively recent origin, formed by hot lava from deep within the earth pushing up through faults and spreading out to form the sea floor. Canadian geophysicist Tuzo Wilson deduced that the earth's crust is divided into a series of plates. The continents of lighter rock float on the heavier plates of solidified magma; their movements are known as plate tectonics (tecton, Greek for building).

Begin by coloring the continental positions in the present day. Use these colors for the rest of the plate. Iceland is colored with Greenland; Australia with the surrounding islands.

Next, color the continents at the end of the Triassic when they formed one supercontinent, Pangea ("all lands"), indicated by the solid line. A single ocean surrounded Pangea.

About 200 mya India was close to Africa with Madagascar wedged between them. Plants and animals on this land mass constituted one continuous living system.

Color the land masses of the Cretaceous indicated within the solid lines. Notice that parts of present day continents were submerged, as indicated by the dotted lines.

Pangea separated into two major land groups, Laurasia to the north, and to the south, Gondwana (land of the Gonds, after an Indian province), each moving away from Africa. India "floated" north and collided with mainland Asia, raising the Himalayan mountains. Madagascar became an island (4-6). South America and Africa were apart, but they remained close enough to exchange plants and animals.

Continental drift answers questions that previously baffled zoologists, botanists, and paleontologists. Dinosaur fossils, for example, are found on all major land masses. How did dinosaurs cross the oceans? The answer is that they did not. They evolved during the Triassic on the single continent of Pangea.

Darwin and his contemporary Alfred Russel Wallace wondered about how the ratites, giant flightless birds, came to be widely distributed: ostriches in Africa; elephant birds (now extinct) in Madagascar; rheas in South America; emus and cassowaries in Australia and New Guinea; and kiwis and extinct moas in New Zealand. Some orthnithologists proposed convergent evolution, that each ratite evolved from a different flying ancestor.

The combination of information from plate tectonics and molecular biology renders the idea of convergence incorrect. Using DNA hybridization (2-7), Charles Sibley and Jon Ahlquist demonstrated that the ratite birds are all genetically related and had a common ancestor resembling the South American tinamou, a bird that flies but shares with the ratites a distinctive "paleognathic" palate. Ratites most likely evolved on Gondwana and took separate evolutionary courses when the giant continent broke up into the southern continents of today.

Reptilian and mammalian evolution also followed the changing globe. The Age of Reptiles lasted 200 million years and gave rise to 20 orders (1-21). The Age of Mammals during the last 65 million years (the Cenozoic, 1-22) diversified much faster, giving rise to 35 orders. When reptiles evolved, there were fewer land masses and climates were more uniform than when mammals evolved. These differences account for the more rapid and extensive diversification of mammals, according to Finnish paleontologist Björn Kurtén. The breakup of the Laurasia and Gondwana supercontinents produced more geographic isolation and therefore more possibilities for independent evolution of species, including marsupials and placentals in Australia and North America (1-9), and lemurs in Madagascar (4-6).

Modern geography is best understood through its geological history. The Mediterranean Sea, separating Africa and Eurasia, is a remnant of the once more widespread Tethys Sea. The Indian Ocean divides India from Africa. The Mid-Atlantic Ridge, a huge submarine mountain chain, separates South America from Africa (4-11). North America and South America became connected only three million years ago through the Isthmus of Panama, permitting interchange of plants and animals between the two continents while isolating the once continuous marine life.

Far from being a fixed monument, our globe has been in flux for more than four billion years. Continents merge, fragment, and sometimes collide with each other. Such movements impact ocean currents, atmospheric circulation, and continental temperature and rainfall patterns. These motions account for how mountains form and why volcanos and earthquakes are most active at the edge of plates. Plate tectonics provide a missing piece of the biogeography puzzle that Darwin tried to solve—the mystery of how innumerable species that have lived on this planet came to be in the particular places where we find them living today or as fossils.

CONTINENTAL DRIFT

EURASIA a
NORTH
  AMERICA b
    GREENLAND b¹
SOUTH
  AMERICA c
AFRICA d
MADAGASCAR e
INDIA f
AUSTRALIA g
NEW ZEALAND h
ANTARCTICA i

200 MYA
TRIASSIC ✲

PANGEA ✲

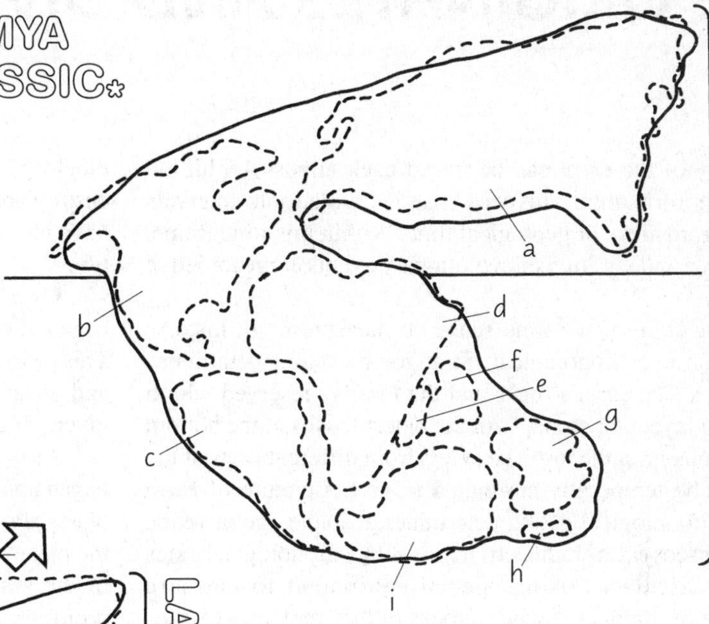

100 MYA
CRETACEOUS ✲

LAURASIA ✲

GONDWANA ✲

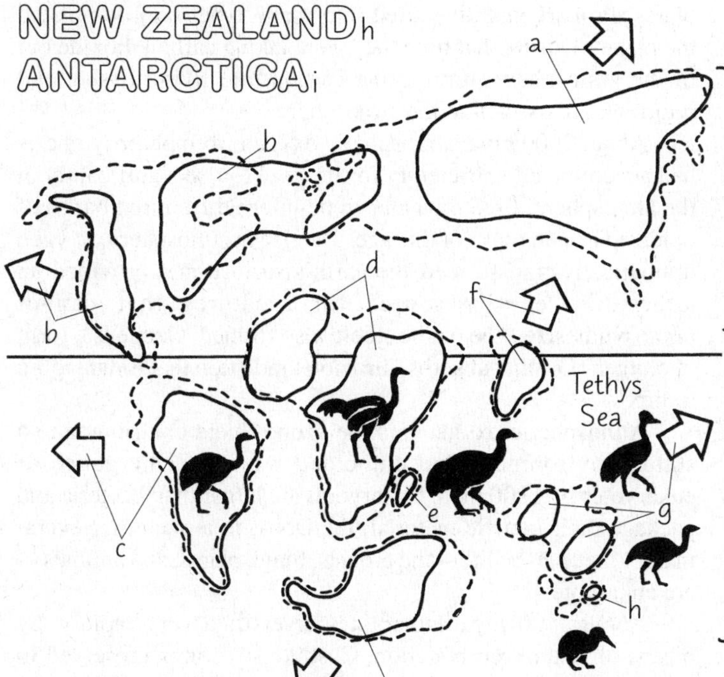

Tethys
Sea

North Pole

PRESENT DAY ✲

Equator

South Pole

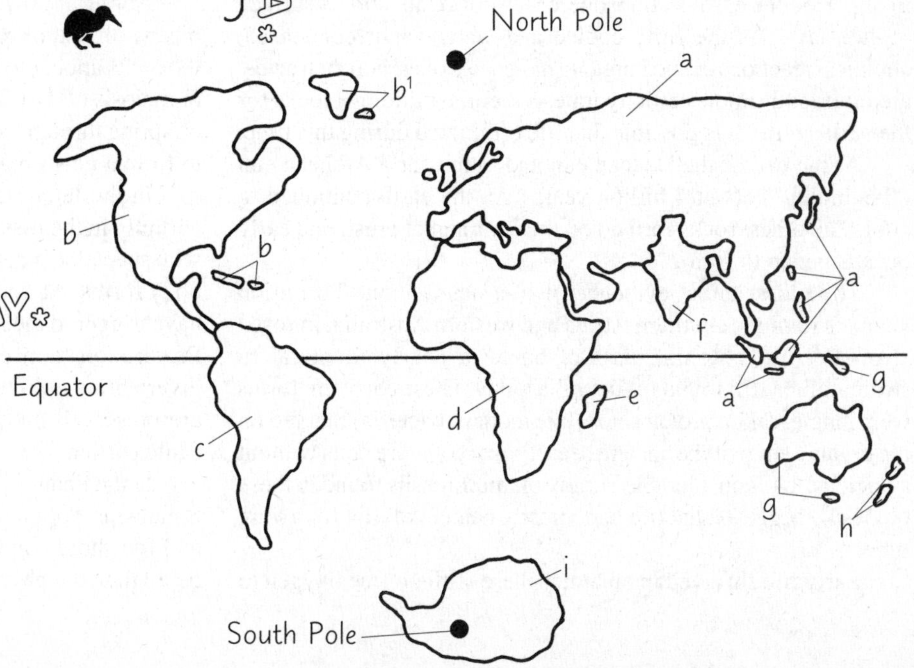

1-19
LIFE ORIGINATES AND DIVERSIFIES

The history of the earth can be traced back almost 4.6 billion years, to its formation. This vast span is divided into intervals that form yardsticks of geological time. Within this time frame, the sequence and duration of evolutionary events are recorded in the rocks.

Geologists use two time scales to measure earth history: stratigraphic and chronological. Stratigraphic dating determines relative age. The earth's rocks and the fossils preserved within them are in layers, or strata, with the oldest fossils at the bottom and the youngest at the top. The layers from different parts of the world can be temporally correlated to give a picture of earth history. Chronological dating determines absolute age in years. After the discovery of radioactivity in 1896, chronological dates could be calculated using special equipment to measure radioactive by-products found in rocks of different ages (5-4).

In this plate, and the following three plates, the art is worked from the bottom of the plate to the top. This reflects stratigraphic dating, where the oldest information is in the lowest stratum. Choose four colors for the four eons: Hadean, Archean, Proterozoic, and Phanerozoic. Color the title for each eon as it is discussed in the text, the corresponding section of the time scale, the chronological date, and the events in that eon. Choose light blue for the representation of atmospheric oxygen (f). The Hadean, Archean, and Proterozoic together are called the Precambrian.

The Hadean eon, (Greek for hell), began nearly 4.6 billion years before the present, when the earth began to form by condensation of dust particles into a molten mass. During this time period the earth's atmosphere was hot steam and its surface molten lava. As the earth cooled and water vapor condensed, chemical reactions created organic molecules of carbon-rich acids, alcohols, and simple carbohydrates, essential building blocks for the earliest life. It is possible that life originated during this time.

At the end of the Hadean eon and in the early Archean eon ("beginning") about 4 billion years ago, the earth continued to cool. The oldest rocks formed on the continental crust, and early oceans began to form.

The oldest direct evidence of life, dated about 3.8 billion years, is found in southern Africa and western Australia, in fossil stromatolites, colonial mats of bacteria nearly identical to stromatolites still found in Australia today. These early life forms were single-celled prokaryotes (like modern bacteria) that fed on the organic soup of the ancient seas. Prokaryotes are cells without a nucleus. The considerable variety of microfossils found in these old rocks suggests that life had already been evolving for a long time.

Early life survived in an atmosphere with no free oxygen to block the lethal ultraviolet radiation from the sun, which can destroy organic molecules. Sulfur compounds from volcanos may have blocked these rays and also served as an energy source for life.

Over 3 billion years ago, prokaryotes such as cyanobacteria began to manufacture their own energy through photosynthesis. This process uses energy from the sun to combine carbon dioxide and water to form simple sugars for energy storage. Oxygen is given off as a by-product.

As the Archean ended and the Proterozoic ("proto-life") eon began about 2500 mya, the land surfaces formed the continental plates. Prokaryotes diversifed into many types and dominated the planet. During that time they were taking carbon dioxide out of the atmosphere, turning the carbon into living tissue, and returning the oxygen to the atmosphere.

About 2000 mya, atmospheric oxygen from photosynthesis had accumulated sufficiently for its level to rise significantly in the atmosphere. Free oxygen can be inferred from red bands of oxidized iron in rocks of this age. The rise in atmospheric oxygen dramatically transformed the earth's surface and provided an alternative energy source for creatures that cannot photosynthesize. The ozone shield also formed. Ozone is a form of oxygen (O_3) that absorbs ultraviolet radiation that is damaging to life.

Atmospheric oxygen and the ozone shield contributed to a stable environment and coincided with the emergence of eukaryotes by 1800 mya. Eukaryotes are larger than bacteria and package their genetic material, the DNA, in a nucleus. Several major kingdoms of life—the protists, fungi, plants, and animals—are eukaryotes.

About 1100 mya, eukaryotes diversified very rapidly, by means of sexual reproduction. Cystlike structures preserved in the rocks appear to be phases of a life cycle with sex cell division, or meiosis (1-14). This important biological innovation produces offspring through combining hereditary material from two parents to form a new organism, and so enhances genetic diversity.

In the later stages of the Proterozoic, metazoans appeared abruptly in the fossil record. Metazoans are multicellular animals with specialized cells and tissue systems and structurally complex body forms. At this time a further increase in oxygen levels may have triggered the later "Cambrian explosion" of metazoans. The Proterozoic eon ended with the appearance of hard-shelled invertebrate animals and an expanded fossil record, since shells are preserved much better than the soft-bodied animals which came earlier.

In the Phanerozoic eon (phaneros=evident, visible; zoe=life), organisms populate the globe and their descendents gain root- and foot-holds on land. This most recent eon, known in greater detail than the previous three, is explored in the next three plates.

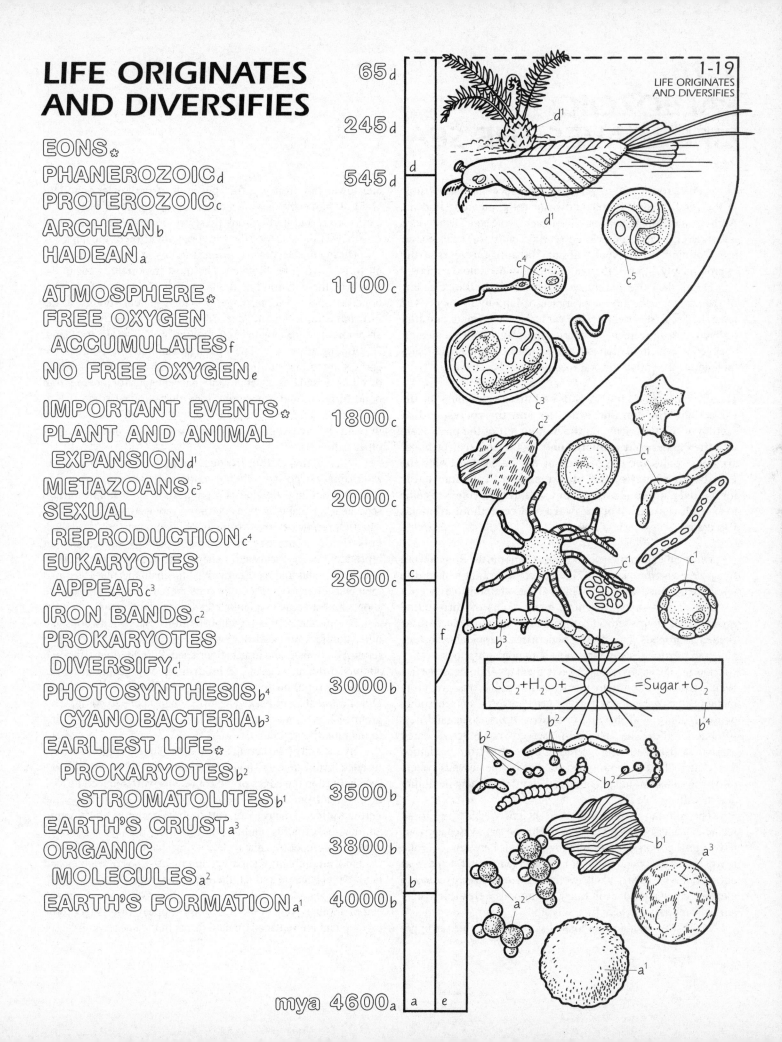

LIFE ORIGINATES AND DIVERSIFIES

EONS *

PHANEROZOIC d

PROTEROZOIC c

ARCHEAN b

HADEAN a

ATMOSPHERE *

FREE OXYGEN
  ACCUMULATES f

NO FREE OXYGEN e

IMPORTANT EVENTS *

PLANT AND ANIMAL
  EXPANSION d1

METAZOANS c5

SEXUAL
  REPRODUCTION c4

EUKARYOTES
  APPEAR c3

IRON BANDS c2

PROKARYOTES
  DIVERSIFY c1

PHOTOSYNTHESIS b4

  CYANOBACTERIA b3

EARLIEST LIFE *

  PROKARYOTES b2

    STROMATOLITES b1

EARTH'S CRUST a3

ORGANIC
  MOLECULES a2

EARTH'S FORMATION a1

65 d

245 d

545 d

1100 c

1800 c

2000 c

2500 c

3000 b

3500 b

3800 b

4000 b

mya 4600 a

$CO_2 + H_2O +$ =Sugar + O_2

1-20
PALEOZOIC:
LIFE LEAVES THE SEA

In the Phanerozoic eon, diverse life forms become more visible in the fossil record. Better known than the previous Hadean, Archean, and Proterozoic eons, the Phanerozoic eon is subdivided into three eras: Paleozoic, Mesozoic, and Cenozoic. The Paleozoic era ("ancient life") spans about 300 million years, from approximately 545 to 245 mya; it is subdivided into 6 periods.

During the Paleozoic era, we find multicellular life expanding in the seas and the first appearance of land-living plants and animals. The first vertebrates appear in the oceans, and soon after on land. The movement of continental plates built mountains, changed ocean circulation and temperature, and altered climates on land. At the end of the era, many species became extinct.

Use the same colors for the eons and three new colors for the eras. Color the eon and era titles and the corresponding section of the time scale on the bottom left of the page. Note that the Phanerozoic is colored only on the time scale. Choose six light colors for the periods of the Paleozoic. Color the Cambrian vignette, the oldest period. You may color individual plants and animals or use your light colors to color over each vignette. Work upward and read about events as you color.

During the Cambrian period, after Cambria, the Roman word for Wales where rocks from that period were first named, life remained confined to the seas. Green algae—the probable ancestor of land plants—appeared, and many kinds of soft-bodied invertebrates flourished. This time marks the appearance of the shelled arthropods, ancestral to modern insects, spiders, lobsters, and crabs. Trilobites were the most common arthropods.

During the Ordovician period (named for Ordovices, the last Welsh tribe to submit to the Romans) numerous predators including the cephalopods, represented here by the ancient squid, evolved, along with the first crinoids and bryozoans and new trilobite families. The first well-preserved vertebrates appeared as jawless fish with armor offering protection from predators. Their internal skeleton provided support for the nervous system (1-4), musculature, and gut organs, without sacrificing flexibility and mobility.

The Silurian (Silures, another ancient Welsh tribe) fossil record contains the earliest evidence of life on land. Vascular plants have a transport system for moving nutrients between roots and leaves, and a waxy cuticle layer to protect leaves and stems from drying out. These early plants were confined to swampy areas so that they could reproduce in water. Arthropods were the first land animals, represented here by a scorpion.

In the seas, placoderms ("plated-skin fish") evolved an upper and lower jaw from the first gill arch of the jawless ancestor (1-5). A moveable jaw opened up many possibilities for new carnivorous and herbivorous lifestyles. Placoderms had paired fins that set the stage for the vertebrate invasion of the land.

During the Devonian (Devon, a county in southern England) all forms of fish proliferated. The most important event in the seas was the evolution of the bony fish, the teleost fish. True bone, as opposed to cartilage, provided greater rigidity in the internal skeleton, and descendants of the bony fish, the amphibians, were soon to begin moving around on swampy land.

Taking advantage of new plant and animal food sources, the earliest amphibians utilized two earlier fish adaptations for land dwelling: lobed fins with bony internal skeletons for moving from pond to pond; and a primitive lung that allowed some fish to come to the surface to gulp air. These "lung fish" could survive in ponds where oxygen levels in the water were insufficient for other fish.

During the Carboniferous, named for the coal in its sedimentary deposits, colliding continental plates contributed to mountain building. Gymnosperms ("naked seed"), nonflowering, seed-bearing plants such as conifers, replaced seedless plants. The first reptiles evolved from amphibian ancestors. A shelled, yolk-rich amniote egg laid on land became their mode of reproduction. Dry, scaly skin retained the body's moisture. Thus both seed plants and reptiles evolved mechanisms that alleviated their restriction to watery environments, and they advanced from shores and streams to populate the drier upland areas.

During the Permian, gymnosperm forests of redwoods and other conifers replaced the swampy primitive forests of giant ferns. Amphibians and insects flourished. Reptiles diversified and adopted different ways of life. From this geological period comes the oldest reptilian fossil egg. The emerging reptiles include *Dimetrodon*, the sail-backed lizard, a synapsid or pelycosaur. This group of animals marks the branch of the evolutionary tree leading to mammallike reptiles.

By the end of the Permian period, the largest continents were fused to form Pangea, a single supercontinent (1-18). The shallow sea shelves on the edges of the continents were reduced to 15% of the area from the early Permian. The mass extinction of the Permian affected many marine invertebrates, such as brachiopods, ammonites, crinoids, and all the trilobites, perhaps a result of increased competition due to decreasing shallow marine habitats. On land, amphibians decreased, and many types of reptiles and land plants became extinct, though at the same time new insect groups appeared. At the close of the Paleozoic era, we see the end of another cycle of life. Life forms appear, flourish, become extinct, and are replaced by new forms in the succeeding eras.

LIFE LEAVES THE SEA

PHANEROZOIC EON d
ERAS ✲
   CENOZOIC g
   MESOZOIC f
   PALEOZOIC e
PROTEROZOIC EON c
ARCHEAN EON b
HADEAN EON a

PALEOZOIC ERA e
PERIODS ✲
   PERMIAN m
   CARBONIFEROUS l
   DEVONIAN k
   SILURIAN j
   ORDOVICIAN i
   CAMBRIAN h

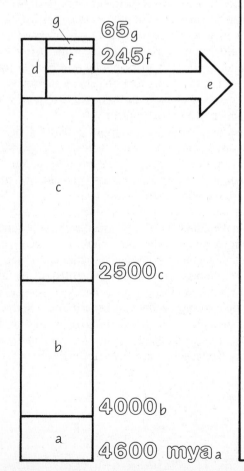

g
65 g

f
245 f

d

e

c

2500 c

b

4000 b

a
4600 mya a

245 f
Reptiles radiate

Amphibians and
  insects expand

Redwood forests m

285 m

First reptiles

Gymnosperms

l

360 l

Teleost fish expand
Amphibians
Forests
Insects

k

410 k

Land plants
  Giant ferns
Arthropods invade
  land
Jawed fish j
Armored fish
  dominate 435 j

Armored, jawless
  fish
Vertebrates
Shell-bearing
  marine inverte-
  brates dominate

i

505 i

Shelled
  arthropods

Trilobites

h

545 h

1-21
MESOZOIC:
REPTILES REIGN, MAMMALS EMERGE

The Mesozoic era ("middle life") from the Phanerozoic eon spans about 180 million years and is divided into three periods: Triassic, Jurassic, and Cretaceous. This era, called the Age of Reptiles, reflects the radiation of a great variety of reptiles, especially the dinosaurs. Many familiar forms of life emerged for the first time: birds, mammals, flowering plants, and many modern insects. Cycad and conifer trees were common, and angiosperms, broadleaf flowering plants such as elm, oak, and maple trees, became evident. Although the era began with the land masses joined together, the breakup of the supercontinent Pangea fragmented the land masses, and climates became more diverse. Many reptiles, including the dinosaurs, became extinct by the end of the era and set the stage for the expansion of mammals and birds during the Cenozoic.

Continue to use your colors for the eons and your three colors for the eras; color those first. Then proceed to the Triassic, Jurassic, and Cretaceous periods, using three new light colors and the coloring plan of the previous plate.

The Triassic period, named for the threefold division of the rocks as seen in Germany, began around 245 mya and lasted for about 40 million years. During this time new amphibians and a variety of reptiles appeared and became successful. Biological innovations, such as the protective eggshell helped offspring to survive, and advanced body structure facilitated locomotor mobility on land. Mammallike reptiles (therapsids) were diverse and abundant. Dinosaurs first appeared at the end of the Triassic period, and the alligatorlike phytosaur was an early dinosaur relative.

Great forests of pine, fir, and cedar trees arose in the Triassic. Today's redwood forests closely approximate the great conifer-cycad forests of the Triassic and Jurassic. At the end of the Triassic, the first true mammals appeared. Small, with shrew-sized jaws and teeth, their fossil remains are found in the western United States, Britain, Europe, and South Africa.

During the Jurassic period, named for the Jura mountains in eastern France and beginning about 200 mya, conifer-cycad-gingko forests were widespread and ferns common. Ammonites dominated the open seas. Reptiles expanded into the air and seas, and on the land. Winged reptiles ranged in size from those smaller than a sparrow to those with 4-foot wingspans. Streamlined marine carnivores, the ichthyosaurs ("fish reptiles") (1-8) and plesiosaurs ("near reptiles") flourished. Reptiles dominated the land; an *Apatosaurus* shown here, is one of the three groups of dinosaurs. The oldest known bird *Archaeopteryx* ("old bird") had feathers like modern birds, but teeth and a skeleton like reptiles, and short wings relative to body length.

Several distinct groups of primitive mammals, known as Mesozoic mammals, emerged. The largest was the size of a cat. The multituberculates, named for having teeth with many simple, pointed cusps ("many tubercles"), were probably plant-eaters and had large chisel-shaped incisors, like rodents. The pantotheres were mostly insectivorous; this group probably gave rise to most of the later mammalian groups. These small mammals did not constitute an abundant or important part of animal life on land at that time.

The Cretaceous period, named for its chalky deposits in England and France, began approximately 145 mya. At this time, Pangea was breaking up into smaller continents. The Andes and Rocky mountains were uplifted. Many varieties of dinosaurs, such as the horned dinosaur *Tricerotops,* continued to be widespread on every continent. The carnivorous *Tyrannosaurus rex* stood 6 meters high, with a skull 1 meter long. There were giant turtles and sea-going mosasaurs. Large flying reptiles such as *Pteranodon* still flourished.

The Mesozoic mammals diversified into several orders during the late Cretaceous, though they remained small-bodied and an insignificant part of animal life on land. Of the 13 families of mammals, 6 were multituberculates, 1 was marsupial, and 3 families were insectivorous.

The most important new arrivals in this era were the flowering (seed-bearing) plants, the angiosperms ("covered seeds"). (Today 96% of vascular plants are angiosperms.) An enclosed seed permits the development of fleshy, edible fruit. Birds and mammals facilitated the spread of plants by transporting their pollens, and by eating the fruits and dispersing the seeds. In contrast, gymnosperms such as ferns and cycads rely on wind for dispersal of pollen from plant to plant.

The angiosperms provided a variety of potential food for birds and mammals. Plant parts such as fruits, seeds, flowers, shoots, and leaves and the associated insects fueled the mammalian radiation. The angiosperms also play an important role in the adaptive radiation of primates (4-1).

The close of the Cretaceous period, like the close of the Permian period in the Paleozoic era, was marked by widespread extinction that wiped out all of the ammonites in the oceans and many of the land-living reptiles, especially the dinosaurs. Probably several events contributed to this dramatic reptilian extinction. Continental uplift reduced swampy areas and lush vegetation; cooler climatic conditions prevailed, influenced by the northern drift of the continental plates; the rise of the angiosperms further altered the food sources of the land reptiles. An asteroid impact at the close of the Cretaceous may have finished off the large reptiles.

REPTILES REIGN, MAMMALS EMERGE

PHANEROZOIC EON d
ERAS ∗
 CENOZOIC g
 MESOZOIC f
 PALEOZOIC e
PROTEROZOIC EON c
ARCHEAN EON b
HADEAN EON a

MESOZOIC ERA f
PERIODS ∗
 CRETACEOUS p
 JURASSIC o
 TRIASSIC n

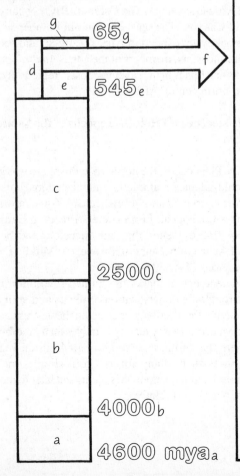

g   65 g
d
e   545 e

f

c

2500 c

b

4000 b

a   4600 mya a

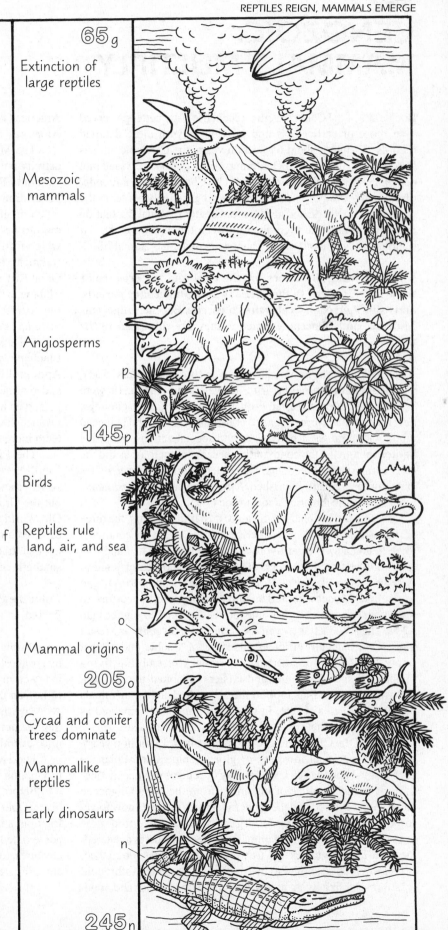

65 g

Extinction of large reptiles

Mesozoic mammals

Angiosperms

p

145 p

Birds

f   Reptiles rule land, air, and sea

o

Mammal origins

205 o

Cycad and conifer trees dominate

Mammallike reptiles

Early dinosaurs

n

245 n

1-22
CENOZOIC:
MAMMALS MULTIPLY

Rock units of the Cenozoic era ("recent life") are better preserved than those of earlier eras and provide us with more detailed records. Spanning about 65 million years, the Cenozoic era has two periods, Tertiary and Quaternary; each period is divided into epochs, many of which were named by Charles Lyell, a founder of modern geology. Climates became progressively cooler as the continents slowly drifted northward. Greater seasonal fluctuation and wider temperature gradient between the equator and polar regions brought about major changes in plant and animal life.

Continue using the colors for the eons and the eras; color those first. Proceed to the Tertiary and Quaternary periods, and using light colors, color the Paleocene, Eocene, Oligocene, Miocene, and Pliocene epochs as they are discussed in the text.

The Paleocene epoch, lasting over 10 million years, was a warm and humid time. Prior to the Paleocene, mammals were small, none larger than a cat. From their insignificant beginnings, new mammalian forms began to constitute a varied and balanced fauna with a range of body sizes and specializations. Primitive hoofed mammals, the condylarths, became numerous, as did the early carnivorelike creodonts. True rodents appeared, insectivores and multituberculates flourished. A primitive primate, *Plesiadapis* inhabited North America and Europe (4-2).

During the Eocene, lasting almost 20 million years, the three northern continents, North America, Europe, and Asia, continued to be in contact. The carnivorous creodonts dominated and true carnivores appeared: members of the cat, dog, and weasel families. Archaic groups like the multituberculates and condylarths began to decline. Modern hoofed mammals appeared. Ancestors to horses, the perissodactyls ("uneven toes") were no bigger than foxes. The artiodactyls ("even-toes") began to diversify as a result of their mechanically efficient ankle joint, a "double-pulley" that improved locomotor efficiency. Primates resembling living prosimians such as lemurs and tarsiers inhabited the northern hemisphere (4-3). Bats took to the air, and whalelike mammals began a marine existence. In this epoch, mammals emerged as the dominant animals on land, in the air, and in the seas.

During the Oligocene epoch, lasting about 13 million years, there was a gradual lowering of global temperature. Polar ice caps formed and the sea level fell. By the end of this epoch, one-third of the 95 families of mammals from the early Oligocene had become extinct, and the modern families that we know today took over. Grasslands emerged, which presented new opportunities for grazing mammals. Three-toed horses appeared; the even-toed ungulates, the true pigs and peccaries, flourished. Primate evolution shifted to the southern continents. Anthropoid fossils resembling living monkeys showed up in Africa and South America (4-10, 4-11). Some prosimian families persisted in North America.

The Miocene epoch lasted over 15 million years. Volcanic activity built mountain ranges in North America and uplifted the Colorado Plateau. The African plate collided with the Eurasian plate, diminishing the intervening Tethys Sea and leaving the much smaller Mediterranean Sea. Seasonality in temperature and rainfall became more pronounced. The African lowland forest, which formerly extended across the equatorial region, began to fragment due to uplift and faulting. This activity resulted in the Great Rift Valley, seen today in a chain of lakes extending from Malawi in the south to the Red Sea in the north. In eastern Africa, the forests became more discontinuous; mixed vegetation, including grasslands, formed the savanna mosaic. Pigs and bovids invaded this newly forming habitat and speciated into many forms. Elephants successfully spread from Africa throughout Eurasia. Apes proliferated into numerous families; carnivores flourished and marine mammals such as seals, sea lions, and whales are preserved in the fossil record. In North America, the horse family invaded the expanding grassy plains and diversified. Longer cheek teeth increased their ability to grind silicon-rich grasses.

The Pliocene epoch was a serene interval lasting about 3 million years. Species continued to expand into plains of North America and African savannas. The Colorado River began carving out the Grand Canyon. The apes declined in number while the Old World monkeys expanded in Africa, Europe, and Asia. The earliest human ancestors, members of the genus *Australopithecus*, left their tracks and bones in the savanna mosaic regions of eastern, southern, and north central Africa (5-2).

Color the Pleistocene and Holocene epochs of the Quaternary period.

During the Pleistocene, the northern hemisphere was gripped by ice ages; cold-adapted mammoths and mastodons, horses, and many carnivores survived and flourished. In Africa, new species of human ancestors appear. From stone artifacts in Europe and Asia, we now find evidence that our ancestors had begun to migrate out of Africa into southern Europe, the Middle East, and into several regions of Asia (5-24).

The Holocene epoch marks the human revolution in food production through the domestication of plants and animals.

Before leaving this section, notice again the vast time of earth history. Our own evolutionary history occupies an incredibly small fraction, a mere five million years. Through 4 billion years, life has existed on earth in many forms, from simple one-celled creatures, to multicellular, vertebrate species and later to mammals and primates, our closest relatives.

MAMMALS MULTIPLY

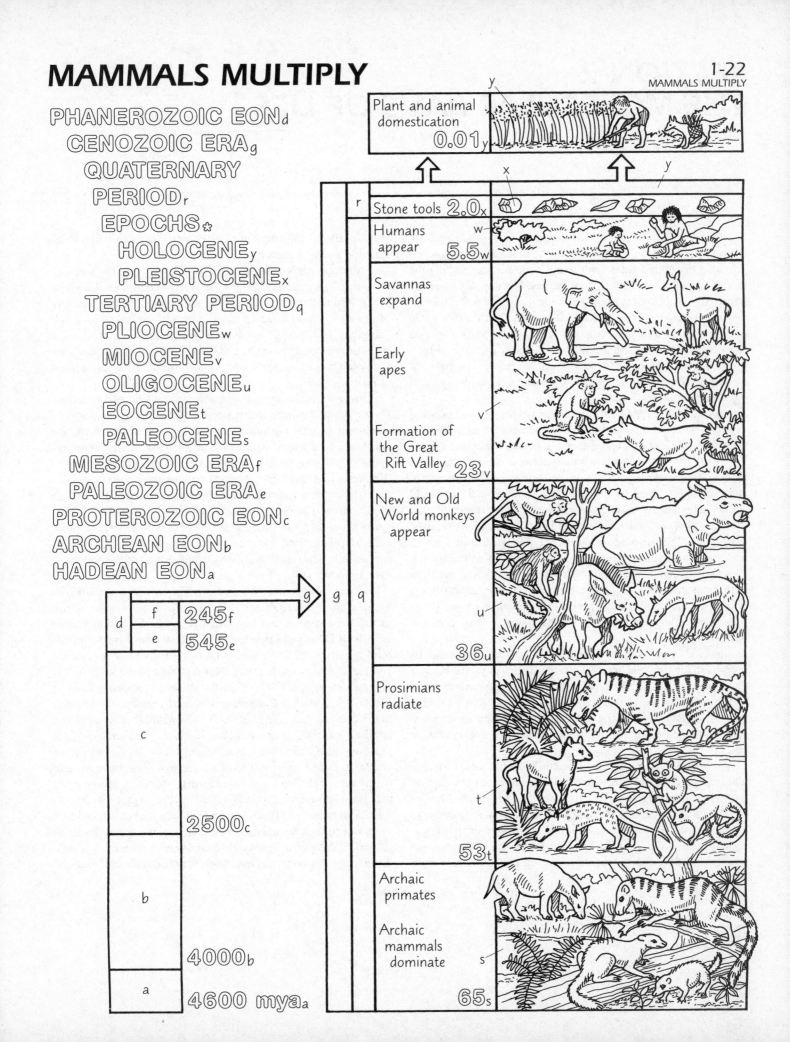

PHANEROZOIC EON_d
CENOZOIC ERA_g
QUATERNARY
PERIOD_r
EPOCHS✷
HOLOCENE_y
PLEISTOCENE_x
TERTIARY PERIOD_q
PLIOCENE_w
MIOCENE_v
OLIGOCENE_u
EOCENE_t
PALEOCENE_s
MESOZOIC ERA_f
PALEOZOIC ERA_e
PROTEROZOIC EON_c
ARCHEAN EON_b
HADEAN EON_a

d
f 245f
e 545e
c 2500c
b 4000b
a 4600 mya a
g

Plant and animal domestication 0.01y

r Stone tools 2.0x
Humans appear 5.5w
Savannas expand
Early apes
Formation of the Great Rift Valley 23v
New and Old World monkeys appear 36u
Prosimians radiate 53t
Archaic primates
Archaic mammals dominate 65s

g q

SECTION 2
THE MOLECULAR BASIS OF LIFE

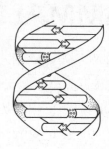

For Charles Darwin and the generations that followed him, comparative anatomy, biogeography, and the fossil record provided three kinds of scientific evidence for establishing the fact of organic evolution. During the past few decades, growing knowledge of the molecular basis of life has added powerful new data to evolutionary studies. Molecular methods make it possible to quantitate genetic and temporal relationships among species to a degree undreamed of a century ago. Today it is as vital for a physical anthropologist to understand the molecular basis of evolution as it is for a physician to understand the biochemical basis for health and disease.

As we look at the scientific advances of the past one hundred years, we see that this has been the Molecular Century. In 1900 very few scientists believed that molecules were real things. Wilhelm Ostwald, a Nobel-winning chemist, strongly opposed the concept of molecules. It was only after Einstein's mathematical analysis of Brownian motion in 1905, showing that one could count molecules by simple observation and measurement, that this reality became generally accepted by physicists and chemists. Since then, the molecular concept has dominated basic understanding in those fields, as well as in biology and medicine. This framework increasingly replaces guesswork and intuition with measurement and quantitative analysis and establishes a common molecular underpinning for the different fields of science, including primate social behavior, primate evolution, and human origins.

In 1953 James Watson, a young American molecular biologist researching in England, teamed up with British physicist Francis Crick, and together they discovered that DNA, the genetic material of life on earth, has the structure of a double helix (2-1). This geometrical structure was the key to deciphering the long-standing secrets of reproduction, inheritance, mutation, and evolution (2-2).

A hundred years earlier, Darwin had observed variation within populations of plants and animals but could not explain the source of the variation. From research on pea plants, Mendel deduced that hereditary "particles" determine such features as the shape and color of plants but had no idea of the particles' composition. As a result of Watson and Crick's discovery, we now know that these "particles" make up the cell nucleus and contain all the information that the cell needs to perform its function and to replicate.

An organism's genome consists of all its genetic material. For most, this material is DNA, but for some viruses it is RNA (2-3). Within the cell nucleus, DNA programs the manufacture of proteins, which make up most tissues in the body (2-4). The "language of DNA" is a universal genetic code. Its alphabet is the four nucleotide bases A, C, G, and T. Three-base codons are translated into amino acids, which constitute the 20-letter alphabet of proteins (2-5).

Proteins make up an organism's structure and function. Hemoglobin, for instance, the red oxygen-bearing pigment of our blood, is vital for human survival at high altitudes and for resistance to diseases such as malaria (6-14). Hemoglobin has evolved, and along with the changes, new forms of life appeared— life forms that no longer obtained oxygen from water but from the air; mammals with higher levels of energy; and primates with larger brains. The fascinating evolutionary history of the globin genes provides a case study to learn about how genes, over long eons, duplicate into families of related genes in a variety of species, add new functions, undergo mutations, and in some cases even become extinct (2-6)!

Comparisons of DNA and proteins make it possible to measure the similarities and differences between species. DNA of different species can be compared by DNA hybridization; strands of DNA from two species are tested for how well they bind together. In DNA sequencing, base pair sequences are compared among species, and their differences counted (2-7).

As long ago as 1900, before we knew the molecular basis of life, G.H.F. Nuttall at Cambridge University studied the proteins of different species. He injected rabbits with blood serum from hundreds of kinds of animals and compared the immunological reactions (2-8). He found that human blood serum was most similar to that of apes, next most similar to that of monkeys, and hardly similar at all to that of other animals. Nuttall was convinced that these immune reactions reflected the degree of genetic relationship between species, as indeed they do, but one hundred years ago, the molecular basis of immunology was not understood.

All of these techniques yield quantitative measures of genetic differences between species, from which family trees can be constructed. Unlike anatomical comparisons, molecular comparisons of living species do provide estimates of time of descent from a common ancestor when combined with information from the fossil record. In the 1960s, Emil Zuckerkandl and Linus Pauling noticed that in family trees constructed from amino acid differences, the branch lengths were roughly proportional to divergence times deduced from the fossil record (2-9). When the molecular clock was first applied to human evolution, it challenged the prevailing interpretation of the time of separation of humans and ape ancestors. Proteins and DNA serve as molecular clocks, with each mutation of a nucleotide or amino acid ticking off the passage of thousands or millions of years (2-10).

Mitochondrial DNA acts as a fast clock that has shed light on the human connection with chimpanzees and on the origin of our species, *Homo sapiens* (2-11). Because mitochondrial DNA is inherited only from the mother and passed via the female line, it has been used to study the interchange and dispersal of female and male primates in the social groups of different species.

DNA is a versatile molecule. It not only measures the genetic relatedness of species and times of their origin, it also serves as an ID, distinguishing every organism on earth from every other, unless it has an identical twin. DNA sequences that encode proteins are virtually identical for different members of the same species. However, noncoding stretches of DNA, called mini-satellites or microsatellites, evolve so rapidly that they are significantly different for every individual. The new techniques of DNA "fingerprinting," which detect heritable DNA differences, take the guesswork out of identifying genetic relationships. For example, DNA fingerprinting can connect an individual with its mother or father, if their DNA is available for comparison (2-12). Uncertainty about primate paternity has been a long-standing problem, and DNA fingerprinting necessitates revisions about the correlation between dominance, social pairing, copulation, and paternity.

It came as a big surprise that molecular differences between species often did not correlate at all with differences in appearance! Species that are nearly identical in external features, like the mouse lemur and demidoff galago, may be very distantly related, whereas species that look very different, like chimpanzees and ourselves may be quite closely related (2-13). Morphological and molecular genetic evidence complement each other, providing information on adaptation and on genetic relatedness and times of divergence; both approaches together contribute to a more complete evolutionary picture than either does alone.

On the frontiers of new knowledge, there is research on homeotic genes that determine the development and body plan of multicellular animals. These genes control the process of development of animal form into body segments, limbs, and head. The small number of homeotic genes of fruit flies, mice, and humans are remarkably similar, showing the continuity of molecular genetic entities over hundreds of millions of years (2-14). Homeotic gene research promises to help bridge the gap between molecules and morphology that until recently was an area of which we had little knowledge or understanding.

In our look at new frontiers of molecular exploration and application, techniques such as radioimmunoassay, a hi-tech version of Nuttall's serum-antiserum experiments, and DNA sequencing have been applied to fossils as well as to living organisms. These techniques have shed light on evolutionary relationships between extinct and living species: for example, the extinct Siberian mammoth and living African and Asian elephants, as well as the extinct South African quaggas and living zebras and horses (2-15).

The human genome, like most animal genomes, consists of all of an organism's genetic material; it is a genetic message of about 3 billion base pairs, containing about 100,000 genes. We are in the process of deciphering the immense complexity of this tiny but voluminous encyclopedia of information about our appearance, function, health, behavior, and evolutionary history. Numerous surprises have leapt at us out of this twisted thicket of DNA. About 95% of it is noncoding DNA, "selfish" or "junk" DNA, that seems to serve no useful purpose for the organism. And there are "pseudogenes," dead, fossil genes that once encoded proteins but now are buried in the genome.

We have a clock-shop of molecular timepieces ticking at different speeds, some so fast that they fingerprint individuals of the same species, others so slow that they hardly distinguish between a cow and a pea.

Welcome to the molecular wonderland!

2-1
THE MOLECULAR BASIS OF LIFE: DNA: THE DOUBLE HELIX

Cells are the fundamental units of living things, the "atoms" of biology. They were discovered and given a name in the 1660s when Robert Hooke examined thin slices of cork under the newly invented microscope. All forms of life consist of cells, claimed Theodor Schwann in 1839.

Most plants, animals, and fungi have large numbers of cells. Each cell constitutes the smallest and simplest unit of life and is specialized for its own role: white blood cells fight infectious disease; nerve cells transmit electrical signals; cells lining the stomach and intestine secrete enzymes to process food. Despite their specialized function, most cells carry all the hereditary material needed to direct the processes of life, such as growth, development, reproduction, and metabolism. Chromosomal DNA inside the cells determines their shape and function.

Gregor Mendel's experiments with peas established that "particles," or genes, transmitted the hereditary material from parent to offspring (1-11). However, the nature of his "particles" remained a mystery. For a long time, genes were thought to consist of some kind of protein. Finally, in 1939, Oswald Avery made the connection between a gene and a molecule called DNA, short for deoxyribonucleic acid. He studied two forms of the *Pneumococcus* bacterium; the smooth form has a coat that makes it active so that it causes pneumonia, whereas the rough form, without that coat, is harmless. The smooth form has an extra gene that transforms rough to smooth. Avery's research showed that this gene was not a protein—it was DNA. This experiment was the first scientific proof that the genetic material is DNA.

After Avery's discovery, the next two decades were a race among researchers to unravel the secrets of DNA: how DNA carries the genetic message from one generation to another; how it interacts with the cellular machinery; how it replicates itself; and how its "message" is "read" and "translated" into proteins. The big breakthrough came in 1953 when James Watson and Francis Crick discovered that DNA is a double helix. Their discovery earned them a Nobel Prize in 1962, along with Maurice Wilkins whose x-ray analysis corroborated the molecular structure. Watson's book *The Double Helix* describes the excitement surrounding the discovery and the competition that led up to it.

On the cutaway drawing of the cell, color the cell membrane, the structure that encloses and protects the cell's components and controls what enters the cell. Color the labeled components of the cell.

Here we picture a typical eukaryotic or nucleated cell. In eukaryotic cells, such as yeast, the DNA is packaged in chromosomes located within the nucleus. The porous nuclear membrane permits selected molecules to pass between the nucleus and cytoplasm. In prokaryotic cells, such as bacteria, which lack a nucleus, the DNA is located in the cytoplasm.

Notice the nucleolus, a nuclear organelle that produces ribosomes (2-4). Mitochondria, the structures pictured in the cytoplasm, provide the power for the activities of the cell. They are discussed in detail on 2-11.

Color the enlarged chromosome. Color the DNA double helix in the sister chromatid.

Most of the time, the nuclear DNA is a loosely tangled mass, not neatly bundled into chromosomes. However, when the cell prepares to divide in prophase (1-13), the DNA forms two duplicate chromosomes, called sister chromatids, joined by a centromere. Chromosomes can be seen readily with a light reflecting microscope.

Color the parts of the double helix, including the strands, base pairs, and hydrogen bonds.

With an electron microscope and a higher level of magnification, the DNA molecule, a double helix, looks like a twisted ladder. The sides of the ladder, Strand 1 and Strand 2, wind around each other in opposite directions.

The backbones of these two strands are held together by a base pair. Base pairs are linked by hydrogen bonds. A single hydrogen bond is weak, but large numbers of them along the double helix give strength yet allow the DNA molecule to open and close like a zipper, an important step in replication.

Genes, composed of DNA, control the synthesis of proteins. Proteins make up most of bodily tissues, and protein enzymes are needed for the thousands of chemical reactions that take place within the cell. An organism's total DNA message, known as the genome, contains the complete instructions for making a new organism.

DNA: THE DOUBLE HELIX

LOCATION IN THE CELL*
CELL MEMBRANE a
CYTOPLASM b
NUCLEAR MEMBRANE c
NUCLEOLUS d
CHROMOSOME e
    CENTROMERE e¹
    SISTER CHROMATIDS e²

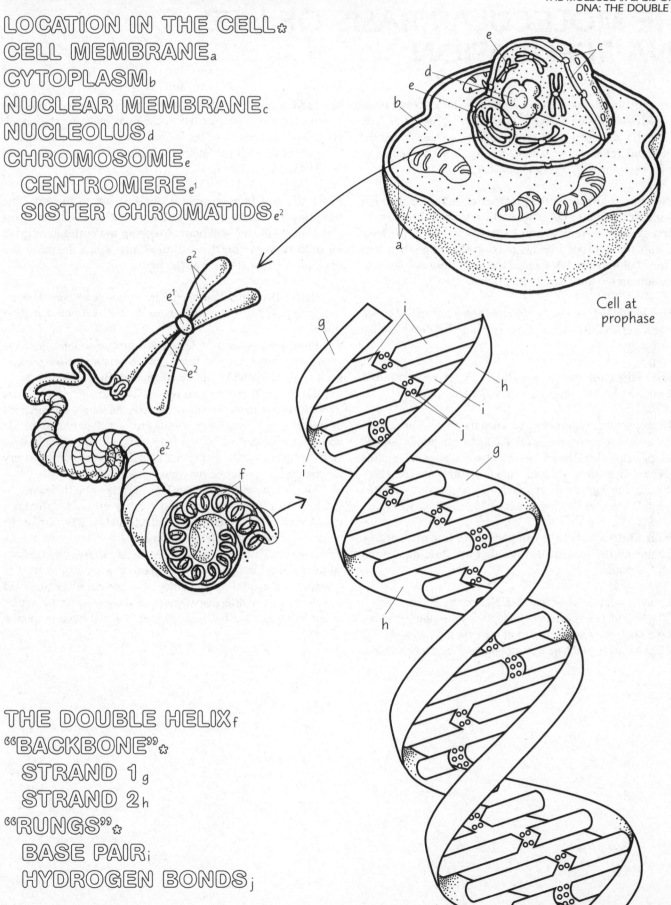

Cell at prophase

THE DOUBLE HELIX f
"BACKBONE" *
    STRAND 1 g
    STRAND 2 h
"RUNGS" *
    BASE PAIR i
    HYDROGEN BONDS j

2-2
THE MOLECULAR BASIS OF LIFE: DNA REPLICATION

The secret of how living creatures reproduce almost exact copies of themselves has been one of nature's deepest mysteries. The double helix revealed how replication works on the most fundamental level—how a molecule of DNA manages to duplicate itself into two identical molecules.

Use the same colors as on the previous plate for (g) through (j). Begin at the top of the plate and color each structure in the first section: parent strand 1, parent strand 2, the base pairs, and the hydrogen bonds holding them together. You have now colored the DNA molecule, as it appears prior to replication, in its double helix formation.

The double helix consists of a right and a left strand coiled around each other. The base pairs act as "rungs" of the ladderlike DNA molecule.

Proceed to the middle of the plate and color parent strands 1 and 2 and the bases, where they have pulled apart.

The replication process begins when the two parent strands "unzip" as specific enzymes break the hydrogen bonds holding the base pairs together. The arrows show the parent strands pulling apart. The coiled strands "unzip" into two single helices where each base of the pair is now exposed and may interact with free nucleotide molecules floating around in the cell nucleus.

Color the illustration of the components of free nucleotides. Next, color all the free nucleotides that are floating around the DNA strands.

A nucleotide has three parts: a phosphate, a sugar, and a base. The base of a free nucleotide connects with a complementary base on a nucleotide which is part of the exposed parent strand. Hydrogen bonds hold the nucleotides in place, and a new ladder begins to assemble. In the twisted ladder structure of DNA, the phosphates and sugars of the nucleotides make up the lateral supports ("backbone") of the ladder. The base pairs match up to form rungs as each parent strand gathers new nucleotides and completes a "daughter strand."

Color the daughter strand on the diagram to the left. The stippling indicates the actual position of the structural components of the backbone. Coloring the entire area gives an indication of the three-dimensional space forming the backbone. Color the rest of the plate.

Replication is finished when there are two new double helices, each composed of one original parent and one new daughter strand.

From one DNA molecule, two identical new molecules have been formed carrying the same genetic message. Now the cell itself is ready to divide into two daughter cells (1-13).

The replication process is remarkably accurate, so that most organisms seem to remain almost exactly the same over hundreds of thousands of generations. Some errors, called mutations, do occur in the process of copying this same genetic message over and over again. Mutations provide the genetic variation necessary for change and evolution over long periods of time.

Most of these "copy errors" make little or no difference to the health of the organism, and so they are called "neutral mutations." Some mutations do affect vital structures like the brain, or impair enzymes necessary to life. These are mostly damaging or lethal. A few may be beneficial and give the organism an advantage for surviving in a particular environment. For example, a mutation in the hemoglobin protein that causes red cells to become sickle-shaped gives its possessors an advantage in surviving malaria but is a liability in a non-malarial region (6-14).

DNA REPLICATION

PARENT STRAND 1 g
PARENT STRAND 2 h
BASE PAIR i
HYDROGEN BONDS j

UNZIPPING *
FREE NUCLEOTIDE k
  PHOSPHATE k¹
  SUGAR k²
  BASE k³

REPLICATION *
DAUGHTER STRAND k⁴

Backbone

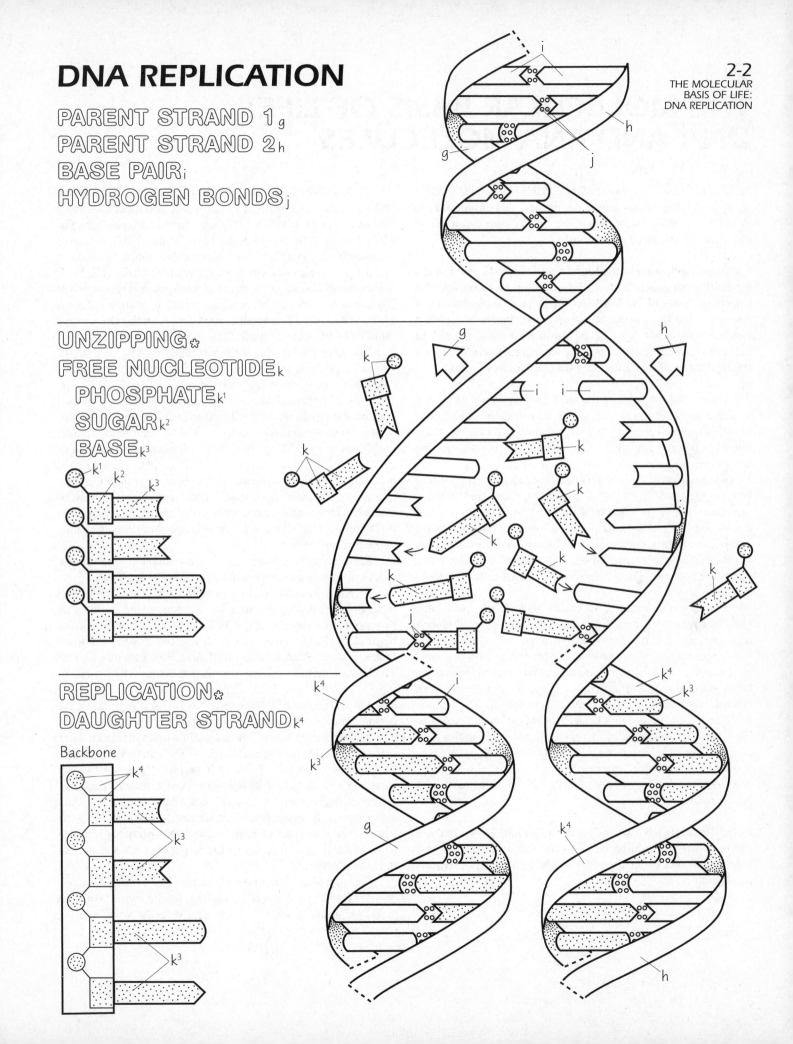

2-3
THE MOLECULAR BASIS OF LIFE: DNA AND RNA MOLECULES

In the last plate, we saw how the DNA double helix is held together by hydrogen bonds and how it unzips and zips to replicate. In this plate we take a closer look at the smaller units that make up this versatile and essential molecule.

Color the nucleotide at the top of the plate. Note again that a nucleotide consists of a phosphate, a sugar, and a base. Color the components of the DNA double helix. Use two shades of one color for the purine bases and two shades of another, contrasting color for the pyrimidine bases. To aid in recognition of the molecular components, each is labeled with the first letter of its name, for example, nucleotide (n).

Recall that the sides of the ladder or backbones of strands 1 and 2 are alternating phosphate and sugar subunits. The phosphates are all alike, and the deoxyribose sugars are all alike, but the particular sequence of the four bases is different and determines the genetic message of each gene.

The simple alphabet of the DNA "message" consists of four bases A, G, C, and T—adenine, guanine, cytosine, and thymine. The bases are of two chemical types: purines (A and G) and pyrimidines (C and T). One purine is joined to one pyrimidine by hydrogen bonds. Purines are the longer molecules whose ends point outward in the illustration. Pyrimidines are shorter and shown with notches. The notches and points fit together like locks and keys.

Before the structure of DNA was understood, biochemist Erwin Chargaff discovered that any DNA he analyzed always had equal amounts of adenine and thymine, and equal amounts of cytosine and guanine. These equalities, A=T and C=G, known as "Chargaff's Rules," provided a clue to Watson and Crick about DNA structure. The significance of these equalities did not become clear until the double helix was revealed.

The "rungs" of the DNA ladder are either an adenine-thymine (A–T) or a cytosine-guanine (C–G) combination. Note that each combination has one purine (A or G) and one pyrimidine (C or T) and explains Chargaff's Rules. We never observe A–C, A–G, or C–T. We therefore say that A and T are complementary bases, as are C and G.

Color the single DNA strand on the lower left. Then, choose a shade of the pyrimidine color to use for uracil and a new color for ribose. Color the RNA strand and the RNA strands in the cell.

An RNA (ribose nucleic acid) molecule has the sugar subunit ribose (instead of deoxyribose), a phosphate, and four bases. Three bases are identical with those of DNA—namely, adenine, guanine, and cytosine. The fourth RNA base is uracil (U), which is chemically very similar to thymine and also similar in shape.

To get its message out from the nucleus of the cell, DNA makes use of RNA as a courier or messenger. A single strand of DNA makes a "transcript" of itself onto a single strand of RNA as illustrated here. T transcribes an A, but A on the DNA strand transcribes a U instead of a T. G on DNA transcribes a C.

The RNA transcript (called messenger RNA) goes from the nucleus to the cytoplasm. In the cytoplasm, ribosomes eventually "translate" the message into molecules of proteins (2-4).

This complicated information system, which resembles a busy international law office with dictation machines, messengers, transcriptionists, and translators, may have been much simpler in the remote past. Many molecular biologists now think that an "RNA world" preceded the present DNA world as life developed on earth. In order to replicate, DNA requires protein enzymes like deoxyribonuclease (DNase). These enzymes can only be created by the complex machinery of DNA, RNA, and ribosomes. It is hard to image all these different kinds of molecules coming into existence at once.

RNA, on the other hand, can take on a number of enzymatic functions as well as carrying the genetic message. Thus we can conceive of a simpler world in which a single self-replicating molecule spawned by the hot chemical soup of the early earth, like a single-person office, got the business of life off to a shaky beginning. Some viruses, which are the simplest known organisms, use RNA instead of DNA as their genetic material. The human immunodeficiency virus that causes AIDS is one of these.

The advantage of DNA over RNA is that it reproduces the genetic message much more accurately when it replicates. RNA is less stable and undergoes about a million times more mutations in the same period of time as DNA does. This can be an advantage in pathogens like HIV, because it permits the virus to keep changing and so escape its host's immune response. For large creatures like ourselves, though, that rate of mutation would almost certainly lead to rapid extinction. Sometime during the first billion or so years of earth history, DNA probably replaced RNA as the boss of the cellular office but kept RNA around to run vital messages.

The next plate shows how messenger RNA (mRNA) relays information from the cell's nucleus to the cytoplasm—in particular to the ribosomes—where it provides the manufacturing plans for protein production.

DNA AND RNA MOLECULES

NUCLEOTIDE n
PHOSPHATE p
SUGAR *
    DEOXYRIBOSE d
    RIBOSE r
BASE b

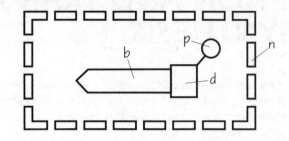

DNA DOUBLE HELIX *

BASE *
    PURINE *
        ADENINE a
        GUANINE g

PYRIMIDINE *
    CYTOSINE c
    THYMINE t
    URACIL u

HYDROGEN BOND h

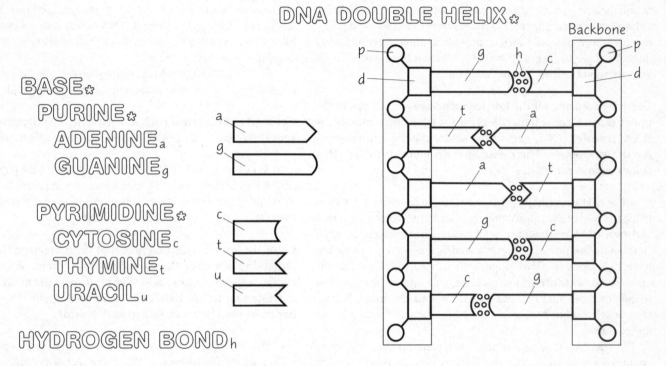

Backbone

TRANSCRIPTION OF DNA TO RNA *
DNA STRAND *   RNA STRAND s

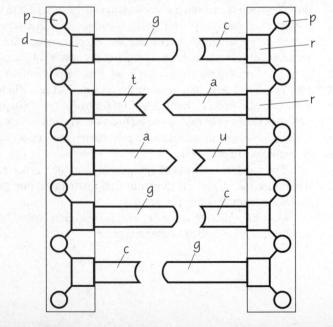

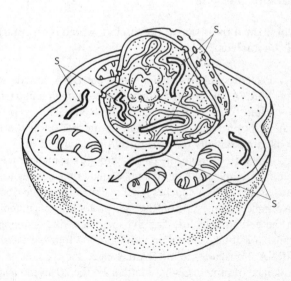

2-4
TRANSCRIPTION AND TRANSLATION: PROTEIN SYNTHESIS

In the three previous plates we learned that the genetic message necessary to direct all the processes of life is coded within the DNA. Genes strung along the double helix provide the instructions for the synthesis or manufacture of proteins. There are about 100,000 proteins in the human body. Proteins (Greek for primary), are molecules that perform many functions in the body. They are the major components of skin, muscle, and organs like the heart, kidneys, and liver. Enzymes, which control the rates of chemical reactions, and antibodies, which provide immune defense against infectious agents, are also proteins. Protein hormones control growth, reproduction, and metabolism.

Begin by coloring all the labeled structures in the cell in the upper right. Choose light colors for the ribosomes, messenger RNA, transfer RNA, and amino acids. Use the lightest color for the ribosomes. The messenger RNA and transfer RNA colors should contrast.

The first stage in the process of protein production happens in the nucleus of the cell. Within the nuclear membrane, the DNA and free RNA nucleotides combine to form messenger RNA (mRNA). (This process is complicated by the fact that most genes have two kinds of DNA sequences: exons, which encode the amino acid sequence of the proteins, and introns, meaningless strings of bases that must be edited out and discarded. Introns are transcribed but not translated [2-6]). The mRNA then leaves the nucleus.

In the second stage, which takes place in the cytoplasm, special enzymes clip out the introns (not shown), and the shortened "edited" mRNA combines with ribosomes, transfer RNA (tRNA), and amino acids to construct the amino acid chains that form proteins.

Color the illustration at the top left, which is an enlargement of the nucleus.

Protein synthesis begins when the DNA strands separate. Free mRNA nucleotides attach to the complementary bases of DNA and form a single strand of mRNA. This step is called transcription because the order of the bases on the DNA is transcribed directly onto the mRNA molecule (2-3).

The mRNA molecule passes through the nuclear membrane into the cytoplasm. After being "edited" by enzymes to remove introns, the mRNA attaches itself to a ribosome. The ribosome is an organelle consisting of RNA and proteins and is manufactured in the cell's nucleolus. The ribosome acts like a stenographer/ translator. It takes dictation written in the four-base alphabet of mRNA, translates the mRNA message, and types it up into the language of proteins, whose letters are the 20 amino acids.

Now color the enlarged ribosome and the mRNA, including the codons that run through the ribosome. It is important to use a very light shade of the mRNA color for the codons.

As the mRNA attaches to the ribosome, a "docking station" is formed where the mRNA bases are exposed three at a time, as the patterns indicate. This step of protein synthesis is called translation. Each set of three mRNA bases, called a codon, acts like a code word that translates into a particular amino acid in the developing "protein necklace."

Transfer RNA (tRNA) accomplishes this translation process by matching each codon to the appropriate amino acid.

Color all of the transfer RNA, each with its anticodon. Use a very light shade of the tRNA color for the anticodon.

At one end, each tRNA molecule has three base pairs called anticodons because they are complementary to an mRNA codon. At the other end of the tRNA, a specific amino acid corresponding to the tRNA anticodon becomes attached.

Color the amino acids and note that the pattern on the tRNA anticodon matches the attached amino acid. Each tRNA carries a specific amino acid. The pattern on the mRNA codon corresponds to the tRNA codon as well. Color the peptide bonds formed between linked amino acids.

The job of the tRNA molecule is to transport its particular amino acid to the ribosome. There, the tRNA molecule attaches by hydrogen bonds to its complementary codon on the mRNA molecule.

When two tRNAs are attached to the mRNA, a peptide bond is formed between the adjacent amino acids. The tRNA then detaches itself from both the amino acid and the mRNA and leaves the docking station to find another amino acid. The ribosome moves along the mRNA, reading the codons sequentially and forming the growing amino acid chain at the bottom of the picture. When the message is completely read, the chain of amino acids, like pearls on a string, form a protein molecule. When it is released, the protein molecule folds into its final shape and proceeds to carry out its designated function. The mRNA molecule is short-lived: it disintegrates through enzyme action and its nucleotides are recycled.

The number and kind of amino acids and their precise order determine the shape and function that distinguish one protein molecule from another.

How the exact sequence of bases in the codons specifies each amino acid is described in the next plate.

PROTEIN SYNTHESIS

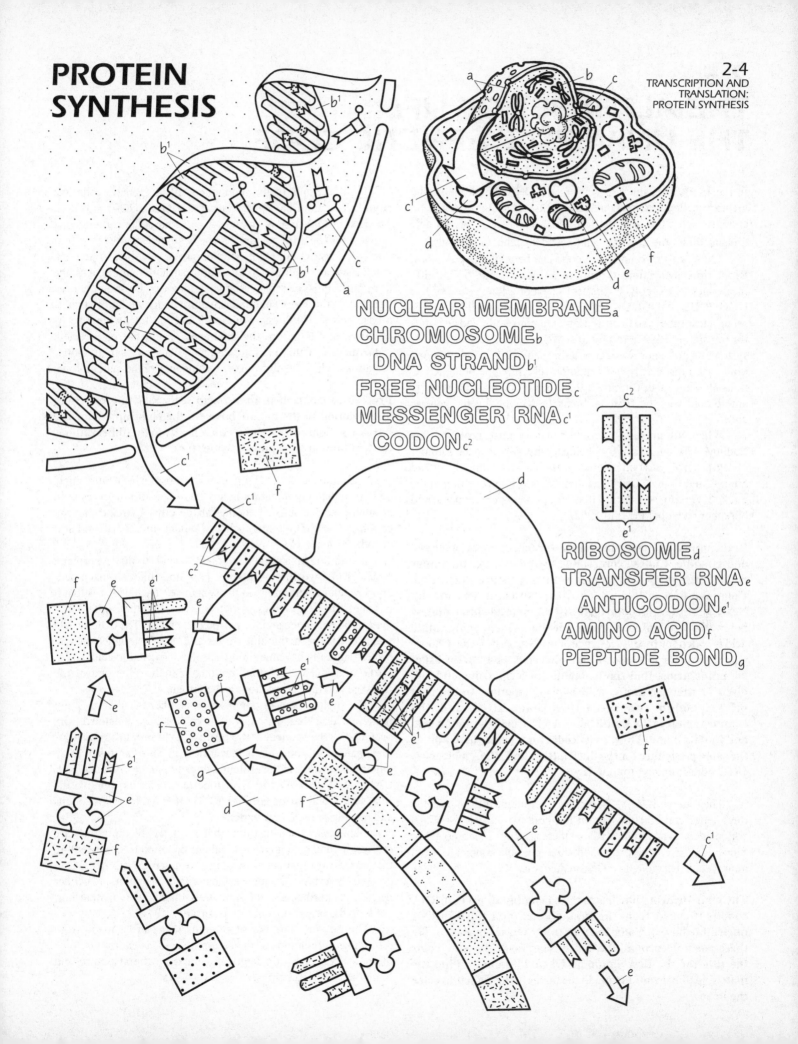

NUCLEAR MEMBRANE$_a$
CHROMOSOME$_b$
DNA STRAND$_{b^1}$
FREE NUCLEOTIDE$_c$
MESSENGER RNA$_{c^1}$
CODON$_{c^2}$

RIBOSOME$_d$
TRANSFER RNA$_e$
ANTICODON$_{e^1}$
AMINO ACID$_f$
PEPTIDE BOND$_g$

2-5
THE ALPHABET OF LIFE: THE UNIVERSAL GENETIC CODE

In the 1950s after the discovery of the DNA double helix, the greatest challenge to molecular biologists was to crack the genetic code, to figure out how the four-letter alphabet of mRNA gets translated into the 20-letter amino acid alphabet of proteins.

The key to a complicated code can be a simple password. Biochemist Marianne Grunberg-Manago made a "stupid" messenger RNA, poly-U, that consisted of a long string of Us: UUUUUUUUUUUUU... Later, biochemist Marshall Nirenberg set up a test-tube system of ribosomes, amino acids, and enzymes for translating RNA into proteins. When he fed poly-U into his system, he got a nonsensical protein chain made up of only one kind of amino acid, phenylalanine: phe.phe.phe.phe... UUU translates into phe. Linking a three base "codon" to a specific amino acid was the first big break in deciphering the genetic code.

When Nirenberg, a then unknown scientist, presented his findings at a Congress of Biochemistry in Moscow in the summer of 1961, hardly anybody attended. But the word quickly spread around, and Francis Crick had him repeat his presentation to the packed closing session. This "simple" experiment earned Nirenberg a Nobel Prize in 1968.

In the upper left, color the bases—uracil, cytosine, adenine, and guanine. Choose contrasting light colors. In the upper right, three mRNA molecules with codons are illustrated. Color the first mRNA codon, UUU (uracil, uracil, uracil). Next, color the anticodon on the tRNA molecule immediately below, AAA (adenine, adenine, adenine). One specific amino acid is coded for by the sequence of mRNA bases UUU. Choose a light color for this associated amino acid (phe). In the list of 20 amino acids, find the matching subscript, phe, and you discover that the amino acid is phenylalanine. In the next mRNA codon you see UUG. Color UUG and the complementary tRNA anticodon, AAC. Color the amino acid and find its name. Thus, UUG codes for leucine (leu). Follow the same procedure for the third mRNA and tRNA molecules. UGG codes for tryptophan (try).

The four bases (U, C, A, and G) can combine into 64 possible three-letter combinations or mRNA codons: 4x4x4=64. Each codon encodes an amino acid, but there are only 20 amino acids. Since 64/20=3.2, there are about three possible codons for each amino acid. The genetic code is redundant.

The main drawing illustrates the 64 combinations of mRNA codons (formed from the first, second, and third mRNA nucleotide bases). Color the four mRNA bases in each of the three positions around the boxes of amino acids. Now, color the title for the first amino acid listed (alanine). Find the matching abbreviation (ala) in the boxes to the right and color the boxes.

In an example of the redundancy of the genetic code, the amino acid alanine has four codons, GCU, GCC, GCA, and GCG. The first mRNA base is guanine for all four codons, the second is cytosine. The third position can be occupied by any of the four mRNA bases: uracil, cytosine, alanine, or guanine. In general, when there are multiple codons for a particular amino acid, the third position is the most variable and the first position the least variable. In the case of alanine, any third codon mutation (that is, a base pair substitution) would still encode for alanine, so its function, and therefore the organism, would not be affected. Substitutions of this kind are called "silent" or "synonymous" mutations, which result from the redundancy of the genetic code.

Proceed to color each amino acid title. Find the matching abbreviation in the box or boxes to the right and color the boxes. Use light colors. Note the similarity in the abbreviations for tryptophan (try) and tyrosine (tyr).

The amino acids methionine and tryptophan have but a single codon, so that any mutation in any codon position will result in an amino acid change. Leucine, at the other extreme, has six codons, which may undergo many "silent mutations" and still encode for leucine.

In building up a sequence of amino acids to make a protein, which is like writing a sentence, how does the cell machinery know when to start and stop the sequence? The answer is that it has start and stop codons, which function like the capital letter that starts a sentence and the period that ends it. The codon AUG which codes for methionine serves as a "start" signal, so that all proteins initially have methionine as their first amino acid. UAA, UAG, and UGA are "stop" codons, signaling the end of the message and the completion of the protein.

The replacement of one base by another is called a "point mutation" or a "base pair substitution." If a base is deleted from or added to the sequence, the result is a "frameshift mutation" that changes all the codons that follow it. This can result in an amino acid change in the protein. For example, the sentence THE CAT ATE THE HAT has five three-letter codons; remove the first letter T, and we get HEC ATA TET HEH AT, four new codons and one incomplete new codon.

Geneticists used to think that virtually all mutations are deleterious and only an occasional one beneficial. As we explore the jungles of organismal genomes, it has been discovered, to everyone's surprise, that the vast majority of mutations are neither deleterious nor beneficial but neutral—that is, they neither hurt nor help the organism's ability to survive.

The possible number of proteins that can be made from different combinations of the 20 amino acids is enormous. Tens of thousands of proteins go into creating the structure and functions of living beings.

THE GENETIC CODE

BASES FOR CODON*

URACILᵤ   U
CYTOSINE_c   C
ADENINEₐ   A
GUANINE_g   G

mRNA with codons

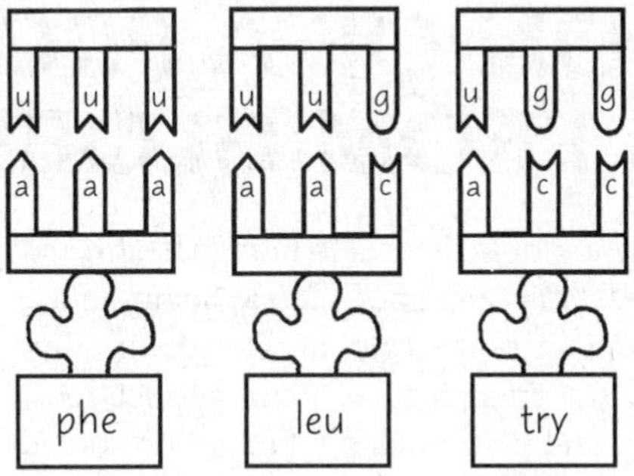

tRNA with anticodons

phe   leu   try   Amino acids

20 AMINO ACIDS*

ALANINE ala
ARGININE arg
ASPARAGINE asn
ASPARTIC ACID asp
CYSTEINE cys
GLUTAMIC ACID glu
GLUTAMINE gln
GLYCINE gly
HISTIDINE his
ISOLEUCINE ile
LEUCINE leu
LYSINE lys
METHIONINE met
PHENYLALANINE phe
PROLINE pro
SERINE ser
THREONINE thr
TRYPTOPHAN try
TYROSINE tyr
VALINE val

Second mRNA nucleotide base

First mRNA nucleotide base

Third mRNA nucleotide base

First	U	C	A	G	Third
U	phe	ser	tyr	cys	U
U	phe	ser	tyr	cys	C
U	leu	ser	Stop	Stop	A
U	leu	ser	Stop	try	G
C	leu	pro	his	arg	U
C	leu	pro	his	arg	C
C	leu	pro	gln	arg	A
C	leu	pro	gln	arg	G
A	ile	thr	asn	ser	U
A	ile	thr	asn	ser	C
A	ile	thr	lys	arg	A
A	met	thr	lys	arg	G
G	val	ala	asp	gly	U
G	val	ala	asp	gly	C
G	val	ala	glu	gly	A
G	val	ala	glu	gly	G

64 CODON POSSIBILITIES*

2-6
EVOLUTION OF A PROTEIN: LESSONS FROM GLOBIN GENES

The red blood pigment, hemoglobin, is vital to human health and has been studied intensively. Globin genes encode hemoglobin, which is made up of iron and the protein globin. The globin story illustrates gene structure, the frequency of gene duplications, changing protein function, and genes that die but are preserved in a recognizable form in the mausoleum of the genome.

Begin by coloring gene structure at the bottom of the plate and the illustration of plant globin (leghemoglobin).

Genes consist of a long sequence of DNA base pairs with alternating stretches called exons and introns. The exons encode the amino acids, which are translated into proteins (2-4, 2-5). The introns do not code for amino acids; they seem to act as spacers, and are taken out during translation and discarded.

Globin proteins are present in some plants and in all animals. A plant globin gene has four exons and three introns. The middle intron was lost in animal lineages, which have only two. The two adjacent exons are now combined into one longer sequence. Therefore, the first globin gene must have originated before plants and animals diverged from a common ancestor a billion years ago. The original globin in animals was myoglobin, the muscle pigment that binds oxygen.

Starting just above the animal globin, color the myoglobin line up to 700 mya. Color the invertebrates, represented by a sea star and anemone. Next, color the myoglobin and hemoglobin up to 450 mya. Early vertebrates are represented by a hagfish, a primitive jawless fish. The rectangle enclosing the two jawless fish is to remind you that both myoglobin and hemoglobin are present in early vertebrates.

During evolution, genes often duplicate into two identical copies. Invertebrates have myoglobin but no hemoglobin. Vertebrates have both. The original myoglobin gene must have duplicated after invertebrates and vertebrates separated about 700 mya (1-19).

When the myoglobin gene duplicated, one gene continued to code for myoglobin, the other became the hemoglobin gene. Usually, one gene product retains the original function, while the second evolves and takes on a complementary function. In animals, the hemoglobin molecule carries oxygen from the water or air to the tissues, and carbon dioxide from the tissues back to the external environment. (Plant globin probably helps to eliminate oxygen from plant tissues, since oxygen, not carbon dioxide, is the waste product of plant metabolism.)

Continue coloring the myoglobin gene up to 300 mya. Color the alpha and beta hemoglobin genes up to 300 mya. Color the jawed fish.

About 450 mya, not long after the origin of the jawed fish, the hemoglobin gene duplicated again into the alpha and beta hemoglobin. Jawed fish have myoglobin and alpha and beta hemoglobin.

Finish coloring the myoglobin. Next, color the rest of the alpha, theta, zeta, beta, and gamma hemoglobins.

Around 300 mya, about the time of the land vertebrates (represented here by the extinct amphibian *Eryops*), the alpha gene duplicated into theta and zeta globin genes. About 150 mya, the time of the early mammals (represented here by the tree shrew), the beta gene duplicated, giving rise to the gamma gene. New World monkeys have a single gamma globin gene. Old World monkeys and humans have two—gamma G and gamma A. Therefore, the gamma gene must have duplicated after the New World monkey and Old World monkey lineages separated about 35 mya.

Color the pseudogenes. Color the human chromosome numbers and associated figures.

If a duplicated gene undergoes damaging mutations, it may not be able to translate itself into a protein product and thus becomes nonfunctional. These nonfunctional "pseudogenes" undergo further mutations at a rapid rate because natural selection does not constrain these changes, as it would constrain a functioning gene (2-10). Pseudogenes have identifiable sequences but, for all practical purposes, are dead and buried in the genome. Like fossils, they may be useful in reconstructing evolutionary history. After all the duplications, the alpha hemoglobin family in humans consists of four functional genes and three pseudogenes (not all illustrated) on chromosome 16. The beta hemoglobin family on chromosome 11 has five functional genes and one pseudogene. Myoglobin is on chromosome 22.

The myriad of duplicated globin genes in humans provide a sophisticated physiological system for different stages of life. For example, the embryo growing in the low oxygen environment of the uterus needs to make the most of the little oxygen it has. Some combinations of hemoglobin chains have higher affinity for oxygen than others. The highest oxygen binders are active in the embryo; the next highest appears in the fetus; and lower affinity hemoglobin emerges during childhood and adulthood, when the ambient air is high in oxygen. The situation changes for people living in malarial regions or in the high Himalayas and this requires further genetic adaptations (6-12, 6-14).

The billion-year history of the globin superfamily shows how: 1) a single gene can duplicate and take on new functions; 2) a gene can become a nonfunctional pseudogene; 3) related members of a family of genes can help the organism to survive different developmental stages; and 4) the presence or absence of genes in lineages helps reconstruct the evolutionary history of the gene family, and when lineages of animals separated from each other in geological time.

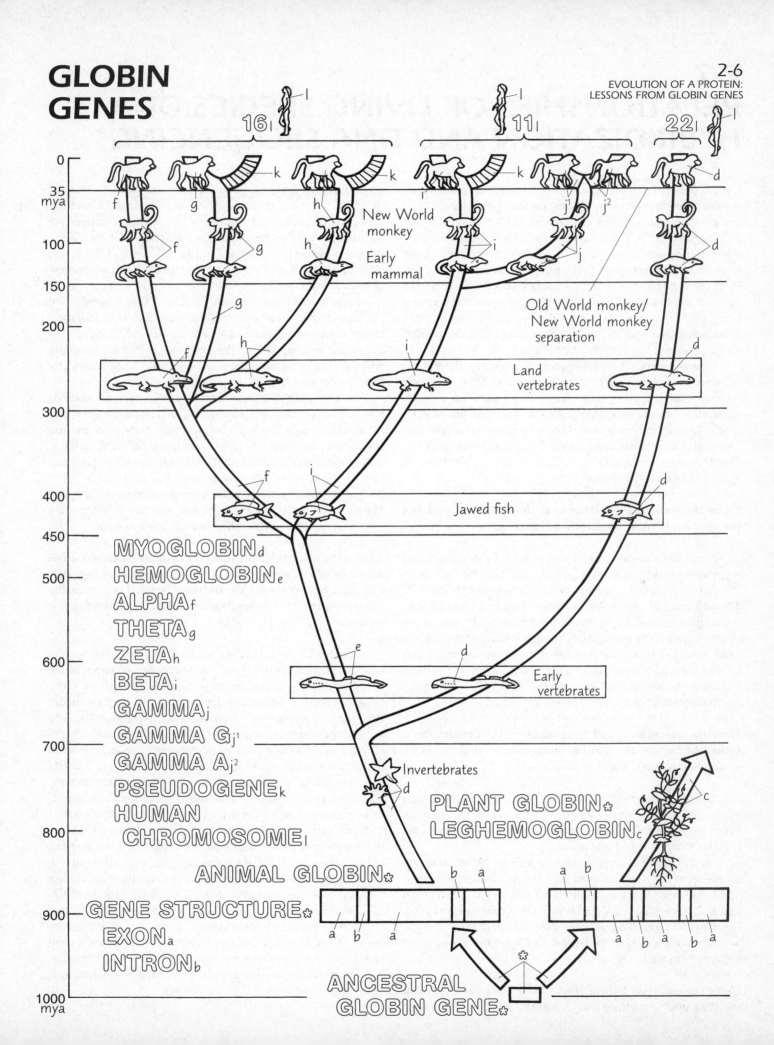

GLOBIN GENES

16ι

11ι

22ι

k

k

k

d

f

g

h

i

j¹   j²

d

New World monkey

Early mammal

f

g

h

i

j

d

g

h

Old World monkey/
New World monkey
separation

f

h

i

d

Land vertebrates

f

i

d

Jawed fish

MYOGLOBIN_d
HEMOGLOBIN_e
ALPHA_f
THETA_g
ZETA_h
BETA_i
GAMMA_j
GAMMA G_j¹
GAMMA A_j²
PSEUDOGENE_k
HUMAN
CHROMOSOME_ι

e

d

Early vertebrates

Invertebrates

d

PLANT GLOBIN*
LEGHEMOGLOBIN_c

c

ANIMAL GLOBIN*

GENE STRUCTURE*
EXON_a
INTRON_b

b   a

a   b

a   b   a

a   b   a   b   a

ANCESTRAL
GLOBIN GENE*

2-7
RELATIONSHIPS OF LIVING SPECIES:DNA HYBRIDIZATION AND DNA SEQUENCING

Darwin deduced that over time all species have descended with modification from previous species. He relied on evidence from comparative anatomy and embryology, the fossil record, and biogeography (1-2). The discovery of DNA and the genetic code made it possible to directly and quantitatively establish relationships among species. The genetic code is universal, that is, all life forms on earth use the same DNA codons to determine the same amino acids, and bacteria and elephants have in common many of the same genes. These discoveries prove Darwin's deduction that all species on earth, living and extinct, stem from the same ancestor and form a "tree of life."

Genes consist of DNA sequences. Genetic differences between species consist of differences in the DNA base pair sequences, which can be counted. The more closely related species are, the more similar are the DNA sequences between homologous genes, like the globin genes. The more distantly related two species are, the more differences there are in homologous genes. One technique for measuring "genetic distance" between two species is DNA hybridization.

Color the human DNA strands at the top left. Color the chimpanzee DNA, using a contrasting color.

Since DNA is made up of two helices, or strands, bound together by hydrogen bonds (2-1), we can take one helix each from two different species and make an artificial hybrid DNA. The base pairs in these hybrid helices will not match exactly, as the original helices did, so they will not bind together as tightly as the originals. The more genetically distant the two species, the more mismatches, and the more weakly the hybrid strands will bind to each other. Binding strength is reflected in the melting temperature, the minimum temperature required in a laboratory to separate a double helix into two single helices.

Color the human DNA and the chimpanzee DNA in each flask. Color the flames, the melting temperatures, and the DNA strands in the petri dish.

To carry out hybridization, DNA is extracted from the cells of the species to be tested—for instance, human and chimpanzee. When the DNA solutions are heated to about 86°C, the double helix melts apart into single strands.

Next, the biochemist uses enzymes to "snip" a single homologous DNA strand from each species into fragments of about 500 nucleotides in length. If we mix single strands from human DNA solutions and chimpanzee DNA solutions, and allow the solution to cool, the single strands bind to other single strands. We then have a double strand that is a hybrid of chimpanzee DNA and human DNA.

Color the enlarged hybrid DNA. Color the hybrid DNA in the flask and its melting temperature.

When heated, the hybrid helices melt apart at 84.4°C instead of 86°C, a 1.6° difference. Each degree drop in melting temperature indicates approximately 1% mismatch between the two strands. The human-chimpanzee difference is 1.6%. Using the same method, the human-gorilla difference is 2.4%, the chimpanzee-gorilla difference, 2.1%, and the orangutan's average difference from this trio is 3.6%.

From these data we can conclude that humans and chimpanzees are most closely related, and therefore had the most recent common ancestor. The gorilla lineage branches off somewhat earlier, before the chimpanzee-human common ancestor. The orangutans are about twice as distant genetically from the human-chimpanzee-gorilla trio.

As a measure of genetic distance, DNA hybridization has both advantages and disadvantages. The main advantage is that by working with extracts from whole cells, the method simultaneously compares DNA from many different genes as well as the noncoding DNA (2-6) and so gives a kind of average genetic distance of the whole genomes of species being compared. (The genome is the total genetic material of a species.) The disadvantage is that hybridization does not yield the exact base-pair sequences of the DNA strands that are tested.

At the lower left, color the differences in the bases of a small sequence of the hemoglobin gene in four hominoid species. Choose a light color for the different bases. Then color the comparison of DNA hybridization and DNA sequencing test results.

Using a DNA-sequencing method, Morris Goodman and his colleagues determined the exact sequence of bases of the beta globin genes (2-6) in humans and three ape species. Once DNA sequences are determined, they can be lined up, one under the other, like sentences from different editions of an old manuscript, and the base-pairs that differ can be counted.

In a small portion of the beta globin gene sequence shown here, human and chimpanzee differ in only 1 base; gorilla differs from human and chimpanzee in 2 bases, and orangutan from the other species in 3 bases. Comparison of sequences of thousands of beta globin bases gives a human-chimpanzee difference of 1.7%, almost exactly the same as the hybridization results. By this method, the human-gorilla difference is 2.0% and the chimpanzee-gorilla difference is 1.9% (not illustrated), confirming that human and chimpanzee are the most closely related pair. Again, orangutan differs from these 3 by about 4%.

These quantitative comparisons of hominoid DNA by two different methods, hybridization and sequencing, give the same results. They show that humans and chimpanzees are the most closely related "sister species," that the gorilla is a slightly older step-brother to the two sisters, and the orangutan is a more distant Asian cousin to the three African siblings.

DNA HYBRIDIZATION

HUMAN DNA*a*
CHIMPANZEE DNA*b*
MELTING TEMPERATURE*c*
HYBRID DNA*d*
MATCHING BASE*e*
MISMATCHED BASE*f*

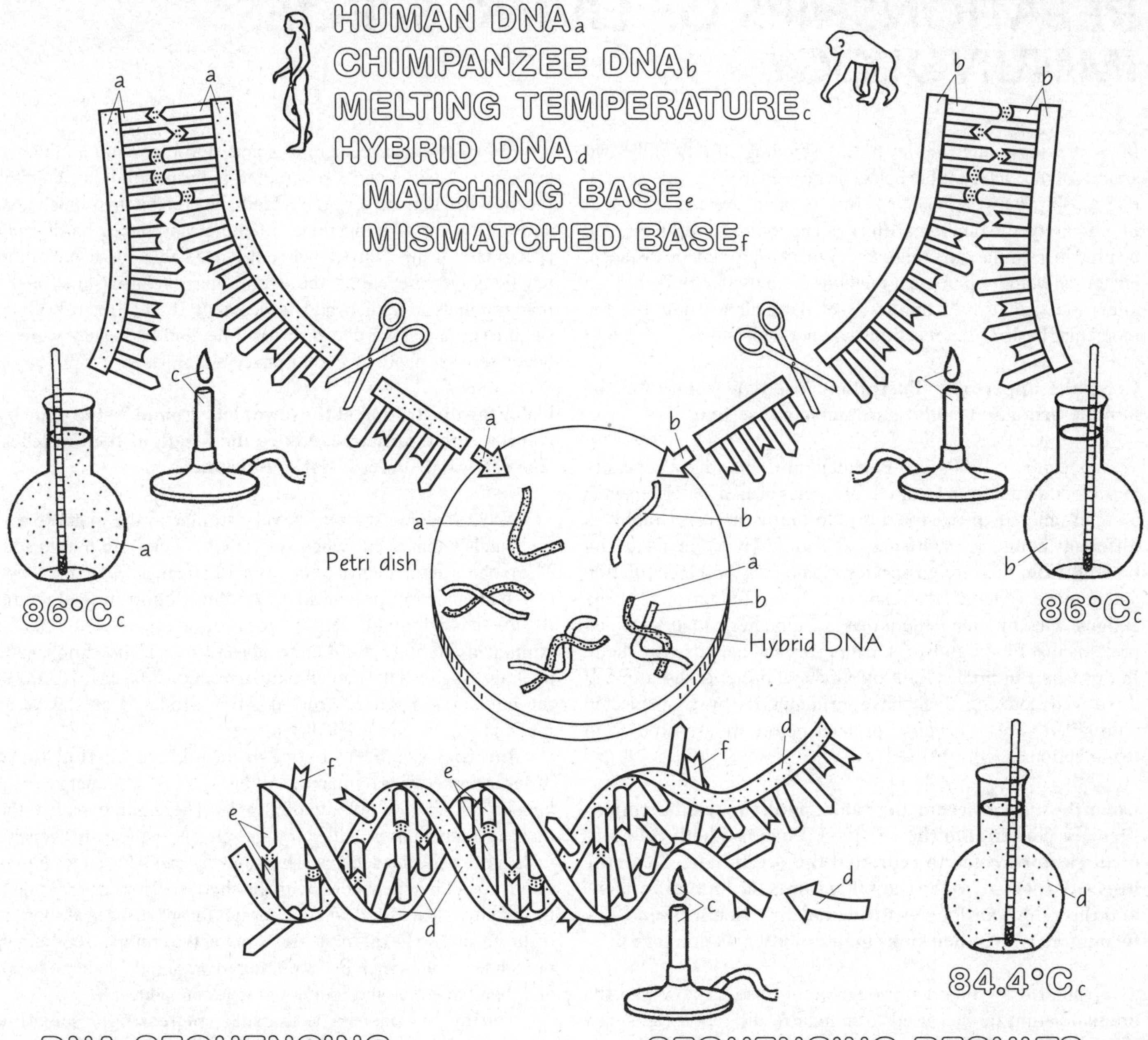

Petri dish

Hybrid DNA

86°C*c*

86°C*c*

84.4°C*c*

DNA SEQUENCING*
DIFFERENT BASE*g*

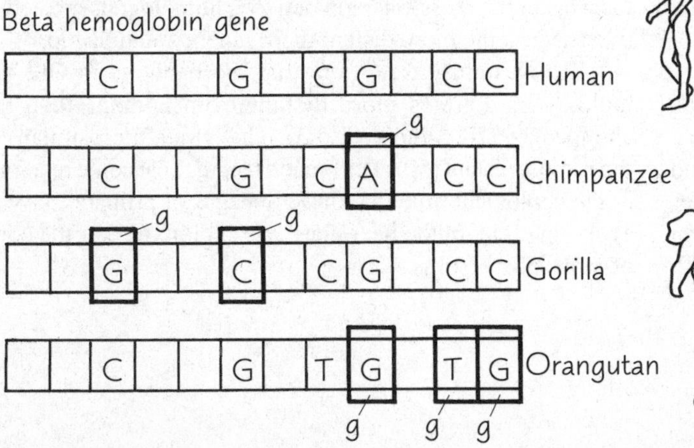

Beta hemoglobin gene

| | | C | | G | | C G | | C C | Human |

| | | C | | G | | C A | | C C | Chimpanzee |

| | G | | C | | C G | | C C | Gorilla |

| | | C | | G | T G | | T G | Orangutan |

SEQUENCING RESULTS*g¹*
HYBRIDIZATION RESULTS*h*

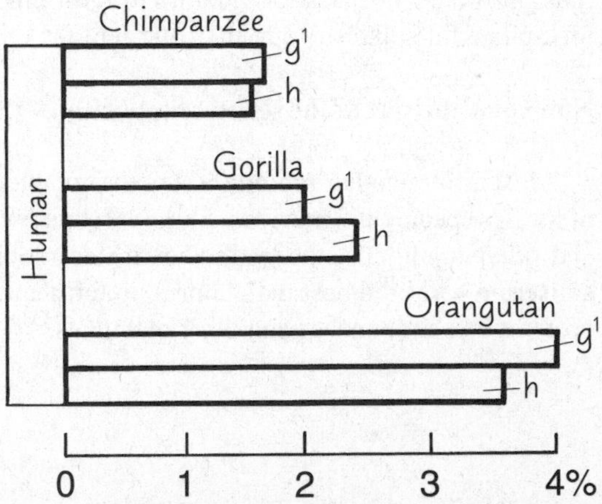

Chimpanzee

Human

Gorilla

Orangutan

0   1   2   3   4%

2-8
RELATIONSHIPS OF LIVING SPECIES: IMMUNOLOGY

In the previous plate, we saw how the binding affinity of the two strands of the DNA double helix can be used to assess the genetic relationship between species. In this plate, we illustrate that immunology, the binding affinity of antibodies for proteins, can be used in a similar quantitative way to measure genetic distance. Historically, immunological methods were used long before we knew the structure of the genes or the genetic code, but the molecular basis of the reactions was not understood.

Color the uppermost illustration. Use light colors for the human serum and rabbit antihuman antiserum.

As early as 1900, G.H.F. Nuttall at Cambridge University took blood serum from hundreds of species of animals. He injected a small amount of each serum into the tissues of a rabbit, a different rabbit for each species. The rabbit is "invaded" by proteins from the foreign species. Some cells in the circulation and immune system of the rabbit react to this foreign protein, the antigen. The immune system makes antibodies, small Y-shaped proteins that bind tightly to the antigens and help destroy them. In this way, our bodies fight off viral and bacterial disease, and do so even more effectively if we are immunized by being injected with killed viral or bacterial proteins before we are exposed to the infectious agents themselves.

Color the human serum and rabbit antihuman antiserum as they are poured into the test tube. Then use both colors to create a third color to represent the precipitate. Color the inset enlargement to the right that shows the human antigens and the rabbit antibodies fitting together in a lock-and-key formation, which then sinks out of solution as precipitate.

Nuttall drew blood from each rabbit, so he now had the original serum he had used to immunize the rabbit (let's say, human serum) plus rabbit antiserum against human serum proteins. When human serum is added in a test tube to rabbit antiserum, the binding of the rabbit antibody with its antigen (human protein) causes the mixture to turn milky, and a white precipitate falls like snow to the bottom of the tube.

Now color the rest of the serum comparisons. Use light colors.

Just as human DNA binds best to the complementary strand of its own species and more weakly to the strands of chimpanzees and other mammals, the antibodies in the rabbit's antihuman antiserum will bind best with human proteins and less well with proteins of chimpanzees and other mammals.

When chimpanzee serum is added to the rabbit antihuman antiserum, again a white precipitate is formed, but not quite as much. When baboon serum is added, the precipitate is much less, and the serum of nonprimate mammals produces hardly any precipitate at all. Nuttall was convinced that these precipitin reactions were revealing the evolutionary relationships of the many animals he studied, and he was right. But like many brilliant scientists, he was far ahead of his time, and his results weren't taken very seriously by evolutionary biologists.

Color the illustration at the lower left. Complete the plate by coloring the family tree. Notice the length of the branches. The vertical distance is not significant.

What is going on here is very similar to the matches and mismatches that occur when two DNA species are hybridized. The rabbit's antihuman antibody is perfectly matched to the shape of a human serum protein like albumin. Chimpanzee albumin, though, is slightly different in shape from human albumin, and so human antibody to albumin doesn't match the chimpanzee albumin exactly. If the human-human reaction is taken to be 100%, the human-chimpanzee cross-reaction produces only 95% as much precipitate, or a 5% difference.

In cross-reactions between albumins, we find these differences between humans and other species: chimpanzee 5%; baboon 20%, lemur 50%, and rat 65%. These numbers, like the melting temperatures in the previous plate, can measure "genetic distances" between species. The numbers can be used to draw a family tree. First the species with the shortest distances are joined; this group is then joined with the species that have the next shortest distance, and so forth. In the tree shown, the chimpanzee-human branch is 5, the branch between these two and the baboon is 20, and then the lemur and rodent branches are added.

During the past three decades, increasingly sensitive immunological tests have been used for deriving family trees—immunodiffusion, complement fixation, and radioimmunoassay. The principles are still the same as those discovered by Nuttall: the weaker the cross-reaction between homologous molecules of two species, the more distant their genetic relationship.

In this family tree, note that the baboon, an Old World monkey, is 4 times more distant from humans than is the chimpanzee (20 compared to 5). The lemur, a prosimian, is 10 times more distant (50). The branch lengths bear some relationship to the geological time that these lineages of primates have been evolving (3-1). In the next plate, we explore further the concept of molecular clocks.

IMMUNOLOGY

HUMAN SERUM$_a$
  HUMAN PROTEIN/
  ANTIGEN$_{a^1}$
RABBIT$_b$
  RABBIT ANTIHUMAN
  ANTISERUM$_c$
  ANTIBODY$_{c^1}$
CHIMPANZEE SERUM$_d$
BABOON SERUM$_e$
LEMUR SERUM$_f$
RAT SERUM$_g$
  RAT ANTIGEN$_{g^1}$

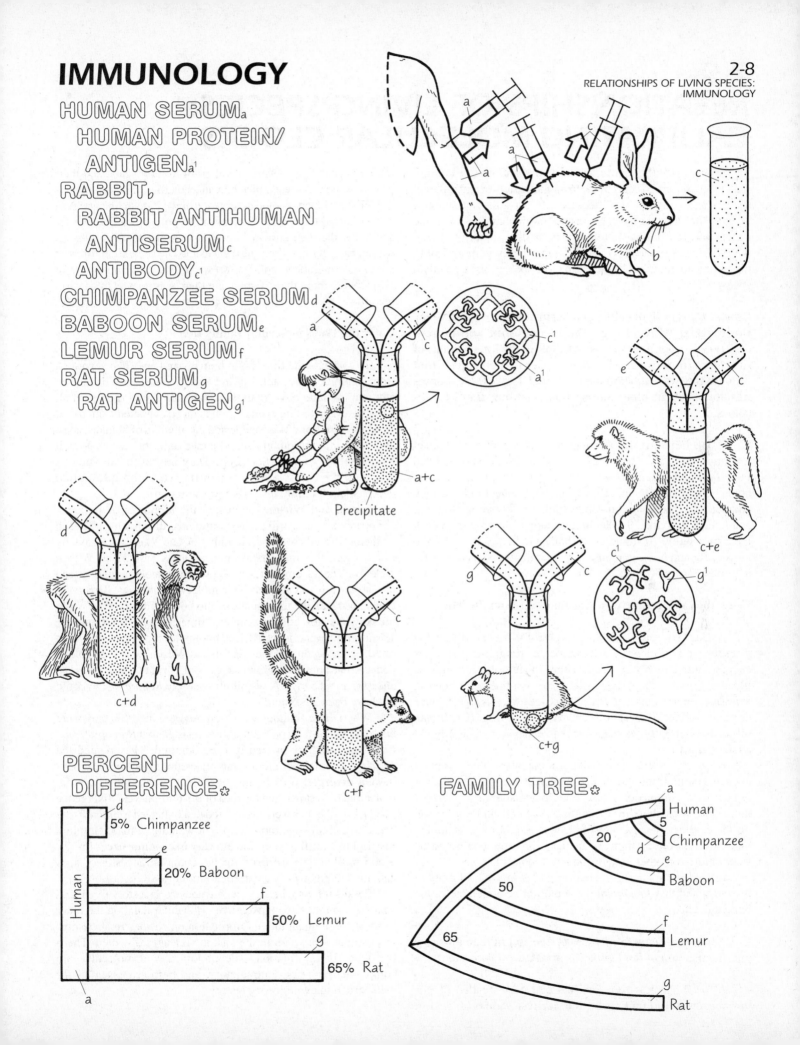

a+c
Precipitate

c+e

c+d

c+f

c+g

PERCENT DIFFERENCE *

5% Chimpanzee
20% Baboon
50% Lemur
65% Rat

Human

FAMILY TREE *

a
Human
5
20
Chimpanzee
d
e
Baboon
50
f
65
Lemur
g
Rat

RELATIONSHIPS OF LIVING SPECIES: CALIBRATING MOLECULAR CLOCKS

In the early 1960s, Emile Zuckerkandl and Linus Pauling sequenced the amino acids of the hemoglobins of several different species and counted the differences. In a significant show of insight, they juxtaposed their results in biochemistry with the history of life from paleontology. The findings surprised them: the differences in the amino acids were roughly proportional to the estimated geological time since these species had a common ancestor!

Choose six very light colors and begin at the top right. Color the matrix, which shows the hemoglobin amino acid differences among six species. At some of the intersections of the colors from two species, the number of amino acids that differ in the two hemoglobins is recorded. Leave these squares uncolored. At the other intersections, combine the two light colors.

Using the matrix we can compare species. Follow the human row until it intersects with the horse row at 18. Zuckerkandl and Pauling found 18 amino acid differences between human and horse hemoglobins. Similarly, comparing human to mouse they counted 16; comparing human to bird, 35; human to frog, 62; and human to shark, 79. The three mammals differed from each other by roughly 20 amino acids (human to horse, 18; human to mouse, 16; and horse to mouse, 22). Mammals and sharks differ in almost 80 amino acids (79, 77, 79).

Using the same colors, color the family tree on the left.

Zuckerkandl and Pauling insightfully observed that the number of amino acid differences among these species corresponded in rough proportions to geological time (as illustrated) when they juxtaposed these two lines of evidence. Primate (human), horse, and mouse lineages were thought to have originated about 70 mya, birds about 270 mya, frogs (amphibian origins) about 350 mya, and sharks (cartilaginous fish origins) about 450 mya.

Hemoglobin was acting like a molecular clock! Nobody expected biomolecules to change at a somewhat regular rate over hundreds of millions of years. Many paleontologists criticized molecular researchers for "assuming" such clocklike behavior. To the contrary, steady rates of change are not an assumption, but, based on observations of the data, are now confirmed by more studies on other protein and DNA molecules.

In their first application to human evolution, molecular clocks demonstrated that *Ramapithecus* could not be a member of the human lineage.

Color the traditional family tree of ape and human ancestry and the position of *Ramapithecus* and *Australopithecus*.

A fossil species from Pakistan and Africa called *Ramapithecus* was thought to be the earliest human ancestor.

Ramapithecus fossils were as old as 14 million years, and their teeth in some ways resembled human teeth. Many anthropologists therefore assumed that the divergence of the human lineage from apes occurred more than 20 mya. Anthropologists did, however, agree that the then-known 2-million-year-old *Australopithecus* was an early human (hominid) ancestor. The separation times of gibbons, orangutans, chimpanzees, gorillas, and humans were estimated to more than 20 mya, but there was no way to confirm the time.

Color the 1960s molecular family tree.

To estimate the time when humans and apes had separated from a common ancestor, Vincent Sarich and Allan Wilson used albumin immunology. Albumin is the main serum protein of all vertebrates, including primates, and can be extracted from blood samples. Sarich and Wilson injected the albumin of humans, apes, and monkeys into rabbits and obtained antisera, just as Nuttall had done 60 years earlier (2-8). They improved on Nuttall's methods by using a more quantitative technique called complement fixation, instead of precipitation.

Sarich and Wilson found that the albumins of humans, chimpanzees, and gorillas (the hominoids) differed by 1%; each of them differed from the albumins of Old World monkeys by 6%. To turn this information into a clock, Sarich and Wilson picked an event from the fossil record that paleontologists agreed on and used it to calibrate their molecular findings. The event they chose was the divergence of the hominoids and Old World monkey lineages, and the estimated time, 30 mya. Therefore, the 1% difference among the African hominoids represents one-sixth of 30, or 5. As you can see, Sarich and Wilson were then able to deduce that humans, chimpanzees, and gorillas had a common ancestor about 5 mya. A 14-million-year-old *Ramapithecus* could not have been a hominid!

When these findings were first reported in 1967, they were controversial. Many paleontologists insisted that *Ramapithecus'* dental morphology proved it to be hominid. They denied the validity of molecular clocks and rejected a 5-million-year ape-human divergence as being too recent. Subsequently, more molecular data supported the idea of a 5-million-year divergence (2-11). Fossil bones were discovered that indicated *Ramapithecus* was a tree-living ape, not an upright walking human. Hominid fossils 3 to 4 million years old are very like chimpanzees (5-17). The 5-million-year estimate for the common ancestor of apes and humans fits with the current hominid fossil record.

Fossils tell us when and where ancient ancestors lived, and what they might have looked like. Molecular data, on the other hand, provide quantitative information on species relationships and estimates of when in the past the lineages diverged. These two kinds of information, paleontological and molecular, are complementary, not contradictory, and both are essential for reconstructing evolutionary history.

MOLECULAR CLOCKS

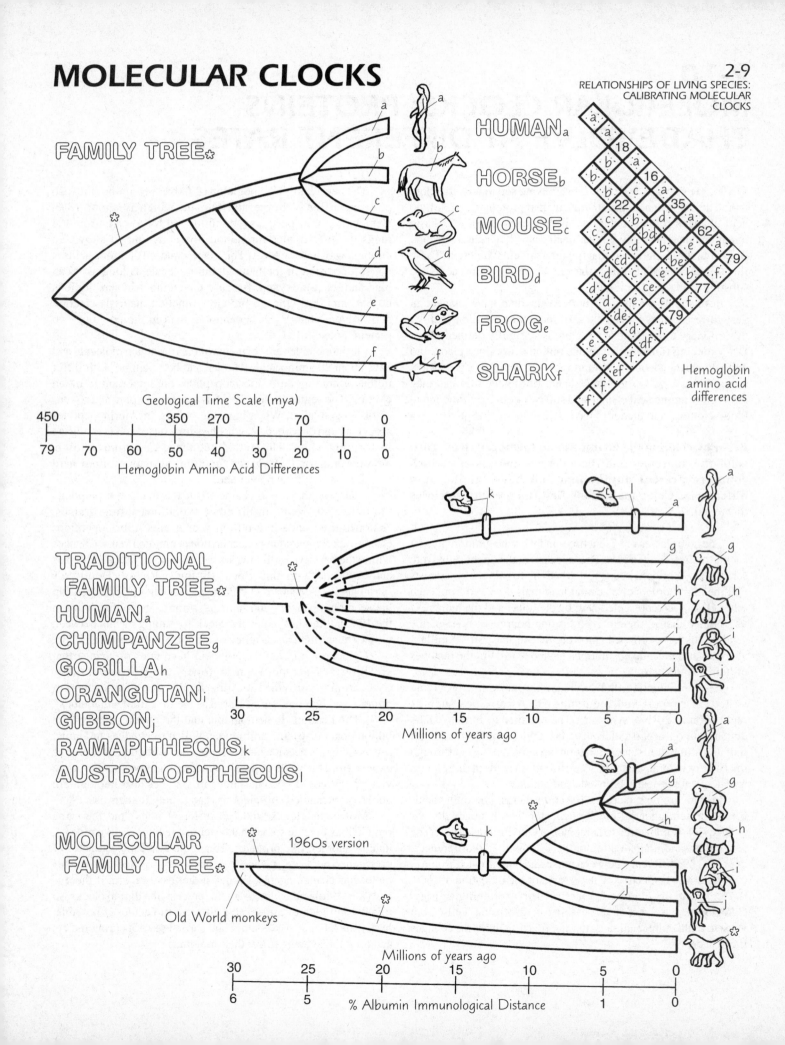

FAMILY TREE

HUMAN_a

HORSE_b

MOUSE_c

BIRD_d

FROG_e

SHARK_f

Hemoglobin
amino acid
differences

Geological Time Scale (mya)

450 350 270 70 0

79 70 60 50 40 30 20 10 0

Hemoglobin Amino Acid Differences

**TRADITIONAL
FAMILY TREE**
HUMAN_a
CHIMPANZEE_g
GORILLA_h
ORANGUTAN_i
GIBBON_j
RAMAPITHECUS_k
AUSTRALOPITHECUS_l

30 25 20 15 10 5 0

Millions of years ago

**MOLECULAR
FAMILY TREE**

1960s version

Old World monkeys

Millions of years ago

30 25 20 15 10 5 0

6 5 1 0

% Albumin Immunological Distance

MOLECULAR CLOCKS: PROTEINS THAT EVOLVE AT DIFFERENT RATES

The longer two species have been evolving separately, the more amino acid differences accumulate in their proteins (2-9). Amino acid changes reflect mutations in the genes (2-5). The basic mutation rate is probably similar for all genes, but natural selection filters out those mutations that impair a protein's function. These functional constraints affect the rate at which amino acids are substituted in a given protein.

In this plate we look at four proteins that have changed at very different rates in the course of more than a billion years of evolutionary time. Histone structure is so rigidly defined for its DNA-binding function that in one billion years since plants and animals separated, only one amino acid difference exists between a pea and a cow. On the other hand, fibrinopeptides can take almost any amino acid change and still carry out their function in blood clotting, and therefore have a fast rate of change.

Begin by coloring the hourglasses in the upper right. Then color the molecules and the enlarged hourglasses, which compare present day human and horse amino acid differences. Color the histone first, then each protein as discussed.

The hourglasses represent time, and the sand grains represent each protein's amino acids. The "clocks" in the upper right were set at zero 90 million years ago, when the fossil record suggests that the major orders of placental mammals diverged from each other (1-22), as represented here by the horse and the human.

Notice that in the enlarged histone hourglass, none of the sand grains have dropped, showing that in the past 90 million years no amino acid substitutions have occurred in the histones of human and horse.

Histones interact with DNA in the chromosomes, providing structural support and regulating DNA activities such as replication and RNA synthesis. Their ability to bind to DNA depends upon a particular structure and shape. Virtually all mutations impair histone's function, so almost none get through the filter of natural selection. The 103 amino acids in this protein are identical for nearly all plants and animals.

In cytochrome c, there are 104 amino acids. The amino acids in this protein undergo mutations faster than histones do, but change slowly compared to hemoglobin and fibrinopeptides. The few fallen sand grains represent the 12 amino acid differences, or about 12% difference between horse and human cytochrome c. Cytochrome c is an enzyme necessary for the oxidation of food, the cell's main chemical reaction for producing energy. Cytochrome c is found in all aerobic (oxygen-using) cells, from yeast to multicellular animals. Its vital function limits the changes it can accept.

The beta chain of hemoglobin (2-6) has 146 amino acids; 26 of them differ in horse and human, which is about 18%. Hemoglobin transports oxygen in the red blood cells from the lungs to other tissues throughout the body and so allows an efficient way to use energy. The exact sequence of amino acids is not so important in the hemoglobin molecule as long as it can bind and release oxygen. Because the amino acid substitutions do not interfere with the protein's function, natural selection allows more changes in hemoglobin than in the previous two protein molecules.

Fibrinopeptides are segments of the fibrinogen molecule and have about 20 amino acids. Human and horse amino acids differ in this protein by 86%. Fibrinopeptides are important in blood clotting. The segments simply act as spacers, keeping active sites of fibrinogen apart. When bleeding occurs, the fibrinopeptides are cut out and discarded, leaving the sticky surfaces free to engage in forming clots. The actual sequence of amino acids is unimportant for this spacer function, so many amino acid substitutions have been tolerated.

Each protein, with its characteristic rate of change, pinpoints the timing of events in different evolutionary time frames. Histones time once-in-a-billion year events. Fibrinopeptides change rapidly, averaging one mutation per million years. Changes within the past five million years between closely related species can be timed with this clock. Biologist Russell Doolittle's fibrinopeptide sequences in 1970 pointed out the close relationship between chimpanzees and humans, prior to its confirmation in the 1980s. (Another molecular clock for timing events between closely related species is mitochondrial DNA discussed in 2-11).

Cytochrome c and hemoglobin have rates of change that are intermediate between histones and fibrinopeptides. Cytochrome c provided the first family tree of a sequenced protein, and hemoglobin was used as the first "molecular clock" (2-9). Duplications in hemoglobin and the globin genes span a billion years (2-6) and are intimately tied to changes in animal life. As animals became land dwelling and shifted their source of oxygen from the water to the air, changes in globin structure were vital. They could become larger in size because hemoglobin duplication enabled sufficient oxygen supply to their tissues.

Molecular clocks "tick" at different rates, and the same protein may change somewhat faster in one lineage, like rodents, than in another, like primates. To get the best time estimates of divergence between species, it is necessary to check the rate of molecular change against events in the fossil record, if there is one (2-9). Molecular clocks are not precise like digital clocks, so it is a good idea to use several different molecules if possible, just as the navigators a century ago carried several chronometers and took the average to get their longitude.

PROTEINS THAT EVOLVE AT DIFFERENT RATES

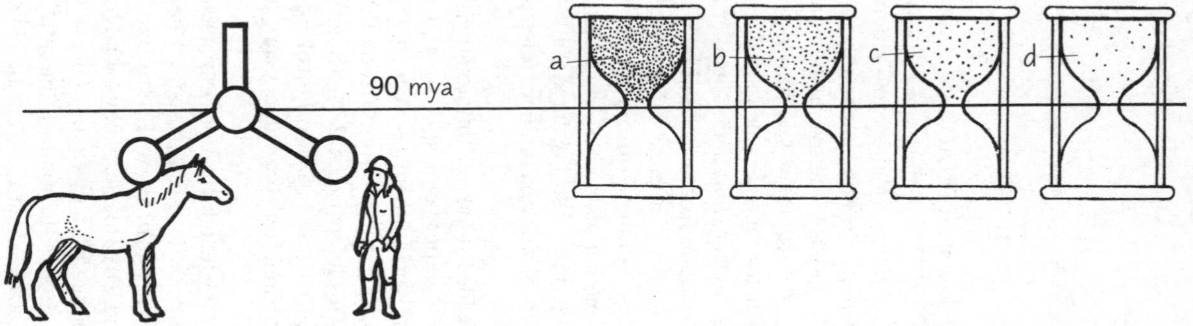

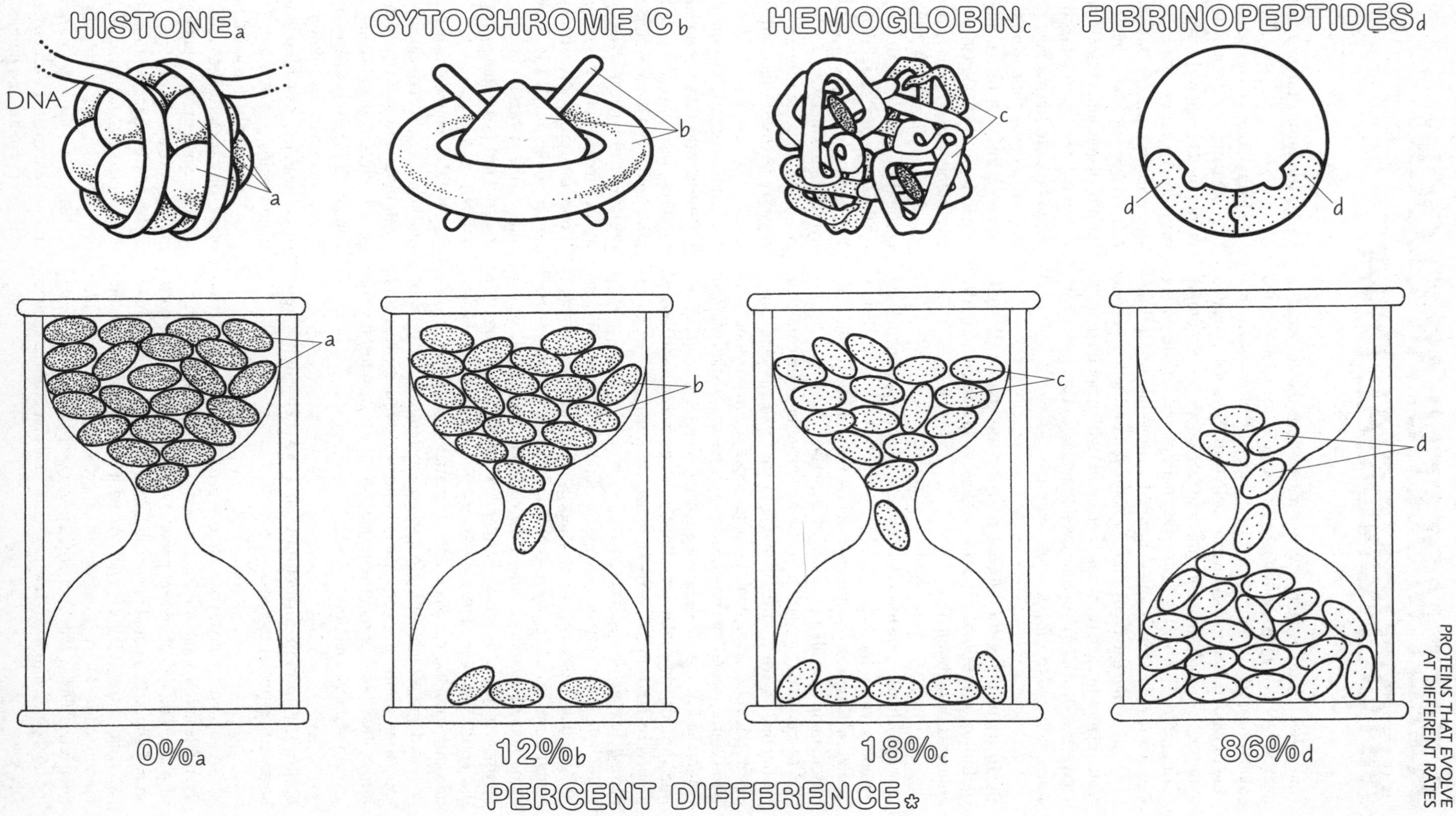

90 mya

HISTONE a

DNA

CYTOCHROME C b

HEMOGLOBIN c

FIBRINOPEPTIDES d

0% a

12% b

18% c

86% d

PERCENT DIFFERENCE *

2-11
A FAST MOLECULAR CLOCK: MITOCHONDRIAL DNA

Until now our discussion of genes and proteins has referred to nuclear DNA (2-1). Although most of the genetic material of the eukaryotic cell is concentrated in its nucleus, there is another kind of DNA called mitochondrial DNA (mtDNA) that is located in the cell's cytoplasm. Mitochondrial DNA does not recombine during mitosis (1-13) and is carried only by the female during meiosis (1-14). In mammals, mtDNA evolves about 10 times faster than nuclear DNA and is useful for evaluating genetic relationships in closely related species and within populations. It serves as a "fast clock" to time events that have taken place from a few thousand to a few million years ago.

Begin by coloring the labeled parts of the eukaryotic cell, including the mitochrondria in the cytoplasm. Color the enlarged mitochondrion.

Mitochondria are tiny oval organelles that are present in large numbers within the cytoplasm of eukaryotic cells. They act as miniature batteries, providing power for the activities of the cell. Mitochondria are about the size of bacteria.

More than 20 years ago, Lynn Margulis suspected that mitochondria were, in fact, bacteria that had invaded early eukaryotic cells, set up housekeeping, and in return provided their hosts with enzymes that produce energy. This speculation seemed far-fetched at the time, but sequencing DNA and comparing mitochrondria to prokaryotic life forms suggest that mtDNA is related to, and undoubtedly derived from, certain species of aerobic (oxygen-using) bacteria.

Though the earth's atmosphere about 2000 mya had less oxygen than today (1-19), these ancestral bacteria had already found a way to use oxygen to produce energy. Before bacteria came aboard as mitochondria, the early eukaryotic cell was a "fermenter" living on relatively inefficient chemical reactions that did not use oxygen. The long association between eukaryotes and mitochondria has been one of mutual benefit. Eukaryotes acquired a new and more effective power source in the form of reactions using oxygen. Mitochondria found a protected intracellular environment with an abundance of nutrients for growth and reproduction.

Color the human mitochondrial DNA. The delineated segments represent genes.

As with other eukaryotes, the two parts of the human genome, the nuclear DNA and the mitochondrial DNA, differ in several respects. The mitochondrial genome has only 16,500 base pairs and 37 genes, compared to nuclear DNA which has 3 billion base pairs and about 100,000 genes. As with bacterial genomes, the mitochondrial DNA is circular in shape, rather than linear like the nuclear DNA. Mitochondrial DNA is very compact, lacking the noncoding introns and excess "junk" that characterize nuclear DNA.

Color the inheritance of mitochondrial DNA.

Unlike the nuclear genome, which contains equal amounts of genetic material from both parents, the mitochondrial genome is inherited exclusively from the mother. The ovum, the female reproductive cell, has lots of cytoplasm swarming with mitochondria, whereas the spermatozoon, the male reproductive cell, consists of a head made of nuclear DNA and a flagellar tail for propulsion, and virtually no cytoplasm or mitochondria. When the ovum and spermatozoon join, the nuclear DNA of each recombines to form a new genome in the fertilized zygote that has about equal parts from the mother and father. Since there is no male mtDNA to recombine, the offspring have only the maternal mtDNA. Genetically then, we are a bit more related to our mothers than to our fathers.

Studies of mtDNA have added important information for estimating times of divergences between species and for establishing genetic relationships within and between species. For example, mtDNA confirmed the findings from DNA hybridization that we are closest to chimpanzees (2-7). Sequences of mtDNA provide strong evidence for an African origin of *Homo sapiens* between one and two hundred thousand years ago (5-27).

Studies of mtDNA combined with information from nuclear DNA can reflect dispersal patterns of females and males. Rhesus monkey populations (*Macaca mulatta*) were studied by primatologists Don Melnick and Guy Hoezler. They found little difference in nuclear DNA among different groups. Dispersing males mix up the genes of the groups. In contrast, the mtDNA shows intergroup differences. The females stay in their natal group, so the mtDNA is passed down and evolves separately in individual groups. Though the males disperse, they cannot transmit mtDNA to their offspring, so little intergroup mixing of mtDNA occurs.

MtDNA studies also test the genetic relationship among individuals who are closely associated. Primatologist Chie Hashimoto and colleagues at Kyoto University confirmed that genetic closeness and social closeness are not connected among female chimpanzees (*Pan paniscus*) in Wamba, Zaire. Young female chimpanzees immigrate into new groups and form close social associations with senior females without regard to genetic relationships.

These newly translated family histories written in the DNA of the tiny bacterialike residents within our cells have wrought startling changes in our understanding of human evolution. Some anthropologists who relied exclusively on anatomy for understanding our evolutionary history have been resistant to the unexpected molecular findings, and the surprising finding that the molecular and morphological levels do not evolve together (2-13). As we see in Sections 4 and 5, taken together, molecular and morphological data provide a more complete picture of the course of primate and human evolution.

MITOCHONDRIAL DNA

STRUCTURE*
 CELL NUCLEUS_a
 CYTOPLASM_b
 MITOCHONDRION_c
 MITOCHONDRIAL DNA_d

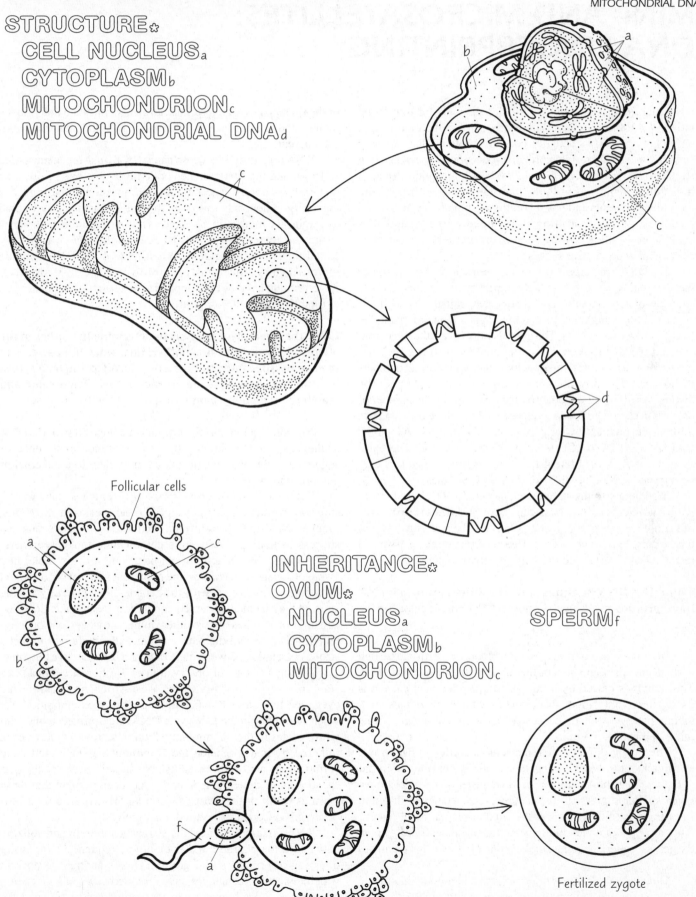

Follicular cells

INHERITANCE*
OVUM*
 NUCLEUS_a
 CYTOPLASM_b
 MITOCHONDRION_c

SPERM_f

Fertilized zygote

2-12
MINI- AND MICROSATELLITES: DNA FINGERPRINTING

DNA makes up the genome and holds the code for translating into about 100,000 genes. With more than 3 billion base pairs, only about 5 to 10% actually code for proteins, leaving long stretches that do not result in protein production. Some noncoding stretches of DNA change so rapidly that they are unique for each individual. This individual "barcode" also identifies the individual's parents and has revolutionized the fields of law and forensics, as fingerprinting did a hundred years ago. For evolutionary studies, identifying males as sires is shaping theories about male reproductive success.

The DNA "fingerprints" refer to regions on the chromosomes that have noncoding DNA units that repeat many times over. These stretches of hypervariable DNA sequences, called minisatellites, consist of repeating units 16 to 64 base pairs long. For example, CATTAGGATTATAACC. The units themselves are the same from one individual to another, but the number of times they are repeated varies. Minisatellites are like trains with varying numbers of boxcars. The boxcars are all alike, but the trains can be distinguished from each other by their lengths, by the number of boxcars in each. The above sequence repeated three times (a train with three boxcars) would read: CATTAGGATTATAACC CATTAGGATTATAACC CATTAGGATTATAACC. The basic sequence, which is different from one satellite to another, may be repeated tens or hundreds or thousands of times.

In addition to minisatellites, another group of DNA sequences known as microsatellites has been discovered. These also consist of variable numbers of repeating units, but the units are only 3 to 6 base pairs long, such as CAT. Repeated three times this would read CAT CAT CAT, and there may be many repetitions.

Color the DNA samples and the illustration of DNA fingerprinting using electrophoresis. Use a light color for the gel.

DNA is extracted from hair, skin, blood, or sperm and treated with an enzyme that cuts out the minisatellite or microsatellite. The sample is placed on a thin gel and an electrical current is passed through it. Notice that each of the three individuals has a unique pattern of bands because of the different length of one minisatellite of DNA units.

The lengths differ because molecules of different sizes travel at different rates. What is happening might be considered similar to the fact that shorter trains can travel faster than longer trains, given similar engines. In the same way, molecules of different sizes travel at different rates; the smaller pieces travel fastest. After a couple of hours, the separated segments will show up on the gel as a pattern of bands, looking like a barcode that identifies items in a supermarket.

Three or four different minisatellites will produce a barcode ID unique for any human or bird or yeast cell unless it has an identical twin. Unlike the print made from the whorls and ridges of the fingers, DNA fingerprints can also identify the individual's mother and father, since its inheritance is Mendelian, half from each parent.

DNA fingerprinting was so named by British biochemist Alec Jeffreys, and the first case he applied it to was one of disputed maternity. A child's paternity is often questioned, but rarely is maternity in doubt. In this case, though, a Ghanian boy wanted to rejoin his mother in England. The immigration authorities suspected that she was not the real mother but was merely expediting his immigration. When half of his DNA barcode matched hers, the family reunion was permitted. DNA fingerprinting has now been applied to thousands of criminal cases to establish innocence or guilt.

Color the fingerprint analysis to determine the father of the offspring. Begin with the mother, then color the patterns of the two possible fathers. Now color the offspring bands, first by coloring those that match the mother. Then color and match the remaining bands with one of the two males.

An individual's DNA fingerprint is a composition of the DNA sequences of both parents. It is the presence or absence of segments in the pattern that link an individual to a maternal or paternal parent.

Before we had DNA fingerprinting techniques, there was no sure way to establish paternity among other species, such as birds, monkeys, and apes. Paternity was deduced by a male's rank and success in mating. The results demonstrate that researchers' observations and deductions can be wrong. For example, in a group of Japanese macaques, the dominant males were observed to copulate most often with the females, but paternity testing showed that the male observed copulating was not the identified sire in 11 of 15 cases. In two other studies, however, one on long-tailed macaques and the other on mandrills, there was in fact a strong correlation between male rank and reproductive outcome.

During 17 years of observation of Taï Forest chimpanzees (*Pan troglodytes*) in Ivory Coast, West Africa, no females were ever seen to approach males in neighboring communities. Yet when 21 mother-infant pairs were DNA fingerprinted, along with all the males in their community, 7 infants proved to have been fathered by males outside the community. Female and male chimpanzees also form consortships, situations where the pair spend a lot of time together, and it has been thought that these pairings result in the most conceptions. However, only 2 of 6 observed consortships resulted in paternity.

DNA fingerprinting results suggest caution in generalizing between a male's rank and copulation frequency with siring offspring in primate social groups. This is another instance in which molecular techniques have provided new tools for testing hypotheses about human and other primate societies and for arriving at new insights into social and reproductive behavior.

DNA FINGERPRINTING

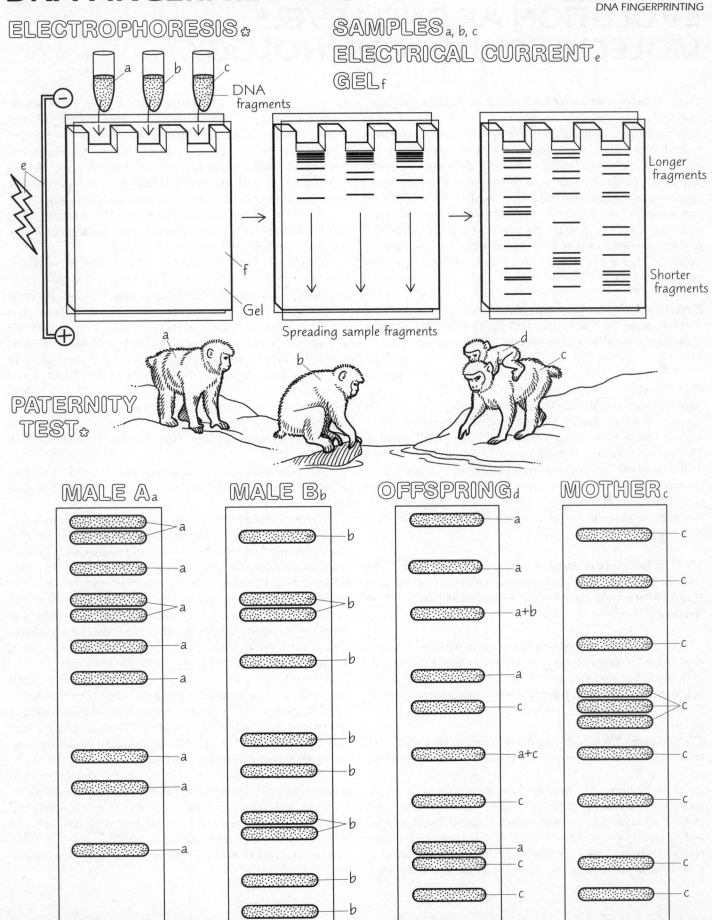

ELECTROPHORESIS ✲

SAMPLES a, b, c
ELECTRICAL CURRENT e
GEL f

a   b   c

DNA fragments

e

f

Gel

Longer fragments

Shorter fragments

Spreading sample fragments

PATERNITY TEST ✲

a

b

d   c

MALE A a

a
a
a
a
a
a
a
a
a

MALE B b

b
b
b
b
b
b
b
b
b
b

OFFSPRING d

a
a
a+b
a
c
a+c
c
a
c
c

MOTHER c

c
c
c
c
c
c
c
c

2-13
EVOLUTION AT TWO LEVELS: MOLECULES AND MORPHOLOGY

Close relatives generally look more alike than unrelated individuals, but looks can be deceiving. Before molecular data were available, evolutionary relationships and times of separation were deduced from morphological similarities and differences among living and fossil species. With the addition of molecular data into evolutionary studies, a number of earlier ideas about species' relationships have had to be revised. Using three pairs of primate species, we contrast the molecular determination of when each pair separated against the impression based upon their physical appearances. The contrast illustrates the limitations of using morphology to estimate how closely or distantly related two species are.

Begin by coloring the demidoff galago and mouse lemur. Color their place on the family tree and the time indicating when these two prosimian species diverged from each other.

Two species can look very much alike and yet be very distantly related. Primatologists Pierre Charles-Dominique and Robert Martin noticed many behavioral and ecological similarities between demidoff galago (*Galago demidoff*) from West Africa and the mouse lemur (*Microcebus murinus*) from Madagascar. The two species resemble each other, for example, in overall size and appearance, locomotion, fruit and insect diet, pattern of ranging and urine washing, and adult vocalizations. These marked resemblances would suggest a close kinship. Molecular data, however, indicate the two species have been separated for over 60 million years (4-4).

Move to the middle of the plate and color the South American (New World) monkey *Cebus capucinus* and the blue monkey (*Cercopithecus mitis*) that lives in Africa. Color their place on the family tree.

Whether they live in New or Old World rain forests, monkeys look and act alike, implying a close relationship. However, the molecular and fossil data as well as continental drift tell us that although New and Old World monkeys shared a common ancestor, the two lineages separated about 35 mya (4-11).

Complete the plate by coloring the chimpanzee (*Pan paniscus*), the human (*Homo sapiens*), and their place on the family tree.

The discrepancy between external appearance and evolutionary distance is particularly marked between the apes and humans. Chimpanzees resemble other apes—the African gorillas and Asian orangutans. Apes climb, feed, and sleep in trees in the forest. In their morphology they share similarities in brain size, long arms and short legs, prominent canine teeth, and abundant hair. A trip to the zoo reveals that these three kinds of apes resemble each other in appearance and behavior more than any of them resembles their zoo-keepers. Humans have brains that are three times as large as ape brains, have small canine teeth, are relatively hairless, and walk on only two limbs. "Common sense" as well as comparative anatomy would declare that the three apes are genetically closer to each other than any one is to humans.

Therefore it came as a surprise when DNA studies (2-7) showed that chimpanzees are closer to humans than either is to gorillas or orangutans.

Geneticist Mary-Claire King and biochemist Allan Wilson noted that evolution at the level of the genes and at the level of morphology proceeds at different rates. Morphology reflects the species adaptation and can evolve either slower or faster than DNA and proteins. Some species retain traits of their common ancestor that are adaptive (galago and lemur; Old and New World monkey), whereas other species change dramatically in morphology in adapting to a new way of life. Gorillas and chimpanzees, for example, have maintained a similar lifestyle in the forest and still climb trees; they resemble their common ancestor far more than do humans, who moved into a new environment beginning about 5 mya and committed to a life on the ground (5-2).

The prosimian, monkey, and hominoid stories illustrate four differences between evolution at the molecular and morphological levels.

1) Molecules are direct expressions of the genetic message. In contrast, morphology is separated by many steps from the DNA and the proteins encoded by it. External features, such as body proportions, tooth size and shape, and even vocalizations, may be determined by many different genes and may be subject to modification through natural selection for a particular way of life.

2) Molecular data are quantitative and replicable, and therefore are easily compared. Different laboratories almost always get similar results. In contrast, assessments of species relationships based on morphology often do not agree.

3) Molecules, consisting of thousands or millions of nucleotide base pairs, do not "converge" significantly, whereas morphology often does. Unrelated or only distantly related animals that live similar lifestyles in similar environments may come to look a lot alike (1-8, 1-9), but their reproductive modes and their molecules reflect evolutionary distance.

4) Molecules change by mutation in rough proportion to divergence times and can be used as clocks (2-9). Morphological evolution can take place slowly, as with the mouse lemur and demidoff galago, or rapidly, as it has with humans and chimpanzees. Consequently, morphology alone cannot provide a reliable estimate of time, rate, and degree of change between two or more species.

MOLECULES AND MORPHOLOGY

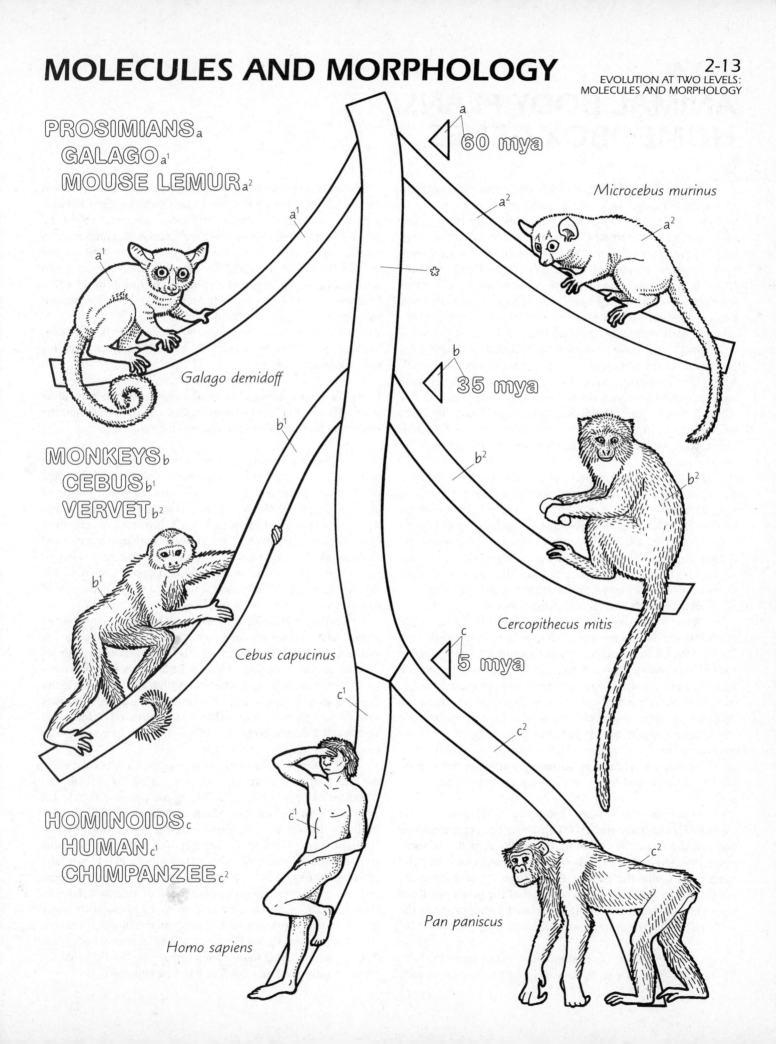

PROSIMIANS_a
GALAGO_{a^1}
MOUSE LEMUR_{a^2}

a
60 mya

Microcebus murinus

a^1

a^2

Galago demidoff

b^1

b
35 mya

b^2

MONKEYS_b
CEBUS_{b^1}
VERVET_{b^2}

b^1

b^2

Cercopithecus mitis

Cebus capucinus

c
5 mya

c^1

c^2

HOMINOIDS_c
HUMAN_{c^1}
CHIMPANZEE_{c^2}

c^1

Homo sapiens

Pan paniscus

c^2

2-14
ANIMAL BODY PLANS: HOMEOBOX GENES

How a single fertilized cell develops into a complex organism like a fly, a mouse, or a human being has long been one of biology's greatest mysteries. Von Baer in the early 19th century observed that all vertebrates, from salamanders to humans, look very similar in the early stages of their embryonic development (1-3). At about the same time, French zoologist Geoffroy Saint-Hilaire declared that all animals have the same body plan. Because the main nerve cord is in the front part of insects and in the back part of vertebrates, Saint-Hilaire hypothesized that vertebrates are essentially upside-down invertebrates!

Now the molecular revolution that revealed the double helix has taken on the conundrum of animal development as well. Molecular biologists have discovered remarkable genetic connections between very diverse animal species. Certain genes called homeotic genes (homeo=alike) are amazingly similar in structure and function in all animals; they serve as molecular architects and direct the building of bodies according to definite detailed plans.

Like so many breakthroughs in genetics, this one came from the humble fruit fly, *Drosophila melanogaster,* a laboratory favorite because it reproduces rapidly, has only 4 chromosomes, and readily exhibits mutations induced by inbreeding and x-rays (1-15). Fruit flies are highly specialized insects with 2 wings and 3 body segments. Their ancestors had 4 wings and many body segments. The fruit fly embryo starts out with a series of 16 equal-sized segments. Various segments merge to make the 3 segments we recognize as the head, thorax, and abdomen.

In the 1940s, American biologist Edward B. Lewis began studying the homeotic genes that affect segmentation in *Drosophila.* He found that mutations in a cluster of genes, called the *bithorax* complex, caused duplication of a body segment with an extra pair of wings. These mutations were weird and hard to explain because hundreds of different genes participate in the formation of a body segment and wings. Yet here were single mutations creating new body parts and eliminating others. These genes were acting as master switches, turning on and off arrays of other genes involved in body shape, and controlling the number, pattern, position, and fusion of segments and appendages.

Choose a color for (a) and color the "lab" gene on the *Drosophila* chromosome, HOM C. Color the corresponding part on the embryo (a) and on the adult (a) with the same color. Proceed in this way; choose color (b) and color the "pb" gene next. Color the part of the embryo (b) and adult (b) controlled by the "pb" gene. Notice that the genes are lined up on one chromosome in the same head-to-tail order as the body parts that the genes control. Choose a light color for (f).

In the late 1970s, German biologists Christiane Nüsslein-Volhard and Eric F. Wieschaus sequenced the homeotic genes controlling the development of the fruit fly's body. They observed that in each of these genes a particular DNA segment 180 bases long was virtually identical. This DNA sequence, called the homeobox, translates into a protein sequence 60 amino acids in length. This protein sequence binds to DNA and switches on and off the process of transcription, the expression of genes into proteins (2-4). By controlling the transcription in all cells, homeobox (Hox) genes act as master switches determining cell fates, growth, and development.

For their work on the homeobox genes, Lewis, Nüsslein-Volhard, and Wieschaus received the 1995 Nobel Prize for physiology or medicine.

Using the same colors and method, color the mouse homeobox genes (Hox A, B, C, D) lined up on four chromosomes and the matching body parts on the mouse embryo.

Hox genes evidently duplicated twice during the evolution of invertebrates into vertebrates, just as there were multiple duplications of the globin gene (2-6). Instead of one cluster of about 10 genes on 1 chromosome like the fruit fly, the mouse has 4 clusters of about 10 genes each, on 4 different chromosomes. Hox genes in mice and humans are very similar in number and chromosomal arrangement. It is remarkable that only about 40 genes out of a total of about 100,000 control most of the development, architecture, and appearance of the body plan of complex mammalian species.

As different as the adult fly and mouse appear, their homeotic genes had a common evolutionary origin, shown by the marked similarity in homeobox sequences. Fly and mouse had a common ancestor half a billion years ago, but the homeobox sequence has hardly changed during that long time period. The same Hox genes that determine the belly side of invertebrates establish the back side of vertebrates. Saint-Hilaire's "ridiculous" idea that vertebrates have the body plan of upside-down insects has also proved to be true.

Hox genes provide spectacular insight into the evolution of the eye. Different kinds of eyes in a variety of animals, for instance, octopuses, flies, and humans, posed a puzzle for evolutionary biologists. Ernst Mayr concluded that eyes may have evolved independently 40 different times. In 1994, however, Swiss biologist Walter Gehring and his team found that the Hox gene responsible for induction of the *Drosophilia* eye is virtually identical to the one that induces the mouse eye. This Hox gene switches on eye formation in the myriad of creatures that see. Hence, it appears that all eyes, no matter how differently constructed they appear now, had a common evolutionary origin.

Hox genes are the molecular architects for animal body plans that von Baer studied more than a century ago and provide the intrinsic unity of design that Saint-Hilaire supposed.

HOMEOBOX GENES

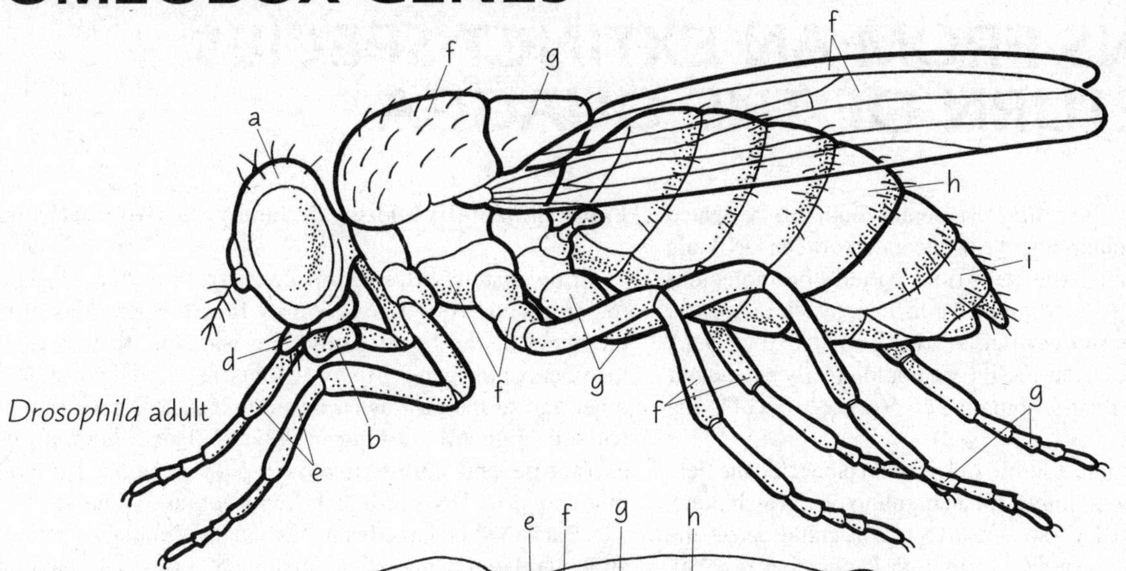

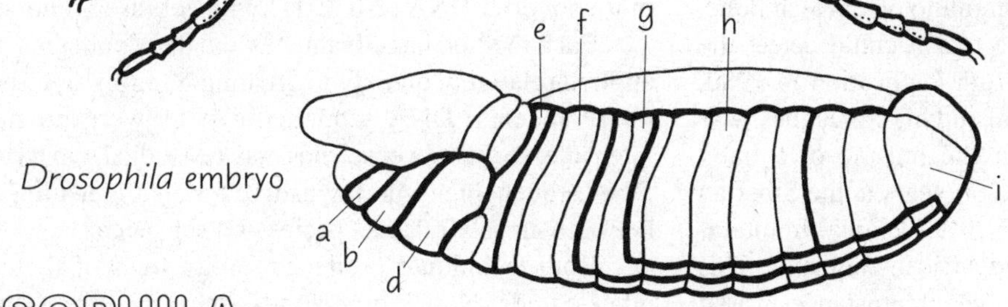

Drosophila adult

Drosophila embryo

DROSOPHILA ✸

HOM C

lab   pb   Dfd   Scr   Antp   Ubx   abd-A   Abd-B

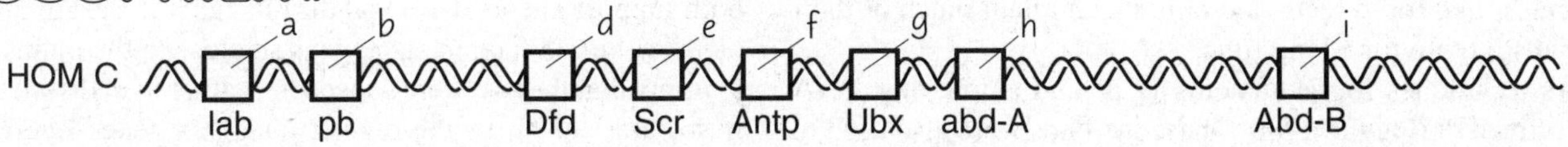

MOUSE ✸

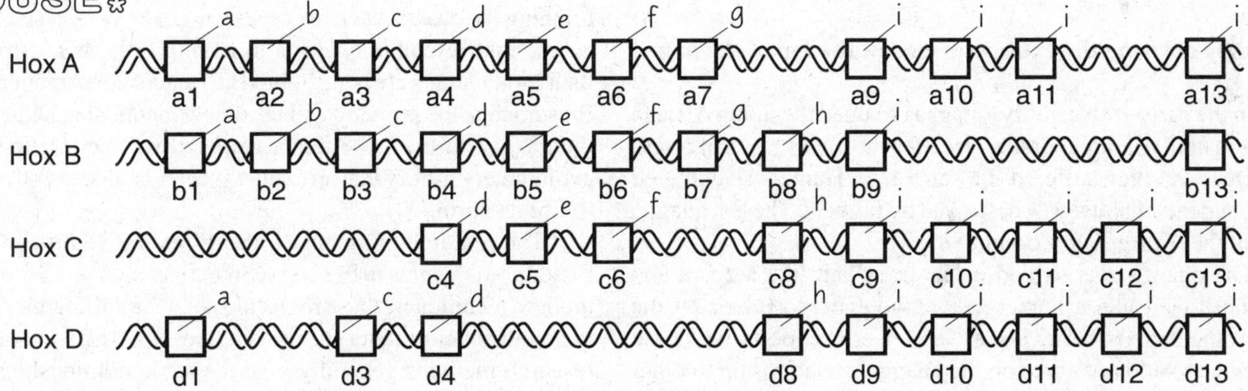

Hox A

a1   a2   a3   a4   a5   a6   a7   a9   a10   a11   a13

Hox B

b1   b2   b3   b4   b5   b6   b7   b8   b9   b13

Hox C

c4   c5   c6   c8   c9   c10   c11   c12   c13

Hox D

d1   d3   d4   d8   d9   d10   d11   d12   d13

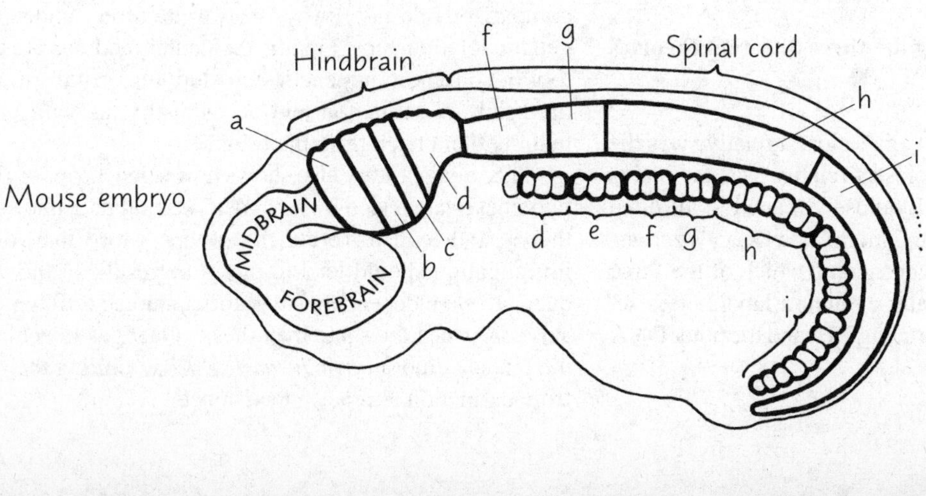

Hindbrain   Spinal cord

MIDBRAIN   FOREBRAIN

Mouse embryo

2-15
LESSONS FROM AN EXTINCT SPECIES: THE RETURN OF THE QUAGGA

The book and movie *Jurassic Park* depict dinosaurs recreated from fossil DNA, popularizing the connection between DNA and fossils and publicizing the new field called "biomolecular paleontology." Among life forms on earth, those that have become extinct far outnumber those still living. If we could extract DNA and protein molecules from fossils, we could greatly extend our knowledge about the relationships and divergence times of living and extinct species.

Molecular evolutionist Jerold Lowenstein pioneered the field of biomolecular paleontology with an immunological technique, radioimmunoassay (RIA), so sensitive that it could detect the presence of proteins in fossils. In its first application in 1980, Lowenstein, together with Allan Wilson and his colleagues, was able to detect albumin molecules in the muscle of a baby mammoth that had been frozen for 40,000 years in the Siberian permafrost. This ancient albumin was 99% identical immunologically to that of the living Asian and African elephants. This finding demonstrated that under favorable circumstances, fossil molecules, like fossil teeth and bones, can retain much of their original structure for a long time.

As techniques for sequencing (2-8) and amplifying DNA were refined during the 1980s, these methods were also used to identify DNA in the fossils of extinct species. The new method of sequencing mitochondrial DNA (2-11) was first applied to the evolutionary puzzle of the extinct quagga.

Begin by coloring the extinct quagga at the top of the page.

In the early 19th century, quaggas roamed the South African plains in herds of innumerable size, like the plains bison of North America, and they suffered the same fate. Hunters slaughtered them, and their habitat was destroyed by farmers. The last quagga died in the Amsterdam Zoo in 1887.

The quagga was striped on its front half like a zebra and chestnut-toned like a horse on its hindquarters. Based on the appearance of its skin, bones, and teeth, experts on horse phylogeny could not agree on the quagga's relationship to other equids. Three different theories vied for acceptance.

Color the drawings representing the three different theories about quagga relationships.

Theory One stated that the quagga's closest relative was the domestic horse. Theory Two: its closest relative was the plains zebra. Theory Three: it was equally closely related to all three African zebra species, the plains, mountain, and Grevy's zebras. Morphology alone was unable to determine which of the three theories was correct. Two molecular evolution laboratories set out to solve the quagga puzzle, one using RIA and the other DNA sequencing methods.

Finish the plate by coloring the family trees from each method.

Lowenstein extracted proteins from a quagga skin in a museum and, using RIA, compared them to proteins of extant members of the horse family. He was able to test all living members of the genus *Equus:* (zebras, asses, and horses) to each other and to the cow as an outside referent. At the same time, Russell Higuchi, working in Allan Wilson's laboratory, was extracting and comparing base-pair sequences of quagga mitochondrial DNA (2-8, 2-11) with zebras and horses.

Each method has advantages and disadvantages. RIA can be applied relatively quickly to creating a family tree that includes many species. DNA sequencing is slower and more labor-intensive, so that fewer species may be studied. On the other hand, DNA sequencing is more sensitive for distinguishing differences between closely related species and subspecies.

Both techniques produced family trees of the quagga and other equids. Notice how similar these two trees are and how both support Theory Two, that the quagga's closest relative is the plains zebra. In fact, the quagga is so close to the plains zebra as to imply that the two were subspecies rather than distinct species. If so, most or all of the extinct quagga's genes live on in the plains zebra.

On this assumption, the South African Museum in Cape Town has instituted a selective breeding program with the goal of bringing the quagga back from extinction, in a certain sense. Plains zebras that resemble quaggas in having little or no striping on their hindquarters are being inbred at a nature conservation station. Presumably, the progeny will be almost identical genetically with the quagga. If this experiment works, it will be the first time in evolutionary history that an extinct species is successfully restored to life on earth.

The research on quaggas makes several significant points. First, biomolecules may survive in extinct species. Second, with modern techniques, these molecules may be sufficiently intact to yield information about species relationships; different molecular research methods generally give the same relationships. Third, in extinct as well as in living organisms, morphological comparisons do not always lead to a correct understanding of genetic relationships. Finally, molecular methods are a powerful tool in conservation genetics, in studying groups of animals on the brink of extinction and occasionally, as with the quagga, helping them back from the brink.

The quagga story also shows how science works. Competing hypotheses are tested by new methods and data that support one theory and tend to refute the others. More than one line of investigation should lead to the same result. In the case of the quagga, two independent laboratories studied different molecules and confirmed the same hypothesis. Quaggas in actuality outdo the fantasy dinosaurs of *Jurassic Park* in finding their way back from extinction to renewed existence.

THE RETURN OF THE QUAGGA

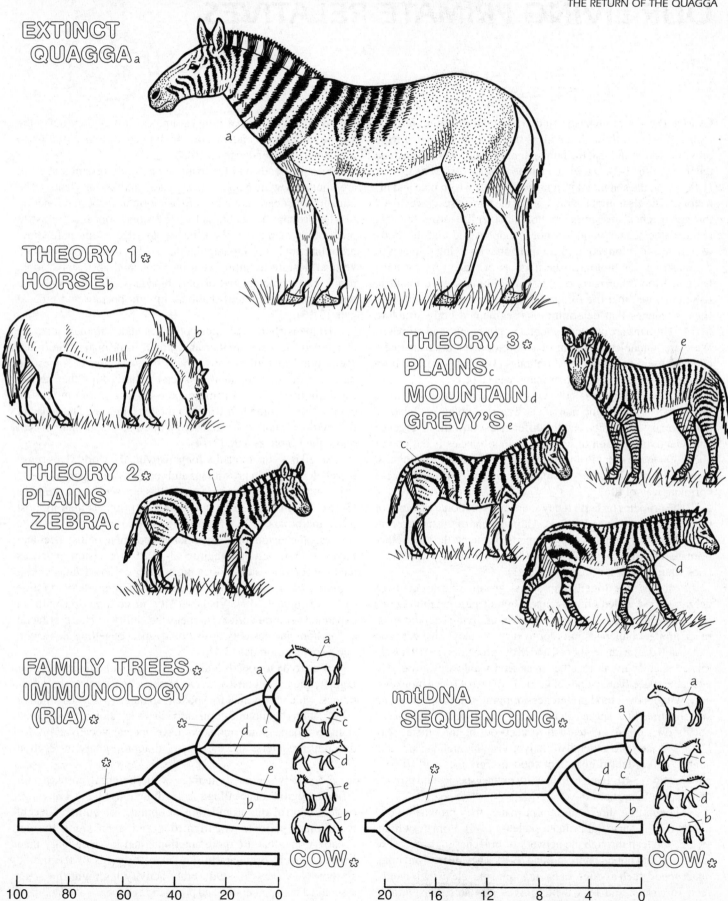

EXTINCT QUAGGA a

THEORY 1 *
HORSE b

THEORY 2 *
PLAINS
ZEBRA c

THEORY 3 *
PLAINS c
MOUNTAIN d
GREVY'S e

FAMILY TREES *
IMMUNOLOGY
(RIA) *

COW *

Immunological Distance

mtDNA
SEQUENCING *

COW *

Base Substitutions (mtDNA)

SECTION 3
OUR LIVING PRIMATE RELATIVES

Charles Darwin brought the study of human evolution into the realm of science through his ideas that all life descended from previous forms and that the human family was but one branch on the tree of life (1-2). Darwin concluded *On the Origin of Species* (1859) with the statement "Light shall be thrown on man and his history." The clear implication was that the human species evolved through mechanisms similar to those of other life forms. In 1950, anthropologist Sherwood Washburn emphasized that the study of human evolution required comparison with living primates to demonstrate our biological heritage as primates. As we have learned from other parts of this book, humans have much in common with other life forms; for example, we share with fruit flies the genes that determine our segmented body structure (2-14). Humans are at once vertebrates, mammals, and primates. We share fundamentals of physical development, brain anatomy, and ear structure with other vertebrates (1-3, 1-4, 1-5), and limb and dental structure with other mammals (1-6, 1-7).

Section 3 illustrates how we resemble and how we differ from other primates and mammals. The resemblances illustrate evolutionary continuity, and the differences show the divergence and adaptive radiation of life. The human species is but one of about 300 in the order Primates. A number of features distinguish primates from the other 17 mammalian orders and define a "primate way of life."

The primates on earth today share an evolutionary history of more than 60 million years (3-1). Although one of the more recent arrivals, humans now occupy all parts of the earth. Most other primates live in tropical rain forests (3-2), three-dimensional high-rises where many species coexist (3-3).

Primates live together in social groups that a occupy a neighborhood, called a home range. Though these neighborhoods differ, forest-dwelling gibbons and savanna-living baboons must meet similar challenges in order to survive; they must get food and water, deal with neighbors, and avoid predators (3-4). Closely related species living together must find viable ways to divide available space. Three kinds of ground-adapted African monkeys, each with its own food preferences, ranging patterns, and group size illustrate how space can be shared. Each species has carved out its own niche and learned to keep out of the others' way (3-5). Primates are generally omnivorous, although the size and shape of the dentition reflect food preferences and dietary composition (3-6). Teeth help identify extinct species and provide clues about their diet.

Though tree shrews are not primates, they provide a good model for the ancestral primate skeleton (3-7). Primates climb, swing, and leap through the network of branches in the forest or walk, run, and bound on the ground (3-8). They differ from other quadrupeds, such as dogs, in having more muscle in their hands, feet, forearms, and legs, which gives primates considerable flexibility and mobility (3-9). During growth and development, the body proportions of infant primates shift as they make the transition from dependence on the mother for transportation to locomotor independence (3-10).

Primate hands and feet maintain a family resemblance. All are equipped with nails, sensory pads, and sweat glands. The human foot departs notably from the norm in shape and function (3-11). Primate hands are active in locomotion. In contrast to most other mammals, these hands are also adept at feeding, grooming, and object manipulation (3-12). Hand use promotes a vertical posture in sitting, and monkeys and apes stand, look, reach, carry objects, and display bipedally, although only the human species maintains habitual upright posture and bipedal gait (3-13).

Humans share with other primates and mammals a strong attachment between mother and infant; in primates, the initial social bond that an infant forms with its mother becomes the basis for the development of social relationships that persist throughout its life. Intimate face-to-face communication commences as infants feed at their mothers' breasts. The capacity for emotional attachment stems from a new part of the mammalian brain, the limbic system (3-14).

Smell is a vital modality for perceiving the world. This sense is well developed in prosimians and serves as an important mode of communication. The sense of smell is less sensitive in humans (3-15). Vision tends to be more acute in primates than in most other mammals. The overlapping fields that make possible stereoscopic vision improve primates' judgment of distances and facilitate their acrobatic agility (3-16). Color vision enhances daytime activities such as locating brightly colored fruit, sighting members of neighboring groups, and spotting predators in time to avoid them (3-17). Visual acuity, in conjunction with an expanded cerebral cortex, sharpens the ability to interpret facial expressions and gestures, an essential aspect of getting along with one's social comrades (3-18).

Sensitivity to sounds is also vital to survival. Prosimians hear high-frequency sounds, whereas humans hear best in the lower ranges, which is optimal for spoken language (3-19). Distinctive vocalizations communicate an individual's location and emotional state to others. Some monkeys have special vocalizations for different predators, and they respond appropriately in reaction (3-20).

The body's great organizer is the cerebral cortex, with different regions controlling specific functions (3-21). Language centers control the articulation of sounds for human speech. Nonhuman primate vocalizations and even some human vocalizations, that are more emotional and less voluntary than normal speech, originate in the cingulate gyrus of the limbic system. New ways to study brain activity highlight the areas associated with perception and production of speech and language (3-22).

Primates live their entire lives in close association with other members of their species. Group size and composition vary between and within species, as does the strength of social bonds among different members of the group. This variation accounts for the flexibility that primates exhibit in surviving under a wide range of conditions (3-23). Primates mature more slowly and live longer than most other mammals. Like other mammals, they pass through defined stages from infancy to old age. The timing and duration of each stage comprise an individual's life history. Each species has its characteristic life history pattern that is not simply a reflection of the body size of the species (3-24).

When we take a closer look at different age-sex classes that make up primate social groups and populations, we see that female primates spend most of their lives pregnant and lactating. Long-term studies on individuals reveal what contributes to a female's lifetime reproductive success (3-25). Individual differences in physical condition and amount of body fat affect the time to conception, success of lactation, and, ultimately, infant survival. A female's access to food and her activity level affect body mass and amount of body fat. These, in turn, affect her rate of physical maturation, age when she first gives birth, and the interval between births (3-26).

Life, from an infant's point of view, is about surviving. Infants are dependent and vulnerable during this time of rapid brain growth. From day one, infants are involved socially, reacting to their mothers and other group members, and learning the "primate way." Their survival depends a great deal on the health and well being of their mothers (3-27). As juveniles, they become more physically independent, foraging on their own and playing for extended periods, but they are still small and vulnerable, learning their place in the social group while relying upon its cohesion and protection (3-28).

The behavior and lives of males remains enigmatic. There is a tendency to stereotype male behavior as aggressive and competitive, occupied only with seeking females or dominating other males. This view is disputed by primatologist Thelma Rowell who emphasizes instead that males lead long and complex lives. Baboon males provide one example of the range of male social behaviors, from nurturance to lethal aggression. We know very little about male lifetime reproductive success, though being popular with females and living a long time are obvious pluses (3-29). Female and male primates differ from each other in a number of ways—coloration, vocalizations, and body and tooth size. In species with pronounced sex differences, males grow for a longer time and reach physical and social maturity later than females (3-30).

When Jane Goodall began what was to become a long-term study on the lives of Gombe chimpanzees, under the sponsorship of L.S.B. Leakey, she recorded events in individual lives. The skeleton of each chimpanzee tells its own story about the individual's life and death (3-31).

Primates have relatively large brains and seem "intelligent" by human standards. Primatologist Alison Jolly, who studied lemurs, points out that primate intelligence is manifested in meeting the challenges of social living and solving problems, not necessarily in tool using, which some people use as a definition of intelligence. Monkeys and apes show considerable ingenuity in solving their everyday problems and in communicating with each other. However, when attempting to solve nonsocial problems, monkeys and apes differ in their abilities (3-32).

Although other animals use tools—sea otters use rocks to crack open clams, finches use cactus spines to probe for grubs, and monkeys occasionally use objects—only chimpanzees, gorillas, and orangutans approach the highly developed manipulative abilities of humans. For example, chimpanzees use a variety of objects for many practical purposes. These skills often require many years of learning and practice (3-33). Tool use among wild chimpanzees is now well known from several populations, findings summarized by field psychologist William McGrew.

Long-term studies on wild chimpanzees also document the variation and individual character of behavior patterns among populations. Some of these behaviors become established traditions and are passed on to the next generation. Behaviors may also be transferred from one chimpanzee community to another, as was documented when an older female emigrated to a neighboring group, bringing her experience and memory with her. Social traditions are not unique to chimpanzees. Other large-brained, long-lived social mammals can transmit information socially, thus enabling preservation of innovations that contribute to survival. Social traditions do not constitute culture in the human sense of the word, but they seem to be precursors to the arts and sciences which characterize the uniqueness of our own species (3-34).

Chimpanzees' struggle with the Candy Game, which human children over the age of four can master, illustrates how abstract symbols may free one from the "biological destiny" of hard-wired reactions (3-35). Our facility for learning language—spoken, signed, and written—provides the basis of the cultural divide, the narrow but very deep gorge that separates us from the apes that are so closely akin to us on the genetic level.

As Darwin deduced, we humans are but one twig on the giant sequoia of life. The nearby branches are our primate relatives. The nearest of all are the African apes, so close that when we watch them in action we often marvel at how "human" they seem. And yet the differences too are fascinating. Much light has been thrown on the ways that different primate species live, and the reflected light tells us a great deal about ourselves.

3-1
PRIMATE LINEAGES: KINDS OF PRIMATES

Primates comprise one of 16 orders of living placental mammals that appear in the early Cenozoic fossil record (1-22) and have now diversified into about 300 species. Primates are distinct from other mammals in their range of locomotor and feeding patterns, which evolved for living in tropical rain forests (4-1). The basic primate adaptation centers around the ability of early primates to climb by grasping, as noted by primatologist Sherwood Washburn.

This plate introduces the major primate lineages and the times of their divergence, drawing on molecular, fossil, and anatomical information. We also introduce a few scientific terms that help to group the many species according to their relationships and adaptations. In the appendix, you will find a scientific classification of primates.

The primate order consists of two major branches, prosimians and anthropoids, which differ in their sensory anatomy and physiology (4-9). The older prosimian group bears the hallmarks of a long nocturnal history: large eyes well suited for night vision and continued reliance on the sense of smell. The later anthropoids, on the other hand, have eyes that function best in daylight and depend less on a sense of smell to locate food or to communicate socially.

Begin with the prosimian group. Color the lemur branch as well as the loris and galago branches as they are discussed.

Within the prosimians, two major lineages shared a common ancestor for a few million years and then separated about 60 mya. The lemur group consists of a diversity of nocturnal and diurnal (day-living) species, from the small mouse lemur to the cat-sized ringtailed lemur to the large-bodied indri (4-4). Lemurs, found only on Madagscar, evolved independently from other prosimians as a result of Madagascar's isolation from the African and Indian continents (1-18).

The other lineage, the lorises and galagos or bush-babies, are small-bodied and nocturnal. The loris family (Lorisidae) consists of slow climbers and includes the pottos of Africa and the slender and slow lorises of Asia (4-5). The galago family (Galagidae) consists of species found only in Africa. Their specialized legs equip them for impressive feats of jumping and leaping. Slow-climbing pottos and quick-leaping galagos live together (are sympatric) in West African rain forests (4-5). The loris and galago groups separated from each other about 55 mya.

Color the tarsier branch.

Tarsiers consist of three species and occupy an interesting place in the primate family tree. They resemble prosimians in overall anatomy and behavior: they are small-bodied, nocturnal,

and prey upon insects and small vertebrates. In the tropical island forests of Southeast Asia, they leap expertly from one vertical support to the next.

Tarsiers also show affinities to the anthropoids in having independent control of the fingers, a fovea in the eye, partially closed eye orbit, dry rhinarium (nose, 3-15), and a muscular upper lip used in facial expressions. Molecular data indicate that the tarsiers shared a brief period of evolutionary history with the anthropoids before following their own divergent path about 50 mya. The technical term, haplorhine, (haplo=single or simple, rhine=nose) unites tarsiers and anthropoids, reflecting this shared evolutionary history. The term strepsirhine ("split nose") distinguishes the lemurs, lorises, and galagos from the tarsier-anthropoid group (4-8, 4-9).

Color the anthropoid branch, which originated from an ancient prosimianlike ancestor and later separated into New World monkeys, Old World monkeys, and apes and humans.

The anthropoids are day-living, fruit-eating primates with specialized color vision and generalized quadrupedal locomotion. Each of the two lineages of anthropoids, the platyrrhines ("flat nose") and the catarrhines ("hook nose") began its own adaptive radiation 35 to 40 mya.

The platyrrhine monkeys, or New World monkeys, live in the neotropical forests of Central and South America. They vary from the tiny marmosets and tamarins to the larger-bodied species, such as howler and woolly monkeys, which have prehensile tails.

The catarrhine primates include two major branches; one led to and includes the Old World monkeys, the other diverged between 20 and 25 mya and led to apes and humans.

The Old World monkeys live in Africa and Asia and include two families, the leaf monkeys, including the colobus and langur, and the cheek pouch monkeys, including baboons, mangabeys, guenons, and macaques (4-19). Of all primates, the Old World monkeys live in the widest variety of habitats, from tropical forests to savannas and from semidesert to snow-covered mountains.

The apes are distinct from the Old World monkeys in their locomotor abilities. With long mobile arms, they hang under branches to reach to the ends and pluck new leaves and fruits (4-26). The Asian apes include the small-bodied gibbons and siamangs, and the large-bodied orangutans. The Asian apes separated from the African apes 10 to 14 mya (4-30). The African apes inhabit the central and western rain forests and include two species of chimpanzees (*Pan paniscus* and *Pan troglodytes*) and two gorilla subspecies, the lowland and mountain (4-34).

Humans (hominids) and modern African apes descended from a common ancestor that lived about five mya.

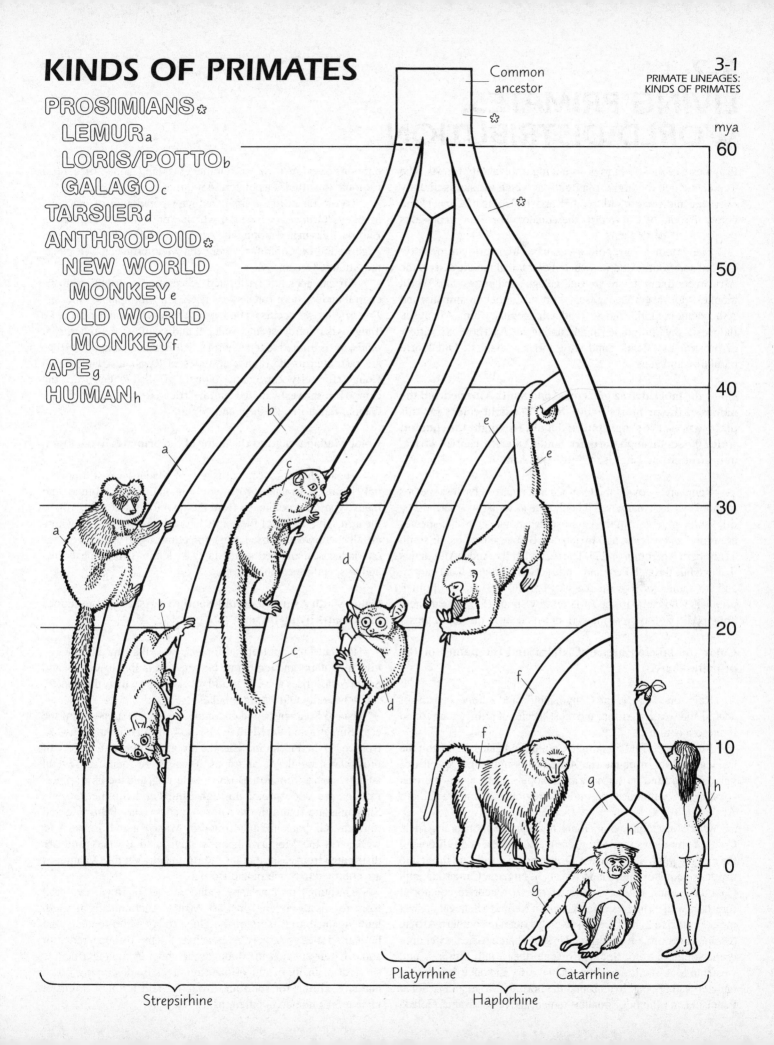

KINDS OF PRIMATES

PROSIMIANS*
  LEMURₐ
  LORIS/POTTO_b
  GALAGO_c
  TARSIER_d
ANTHROPOID*
  NEW WORLD
    MONKEY_e
  OLD WORLD
    MONKEY_f
  APE_g
  HUMAN_h

Common
ancestor

mya
60
50
40
30
20
10
0

Strepsirhine

Platyrrhine Catarrhine
Haplorhine

3-2
LIVING PRIMATES: WORLD DISTRIBUTION

Primates live mostly in regions having tropical rain forests. The tropics include the highest latitudes at which the sun is directly overhead and correspond to 23.5° above (Tropic of Cancer) and below (Tropic of Capricorn) the equator. The 23.5° represents the tilt of the earth's axis.

Four main geographic areas have high primate density: Central and South America where neotropical monkeys live; the African continent where we find galagos and pottos, Old World monkeys, and apes; Madagascar with only lemur prosimians; and Asia, including India and Sri Lanka, Indochina, China, Malaysia, Indonesia, the Philippine Islands, and Japan. Asia houses a variety of prosimians (slender and slow lorises, tarsiers), Old World monkeys, and apes.

Color the labeled area of Central and South America and the names of the primates living there. Use light colors for this plate to preserve geographical details. Highlight the equator, which passes through northern South America, central Africa, and through the islands of Southeast Asia.

Rain forest covers the Orinoco and Amazon basins; species of monkeys are concentrated here, such as tamarins, marmosets, titi, saki, capuchin, squirrel, and spider monkeys. Some species are found as far north as Mexico and Belize, others as far south as northern Argentina (4-12). The section of the Andes Mountains that extends through Peru and Chile acts as a geographical barrier, and no monkeys live on the west coast. Besides the human primates who came to the Americas by about 15,000 years ago, only monkeys (no prosimians or apes) occur in the neotropics.

Color the labeled areas of Africa and the names of the primates there.

Rain forest covers the Congo, Niger, and Zambezi basins of central and western Africa, and most species of primates are found in these locations.

Small, nocturnal prosimians, pottos and galagos, inhabit the tropical forests of equatorial Africa, although some species of galago are found as far east as Ethiopia, south along the east coast to Mozambique, and into arid regions of central southern Africa.

Old World monkeys are found throughout subSaharan Africa. Colobine monkeys range from Kenya, Zanzibar, and Ethiopia in the east to Gambia in the west. Drills and mandrills are limited to the dense equatorial lowland forests in Nigeria, Cameroon, and Gabon. Guenon monkeys (*Cercopithecus*) occur in equatorial forests as well as in mixed habitats from Kenya to Senegal. Vervet monkeys thrive in arid regions, which extend to southern Africa. Savanna baboons are widespread in subSaharan Africa, extending to the southern tip of South Africa, northeast into Ethiopia, and west into Mauritania and Senegal. In the dry and open semidesert, hamadryas baboons live around the horn of Africa and Arabian Peninsula, in Ethiopia, Somalia, Yemen, and Saudi Arabia. Gelada baboons survive in the montane grassland zones of central Ethiopia to altitudes as high as 4500 meters.

To the far north, a small remnant population of macaque monkeys (*Macaca sylvanus*), which were once widespread in Europe, lives in and around the Atlas Mountains of Morocco and Algeria and on Gibraltar, where the Mediterranean Sea meets the Atlantic Ocean.

African apes have a limited geographic distribution in the central and western forests of Africa. One chimpanzee species, *Pan troglodytes* occurs as far east as western Tanzania near Lake Tanganyika and west into Senegal and Gambia; the other, *Pan paniscus* is limited to the Congo River Basin. Mountain gorillas are restricted to the higher altitudes in Rwanda, Uganda, and Congo (formerly Zaire); the lowland gorillas extend from the Congo forests westward to Central African Republic, Cameroon, Gabon, Equatorial Guinea, and Nigeria.

Color Madagascar and the name of the primates living there.

Today, the large tropical island of Madagascar still houses only lemur prosimians. Prosimians inhabit different altitudes and many types of woodlands, from the lush forests of the north, to the arid spiny forest of the south. Though prosimians elsewhere are all nocturnal, the absence of competing day-living anthropoids on Madagascar allowed some Malagasy lemurs to become diurnal and to spend time on the ground.

Color South Asia and Island Southeast Asia and the names of primates living there.

Primates inhabit tropical forests, as well as the extremes of high mountains and temperate climates. In India, Sri Lanka, and South Asia, lorises and Old World monkeys are widely distributed. Japan has only Old World monkeys.

Island Southeast Asia encompasses a wide area—from the east, Sumatra and the Mentawi Islands, through Java, Suluwasi, Borneo, to the Philippine Islands, a region home to a variety of prosimians, monkeys, and apes. Tarsiers are found on several islands, such as Sumatra, Borneo, Suluwasi, and the Philippines. Lorises are widespread through South and Southeast Asia. Siamangs are found in the forests of the Malay Peninsula and Sumatra. Gibbons are also found in Malaysia and Sumatra, as well as in the Mentawi Islands, Java, and Borneo, and are distributed from eastern India and Burma into China. Orangutans are confined to Sumatra and Borneo.

The human primate appeared more than four mya, identified from fossils discovered in East Africa. Anatomically modern humans inhabit all parts of the globe today. Unfortunately, the human species is largely responsible for the disappearance of some lemur species in Madagascar and for endangering the survival of many of our primate relatives by destroying forest habitats, killing for food and trophies, and through dramatic increases in human populations.

WORLD DISTRIBUTION

CENTRAL, SOUTH AMERICA$_a$ · SOUTH ASIA, JAPAN$_d$

NEW WORLD MONKEYS$_a$ · LORISES$_d$

AFRICA$_b$ · OLD WORLD MONKEYS$_d$

POTTOS, GALAGOS$_b$ · GIBBONS$_d$

OLD WORLD MONKEYS$_b$ · ISLAND SOUTHEAST ASIA$_e$

CHIMPANZEES, GORILLAS$_b$ · LORISES, TARSIERS$_e$

MADAGASCAR$_c$ · OLD WORLD MONKEYS$_e$

LEMURS$_c$ · GIBBONS, ORANGUTANS$_e$

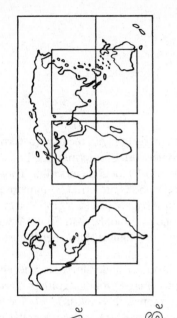

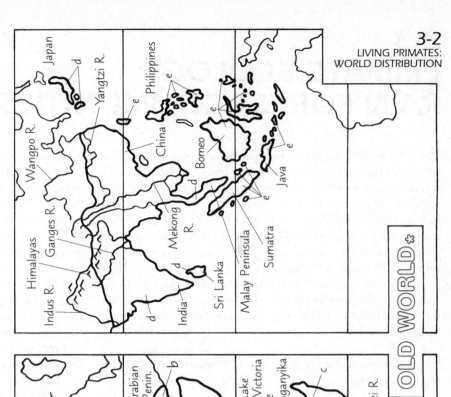

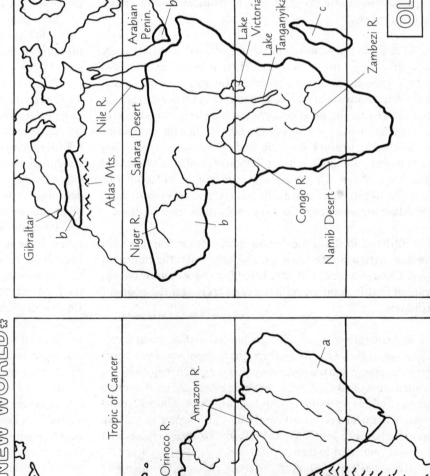

NEW WORLD ✴

OLD WORLD ✴

3-3
PRIMATE ECOLOGY: RAIN FOREST COMMUNITIES

The remarkable tropical rain forests represent only about 6% of the earth's land surface but house nearly half of all living species on earth and about 90% of primate species. Five times more light and heat from the sun fall at the equator than at higher latitudes; this is why tropical regions are warm (25°C average annual temperature), moist (200–400 cm annual rainfall), and produce abundant plant growth and great plant diversity. Tropical rain forests of the Malay peninsula, for example, contain at least 2500 trees and 5400 species of seed-producing plants (angiosperms). This richness of plant life, the primary producers, in turn supports the animals that consume and decompose them, the primary consumers (4-1).

Color the schematic cross section of tropical biomes at the top of the plate.

Most primates inhabit primary rain forests that are relatively undisturbed by human activity. Their habitats extend into secondary forests that are regenerating from natural or man-made disturbance. Primates are also found in gallery forests that border lakes and rivers, and in woodlands that may be continuous with the savanna mosaic. A few primate species inhabit semidesert scrub. Forests are not uniform and show many gradations depending upon amount and distribution of rainfall, altitude, soil condition, and age. They range, for example, from seasonal or deciduous forests, montane rain forests at higher elevations, thorn or montane woodlands, to mixed vegetation of the savanna mosaic.

This illustration depicts primate species from tropical rain forests in Africa, South America, and Asia. Color the emergent layer. Choose a shade of this color for the woolly monkey. Proceed in this manner, coloring each layer and the resident primates.

The struggle of plants for light has led to three main levels of vegetation above the forest floor: the upper story or emergent layer, the canopy, and the understory. Primates, with their climbing abilities, easily make their way through tangled and cross-cutting pathways of this three-dimensional environment. Although most primates frequent a preferred height, they are capable of moving vertically between levels to exploit dozens of plant species and the insects attracted to them.

Trees that reach 40 meters or more characterize the upper story or emergent layer and capture direct sunlight. They emerge so high that vertical gaps separate their enormous crowns from the surrounding vegetation of the canopy below. Woolly monkeys in the neotropics, guenons in Africa, and leaf monkeys in Southeast Asia frequent the upper forest layer. Many other species of primates climb up to this level to bask in the sun, though they are more vulnerable to aerial predators when they do so.

Beneath the emergent layer, the canopy forms a dense leaf- and vine-covered network of intermingled branches connecting large trees at levels of 10 to 25 meters high. This middle layer is the most productive and is preferred by numerous species, such as mangabeys in African forests, gibbons in the forests of Southeast Asia, and saki monkeys in South America. This layer is so dense that only dim light is able to penetrate to the understory below.

The lowest layer, or understory, rises to about 10 meters, with shade-adapted herbs, young saplings, shrubs, and vines. Goeldi's monkey prefers the lowest levels for insect foraging. Tarsiers in Southeast Asian forests also prefer the low levels where they feed on insects and small vertebrates and occasionally forage on the forest floor.

Less than 2% of sunlight filters onto the forest floor, and only a few primate species travel there. Mandrills, both species of chimpanzees, and lowland gorillas feed and sleep on the ground and in trees.

Primates are mostly primary consumers at the low end of the food chain; they take advantage of the abundant energy source provided by plants and their many edible parts. A dozen or more primate species can live in the same forests sympatrically. Closely related species establish unique niches by using slightly different combinations of food and different levels of the forests (4-5). Consequently, the forest supports high primate population densities compared to carnivores (secondary consumers eating other animals) of the same body size.

Primates are adaptable and their opportunistic tendencies enable some species to survive in marginal habitats: for example, hamadryas baboons sleep on rocky ledges or cliff faces in the semidesert region in Ethiopia; macaques in northern Japan forage for food beneath the winter's snow; and snub-nosed monkeys survive on lichens in the coniferous forests of China (1-16). Quadrupedal locomotion and the ability to move in trees as well as travel on the ground equip them for surviving in habitats that challenge even human populations.

French primatologist François Bourlière attributes the evolutionary success of primates to their predominantly vegetarian diet, arboreal tendencies, and the primate flexibility in seizing available opportunities. Primates contribute significantly to the health, maintenance, and regeneration of the rain forests. Rain forest plants cannot rely on the wind to disperse their seeds because the air in the forest is still; they must rely upon animals for spreading their seeds to new areas. As primary consumers, primates help to disperse seeds by releasing them from their hard covering after eating the flesh, by spitting them out, or dropping them after a journey through the digestive tract. Therefore, primates play a dominant role in rain forest communities (4-1).

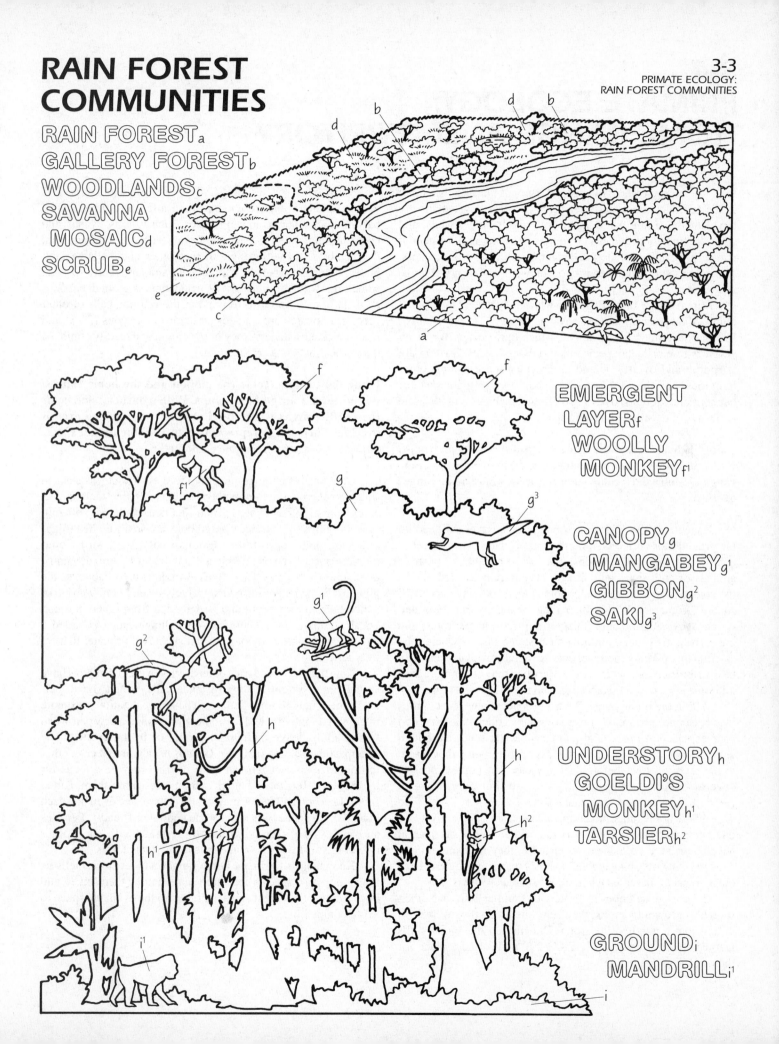

RAIN FOREST COMMUNITIES

RAIN FOREST_a
GALLERY FOREST_b
WOODLANDS_c
SAVANNA
MOSAIC_d
SCRUB_e

EMERGENT
LAYER_f
WOOLLY
MONKEY_f1

CANOPY_g
MANGABEY_g1
GIBBON_g2
SAKI_g3

UNDERSTORY_h
GOELDI'S
MONKEY_h1
TARSIER_h2

GROUND_i
MANDRILL_i1

3-4
PRIMATE ECOLOGY: HOME RANGE AND TERRITORY

Primates live their whole lives in social groups that usually remain in the same location year after year. The group systematically travels within a familiar area and collectively knows where and when to find food and water sources, how to avoid potential competitors, and to be alert to danger, especially from predators. The group's survival depends upon knowledge of its home range and territory.

Primates vary in the degree to which they defend their home range. Most species, like the savanna baboons (*Papio anubis*), live in undefended home ranges, which they occupy for many years. A few primate species like gibbons (*Hylobates lar*) are territorial and overtly defend a particular space against other individuals of the same species. These two primate species, baboons and gibbons, live in two different habitats and illustrate two ways of defining and using space.

Color the baboon and the home range of four baboon troops. Use light colors. Then color the core areas within the home ranges. Using a dark color, color the areas where home ranges overlap.

Baboons in the African savanna mosaic travel and feed on the ground more often than most other primates. They travel in cohesive groups, called troops, that consist of 20 to 80 or more animals of both sexes and all ages. The terrain covered during the course of a year is called a home range and may exceed 20 square kilometers. Within their range, baboons find food and water. They eat fruits and foliage from trees; herbs, roots, and bulbs from the ground and low bushes; and insects where they can find them. Many foods are only seasonally available and may be distributed over a wide area, so the troop may cover more than 4 kilometers a day, a distance referred to as their day range.

Within the home range, the troop concentrates its activities in at least one core area. Core areas usually contain the best food sources, sleeping trees, and permanent water holes. Although anubis baboons spend much of the day on the ground, they return to the safety of trees before dusk to sleep. The home ranges of several baboon troops usually overlap, but core areas of neighboring groups overlap much less.

Where home ranges overlap, baboon troops generally avoid one another, so overt conflict is rare. When troops do meet at streams or large permanent water holes, they may intermingle and the young may play together; or they may simply ignore each other. Tension increases when troops share core areas.

Baboons in neighboring groups are familiar with each other. As males grow into adults, they leave the group they were born in and join a neighboring troop. Drawing on the social skills learned while growing up (3-28, 3-29), males find a place for themselves in the new group.

Many other species, especially large browsers and grazers such as impala, wildebeest, elephant, giraffe, and buffalo share a baboon troop's home range. Predators such as lions, hyenas, and cheetahs sometimes menace the troop. Safety lies in numbers; the members stay within sight of each other, and the large adult males with their saberlike canine teeth and large body size can sometimes warn off predators. When danger is spotted, baboons give alarm calls and also respond to the warning calls of other species. Leopards are a major predator on baboons (5-12) and pose the greatest danger; they hunt at night and readily climb the trees where baboons are sleeping.

Using light colors, color the gibbon and the home ranges/ territories of four gibbon groups. With a darker color, color the conflict areas where territories of neighboring groups overlap. Each range represents a three-dimensional space, about one-seventh of a square kilometer.

Gibbons live in the tropical rain forests of Southeast Asia in small social groups of minimally one adult male, one adult female, and young of different ages. Their diet consists largely of fruit, especially figs (4-31). Because gibbons are small-bodied (5 kg) and their habitat is three-dimensional (3-3), nutritional requirements can be met within a small (about 1.5 km) day range containing a few key food trees. In contrast to baboons, the gibbons' home range is used exclusively by one family group or mated pair and offspring and is defended from others through vocalizations (3-30). Therefore, their home range is called a territory. Gibbons are among the few species of primates that are truly territorial.

Note that the boundaries of territories overlap. Gibbons have an elaborate system of long distance calls, which signal their location to neighboring groups. These vocalizations promote intergroup familiarity and facilitate formation of a new pair when young adults leave their natal group, or in the event of the disappearance of one in a pair. Groups usually avoid each other to minimize contact. The areas of overlap may be a focus for interaction. "Territorial battles" take place within them. Ritual fights do occur, and males may charge, chase, and even bite each other. Group encounters can also be neutral or friendly. Females and males of different groups may mate with each other opportunistically at the boundaries of their territories.

Knowledge of primate home ranges and territories tells us how groups of a species apportion space among themselves, and how groups of different species divide up the available space to avoid competition.

HOME RANGE AND TERRITORY

BABOON_a
HOME RANGE_b
CORE AREA_c
OVERLAP AREA_d

GIBBON_e
HOME RANGE/TERRITORY_f
CONFLICT AREA_g

3-5
PRIMATE ECOLOGY: HABITAT AND NICHE SEPARATION

Several primate species often live together in the same habitat but occupy different niches (French for nest, from Latin, nidus). Each species has evolved a distinct pattern of using space and feeding that avoids direct competition with other primates. Drawing on the research of British primatologists Robin and Patsy Dunbar, we focus on three species of sympatric monkeys living in the Bole Valley in Ethiopia.

The Bole Valley is part of the Blue Nile drainage system and forms a canyon 600 meters deep, divided into 4 vertical strata. Zone 1 is river and gallery forest with high trees (30 m) and dense understory where a variety of shrubs, herbs, and grasses grow. Zone 2 lies above the gallery forest and supports a dense cover of trees, shrubs, and herbs interspersed with several grasses. The steep upper slopes of the valley in zone 3 consist almost exclusively of open grassland with scattered bushes and small trees. Zone 4, at the top of the plateau, is open grassland with scattered thickets and occasional trees.

Color the anubis baboon and its home range through the zones on the main drawing. Use a light color for the home range. At the lower left, color the anubis baboon's home range size and day range length. Repeat this process for the gelada baboon and the vervet monkey. Use both colors where the home ranges overlap.

The Bole Valley supports 7 troops of anubis baboons (*Papio anubis*) (140 individuals); 3 to 5 bands of gelada baboons (*Theropithecus gelada*) (240) divided into 17 reproductive units and a few all male groups; and 4 groups of vervet monkeys (*Cercopithecus aethiops*) (75).

Anubis baboon groups occupy all 4 vegetation zones with an annual home range size averaging about 94 hectares (940,000 m²). They use mostly zones 1 and 2, and the average day range is 1200 meters. Gelada baboons forage exclusively in zones 3 and 4 and have a home range size of 84 hectares and a day range average of 630 meters. Vervet monkeys confine their travel to zones 1 and 2, with a home range size of 30 hectares and a day range average of 700 meters.

Color the pie charts representing the dietary composition of each monkey species. Color the bar graphs representing the layers of vegetation on which each monkey forages.

Anubis baboons' diet consists of fruits and seeds (55%), leaves (grasses and herbs)(33%), flowers (7%), insects (3%), and roots and bulbs (2%). Gelada baboons' largest dietary component is leaves (92%), and includes fruits and seeds (7%), flowers and occasional roots and bulbs (1%), but no insects. Vervet monkeys consume mostly fruits and seeds (50%), fewer leaves (19%),

flowers (18%), insects (7%), and bark (6%), an item not found in the diet of the other two species.

The dietary composition of each species is associated with the height of the plants. Anubis baboon food items are distributed about equally through the layers of vegetation: 39% from the ground (grasses and herbs), 25% from the middle layer of shrubs and bushes, and 35% from the trees. Gelada baboons get more than 97% of their food from the ground, only 2% from shrubs and bushes, and less than 1% from trees. Vervet monkeys feed mostly in trees (64%), on the ground (28%), and from shrubs and bushes (8%).

Feeding methods differ among the three species. Anubis baboons stand on three limbs when harvesting grass, and dig for rhizomes by scraping away the earth and pulling the pieces from the ground. Geladas are quick and efficient. They sit on their haunches, harvesting grass blades with both hands, and while still sitting, shuffle forward a meter or so at a time; both hands dig into the earth to obtain roots and bulbs. Vervet monkeys feed by plucking a single food item, such as a fig, then sit and bite small pieces from it. (Anubis baboons place all or most of the fruit in their mouths at once.)

Although these species are sympatric throughout their geographical ranges, there is little overlap between them in areas where they coexist. Geladas are clearly differentiated from the other two in habitat zone and dietary preference. Geladas (11–20 kg) have a smaller home range and day range half the length of the anubis (14–28 kg). Geladas rarely climb trees. Their preference for sitting while feeding might account for the unusual markings on gelada baboon chests—bright pink skin in an hourglass shaped area on the neck and chest. In females, this chest skin blisters during estrus, acting as a signal of her sexual state (3-25).

Vervet monkeys are the smallest (3–5 kg), most arboreal, and feed at greater heights than the other two primates. The length of their day range, longer than that of gelada baboons, correlates with the large dietary component of fruit and seeds, food items that are patchily distributed. Anubis baboons feed on low-level vegetation and utilize resources of the more open parts of the habitat in zones 3 and 4, which vervets do not occupy. As a result, even though both species eat a high percent of fruits and seeds, direct competition is minimal.

Now, return to the colored plate. Notice the connections between dietary composition, home range size, ecological zones, and distance traveled each day. Although these monkey species share the same three-dimensional space in Bole Valley, they use space differently. The job of making a living is unique to each group and the niche it occupies. By analyzing food preferences and foraging and ranging patterns, primatologists identify how several primate species live together in the same habitat.

HABITAT AND NICHE SEPARATION

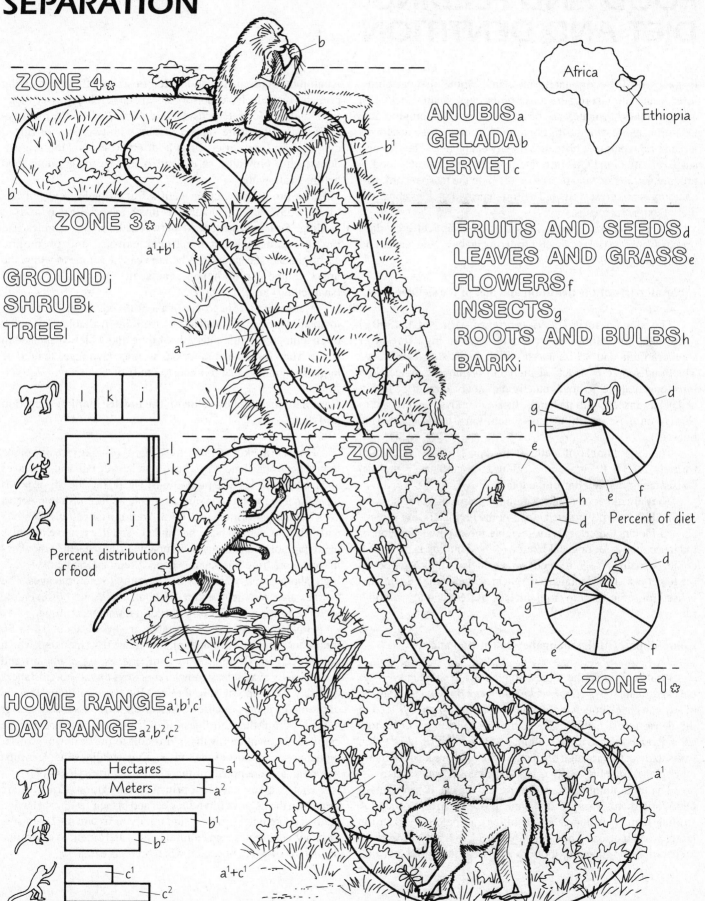

ZONE 4✲

ZONE 3✲

ZONE 2✲

ZONE 1✲

Africa

Ethiopia

ANUBIS$_a$
GELADA$_b$
VERVET$_c$

FRUITS AND SEEDS$_d$
LEAVES AND GRASS$_e$
FLOWERS$_f$
INSECTS$_g$
ROOTS AND BULBS$_h$
BARK$_i$

GROUND$_j$
SHRUB$_k$
TREE$_l$

Percent distribution
of food

Percent of diet

HOME RANGE$_{a^1, b^1, c^1}$
DAY RANGE$_{a^2, b^2, c^2}$

Hectares
Meters

3-6
FOOD AND FEEDING: DIET AND DENTITION

Primates feed predominately on plants. Some also eat gums, insects, and animal protein such as birds' eggs, small vertebrates, and mammals. Primates are best characterized as omnivorous. Dentition, along with the digestive and locomotor systems, forms an important part of a primate's dietary adaptation. The size and shape of an animal's teeth relate to the ways in which food is procured, prepared, and processed (1-7). In the fossil record, soft anatomy is not preserved, and dentition provides clues about the diet of extinct primates.

Each of the three species illustrated here has a different diet: primarily insects (loris), mostly fruit (mangabey), and leaves and fruit (howler monkey).

Color all parts of the dentition and diet of the slender loris.

The slender loris (*Loris tardigradus*), a small (300 g) nocturnal, slow-climbing prosimian, lives in high forests of southern India and Sri Lanka. It prefers to eat sluggish insects. This food source is widely scattered throughout its range, so a loris forages alone. It moves quietly and slowly through the forest, and seizes insects with its hands. Its small body size allows it to survive on these small but highly nutritional food packets (i.e. bugs!).

The total number of teeth, 36, is represented by the dental formula 2.1.3.3 (2 incisors, 1 canine, 3 premolars, 3 molars) consisting of one-quarter of the total.

The animal's food requires minimal preparation. Incisors are small. High, sharply pointed cusps of the premolars and square-shaped molars "interlock" for piercing the external skeleton of the insect body. An unusual feature of the dentition is the dental comb, or tooth scraper, formed by the 4 incisors and 2 canines of the lower jaw. This dental arrangement, found in the prosimians, is used for scraping gum from the bark of trees and for combing fur.

Color all parts of the mangabey's dentition and diet.

Fruits comprise the largest single item in the diet of gray-cheeked mangabeys (*Lophocebus albigena*) (6–7 kg), a group of African cheek pouch monkeys (4-20). These monkeys feed in the dense forest canopy and using color vision (3-17), show considerable selectivity in feeling, sniffing, or biting large green fruits to detect their stage of ripeness. Mangabeys also eat many other plant parts, birds' eggs, and vertebrates, such as snakes.

The tooth number, 32, (formula: 2.1.2.3) is the same in all Old World monkeys, apes, and humans (the catarrhine group). A striking feature of mangabey dentition can be observed in the large, broad incisors. These teeth bite, peel, or tear large fruits in preparation for chewing, motions that wear down the incisors.

Anatomist William Hylander demonstrated that fruit-eating primates typically have incisors that are large relative to the molar teeth and can tolerate considerable wear. Old World monkeys have distinctly square-shaped molars with two pairs of ridged cusps, a feature called bilophodonty (bi=two, loph=crest, dont=teeth), providing an expanded surface for grinding food before swallowing.

The prominent canine teeth differ in males and females (3-30, 4-33) and may function as much in social behavior as in feeding. Spaces (diastemas) between the upper canines and incisors and between the lower canines and premolars accommodate the canines. When the canines come together, the upper canine can be honed against the specialized sectorial (sharpening) lower premolar.

Mangabeys live in groups of about 15 individuals, and forage in smaller subgroups. Patches of fruit are available seasonally, often at unpredictable intervals of time and widely dispersed in space. Therefore, home ranges as well as day ranges tend to be larger in monkeys that rely mostly on fruit.

Complete the plate by coloring the howler monkey dentition and diet.

Howler monkeys (*Alouatta palliata*) (4–8 kg) are one of the largest neotropical monkeys, have a prehensile tail, and eat leaves and fruits in nearly equal proportions. The prehensile tail suspends the animal to reach food items available at the ends of branches.

The dental formula is 2.1.3.3. Well-developed incisors bite and strip leaves from branches and are smaller relative to cheek teeth (premolars and molars), compared to those teeth in monkeys that eat more fruit. The square-shaped premolars and molars have high, sharp cusps, which act like scissors to cut up leaves. The canines are prominent, and a diastema is present; however, the sectorial lower premolar of Old World monkeys is absent.

Howler monkeys live in stable groups of about 18 to 30 individuals and have a smaller home range than monkeys which eat more fruit. Compared to fruit, leaves are abundant and continuously available, so howler monkeys travel short distances each day. Anthropologist Katherine Milton demonstrated that the digestion of leaves requires a longer digestive tract and greater passage of time than the digestion of fruits or protein because the cellulose of plant cell walls is difficult to break down. Howler monkeys spend most of the time resting and digesting, less time traveling, and are noted for their laid-back lifestyle (4-17).

Diet is a key part of a primate's adaptation. Primates are flexible in the range of foods they eat and in their feeding behavior. Humans, like other primates, are omnivorous and opportunistic. Ecology, economics, and cultural beliefs and practices determine the details of what, how, and when humans eat.

DIET AND DENTITION

TEETH *
  INCISOR a
  CANINE b
  PREMOLAR c
  MOLAR d

DIET *
  INSECTS e
  FRUIT f
  LEAVES g

SLENDER LORIS *

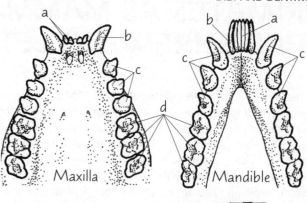

Maxilla

Mandible

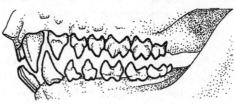

Side view

MANGABEY *

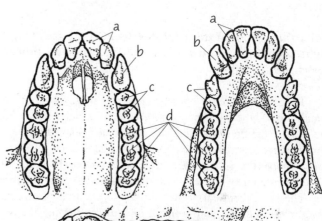

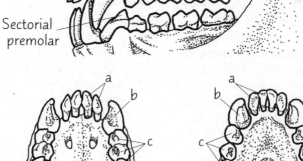

Sectorial premolar

HOWLER MONKEY *

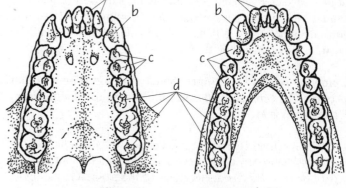

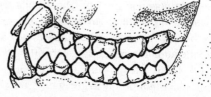

PRIMATES AS MAMMALS: TREE SHREW SKELETON

Primates descended from a mammalian ancestor similar in body form to that of the modern tree shrew (*Tupaia glis*). This small, insect-eating mammal guides our discussion of the major bones of the skeleton, its overall construction, and its functional capacities. The mammalian skeleton provides a stable, but flexible, framework that departs significantly from the more rigid reptilian skeleton. The agility of tree shrews, and of primates, depends upon the construction of the axial and appendicular skeletons. Grasping hands and feet and variations in limb proportions further increase primate mobility. Anatomist and paleontologist Farish Jenkins studied the anatomy and behavior of tree shrews and the anatomy of early fossil mammals to address the question of whether primates had an "arboreal" or "terrestrial" ancestor.

Color the regions of the axial skeleton. On the skeleton, the right scapula is drawn as an outline, and the thoracic vertebrae are visible.

The axial skeleton encompasses the skull (cranium and mandible) and the spinal or vertebral column, which extends from the neck to the tip of the tail. The individual bones of the spine, the vertebrae, comprise five regions. Each region has differently shaped bones that reflect their different functions. (In reptiles the vertebrae are fairly uniform with ribs attached to each vertebra.)

The neck (cervical) vertebrae (C_1–C_7) of tree shrews lack ribs, unlike reptiles, and promote mobility in turning the head from side to side and up and down. The thoracic vertebrae (T_1–T_{13}) support ribs which enclose and protect the "vital organs," the heart and lungs. The lumbar vertebrae (L_1–L_6) lack ribs and support the pelvic girdle, which is part of the appendicular skeleton. The sacral vertebrae are fused and, with the two innominate bones, form the pelvic girdle; only the neural spine of the last sacral vertebra is visible in this side view. The tail or caudal vertebrae vary considerably in number and provide attachment points for tail muscles, or in the absence of a tail, for the muscles of the pelvic floor.

Color the parts of the appendicular skeleton. The reptilian pelvic and pectoral girdles are illustrated for comparison. Color them gray.

The forelimb consists of three regions: the arm having the humerus; the forearm, the radius and ulna; and the paw, having wrist bones or carpals, metacarpals of the palm, and the digits having phalanges or "finger bones" (1-6). The scapula and clavicle comprise the mammalian pectoral girdle, two bones rather than the reptile's six bones. Muscles rather than bones attach the pectoral girdle to the humerus and thorax, permitting the scapula to move relatively freely on the rib cage. Scapular mobility, combined with shoulder motion, add a greater arc and potentially longer length to the stride. The socket for the humerus points

downward, allowing the forelimb to be drawn up under the body. The wrist joint rotates inward and outward (pronation and supination).

The hindlimb consists of three regions: the thigh, having the femur; the leg, the tibia and fibula; and the foot, consisting of the ankle and heel or tarsal bones, the metatarsal bones of the sole, and the phalanges or toe bones.

The pelvic girdle consists of a pair of innominate bones connected by the sacrum. The adult innominate bone, or os coxae, is comprised of three bones that fuse during growth: the ilium, ischium, and pubis. (In contrast, the reptilian innominate has a different shape and the bones do not fuse.) The ilium is long and lies parallel to the spinal column; the hip joint (acetabulum) faces downward, and the muscles crossing this joint promote flexion and extension of the lower limb. This construction makes possible a stable and flexible hip joint. The ankle joint has the ability to rotate inward and outward (inversion and eversion).

Color the flexion-extension spinal motion of the mammal and the enlarged anticlinal region. Color the reptile's lateral spinal motion.

When the tree shrew runs, its spine flexes and extends, a motion which increases the length of each stride while the limbs move backward and forward under the body. The flexion-extension point of motion, called the anticlinal region, takes in the lower thoracic area between T_{11} and L_1. The diaphragm is also located in the anticlinal region. The diaphragm separates the heart and lungs from the viscera and the motion in the lumbar region, thus reflecting the increased activity of the locomotor mechanism. Flexion of the spine displaces the body vertically and permits variation in the motions of the shoulder and hip joints, which, in turn, affects the placement of the forefeet and hindfeet. In contrast, reptilian movement is restricted to rotation in the side-to-side plane.

Jenkins concluded that tree shrews, probably like the early primates, are not exclusively "arboreal" or "terrestrial." The significant point is that with the combination of spinal flexibility and forefeet and hindfeet mobility, tree shrews are both stable and agile for moving on uneven, disordered surfaces which might occur in low vegetation or higher above the forest floor.

The mammalian skeleton contributes to the diversity of mammalian adaptations (1-6). Bones provide the anchor for the muscles of the locomotor system. Mammalian bones, unlike reptilian ones, have a defined period of growth; marrow cavities produce red blood cells, and the bone cells act as reservoirs of calcium. The skeleton also serves reproductive functions. During pregnancy, calcium is transferred from the female to the fetus to form its teeth and bones. In evolutionary studies, variation in the size and shape of individual bones and their proportions to each other guide the identification of extinct species and the interpretation of locomotor behavior.

TREE SHREW SKELETON

AXIAL SKELETON ✱
  SKULL ✱
    CRANIUM a MANDIBLE a¹
  VERTEBRAL COLUMN REGIONS ✱
    CERVICAL b
    THORACIC c
      RIB CAGE c¹
    LUMBAR d
    SACRAL e
    CAUDAL f

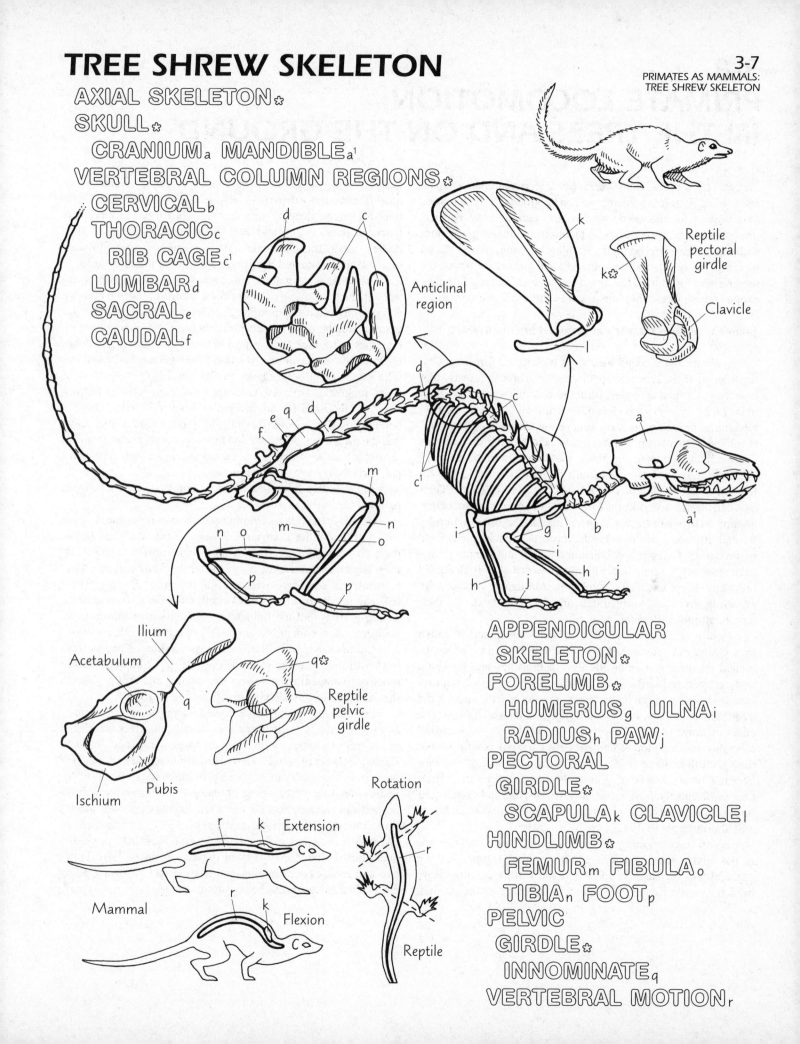

Anticlinal region

Reptile pectoral girdle

Clavicle

Ilium

Acetabulum

Reptile pelvic girdle

Ischium

Pubis

Rotation

Extension

Mammal

Flexion

Reptile

APPENDICULAR
  SKELETON ✱
  FORELIMB ✱
    HUMERUS g ULNA i
    RADIUS h PAW j
  PECTORAL
    GIRDLE ✱
      SCAPULA k CLAVICLE l
  HINDLIMB ✱
    FEMUR m FIBULA o
    TIBIA n FOOT p
  PELVIC
    GIRDLE ✱
      INNOMINATE q
VERTEBRAL MOTION r

3-8
PRIMATE LOCOMOTION:
IN THE TREES AND ON THE GROUND

Primates show considerable versatility in locomotor performance and feeding postures in the trees and on the ground. It is impossible to describe with one word a species' locomotor pattern because primate movements include combinations of climbing, running, walking, scampering, bounding, leaping, bridging, swinging, and hanging. Many species use both trees and ground for travel, for feeding, and for socializing. Some species confine their activities exclusively to trees; only humans are confined to the ground.

Color the plate as the various primates are discussed.

Some primates spend their lives high in the forest canopy, feeding on fruit, leaves, and insects. In tropical forests, tree branches, oriented at angles, form discontinuous pathways high in the forest. Primates traveling through this tangled network must be agile in grabbing the leafy supports at the ends of branches, climbing vertically up tall tree trunks, and judging distances as they jump or leap from one network of branches to the next.

Pottos are slow-moving and deliberate climbers, with forelimbs and hindlimbs that are nearly equal in length. Their broad hands and feet, like the loris' (3-11), clamp about branches, holding on to two or three supports at once as they move carefully through the trees; stealth helps these animals remain undetected by predators. Galagos specialize in hopping and jumping; they have relatively long and heavy hindlimbs with noticably elongated feet, and short and light forelimbs. Malagasy sifakas leap gracefully from one vertical tree support to the next, and their long hindlimbs reflect this pattern.

Neotropical monkeys of Central and South America, unlike their Old World cousins, seldom come to the ground. The small-bodied tamarins run along the tops of branches and feed in a vertical posture (4-13). Talented leapers and jumpers, squirrel monkeys walk and run on branches, moving swiftly through the trees in large groups, stirring up flying insects, which they catch and consume (4-16). Woolly spider monkeys, also called muriquis, move on top of branches using the tail as a fifth limb; they hold their large bodies close to the supporting branches, keeping their centers of gravity low to the supports. Their prehensile tails wrap around branches to suspend and stretch their bodies toward leaves and fruit and to bridge across branches of neighboring trees (4-17).

Asian langur monkeys make spectacular leaps from one tree to the next, using their long hindlimbs for propulsion, long graceful tails for balance, and hands and feet for catching leafy branches as they land. They sometimes come to the ground.

Guenon monkeys live high in the central African forests and move quickly and quietly there (4-21). Macaques, like baboons, climb trees for safety, sleeping, and feeding. They travel around their home range on the ground, and mothers carry infants on their bodies, as do most primates. Patas monkeys, accomplished runners, are considered the greyhounds of the primate world.

Gibbons, the smallest apes, are star aerialists, whipping through the trees by a gymnastic combination of bipedal running and pushing off, rapid climbing, and leaping. They illustrate the extreme adaptation of suspension, hanging and swinging beneath branches using their long arms and hands and mobile shoulders (4-26). This is in contrast to some of the neotropical monkeys who suspend themselves using prehensile tails (4-17).

Orangutans, large red Asian apes, range in body weight from over 30 kilograms for adult females to over 75 kilograms for adult males. Large, hooklike grasping hands and feet, long arms, and the mobile ape shoulder and hip joints enable orangutans to distribute their weight over several supports in the trees. The males are particularly adept at using their considerable upper body strength to sway branches and tree trunks together to form pathways between trees (4-32).

Gorillas, as well as chimpanzees, spend less time in trees than do either of the Asian apes. When walking on all four limbs, their fingers are flexed, and they walk on their knuckles. Prominent muscle attachments on the forelimb and scapula reflect adaptations for terrestrial weight bearing. Despite their considerable body size, gorillas climb into trees to feed on fruit. Young gorillas and the lighter females can climb out on more slender branches for fruit than can the weightier males (4-34).

Chimpanzees (not illustrated) also feed and sleep in trees but travel from place to place on the ground. Chimpanzees, like other primates, utilize a variety of postures and motor patterns that include bipedal carrying and throwing (3-13).

Primates are the only large-bodied mammals that live in trees. Body size usually limits where an animal can safely travel in a given tree. Primates, with their grasping hands and feet and flexible joints in the forelimbs and hindlimbs, can distribute body mass over several branches and provide a stable position for resting, feeding, or escaping predators. The variation in body proportions and length of the limbs reflects the ways each species "fine tunes" its locomotor skills. The agility and success of primates in trees and on the ground depends upon limb flexibility and is further enhanced by having depth perception (3-16), hand-eye and motor coordination, and a good memory for finding established routes throughout its home range (3-4).

IN THE TREES AND ON THE GROUND

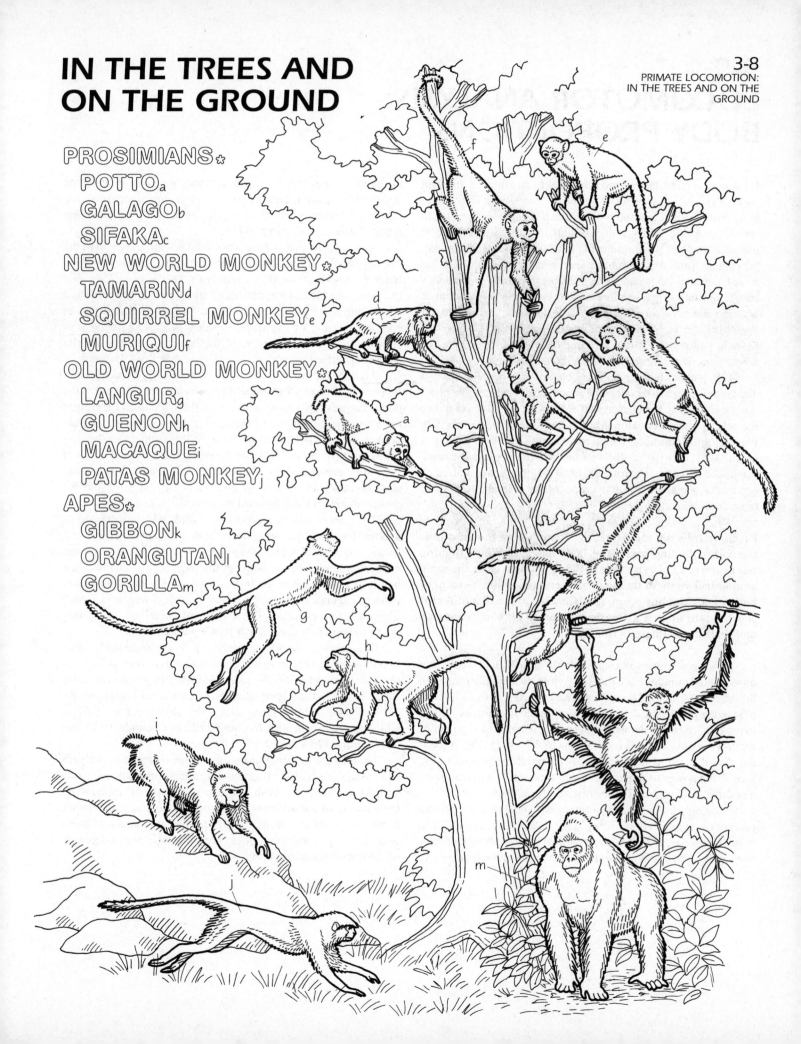

PROSIMIANS*
  POTTOa
  GALAGOb
  SIFAKAc
NEW WORLD MONKEY*
  TAMARINd
  SQUIRREL MONKEYe
  MURIQUIf
OLD WORLD MONKEY*
  LANGURg
  GUENONh
  MACAQUEi
  PATAS MONKEYj
APES*
  GIBBONk
  ORANGUTANl
  GORILLAm

3-9
LOCOMOTOR ANALYSIS: BODY PROPORTIONS

Locomotion contributes fundamentally to an animal's survival and is a central component of a species' adaptation. The whole-body nature of the locomotor adaptation becomes clearer when we compare the limbs and muscular masses of a primate, a macaque monkey, with another mammal, the domesticated racing greyhound. Both species move quadrupedally (on four legs), but there the resemblance ends! The macaque runs, jumps, and walks on the ground, but also climbs in trees, and is quite adept at walking along the tops of slender branches. The greyhound, on the other hand, is a ground-running machine. Analysis of the soft tissues demonstrates how we might compare the locomotor adaptations of a wide variety of animals.

This plate draws on the research of comparative anatomist Ted Grand, who has developed a way to analyze the whole body, not just the bones. He measures all anatomical parts and compares the relationship between the bones and soft tissues, especially muscle, and locomotor behavior. Grand's method, which is quantitative, consists of dividing the body into segments: head, trunk, and tail; arm, forearm, and hand; thigh, leg, and foot. Each segment is weighed, and its percent of the animal's total body mass is calculated.

Begin by coloring the trunk, head, and tail of the macaque, the corresponding percent of body mass, and the adjoining bar graph (a). Using a shade of the same color, color the same anatomical segment on the dog, its corresponding percent of body mass, and bar graph (a^1). Choose shades of a different color for (b) and (b^1). Continue coloring all body segments and their percentages in this way.

When you finish coloring, study the similarities. Notice that overall, both animals have most of their body mass distributed in the head and trunk (62% in the monkey vs. 70% in the dog), and next in the hindlimbs (a total of 24.8% in the monkey vs. 20.6% in the dog). Besides the head and trunk, the heaviest segment of the body in both animals is the thigh (16.4% vs. 15.8%). A well-developed thigh in both species is essential for providing the propulsive power to move the animal forward. The two animals also have similar mass in the arms: (6.8% vs. 6.0%).

Now notice the specific differences. The dog has a greater percent of its body mass (70%) in the head, trunk, and tail than does the monkey (62%). Correspondingly, the monkey has more mass distributed to both limbs. A significant difference lies in the monkey's forearm, which is over twice the mass of that in the dog (5.2% vs. 2.4%)! This difference reflects function; macaques, like other primates, use their forelimbs skillfully in grasping, manipulation, and feeding (3-11).

Although the mass of the hindlimbs is similar overall in the two animals (24.8% vs. 20.6%), the macaque's feet are relatively twice as heavy as the dog's hind paw (2.4% vs. 1.2%). The macaque's hands and feet consist of about one-third muscle and are mobile and flexible for holding on to arboreal supports. In contrast, the dog's paws consist mostly of skin and bone with almost no muscle and are used for bearing weight on a flat terrestrial surface only.

Adapted for life in the trees, the macaque has a much greater range of joint movement in the forelimbs and hindlimbs than the dog. Primates have more rotation in their joints and therefore have correspondingly more muscle for this rotating action than does the dog. Monkeys move well on the ground, but heavier limbs prevent monkeys from running fast. Instead of joint flexibility, greyhound dogs have restricted joint motion. Muscle action is channeled into one plane, that of flexion-extension, for powerful and efficient forward movement.

The greater relative weight in the trunk, with less mass in its legs and forearms, directly reflects the dog's adaptation for speed. In the dog, muscles providing the power for locomotion are concentrated high in the body, in the back region, and near the points of movement at the hip and shoulder joints. The lighter paws at the ends of the dog's limbs mean less weight is swung forward with each stride. The longer paws and limbs of the dog give a longer stride and greater running efficiency.

This kind of anatomical analysis provides quantitative data to compare individuals of different body mass, age (3-10), sex (6-8), or species (4-36). For example (4-5), the potto, which is a slow climber, has nearly equal mass in its forelimbs and hindlimbs (12% of total body mass vs. 14%). The closely-related galago, which is an adept leaper, has notably light forelimbs (9%), but its hindlimbs (23%) are 2.5 times as heavy.

Grand's method emphasizes the whole animal and analyzes soft tissue along with the skeleton. Information on body soft tissue and the skeleton are both necessary in order to understand locomotion. In our attempts to interpret the locomotor behavior of an extinct species from fossilized, often fragmentary bones, we must keep in mind that bones represent only one component of the locomotor adaptation.

BODY PROPORTIONS

MACAQUE✴

62%a

6.8%b
5.2%c
1.2%d

16.4%e
6.0%f
2.4%g

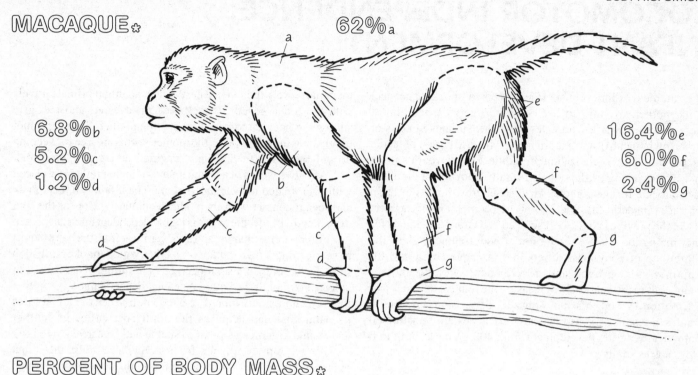

PERCENT OF BODY MASS✴

TRUNK,
HEAD,
TAIL a,a¹

ARM b,b¹
FOREARM c,c¹
HAND/PAW d,d¹

THIGH e,e¹
LEG f,f¹
FOOT g,g¹

Monkey   Dog

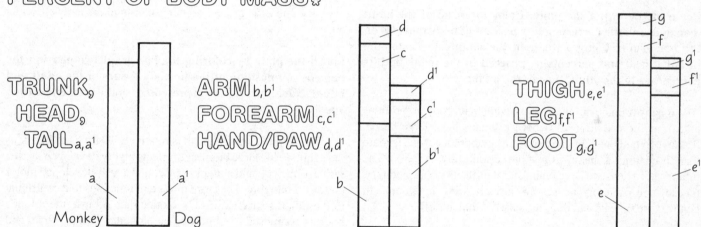

GREYHOUND✴

70%a¹

6.0%b¹
2.4%c¹
1.0%d¹

15.8%e¹
3.6%f¹
1.2%g¹

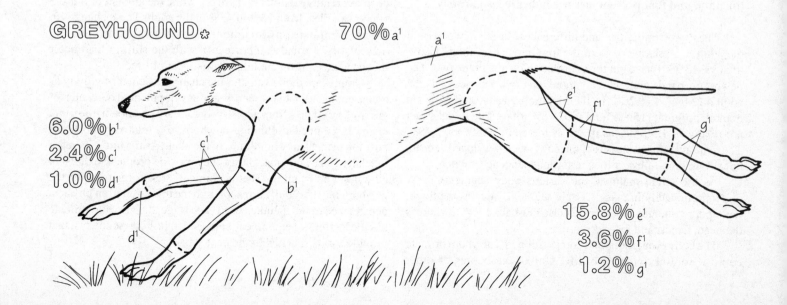

3-10
LOCOMOTOR INDEPENDENCE: INFANT DEVELOPMENT

At birth, the newborn primate is not prepared to be independent of its mother. It clings to her body hair, gets carried almost everywhere (only a few primates leave their infants in nests or parked on branches), and experiences an intense period of tactile and psychological socialization. In addition, the newborn's shape (and size, of course) differs fundamentally from that of the adult. The schedule for the complex changes in growth rates of brain and muscle underlie the progress toward locomotor independence.

In the previous plate, we discussed Ted Grand's methods for determining the relative proportion of body segments: how the distribution of body mass differs in a macaque and a dog. To examine infant growth and development, we add another component to the analysis. We measure the relative amounts and distribution of body tissues—muscle, bone, skin, and brain. Grand's research demonstrates how macaques are transformed anatomically during development from 400 grams at birth to 8 kilograms as adults.

Begin at the top of the plate. Color the head of the adult macaque and the corresponding percent of body mass (a) on the bar graph. Using a shade of the same color, color the infant's head and percentage. Proceed to the trunk and its percentage in the adult, then in the infant.

A baby primate differs from the adult in its body proportions and tissue composition. Newborn primates have large heads. Relative to body weight, the head of a newborn macaque is more than three times as heavy as that of the adult (20% vs. 6%). The infant's head houses a large brain, and at birth, its visual, auditory, tactile, and olfactory senses are already well developed. In contrast, infant cats and dogs are nearly blind at birth.

Now color the forelimb and hindlimb segments. Notice that the hand and foot percentages are indicated separately.

There are similarities and differences. In the newborn and the adult, the relative mass of the forelimbs are similar (11.6% total vs. 13.2% total), but the distribution differs in the two. The newborn's hands are relatively more than twice as heavy as the adult's (2.6% vs. 1.2%). In the hindlimbs, baby and adult are notably different (15.8% total vs. 24.8% total). The infant's feet are relatively 1.5 times as heavy as the adult (3.8% vs. 2.4%). Thus, the anatomical basis for grasping is well developed at birth, but strong hindlimbs for locomotor independence are not.

As the infant matures, the various body segments grow disproportionately in mass. Certain segments such as the thigh, leg, upper arm, and shoulder increase in relative mass, whereas the head, hands, and feet decrease.

The body proportions and composition of a newborn primate equip it for surviving early life. Unlike the babies of other mammals safely hidden in a nest or den, an infant primate travels with the social group. Its well-developed hands and feet grip strongly to hang on to its active, mobile mother. With the infant tightly clinging to her body, the mother's arms are free for keeping up with the group, feeding and foraging, and escaping predators.

After two weeks of age, the infant's clinging reflex is replaced with coordinated muscle movements. The infant can then break and regain contact with its mother voluntarily. But for the first three months of life, the infant is totally dependent upon its mother.

After several months, and awkwardly at first, the baby begins to venture on its own to play with other young monkeys. It soon shifts from riding on its mother's belly to riding on her back. For at least six months, a young macaque depends upon its mother for protection, nourishment, and locomotion. As the infant loses its natal coat and acquires the adult coat color, its mother increasingly ignores its pleas to suckle and be carried.

As it is slowly weaned from its mother's milk, the infant practices the skillful movements for adult locomotion through play. By one year of age, a young macaque moves well on its own.

Finish the plate by coloring the bar graphs comparing the percent composition of major body tissues of the adult and infant. Not all tissues are represented, so the total is less than 100%.

The infant's brain at birth is relatively 10 times as heavy as the adult's. This large brain size reflects highly developed tactile, visual, olfactory, and auditory senses and a well-developed motor cortex for clinging. These are important functions that contribute to the infant's survival (3-27). Notice that at birth, the infant's body is composed of almost equal amounts of skin, bone, and muscle (20%, 15%, 25%). During development, skin and bone decrease relative to total body mass, while the amount of muscle almost doubles, from 25% to 43% in the adult. These changes in tissue composition document a trend toward increasing muscularity, a trend that correlates with the shift to locomotor independence during an infant's first year of life.

Grand's method evaluates the change in center of gravity as a consequence of tissue and brain development. The center of gravity "migrates" from a relatively forward position in the trunk of the large-headed clinging newborn to a relatively posterior position in the heavy hindlimbs of the adult. As the limbs increase in relative size and muscularity, they provide propulsive thrust in climbing and running. The anatomical "transformation" of the newborn into the adult corresponds to the transition from physical dependence to independence. At each stage, the growing primate has the locomotor equipment, reflected in its body segments, that provide for its survival to the next stage.

INFANT DEVELOPMENT

PERCENT OF BODY MASS*

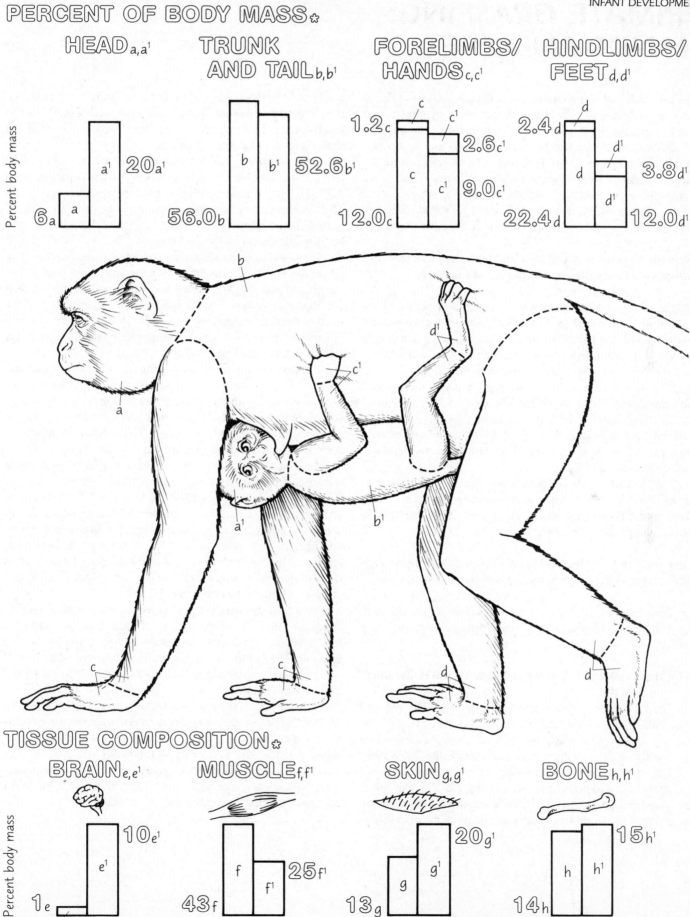

HEAD $_{a,a^1}$

TRUNK AND TAIL $_{b,b^1}$

FORELIMBS/ HANDS $_{c,c^1}$

HINDLIMBS/ FEET $_{d,d^1}$

Percent body mass

20_{a^1}

6_a

52.6_{b^1}

56.0_b

1.2_c

2.6_{c^1}

9.0_{c^1}

12.0_c

2.4_d

3.8_{d^1}

22.4_d

12.0_{d^1}

TISSUE COMPOSITION*

BRAIN $_{e,e^1}$

MUSCLE $_{f,f^1}$

SKIN $_{g,g^1}$

BONE $_{h,h^1}$

Percent body mass

10_{e^1}

1_e

43_f

25_{f^1}

20_{g^1}

13_g

15_{h^1}

14_h

3-11
PRIMATE GRASPING: HANDS AND FEET

Primate hands and feet are remarkable in their ability to grip, to feel and touch, and to control the movements of the fingers and toes. In this plate, we explore the unique structures that underlie the sensory and motor functions of the hands and feet: long, straight digits equipped with flattened nails; sensory pads at the ends of the digits, richly supplied with blood vessels and nerve endings that enhance touch; thick friction skin on the palms and soles with sweat glands that keep the skin clean and pliable; and, most notably, opposable thumbs (pollex) and big toes (hallux).

Color the structures of the claw and nail, shown in side and bottom view in the diagram at the top of the plate.

The structure of primate nails is a departure from the claws of most other mammals. A claw has two layers: a deep stratum fits tightly over the laterally compressed terminal phalanx and a superficial stratum provides a protective cover. The joint between the terminal and middle phalanx is sharply flexed.

Nails lack a deep stratum. The superficial stratum provides structural support for the tactile pad. The terminal phalanx is broad and flat, and the joint with the middle phalanx is straight or unflexed. Tactile pads on the ends of the digits and toes contain numerous touch receptors, which discriminate temperature, texture, pressure, and shape.

The skin of the digits, palms, and soles forms a hairless surface. This friction skin has abundant sweat glands to keep it moist and pliable, essential conditions for fine tactile discrimination and for a firm grip.

Color the hand and foot of the tree shrew, which represents the ancestor to primates. Choose contrasting colors.

The tree shrew (3-7) retains claws on all its digits, although like primates, it uses its hands for holding and manipulating objects.

Color the hands and feet of the primates as each is discussed.

The loris uses its hands and feet as clamps. The reduced second digit helps maximize the loris' reach, which is the widest of any primate's. One claw, used for scratching, is retained on the second toe; all other digits have nails, not visible in this view.

Tarsier hands are splayed in order to grasp prey securely and to grab and cling to branches when landing a spectacular jump. The long, extended digits and well-developed tactile pads are distinctive. The thumb lies in the same plane as the other digits and is not very opposable. With its pronounced big toe, the foot is as long as the tibia and femur, each contributing one-third the length of the hindlimb (4-8). This limb structure reflects the tarsier's remarkable leaping abilities.

Long, slim hands and feet characterize howler monkeys. The index finger and thumb move independently, a departure from the "whole hand" motor control characteristic of the prosimians. The howler monkey hand is distinctive among primates in that it grasps branches between its second and third digits, rather than between the thumb and second digit (4-17).

Baboons have somewhat shorter digits and toes than the more arboreal monkeys because they spend so much time walking on the ground and digging. Palms and soles have thick skin. The thumb can be opposed to the index finger. Fine control of the hand is further enhanced by the ability for each digit to move independently of the others. The basis for this ability lies in the motor cortex of the brain (3-21).

Orangutans are sometimes referred to as "quadrumanus" (quad=four, manus=hand). They can extend their limbs in all directions and distribute the weight of a large body by grasping several branches (4-32). Their hands and feet have long palms, soles, and digits. The thumb and big toe are relatively short, but are well muscled and can be opposed in a strong grip.

Human hands and feet differ from those of other primates in features of bone and muscle arrangement. The human foot is well adapted for weight bearing; it has a broad heel for striking the ground, a thick-skinned ball cushioned by a foot pad, and arches across and down the foot to give it spring. The human foot departs noticably from all other primate feet in having a nonopposable and robust big toe (hallux) aligned with the other, extremely short toes; this arrangement is well suited for weight bearing and pushing off during walking (5-14).

Adult human hands serve no locomotor function. Human hands are similar in shape to those of other primates and have relatively long, well-muscled thumbs with the capacity for fine manipulation. The thumb-to-finger grip and the individual control of fingers underlie the unusual ability to have both precision and power grips (5-23).

Primate hands perform complex sensory and motor functions (3-12). The primate brain is specialized to interpret information about the environment transmitted by the hand's discriminating sense of touch, and to coordinate the hands and eyes. A large area in the human cerebral cortex processes incoming information from the hands and generates appropriate responses for fine motor control of the fingers and thumb.

HANDS AND FEET

CLAW a
NAIL b
SUPERFICIAL
  STRATUM c
DEEP
  STRATUM d
TERMINAL
  PHALANX e
THUMB f
PALM g
BIG TOE h
SOLE i
DIGIT j

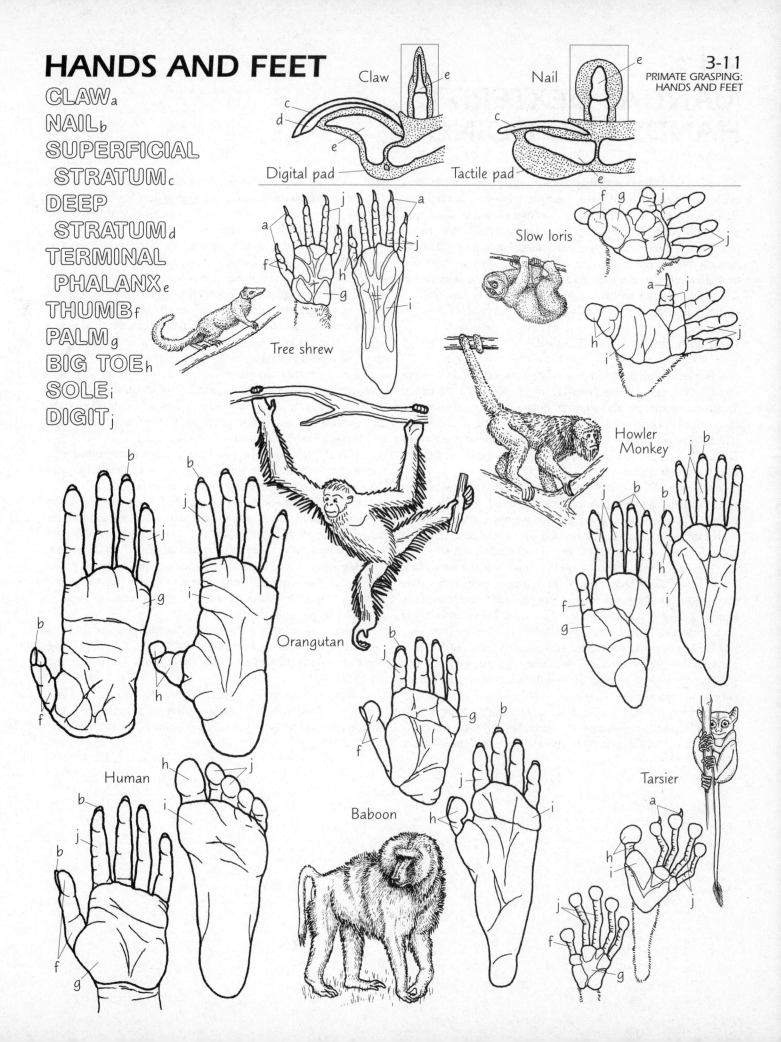

Claw
Nail

Digital pad
Tactile pad

Tree shrew

Slow loris

Orangutan

Howler Monkey

Human

Baboon

Tarsier

3-12
MANUAL DEXTERITY: HANDS AND DOING

Primates grasp things with their hands and feet, something most other mammals cannot do with their paws, hooves, and flippers. Hands are useful for preparing food, exploring and manipulating the environment, and engaging in social contact. Primate hands rely for their skills on good visual and motor coordination. Manual dexterity would not be possible without the mobility inherent in primate forelimbs. Here we investigate some of the activities in which hands are employed, not only to satisfy an animal's curiosity but also to improve its chances of survival.

Color each activity as it is discussed.

Primate hands are used in various ways in their movement through the forest. The long flexible fingers and toes of the tarsier encircle a slender vertical support. Gibbons hang and swing by their hands and long arms as they swish through the air. Monkeys like this langur need all four limbs to walk along the tops of branches or on the ground, and their hands assist in bearing the weight of their bodies.

At birth and for its first few months a baby primate must cling fast to its mother's hair as she moves along. To let go might mean death by falling or exposure. Even human babies are born with a strong grasping reflex, and baby primates' hands and feet have relatively more muscle than those of adults (3-10).

Primates differ from most other mammals in the use of their hands for feeding. They bring food to their mouths rather than taking their mouths to the food, as bobcats and beavers do (1-7). Hand feeding is not as simple as it looks. It entails multiple separate tasks: finding, reaching, plucking, picking, seizing, and holding. Forearm mobility and good visual and motor coordination are required. When feeding, primates typically sit in a stable vertical posture, so that their hands are freed from support activities (3-13).

Primates are by nature curious creatures, constantly taking in stimuli from the environment, often exploring and searching for food that is not immediately visible. This search may require moving leaves or rocks aside, as this baboon is doing, to expose lizards or luscious insect snacks. Digging deeper may also bring up hidden treasures: corms for baboons or earthworms for chimpanzees.

We humans are not alone in washing our vegetables before eating them. Some years ago, a young Japanese macaque called Imo was observed taking her sandy sweet potato down to the ocean to wash it off. This seemed such a good idea that others in her play group took it up. Next the mothers began washing their sweet potatoes, and finally the adult males did it too. In this way Imo's novel behavior initiated a tradition that is still carried on by these monkeys today.

The primate manual skills and coordination shown in foraging can also be turned to using tools, as illustrated here by the human hand with the pencil. Capuchin monkeys and chimpanzees are also adept at tool use. Chimpanzees modify and put to use a variety of materials (3-33).

Hands play an important role in social communication between members of a primate group. Bodily contact is frequent. Newborns instinctively cling to their mothers, and her touches are the very first social messages the babies receive. Older individuals hold, touch, and groom each other. Grooming can be an expression of friendship, a prelude to mating, or an indication of social rank, as higher status attracts more activity. Grooming also seems to relieve tensions, as when competing males groom rather than fight with each other. There is also the practical aspect of grooming, as the process removes dead skin, dirt, and parasites and may help clean wounds.

Humans are not the only primates that use gestures for social messages. Chimpanzees may hold out a hand, palm up, to beg for food or pat a troubled friend on the back for reassurance (3-18).

Manual dexterity, expressed in many ways, is a vital component of the primate evolutionary heritage and a distinguishing characteristic of the primate adaptation.

HANDS AND DOING

GRASPING.ₐ
HANGING AND SWINGING.ᵦ
WEIGHT BEARING.c
CLINGING.d
FEEDING.e
EXPLORING.f
DIGGING.g
POTATO WASHING.h
TOOL USING.ᵢ
GROOMING.ⱼ
GESTURING.ₖ

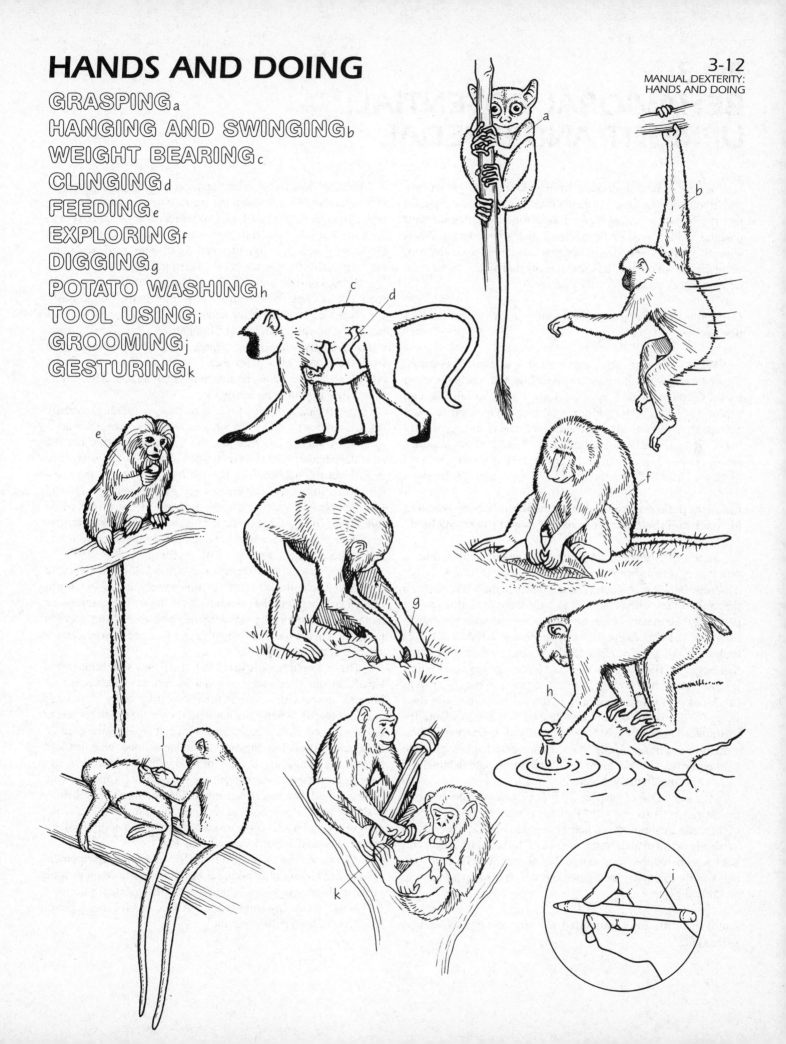

3-13
BEHAVIORAL POTENTIAL: UPRIGHT AND BIPEDAL

Humans are distinct from other primates in their upright posture and bipedal locomotion. Although often regarded as unique, in fact the human mode of locomotion forms a continuum with postural and locomotor adaptations of monkeys and apes. When viewed comparatively, we notice that nonhuman primates, too, stand and move on two legs, and it is instructive to examine the circumstances under which they do so.

Color the sitting dog and the monkey in a typical feeding posture.

When sitting, primates are oriented in an upright position. This posture makes it easier for the hands and forelimbs to be useful for plucking and preparing food, eating, socializing, and exploring (3-12). While performing these activities, the monkey and ape trunk is vertically situated, with the head and upper body balanced above the broadened pelvis (4-25). In contrast, the dog's sitting posture requires support from its forelimbs and paws, and its head is held in front of, rather than over, the narrow pelvis.

Color the patas monkey looking around, the baboon reaching for food, and the Japanese macaque monkey carrying food.

In a way, primate hand feeding and manipulation forms a "first step" toward bipedal behavior. Although monkeys are quadrupedal walkers, runners, and jumpers in the trees, while on the ground they often stand up to look around. In this upright position, their greater height off the ground increases their range of vision. Patas monkeys living in savanna woodlands of Africa look over tall grass to spot food sources, predators, or other monkeys (c). Baboons, as well as vervet monkeys and chimpanzees, stand on two legs to reach for food in bushes or trees (d). Monkeys may run bipedally, as this Japanese macaque does when its hands are occupied with food and not available for locomotor support (e). Monkeys' ability to orient themselves vertically and move bipedally is, to some extent, made possible by their broader pelvis, more mobile hip joints, and habitual use of flexible, manipulative forelimbs.

The evolution of suspensory behavior of hominoids might be viewed as "a second step" that contributed to the emergence of bipedal locomotion. When suspended, the ape's body is vertically oriented under branches (4-26). Its broad rib cage, short back region, reduced lumbar mobility, absence of a tail, and long and mobile forelimbs are adaptations which predispose them to an upright posture.

Color the title and associated activity of apes as each is discussed.

Gibbons live in the forest and rarely come to the ground; they swing and leap through the trees. When moving along the tops of branches, they walk on two legs with arms held over the head or out to the side, tightrope-walker style (f). Gibbon arms are so long and their shoulder and wrist joints so flexible that they are unable to bear weight on their forelimbs.

Bipedal posture and behavior enhance tasks associated with food. For example, chimpanzees at Wamba in the Congo Basin sometimes collect and carry sugar cane, and a female's infant must hold on for the ride (e[1])! Chimpanzees at Bossou, Guinea, stand bipedally while using a large pestle-stick to pound pulp from the center of a palm tree (g). Taï Forest, Ivory Coast chimpanzees carry stone hammers to crack nuts, and 8% of the time they carry them bipedally.

Apes typically display while standing up or running bipedally (h). Chimpanzees at Gombe Stream, Tanzania, wave their arms to threaten their baboon rivals; the taller chimpanzee has the advantage both in size and reach when it stands, swings its arms, or kicks at the baboon. The baboon tries to bite, but the ape's long arms effectively keep the monkey's sharp teeth out of range. Chimpanzees at Wamba display in front of the group while running bipedally, dragging large branches behind them. Gorillas beat their chests in play, to get attention, to assert dominance, intimidate strangers, or to scare off predators.

Chimpanzees and gorillas can throw with considerable accuracy. Their limited trunk rotation affects the shoulder-arm motion and therefore the precision of the throw. The chimpanzee method of throwing contrasts with the pronounced trunk rotation involved when a baseball player fires a fast ball or when an ice skater prepares for a jump.

These examples illustrate activities and situations when bipedal locomotion is advantageous for monkeys and apes. This information provides a basis for speculating "why" hominids became bipedal. When early hominids began to exploit resources in the savanna mosaic regions of Africa, it would have been an advantage to look into the distance to locate food, enemies, and friends. Standing and reaching for food in bushes or trees would have increased their foraging range. Upright displays and throwing objects would have effectively intimidated strangers or predators. Walking bipedally would have freed the arms and hands for carrying a variety of objects, such as food and tools, and for traveling considerable distances each day.

All of these "steps" probably contributed to the development of hominid locomotion, taking it beyond an occasional posture or short-distance movement, into a sustained, habitual gait (5-2). It is unlikely that any single behavior accounts for the origin or evolution of human locomotion.

UPRIGHT AND BIPEDAL

SITTING*
  DOG$_a$
   MONKEY$_b$
LOOKING$_c$
REACHING$_d$
CARRYING$_{e,e^1}$
WALKING$_f$
TOOL USING$_g$
DISPLAYING$_h$

3-14
THE SOCIAL REVOLUTION AND THE MAMMALIAN BRAIN

In the evolution of placental mammals, new forebrain structures made possible three behavioral innovations: nursing in conjunction with infant care; audiovocal communication for maintaining maternal-infant contact; and playful behavior, originating in the nest among litter mates. These innovations, as explained by psychiatrist Paul MacLean, comprised a revolution in mammalian, and later primate, social behavior. Emotional attachments develop early in life between an infant, its mother, and litter mates and lay the foundation for adult interaction and communication. The limbic system underpins the emotions that guide and motivate social behavior.

Color the infant's behaviors as they are discussed.

Suckling was an important innovation in mammals. Infant mammals concentrate suckling, swallowing, breathing, smelling, and vocalizing within a small region of the nose, mouth, and throat. A novel neural and muscular apparatus accommodates this complex set of functions according to biologist Kathleen K. Smith. Motor control of the facial muscles (especially the buccinator) creates a vacuum in the mouth, making suckling possible. The mammalian hard palate separates the pathways of breathing and swallowing. Vocalizations from the infant's larynx communicate its location and emotional state. Infant mammals often vocalize at birth and emit what MacLean labels the isolation or separation call, the most primitive and basic mammalian vocalization. The new mammalian ear bones indicate a hearing mechanism refined over that of reptilian ancestors (1-5, 3-19). The infant's sense of smell helps identify its mother. Its gaze into her eyes promotes visual communication as it learns to read facial expressions. Touching its mother provides a sense of security and well being.

Color the corresponding behaviors of the adult female (placental) mammal as they are discussed.

Parental care in birds involves both parents. In contrast, female mammals provide all the nourishment for the young, initially through the placenta to the fetus (for which placental mammals are named), and after birth, through the production of milk from the mammary glands. Mothers touch, lick, and groom their infants; these activities contribute to infant survival and well being (3-27). Enhanced mammalian senses ensure a mother's contact with her infants, through smelling, seeing, hearing distress calls, and vocalizing in return.

Locomotor mobility (3-7) enables mammalian females to maintain a high level of activity for effective foraging and avoidance of predators during pregnancy and lactation. (The maintenance of a high, constant body temperature characteristic of mammals helps sustain locomotor activity.) Bone growth of female mammals is usually completed prior to reproduction, therefore energy can be diverted from growth to pregnancy and lactation. Fat stored in body tissues and calcium in the bones are utilized during lactation (3-26). Calcium reserves are mobilized and transferred through the placenta to promote bone and tooth formation in the fetus. After birth, calcium is transferred to the infant through milk to promote its skeletal and dental growth.

Color the structures of the limbic system.

The behavioral innovations of mammals have a neural basis in the limbic system, the part of the forebrain not present in reptiles. The forebrain or cerebrum expanded in early phases of mammalian evolution (1-4). The limbic system is sometimes known as the primitive brain or the "smell brain" because it includes the olfactory bulb and tract, a major brain system in primitive mammals.

The limbic system is a group of structures associated with almost all parts of the forebrain except the neocortex; it wraps around the brain stem and forms a border which links cortical and midbrain areas with those that control internal body systems, hence limbic (limbus=border or margin). The components of this ring-shaped system include the amgydala (Latin for almond), which influences feeding, sexual behavior, and emotional reactions such as fear and anger; the hippocampus, which is involved in learning and memory; and the hypothalamus. The hypothalamus is the size of a small, flat grape. It acts as a master control for regulating hormones secreted by the pituitary gland (not illustrated) and in turn affects, for example, lactation, ovulation, licking, and suckling. The angular cingulate cortex and parahippocampus comprise part of the limbic cortex which modifies the animal's expression of rage and fright.

The limbic system plays a complex and important role in the expression of instincts, drives, and emotions. The association of feelings with sensations, such as smell and sight, and the formation of memories are also influenced by the limbic system. MacLean's research illustrates the neural basis for maternal care, play, and vocalizations. If the limbic cortex does not develop in hamsters for instance, play is absent in the young, and appropriate nesting and caretaking behaviors do not develop in adult females. Without limbic cortex, squirrel monkeys fail to emit spontaneous isolation calls. In humans, many of these innate or primitive behaviors are moderated by the cerebral cortex.

In the evolution from reptiles to mammals, anatomical and functional changes in the brain correspond to a reorganization of the senses (smell, hearing, touch) and a new repertoire of social behaviors (nursing, separation call of infants, play) that are rooted in the emotional brain. The extended association between adults and young provides the time for establishing emotional ties and for learning and practicing necessary social skills. These skills form the foundation for the diversity, complexity, and adaptive significance in social behavior that we find among primate species (3-23).

THE SOCIAL REVOLUTION AND THE MAMMALIAN BRAIN

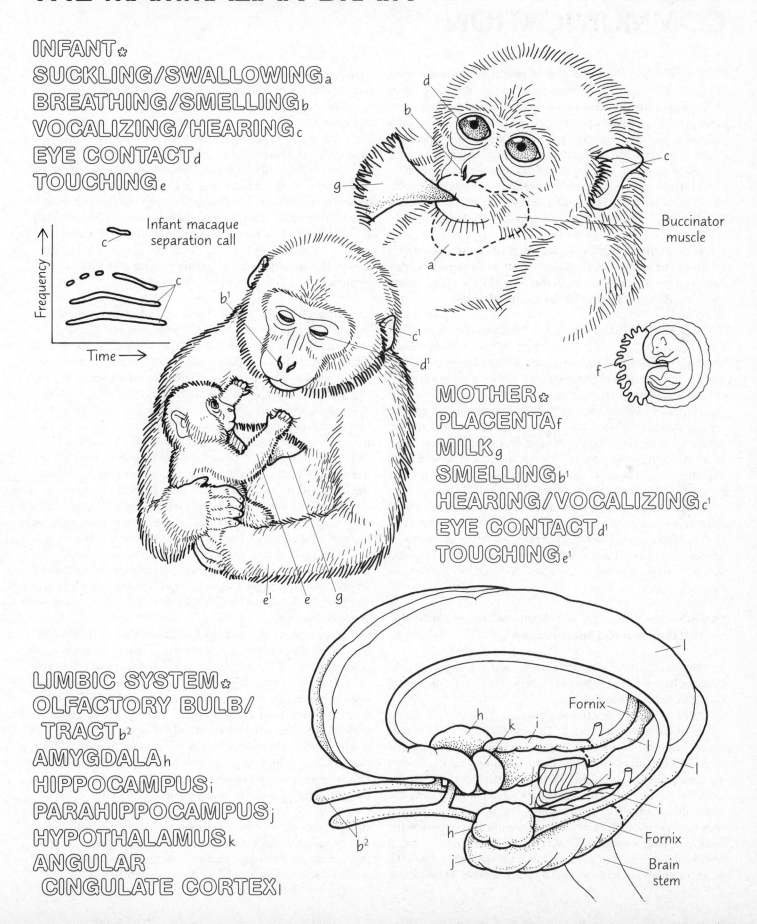

INFANT⋆
SUCKLING/SWALLOWING$_a$
BREATHING/SMELLING$_b$
VOCALIZING/HEARING$_c$
EYE CONTACT$_d$
TOUCHING$_e$

Infant macaque
separation call

Frequency →

Time →

Buccinator
muscle

MOTHER⋆
PLACENTA$_f$
MILK$_g$
SMELLING$_{b^1}$
HEARING/VOCALIZING$_{c^1}$
EYE CONTACT$_{d^1}$
TOUCHING$_{e^1}$

LIMBIC SYSTEM⋆
OLFACTORY BULB/
 TRACT$_{b^2}$
AMYGDALA$_h$
HIPPOCAMPUS$_i$
PARAHIPPOCAMPUS$_j$
HYPOTHALAMUS$_k$
ANGULAR
 CINGULATE CORTEX$_l$

Fornix

Fornix

Brain
stem

3-15
OLFACTION: NOSES AND SMELLING: COMMUNICATION

Early mammals evolved as nocturnal creatures, dependent upon the sense of smell for locating their young, detecting food, avoiding predators, and organizing social behavior. Lemurs and other prosimians retain a keen sense of smell from mammalian ancestors and rely on it for perception and communication. Anthropoids, including humans, depend less on the sense of smell than do prosimians. Consequently, the structures that perceive odors differ in the two groups. In a prosimian and an anthropoid, we illustrate the nasal region that receives the chemical signals and the neural center in the brain that processes them.

Color the rhinarium at the top of the plate. Color Jacobson's organ in the septum of the nasal cavity of the lemur. Color the nasal cavity and septum in the frontal view of the lemur and human. Use a light color for the nasal cavity.

In lemurs, galagos, and lorises, a rhinarium (Greek for nose) surrounds the nostrils and contains many mucus-secreting glands. This "wet muzzle" appearance is characteristic of many mammals. The rhinarium comes in contact with Jacobsen's organ via a pair of tiny canals in the roof of the mouth. Jacobsen's organ, inherited from reptilian forebears, lies embedded in the nasal septum. The septum divides the nasal cavity in half and accounts for the separation of the two middle upper incisors in strepsirhines. These features identify prosimians as "strepsirhine," meaning split nose, to distinguish them from "haplorhine" tarsiers and anthropoids (3-1).

When chemical substances in the air come in contact with the lemur's moist nose, they dissolve in mucus and are analyzed in Jacobsen's organ. Inside the organ, olfactory receptors in specialized sensory tissue respond to the dissolved molecules and send electrical impulses to the accessory olfactory bulb in the brain.

Color the cribriform plate and olfactory structures in the side views of the lemur and human crania.

In lemurs, the snout projects beyond the eye orbits. In humans, the eye orbits, sinuses (cavities in the facial bones), and nasal cavity lie in the same plane.

Within the nasal cavity, mucus-secreting tissue (epithelium) covers the turbinates or conchae. These tiny, bony scrolls increase the surface area of the overlying tissue, which humidifies and warms the incoming air passing through the nasal cavity. Toward the back of the nose, olfactory receptors in the turbinates analyze the dissolved chemicals based on the size and shape of the molecules. Each olfactory receptor is specialized to respond to only one specific molecular shape. When this shape contacts the odor receptor, chemical information is translated into electrical impulses and carried by olfactory neurons through holes in the skull, the cribriform (cribr=sieve) plate, to the brain. The olfactory

bulb processes the smell information and relays it via the olfactory tract to other parts of the brain for further analysis.

The size of the nasal cavity, number of turbinates, the extent of olfactory epithelium, the number of olfactory receptors, and the relative size of the olfactory bulbs are larger in prosimians than in humans and other anthropoids. In particular, note the much larger perforated cribriform plate of the lemur. These anatomical differences, along with the loss of the rhinarium, indicate that the sense of smell is less emphasized among anthropoid primates. When preserved in fossil crania, the size of the cribriform plate is one way to assess the sense of smell in extinct primates.

Color the examples of olfactory communication among lemurs.

Ringtailed lemurs have specialized scent glands (enlarged sebaceous glands) on the chest, forearms, and ano-genital areas. When rubbed against branches and tree trunks, the glands emit odorous secretions. When females mark on tree trunks, their glands emit a specialized scent indicating their willingness to mate. Males take immediate notice because their chance to breed is restricted to one month-long breeding season each year (4-7). Lemur males also spread scent from the forearm glands onto their tails, which they then wave at each other during confrontations, called "stink fights"! To communicate between social groups, males rub branches with scent to map out their exclusive area of the forest and to signal that others must keep out.

Many prosimians and some monkeys regularly urinate over their hands and feet and then spread the scent around, marking their trails chemically. By sniffing the sites where others have scent-marked, these primates gather information on the whereabouts of group members and neighbors and about sexual identity and receptivity. Chemical signals may be so subtle as to identify the "scent marker" as a specific individual whom the sniffer knows well.

Even without specialized scent glands, Old World monkeys and apes use chemical information as one method of communication. For example, when threatened, male gorillas give off a strong odor from the axillary glands. Female monkeys and apes emit pheromones (volatile organic substances) from their vaginas when they are ovulating. These chemical signals communicate that a female is sexually receptive, whether or not brightly colored sexual swellings are present. Human females may also emit pheromones, which may be perceived at an unconscious level and may synchronize menstrual schedules of women living in the same social group.

Although the sense of smell is less acute in anthropoids than in prosimians, it remains important in perception and in communication. Because the olfactory nerve network is part of the limbic system, the seat of the emotions, strong memories and feelings are often associated with specific odors.

NOSES AND SMELLING

RHINARIUM a
JACOBSEN'S ORGAN b
NASAL CAVITY c
   SEPTUM d
CRIBRIFORM PLATE e
OLFACTORY
   RECEPTORS/NERVES f
   BULB/TRACT f¹

OLFACTORY
   COMMUNICATION *
SCENT GLANDS g

MARKING h

SNIFFING i

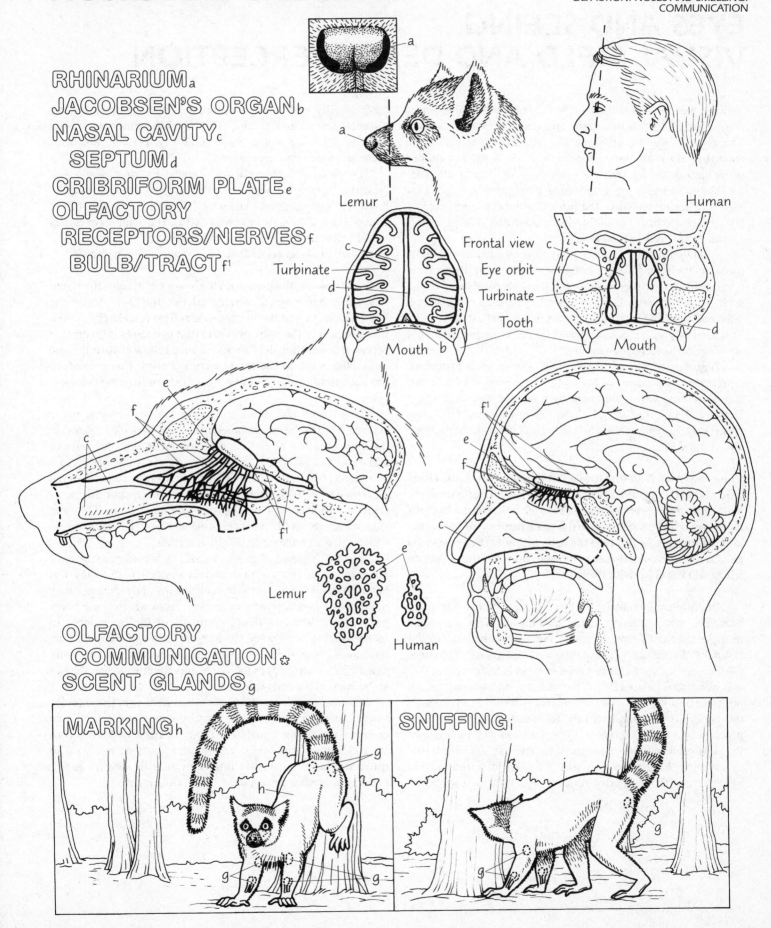

Lemur

Human

Turbinate

Frontal view
Eye orbit
Turbinate
Tooth
Mouth

Mouth
b

Lemur

Human

3-16
EYES AND SEEING: VISUAL FIELD AND DEPTH PERCEPTION

Vision is the most specialized and most complex of the five senses (vision, olfaction, audition, taste, and somatosensory or tactile). The primate way of life depends upon excellent vision for traveling through the rain forests (3-8, 4-1), for object manipulation, and for hand-eye coordination (3-12). In this plate, we discuss stereoscopy, or binocular ("two eyes") vision. This aspect of seeing underlies the primate ability to catch hold of leafy twigs and branches during locomotion and to locate, seize, examine, and prepare food items.

Although stereoscopy has evolved in cats and in species of predatory birds, most vertebrates survey the world in all directions (even behind them) with eyes placed on opposite sides of the head. In species with laterally placed eyes, each eye covers a different visual field and can detect even the smallest movement. This kind of vision is advantageous for detecting predators, but is not suited for depth perception.

Here we compare the visual fields of nonprimate mammals, represented by a rabbit; of prosimians, represented by a lemur; and of anthropoids, represented by a human. Two anatomical features affect this aspect of vision: the orientation of the bony sockets and the eyes within; and the neural networks in the optic and visual wiring.

Color the visual field that the rabbit's right eye sees, the visual field of the left eye, and the overlapping field. Use light colors. Color the arrows representing the orientation of the rabbit's right and left eye sockets. Use the same process for the lemur and the human. Notice that the orientation of the eye sockets results in different degrees of overlap between the right and left visual fields in these three species.

In primitive mammals, the eye orbits are on the side of the head. The zone of overlap, called the binocular field, is minimal in these mammals, represented by the rabbit where overlap is about 30°. In primates, the eye orbits shifted toward the front of the face, so that the fields of vision overlap in lemurs about 90°, and in humans about 120°. A bar of bone surrounding the eye orbit (the postorbital bar) is present in prosimians; in anthropoids the eye orbits are completely encircled in bone (4-9). In fossil primates and other mammals, the orientation and enclosure of the bony orbits provide clues about their visual abilities (4-10).

Although each eye collects slightly different visual information from nearby objects, the area of overlap is automatically analyzed by visual centers in the brain to produce a three-dimensional picture. This resulting binocular vision permits depth perception and the ability to judge distances between objects and the observer.

The second anatomical requirement for stereoscopy is a "rewiring" of nerve fibers. The retina, at the back of the eyeball, holds the light-sensitive cells which detect light rays that have entered the eye through the cornea (3-17). The optic nerve carries visual information from the retina to the visual cortex (3-21). Each section of the visual field has its own neural pathway.

In the schematic illustration on the lower right, color the visual fields and their areas of overlap (a), (b), and (a+b). Color the left-most section of the human visual field (c). On the retina, find the part of the optic nerve (c) that processes information received from that field of vision and follow it through the optic chiasma into the visual cortex. Follow this procedure for each field (d), (e), (f), and (g), using contrasting colors.

In nonbinocular animals like the rabbit, the optic nerve coming from the retina completely crosses over (decussates) at the optic chiasma. Therefore, all information from the left eye and the left visual field is processed by the right side of the brain and vice versa. In primates, the inner half of the retina sees the outer-most fields of vision, (c) and (g). These optic fibers, as with the rabbit, cross to the opposite side of the brain. The outer side of each retina (d) and (f) sees the world on the opposite side and the fibers on the outer side do not cross.

So, the right half of each eye sends its messages to the right hemisphere of the cerebral cortex, the left half to the left hemisphere. When the optic tracts leave the optic chiasma, they travel to the lateral geniculate nucleus from which some fibers go to the superior colliculi, remnants of the optic lobes in mammals that localize objects in space. Most of the optic tract continues from the lateral geniculate nucleus as the optic radiations and projects to the visual cortex in the occipital lobes at the back of the cerebrum.

Compare the colors from the visual field with those on the visual cortex to note how the sensory cortex is essentially an orderly "map" of the visual field. From the visual cortex, neurons send electrical impulses to many other parts of the brain to integrate incoming visual information with sensory input, memories, motivations, and motor activity patterns.

VISUAL FIELD AND DEPTH PERCEPTION

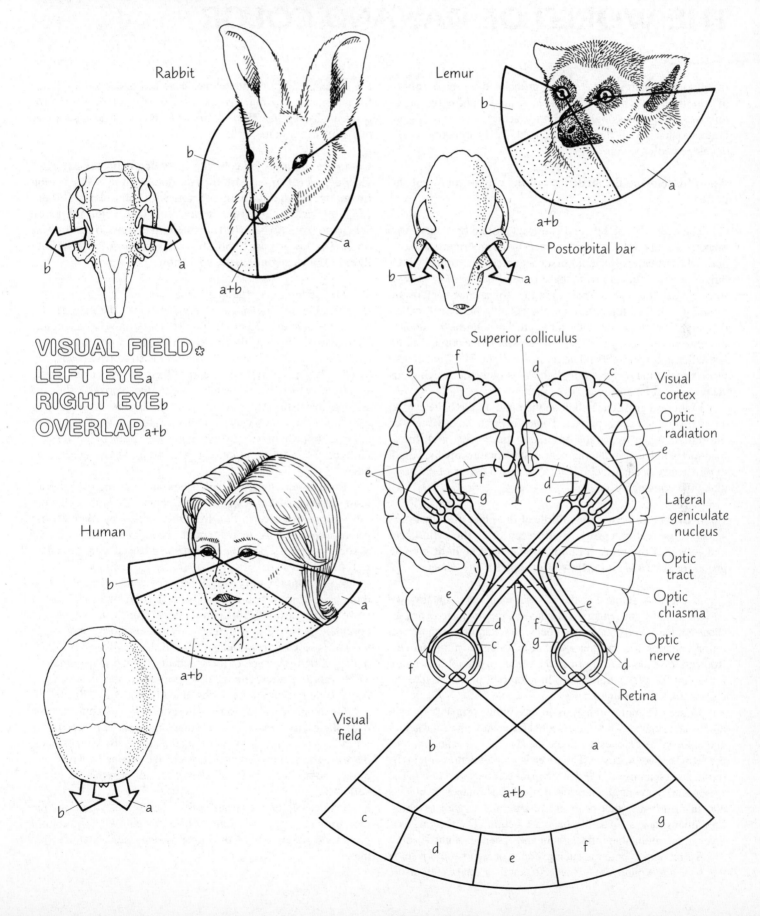

Rabbit

Lemur

Postorbital bar

VISUAL FIELD*
LEFT EYE a
RIGHT EYE b
OVERLAP a+b

Human

Superior colliculus

Visual cortex

Optic radiation

Lateral geniculate nucleus

Optic tract

Optic chiasma

Optic nerve

Retina

Visual field

EYES AND SEEING: THE WORLD OF DAY AND COLOR

In addition to stereoscopic vision, primates have the ability to discriminate colors in the environment. In this second of two plates on vision, we discuss light sensitivity, acuity, and color vision. Humans share with the apes and Old World monkeys well-developed color vision.

Begin by coloring the structures of the eye at the top of the plate.

The eyeball is mobile and is moved around by a set of eye muscles. Light reflected from an object in the environment, (seen here schematically as an ape) first encounters the cornea, which bulges slightly outward from the surface of the white of the eye (the sclera). The cornea bends light rays toward the back of the retina, which then travel through the opening in the iris, called the pupil. The iris is a muscular structure that controls the amount of light entering the eye by changing the size of the pupil, making it smaller in bright light and larger in dim light. The iris can also protect the retina by absorbing light in its pigment, which gives each of us our characteristic eye color.

Light rays cross each other on their path through the eye, so a tiny inverted image is projected onto the light-sensitive cells of the retina. When light falls on one of these cells, a chemical reaction is induced in the pigment of the photoreceptors, which in turn sends an electrical signal to the visual cortex of the brain along the optic nerve.

Color the retina across the middle of the plate and the light-sensitive neural receptors (photoreceptors): the cylindrical rod cells and the more bulbous cone cells. Use light blue or green for the rods and yellow or orange for the cones.

The primate retina, like that of other mammals, contains two basic kinds of light sensitive photoreceptors: rods and cones. In sheer numbers, rods far exceed cones; for example, each human retina contains 125 million rods but less than 7 million cones. Rods are distributed away from the center of the retina and are important for peripheral vision. In nocturnal primates, like the galago, rods predominate.

Cones are more numerous in day-living primates than in nocturnal primates. They are essential for achieving visual acuity and color vision. Cones dominate the specialized central part of the retina called the fovea. The fovea is a small depression in the retina and contains 30,000 densely packed cones (no rods). The fovea is like a central analyzer; it magnifies images of objects and discriminates shapes in greatest detail, as well as color. Prosimians lack a fovea but have a tapetum. The tapetum is a layer in the retina that reflects light and enhances night vision.

To recognize patterns such as faces or words on a printed page, we move our eyes and heads so that their images fall on the fovea. People born without cones have achromatopsia (a, Latin for without; chroma, Greek for color). When cones are congenitally absent and do not fill the fovea, visual acuity is about one-tenth of normal.

Complete the plate by coloring the galago and the range of visible light it can see with the rod-dominant eye. Then color the mangabey, a day-living primate with color vision and the range of visible light that it can see. Next, color the color spectrum from the shortest wavelength (violet) to the longest (red). The lowermost band illustrates the position of visible light in the electromagnetic spectrum.

The galago's best vision is in the blue and blue-green wavelengths, although it can see in a wider range. The mangabey's best range is in the higher red, orange, and yellow wavelengths. Vision involves the ability to sense energy in part of the electromagnetic spectrum. Visible light is so called because we "see" it. Light is only a small part of the entire electromagnetic spectrum, which has wavelengths ranging from the shortest gamma rays to the longest radio waves. The color we perceive is determined by which wavelengths of light an object reflects to our eyes and which wavelengths it absorbs. If the object reflects all light, we see it as white; if it absorbs all light, we see it as black.

Rods discern light and dark, shape and movement. They are most sensitive to light of shorter wavelengths. Rods are a hundred times more sensitive to dim light than cones, but they do not perceive color. We use them for night vision, where images appear as shades of gray. Cones, on the other hand, need more light than rods to be activated.

Rods contain only one light-sensitive pigment called rhodopsin, which is optimally activated by light of the blue-green wavelengths around 500 nanometers. Cones, however, are optimally sensitive to different wavelengths, corresponding to the colors violet, green, and yellow-red. They are most sensitive in the yellow-green end of the spectrum, about 555 nanometers. Their relative photochemical responses to visible light are responsible for our ability to perceive the world in color.

Other animals also discriminate colors. For example, lizards mark their territories with a substance that can be perceived by other lizards in the ultraviolet range, and insects, such as bees, perceive the yellow center of flowers. The retina of day-living birds is composed largely of cones, which discriminate colors in yellow and red ranges.

Primate color vision and visual acuity contribute to fine discrimination of food items, arboreal pathways, potential predators, neighbors of the same species, and social group members.

THE WORLD OF DAY AND COLOR

EYE MUSCLE a
LENS b
RETINA c
OPTIC NERVE d

LIGHT ✳
DIM e¹
BRIGHT f¹

RODS e

CONES f

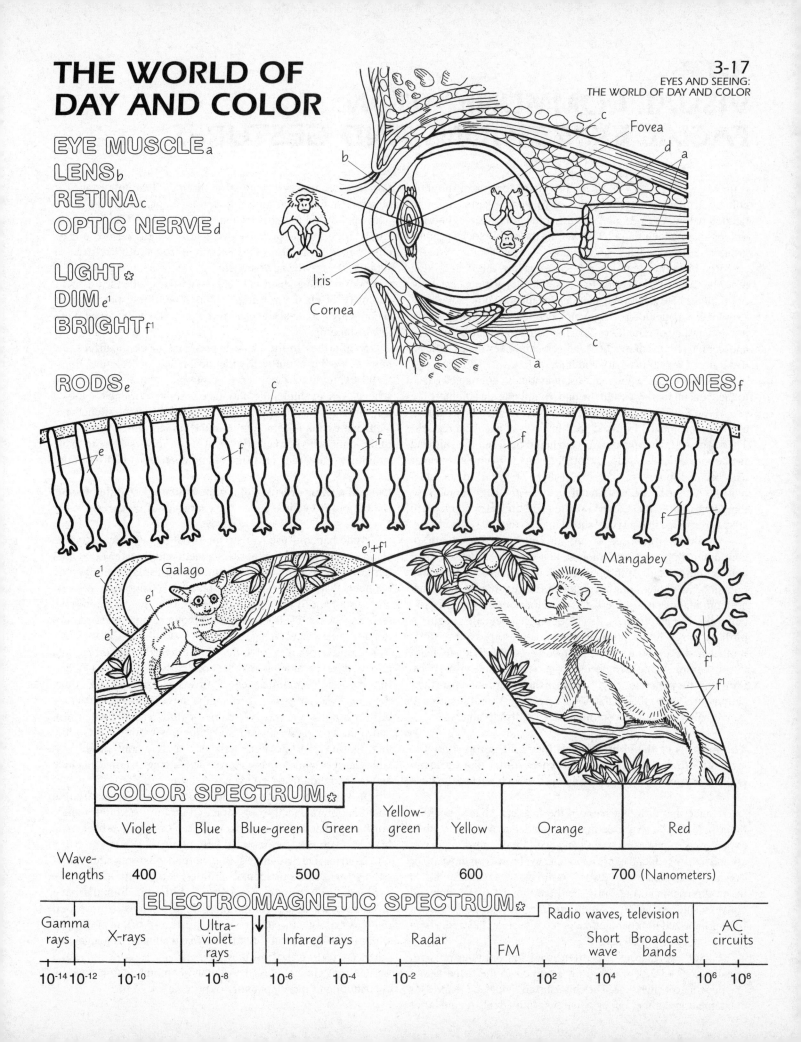

Fovea

Iris

Cornea

Galago

e¹+f¹

Mangabey

COLOR SPECTRUM ✳

Violet	Blue	Blue-green	Green	Yellow-green	Yellow	Orange	Red

Wave-lengths   400   500   600   700 (Nanometers)

ELECTROMAGNETIC SPECTRUM ✳

Gamma rays	X-rays	Ultra-violet rays	Infared rays	Radar	FM	Radio waves, television Short wave Broadcast bands	AC circuits

10^{-14} 10^{-12} 10^{-10} 10^{-8} 10^{-6} 10^{-4} 10^{-2} 10^{2} 10^{4} 10^{6} 10^{8}

3-18
VISUAL COMMUNICATION: FACIAL EXPRESSIONS AND GESTURES

Primates depend upon well-developed vision for locating brightly colored fruit in the green forest (3-6), maneuvering through tangled pathways (3-3), and spotting predators and neighboring groups sharing their range (3-4). Within the highly social primate group (3-23), individuals communicate with one another visually.

Visual signals may carry information about age, sex, reproductive state, and rank. For example, the distinct coat color of infant primates identifies their dependent and vulnerable status to other group members. Bright pink perineal swellings advertise the sexual state of females (3-25). Lavender or turquoise-colored ano-genital regions of mandrill and vervet monkey males indicate the signs of sexual maturity and high rank.

In close-up social interactions, individuals communicate face to face. Facial markings and the underlying muscles promote the use of the face for expression. Muscles of the mammalian face and scalp originated from the neck muscles of ancestral reptiles. These "new" facial muscles are anchored between the skin and facial bones. On the scalp, the newly evolved mammalian outer ears became mobile for hearing at night (3-19). Primate facial muscles are more differentiated than those in other mammals, so that facial expressions can be used to communicate complex and subtle meanings in everyday social interaction.

Facial expressions serve an important function in communicating emotions, moods, and intentions between and among individuals. Anthropologist Paul Ekman maintains that human facial expressions accurately reflect emotional states that are communicated to others and therefore are universal cross-culturally. For all primates, this face-to-face interaction begins at birth, when an infant primate maintains close proximity to its mother and often looks into her face (3-14). Individuals learn how to communicate their needs through appropriate visual cues. Similarly, they learn to "read" others in the group, anticipate their actions, and adjust their behavior accordingly. Visual signals and nonverbal behavior can communicate "loudly" to others!

The muscles of the chimpanzee's face on the top show the structures that generate the facial expressions. Color the facial expressions, using contrasting colors for each part of the face.

Notice that different parts of the face can change position independently, thereby creating an expanded repertoire of subtle expressions. A primate's mouth and eyes are the most important components of a facial expression. The eyebrows can move up or down, to the middle or outward. A direct, wide-eyed stare is a threat expression for most primates; averting the eyes downward conveys submission. The highly mobile lips can be protruded forward, pushed tightly together, or retracted over the teeth while the jaws are open or closed.

Facial expressions are often used in combination with vocalizations (3-22), which draw attention to the facial signal and punctuate its message. The chimpanzee "hoot face" expresses excitement and affection, as when two individuals reunite after foraging separately for most of the day. The "play face" is observed most often among juveniles engaged in rough and tumble play and in infants when they are tickled. The "glare" is easily recognized because we use it when we are angry; chimpanzees do too. The "silent bared teeth" expresses submission, as when a young chimpanzee wishes to express that it intends no antagonism and does not wish to challenge the social authority of an older animal. A crouched body posture may accompany the facial signal and emphasize the younger animal's lower standing.

Similarities in the facial expressions of chimpanzees and humans are due to our nearly identical facial musculature. Some facial expressions even serve common functions for the two species. For example, the play face is thought to have evolved into human laughter. Many researchers think that the silent bared teeth expression is homologous to the human smile. Association of the smile with human enjoyment is not universal, for in many cultures smiling may be a sign of apprehension and discomfort.

Color the canine display of a male baboon. Use pale blue for the baboon's eyelids. Color the examples of gestures.

Male baboons use an extreme facial expression, called the canine display, which exposes the teeth and threatens potential intruders. In other circumstances, the canine display notifies group members that the male can defend his social position if necessary, and to stay out of his way, to move off, or to give a submissive response. Notice the lowered eyelids (color is important here too) as part of the visual signal.

Gestures often involve the face, especially the directional gaze of the eyes, along with other body parts. When Jane Goodall first reported on chimpanzee gestures she observed at Gombe, the world was amazed at their "humanness." Chimpanzees may beg for a morsel of food by leaning forward, reaching out an arm and holding a palm upward under the possessor's chin, while gazing intently between the desired item and possessor. Chimpanzees convey reassurance by extending an arm to encircle another individual and giving a reassuring pat.

Primatologist Joanne Tanner documents a remarkable combination of facial expression and gesture. A young female gorilla uses her hand to hide her play face from a silverback male in order to conceal her motivation to play (3-22).

Charles Darwin noted that human gestures and facial expressions, like our mental abilities, are adaptive and have evolved through natural selection. Although humans have language, we also communicate face to face using facial expressions, gestures, and body postures, often employed simultaneously. The ability to read visual signals, to gauge how others are feeling and how they might act, extends the range and subtlety of primate as well as human communication, thereby contributing to the adaptability of primate social life.

FACIAL EXPRESSIONS AND GESTURES

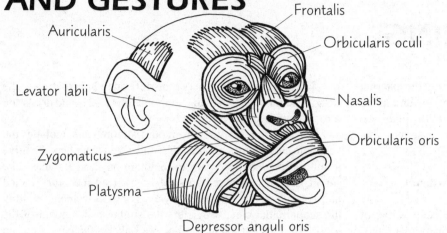

Auricularis
Frontalis
Orbicularis oculi
Levator labii
Nasalis
Zygomaticus
Orbicularis oris
Platysma
Depressor anguli oris

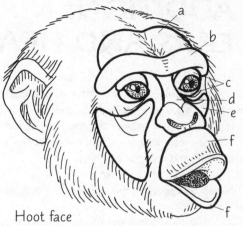

Hoot face

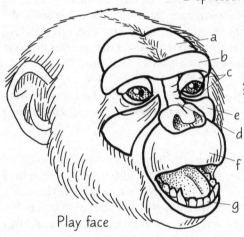

Play face

Glare

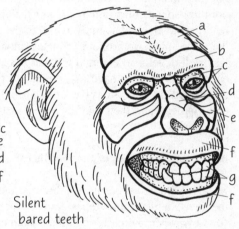

Silent
bared teeth

FOREHEAD a
EYEBROW b
EYELID c
NOSE d

CHEEK e
LIPS/MOUTH f
TEETH g

CANINE
DISPLAY h

GESTURES *

BEGGING i   REASSURING j

CONCEALING
PLAY FACE k

3-19
AUDITION:
EARS AND HEARING

Sounds are an important source of information about the external world. Primates vary in the acuteness of their hearing and in the range of sound frequencies they can perceive. In this plate, we describe ear structure, function, and the range of sounds that humans and galagos can hear.

Begin by coloring the outer ear, canal, and eardrum.

The basic structure of the human ear is the same as that of our mammalian ancestors (1-5). Galagos, like many mammals, optimize sound collection by moving their ears around like radar receivers to channel sound waves into the ear canal and toward the tympanum. Anthropoid primates (monkeys and apes) have less well developed external ear muscles and less mobile outer ears. (Most humans have lost the ability to wiggle their ears.) Anthropoids rely heavily on vision for monitoring the environment, and their hearing is less acute than the nocturnal prosimians.

Next color the bones of the middle ear.

The middle ear consists of three ossicles (little bones) (1-5); the incus, malleus, and stapes. As you color, imagine the path of sound waves moving through the human ear as a succession of high- and low-density packets of air. The number of these pressure waves reaching the ear each second is the frequency. Low frequencies are perceived as deep pitch and high frequencies as shrill. When pressure waves strike it, the tympanum, stretched across the entrance to the middle ear, vibrates like the drum for which it is named. This sets the three middle ear ossicles into motion: the malleus (hammer) strikes the incus (anvil), which in turn strikes the stapes (stirrup).

Color all of the structures of the inner ear and the cochlear canals.

The cochlea, a snail-shaped, triple-barreled tube, is vital for sound perception. Beneath the cochlear canal lies the thick basilar membrane, and on this membrane lies the organ of Corti, with its fine, hairlike projections.

The stapes transmits pressure waves via the flexible oval window to the cochlea. Sound waves go down the vestibular canal to the apex, then travel back through the tympanic canal to the flexible round window, where sound energy passes out of the inner ear. The sounds waves set up vibrations in the basilar membrane, and stimulate the hairs on the organ of Corti. The hairs send nerve impulses to the brain. Different hairs respond to different sound frequencies and are perceived in the brain as different pitches.

The auditory nerve fibers transmit sound information to the sensory auditory cortex in the temporal lobe (3-21) and decussate (cross) completely before reaching it.

The inner ear, a legacy from our fish forebears, includes the vestibule and semicircular canals, fluid-filled chambers sensitive to motion that are necessary to maintain balance. Balance, like sound, depends on stimulation of specialized receptors, called hair cells, that respond to sound waves or to movement. Fluid in the semicircular canals registers the slightest movement of the head. The sense of balance relies not only on the canals but on visual input and on information received from receptors in the body, especially those around the joints. The information, processed by the cerebellum and cerebral cortex, enables the body to adjust with changes in movements of the head.

Color the sound wave frequencies using dark contrasting colors. With light colors, color the hearing range of the galago and human.

High frequencies excite nerve fibers at the base of the cochlea, low frequencies at the apex. The range of frequencies an animal can perceive depends upon the length of the cochlea. Mammals, with a longer cochlea, can hear higher frequencies than reptiles. The human organ of Corti contains more hairs than that of other mammals, reflecting the importance of auditory discrimination for understanding speech.

Prosimians can hear frequencies in the ultrasonic range, up to 60,000 Hertz (cycles per second), sounds which are beyond the perceptual range of monkeys, apes, and humans, whose upper limit is 20,000 to 25,000 Hertz. Galago hearing is most sensitive in the range of 8000 Hertz. Human sensitivity lies between 2000 and 4000 Hertz, the range of the human voice during speaking.

Bats are adept at perceiving sound frequencies of more than 120,000 Hertz. Small mammals with close-set ears, like bats, can hear high-frequency sounds better than species with large heads and wide-set ears. At the other extreme, elephants perceive rumbles in the low frequencies from 10,000 down to 17 Hertz, in the infrasonic range, too low for human hearing. Larger animals can hear low frequencies and can better detect brief sounds from a longer distance.

In our everyday life, we are bombarded with a bewildering array of overlapping sounds, different in intensity, frequency, and rhythm. Our capacity to sort these out and make sense of them, to locate their different sources simultaneously, even to listen to more than one conversation at a time, is truly remarkable. Hearing range diminishes with age, and continual loud sounds over time can damage hearing permanently and speed up hearing loss associated with the normal aging process.

EARS AND HEARING

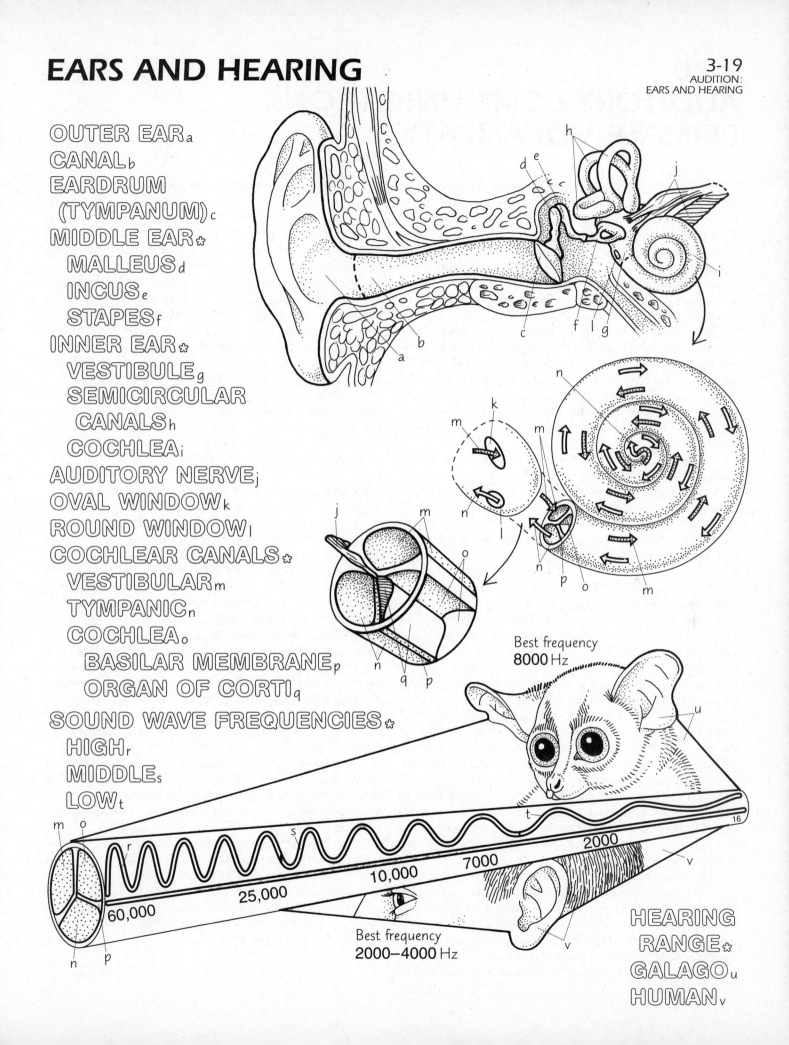

OUTER EAR a
CANAL b
EARDRUM
  (TYMPANUM) c
MIDDLE EAR ✶
  MALLEUS d
  INCUS e
  STAPES f
INNER EAR ✶
  VESTIBULE g
  SEMICIRCULAR
    CANALS h
  COCHLEA i
AUDITORY NERVE j
OVAL WINDOW k
ROUND WINDOW l
COCHLEAR CANALS ✶
  VESTIBULAR m
  TYMPANIC n
  COCHLEA o
    BASILAR MEMBRANE p
  ORGAN OF CORTI q
SOUND WAVE FREQUENCIES ✶
  HIGH r
  MIDDLE s
  LOW t

Best frequency
8000 Hz

Best frequency
2000–4000 Hz

HEARING
RANGE ✶
GALAGO u
HUMAN v

60,000
25,000
10,000
7000
2000
16

3-20
AUDITORY COMMUNICATION:
PRIMATE VOCALIZATIONS

Vocalizations play a prominent role in primate communication. Individual primates typically produce acoustically distinct calls. Different age and sex classes within a population may be distinguished by their calls. Among closely related species, such as within the gibbon genus, *Hylobates* (4-31), and within guenon monkeys, *Cercopithecus* (4-21), vocalizations also serve as a means to identify one species from another. Vocalizations often accompany facial expressions (3-18) in close face-to-face encounters, lending emphasis to the message.

The frequency and types of vocalizations a species uses depends on where it lives. In relatively open habitats, baboons and patas monkeys, for example, forage, rest, and play on the ground and depend upon visual contact. These species tend to be silent in interactions and so remain unobtrusive. In contrast, primates in dense forest with limited visibility depend upon loud vocalizations to maintain contact with each other and neighboring groups.

This plate illustrates specific vocalizations in two species of monkey: the loud vocalizations of forest-living mangabeys, where each male gives an acoustically distinct call, and the alarm calls of savanna-living vervet monkeys.

Color the "whoop-gobble" components as discussed in the text. Color the inflated air sac.

Primatologist Peter Waser studied the distinctive "whoop-gobble" calls given by male gray-cheeked mangabeys living in rain forests north of the Congo River. Taking sound pictures, or "sonograms" of the calls, Waser was able to characterize the pattern of this call and to document subtle differences between individuals.

The call consists of a low-pitched tonal "whoop," followed by a four to five second silence that ends with loud "gobbling" pulses. Notice the different patterns of timing and duration that make it possible to distinguish the call of each individual from the call of the others. When mangabeys hear the whoop-gobbles, they can tell whether the calls are given by a male from their own group or whether a neighboring male is giving the call.

Only males produce the whoop-gobble. The full-fledged version does not appear until sexual maturity. The call is produced by the larynx and air sacs located in the neck region under the jaw, which inflate and add resonance to this low-frequency vocalization of 1000 to 2000 Hertz (3-19).

Other primate species are well known for their unique calls that carry some distance through the tropical forest vegetation: the resonating roars of howler monkeys and the whinney of spider monkeys in the neotropics; the whoops of Asian leaf monkeys; and the duets of gibbon pairs. Forest-living primates also employ other sounds to communicate warnings or to attract others, such as the chest beating of gorillas and tree drumming of chimpanzees.

Color the illustration of alarm calls given by vervet monkeys.

Vocalizations also serve an important function in communicating danger. Primatologist Thomas Struhsaker discovered that vervet monkeys have three discrete warning calls for three different classes of predators.

Each call can be distinguished acoustically by researchers as well as the monkeys. Short tonal chirps indicate "leopard!"; a high-pitched chutter signals python; and low-pitched, staccato grunts—a *r-raup* sound—warn about eagles. The monkeys respond differently to each signal and vary the escape route in accordance with the specific call. Appropriately, to avoid the leopard they rush up into the trees and out on the small branches; to locate the python they look down and around; and to hide from a potential aerial predator, they dive into the center of the tree or into underbrush.

To check out whether the calls really referenced predators rather than indicating levels of fear, Struhsaker's colleagues, Robert Seyfarth, Dorothy Cheney, and Peter Marler carried out experiments. The researchers artificially changed the volume and length of the calls and played them back to the group. The reaction of the monkeys was always specific to the alarm call.

To find out how infant monkeys learn to give the warning calls, the researchers played previously recorded vocalizations of infant monkeys to other vervet monkeys. At first the adults pay little attention to infants' calls, which are given indiscriminately to a wide range of objects. Gradually, as infants learn to vocalize more accurately, their calls elicit the appropriate reaction from others. About the same time, the young animals learn the appropriate behavioral response to each specific call.

Cheney and Seyfarth also discovered that vervet monkeys understand social relationships. They played back a recording of an infant's distress call to females whose infants were out of view. The infant's mother showed agitation and looked in the direction of the call; the other monkeys looked toward the mother of the distressed infant.

Numerous studies document the variety of vocalizations among primates: toque macaques' calls convey the presence of abundant food; trills among capuchin monkeys coordinate group travel; and coos between mother and juvenile Japanese macaques reassure.

Vocalizations provide group members with information about both the external environment and the social environment. Audition is one component of primate communication systems that also include olfactory, tactile, and visual modes, often given in combination. A significant component of human communication is the development of precise vocalizations in the form of spoken language or speech (3-22).

PRIMATE VOCALIZATIONS

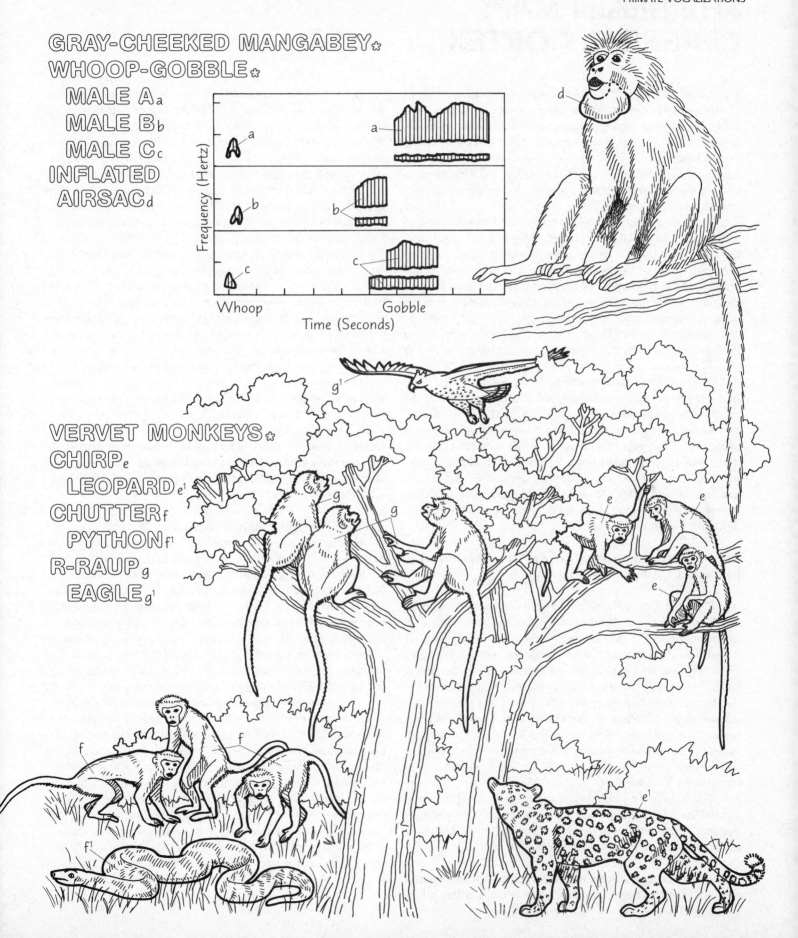

GRAY-CHEEKED MANGABEY☆
WHOOP-GOBBLE☆
  MALE A a
  MALE B b
  MALE C c
  INFLATED
  AIRSAC d

Frequency (Hertz)

Whoop   Gobble
Time (Seconds)

VERVET MONKEYS☆
CHIRP e
  LEOPARD e¹
CHUTTER f
  PYTHON f¹
R-RAUP g
  EAGLE g¹

The primate brain retains the general organization of other vertebrates and mammals but with an expanded forebrain (1-4, 3-14). The large cerebrum and neocortex in primates, especially in humans, corresponds to elaboration of the special senses, of skilled hand movements, and of complex social behavior. The brain integrates incoming sensory information, and then organizes the motor output to ensure that necessary and purposeful actions are carried out efficiently.

The human brain contains more than 12 billion neurons and weighs less than 1.4 kilograms (3 lb). Along with the spinal cord, the brain monitors and regulates many bodily processes, such as heart rate, and coordinates voluntary movements. About half the brain's volume is occupied by the cerebrum, compared to about one-third in most other mammals, and is responsible for complex thought, memory, emotion, and language.

The cerebrum includes two sides, right and left (cerebral) hemispheres joined by the corpus callosum. This tract evolved in placental mammals more than 100 mya. It has more than two million nerve fibers in humans and facilitates the exchange of information between the hemispheres. The outer surface of the cerebrum is covered by a thin layer or cortex (Latin for bark) of gray matter 2 to 6 millimeters thick, which consists of cell bodies of neurons. The gray matter covers the white matter that contains the long processes of the neurons. The cortex folds into distinctive patterns. These convolutions effectively increase the surface area and brain power without requiring an enlarged braincase. Deep fissures or sulci (sulcus, singular) separate the regions or lobes of the cortex from each other.

Color the lobes shown on the left cerebral hemisphere. Use light colors. Color the cerebellum as well.

The lobes of the cerebral cortex generally correspond to the overlying bones of the head. For example, the frontal lobes (a) lie mostly under the frontal bone. Front to back, we encounter the precentral fold or gyrus of the frontal lobe, which is separated from the postcentral gyrus of the parietal lobe (b) by the central sulcus. The occipital lobe (c) is at the back of the brain. The Sylvian or lateral fissure separates the frontal and parietal lobes (above) from the temporal lobe (below) (d). These landmarks frequently leave impressions on the inside of the braincase, and in fossil hominid brains, these fossilized impressions or endocasts show blood circulation patterns (5-21) and brain landmarks associated with language (3-22).

The hindbrain, composed of the pons, medulla, and cerebellum, contains important sensory and motor relay centers that link to other regions of the brain and spinal cord. The human midbrain is very small, as in other mammals (1-4).

Color the functional areas of the cortex, which correspond only generally to regional lobes. Choose contrasting colors for (h) and (i).

Sensory information carried via nerve tracts to the cortex are processed in different parts of the cortex: hearing in the primary auditory cortex (f) in the temporal region; vision in the visual cortex (g) in the occipital region. The primary somato-sensory cortex (h) located in the postcentral gyrus region and its association area nearby receive and process stimuli from the eyes and ears, as well as temperature, pressure, and tactile information from the skin and musculoskeleton. The motor cortex (i) in the precentral gyrus region and its association area control and process movements of the voluntary muscles of different body parts.

The association areas take up large parts of the cortex. These areas analyze and interpret neural information received from the primary sensory areas and integrate it with knowledge stored from past experiences. The premotor cortex (j) promotes skilled movements; the prefrontal cortex (k) is involved in thinking and planning; the areas associated with the visual cortex process and store visual information. Several areas of the neocortex are involved in speech production and comprehension (3-22). This ability to remember and draw upon previous experience enables anthropoid primates to devise novel solutions to problems and is responsible for human "thinking."

Color each segment of the human body and its approximate corresponding neural processing region in the motor and sensory neocortices. Note that (l) through (s) indicate body and brain areas.

Notice the upside down arrangement of body parts on these two neocortical areas. For example, the foot is represented in the top of the sensory and motor strips and the uppermost parts of the body are represented in the lower sections of the neocortex. The extent of cortical representation does not correspond to the size of the body part. The head, mouth, and tongue, for instance, occupy a much larger area than their relative sizes would suggest; this is due to the flow of information in the process of eating, talking, and communicating via facial expression. Likewise in primates, the areas devoted to the hand, particularly the thumb, are large to facilitate the high degree of manual dexterity (3-12).

The sensory and motor cortices work together so we can be aware of and react to what we have touched, heard, and seen. Sensations are carried via nerve tracts to the cortex and processed, bringing them into consciousness. For example, in picking up an object, the hand and eyes perceive the object, which stimulates the sensory neurons in the sensory and visual cortices to relay the message to the motor cortex. The motor nerve cells send instructions to the voluntary muscles of the hand to pick up the object. As visually guided arm and hand movements progress, nerve signals from the cerebellum coordinate and update the actions. The cerebellum controls balance and the body's position in space and so facilitates smooth, precise movements.

CEREBRAL CORTEX

BRAIN MAP*
CEREBRUM*
LOBES*
FRONTAL a
PARIETAL b
OCCIPITAL c
TEMPORAL d
CEREBELLUM e

FUNCTIONAL AREAS*
CORTICES*
AUDITORY f
VISUAL g
SOMATOSENSORY h
MOTOR i
PREMOTOR j
PREFRONTAL k

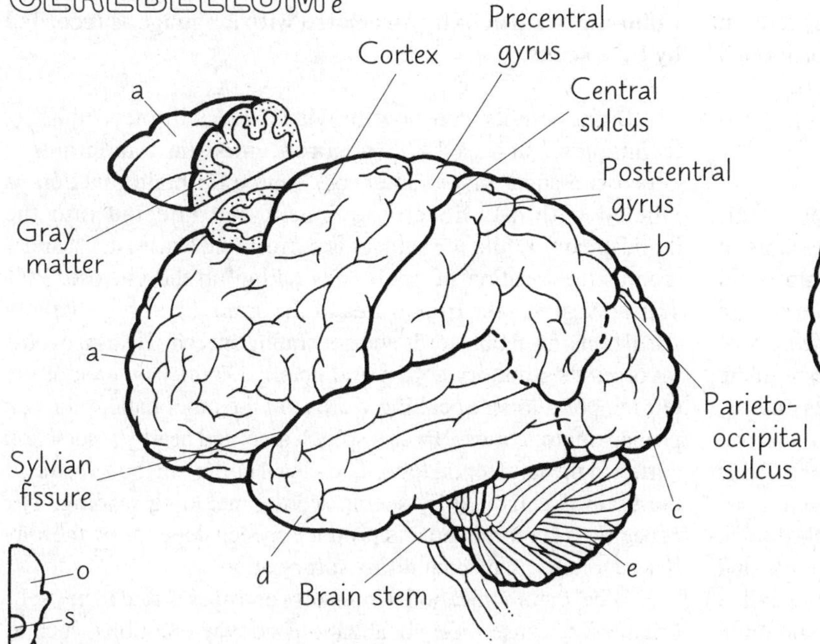

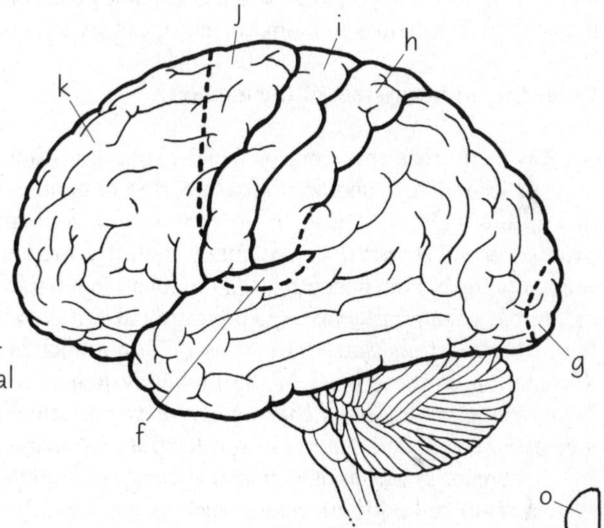

a
Cortex
Precentral gyrus
Central sulcus
Postcentral gyrus
b
Gray matter
a
Sylvian fissure
Parieto-occipital sulcus
c
d
e
Brain stem

j
i
h
k
g
f

MOTOR REGION i

SOMATOSENSORY REGION h

o
s
n
p
r
m
q
l
Gray matter
White matter
h
i
n
m
p
q
r
o
s
l
h
n
h
m
o
p
q
l
r
s

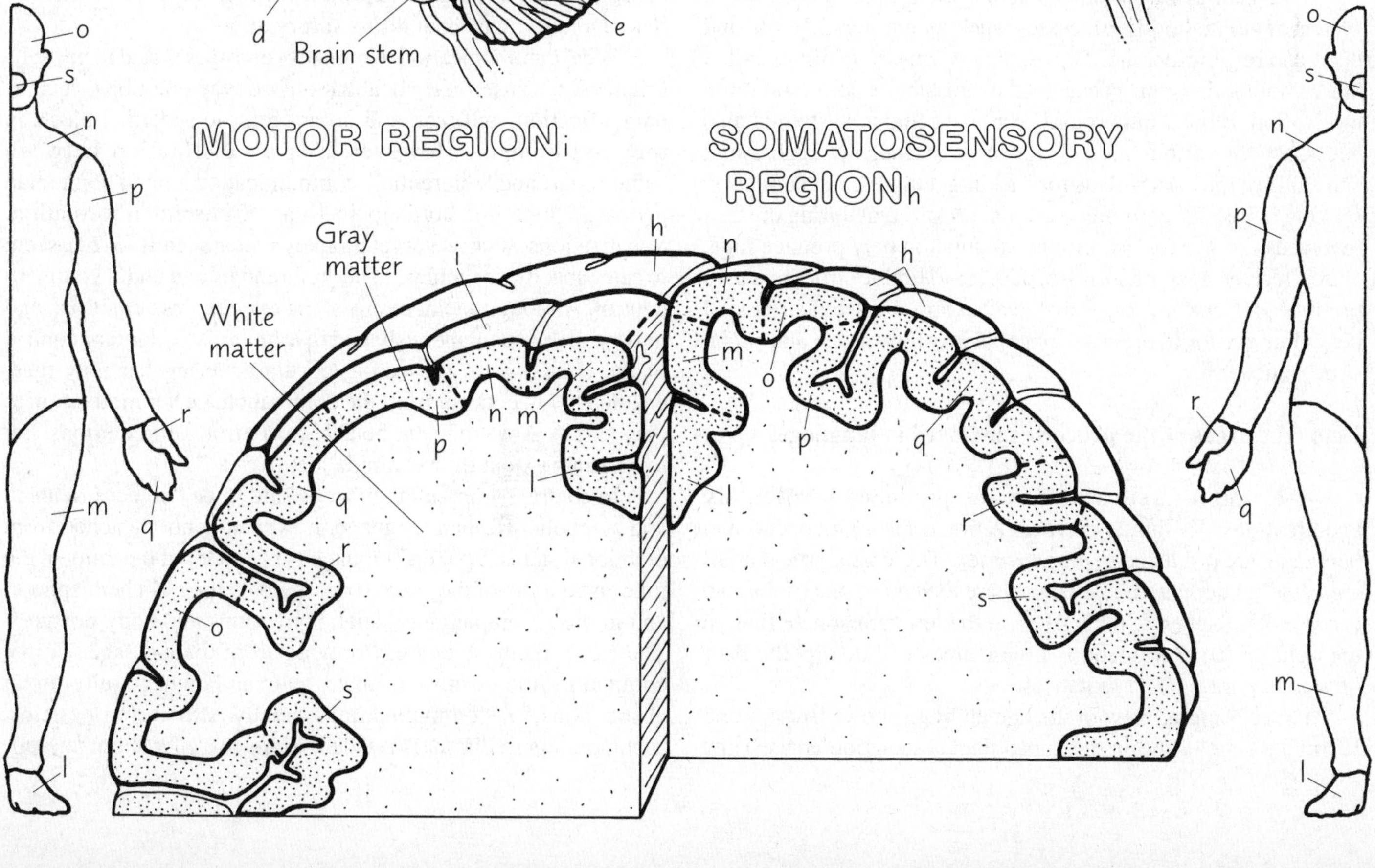

3-22
COMMUNICATION, LANGUAGE, AND THE BRAIN

Communication in monkeys, apes, and humans is multimodal, that is, it relies upon giving and receiving messages involving multiple senses: olfaction, audition, vision, and somatosensory (tactile). The messages are often redundant, that is, they "say" the same thing. For example, a laugh accompanies a play face, a scream accentuates a fear grimace, or a coo is given during grooming. Primate and human communication, although sharing similarities, differ in two interrelated ways: in the extent to which the vocalizations and facial expressions depend upon volition (voluntary control) and in their "control centers" in the brain. In humans, the face and voice can be under voluntary control through the neocortex, whereas in monkeys and apes they are not.

Color the limbic system of the monkey.

Cortical areas that control facial expressions and vocalizations in monkeys and apes are connected to brain centers in the limbic system. These brain centers control emotional expression and are not under voluntary control as are the speech centers in the human neocortex. The angular cingulate cortex of the limbic system influences the orbitofrontal cortex to regulate facial expressions and some calls of nonhuman primates. Stimulation of these parts of the limbic system in a squirrel monkey elicits almost its entire range of vocalizations. If this area is damaged, deficiencies in vocalizations are marked.

In humans as well as other mammals, some parts of the limbic system regulate bodily processes, such as hormonal levels and heart and respiration rate. The limbic system is sometimes called the "emotional" brain because of its possible role in attention, motivation, mood, and arousal. An intact limbic system is also necessary for various social behaviors—friendship, aggression, and submission—as well as for suckling, clinging, and affection seeking in infants, activities essential for survival during the first few weeks of life (3-14). Limbic stimulation may produce rage, alarm, fear, ecstasy, or surprise; damage to limbic structures may produce deficits not only in facial expressions but in sexual behavior, territorial defense, maternal protectiveness, and social communication.

Color the areas of the neocortex involved in language.

The limbic system of humans produces involuntary vocalizations. "Voluntary" vocalizations, through speech and language, are produced in the neocortex. These neocortical areas are usually lateralized, that is, they are located in one of the two cerebral hemispheres, more often in the left hemisphere than in the right (5-30). Stimulation of these areas will disrupt the flow of words, phrases, and sentences.

The left lateral view of the human brain shows Broca's and Wernicke's areas within the neocortical association areas. They are found only in the language-dominant hemisphere and have no obvious counterparts in nonhuman primates. Present on the left side of the brain, but not on the right, Broca's area influences the muscles of the face, tongue, palate, and larynx used in speech. When this area is injured, as with stroke victims, speech becomes slow and labored. Also on the left side, Wernicke's area contains circuits for speech comprehension. When it is damaged, speech may still seem fluent but the message is garbled and confused.

Color the brain activity associated with language as recorded by PET scans.

Brain activity can now be visualized with new imaging techniques, such as PET (positron emission tomography). Glucose, a sugar that is an energy source for brain function, is labeled with a radioactive element and injected into the bloodstream. While the subject is performing a task, the scanner records the location of brain cells taking up the glucose. PET scans reveal that the frontal area of the brain shows high activity when thinking about words and generating speech. Hearing words involves the auditory cortex and nearby Wernicke's area of the left temporal lobe. Speaking words, on the other hand, relies on primary motor cortex, Broca's speech area, and nearby association cortex in the left frontal lobe. The visual cortex on the left side of the brain is activated by seeing words, including reading. The capacity to comprehend and produce speech depends on the way human brains analyze auditory information.

Vocal communication in monkeys and apes is said to be "self-oriented" because their vocalizations convey emotions, such as pain, affection, and fear, and do not refer to specific objects in the environment. However, a strict distinction between "emotional" and "referential" communication among nonhuman primates does not hold up in light of current information. Vocalizations, such as vervet monkey predator calls (3-20), seem to carry specific meanings, to be "referential" and under voluntary control. Although facial expressions may express emotions and may be given spontaneously and involuntarily, voluntary control of the hands, as in the young gorilla covering her play face, enabled her to conceal from the dominant male her motivation to play (3-18). Apes may not be able to control their emotions, but to a certain extent they can hide them!

In contrast, human language is said to be "object-oriented" and symbolic. Human language, however, is not detached from emotional states. Spoken language carries a lot of meaning in the tone and quality of the voice (processed by the right hemisphere) and in the accompanying facial expressions and body postures. The words themselves carry only a part of the message. Unlike communication of other primates, human language relies upon abstractions for communicating socially, structuring systems, accumulating traditional knowledge, and learning about oneself.

COMMUNICATION, LANGUAGE, AND THE BRAIN

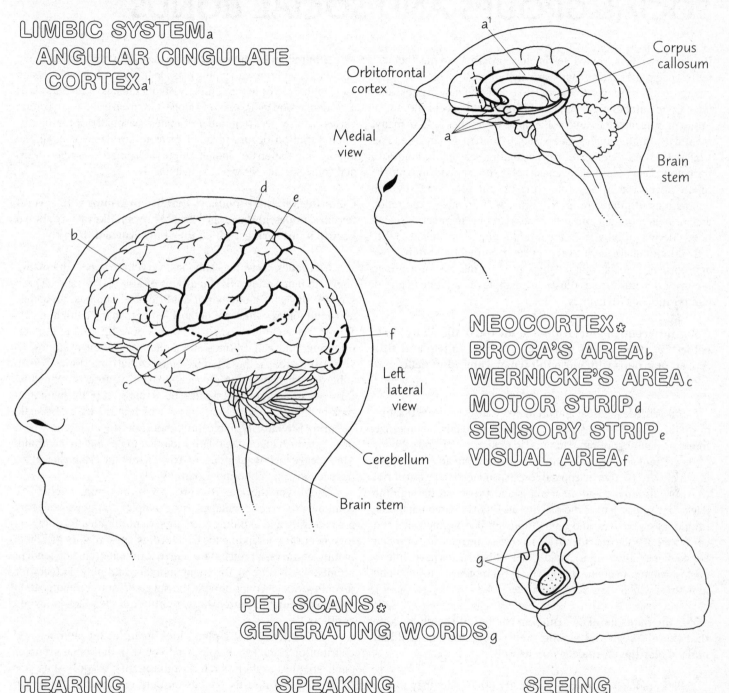

LIMBIC SYSTEM_a
ANGULAR CINGULATE CORTEX_{a¹}

Orbitofrontal cortex

Medial view

a¹

Corpus callosum

a

Brain stem

b

d

e

f

c

Left lateral view

Cerebellum

Brain stem

NEOCORTEX✶
BROCA'S AREA_b
WERNICKE'S AREA_c
MOTOR STRIP_d
SENSORY STRIP_e
VISUAL AREA_f

g

PET SCANS✶
GENERATING WORDS_g

HEARING WORDS_h

h

SPEAKING WORDS_i

i

SEEING WORDS_j

j

PRIMATE SOCIAL LIFE: SOCIAL GROUPS AND SOCIAL BONDS

Primates live their whole lives in close proximity to members of their species. Social groups are dynamic, and membership changes as individuals are born, leave and join new groups, and die. Group number may remain relatively stable over time, and a group may occupy the same home range over time (3-4). In many mammals, adult females and males live apart for most of the year and come together during a mating season. In contrast, primate social groups tend to consist of both sexes and individuals of all ages, and at any one time, might represent several generations. Primate groups vary in size, in female-male ratio, and in degree of genetic relatedness among members. Social bonds derive initially from the infant-mother attachment (3-14, 3-27). Individuals learn to recognize each other and to behave appropriately; social relationships provide the basis for group integrity. Several species illustrate a sample of variation in group composition and dynamics.

Color the group of indri lemurs at the top of the plate. Next, color the titi monkeys lower in the tree. Indris and titis represent groups with one adult female, one adult male, and young.

Indris in Madagascar and titi monkeys in South America live in small groups of between two and five individuals, a group size found in a number of other lemurs, in tarsiers (4-8), and gibbons (4-31). These species have little sexual dimorphism in body size or weight (3-30), live in tropical forests, and tend to be territorial (3-4). Adult female and male indris and titis bond through the duets they sing as part of their territorial defense. Although indris, titi monkeys, tarsiers, and gibbons are similar in group size and composition, they differ from each other in the intensity of social bonds. For example, indri, tarsier, and gibbon males have little to do with young. In contrast, adult male titi monkeys closely bond to infants, which they carry and protect (4-14).

Color the patas monkey group on the left of the plate. Note that there are several females and young and one resident male. Color the all-male group as well.

Patas monkeys are highly sexually dimorphic; they live in female-centered groups of 10 to 30 or more, with 1 adult male during the nonbreeding season. Adult and juvenile females and infants form the core of the group. Juvenile males leave their natal group at 3 years of age and join all-male groups. During the 3-month breeding season in central Kenya, several females come into estrus at the same time (3-25). At this time, other males may challenge and displace the resident male, join the group temporarily to mate, or mate with females on the periphery of the group. Resident male turnover is high.

Adult females and males have short-term relationships, and males interact little with young patas monkeys. Adult males spend most of their lives in the company of other males, with periods as a resident group male, or living alone. Group size and composition varies with respect to number of males seasonally or regionally. Such variation occurs in other primate species, for example, among populations of Indian langurs (*Presbytis entellus*, 4-23) and some species of African guenons (4-21).

Color the Japanese monkeys that live in groups with several females, males, and young. These "snow monkeys" are shown here in a hot springs, which they have learned to enjoy.

Macaques, as well as baboons, vervet monkeys, and mangabeys, to name a few, live in groups of 20 to 50 or more. These groups consist of a number of adult females, infants, juveniles, and adult males, which are notably larger than the adult females. Within macaque groups, strong bonds develop among mother, offspring, and half siblings and endure over their lifetimes. In very large groups, these family units, called "matrilines," form subgroups that maintain physical proximity, groom frequently, form coalitions, and hold similar social ranks. At birth, an infant's rank is based on its mother's rank, which in the case of female offspring is relatively stable throughout her life; males, however, must establish their rank relative to other males and to the group. Males leave their natal group, and over a lifetime establish a place in successive neighboring groups (3-29).

Whatever the specific group composition, social life combines several advantages, for example: extra eyes and ears for detecting and avoiding predators; opportunities for foraging together or for defending the best feeding sites; readily available mating partners; a protective enclave for females and dependent infants; "baby sitters" for young animals; and play partners for juveniles. Social bonds provide "social glue," and communication systems mediate relationships, reinforce bonds, and alleviate conflicts.

Before leaving the plate, look again at the number and distribution of males, females, and young in the social group of each species. Labels such as monogamy or polygyny are misleading because they focus on only one function of group living, that of mating, and on only one social bond, that between adult females and males. Classifications, such as "one-male" groups, emphasize one age-sex class and exclude the others. Social structures in primate species are difficult to label and classify definitively: the intensity of social bonds, size of group, and composition of local populations vary within and between species. Such variation, however, offers primates considerable flexibility and adaptability in surviving, mating, and rearing young under a wide range of conditions.

SOCIAL GROUPS AND SOCIAL BONDS

INFANT_a
JUVENILE_b
ADULT FEMALE_c
ADULT MALE_d

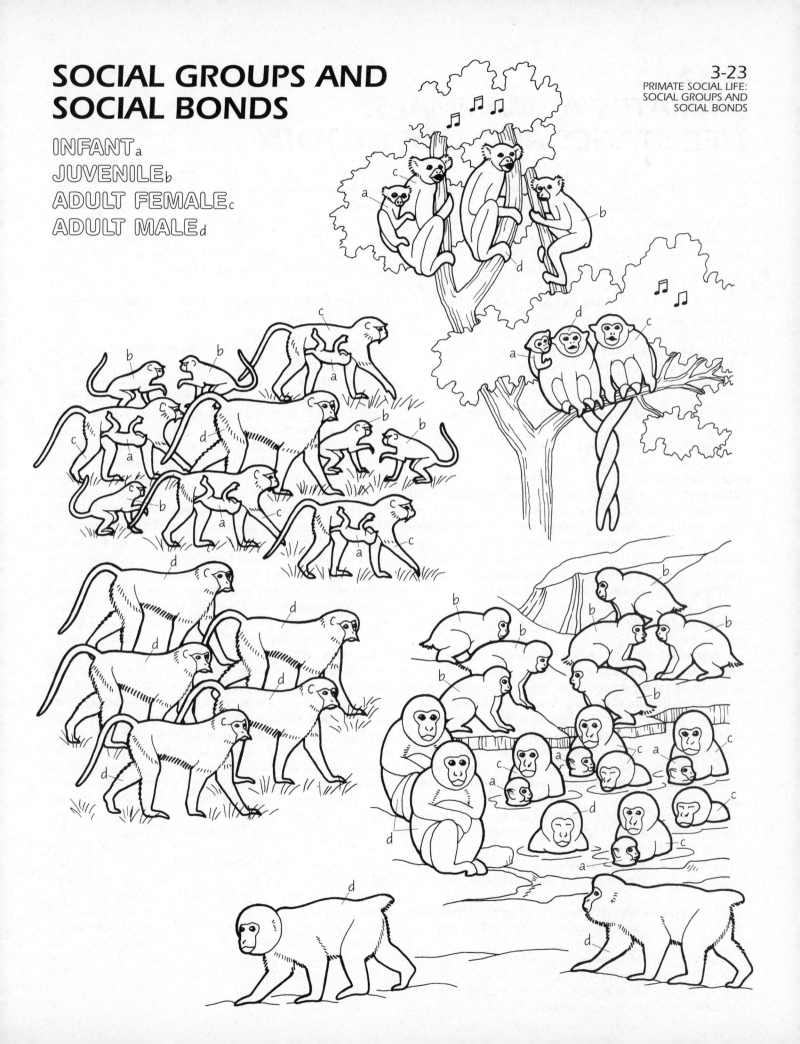

3-24
PRIMATES AS MAMMALS: LIFE STAGES AND LIFE HISTORY

Mammals have distinct life stages. Major events mark the transition from one stage to the next: birth ends gestation and begins infancy; weaning ends infant dependency and initiates juvenile independence; sexual maturity launches reproduction and adult life. Compared to other mammals, primates, and especially apes and humans, have longer life stages. Primates have relatively large brains, which grow for an extended time after birth. Relative brain size and species lineage (3-1) influence length of life stages more than does body size alone. In order to highlight the variation among primates and contrast with nonprimates, we compare a small nonprimate with four small-bodied primate species: domestic cat (3 kg), ringtailed lemur (3 kg), capuchin monkey (3 kg), vervet monkey (3–5 kg), and lar gibbon (5–6 kg).

Color the gestation periods (in weeks) for all species.

The fetus, protected from the external environment, receives nutrients from the mother through the placenta. Placental mammals have more developmental time within the uterus than do marsupial mammals and therefore are more developed at birth (1-9). The gestation length of cats (6 weeks) is one-third the length of lemurs (18.5 weeks), even though they share similar body weights. Gestation in capuchins extends about 23 weeks, in vervet monkeys, 27 weeks, and in gibbons a little longer (30 weeks). The longer gestation time of primates compared to other mammals correlates with a relatively larger brain at birth.

Color the infancy period (in months) for all species.

Kittens are born as part of a litter and are kept in a nest. Their eyes are closed, and they rely on smell, hearing, and touch to locate the mother's nipple. They must also rely upon these senses for finding the body warmth of litter mates and mother. Most primates give birth to a single infant. When born, primate infants have well-developed vision, smell, touch, and hearing, and a large brain that grows rapidly during infancy (3-27). Infants actively cling to mother's hair with grasping hands and feet (3-10) and rely on mother for transportation, nutrition, warmth, and protection.

Kittens are weaned at 1.5 months. In lemurs, weaning takes place at about 4 months, 12 months in capuchins, 10 months in vervets, and 3 times longer in gibbons, about 30 months. Weaning in primates is usually gradual over a period of weeks or months as the infant develops locomotor and feeding independence.

Color the juvenile period (in months and years). The hatched lines denote the transition period from juvenile to adult.

Kittens are juveniles by 2 months of age; they grow quickly, play, and practice hunting skills. Among primates, the juvenile period lasts at least 20 months in lemurs, over 36 months in capuchins, 36 months in vervet monkeys, and is at least 48 months

in gibbons. Juvenile primates grow in body size and weight; they play, practice motor skills, and establish social networks (3-28). Juveniles continue to rely on mother, older siblings, and other adults for protection, social interaction, and emotional well being. During the late juvenile period, male vervets disperse from their natal group. Gibbons have a defined subadult stage during which they look for a mate and establish a territory.

Color the period of adult reproductive life and life span (in months and years).

The transition to reproductive life occurs quickly in cats and many other mammals, but the transition in primates is gradual, as indicated by the hatched lines: lasting about 6 months in lemurs, about 1 year in capuchin and vervet monkeys, and in gibbons about 2 years. Note that on the illustration, the gibbon transition period is in years, not months.

The timing of sexual maturity for female mammals occurs at first estrus (3-25) and can be more easily established than can the timing of male sexual maturity. Males have viable sperm before they reach adult size, but have few opportunities to mate, as they are immature and not yet established socially. When females first give birth they have reached adulthood. At sexual maturity, at about 1 year of age, a cat bears her first litter of kittens. Lemur females give birth at about 3 years of age, capuchins at 5 years, and vervets at 4 years. Gibbons do not have their first offspring until nearly 9 years of age. Most female mammals reproduce throughout their lives. Humans experience a significant exception from this reproductive pattern; the potential life span extends well beyond a woman's reproductive capacities, which cease during her 40s.

Life span measures the maximum amount of time between birth and death. Life span is difficult to establish; few data are available and there is a large range. Domestic cats usually do not live beyond 12 years, although they can exceed 20. Ringtailed lemurs may live more than 20 years. Capuchins in captivity live into their 40s; wild vervets more than 20 years. Gibbons live into their 30s and may reach 40 in captivity. Because primates live a long time, their social groups may consist of individuals of several generations where younger members learn from the experience of older individuals (3-33).

Individuals face different challenges in order to survive and reproduce. From an evolutionary point of view, natural selection operates at each stage of life, not just at the point of mating or in giving birth to a live infant. Natural selection encompasses individual survival, reaching maturity, finding mates and reproducing, and ensuring the survival of one's offspring. Each individual experiences life events differently, and this lends a complexity and collective knowledge to primate groups. Human life stages are more prolonged than are those of other primates. Childhood comprises a new stage that is prior to and separate from the juvenile stage (6-3).

LIFE STAGES AND LIFE HISTORY

GESTATION_a
INFANCY_b
JUVENILE_c
ADULT REPRODUCTIVE LIFE_d
LIFE SPAN_e

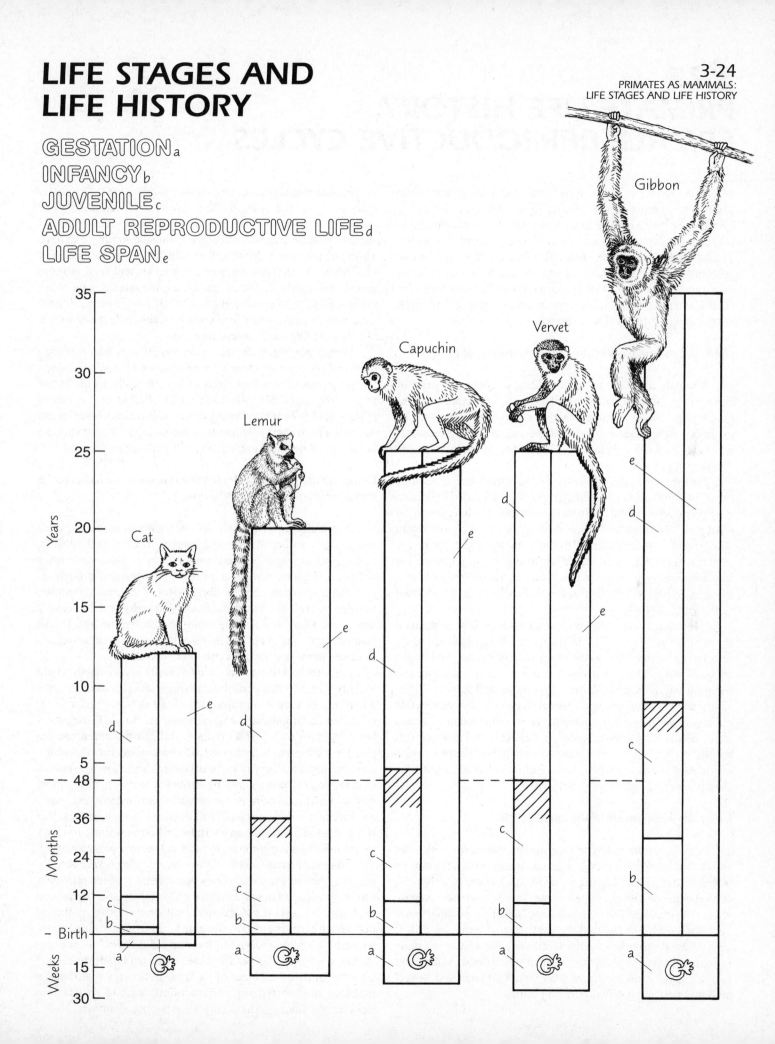

3-25
PRIMATE LIFE HISTORY: FEMALE REPRODUCTIVE CYCLES

A female primate spends a significant proportion of her life in some stage of reproduction. Producing offspring that survive to maturity involves a number of components: ovulation, conception, pregnancy, lactation, and investment in offspring after weaning. The length of each of these events affects the lifetime reproductive outcome of individual females, and consequently, of the social group and population. Using macaque monkeys to represent catarrhine primates (3-1), we illustrate female primates' monthly, yearly, and lifetime cycles of reproduction.

Color the components of the monthly menstrual cycle.

A female macaque begins ovulating at about 3.5 years of age and ovulates monthly unless pregnant or lactating. Other nonprimate female mammals ovulate once or twice a year. The ovulatory cycle is under the control of estrogen and progesterone, which in turn are regulated by hormones released from the pituitary gland in the brain.

During each cycle, one ovarian follicle matures and releases estrogen into the bloodstream. Around day 14, ovulation occurs: the follicle releases the ovum into the oviducts, where it may be fertilized. The ruptured follicle develops into a secretory organ which releases progesterone. This hormone stimulates the uterus to build up a vascular, nutritive lining in preparation for implantation. If the ripe ovum is not fertilized, progesterone release declines and the uterine lining sloughs off in a menstrual flow by day 28 (6-1).

In macaques and other primates, ovulation is accompanied by estrus, that is, marked physical and behavioral changes. Specialized sexual skin on the rump, base of the tail, and thighs enlarges and reddens. Females in estrus increase grooming and foraging activities, become more aggressive, and actively solicit sexual activity from males. Chemical changes in the vagina yield olfactory cues that inform group members of the female's sexual state. Estrus lasts approximately seven days and ensures that mating occurs when conception is most likely. Estrous cycles continue monthly until pregnancy and do not resume until the time when the infant approaches weaning.

Color the components of the annual cycle.

Female macaques live in year around association with adult males (3-23). When cycling, a female mates with one or more males in the group. Mating behavior may occur briefly with several males or with one male for hours or a day. Females exercise choice in mating. They prefer some males over others, not necessarily the highest ranking ones. Sexual behavior differs significantly among species. Gibbons, for example, mate infrequently except when forming their initial bond. At the other extreme, pygmy chimpanzees (*Pan paniscus*) engage in sexual activity often and not always during estrus.

Female macaques usually conceive within three cycles. Some macaques are seasonal in their reproductive behavior. For example, in temperate regions of Japan, macaques (*Macaca fuscata*) mate and females conceive during the autumn, and have a 6-month pregnancy. Most births are in the spring; 75% occur in March and April. Temperatures are warmer and food is more varied and readily available. By winter, the infants, now older, are more likely to survive the cold and snow. Some primates have a birth peak, when births are concentrated, rather than a birth season like the Japanese macaques.

During pregnancy, females gain weight; they also may feed more and socialize less than cycling females. During lactation, a female produces small amounts of low-fat milk, so the infant nurses frequently. She also carries the infant until it becomes independent at weaning. During this period, females lose weight, due to the high energy demands of producing milk, carrying the infant, traveling and foraging, and self-maintenance (3-26).

Complete the plate by coloring the reproductive pattern of a female macaque over her lifetime.

As weaning approaches, a female resumes her sexual cycles and is likely to become pregnant again. The interval between births, that is gestation time plus length of lactation, varies between females within a group and between groups or populations. When food is abundant and climate moderate, females are well nourished and healthy and may give birth every one to two years. If a nursing infant should die, the female will resume her sexual cycle and is likely to become pregnant again. In these circumstances, the birth interval is shorter.

Long-term observations on individually known females help identify variables that contribute to successful reproduction over a lifetime. In a study on Japanese macaques living under food-enhanced conditions in Texas, primatologist Linda Fedigan and her colleagues followed 48 females through life and noted the number of offspring that survived to 5 years of age. Females varied from having no offspring to 14 offspring! Variation in numbers of surviving offspring could be attributed to living a long time, and so having numerous opportunities to become pregnant. Another factor is the pace of reproduction—a birth interval that is too short increases infant mortality, whereas waiting too long means missing an opportunity to mate and become pregnant again.

Long-term studies also clarify the role that sexual activity plays in maintaining social bonds. Adult females spend relatively little time engaged in sexual activity. This information disproved the hypothesis of Solly Zuckerman, who in the 1930s, proposed that sexual activity acted as the glue keeping males and females together. We now understand that the "social glue" is not sex. Rather, the "glue" derives from the emotional bonds developed from the initial investment of the time and energy that females make in their offspring. These bonds extend to lifetime associations among individually known group members.

FEMALE REPRODUCTIVE CYCLES

MONTHLY CYCLE
(28 DAYS) *
ESTROGEN a
PROGESTERONE b
OVULATION c
MENSES d
  SEXUAL SKIN d1
ESTRUS e
  SEXUAL SKIN e1

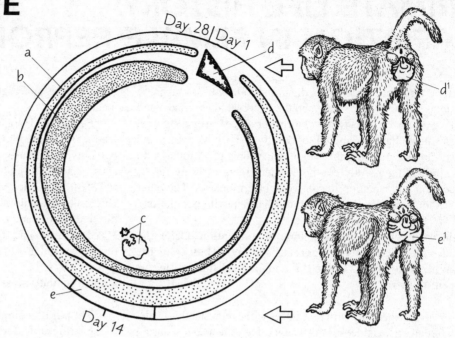

ANNUAL CYCLE
(12 MONTHS) *
MATING SEASON f
BIRTH SEASON g

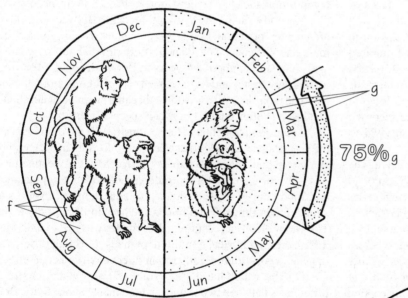

75% g

LIFETIME PATTERN
(25 YEARS) *
INFANT/JUVENILE h
CYCLING ADULT i
PREGNANT j
LACTATING k

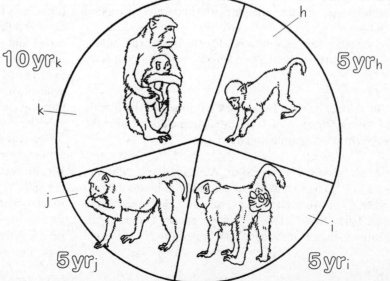

10 yr k

5 yr h

5 yr j

5 yr i

3-26
PRIMATE LIFE HISTORY: VARIATION IN FEMALE REPRODUCTION

The long-term study of Linda Fedigan and colleagues on Japanese macaque females (3-25) analyzed the factors that are associated with the number of surviving offspring produced over a lifetime. Other studies have attempted to identify specific variables and their influence on reproductive outcome. This plate focuses on two studies. One study examined the effects of body fat on conception and lactation in captive female monkeys. The other focused on access to food among females in a wild population.

Begin with reproductive outcome in conception. Color the females and their different percent body fat. Then color the outcome of lactation. Color the females and their different percent body fat.

As they experience different stages of the reproductive cycle, adult females gain and lose body weight. They are heaviest during the late stages of pregnancy and lightest in the later stages of lactation, when energy output for milk production and carrying an infant is greatest. To study in more detail this fluctuation in body mass, anthropologist Robin McFarland documented changing body composition in captive pigtail macaques (*Macaca nemestrina*) housed in social groups with adult males. At intervals over a 15-month period, McFarland weighed each of 76 adult females and measured the amount of body fat. She recorded reproductive condition and outcome of offspring survival to 6 months of age.

During the study, 14 of the 76 females did not conceive. The amount of body fat was significantly lower in this group (9%) compared to the group that did conceive (13%). Of those females who did become pregnant and gave birth to live offspring, fatness correlated with successful lactation. Females that were unable to lactate had only 10.2% body fat prior to conception, whereas those that did lactate had 13.8% body fat. Food was readily available to all, so they did not have to compete for food; but body fat still varied, and the variation had an impact on conception and lactation.

In contrast, a study of yellow baboons focused on the effects of food availability and activity on female body mass and body fat.

Color the female baboon from Hook's group and the female baboon from Lodge group. Use contrasting colors. Color the differences in feeding time and day range.

Primatologists Jeanne and Stuart Altmann, Philip Muruthi, and their colleagues studied adult female baboons (*Papio cynocephalus*) in two social groups from a single population in Amboseli Park, Kenya. Hook's group depended upon foods foraged around their home range (3-4). Lodge group lived near a tourist lodge and regularly foraged on leftovers from human meals.

Females in Hook's group spent twice as much time each day feeding as did the females in Lodge group (45% vs. 22.5%). The two sets of females, however, had similar caloric intake: on average 3450 kilojoules with 21 grams of protein (Hook's group) vs. 3830 kilojoules with 31 grams of protein (Lodge group). Kilojoules is a caloric measure. The distance traveled each day differed significantly. Those who foraged for food covered 8 to 10 kilometers a day. Those who fed from the accessible garbage dump traveled less than 4 kilometers a day.

Color the body mass and body fat.

The wild-feeding females averaged 11 kilograms compared to 16 kilograms for the garbage-feeding females. In body composition, the wild-feeding females had 2% body fat compared to 23% body fat in the garbage-feeders! Body mass and fat affected reproduction. Lodge group females, having greater body mass and fat, conceived their first offspring about 4.5 years of age, compared to about 5.5 years in Hook's group. Lodge group infants grew faster and were weaned earlier. Lodge group females resumed their sexual cycle sooner, became pregnant again sooner, and had a shorter interval between successive births.

These complementary studies illustrate, at the individual and the group level, variables that affect reproduction. In McFarland's study of pigtail macaque females, a female's relative amount of body fat correlated with the outcome of conception, lactation, and infant survival. The pigtail macaque females lived under similar environmental conditions and had similar activity levels. The variation observed among the females was tied to individual differences in physical condition, perhaps reflecting differences in genetic constitution, rather than direct environmental effects.

On the other hand, the Amboseli study demonstrated differences between two groups in food intake and activity. Body mass and fat were inversely correlated with effort expended in travel and foraging for food. Increased access to food and decreased amount of daily travel in Lodge group females resulted in increased body mass and body fat. The quantity and quality of available food combined with activity level influence the females' physical condition and, in turn, components of reproduction.

The existence of variation among individuals is a prerequisite for natural selection to operate. In one example, females with similar access to food nonetheless differed in amount of body fat which affected reproduction. In the other example, females from the same wild population but living in two social groups differed in reproductive condition. Variation is a fundamental condition for evolutionary change, seen here in the former case due to genetic differences in individuals, and in the latter case, to chance factors associated with group membership and home range.

VARIATION IN FEMALE REPRODUCTION

REPRODUCTIVE OUTCOME ✱
NO CONCEPTION/LESS FAT a
CONCEPTION/MORE FAT a¹

NO LACTATION/LESS FAT b
LACTATION/MORE FAT b¹

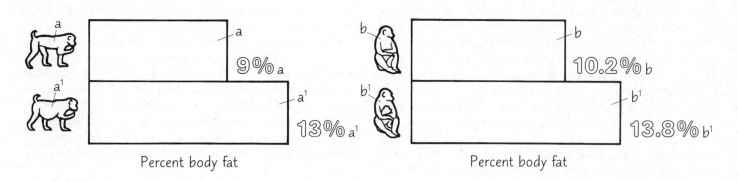

a

a

9% a

a¹

a¹

13% a¹

Percent body fat

b

b

10.2% b

b¹

b¹

13.8% b¹

Percent body fat

GROUP VARIATION ✱
HOOK'S GROUP c
LODGE GROUP d
FEEDING TIME c¹,d¹
DAY RANGE c²,d²
BODY MASS c³,d³
BODY FAT c⁴,d⁴

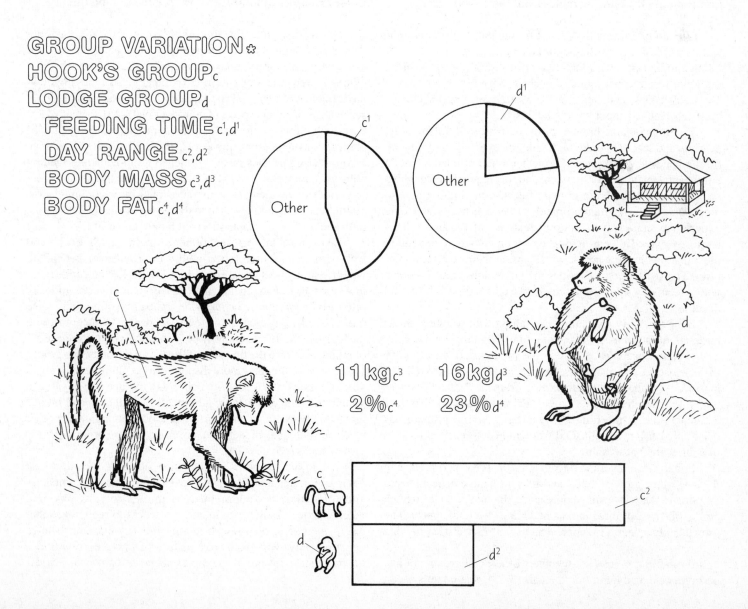

c¹

d¹

Other

Other

c

d

11 kg c³   16 kg d³
2% c⁴   23% d⁴

c

d

c²

d²

3-27
PRIMATE LIFE HISTORY: INFANTS AND SURVIVAL

Infancy is a critical stage in a primate's life, marking the end of a protected fetal life in the womb and the beginning of an independent life outside. At birth, primate infants are completely dependent; they must be fed in order to survive and grow, and they must be protected from climatic extremes, predators, other group members, and hazards encountered in the social and physical environment. Infancy is a precarious time and many factors, especially the contributions of the mother, help ensure that the infant gets a good start in life. The "job" of infants is to grow and develop physically and socially. This plate looks at "life's agenda" and survival from an infant's point of view.

Color the components of physical growth (brain, body mass, dentition) in the newborn infant monkey and the weaned infant monkey. Color the infants and their social group.

Primate brain growth is rapid throughout the first months and years of life. At birth, the infant's brain is 10 times heavier relative to its body mass than that of the adult (3-10). At birth, the brain of an infant monkey is about 65% of adult size; (an ape's, about 45%; a human's, about 25%). At weaning, the infant's brain has reached about 95% of adult size.

The infant's large brain at birth equips it well for smelling, hearing, and seeing in order to monitor its external environment. Strong hands and feet grasp the mother's hair. It must maintain close contact with her for transport and for frequent suckling that promotes continued brain growth. Because the brain grows so much *after* birth, an infant primate's behavior is not "preset" and experience shapes even internal features of the brain. This relatively extended neurological development would be fatal to most mammalian newborns, which are on their own soon after birth. The social group provides the vulnerable primate infants with a relatively safe haven, which gives them time to learn and develop.

Bone and body growth increase along with weight gain. At birth, infant catarrhine monkeys are about 5% of maternal weight. The skeleton becomes robust as the bones continue to ossify (6-5). Muscle tissue increases, and the hindlimbs gain in relative mass (3-10) as the infant ventures away from the mother to explore under its own locomotor power. Primatologist Phyllis Lee estimates that at the time of weaning, a young primate has quadrupled its birth weight. Old World monkeys reach about 20% of adult weight at weaning.

Infants have no erupted teeth at birth. Tooth germs form in the jaws of the growing fetus, and after birth the milk teeth begin erupting (6-4). As weaning approaches, the first permanent teeth erupt—the first of three molars or 12% of the total appear. The growing infant begins to supplement its milk diet as it learns what to eat.

From birth, infants are members of a social group, not just part of an isolated infant/mother pair (3-23). The infant's social life begins with its mother, initially through their physical proximity and the emotional attachment between them. Carried and held, an infant becomes familiar with its mother's social network. Interaction with siblings is an important component of this network.

The infant is by no means passive, along for a free ride and meal! To the contrary, as it matures, the infant takes an increasingly active role in maintaining contact with its mother, keeping track of her location, and attending to her activities. The infant gives and responds to vocalizations and facial expressions in communicating with its mother and others. By coordinating activity with its mother and observing her interactions, the infant learns social skills, thereby becoming integrated into the group.

Color examples of infant survival related to food quality.

During this vulnerable time of life, an infant's survival is not guaranteed. Infants fail to survive for a number of reasons, for example, weak inborn constitution, infections, accidents, fatal injury, or predation. Long-term and comparative studies highlight the influence of maternal food quality and availability on infant survival, as on other aspects of reproduction (3-26). Primatologist Kunio Watanabe and colleagues summarized 34 years of observation on macaque monkeys (*Macaca fuscata*) in Koshima, Japan. During periods of fairly intensive supplemental feeding with artificial foods (1952–1972), about 80% of infants survived. In periods of restricted or only occasional provisioning (1972–1986), when the monkeys had to forage for available wild foods, only about 55% of infants survived the first year of life.

Environmental features influence the mother's health and well being, and therefore her ability to provide for her infant, which in turn, affect its survival (4-7). Phyllis Lee and colleagues in Amboseli, Kenya, documented the survival of vervet monkey infants (*Cercopithecus aethiops)* in three groups living in home ranges of differing quality and food abundance. In the group with the highest quality and quantity of food in their home range, 60% of infants survived the first year of life. From the other two groups with lower quality and more dispersed food clumps, only about 40% of infants survived. With poor food, mothers are not able to sustain the high energetic requirements of lactation, and infants grow slowly or die. In contrast, when food is abundant, a mother meets the demands of lactation, promoting infant brain and body growth and survival.

The infant increases in body size, acquires the adult coat color and permanent teeth, and develops physical coordination and muscular development as it moves toward physical independence. As its brain matures, it learns to recognize other group members, distinguish among individuals, and behave discriminately. This distinctive pattern of primate growth lays the foundation for life in a complex social and physical world.

INFANTS AND SURVIVAL

NEWBORN INFANT*
 BRAIN SIZE$_a$
 BODY MASS$_b$
 DENTITION$_c$

WEANED INFANT*
 BRAIN SIZE$_{a^1}$
 BODY MASS$_{b^1}$
 DENTITION$_{c^1}$

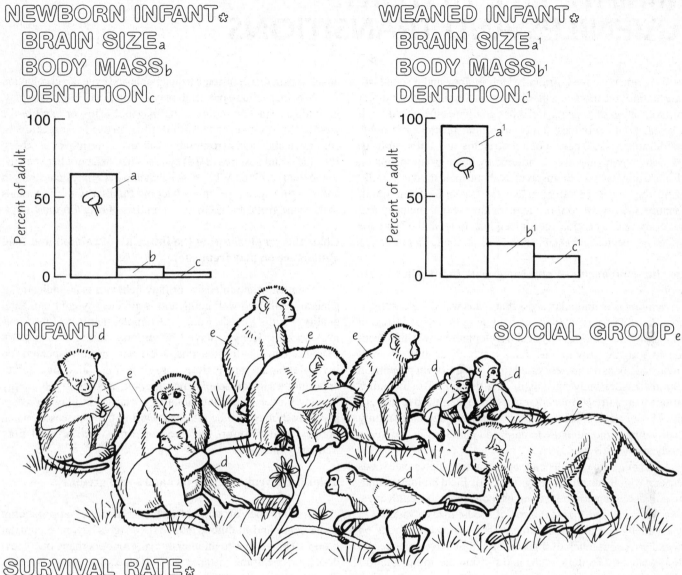

INFANT$_d$

SOCIAL GROUP$_e$

SURVIVAL RATE*
 FOOD ABUNDANCE$_f$
 FOOD SCARCITY$_g$

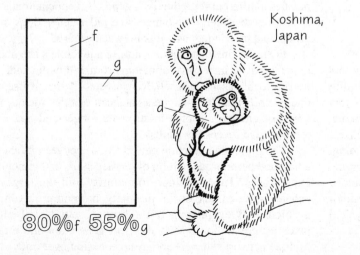

Koshima, Japan

80%$_f$ 55%$_g$

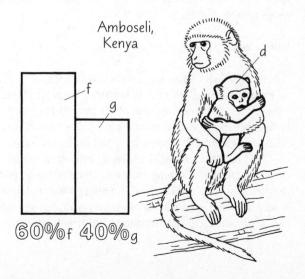

Amboseli, Kenya

60%$_f$ 40%$_g$

PRIMATE LIFE HISTORY: JUVENILES AND TRANSITIONS

Juvenile primates have "officially" left infancy and a social life centering around mother and siblings. Increasingly they direct their lives outward to peers and other group members. Although the social group provides some protection, juvenile life holds considerable risk. These young primates are vulnerable to predation, may be harassed or injured by other group members, and must now sustain themselves without their mother's milk. During this stage, juveniles make the transition from small, immature individuals to those approaching sexual maturity and adult body size. The "job" of a juvenile is to learn the "primate way" of its species and establish the foundation for its future.

Color the components of physical growth in juveniles.

Weaning is a gradual process that spans weeks or months; it marks the end of infancy and the beginning of independence in feeding and locomotion. Physical development now shifts from brain to somatic growth. Juveniles reach about 80% of adult weight, and bones are mostly fused (6-5). A significant proportion of the increasing body mass is muscle tissue (3-10). Juveniles continue to acquire permanent molars up to their third molars, or about 85% of adult number. In species in which adults are highly sexually dimorphic, juvenile females and males begin to diverge in body size (3-30).

A juvenile's survival depends upon learning appropriate foods to eat and which poisonous things to avoid. Field biologist Stuart Altmann documented how young baboons in Amboseli, Kenya, locate, prepare, and ingest dozens of foods, many available in few locations and at limited times. They learn some foods by trial and error, but much of their dietary knowledge comes from closely watching feeding adults and sniffing the adults' mouths as they chew. Judging by experiments on other mammals, infant primates may be sensitized to certain food flavors in their mother's milk or even via the placenta before birth! Thus in various ways, knowledge of what to eat and what not to eat is passed from one generation to the next.

Color social play.

Play activity begins in infancy, increases in frequency and intensity among young juveniles, then declines among adolescents. Juvenile life revolves around play activities that provide a benign context in which to learn and practice caretaking, sexual and aggressive behaviors, and social communication.

Play is also physical training. The exertion of jumping, running, chasing, climbing, wrestling, manipulating, and carrying exercises muscles and bones, promoting growth and development. Visual and motor coordination, reaction speed, and other motor skills improve. Play stimulates brain activity and physical development that contribute to adaptable and even novel behavior.

Whether solitary or social, play is beneficial. In solitary play, individuals practice motor skills like tool using or explore the world for themselves. Social play provides practice in communication and in responding quickly to the moves of others. Play faces and gestures (3-18) synchronize behavior between the sender and receiver. While testing each other's physical strength and reaction speed, juveniles become familiar with individuals of the same group and recognize members of neighboring groups.

Color the graph showing the influence of rainfall and food abundance on play frequency.

Frequency and intensity of play behavior is an indicator of general health and well being and is affected by environmental quality. Phyllis Lee showed, for example, that vervet monkeys in Amboseli, Kenya, played differently during wet and dry seasons. During dry seasons, food was more dispersed, so juveniles spent more time foraging; they also had fewer opportunities to contact play partners and apparently less energy for play. Under severe nutritional or social stress, play decreases and growth may also be retarded. During the wet season, when dietary quality improves, feeding time declines and play frequency increases.

Color the juvenile leaving its natal social group.

In a number of primate species, juveniles approaching adolescence and adulthood extend their sights beyond their natal group. They move to another social group, perhaps one "next door," or one some distance away. Depending on the species, dispersers may be females, males, or members of both sexes. Traveling to another group requires energy and social skills for interacting with new associates. As juveniles approach sexual maturity, female and male lives begin to diverge, as each sex pursues a different reproductive agenda. Juvenile animals serve as a bridge between the younger and older generations in their group, and by leaving, as a link between groups.

Focusing on what happens during a juvenile's life helps us understand its later development. From following individual juvenile baboons in Amboseli, Kenya, Stuart Altmann discovered that juvenile females who ate a balanced diet that included high levels of energy and protein survived longer and had greater reproductive success as adults.

The prolonged juvenile period (3-24) between infancy and adulthood permits acquisition of learned skills and remembered experiences. This extended immaturity and the large brain enhance physical and social plasticity, promoting flexibility in problem solving later in life. Through social explorations, juveniles create bonds with the next generation and establish lifetime networks that ensure group cohesion over time.

JUVENILES AND TRANSITIONS

PHYSICAL CHANGES*
WEANED INFANT$_a$
JUVENILE$_b$
PERCENT OF ADULT*
BRAIN SIZE$_{a^1,b^1}$
BODY SIZE$_{a^2,b^2}$
TEETH$_{a^3,b^3}$

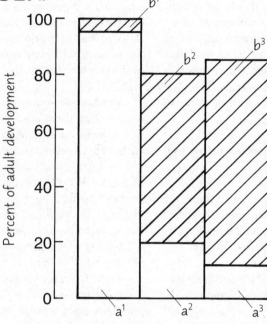

Percent of adult development

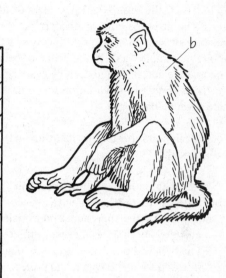

RAINFALL, FOOD ABUNDANCE$_c$
PLAY FREQUENCY$_d$
  HIGH$_{d^1}$ LOW$_{d^2}$

SOCIAL PLAY$_e$

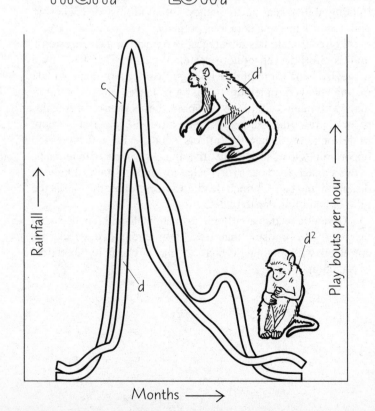

Rainfall

Play bouts per hour

Months

DISPERSAL$_f$

3-29
PRIMATE LIFE HISTORY: MALES AND SOCIAL LIVING

On the stage of primate social life, adult males play many roles (3-23). They act as mates, protectors of mothers and infants, defenders of the group, and patrollers of the boundaries of the group's home range. They even learn to tolerate each other in the presence of sexually receptive females, a rare accommodation among mammals. In different primate species, and even within the same species, male activities can vary considerably. This plate illustrates some of the variation found in the social behavior of male savanna baboons.

Color each behavior and its location on the graph below, as it is discussed.

Male behavior spans the spectrum from nurturance and protectiveness to aggression and violence. They guard and care for the young. Yet they may attack other males, sometimes females or youngsters, and in rare instances inflict serious injuries.

Male baboons pay close attention to new mothers to ensure their access to food and water, and protect and play with infants. Friendships often develop between an adult male and female. The male will sit with his friend, groom her, and play with her offspring. He has a high tolerance for the little ones, even when they are pesky and crawl all over him. High-ranking males may act as peacemakers and break up fights.

But all is not friendliness in baboon social life. Adult males can be menacing and dangerous. Competing males may fight and inflict serious injuries. Males sometimes batter adult females or kill infants. They have twice the body mass of females and are equipped with saberlike canine teeth (3-30). Conflict is often avoided by communicating with facial expressions, body postures, or flashing canines. But when these signals fail, threatening encounters and physical aggression may ensue.

Interspecies variation is great. Titi monkey males are usually intense caretakers of the young (4-14). Patas monkeys sometimes live easily in all-male groups (3-23), but at other times avoid each other. In some species, males groom each other frequently as a way of reducing interpersonal tension. They may vie vigorously with each other for high rank or access to females, but they may also form coalitions, cooperate in hunting, and keep aggression under control by touching, gesturing, or vocalizing.

Color the male entering the baboon group.

Older juveniles, adolescents, or young males of many species leave their natal group to take residence in other groups. They thus avoid competition with older males at home and find unrelated sex partners in a nearby troop. Successful integration into the new group depends heavily on the male individual's social skills, according to primatologist Shirley Strum. A baboon emigré, for instance, will often make friends with a female first, in order to smooth his acceptance by her family and then by the rest of the troop.

Females of some species do change groups, usually only once in their lives, prior to having their first offspring. Without the energetic constraints involved in female reproduction, males are freer to travel and seek adventure and new social relationships.

Male reproductive success has been the theme of much theorizing. What factors determine the number of offspring a male sires during his lifetime? Minimally, he must be able to produce viable sperm, gain access to females, and complete copulations. Unlike females, male primates other than humans have no way of knowing which infants are their own, and they have no concept of "paternity" or "biological" offspring.

Until DNA testing became available (2-12), primatologists had no certain way to assign paternity. It now turns out that many pre-DNA notions were incorrect. For instance, it was widely believed that the highest ranking male sired most of the offspring, and that females rarely or never mated outside their group. Wrong on both counts. By DNA testing, we now know that lower-ranking males father offspring, and female matings outside the group can be common, though they are rarely observed by field workers. Contrary to theory, it is no longer axiomatic that a male's rank, fighting ability, mating frequency, infant-killing, or friendship with females insure a populous progeny.

Long-term studies do suggest two positive influences on a male's lifetime reproduction: female choice, and his own longevity. Female preference is a significant determinant of male mating behavior. In lemurs (4-7), for instance, females prefer to mate with males within the group. In rhesus monkeys, females seem to prefer the "new guys" who have just joined the group. Male longevity generally reflects good health and increased opportunities to mate and sire offspring. As compared to females, males engage in more risky behavior and are more likely to disappear and be presumed dead. In some groups, this raises the ratio of adult females to males.

Given the wide variation in primate male and female social behaviors, it is unlikely that male lifetime reproductive success correlates with any single factor or has any simple theoretical explanation.

MALES AND SOCIAL LIVING

NURTURANCE_a   TOLERANCE_c   INJURY_e
       FRIENDSHIP_b   AGGRESSION_d
NEW MALE_f

3-30
SEX DIFFERENCES:
FEMALE AND MALE VARIATION

Adult females and males differ in their reproductive anatomy, and males in many species are larger in size and have longer canine teeth. However, in other species it is not easy to tell the two sexes apart. In some species, females and males differ in unusual and subtle ways. This plate illustrates examples of three patterns of sex differences: sexual dichromatism, sexual divocalism, and sexual bimaturism.

Color the body mass and canine teeth of *Lemur macaco*. Be sure to color the female and male according to the colors described in the text.

Like most prosimians, female and male lemurs of Madagascar differ very little in body or tooth size. *Lemur macaco* females and males weigh the same; their upper canines are similar in size and shape. The striking sex difference in this species, called the black lemur, is that the two sexes differ in hair color and pattern, an example of sexual dichromatism (di=two, chroma= color). The male is jet black all over—face and head, back, tail, and belly. In contrast, the female has a brown back and tail, white belly, gray head, and long tufts of white hair around the ears and jaws. Males and females are so different in coloration that they appear to be two separate species!

"Black lemurs" are fruit-eaters and live in groups averaging 7 to 10 members in northwestern Madagascar. Females are dominant over males, a pattern common among lemurs (4-7). Their distinct coloration easily distinguishes females from males.

Color the lar gibbons and their characteristics.

Some species of gibbons are sexually dichromatic, but lar gibbons are not, and it is difficult to distinguish among males, females without young, and adolescents. Adults are similar in body mass, and both sexes have well-developed canine teeth. Reproductive anatomy is not prominent. Gibbons live in small family groups that defend a territory (3-4, 4-31). The two sexes are co-dominant; both are aggressive and intolerant of other, same-sex adults encountered in neighboring groups, so that territorial skirmishes take place. As a result, males may have facial cuts, and anthropologist John Frisch reported that 41% of male lar gibbons compared to 20% of females had lost or broken canines.

Within each species of gibbon, vocalizations distinguish adult females from males. The gibbon pair sings duets; each sex sings a slightly different part. The "great call" of the females is the most easily identified part of the gibbon songs and is distinct from that of the male's. Among gibbons, vocalizations are a key part of their adaptation and serve a number of functions: as a means to distinguish each species from all others; to locate, define and maintain territorial boundaries; to attract mates; to reinforce the group's female-male bond; and to identify the sex of the caller to neighboring groups.

Color the characteristics of anubis baboon females and males that illustrate bimaturism.

Female and male savanna baboons could hardly be more different. Males have almost twice the body mass of females and saberlike canine teeth seven centimeters long. The massive root requires supporting bone and muscles, resulting in a robust head and extended muzzle that give male baboons a doglike appearance. Females have smaller heads, shorter muzzles, and more slender bodies. They exhibit bright red sexual swellings when they come into estrus (3-25).

The marked sex difference in both body and canine size emerges from different patterns of growth and development. Females begin having sexual swellings at about 4.5 years of age and reach sexual maturity about 6 years. They give birth to their first offspring at about 6.5 years. At this age, they have reached adult body size, their canines are fully erupted, and bone growth is almost complete. With the birth of her first infant, a baboon female achieves all levels of maturity—sexual, physical, and social—about the same time.

The male pattern is quite different. A male produces viable sperm perhaps about age 5. At that time, he is only half the size of the adult males and so finds few mating opportunities. He continues to grow and develop for several years, gaining body mass and growing larger canines. He begins to dominate all adult females, and gradually makes the transition to adult status. Physical maturity is finally reached about age 10. By then a male is equipped to compete with other fully grown males, to test his strength against them, to form coalitions, and to be accepted by mating females. In contrast with the female pattern, males reach social maturity long after they are sexually and physically mature.

Gorillas, orangutans, and patas monkeys also have pronounced sexual dimorphism like the baboons. The males all achieve their larger size by sexual bimaturism. They continue to grow beyond the age when females have reached their full size.

Primates, of course, have no trouble telling males from females in their own species, but it's not always that easy for the rest of us. Primatologists must often play detective and pick up on the less obvious clues that distinguish females from males. It would be embarrassing to call male and female black lemurs two separate species because of their dramatically different coloration, to mistake an immature male baboon for a full-grown female, or to have such a tin ear as not to recognize the male and female parts in a gibbon duet.

FEMALE AND MALE VARIATION

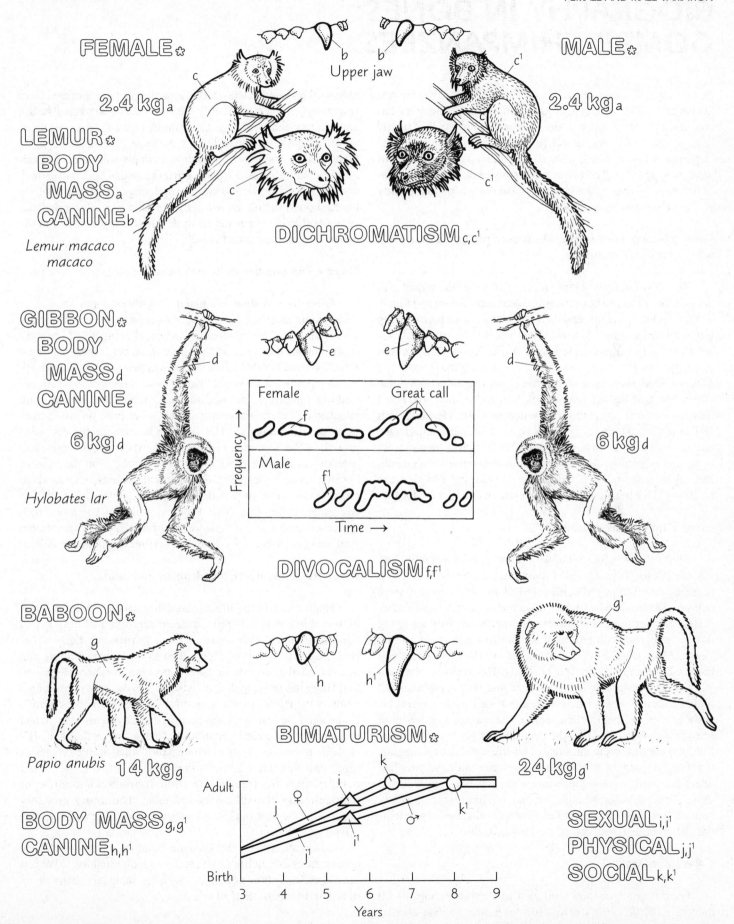

FEMALE ✳

2.4 kg a

LEMUR ✳
BODY
MASS a
CANINE b

Lemur macaco
macaco

Upper jaw

b   b

DICHROMATISM c,c¹

MALE ✳

2.4 kg a

GIBBON ✳
BODY
MASS d
CANINE e

6 kg d

Hylobates lar

e   e

Female   Great call

f

Male

f¹

Frequency →

Time →

DIVOCALISM f,f¹

6 kg d

BABOON ✳

g

Papio anubis   14 kg g

h   h¹

BIMATURISM ✳

g¹

24 kg g¹

BODY MASS g,g¹
CANINE h,h¹

Adult

Birth

♀
j   i
          k

♂
          k¹
j¹   i¹

3   4   5   6   7   8   9
Years

SEXUAL i,i¹
PHYSICAL j,j¹
SOCIAL k,k¹

3-31
BIOGRAPHY IN BONES: GOMBE CHIMPANZEES

In 1960 Jane Goodall began to observe chimpanzees at Gombe in Tanzania. The research of Goodall and her colleagues has continued for more than four decades, revealing details of family life, social networks, and life experiences. Aware of the importance of the whole animal, Goodall saved the skeletons whenever possible. The bones tell a story about the uniqueness of individuals' lives and add a biological dimension to the study of this chimpanzee population.

Color Flo and Flint in the Flo family picture. Color Flo's portrait and her mandible.

The first family of chimpanzees that Goodall studied was the matriarch Flo and her offspring: older sons, Faben and Figan, adolescent Fifi, son Flint, and daughter Flame. Flo, a high-ranking female, lived a long life until about age 45. As Flo aged, she became frail and emaciated, had difficulty in walking and climbing, and given her worn teeth, in obtaining and processing adequate food. Flo's skeleton records a story of a robust individual during most of her life. Her bones were large and show some mineral loss with age, but no joint degeneration. Her tooth loss and wear were extreme and evident years before her death. Healed fractures seemed not to have affected her growth or later success in rearing offspring. Daughter Fifi, a mother before Flo's death, had eight offspring. Fifi's daughters Fanni and Flossie have offspring. This translates into high reproductive success for Flo.

Color Flint and his mandible.

Flint was Flo's fourth known offspring, born when Flo was already 35 to 40 years old. Infant Flint appeared to develop normally, but as a juvenile, his physical and social growth were delayed. He remained with Flo rather than venture off with other males. His foraging and travel patterns, limited by an aging mother, may have compromised his nutritional state. At age 8.5 years, Flint died 3 weeks after his mother; he had been inconsolable and had not left her body. His skeleton reveals a story of growth problems. Brain size and dental eruption fall within a normal range, whereas shorter bone lengths suggest his body growth fell below the average. Disjuncture in bone-tooth growth is demonstrated by the crowding of his lower incisors. Flint's skeleton adds to the story of his life and death; it suggests that the milk supply of an aged mother may not have provided adequate nutrition for the infant's normal bone growth and mineralization. After weaning, he may not have foraged widely enough to achieve a balanced diet. Flint's developmental problems and the emotional loss contributed to his death.

Color infant Gyre.

Gyre was a twin and struggled to survive during his 10 months of life. At the time of his birth, his mother Melissa, another high-ranking female whose life Goodall observed, suffered from respiratory problems, possibly pneumonia. Her weakened health and the unusual burden of two infants probably decreased her ability to forage for adequate food and to produce sufficient milk. Gyre died of respiratory problems, perhaps weakened by malnutrition. Gyre's cranium and teeth indicate that his brain growth and tooth eruption were within normal range. However, his long bones show very little growth and mineralization. Gyre's skeleton suggests that his brain and tooth development proceeded at the expense of skeletal growth (3-27).

Color Gilka and her right arm bones.

Gilka lived a short life plagued by disease and loneliness. As an infant and youngster, Gilka was apparently healthy. At age 7 she contracted polio, resulting in partial paralysis of her right limb; her mother died at this time. She contracted a fungal infection that distorted her face. She was low ranking and, except for an older brother Evered, had few social companions. Higher ranking females, a mother and daughter, Passion and Pom, attacked Gilka; she apparently died of a systemic infection from these injuries at age 19. Her skeleton documents the disrupted growth in the asymmetry of her arm bones from the polio, and osteomyelitis in her hand bones, presumably from the bites of her attackers. Although Gilka gave birth to 3 infants, none survived more than a year, in part due to her locomotor difficulties in adequately supporting them. Physical problems combined with the absence of a social network, low rank, and poor emotional well being led to her early death and lifetime reproductive failure.

Color Hugo and his right calcaneus and talus.

Hugo lived a long life of about 40 years as a vigorous and high-ranking male with pronounced leadership qualities; he was quick to threaten others but also quick to reassure. Early in her study, Goodall observed Hugo, then in his prime, limping and accompanied by an estrous female; the circumstances suggested that Hugo fell or jumped from a tree while fighting or chasing a competing male. After a few months, his gait returned to normal. As he aged, he lost teeth and became frail, dying of old age and presumably pneumonia contracted during the wet season. His skeleton reveals the story of a robust individual above average in size who survived a minimum of 8 fractures. A healed compression fracture of the right foot shows significant remodeling of the calcaneus and talus. The injury probably occurred at the time of Goodall's observations. Hugo likely sired offspring.

Information from the skeleton combined with behavioral observations during life gives texture to individual lives. We can see more clearly how population averages represent abstractions of real individuals, none of which are average.

GOMBE CHIMPANZEES

FLO FAMILY PORTRAIT *

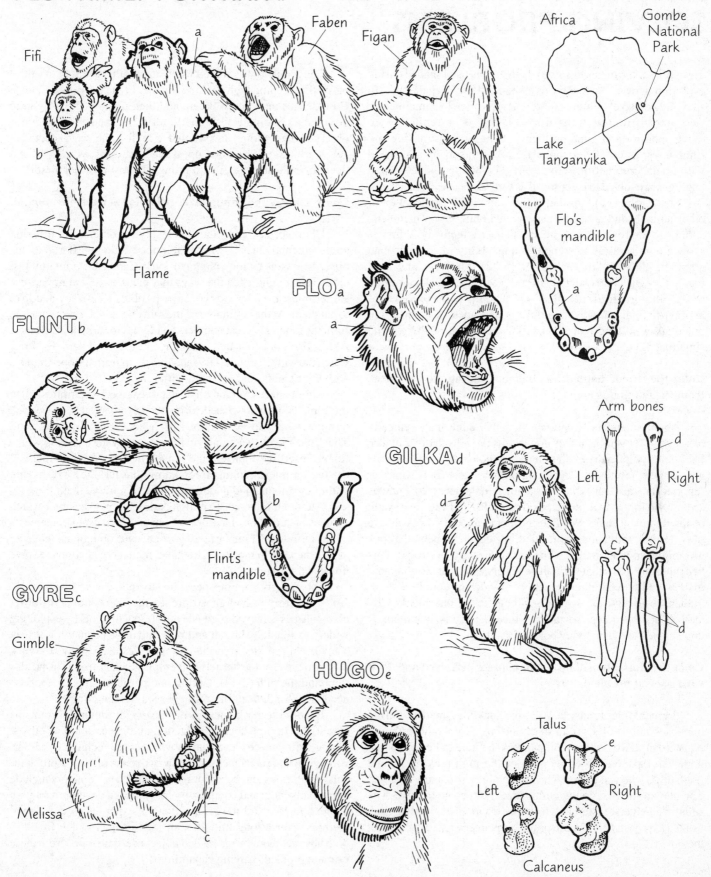

Fifi

a

b

Faben

Figan

Flame

Africa

Gombe National Park

Lake Tanganyika

Flo's mandible

a

FLO a

a

FLINT b

b

b

Flint's mandible

GYRE c

Gimble

Melissa

c

GILKA d

d

d

Arm bones

Left

Right

d

c

d

HUGO e

e

Talus

e

Left

Right

Calcaneus

3-32
PRIMATE INTELLIGENCE: SOLVING PROBLEMS

The ability of primates to solve problems has been shaped during evolution in response to environmental and social challenges. In studying human evolution, anthropologists often link intelligence to object-oriented behaviors. There is a tendency to overemphasize nonsocial problem solving, such as making and using tools, and to underemphasize problem solving associated with social interaction. However, the foundation of human intelligence evolved to meet social as well as nonsocial challenges.

Social living requires that individuals "read" the behavior of other animals and assess situations involving group members, anticipate the reactions of others, and act effectively. Primates show a high level of awareness and an ability to communicate complex messages to each other (3-22). Monkeys and apes manipulate each other socially in complex ways that demonstrate their ability to "read the mind" or "take the point of view" of another animal. However, monkeys and apes show different potential in solving nonsocial problems and in reading social situations.

Color the female hamadryas baboon "hiding the evidence" from the dominant male.

Among hamadryas baboons, a single adult male typically has several females as mates and guards them from other males. In a study compiled by evolutionary psychologists Richard Byrne and Andrew Whiten on deception, primatologist Hans Kummer reported an incident where an adult female spent 20 minutes seeming to forage in a sitting position while shuffling out of sight of the dominant male. With her head and upper body visible to the male but with hands concealed, she ended up behind a rock grooming another male, who was hidden by the rock! This behavior illustrates that the female understands that the dominant male would prevent the interaction provided he could see it. To human observers, the social manipulation of one monkey by another demonstrates "social intelligence"; that is, one monkey understands the visual viewpoint of another.

Color the illustration of how chimpanzees perceived and dealt with a social problem.

Primatologist Frans de Waal recounted an incident during his observations of a group of chimpanzees at Arnhem Zoo in Amsterdam. Two mother chimpanzees (Female A, Female B) sat under an oak tree on either side of the high-ranking female (Female C) who was asleep. Their offspring were playing together. The play of the two young chimpanzees turned aggressive. The situation created tension between the two mothers because each wanted to protect her own offspring, but neither wanted to confront the other.

The problem was solved when one mother brought in a third party, the sleeping high-ranking female. Female A poked Female C in the ribs until she woke up and then pointed at the fighting youngsters. Female C immediately assessed the situation, observed the fighting, and seemed to realize she was expected to act as arbitrator. She stood up, waved her arms, vocalized, and the two youngsters stopped fighting; she resumed her siesta.

Color baboon and chimpanzee behavior at a termite mound.

Chimpanzees and other apes solve problems by utilizing environmental clues in ways that monkeys do not. Based on his observations at Gombe National Park, Tanzania, primatologist Geza Teleki contrasted the ways that baboons and chimpanzees eat termites. Both species consider termites a delicacy and love to eat them. At the beginning of the rainy season, termites emerge from the mound in great numbers and fly off to form new colonies. At this time, baboons take advantage of this food item. Baboons watch the winged termites fly out, grab them from the open tunnels with their hands, and eat them with relish.

Chimpanzees, on the other hand, eat worker termites when the tunnels are still closed, prior to the emergence of winged termites. Chimpanzees fashion a probe from a nearby grass stem. They find and open a tunnel by flicking away the covering with a finger, insert the tool into the tunnel, and carefully extract and eat the termites. Chimpanzees know that termites live hidden within the mound and understand how to retrieve them.

Although baboons live alongside chimpanzees and watch them using tools, they have never been observed using implements to eat termites. Chimpanzees, gorillas, and orangutans have an ability, lacking in monkeys, to make mental connections to solve nonsocial problems.

Tool use gives chimpanzees an advantage in getting food. At Bossou, Guinea, when staple foods were not available, chimpanzees achieved adequate nutrition with tools by exploiting widely available palm nut and pith. Japanese primatologist Gen Yamakoshi reported that the chimpanzees used stones to crack oil palm nuts for the kernels and employed leaf fronds as pestles to pound the pith (3-13). During one particular month, tool use accounted for 32% of the chimpanzees' feeding time.

Even with mechanical skill, the social dimension remains essential. Through social interaction and observation of others, young chimpanzees learn and practice these techniques (3-33). Biological and social factors are interwoven in primates' problem-solving abilities and behavioral flexibility. These factors include a relatively large and complex brain, extended development with a long time for learning, a rich variety of experiences, and a good memory over a long life. Human intelligence, which involves both abstract thought and skilled object use, developed from these primate problem-solving capabilities.

SOLVING PROBLEMS

SOCIAL MANIPULATION∗
FEMALE a
  VISUAL VIEWPOINT a¹
DOMINANT MALE b
  VISUAL VIEWPOINT b¹
NONDOMINANT MALE/
  EVIDENCE c

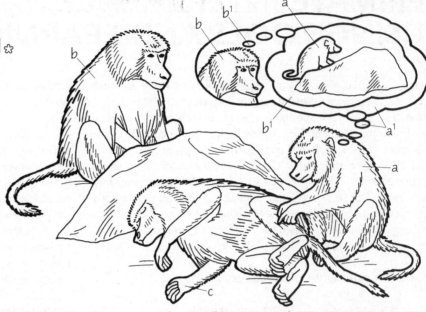

SOCIAL PROBLEM
  SOLVING∗
FEMALE A d
OFFSPRING A d¹
VIEWPOINT d²

FEMALE B e
OFFSPRING B e¹

DOMINANT FEMALE f
VIEWPOINT f¹

NONSOCIAL PROBLEM SOLVING∗
BABOON g   CHIMPANZEE h
  GRAB g¹   TOOL/PROBE h¹
  WINGED   WORKER
    TERMITE g²   TERMITE h²

3-33
PRIMATE INTELLIGENCE: USING TOOLS AND LEARNING SKILLS

Jane Goodall's discovery of spontaneous tool using in chimpanzees, first reported in the scientific literature in 1965, showed that the gap between ape and human behavior was narrower than had been thought. The "moving evidence" provided by the films of nature photographer Hugo van Lawick left no doubt in the scientific community that Goodall's observations were as she reported them. Chimpanzees use materials in nest building, grooming (sticks as toothpicks, leaves as towels), playing, and displaying to intimidate others. Drawing on research from several study sites, this plate illustrates examples of chimpanzee skill in using tools that enhance their ability to get food.

Color the skills and tools as discussed.

Chimpanzees probe for termites and ants using grass stalks, twigs, vines, and bark strips to enter mounds or nests. At Gombe, Tanzania, the chimpanzees "fish" for termites (shown here), and at Mahale, Tanzania, (3-34) the chimpanzees "dip" for ants using long "wands." A chimpanzee usually digs into a safari ant nest with its hands. Then it inserts a slender "wand" and the disturbed ants rush up the stick. Just as the ants reach its hand, the chimpanzee sweeps the mass of biting ants off with the other hand, stuffs them into its mouth, and chews quickly to minimize the bites! Occasionally, however, chimpanzees dig with a thick, long stick, to get deeper into an ant nest or termite mound before inserting a second implement. The use of more than one kind of tool for a single task exemplifies a "tool composite" and emphasizes the innovative and problem-solving abilities of these apes.

Chimpanzees chew leaves and use them to sponge water from the bowls of trees. Chewing makes the leaves more absorbent, and the method is more effective than just dipping the fingers in the water. Chimpanzees also use wads of crumpled leaves to sponge up brain tissue when eating animal prey, or leaves to mop up swarming ants. Chimpanzees pound hard items such as nuts or fleshy fruits which have tough outer coverings, using sticks and stones as hammers and anvils; they use large sticks as pestles to pound up the pulp of palm trees (3-13).

Adult females are the most skillful tool users and engage in these activities more frequently than do males. Young chimpanzees require four to five years to gain proficiency at fishing for termites. Chimpanzees learn through observation and practice, utilizing their mothers' open termite tunnel or tools left beside the mound. Geza Teleki observed chimpanzees' seemingly effortless tool use and investigated how chimpanzees learn the components of termite fishing: finding entry to termite tunnels without obvious external clues on the mounds; selecting a "Goldilocks" implement for probing, one that is not too stiff or too flexible but just right; and mastering the actions required for a successful outcome—the taste of delicious termites. The skilled chimpanzee named Leakey served as Teleki's model.

Color the components of termite fishing that Geza Teleki attempted to copy.

Gombe chimpanzees fish for termites most productively during two months at the onset of the rainy season, when winged termites prepare to leave the mound on their nuptial flight to start a new colony. Termites are nocturnal and any disturbance to the mound is repaired at night, so chimpanzees must locate tunnel openings each day.

Chimpanzees select their tool materials with ease, speed, and accuracy. After a brief visual scan, the individual deftly tears off two or three grass stalks, then discards or modifies the stalk by stripping leaves or biting to achieve the proper length (8–16 cm) and flexibility. With obvious premeditation, they may carry potential tools for more than an hour and for considerable distances to a mound. After months of observing and aping the apes, Teleki managed to achieve the meager skill level of a three-year-old chimpanzee in selecting a proper tool.

At the termite mound, chimpanzees quickly examine the surface, then reach out decisively and uncover a tunnel by scraping away the soil layer. In an attempt to learn how to do this, Teleki minutely examined every crack on the mound but could not figure out how the chimpanzees detected the hidden tunnels. Eventually, he resorted to scraping the surface with his jackknife until he found a tunnel! After extensive observations, Teleki concluded that chimpanzees memorize the precise location of 100 or more tunnels on a familiar set of 10 to 25 mounds which they visit and check out routinely.

Having located a tunnel and a suitable implement, the chimpanzee carefully navigates the probe through the twisted channel, then gently taps the tool; the vibration stimulates the termites to bite. With a fluid and graceful movement, the chimpanzee slowly twists its wrist to extract the insects. If this move is performed too rapidly or clumsily, the termites are dislodged as they go through the tunnel. The chimpanzee stabilizes the probe on its forearm, withdraws it, and gently picks off each termite with its lips. Failing to meet the standards of the preceding stages, Teleki spent hours inserting probes, pausing for the designated interval, and pulling out the tool—without ever getting a termite!

Prior to Goodall's studies, anthropologists had underestimated the technical skills of apes and, implicitly, misjudged the starting point of early hominid tool use. Chimpanzee tools such as the grass stems used for termite fishing are highly perishable and, even if preserved, would not be recognized as implements. The relatively unmodified stone hammers and anvils for cracking nuts would also be difficult to identify as tools in the prehistoric record. It is probable that the very early hominids used tools made of similar materials well before the 2 to 2.5 million year date when stone artifacts are recognized in the archaeological record (5-24).

USING TOOLS AND LEARNING SKILLS

SKILL*
  PROBINGₐ
  DIGGING_b
  SPONGING_c
  POUNDING_d

TOOL*
  GRASS STALK_{a¹}
  STICK_{b¹}
  LEAF SPONGE_{c¹}
  STONES_{d¹}

FISHING FOR TERMITES*
  SELECTING TOOL_e
  LOCATING TUNNEL_f
  UTILIZING PROBE_g

POPULATION VARIATION: BEHAVIOR, TRADITIONS, AND TRANSMISSION

After Goodall began her studies on wild chimpanzees at Gombe in Tanzania, research sites on *Pan troglodytes* were established at several locations, for example, Mahale, Tanzania, by Japanese primatologist Toshisada Nishida; Budongo Forest, Uganda, by British primatologist Vernon Reynolds; and Bossou, Guinea, by Japanese primatologist Yukimaru Sugiyama. These and other ongoing studies reveal that each chimpanzee population differs from the others in its combination and frequency of behavior patterns. Observations that span chimpanzee lifetimes (3-31) permit researchers to discover how variation arises, continues, and spreads.

Color the six chimpanzee study sites and a behavior from each population as it is discussed.

These long-term studies taken together represent over 150 years of observation! Andrew Whiten and his chimpanzee-researcher colleagues compiled the data and documented 39 different behavior patterns that itemize variables such as tool using, grooming, and courtship. Pestle pounding has been observed only at Bossou. Chimpanzees use leaves for grooming, but only at Budongo do they use leaves to remove insects from the body and then closely inspect them.

Levers are used habitually at Gombe, occasionally at Taï Forest, Ivory Coast, and never at the other sites. At Kibale, Uganda, chimpanzees use leaves to daub at blood on their wounds, a behavior not seen elsewhere. Fishing for ants is common at Mahale but not elsewhere, and bees are probed for only at Taï Forest. Each behavior observed does not necessarily become a tradition. Like a mutation in the genes, not every innovation becomes fixed in the population. Some are lost after one generation, others persist for many generations.

Color the transmission of nut cracking through generations by observation and facilitation.

Older individuals are a repository of experience and memory; younger individuals learn through social interaction and observation. Ethologists Christophe and Hedwige Boesch studied chimpanzee tool use in Taï Forest for over a decade. Chimpanzees employ wood and stone hammers and anvils to crack open several species of nuts having very hard shells. They require 10 years to master the skill, as measured by how many hits are needed to crack open one nut. Adult females achieve the highest level of skill, in the number of nuts that can be processed per minute.

Chimpanzees take a long time to grow up. Close association with their mothers promotes acquisition of tool using through observation and practice. The apprenticeship involves watching their mothers closely, who in turn. leave nuts on the platform and

implements nearby, in what C. Boesch describes as facilitation. Boesch documented an instance of active instruction, when a mother carefully demonstrated to her 5-year-old daughter how to hold and position the hammer to effectively pound the nut.

Color the transmission of coula eating from one chimpanzee community to another through migration.

Among chimpanzees, females, but not males, visit or transfer permanently to neighboring communities. At Bossou, chimpanzees crack oil-palm nuts but not coula nuts. Their neighbors at Mt. Nimba, 10 kilometers away, crack coula nuts. In a series of field experiments, primatologist Tetsuro Matsuzawa provided the unfamiliar coula nuts to 18 Bossou chimpanzees. The chimpanzees at first ignored the nuts except for one adult female, Yo, estimated to be about 30 years of age. She immediately placed the coula nuts on a stone anvil, cracked them, and ate the kernels. Two juveniles 6 years old, one female, one male, adopted the cracking of the coula nuts. Matsuzawa hypothesized that Yo had immigrated to Bossou from the Mt. Nimba community, where she had learned the tradition and remembered it. Two young members of the community, but no adults, copied the behavior of this older female.

Observations on the same population year after year provide a vivid picture of social traditions. When a behavioral innovation by one individual is copied by others, it might then be transmitted to younger individuals by example. Over time, each population becomes a little different from the others. The transmission of learned behavior through time and space constitutes a tradition. Primates are endowed with relatively large brains, as well as good memories and problem-solving abilities; they live a long life, in social groups with both sexes and all ages. Three generations might reside in the same community or even within the same family. These conditions, according to zoologist John Eisenberg, are essential for fostering the transmission of behavior socially rather than genetically.

Traditions for chimpanzees must be learned during an individual's lifetime by direct example. Humans learn in this way, but can also absorb information without direct observation. Humans, but not chimpanzees, spontaneously learn to communicate symbolically in the early years of life and have specialized brain centers which makes this possible (3-22). Through the development of abstract conceptual thought and symbolic communication, humans are freed from the immediacy of situations. They have available to them cultural information about the past and future that has the potential to make a difference in survival and reproduction. Although social traditions are a necessary prerequisite for what we anthropologists call culture, traditions by themselves do not constitute culture.

BEHAVIOR, TRADITIONS, AND TRANSMISSION

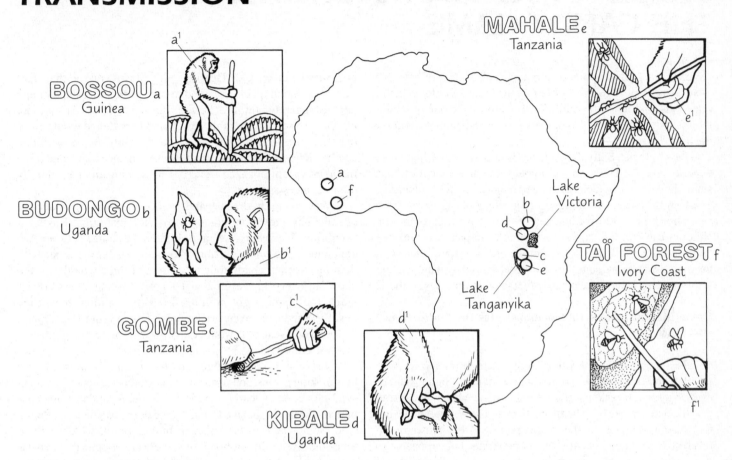

BOSSOU_a
Guinea

BUDONGO_b
Uganda

GOMBE_c
Tanzania

KIBALE_d
Uganda

MAHALE_e
Tanzania

TAÏ FOREST_f
Ivory Coast

Lake
Victoria

Lake
Tanganyika

TRANSMISSION*
 THROUGH MIGRATION*
YO_i
COULA NUT_{i^1}
MT. NIMBA_{i^2}
BOSSOU/PALM NUT_j
JUVENILE_{j^1}

THROUGH GENERATIONS*
OBSERVATION_g
FACILITATION_h

3-35
SYMBOLS AND ABSTRACTIONS: THE CANDY GAME

Humans incorporate symbols into almost all aspects of behavior —solving problems and considering past events, present dilemmas, and future possibilities. But are we the only primates who think symbolically? What advantages do symbols hold for the users?

Psychologist Sally Boysen devised a series of ingenious experiments that show how chimpanzees can be taught to use symbols to transcend their hard-wired biology, if only temporarily. The Candy Game is a simple test requiring a player to make the best choice between two batches of candy. By four years old, children can win the game every time. Chimpanzees flunk out with uncanny consistency, as long as they are confronted with the mouth-watering tidbits they must choose. But by manipulating symbols, even chimpanzees can learn that sometimes less is more.

Color the illustration that demonstrates the "interference effect."

Two chimpanzees play the Candy Game. Boysen offers two unequal arrays of candy to one of them, let's say Sarah. Whichever array Sarah picks is given to her friend Sheba, and Sarah gets the one not chosen. Therefore, the logical choice, if you want more candy, is to point at the smaller portion. Adult humans learn this lesson very quickly, after one or two trials, but chimpanzees don't seem to get it. Even after hundreds of trials, they will still go for the bigger plate of candy and end up with the smaller amount. It is not as though they don't know what is going to happen; they just can't help themselves. They are programmed to go for broke. Their faces have a pained look, as though to say, "Oh no! I didn't do it again!" and they bang on the apparatus in frustration.

Boysen calls this phenomenon the "interference effect," because an uncontrollable impulse to get more candy interferes with the chimpanzees' ability to make the right choice. Here is where the power of symbolic thinking can come to the rescue.

Color the illustration of the "symbol effect."

Boysen taught several chimpanzees to read numbers on plastic chips. They demonstrated their understanding by selecting the correct number corresponding to a specific number of fruits or pieces of candy. In order to be rewarded with these goodies, the chimpanzees can even do some rudimentary addition with the plastic numerals.

Boysen then played the Candy Game with the numerate chimpanzees, presenting them with plastic numbers, for instance 2 and 6, instead of candies. If Sarah picked 6, Sheba got 6 candies

and Sarah got only 2. Dealing with plastic rather than real yummies, Sarah quickly learned to pick the smaller number and get the bigger mouthful for herself. Boysen calls this the "symbol effect." To see whether this new-found knowledge would carry over, Boysen went back to the original Candy Game, with real candies. The "interference effect" kicked in once more, and these math-savvy chimpanzees reverted to making their seemingly dumb choices again.

Very young children behave in this respect like chimpanzees, as shown in studies carried out by psychologist James Russell at Cambridge University. He gave children the choice between two containers, one with a visible chocolate inside, the other with nothing. Normal children up to the age of three would pick the chocolate every time, even though it always went to their partner, while the chooser got nothing. Like the chimpanzees, they never learned from experience to pick less in order to get more. Normal four-year-olds would quickly catch on to this game and pick the empty box.

Between the ages of three and four, a child's brain matures as if making a transition from ape's interference effect to a human symbolic effect. Clearly there is no simple formula for the ape-human difference, but the Candy Game does provide a tantalizing clue. Somewhere in the enlarged human brain, which is three times the size of the chimpanzee's, there are circuits that make it easier for us to learn other ways of behaving and so escape the tyranny of immediate gratification and, some of the time, to make wiser long-range choices. The human brain is hard-wired for learning language spontaneously and thinking symbolically and abstractly, while the chimpanzee's is not.

The Candy Game illustrates the cleverness of chimpanzees and at the same time pinpoints a crucial difference in ape and human mental processes. Chimpanzees can change their built-in responses and counterproductive behavior when numbers are substituted for candy; but when confronted with "the real goods," they can't refuse, and they revert to their compulsion to take the most.

The "symbol effect" illustrates the powerful role that symbols have played, and continue to play, in human evolution and in daily life. Sometime during the past five million years, the human brain evolved the ability to think abstractly and use symbols, an ability that must have made a significant difference in hominids' survival and reproduction. Although chimpanzees and humans share many similarities in anatomy and behavior, the difference between them is profound. How chimpanzees and people play the Candy Game reveals a crucial difference in brain function and in the central role that symbols play in all aspects of human life.

THE CANDY GAME

INTERFERENCE
 EFFECT*
SALLYₐ
SARAH_b
SHEBA_c
CANDY_d

SYMBOL EFFECT*
NUMERALS_e

SECTION 4
PRIMATE DIVERSITY
AND ADAPTATION

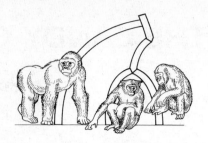

Darwin's Tree of Life depicted relationships among life forms with humans as one twig among many branches. Genetics, the fossil record, and comparative anatomy and behavior confirm these connections and their continuity over evolutionary time. When time passes and the environment changes, species diverge from each other, as the branches and twigs of a growing tree do. Primates are the diverse order of mammals to which we belong and in which we have a particular interest. We can view these nearly 300 species as making up an orchestra, rendering a symphony in which each species plays one variation on the overarching primate theme. In this section, we explore the Mozartian variations on that theme sounded by prosimians, tarsiers, New and Old World monkeys, and our closest relations, the apes.

In another metaphor, originated by biologist Evelyn Hutchinson, primates are mammalian actors playing out their roles in the ecological theater with a backdrop of lianas, multistoried high-rise forests with dispersed treasures of fruits, flowers, new leaves, seeds, insects, and gums. Primates evolved as tropical animals, living in rain forests, moving at all levels in the trees, at times on the ground, and relying on plants for food. Their early appearance coincided with the expansion and success of the angiosperms. New plant life provided food sources for primates, and primates dispersed the seeds, a codependency, each relying on the other (4-1).

Fossils of archaic primates of the North American and Eurasian Paleocene epoch resemble later primates in their dentition and ear region anatomy, but lack the entire suite of characteristics that define later forms. Like tree shrews, these early primates may have lived in the low bushy understory of the developing forests, and their dentition suggests plant foods were a dietary item (4-2). Eocene primates, equipped with grasping hands and feet, likely moved up into the trees and eventually to the canopy and climax forest. These early Eocene primates are recognizable as prosimians. Some of them may be related to living prosimians and tarsiers, and fragmentary fossils from Asia and North Africa may be evidence of anthropoids (4-3).

The family tree of living prosimians and tarsiers is constructed on the basis of molecular, anatomical and fossil, and behavioral evidence. The diversity of species represents a broad adaptive mosaic. Many are nocturnal and small in body size (4-4). Several small nocturnal prosimian species inhabit West African forests. Each of the three galagos and two pottos has a distinct niche based upon locomotion, diet, and predator avoidance. The explosive hopping of the galagos contrasts with the slow climbing and stealth of the pottos (4-5).

Prosimian primates crossed from Africa to Madagascar over water when the land masses were closer. Similar to the finches that arrived in the Galápagos Islands and diversified from a common ancestor into 13 species (1-17), the lemurs evolved into about 45 species without competition from day-living primates like monkeys. Some 15 species of extinct lemurs, slow moving and terrestrial, were easy targets for human hunters who arrived more than 1500 years ago. The living aye-ayes, bamboo-eating lemurs, and the pollinating ruffed lemurs illustrate a sample of these island primates (4-6). Day-living ringtailed lemurs live in large social groups and resemble monkeys in their social organization and behavior. They show little sexual dimorphism, and females are dominant to males. As part of their reproductive pattern, adult females have feeding priority over males, ensuring that they have adequate food for reproduction (4-7).

Tarsiers share some anatomical features with prosimians and some with anthropoids. Their leaping specialization illustrates how locomotion contributes to survival and reproduction (4-8). Anthropoids represent an adaptive radiation of day-living fruit eaters with color vision. They differ from prosimians in anatomy and behavioral expression (4-9). The fossil record of anthropoids is best preserved in the Fayum of Egypt (4-10). Although anthropoids split from prosimians about 50 mya and a few appear in the Eocene, not until the Oligocene are they well represented in the fossil record and recognized morphologically as anthropoids.

In South America, New World monkeys appear suddenly in fossil deposits of Bolivia and Chile with no prior fossil evidence of prosimian ancestors. Molecular and paleontological evidence point to an African origin for the platyrrhines and a subsequent dispersion across Atlantic waters (4-11). In the last 10 to 20 million years platyrrhine monkeys achieved considerable diversity, about 5 subfamilies, with variations in fruit eating and social behavior (4-12). The smallest and most diverse group, the tamarins and marmosets (callithricines), have clawlike nails for clinging to tree trunks to eat sap and insects; infant care is communal and usually only 1 female in the group reproduces (4-13). Among titi monkeys, the adult male specializes in taking care of the relatively large, fast-growing infant while the lactating female spends her time feeding in order to produce sufficient milk (4-14).

Other New World monkeys are larger in body size and show interesting variations on the platyrrhine monkey theme. Saki monkeys (pitheciines) employ unusual dental adaptations for gaining access to the soft seed beneath the hard external covering and are known as seed predators (4-15). Squirrel and capuchin monkeys (cebines) are noted for their curiosity, incessant motion, aggressive foraging, and manipulative skills in their active search for all kinds of prey including insects, frogs, and small mammals (4-16). The largest bodied monkeys (atelines) have prehensile tails. Howler and spider monkeys contrast in their forelimb use and in their level of activity. The laid-back howler monkeys interact with other groups through their howling roars and eat a lower quality leaf diet than the more fruit-eating and higher energy spider monkeys (4-17).

New and Old World monkeys differ in anatomical details of their cranial and dental anatomy, tails, and in range of habitats (4-18). Neotropical monkeys are more strictly arboreal, tropical, and fruit eaters, whereas Old World monkeys successfully live in temperate regions and at high altitudes in the trees and on the ground. Old World monkeys live throughout Africa and Asia (4-19). The two major subfamilies of Old World monkeys differ in their foraging patterns; the cercopithecines have cheek pouches to hold food for later processing; the colobines have specialized stomachs for digesting quantities of lower quality foods, such as leaves and unripe fruit (4-20).

In equatorial Africa, the array of guenons (*Cercopithecus*, about 25 species) with their distinctly marked faces and bodies share similarities in diet and locomotion; it is not unusual to find several species occupying the same forest, separated by slight differences in the composition of their diets (4-21). The leaf monkeys (colobines) of Africa are sympatric but divide up the arboreal habitat by frequenting different levels of the forest and by eating distinct combinations of leaves, seeds, and fruits (4-22). In Asia, the hanuman langur of India is a single species, highly variable in body size, habitat, social organization, and social interaction. The ecological variation of this species has been not been fully studied, partly due to an overemphasis on male killing of infants. The significance of this behavior ("infanticide") needs to be placed into the broader context of ecological and behavioral studies that consider all age and sex classes (4-23). The macaques further illustrate the extreme adaptability of some primates. They have radiated into 15 species, widely distributed across Asia; 4 species live so successfully around human habitation that they are accurately described as "weed species" (4-24).

Old World monkeys as well as apes and humans share a common catarrhine ancestor and many biological features, but the three groups are distinguished by their locomotor-feeding adaptations. Trunk proportions and the position of the shoulder joints illustrate monkey-ape/human differences. In the trunk the ape ancestry of the human species is clearly seen (4-25). The difference between monkeys and apes is further apparent in their feeding postures and in the anatomy of the limb bones and joint motions; apes have a stable above- and below-the-branch reach due to increased range of movement in the shoulder joint. Dentally monkeys and apes also differ. The Old World monkeys' bilophodont or crested molar teeth, contrast with the low, bunodont cusps of apes (4-26).

Monkeys and apes can be distinguished from each other on the basis of their dentition by the early Miocene. When catarrhine monkeys make their appearance in the African fossil record of 15 to 20 million years ago, there are only a few species. At the end of the Miocene and early Pliocene, their numbers and distribution increase greatly (4-27). The fossil record of apes is nearly the opposite. Apes flourish in the middle Miocene in Europe, Africa, and Asia, but their numbers diminish rapidly by the end of the Miocene. Miocene fossil apes reveal little of human forebears (4-28). The Miocene fossil *Proconsul* illustrates how scientific discovery and interpretation can unfold over several decades, with chance events playing a role (4-29).

Living apes, few in species number compared to the diversity of monkeys, nonetheless vary widely in body size and social organization (4-30). The small-bodied gibbons with 11 species are similar in diet and size and composition of their social groups. But when 2 are sympatric, their differences in diet and activity bring out the fine points of each species' adaptation (4-31). Orangutans inhabit the tropical forests of Sumatra and Borneo where their main food item, fruit, fluctuates dramatically. When fruit is abundant, they store fat that helps them through low fruit periods. This ability to survive in a fluctuating environment has resulted in unusual patterns of reproduction: widely spaced birth intervals and two kinds of reproducing males. If orangutans can survive in the face of habitat destruction, we may be able to unravel the puzzle of these fascinating primates (4-32).

The African apes, our closest living relatives, illustrate three patterns of sexual dimorphism. Females and males of a species can differ to varying degrees in body and tooth size, a point that must be kept in mind when trying to assign sex or species based on only fragmentary fossil bones and teeth (4-33). Research on gorillas continues to open new insights on these noble creatures. Altitude is an important determinant of their diet and daily range. Like their cousins the chimpanzees, gorillas prefer fruit when they can get it, but when it is scarce, they turn to the abundant herbs and leaves (4-34).

The two species of chimpanzee, *Pan paniscus* and *Pan troglodytes*, share many anatomical and behavioral features, yet differ dramatically in social relationships within and between communities. *Pan paniscus* females bond closely to each other, whereas male *Pan troglodytes* are closely bonded. The bipedal patterns of each species further illustrate the differences in their social lives (4-35).

Primatologists have had difficulty coming to agreement on nontechnical names for the two species. *Pan troglodytes* has been referred to as "common chimpanzee," but "common" is unsatisfactory because chimpanzees are endangered and are by no means common. The specific name, *Pan paniscus,* was originally assigned based on their gracile skulls and smaller teeth (paniscus, "little Pan") hence, "pygmy chimpanzees." But because the two species overlap in body size (4-33), "pygmy" is a misnomer. The frequently used "bonobo" is even more misleading because the term obscures the anatomical similarities and common evolutionary history of the two chimpanzees. The solution adopted here is also suggested by primatologist Adrian Kortlandt: "chimpanzee" is generic and includes both species. When referring to one species or the other, the terms *Pan troglodytes* or "robust chimpanzee" and *Pan paniscus* or "gracile chimpanzee" are used. These terms accurately reflect the anatomical differences and maintain the integrity of their close genetic relationship.

Chimpanzees and human had a common ancestor about 5 mya and share many physical features. Chimpanzees are our closest living relatives, and the total DNA in our genomes differs by only 1.5%. That small genetic difference, however, blueprints a human brain 3 times larger and a body redesigned by natural selection for bipedal locomotion (4-36). We are linked to our primate past but have departed in significant ways to lead very different lives.

RAIN FORESTS, PLANTS, AND PRIMATES

The diversity of extinct and living primate species can be traced to their adaptations to life in the forests (3-3). The origin and radiation of the primate order likely paralleled the expansion of the angiosperms, the flowering plants, according to anthropologist Robert Sussman. He proposed that primates and tropical rain forests evolved together, each helping to create the other.

As angiosperms began to replace the coniferous forests of the Cretaceous, they constituted new food sources for insects, birds, and mammals. With an agile locomotor system (3-7) and grasping feet and hands (3-11), primates were equipped to move through the trees and forage at the ends of branches on the seasonal flowers, fruits, new leaves, and buds. As they came to rely on these new dietary resources, primates became dispersers of the plants' seeds.

Color the parts of angiosperms at the top of the plate. Then, as you read, color the plant parts and insect as well as the primates eating them in the composite forest.

Flowering plants go through several life phases with structures that primates like to eat: flowers, nectar, fruits, seeds, floral and leaf buds, leaves, woody stems, saps, and gums. Plant parts offer nutritional sources of protein, several forms of carbohydrates, fats, vitamins, minerals, trace elements, and water.

In rain forests, leaves are available all year around; they offer a source of vitamins and minerals such as calcium, phosphorous, and magnesium. For example, sifakas (a[1]) eat young leaves, which are a good source of protein and water and some structural carbohydrates, that is, fiber made up of cell walls or cellulose. Mature leaves contain more protein; older plants also have thicker and less flexible cell walls. Many primates cannot digest mature leaves, although colobine monkeys (b[1]) have specialized stomachs, which help to break down and digest them (4-20).

In general, wood or bark has little nutritional value. Just beneath the bark are the protein-rich phloem and inner cambium. Cambium is the site of new cell growth, with thin cell walls. Gorillas (c[1]) utilize this food by first peeling away the inedible woody outside.

Sap consists of water, minerals, and fruit sugars (one form of carbohydrate). Gum, a product of specialized cells produced by the plant in response to injury or infection, is a valuable source of carbohydrates as well as some protein, fiber, and minerals; it is an important dietary component for primates and is a specialty of marmoset monkeys (d[1], 4-13).

Enjoyed by the mouse lemur (e[1]), flowers contain fruit sugars in the nectar and high water content. Orangutans (f[1]) relish ripe fruits that have highly succulent flesh which provides a rich source of fruit sugars, citric acid, and water. Fruits, though, have little protein, fat, or structural carbohydrates. Figs, with high calcium levels, appear to be a fallback food when other fruits are scarce.

Seeds are high in fat and starch, and some provide protein or vitamins; they contain little water, minerals, or sugars. A protective covering often allows seeds to pass undigested through the gut of an animal. Other seeds are filled with bitter compounds so that animals will spit them out before swallowing the flesh. Some animals, like saki monkeys (g[1]), specialize in eating seeds (4-15). Herbs are a source of water and protein and occur in patches in the light gaps on the forest floor. They are consumed by mandrills (h[1]) and gorillas.

The life cycles of insects are intimately tied to plants, and insects also serve as food for primates, especially for squirrel monkeys (i[1]). Insects provide high-quality protein, fats, fluids, and minerals; insect exoskeletons provide carbohydrates, and animal bodies often contain essential trace elements lacking in many plants.

Because of the many kinds of distinct plant parts made available by the angiosperms and their great number of species, primate diets are diverse enough so that closely related species can share the same environment by eating different combinations of foods or different parts of the same plants (4-5, 4-6).

Color the seedlings germinating on the forest floor.

The seeds of early angiosperms were small, pollinated by unspecialized insects, and dispersed by the wind. As larger trees evolved and formed the upper story canopy and climax vegetation, they could afford to invest more in individual seeds and so produced larger seeds. Larger seeds, however, are more difficult to disperse and require larger bodied animals to scatter them. Forest primates do the job effectively.

Primates easily travel through trees and on to the ends of branches using a variety of postures and movements. With the assistance of color vision, they are attracted to the fruits' bright reds, oranges, and yellows. An animal selects and picks a fruit and consumes the fleshy part. The seeds are usually dropped, spit out, or swallowed. If swallowed, the seeds pass through a primate's gut in hours or days. When eliminated, the seeds are likely to be deposited some distance away from the parent tree. The seeds might germinate if not destroyed during digestion or scavenged by insects or seed predators on the forest floor. Primates further facilitate seed dispersal when they knock down or drop uneaten foods to the forest floor; this allows other animals to consume the fruits and scatter the seeds.

Field studies on fruiting trees demonstrate that primates are responsible for moving large numbers of seeds. In a northern Costa Rican forest, ecologist Colin Chapman reports that 3 species, capuchin, howler, and spider monkeys, disperse over 5000 large seeds a day per square kilometer! Experiments indicate that some seeds germinate better after they have passed through the guts of primates. Large-bodied fruit-eating primates today are central for seed dispersal. This role may have originated in the Paleocene and is essential for maintaining plant health and diversity and for regenerating tropical forests.

RAIN FORESTS, PLANTS, AND PRIMATES

ANGIOSPERM PART/PRIMATE ✳
LEAF BUD/YOUNG LEAF$_{a,a^1}$
MATURE LEAF$_{b,b^1}$
WOODY STEM$_{c,c^1}$
SAP/GUM$_{d,d^1}$
FLOWER/NECTAR$_{e,e^1}$
FLESHY FRUIT$_{f,f^1}$
SEED$_{g,g^1}$
HERB$_{h,h^1}$
INSECT$_i$
SEEDLING$_j$

4-2
ARCHAIC PRIMATES IN THE PALEOCENE

As the large reptiles died out at the end of the Cretaceous, the last period of the Mesozoic era (1-21), the primitive angiosperms were no longer eaten and trampled by the giant herbivores. Angiosperms then began to dominate the landscape. Small nocturnal and insect-eating mammalian ancestors gave rise to many new forms of placental mammals. The molecular data suggest that by the end of the Cretaceous (70–80 mya) primates branched off from primitive placental mammals, presumably from a family within the Insectivora. These primate ancestors began to feed on the high-energy plant parts from the newly evolved flowers and seed coverings. Although the Paleocene is a time of experimentation in mammalian evolution, the origin of most of the modern orders can likely be traced back to this epoch.

The earliest fossil primatelike mammals of the Cenozoic (1-22) are the plesiadapiforms. These Paleocene primates are "archaic" in that they constitute a lineage separate from the later Eocene primates. No single Paleocene primate species has all of the bony characters that define the later true primates. Although the plesiadapiforms lack a postorbital bar (3-18), the structure of the ear region shows affinities with later primates (4-3). In addition, the molar teeth of plesiadapiforms are more similar to those of later primates than to any other mammalian order. Among these early primate experiments, locomotor agility, dental specializations, and diversity in body size indicate continuity with later primates.

Color the Paleocene time range gray. Color Paromomyidae on the family tree of plesiadapiform primates at the lower right. Then color the representative fossil *Purgatorius* and the arrow indicating its position on the map. Proceed in this manner as each fossil is discussed. Color the limb bones of *Plesiadapis* as well. Shading indicates the actual fossil discovered; the remainder is reconstructed.

Early primatelike fossils have been recovered from North American and Eurasian sites. During the Paleocene, the northern continents had a warm, tropical climate. At that time, the modern continents were closely connected to one another and formed what was almost a single continent, separated from the "island" continents in the southern hemisphere, such as Africa and South America. This may explain the "holarctic" distribution (entire northern hemisphere) of the Paleocene primates.

The fossil evidence consists primarily of dental remains with some cranial remains. Dental enamel is the hardest tissue in the mammalian body. Therefore, the early primate fossil record consists mainly of teeth. Five families of Paleocene primates are highlighted here. They include numerous species within the widespread and diverse Plesiadapiformes ("nearly like adapids"): Paromomyidae, Picrodontidae, Carpolestidae, Saxonellidae, and Plesiadapidae. In body size, these small mammals ranged from the size of a mouse lemur to the size of a domestic cat.

The genus *Purgatorius* (family Paromomyidae) is named for Purgatory Hill in Montana and is the oldest primatelike fossil yet discovered. The site is located in what is now the Rocky Mountain region. The Rockies had not yet reached their present heights, and the Paleocene climate was subtropical. This fossil is known only from a few teeth and the mandibular fragment shown here. The limited evidence suggests that *Purgatorius* was primatelike in its diet. In mammals evolving away from a diet of insects with hard exoskeletons to one of fruit or leaves, the molars tend to lose their high, spiky cusps and become broader to provide more grinding or pulping surface (3-6). *Purgatorius'* molars suggest these changes were occurring.

Palaechthon, a member of the same family, was also found in the Rocky Mountain region. A bit younger, 60 mya as compared to 65 to 70 mya, its remains include the earliest known primatelike fossil skull. The face, like that of other early mammals, is long and lies directly in front of the small braincase. However, its molar tooth cusps are even lower than those of *Purgatorius*, suggesting that it too ate fruit and other vegetation.

Picrodus, from western North America, was first thought to be a bat because of the notch on the tongue side of the first molar tooth. However, overall tooth and jaw structure indicates that *Picrodus* is primatelike with a paromomyid ancestor.

The carpolestids ("fruit stealers"), here represented by the genus *Carpodaptes*, have an unusual last premolar with a high, bladelike crest. This unusual premolar is similar to that of some living marsupials, which use the crest to slice through the tough fibrous husk of an avocadolike fruit.

A single species, *Saxonella* (Saxonellidae) from a late Paleocene site in Saxony, Germany, has incisors like the plesiadapids but a bladelike premolar like the carpolestids.

Plesiadapis skulls and skeletons have been found in North America and western Europe. At least 15 species have been identified, making this group the most diverse and best known of early primate fossils. The large rodentlike incisors protrude in front; the lost lower canine and premolar provide a large gap (diastema), and the upper canine is reduced in size.

From the features preserved in these Paleocene fossils, the Paleocene primatelike mammals illustrate the "mosaic" nature of evolution. The characters that we use to distinguish primates from other mammals are not all present in any single fossil. However, this mosaic is typical of any early stage in mammalian evolution, when the modern orders of mammals were evolving. Some paleontologists exclude the plesiadapiforms from the primate order. It is logical, however, to look at the Paleocene primatelike mammals as experiments in becoming primates. The range of specializations, from insect eating to fruit eating and an omnivorous diet, suggests a period of rapid diversification in plant products. What appears certain is that from among these Paleocene "newcomers" the true primates "arrived" by the Eocene.

PALEOCENE PRIMATES

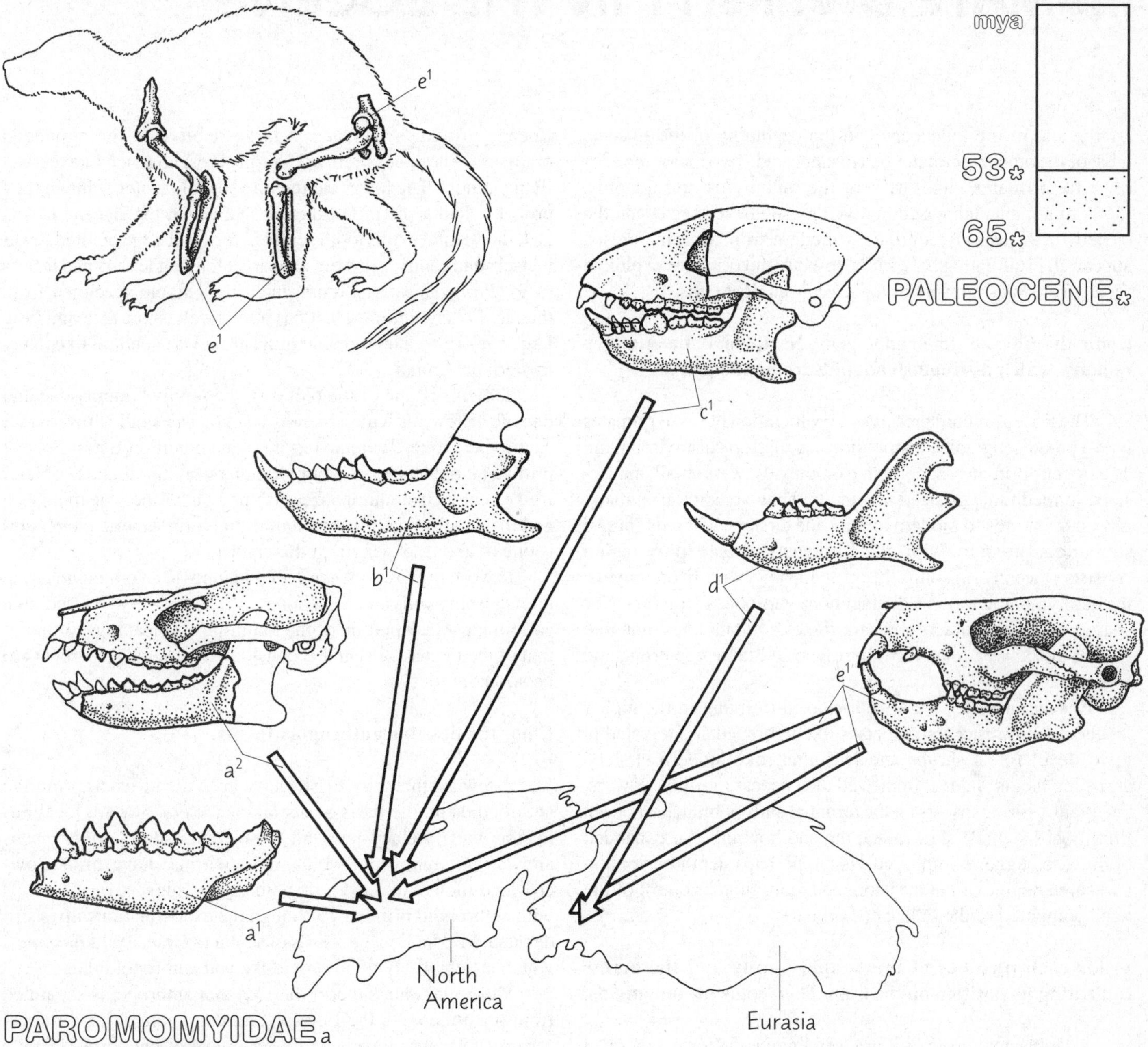

mya

53 ✴

65 ✴

PALEOCENE ✴

e^1

c^1

b^1

d^1

e^1

a^2

a^1

North America

Eurasia

PAROMOMYIDAE $_a$

PURGATORIUS $_{a^1}$

PALAECHTHON $_{a^2}$

PICRODONTIDAE $_b$

PICRODUS $_{b^1}$

CARPOLESTIDAE $_c$

CARPODAPTES $_{c^1}$

SAXONELLIDAE $_d$

SAXONELLA $_{d^1}$

PLESIADAPIDAE $_e$

PLESIADAPIS $_{e^1}$

PLESIADAPIFORMS ✴

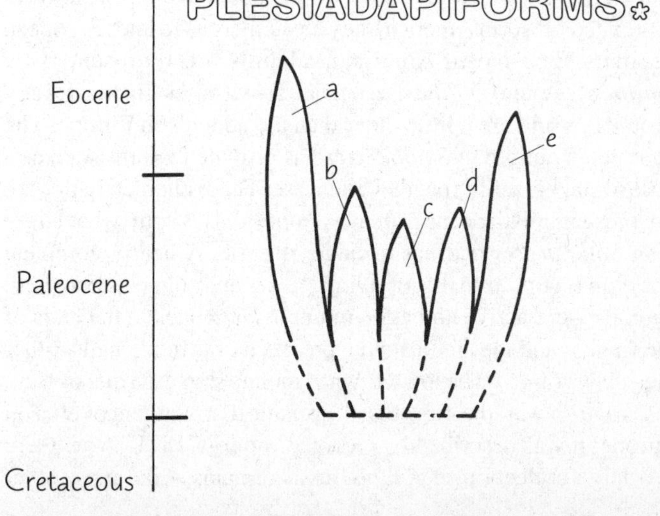

Eocene

Paleocene

Cretaceous

a

b

c

d

e

PRIMATE DIVERSITY IN THE EOCENE

By the end of the Paleocene and the beginning of the Eocene, most of the archaic primates had disappeared. Two major families of "true primates" had arrived, the omomyids and adapids. Flowering plants increased in diversity and in seed size, and the closed forest canopy, similar to modern tropical rain forests, appeared. Fruit-eating bats, birds, insects, and primates exploited seeds, fruits, and flowers of the diverse angiosperms.

Color the Eocene time range gray. Next, color the auditory regions, which distinguish adapids from omomyids.

The Eocene record preserves a proliferation of fossil primates with a broad geographic distribution in a subtropical environment. The Eocene primates, adapids and omomyids, were small, mouse-sized to medium, cat-sized mammals. They are similar in many physical features to modern lemurs and tarsiers. Adapids share a similar ear structure with modern lemurs; the auditory region consists of a bony ring only, the ectotympanic bone. In omomyids, the ectotympanic forms a distinct bony ear tube, a structure they share with living tarsiers and catarrhines. Omomyids, compared to adapids, have a relatively short face and large eye orbits and brain.

Eocene primates were well adapted to living in the higher levels of the forests; some species likely foraged and traveled in lower level forest shrubs and leaf litter, like modern tarsiers. Grasping hands and feet improved their access to fruits, flowers, and plant-visiting insects on the terminal ends of branches. Fossil limb bones suggest skill in leaping and hopping. An expanded brain case suggests improved vision, perhaps depth perception and some degree of color vision, and more motor control of the hand compared to the Paleocene primates.

Color each member of the adapid family and the arrow indicating its position on the map. Then color the omomyids.

Adapids and omomyids are well known in North American and European localities. Although the adapidae appear to have originated in North America, they are numerous in later European deposits. The North American adapids are represented by *Smilodectes* and *Notharctus* from fossil sites in the Rocky Mountains and are a little older than the adapids in Europe. The complete cranium of *Smilodectes* has primate features such as a postorbital bar and expanded braincase. These characteristics are not present in Paleocene primates. *Notharctus* is somewhat larger than *Smilodectes* and has a longer muzzle. A nearly complete skeleton is similar to that of living lemurs and suggests that these animals were active and agile in trees. The bones at the ends of the fingers and toes indicate the presence of primate nails rather than claws (3-11). The low-crowned molars suggest a diet of fruit.

Adapis was the first fossil primate that was uncovered in Europe; it was described by George Cuvier in 1821. Now there is a large collection of *Adapis* fossil remains. Like most other Eocene primates, the face is large relative to the expanded braincase. The cheek teeth are sharply crested, much like teeth in living lemurs. The lower canines are spadelike, not pointed: they probably had a scraping function. However, the Eocene fossils lack the "dental comb/tooth scraper" formed by the pointed lower incisors and canines, present in nearly all living lemurs and lorises (4-9). *Pronycticebus* is represented by a single specimen from the late Eocene in France; it has a relatively short face and very large eye orbits, a feature that indicates it was noctural like many modern prosimians (3-17).

Tetonius is one of the oldest of the family Omomyidae and one of the few for which there is a skull. The skull is just over 3 centimeters long. *Tetonius* has a unique dentition for an Eocene primate: large incisors and small molars, similar to those of later fruit eaters such as chimpanzees, some South American monkeys, and the small-bodied mouse lemur. In North America, *Omomys* is one of about 12 genera in this family.

In western Europe, *Necrolemur* belongs to an omomyid group known from skulls and limb bones. *Necrolemur* had a fused tibia and fibula, an adaptation of the hindlimbs for leaping, similar to that of the tarsier (4-8) and is considered by some researchers to be ancestral to it.

Color the possible anthropoid fossils.

A few fragmentary fossils have been identified as primitive anthropoids on the basis of dental characters. Several localities in Asia have yielded jaw and tooth fragments. *Amphipithecus* and *Pondaungia* from Mynanmar (Burma) have broad low-crowned molars and deep mandibles that suggest relationships with anthropoid primates, although the exact relationship is still debated. Middle Eocene fossils of southern China yield *Eosimias*, which is dentally both omomyidlike and anthropoidlike.

Molecular data support the idea that anthropoids separated from prosimians by the Eocene, and that tarsiers (haplorhines) separated from anthropoids by the mid-Eocene about 45 mya (3-1). Therefore, the possibility of anthropoids in the Eocene is not unexpected. However, fossil evidence is restricted to a few fragmentary dental remains that suggest, but do not fully support, their anthropoid status based on morphology.

By the end of the Eocene, the North American primates disappeared along with the few remaining archaic primates and were replaced by rodents. The dental, cranial, and post-cranial remains of Eocene primates suggest that, like their modern lemur and tarsier counterparts, they were fully adapted to feeding on a variety of plants and insects found on terminal branches of the angiosperms. Along with bats and birds, primates were linked in a tight relationship with the plants (4-1). Plants provided food; primates acted as primary seed dispersers. Omomyids may be ancestral to tarsiers and may also have given rise to the monkeylike fossil primates of the Oligocene (4-10).

EOCENE PRIMATES

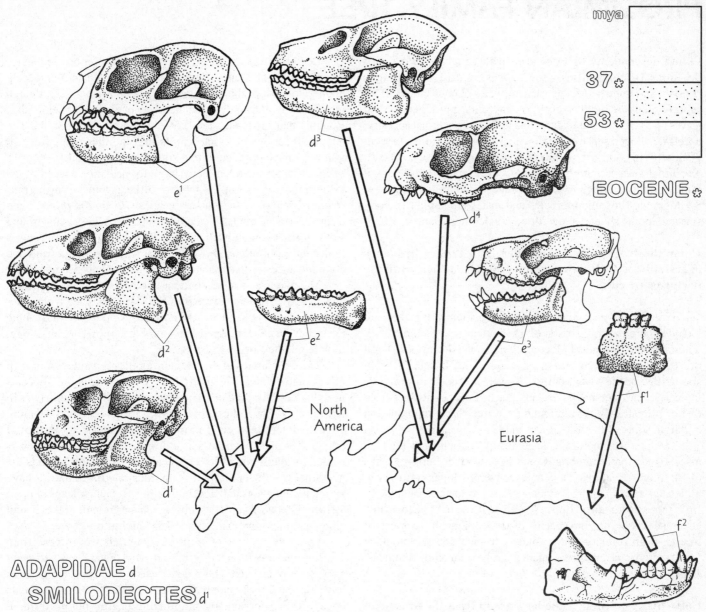

mya

37 ✴

53 ✴

EOCENE ✴

North America

Eurasia

ADAPIDAE d
SMILODECTES d^1
NOTHARCTUS d^2
ADAPIS d^3
PRONYCTICEBUS d^4
OMOMYIDAE e
TETONIUS e^1
OMOMYS e^2
NECROLEMUR e^3
ANTHROPOID? f
AMPHIPITHECUS f^1
EOSIMIAS f^2

AUDITORY REGION ✴
TEMPORAL a ECTOTYMPANIC c
PETROSAL b

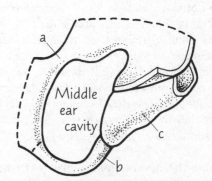

Middle ear cavity

Middle ear cavity

ADAPIDAE d OMOMYIDAE e

4-4
PROSIMIAN FAMILY TREE

Living descendents of Eocene primates include two major divisions (superfamilies): the lorises, pottos, and galagos (Lorisoidea) and the Madagascar primates (Lemuroidea). Both superfamilies are omnivorous; they eat fruits, gums, insects, and leaves (4-5). They share features that indicate a nocturnal ancestry: a well-developed sense of smell with a moist rhinarium and scent glands (3-15) and a tapetum in the retina of the eye (3-17). Nocturnal species tend to be solitary foragers or live in small family groups. Living prosimians range in size from 40 grams to 8 kilograms. Prosimian females and males are similar in body size and tooth size and show little sexual dimorphism (3-30).

Color the tree shrew (Tupaoidea) and tarsier branches (Tarsioidea). Color the moon symbols, which indicate nocturnal species.

Tree shrews and tarsiers are not prosimians, but they are included here for comparison (3-1). Tree shrews resemble early mammals and primates in locomotion (3-7) and dentition. Until the 1980s, they were classified as primates based on brain similarities of the visual cortex. Newer molecular information indicates that tree shrews are an ancient lineage, distinct from that of primates. Behavioral studies of tree shrew reproduction highlight some of the differences in the two lineages.

Tarsiers are nocturnal, specialized jumpers that feed on insects and small vertebrates, and live in small family groups (4-8). In these features, tarsiers resemble prosimians. However, molecular and anatomical evidence, such as the ear canal (4-3), link tarsiers to anthropoids, and the term "haplorhine" encompasses both. Five species of tarsiers inhabit a variety of forests, from primary and secondary tropical forests, montane forest, to coastal mangrove glades on the islands of Southeast Asia.

Color the separation of the loris group from the prosimian ancestral line gray. Color the loris branches (Lorisoidea).

The lorisoids include two nocturnal subgroups (families) that separated from each other about 50 mya. One group, the Galagidae, includes the galagos or bushbabies; the other group, the Lorisidae, includes the lorises and pottos. Both families are nocturnal, omnivorous, and similar in cranial and dental morphology, but differ in their locomotor adaptations (4-5). The Galagidae, found only in sub-Saharan Africa include at least 15 species. Galagos are skilled jumpers and have large mobile ears for hearing insect prey. The Lorisidae are slow climbers; they include slender lorises from India and Sri Lanka (not illustrated here, but see 3-6), pottos from Africa, and slow lorises from Southeast Asia, about 6 species in all.

Color the diverse lemur group (Lemuroidea) as each is discussed.

Lemurs are endemic to Madagascar and are found no place else on earth. The name "lemur" (Latin for "ghost") is loosely applied to most of the primates that live in Madagascar, though technically it refers only to the members of the family Lemuridae. Roughly half the lemurs are active at night, half during the day. About 30 species of living lemurs in 5 families range from 40 grams for the mouse lemur to 8 kilograms for the indri. About 15 extinct species included many large forms, some exceeding 50 kilograms, for example, a baboonlike ground-living lemur (*Hadropithecus*), a suspensory species (*Paleopropithecus*), and a gorilla-sized lemur (*Archaeoindris*), perhaps like a giant ground sloth in its locomotor adaptation. Primatologist Anne Yoder's molecular information shows that the lemurs evolved from one common ancestor that reached Madagascar about 55 mya (4-6).

The aye-aye (Daubentoniidae) consists of 1 living species and an extinct species twice its size. They separated from other lemur lineages about 50 mya. Aye-ayes lack premolars and canine teeth, have well-developed incisors, big floppy ears, and long, mobile middle fingers (4-6).

The remaining 4 of the 5 lemur families separated from each other about 40 mya. The indrid family consist of about 5 species in 3 genera: the indri (*Indri*), the largest of living lemurs, lives in territorial family groups and is known for its eerie and haunting vocalizations given each morning to broadcast its territorial boundaries and location. The diurnal sifaka (*Propithecus*) is named for the sound of its alarm call. The smallest indrid is the nocturnal woolly lemur (*Avahi*, not illustrated). All indrids have extremely long legs and are capable of spectacular leaps of up to 10 meters between vertical supports. On the ground, sifakas bound along in an upright position on their hindlimbs.

Sportive lemurs (*Lepilemur*), which weigh less than 1 kilogram, are found throughout Madagascar in 7 distinct subspecies or species. Their diet consists mainly of leaves (over 90%), unusual for a mammal of such small size. These animals cope with a poor diet by minimizing energy output through inactivity, especially in the cooler season at the time of greatest stress. Dubbed a "vertical clinger and sleeper," lepilemurs are nocturnal, relatively solitary, and communicate with loud screeching calls.

The nocturnal dwarf and mouse lemurs (Cheirogaleidae) consist of about 8 species; the pygmy mouse lemur (40 g) is the smallest living primate. Dwarf lemurs take advantage of abundant fruit during the wet season, and store fat in the tail. During the 6-month dry season, they hole up in hollow tree trunks and sleep.

The family Lemuridae consists of about 10 species, widely distributed throughout the island. Most species are diurnal and arboreal; some species spend time on the ground. The ruffed lemur is the earliest branch and the heaviest species (about 4 kg, 4-6); the bamboo or gentle lemurs (3 species, 4-6) are specialized for eating bamboo and seem to be closest to the ringtailed lemurs, the most terrestrial of the lemurs (4-7). Other lemur species include the brown, black, red-bellied, mongoose, and crowned lemurs (not illustrated). Several species manifest different patterns of fur coloration for each sex, or sexual dichromatism (3-30).

PROSIMIAN FAMILY TREE

TREE SHREW a   LEMUR GROUP ✷   RUFFED LEMUR h

TARSIER b   AYE-AYE d   BAMBOO LEMUR h^1

LORIS GROUP ✷   INDRI e   RINGTAILED LEMUR h^2

GALAGO c   SIFAKA e^1

POTTO c^1

SLOW LORIS c^2 SPORTIVE LEMUR f

DWARF LEMUR g

MOUSE LEMUR g^1

PROSIMIAN ANCESTORS ✷

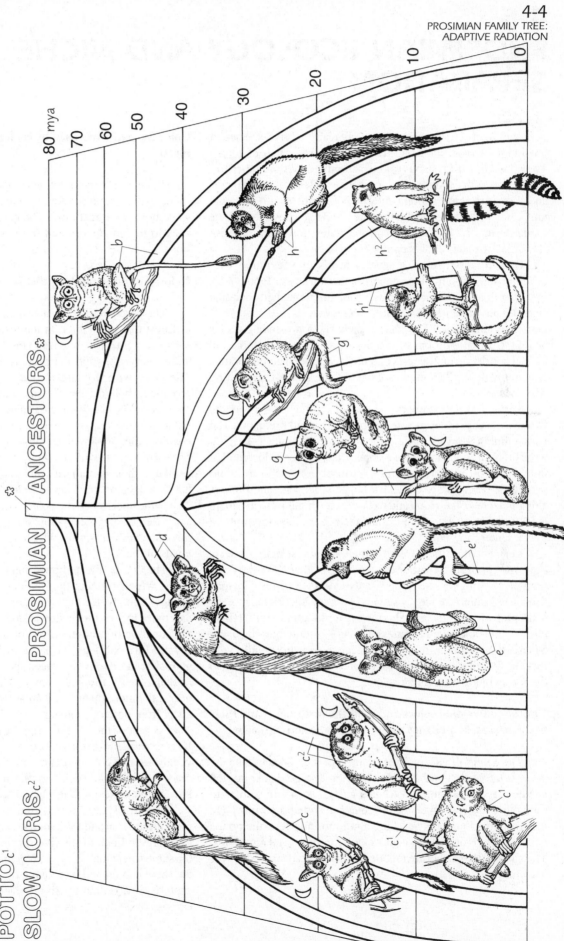

4-4

PROSIMIAN FAMILY TREE:
ADAPTIVE RADIATION

4-5
PROSIMIAN ECOLOGY AND NICHE SEPARATION

In some West African rain forests, as many as five species of prosimians live in the same trees in the same patch of forest. They successfully survive and reproduce without directly competing with each other over resources. Because the galagos and pottos are active at night, they do not compete with birds and monkeys, which also inhabit the forest and eat many of the same foods during the day. This plate illustrates how each of these nocturnal primates avoids competing with the others.

Rain forests comprise several levels of vegetation with different sizes of climbing supports and a variety of foods (3-3). French primatologist Pierre Charles-Dominique studied nocturnal primates in Gabon forests. This habitat houses 120 species of mammals, including 17 primate species. The 5 prosimian species belong to 2 major groups of nocturnal prosimians: the lorises in Gabon consisting of 2 species of pottos (pottos and golden pottos, which are also called angwantibos) and the galagos, consisting of 3 species.

Very different locomotor adaptations influence the way the two groups capture prey, select foods, and avoid predators. The slow-climbing lorises make direct and secure contact, keeping three limbs in contact with the branch. Their deliberate locomotion thus relies on stealth to forage on insect prey and to avoid predators. Galagos are explosive hoppers, leapers, and runners along branches. Their long and well-muscled hindlimbs give them leverage and power in jumping and their short, light forelimbs, a lower center of gravity.

Lorises detect their prey by smell, usually selecting insects that are ignored by other insect eaters: the slow-moving, repugnant, stinging caterpillers, ants, and centipedes. Galagos listen for the high-frequency sounds of the speedier flying insects: orthoptera (crickets, grasshoppers), lepidoptera (butterflies, moths), and coleoptera (beetles). Galagos capture bugs by using a stereotypic motion in which they lunge forward rapidly with feet firmly grasping a branch and hands widely splayed to grab the flying bug with a single swipe.

Choose contrasting colors and color the prosimians and their body masses. Notice they are not drawn exactly to scale.

The demidoff galago is the smallest of the 5 species, and the potto is the largest and 18 times heavier. The golden potto, the needle-clawed galago, and Allen's galago are more similar to each other in size. Notice the difference in body proportions: the galagos have long tails and long hindlimbs and feet; the pottos have short tails and nearly equal length forelimbs and hindlimbs. The galagos' large ears are mobile and act like radar receivers for detecting prey (3-19).

Color the pathways used by each animal moving through the forest.

The potto, the demidoff galago, and the needle-clawed galago spend their time in the forest canopy between 5 and 40 meters, well above the forest floor. The golden potto and Allen's galago stick to the understory and in the low bushes nearer the forest floor.

Color the components of diet for each prosimian.

The potential diet of each species is influenced by the level of forest that it inhabits. In the forest canopy, the three species eat some gums, the thick sap beneath the bark, as well as fruits and insects, although the proportion of each food type varies. The potto with the largest body size eats mainly fruit which provide carbohydrates; the tiny demidoff galago feeds primarily on insects. The needle-clawed galago eats large amounts of gums. Its needlelike "claws" are actually keeled nails, a specialization enabling this prosimian to move along smooth surfaces to find and extract gums without slipping and falling. Their "claws" are similar to those of tamarins and marmosets, which also use their hands to feed on gums and employ a vertical posture (4-13).

In the understory, the golden potto feeds primarily on insects, and Allen's galago eats large amounts of fruits. Neither one of these species eats gums, which are only available in the higher levels of the forest.

The two families of prosimians avoid predators in different ways, which reflects the distinct locomotor pattern of each. Galagos quickly flee from predators with leaps and bounds; pottos and other lorises move slowly and silently or "freeze" to avoid the attention of arboreal carnivores such as the palm civet. The cryptic loris strategy works only in areas where these small animals can effectively screen themselves in the dark shadows of dense, leafy forest coverage. The fast-moving galagos may utilize the more open forest areas because they can quickly leap away from potential danger.

As part of their low profile, being discrete and unobserved, lorises rely more on olfaction and scent marking than on vocalization to communicate with each other. Galagos also scent mark but are more social and noisier than lorises because they have a quick escape route should danger threaten.

This case study illustrates the diversity in locomotor supports, plant production and food sources, and life forms that exist within rain forests. Each of the five species of prosimians that occupy the same forest makes a living by inhabiting different "floors" of the same habitat and by moving in contrasting ways to feed and capture prey. Within the forest, each species with its own niche carries out its own "job."

GALAGOS AND POTTOS

LORISES⁕
POTTOa
GOLDEN
POTTOb

GALAGOS⁕
DEMIDOFFc
NEEDLE-CLAWEDd
ALLEN'Se

DIET⁕
GUMSf
FRUITSg
INSECTSh

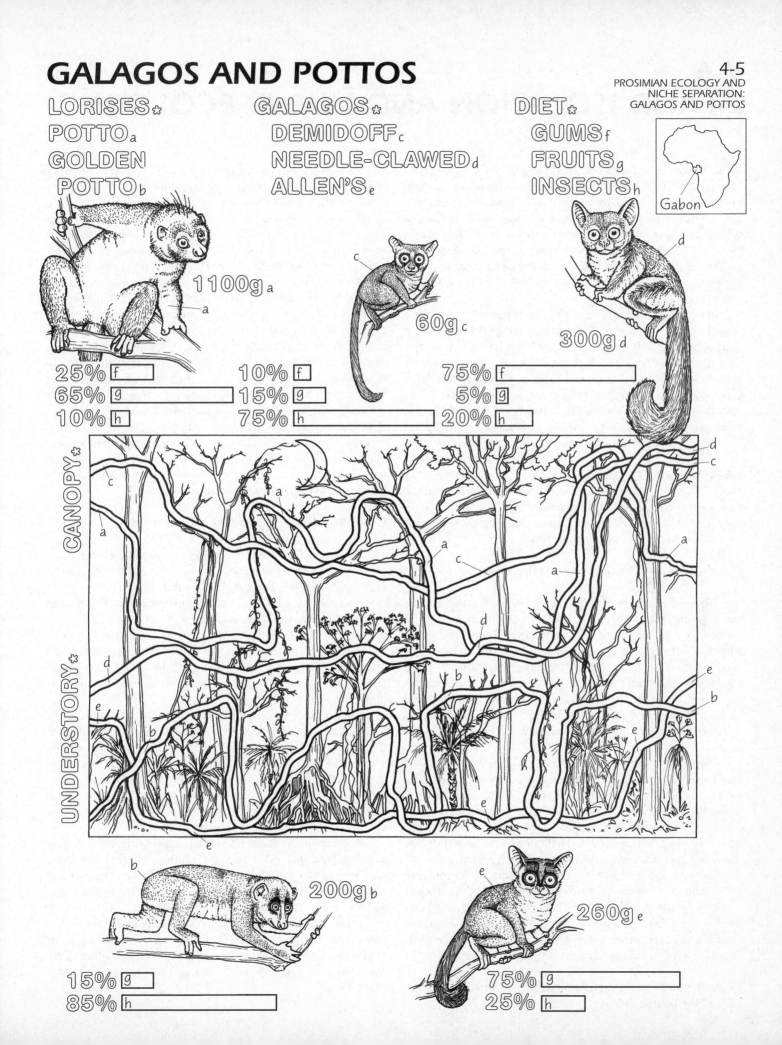

Gabon

1100ga

60gc

300gd

25% f
65% g
10% h

10% f
15% g
75% h

75% f
5% g
20% h

CANOPY⁕

UNDERSTORY⁕

200gb

260ge

15% g
85% h

75% g
25% h

ISLAND ISOLATION AND LEMUR ECOLOGY

Isolated from the African continent more than 100 mya (1-18), Madagascar is an evolutionist's delight. The island is 1700 kilometers long, 575 kilometers at its widest point, and 390 kilometers across the Mozambique Channel from continental Africa. The long central plateau has peaks of over 2000 meters; rainfall is seasonal, alternating with long dry periods in the west, south, and extreme north. The Mozambique Channel probably provided a corridor for colonizing species from the mainland about 60 mya.

Plant life includes a diversity of native palms, 1000 species of orchids, and 7 species of baobab tree, compared to 1 baobab species on the whole African continent! Few of the bird species feed on nectar or fruit, and there are no woodpeckers. Mammals include 3 species of fruit bats, and 7 species of mongoose-related carnivores. In an amazing adaptive radiation, 30 species of tenrec insectivores fill niches that are filled elsewhere by moles, shrews, and hedgehogs. One species of tenrec produces litters with 20 to 30 young! Lemurs dominate mammalian life today as in the past; of the 45 species, 15 are known only from the remains of their bones and teeth. The recently extinct lemurs, referred to as subfossils, were wiped out when people colonized the island more than 1500 years ago, and many species today are threatened or in danger of extinction. Here we illustrate 3 among many unusual adaptations of these fascinating animals.

Color the island of Madagascar and the aye-aye.

Aye-ayes (*Daubentonia madagascariensis*), thought to be extinct, were rediscovered in 1957 by French primatologists and pioneers in lemur studies, Jean-Jacques Petter and Anne Rousseaux-Petter. Aye-ayes have a peculiarly shaped head with prominent floppy ears. Protruding incisors grow continually (note the long root), as with rodent teeth; canine and premolar teeth are absent, and molar teeth are small. The unusual twiglike and mobile middle digit is equipped with a sharp claw. At 3 kilograms, aye-ayes with their long, bushy tails are the largest nocturnal lemurs.

The aye-aye's mobile ears detect the slightest movement of small insects in tree crevices. Its long incisors gnaw through dead wood, peel tough plant coverings as on coconuts, or bite through items like egg shells. The middle finger probes adeptly into crevices to spear insect larvae, and serves as a scoop, flicking liquids like egg yolk and coconut milk into its mouth so fast that the action appears blurred. And it doesn't spill a drop.

Early on, aye-ayes were regarded as specialists for foraging and feeding on insects. Primatologist Eleanor Sterling tracked aye-ayes for two years in the wild; her observations revealed that they also eat kernel meats, nectar, sap, and gums. They are anatomically specialized to forage and feed on a few plant and animal foods that are abundant but difficult to extract.

Color the body mass, diet, and number of food species for each of the bamboo lemurs.

Paralleling the Asian pandas, not 1 but 3 species of lemur thrive on a diet of bamboo, somehow dealing with the bamboo's cyanide that would poison humans! All 3 species live sympatrically in Ranomafana National Park. Primatologist Chia Tan learned how each one varies from the others. The lesser bamboo lemur, *Hapalemur griseus*, 0.9 kilograms, eats the most general diet. Giant bamboo contributes 72% of its diet, which is supplemented with 24 species of other grass species, foliage, and fruit. It has the smallest home range (15 ha), but the widest geographical distribution along the eastern coast. The rare and recently discovered golden bamboo lemur *H. aureus*, 1.5 kilograms, depends on the leaf bases, pith, and growing shoots of the giant bamboo for 78% of its diet, supplemented with 21 other species of grass, foliage, and fruit. Its home range size is 26 hectares. The greater bamboo lemur, *H. simus*, the heaviest at 2.4 kilograms with the largest home range (62 ha), has the most monotonous diet; giant bamboo contributes 95%, supplemented by only 7 other plant species. *H. simus* eats both immature and mature leaves, as well as the pith of the bamboo. The mystery of how these lemurs can avoid or consume quantities of cyanide that would kill humans remains to be solved.

Color the ruffed lemur and the traveler's palm.

The beautiful ruffed lemurs have an unusual evolutionary relationship to the native traveler's palm (*Ravenala madagascariensis*). The traveler's palm is named for its water storing capability. *Ravenala*, an early offshoot of the Streliziaceae family of plants, has close relatives in South America that are pollinated by bats, and in Africa that are pollinated by sunbirds. Its large flowers produce nectar for several months, contain a lot of pollen, and are not easily damaged. In Madagascar ruffed lemurs, found only in undisturbed primary forest, play an important part in pollinating *Ravenala*.

Rarely do large-bodied, nonflying mammals depend on nectar as an important food source; and it is even more unusual for them to serve as pollinators, since large, nonflying animals usually damage or destroy flowers. Although ruffed lemurs weigh about 4 kilograms, they are highly dependent on nectar during certain times of the year. The lemurs manage to enjoy the nectar without hurting the flowers and, in the process, carry pollen on their fur from one flower to another.

Anthropologist Robert Sussman and botanist Peter Raven hypothesized that prior to the evolution of birds and bats, nonflying mammals served as pollinators of flowering plants and contributed to the plant's evolutionary success. The ruffed lemur and traveler's palm apparently retain an ancient pattern of pollination that has mostly disappeared elsewhere. This lemur-palm relationship illustrates one among many wonders in Madagascar; many evolutionary mysteries still lie hidden. This rare ecosystem is endangered and needs to be conserved for future generations.

LEMUR ECOLOGY

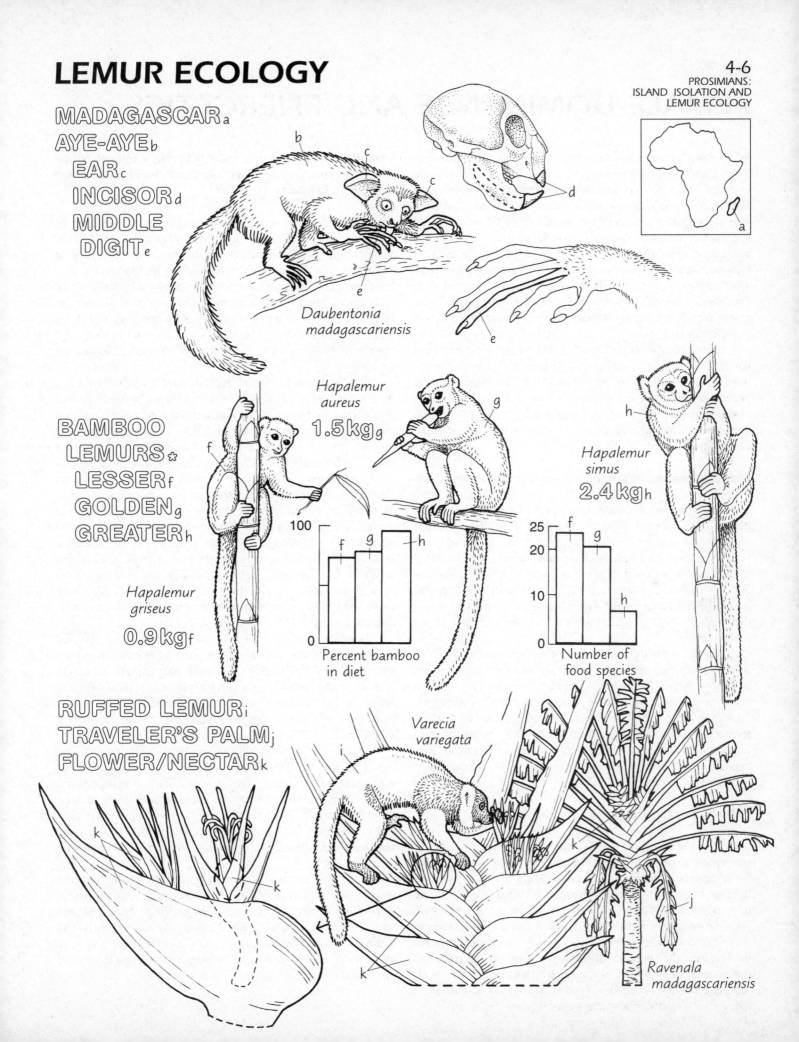

MADAGASCAR a
AYE-AYE b
EAR c
INCISOR d
MIDDLE
DIGIT e

Daubentonia madagascariensis

BAMBOO
LEMURS *
LESSER f
GOLDEN g
GREATER h

Hapalemur aureus
1.5kg g

Hapalemur griseus
0.9kg f

Hapalemur simus
2.4kg h

100

0
Percent bamboo in diet

25
20
10
0
Number of food species

RUFFED LEMUR i
TRAVELER'S PALM j
FLOWER/NECTAR k

Varecia variegata

Ravenala madagascariensis

4-7
FEMALE DOMINANCE AND ENERGETICS

When reporting her research on free-ranging ringtailed lemurs in 1966, primatologist Alison Jolly noted that females were dominant to males. This discovery was rather unexpected. At the time, our understanding of primate social behavior was derived from research on a few species of terrestrial Old World monkeys and apes, where males had priority over females and young. Little was known about prosimian social behavior, and theories about reproductive success almost exclusively took a male point of view. The "primate pattern" was therefore assumed to be one of male dominance. Since Jolly's pioneering studies, subsequent lemur research confirms that adult females are dominant over males in many lemur species.

This plate explores aspects of female dominance in ringtailed lemurs and its wider evolutionary and ecological context. Female dominance should not be viewed as a "trait" or property that is present or absent, like tooth number or cranial capacity. The phenomenon is best understood by considering the intersection of the behavior and biology of the species within a seasonal environment.

Begin by coloring the members of the traveling social group.

Ringtailed lemurs use all levels of the forest but do most of their travel and some feeding on the ground. Their diet is eclectic; they eat a variety of foods, especially fruit, and forage in a relatively large home range. Ringtailed lemurs live in social groups consisting of both sexes in equal number, on average between 10 and 15 members, though occasionally more than 20, a large group size for lemurs. When they travel through the forest, their tails are held high; a convenient way of keeping track of each other.

Females form the stable core of the group; males join or depart for other groups. It is mutually advantageous for the sexes to live together (3-25). For males, social groups provide a known home range and familiarity with its food offerings and some protection against predators. In terms of reproduction, females are more likely to mate with males in the group than with outsiders. The presence of males helps ensure that a female does not miss an opportunity to become pregnant during the extremely restricted breeding period.

Color the two illustrations of female dominance.

Dominance expresses the outcome of numerous social encounters among individuals. Interactions within the group are highly competitive, but males consistently give way to adult females. In lemurs, dominance is expressed when an adult female takes possession of a preferred food item from a male, which he gives up without a fight. Adult females also displace males at feeding or drinking sites. Females exercise strong choice of mates by tolerating the approach of males, by vocalizing to advertise their interest, or by approaching males they are interested in. Adult females and males are similar in body size and color, so that males enjoy no physical size advantage over females.

Color the sunbathing lemur. Using light colors, color all phases of lemur reproduction. Color the rainfall and the seasonal fluctuation in food types.

Ringtailed lemurs live in the southwestern part of Madagascar in scrub, spiny desert, and dry and gallery forests. Temperatures fluctuate daily during the dry winter and may go as low as 14°C. Lemurs are active during the day and have a lower metabolism than anthropoids. They adjust behaviorally to daily temperature fluctuations by sunbathing each morning to take advantage of heat from the sun and by huddling together at night to conserve heat. The lemurs accommodate to seasonal change by focusing on a few critical food resources during the dry season.

Seasonal constraints of reproductive events have been documented at Beza Mahafaly by primatologist Michelle Sauther and colleagues. Females' annual conception, birth, and lactation are timed to correspond with optimum food availability. The mating season occupies the month of May. During her estrous cycle, each female has a 24-hour window when she is able to conceive. If she misses the opportunity, she must wait 40 days for the next cycle, or wait until the next year for another. After an 18-week gestation, births occur at the end of the dry season, so that early lactation coincides with increased rainfall and an initial peak in fruit availability. Infants grow quickly and are weaned at 4 months during a second peak when fruit and young leaves are available. Consequently, if a female conceives during her second cycle in July, 40 days after the breeding season, her infant will be weaned during a time of food scarcity, which decreases its chances of survival.

Therefore, feeding is a high priority for reproducing females; their low metabolism and rapid growth of dependent infants reinforces the need for adequate female caloric intake in order to prepare weaned offspring for survival. Even so, infant mortality is high. Infant survival is influenced by the health of the mother (3-27), and a healthy infant at weaning is more likely to survive as a juvenile (3-28).

Taking into account physiology, behavioral ecology, and environmental context, Sauther presents a compelling case that the system of female dominance ensures that reproducing females have feeding priority during the most critical times of their reproductive lives, especially in the later stages of pregnancy and while lactating. Resident males feed near the females, and female dominance mitigates potential feeding competition with them.

The lemur social system with female dominance evolved within the constraints of lemur ecology and biology: physiologically low metabolism; fast-growing infants and high energy output of lactating females; and tightly constrained annual mating and birth seasons timed to food abundance to maximize infant survival. Female feeding priority is therefore a key part of the reproductive pattern.

LEMUR REPRODUCTION

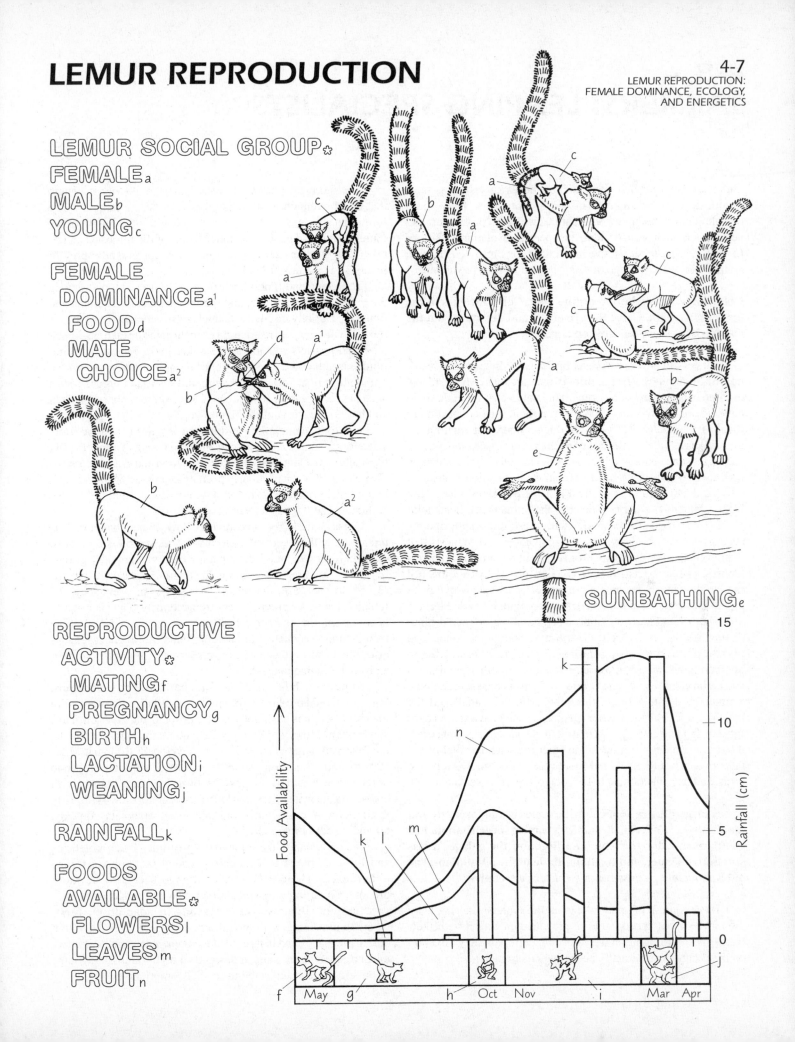

LEMUR SOCIAL GROUP ✳
FEMALE a
MALE b
YOUNG c

FEMALE
DOMINANCE a¹
FOOD d
MATE
CHOICE a²

SUNBATHING e

REPRODUCTIVE
ACTIVITY ✳
MATING f
PREGNANCY g
BIRTH h
LACTATION i
WEANING j

RAINFALL k

FOODS
AVAILABLE ✳
FLOWERS l
LEAVES m
FRUIT n

Food Availability

Rainfall (cm)

15

10

5

0

f   May   g   h   Oct   Nov   i   Mar   Apr

TARSIERS: LEAPING SPECIALISTS

Tarsiers, named for their elongated foot bones (tarsus=foot), have unique locomotor and life history adaptations. They share morphological and behavioral features with both prosimians and anthropoids but have had a long, independent evolutionary history (3-1, 4-4). The tarsier's specializations are illustrated through comparison with a galago, a small-bodied leaping prosimian.

Color tarsier distribution on the map. Color the eyes in the large illustration. Color the eye orbits and dentition, and for comparison, those features on a galago.

Tarsiers live in rain forests of Sumatra, Borneo, Sulawesi, and the Philippines. Their enormous eyes are rotated forward and encased in prominent bony orbits. This approaches the anthropoid condition and led to early controversy about their connection to them (4-9). Anatomist Ted Grand determined that each tarsier eye weighs as much as the brain! Both eyes are twice brain weight and suggest a keenness of vision. A tarsier tracks objects like an owl does; it moves its head 180° in each direction instead of moving the eyes in their orbits. Each eye possesses a fovea but lacks a tapetum lucidum, a layer in the retina that reflects light (3-19). The fovea, also shared with the diurnal anthropoids, accentuates visual acuity served by the cones and suggests that their ancestors were diurnal. From her field research on Sulawesi tarsiers, primatologist Sharon Gursky reports that during full moonlight, tarsiers become more active, in contrast with typical nocturnal species that become less active with increased light.

The dry and narrow flat nose and nasal region (haplorhine) distinguish the tarsier from the wet nose and more pronounced muzzle of prosimians (strepshirines, 3-1, 3-15). Its teeth differ in number and shape from those of galagos and other prosimians and anthropoids (3-6). The two lower incisors are small, and the canines moderately large; the upper canine is small and the incisors large. The molars are equal in size and have sharp cusps for shearing and cutting. By contrast, in the galago's dental comb, the lower canine is similar to the other incisors. The diet of the tarsier consists of insects and small vertebrates, such as reptiles, birds, and bats, in contrast to the galago's more mixed diet (4-5).

In the large illustration, color the bones of the forelimb and hindlimb that underlie the tarsier's leaping specialization. For comparison color the tibia and fibula of the galago, a less specialized leaper, and the tibio-fibula of the 50-million-year old *Necrolemur*, a possible ancient tarsier relative.

Tarsiers are equipped to leap as far as three meters. They move with great speed, ambush prey, and capture it with their hands. While foraging in the forest undergrowth, they also hop on the ground, occasionally becoming quadrupedal.

The short trunk has a relatively hairless tail twice its length that helps maintain balance and direction during jumping. The forelimbs are short. The humerus is about half the length of the femur. The broad hand is the longest part of the forelimb, and its relative size gives strength and dexterity for grasping prey or branches as the tarsier lands.

The elongated hindlimbs are equally proportioned among the femur, the tibio-fibula, and the foot segments. The tibia and fibula are partially fused in a distinct construction that maximizes flexion-extension and restricts movement at the distal tibio-fibular joint and restricts rotation at the ankle joint. This fused tibio-fibula resembles a fragmentary one belonging to *Necrolemur*, an omomyid primate 50 million years old (4-3) and argues for an ancient specialization. The galago's lower limb is not specialized and has no reduction of the fibula.

The foot segment is one-third the length of the total limb. The elongated tarsal bones (calcaneus, navicular) allow the big toe (hallux) to maintain its divergent position and grasping ability. This elongation is a peculiarly primate character. Mammals that hop on the ground (e.g., rabbits) do not require mobility of the hallux, and so the metatarsals elongate.

Gursky's field research reveals how tarsier locomotion is integrated within their total life history. Gestation is 6 months, extremely drawn out for a species of less than 150 grams. Monkeys weighing 3000 grams have similar gestation lengths (3-25). In any case, during the late stages of pregnancy, the female's center of gravity alters tremendously. Thus her agility is compromised, and she relies more on quadrupedal climbing than do nonreproductive or lactating females. Pregnant females also move shorter distances, have shorter nightly path lengths, and smaller home ranges.

At birth the infant is 25% of mother's weight. (In humans, this ratio would produce 30 pound babies!) The ratio of infant to maternal weight is the highest of any primate that gives birth to a single infant. However, although difficult for the pregnant female, the relatively large neonate is more developed. Biologist Miles Roberts notes that, from the infant's point of view, the slow rate of fetal growth has advantages after birth. The large brain at birth enables the neonate to develop locomotor and foraging skills early in life, and infants achieve independence remarkably quickly, around 80 days of age (3-25).

Tarsier females, like some of the prosimians such as galagos and lorises, "park" their suckling young so they can forage unburdened. Their energetic challenge seems to be more pronounced during pregnancy rather than during lactation.

Tarsiers illustrate three lessons in adaptation. First, locomotion is integrated into all aspects of life, in its alteration during pregnancy and in its early development in infancy. Second, the perfection of anatomical design is a myth. Third, each stage of the life cycle is subjected to special compromises.

TARSIERS: LEAPING SPECIALISTS

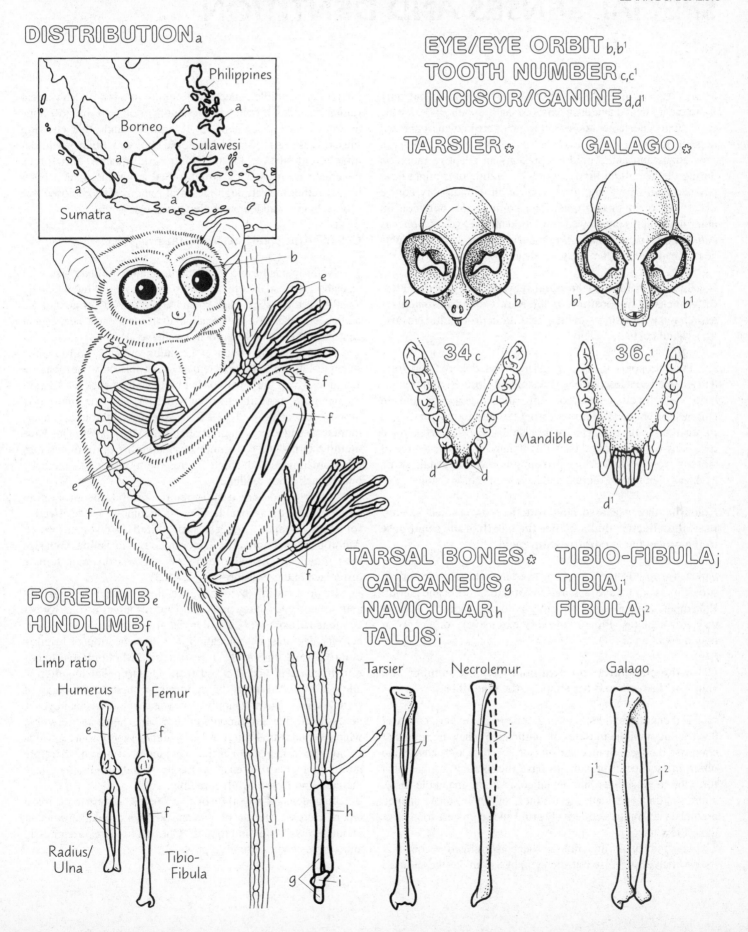

DISTRIBUTION a

Philippines a

Borneo

Sulawesi a

Sumatra a

a

EYE/EYE ORBIT b,b¹
TOOTH NUMBER c,c¹
INCISOR/CANINE d,d¹

TARSIER ✴   GALAGO ✴

b — b

b¹ — b¹

34 c

36 c¹

Mandible

d — d

d¹

FORELIMB e
HINDLIMB f

Limb ratio

Humerus   Femur

e   f

e   f

Radius/   Tibio-
Ulna   Fibula

TARSAL BONES ✴
CALCANEUS g
NAVICULAR h
TALUS i

TIBIO-FIBULA j
TIBIA j¹
FIBULA j²

Tarsier   Necrolemur   Galago

j   j

j¹   j²

h

g   i

4-9
SPECIAL SENSES AND DENTITION

Many fossil prosimians of Eocene age are known but only fragmentary dental evidence exists for anthropoids (4-3). By the early Oligocene, larger bodied anthropoids are known from fossil deposits in Egypt (4-10). Each of the two divisions (suborders), prosimians and anthropoids, represents an adaptive radiation during the last 50 million years (3-1). Anthropoids might have pursued fruit eating and day living in an evolutionary course divergent from prosimians. The comparison between an anthropoid represented by an Old World monkey (*Cercopithecus aethiops*) and a prosimian represented by *Lemur catta*, highlights anatomical features that relate to an anthropoid way of life.

Use light colors for the lemur and vervet monkey faces. Notice differences in the position of the eyes. Color the structures associated with vision—orbit orientation, postorbital closure, and visual cortex.

In anthropoids, the eye orbits are directed more to the front and are totally enclosed in bone (postorbital closure). Anthropoids have well-developed stereoscopic and color vision and an enlarged visual cortex for processing visual information (3-17). In prosimians, the orbits are more laterally placed and encircled by a bony bar (postorbital bar). Prosimians have some degree of stereoscopic vision. Most prosimians are nocturnal; some Malagasy lemurs are diurnal and have some color vision.

Color the structures associated with the sense of smell—snout/ nose and olfactory bulb. Notice the length of the snout/nose in the prosimian versus the anthropoid.

Anthropoids have lost the wet muzzle (rhinarium) of prosimians and have a smaller olfactory bulb and snout. Prosimians have a larger olfactory bulb and snout, and larger cribriform plates. Prosimians rely extensively on scent for communication (3-17).

Color the mandibles and dentition. Note the number and shape of the teeth and the shape of the mandible.

The dentition and supporting bone in the upper and lower jaws, along with the muscles of mastication (chewing) together comprise the feeding mechanism (1-6). Anthropoids have large biting incisor teeth; prosimians have incisors and canines that form the tooth scraper and dental comb in the mandible (3-6). Anthropoid canine teeth are distinct, and their square-shaped premolars and molars effectively grind and so process food prior to swallowing.

The anthropoid mandible is shaped for effective chewing. Its two halves are fused at the symphysis, unlike the unfused prosimian mandible. A deep, wide anthropoid jaw with a vertical ramus provides a firm base for tooth roots; the broad ramus accommodates attachment of the masseter and other chewing muscles (1-6). Anthropoids' enclosed bony eye orbits provide an attachment surface for the temporalis muscle, and forces generated from chewing are absorbed around its lateral bony border rather than through the nasal region. The enclosed eye orbit also gives added protection to the eye itself.

Complete the plate by coloring the neocortex.

Anthropoids have a larger brain relative to body size with an elaborated visual cortex and sensory-motor area, but relatively small olfactory lobes. This expanded sensory-motor area of the brain contributes to refined manipulation and greater independent control of the digits than prosimians have.

Anthropoids have longer gestation, infancy, and juvenile stages (3-24). An anthropoid female usually has only one offspring at a time, which she carries on her body while it suckles. A larger brain requires more time to grow, which increases the time during infancy for learning (3-27). Consequently, anthropoids invest more time and energy in their offspring. Many prosimians have multiple births and sometimes leave their offspring in nests. In other prosimians with single young, the mother parks the baby on a branch while feeding.

Anthropoids are quadrupedal without the prosimian specialization for vertical leaping—a locomotor mode effective for short distances but less well suited to distance travel. Anthropoid males are often larger in body and canine tooth size than females, whereas prosimians show little male-female difference in these features (3-30, 4-33).

From existing evidence, we deduce that the earliest anthropoids intensively exploited fruit resources as rain forests continued to expand (4-1). Color vision, an adaptation to daytime activity, facilitated the location and identification of brightly colored fruits among the forest greens. Manipulative hands effectively held and plucked fruit. Quadrupedal locomotion allowed extended travel through trails in the trees in search of fruit. A changing fruit supply, dependent upon seasonal cycles, necessitated that anthropoids have a large home range within which to find fruit. Fruit provides a higher energy source, which could support larger bodies that were more visible and therefore more vulnerable to predators. Larger social groups may have increased protection while foraging.

To understand the origin of anthropoids, we turn to the fossil record. Here we have only bones and teeth for evaluating whether or not the fossils are "anthropoid." Our best fossil record for early anthropoids comes from Egypt (4-10).

PROSIMIANS AND ANTHROPOIDS

PROSIMIAN $_a$

ORBIT ORIENTATION $_{c,c^1}$
POSTORBITAL BAR $_d$
POSTORBITAL CLOSURE $_{d^1}$
SNOUT $_e$/NOSE $_{e^1}$

ANTHROPOID $_b$

Lemur

Vervet

Cerebellum

Cerebellum

Ramus

MANDIBLE $_{f,f^1}$
DENTITION ✻
NUMBER $_{g,g^1}$
INCISOR/CANINE $_{h,h^1}$
MOLAR $_{i,i^1}$
BRAIN/NEOCORTEX $_{j,j^1}$
VISUAL CORTEX $_{k,k^1}$
OLFACTORY BULB $_{l,l^1}$

Unfused
symphysis

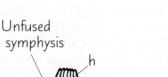

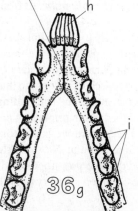

36 $_g$

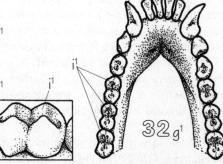

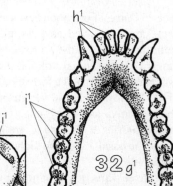

32 $_{g^1}$

ANTHROPOIDS OF THE FAYUM, EGYPT

Our picture of early anthropoid evolution comes primarily from an area in northern Egypt where numerous primate fossils have been preserved. Possible anthropoids have been identified from fragmentary fossils in Asia of Eocene age (4-3), but anthropoid fossils are absent in North America and Europe. In contrast, fossil localities in the Fayum of Egypt yield an abundant and diverse mammalian and primate fauna, from deposits of early Oligocene age, near the Eocene-Oligocene transition at 36 mya. Fossils from the Fayum were first uncovered during expeditions from the American Museum of Natural History in 1906. Excavations were resumed during the 1950s, and during the past several decades, dozens more fossils have been discovered through the efforts of paleontologists Elwyn Simons, John Fleagle, and their colleagues.

Color the Oligocene time range gray and the map, which shows the position of the Fayum depression. Color the bar at the side of the Jebel el Qatrani Formation.

The Fayum depression is an expanse of badlands in northeastern Africa that lies at the eastern edge of the Sahara desert about 100 kilometers southwest of Cairo, below the Nile Delta. During the late Eocene-early Oligocene, when fossils were accumulating, Africa was separated from Eurasia by the warm, shallow Tethys Sea (4-27). The Red Sea had not yet formed, thus Africa and Arabia were still connected and not yet separated by the Arabian Peninsula.

The Jebel el Qatrani Formation of the Fayum is of particular importance to paleontologists because of its dense concentration of fossil primates, and its abundant vertebrate and plant remains, which provide a valuable ecological profile. The fossils paint a picture of this ancient environment around the Tethys Sea. Crocodilian and wading bird fossils indicate a warm, wet habitat. Fossil leaves, vines, roots of mangrovelike plants, and the fruits themselves further document a tropical forest environment. About a dozen orders of African mammals also suggest a rich, tropical fauna. These include species of modern orders such as hyraxes, elephants, dugongs, weasels, insectivores, marsupials, and bats.

Color the Widan el Faras basalt cap and the quarries. Use contrasting colors.

A series of quarries (schematically shown here) within the Jebel el Qatrani Formation have yielded numerous primate fossils; some are identified as prosimians, others are identified as anthropoids, and some do not clearly fall into one group or the other. Paleontologist John Kappelman and colleagues have estimated the ages of the formation based on paleomagnetic dating (5-4). The lowest deposits from the L-41 Quarry are estimated at about 36 mya and the youngest quarries, M and I, at about 33 mya. Quarries E, G, and V are intermediate in age. Widan el Faras, the basalt cap at the highest level, is about 25 to 27 million years old.

Three families of anthropoids are represented: Parapithecidae, Oligopithecidae, and Propliopithecidae. What characteristics distinguish these fossils from prosimians? In prosimians, the two halves of the lower jaw and frontal bone of the cranium are not fused; the posterior part of the eye orbit is not closed (4-9). In contrast, anthropoids and the Fayum fossils have fused jaw bones; the eye orbits are fully oriented toward the front and are completely enclosed in bone. The incisors are broader, and the molars are more square-shaped with lower cusps.

Color the fossil genera belonging to the three families of anthropoids. Use shades of one color for each family. Color the arrows that indicate their quarry of origin.

The parapithecids are represented here by three genera, *Qatrania*, *Apidium*, and *Parapithecus*. Of the three anthropoid families, the parapithecids are more similar to prosimians and New World monkeys in that they possess a third premolar. Their limb bones suggest possible leaping adaptations in *Apidium*. In many respects the parapithecids resemble New World monkeys.

The other two families are similar to the catarrhines (Old World monkeys and apes) in having only two premolars and, in some, canine teeth that appear to be sexually dimorphic. The Oligopithecids are represented here by *Catopithecus*, estimated to be less than a kilogram, and *Oligopithecus*. The Propliopithecids include *Propliopithecus* and *Aegyptopithecus*. The endocast (a mold of the inside of a braincase) of *Aegyptopithecus* shows a brain pattern intermediate between prosimians and New World monkeys; its limb and pelvic bones suggest it was an agile quadruped.

The anthropoid fossils are most numerous from two levels: Quarry L-41, lowest in the formation and the oldest age, and the later Quarries M and I. Quarry L-41 is full of bones; hyrax is the most common mammal specimen. There are also rodents, insectivores, and carnivores. The diversity of anthropoid specimens from the early quarry suggests that anthropoids originated prior to the Fayum record. Several species of prosimians are also present in this early quarry.

Qatrania occurs at three levels: Quarry L-41, Quarry E, and Quarries M and I. Quarries G and V contain the earliest representatives of the propliopithecids as well as the parapithecid, *Apidium*. Quarries M and I have several species from two families, the parapithecids, and *Aegyptopithecus* and *Propliopithecus* from the propliopithecids.

Some of the Fayum primates were thought to be "dental apes" because their molars have low, rounded cusps, more like those of fruit-eating apes than those of the sharper, crested molars of Old World monkeys (4-26). However, researchers recognize that the rounded cusps are also similar to the molars of fruit-eating New World monkeys. This suggests that the Fayum primates were fruit eaters, not that they were apes. The picture we have from the Fayum primates supports the idea that the New World monkeys had already branched off and that the propliopithecids were primitive catarrhines, close to the common ancestry of both apes and Old World monkeys.

ANTHROPOIDS OF THE FAYUM

Mediterranean Sea

Nile Delta

Cairo

El Fayum

Egypt

Arabian Penninsula

Red Sea

JEBEL EL QATRANI
FORMATION a
WIDAN EL FARAS b
QUARRIES M AND I c
QUARRIES G AND V d
QUARRY E e
QUARRY L-41 f

mya

23 ✶
36 ✶

OLIGOCENE ✶

OLIGOPITHECIDAE ✶
CATOPITHECUS g1
OLIGOPITHECUS g2
PROPLIOPITHECIDAE ✶
PROPLIOPITHECUS h1
AEGYPTOPITHECUS h2

PARAPITHECIDAE ✶
QATRANIA i1
APIDIUM i2
PARAPITHECUS i3

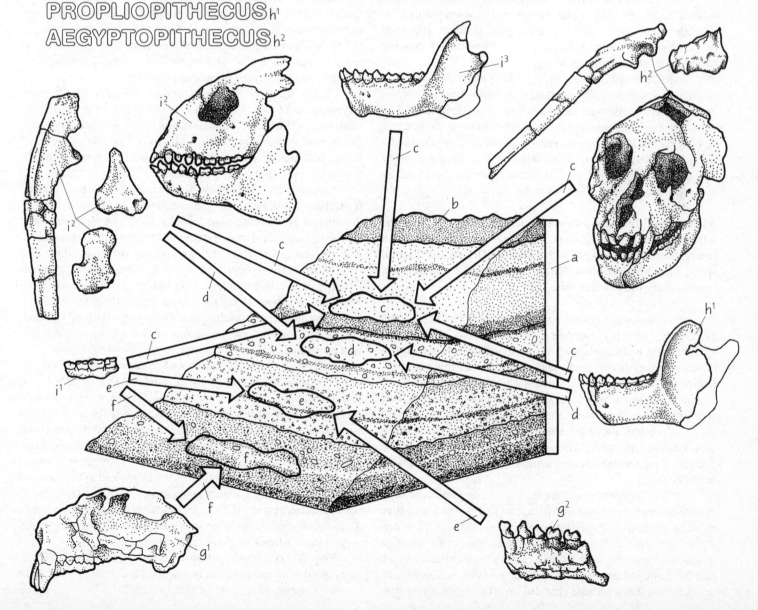

The origin of platyrrhine monkeys puzzled paleontologists for decades. The North American fossil record consists only of Eocene prosimians, adapids and omomyids (4-3), and no identified anthropoids. The South American Oligocene and Miocene fossil record, in contrast, includes only anthropoids. The African fossil record has both prosimians and anthropoids (4-10). When and how did the monkeys get to South America?

Prior to about 1970, paleontologists invoked the concept of parallel evolution. The reasoning went like this: North American Eocene omomyids dispersed south and evolved into South American monkeys, and related Eurasian omomyids evolved in parallel into Old World monkeys, possibly in Africa. It seemed so unlikely that monkeys from Africa could cross a water barrier like the Atlantic Ocean, that by default, a North American origin and an undiscovered ancestor were generally presumed.

Two new lines of evidence independent of the fossils have solved the puzzle. Molecular evidence demonstrated that all monkeys shared a common ancestor prior to their separation (3-1). This evidence fits with the Fayum fossil record showing two kinds of anthropoids at 36 mya.

Evidence from plate tectonics (1-18) clarified the geological history of South America, Africa, and North America. While primates were evolving, South America was an island adrift. The American land masses were not connected through the Isthmus of Panama until 3.5 mya, a time too recent to have provided a route for a prosimian ancestor. Whether New World monkey origins centered in Africa or in North America, the founding ancestors had to cross a body of water.

At the top of the plate, color Africa, South America, and the Atlantic Ocean as they were in the early Oligocene. Then (using shades of blue) color the Atlantic Ocean, continental shelf, and Mid-Atlantic Ridge on the large illustration representing the present time.

Africa and South America were once connected (1-18). But as the deep valley in the middle of the Atlantic Ocean, called the Mid-Atlantic Ridge, released molten material from the earth's mantle, the sea floor spread and pushed the continents apart. During the Oligocene, South America was distant from both North America and Africa, between 2000 and 3000 kilometers. Sea level was at an all-time low. Some mid-Atlantic peaks reached a height of 3.2 kilometers above the sea floor. With a drop in sea level, these peaks on the ocean floor were exposed and created islands. The prevailing winds and ocean currents travel from Africa toward South America.

The "rafting hypothesis" argues that monkeys evolved from prosimians only once and in Africa, and that it was a primitive monkey (parapithecid), and not a prosimian, that made the water-logged trip to South America. We might reconstruct the situation as follows: a few monkeys served as a founding population, much like the mainland finches in the Galápagos Islands. The African ancestral monkeys became stranded on a large rain forest tree, uprooted along a swollen and swiftly moving river during a storm, and thrust out to sea. Clinging to a floating tree with attached branches, vegetation, and soil, monkey ancestors might have "island-hopped," eventually colonizing South America. The credibility of an anthropoid dispersion from Africa is increased by evidence from fossil rodents, which appeared about the same time. Their close living relatives, the porcupines, also reside in Africa. Other species colonizing South America must have arrived in similar ways over millions of years.

Color the representative fossils, listed from oldest to youngest, the geographic location, and place on the time scale.

South American primate fossils compared to those from the Fayum are fragmentary and not well preserved. The earliest fossils in South America are 24 to 27 mya, about 10 million years later than the earliest Fayum fossils (4-10). *Branisella* and *Szalatavus* (not illustrated) come from a single locality in the Bolivian Andes; the mandibular fragments with three premolars and a shallow fused symphysis are similar to those features in present day platyrrhines and Fayum parapithecids (4-10).

Fossils from the early and middle Miocene of southern Argentina and Chile are clearly New World monkeys based on tooth size and shape and cranial anatomy, but may not be ancestral to any modern form. From the Andes of central Chile (about 20 mya) a nearly complete cranium of *Chilecebus* resembles squirrel monkeys in its large upper premolars.

Argentinian sites (15–19 mya) yield several genera. The postorbital closure and ear region found in the fairly complete cranium of *Tremacebus* (and *Dolichocebus,* not illustrated) are typical of New World monkeys; the short face and three premolars and three molars resemble titi and owl monkeys. *Homunculus* (not illustrated) has large enclosed eye orbits. Although about the size of a cebus monkey, it is unlike any living monkey. *Propithecia* (about 15 mya) resembles an early member of the pitheciine monkeys, according to anthropologist Richard Kay and colleagues. A well-preserved genus of two species, *Soriacebus* (not illustrated), might be a primitive saki monkey.

La Venta in Columbia, a rich mid-Miocene site (12–14 mya) yields at least 10 species of fossil monkeys that in dental and facial morphology more closely resemble living species than did earlier fossils. *Neosaimiri* appears to be closely related to living squirrel monkeys. *Cebupithecia* (not illustrated) resembles a saki monkey. *Stirtonia* (not illustrated), the largest La Venta monkey, may have affinities to howler and woolly spider monkeys. *Protopithecus*, the youngest fossil from Brazil and of Pleistocene age is known from a cranium and a nearly complete skeleton; it resembles spider and woolly monkeys but is probably not related. *Xenothrix* from the Caribbean indicates that monkeys found their way to these islands by Pleistocene times.

The diverse fossil primates from South America are anthropoid in morphology; some may be the ancestors of modern monkeys, while others may be side branches.

THE RAFTING HYPOTHESIS

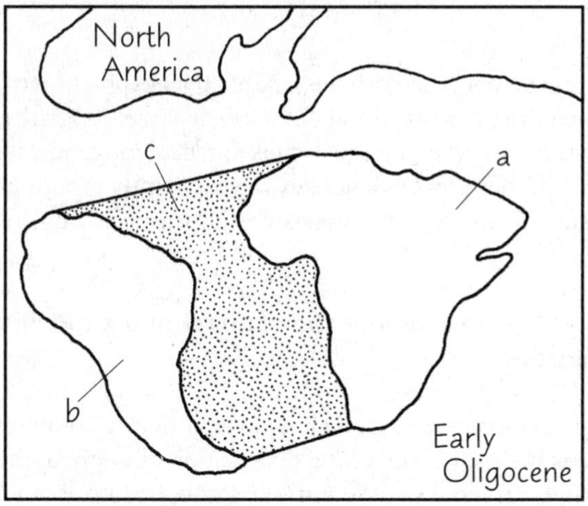

North America

c

a

b

Early Oligocene

AFRICA a
SOUTH AMERICA b
ATLANTIC OCEAN c
CONTINENTAL
SHELF c1
MID-ATLANTIC
RIDGE c2

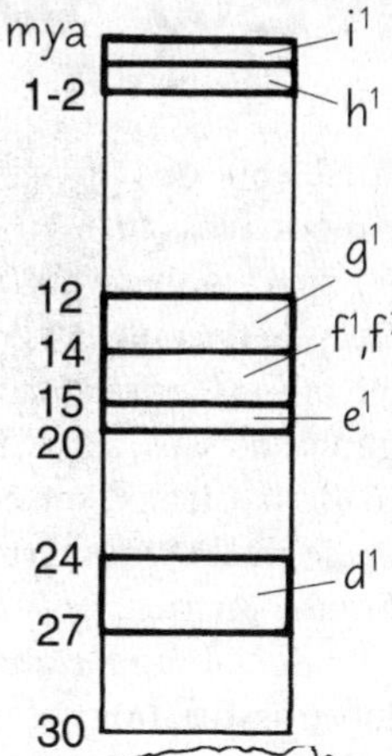

mya
1-2
12
14
15
20
24
27
30

i^1
h^1
g^1
f^1, f^2
e^1
d^1

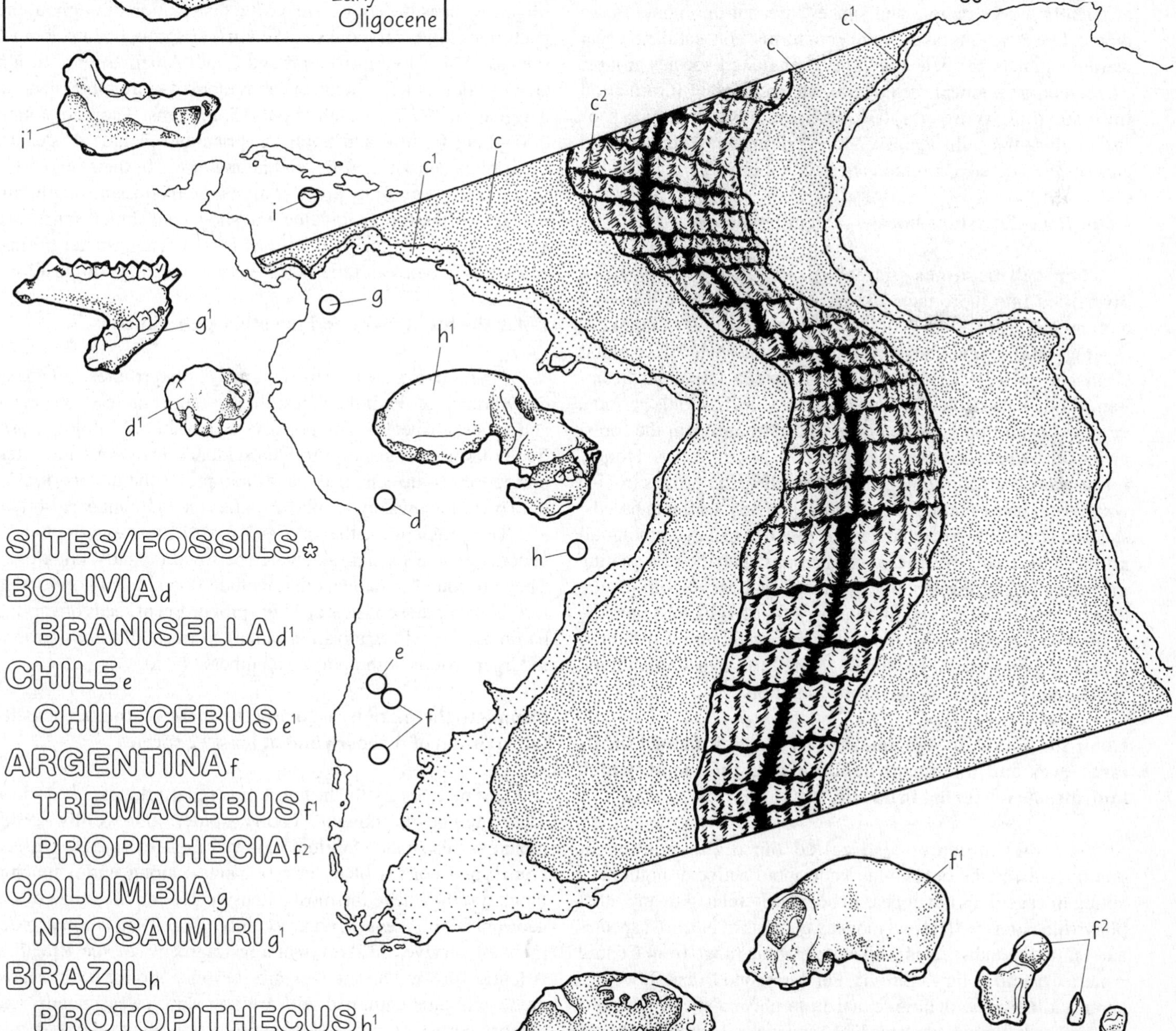

i^1

g^1

d^1

c^1

c^2

c

c^1

c

c^1

i

g

h^1

d

h

SITES/FOSSILS *
BOLIVIA d
   BRANISELLA d1
CHILE e
   CHILECEBUS e1
ARGENTINA f
   TREMACEBUS f1
   PROPITHECIA f2
COLUMBIA g
   NEOSAIMIRI g1
BRAZIL h
   PROTOPITHECUS h1
JAMAICA i
   XENOTHRIX i1

e

f

f^1

f^2

e^1

NEW WORLD MONKEY FAMILY TREE

Ancestors of the living platyrrhine monkeys arrived in South America less than 30 mya (4-11) and diversified into more than 50 species that vary in size from 100 grams to 14 kilograms. Despite the range of body sizes, fruit is the major dietary item for all but a few of them. In addition to fruit, these primates add gums and saps, seeds, leaves, and invertebrate and vertebrate prey to their diets. Consequently, these monkeys occupy diverse ecological niches throughout the tropical regions of Central and South America.

Social organization ranges from cohesive family groups to loose associations of individuals that fragment to find food more efficiently. Large raptors and snakes threaten the monkeys, so their defense systems take a number of forms: concealment; vocal warning signals; residence in large, even mixed-species groups. Molecular, anatomical, behavioral, and ecological information indicate that living platyrrhines comprise 5 lineages or subfamilies: the callitrichines, aotines, pitheciines, cebines, and atelines; all shared a common ancestor about 20 mya.

Color the callitrichine lineage (a) and branches.

The callitrichines—tamarins and marmosets—have diversified into more than 25 species within 5 genera from a common ancestor about 10 mya. They are the smallest monkeys (average 400 grams, range 100–700 g) and have 1 less molar tooth than other platyrrhines. Gums and saps are important dietary items (4-13), particularly for marmosets. Clawlike nails permit a vertical posture on large branches and tree trunks in the forest understory, where marmosets gouge holes, lick the sap, and forage for insects. The callitrichines live in small social groups (8–10) with more than 1 adult male and female. Only 1 female breeds; she gives birth to twins and care of infants is shared among all group members (4-13). These social groups, with their fluctuating membership, are not strictly "families" or bonded pairs as are those of owl monkeys and titi monkeys (4-14). Goeldi's monkey (*Callimico*) belongs with the callitrichines, though it differs in retaining a third molar tooth and giving birth to a single infant, which may represent the ancestral condition.

Color the aotine lineage and the owl monkey, named for its large eyes and nocturnal habits. Color the moon, which indicates its nocturnal behavior.

The owl monkey (also called the night monkey or douroucouli) is the only living anthropoid active at night. The aotine lineage does not appear to be closely related to any other platyrrhine lineage. The owl monkey consists of at least 2 species and numerous subspecies with a geographic range from Central America, south as far as Bolivia, Paraguay, and Brazil. It weighs about 1 kilogram with little sexual dimorphism. Nocturnal habits distinguish it from other platyrrhines and make it possible to avoid daytime predators and competition with larger monkeys for a diet of fruit, leaves, and insects. *Aotus* has no trace of a tapetum lucidum (3-19), which indicates its evolutionary connections to

anthropoids and tarsiers (haplorhines), rather than to prosimians. Its vision is maximally sensitive at 450–500 nanometers (3-18), which takes advantage of contrast cues for detecting objects illuminated by moonlight. Owl monkeys live in family groups of 2 to 6 animals, all related, and males participate in caring for infants.

Color the cebine lineage and the squirrel and capuchin monkey branches.

The squirrel monkey and capuchin monkey share a common Miocene ancestor. They have a wide distribution throughout the neotropics. Squirrel monkeys (*Saimiri*) are grouped into about 4 species, which live in Central and South America; they weigh about 1 kilogram. Capuchin or cebus monkeys (after their generic designation *Cebus*) weigh about 3 kilograms. They are found throughout Central and South America and include 4 species. Their diets consist of fruits and animal prey. In their search for insect and vertebrate prey, squirrel monkeys and capuchin monkeys often forage together and show considerable curiosity and marked manipulative abilities (4-16). Their social groups consist of females and males and vary in size and composition.

Color the titi monkey and the other pitheciines.

Titi monkeys are a distinct branch of platyrrhines, but are an early branch of the pitheciines; they comprise at least 3 species and many subspecies. Titi monkeys weigh about 1 kilogram, and live in family groups of 2 to 6 individuals. They eat fruit, often unripe, seeds, insects, and leaves and prefer the understory. As with owl monkeys, males play a major role in infant care (4-14).

The pitheciines, the saki and uakari monkeys, include 3 genera (about 8 species) and weigh between 1.5 and 4 kilograms. They are found in habitats that include flooded and nonflooded forests. Their diet consists of a high proportion of seeds of varying hardness. Social organization ranges from small family groups to larger groups with up to 25 members (4-15).

Complete the plate by coloring the atelines, the prehensile-tailed group of 4 genera and at least 12 species.

The atelines are the heaviest of the platyrrhines, (4 –14 kg). They include the howler, woolly, spider, and woolly spider monkeys (also called muriqui). Howler monkeys are the earliest branch and consist of at least 6 species; along with capuchin monkeys, they have the most extensive geographic range of the neotropical monkeys. In contrast, only 1 species of woolly spider monkey survives in the remaining fragments of the Brazilian Atlantic forest. The atelines are the only monkeys that have prehensile tails equipped with friction skin, sweat glands, and sensory nerves as well as a large projection on the motor cortex (4-17). They rely on ripe fruit, and also eat young leaves. Social groups are variable in size and composition, though they generally consist of several adult females and males.

NEW WORLD MONKEY FAMILY TREE

CALLITRICHINES_a
GOELDI'S MONKEY_a¹
PYGMY MARMOSET_a²
COMMON
MARMOSET_a³
LION TAMARIN_a⁴
SADDLEBACK
TAMARIN_a⁵

AOTINE_b
OWL MONKEY_b¹

CEBINES_c
SQUIRREL MONKEY_c¹
CAPUCHIN MONKEY_c²

PITHECIINES_d
TITI MONKEY_d¹
SAKI MONKEY_d²
BEARDED SAKI
MONKEY_d³

ATELINES_e
HOWLER MONKEY_e¹
SPIDER MONKEY_e²
WOOLLY SPIDER
MONKEY_e³

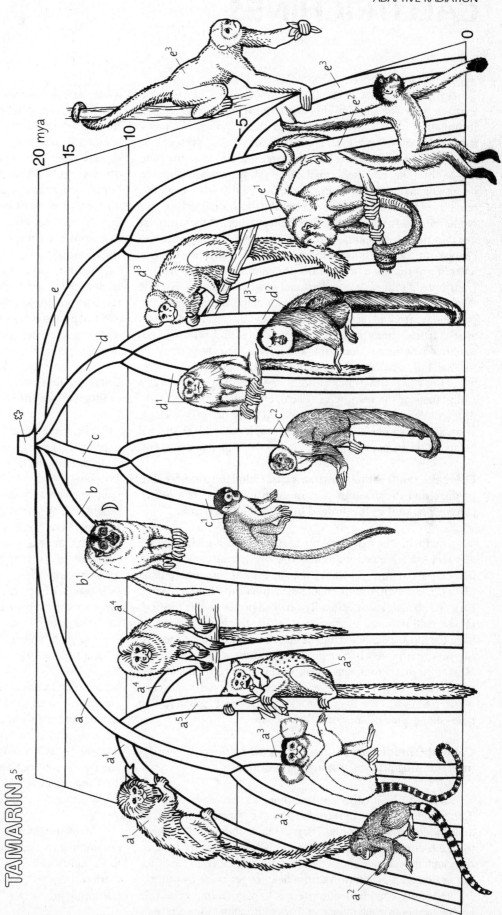

4-13
CALLITRICHINES

Tamarins and marmosets combine a number of unusual features that account for their highly successful radiation. Before information was available from field studies, misconceptions surrounded these primates. Their diminutive size, presence of "claws," and scent-marking behavior were interpreted as primitive and squirrellike, and their small social groups were assumed to be monogamous families. Primatologist Paul Garber began to turn these ideas around when he compared the locomotor behavior of tamarins and tree squirrels. The monkeys, but not the squirrels, use thin flexible supports, take long acrobatic leaps through the canopy, use their grasping ability to forage on interlacing foliage, and cling vertically to tree trunks. Primatologist Warren Kinzey contributed further to our understanding when he discovered that the function of clawlike nails was postural to maintain a vertical position for feeding on tree trunk resins and insects. Field studies also clarified many aspects of their social and reproductive systems; twinning is common, and infants are cared for by all members of these nonmonogamous social groups.

This plate illustrates unique aspects of these monkey Lilliputians of the neotropics. Each genus illustrates a slightly different variation on the theme of small body size (100–700 g), vertical feeding posture in the forest's understory (3-3), dietary composition, scent marking, twinning, and communal infant care.

Color the callitrichine clawlike nails. Color the gum-feeding posture and dentition of the common marmoset (*Callithrix jacchus*) as well as the gouged holes in the tree trunk.

But for the flat nail of the big toe (hallux), callitrichine hands and feet are equipped with nails that are laterally compressed like claws, although they have the anatomical structure of nails (3-11). The clawlike nails enable the animals to dig into the tree bark and so maintain a vertically oriented posture while feeding. Of the callitrichines, marmosets (*Callithrix*, about 11 species) have the most specialized diet of gums and sap, called exudates. In pygmy marmosets (*Cebuella*, 100 g), exudates constitute about 60% of the diet. Prominent incisors, well-enameled canines, and a flaring lower jaw support well-developed masseter muscles, which marmosets use to cut through the tree bark and pith. The holes they gouge promote the flow of sap.

Color the saddleback tamarin (*Saguinus fusicollis*) in its insect-feeding and scent-marking postures.

Saddleback tamarins are 1 of about 15 species of tamarins. Tamarins have a generalized diet and eat insects, gum, nectar, and a wide variety of fruits. They use their sharp clawlike nails to perch comfortably on tree trunks while capturing insects. Although they do not gouge the trees, they do bite into lianas for sap or lick the sap that flows from tree gouges made by others.

Olfactory communication seems to play an important role among the neotropical monkeys. The callitrichines use secretions from various glands or urine to mark territories and convey reproductive state. Marmosets are not territorial but directly mark feeding holes with urine, apparently to express ownership of these resources. Tamarins are territorial and defend the boundaries against neighboring groups. When groups meet, the monkeys often scent mark on branches using their sternal glands, and females may scent mark gum sites. Tamarins also communicate through a variety of vocalizations; during territorial encounters, they have vocal "battles" with high-pitched sounds including twitterings, chirpings, and squeakings that strongly suggest conversation.

Tamarins live in groups of up to 18 members, as many as 4 adult females and 4 adult males. Sometimes tamarin species join together and form larger mixed-species groups. The presence of additional individuals seems to improve detection of predators without increasing competition because the dietary composition of each species is distinct.

Color the lion tamarin (*Leontopithecus rosalia*) social group to illustrate callithrichine communal caretaking.

The social behavior of clawed monkeys has no counterpart in primates. Group membership often includes more than 1 adult male and female, as well as the younger subadults and juveniles. Twinning is the rule, and all group members help care for the young in a communal effort. In the lion tamarin, after a 4-month pregnancy, the newborn twins together comprise 20% of the female's body weight! The males, as well as the younger group members, are eager to hold the infants and within 2 to 3 weeks carry them, freeing the lactating female to forage. Group members, especially males, share insects with infants as young as 9 weeks of age and continue sharing until infants reach the juvenile stage, about 1 year old. Food is offered by holding out the hand or by vocalizing to the infant to come and take it.

Only 1 female in the social group breeds, and she mates with all adult males. The high-ranking, breeding female suppresses the reproductive activity of other females through her dominant behavior and pheromones, so that rarely does more than 1 female breed at a time. Within 10 days of giving birth, lion tamarin females enter a short period of estrus and may be pregnant and lactating at the same time. This results in one of the shortest birth intervals in anthropoids. With short reproductive turn-around time and twins, callitrichines are able to colonize new areas quickly. This reproductive pattern contrasts with the slow breeders like spider monkeys and saki monkeys that give birth once every 2 years.

Many unanswered questions remain, for example, under what environmental conditions did selective pressures operate to lead to the callitrichines' adaptations? Like so much in primatology, there is more to learn about the behavior and evolution of these intriguing primates.

TAMARINS AND MARMOSETS

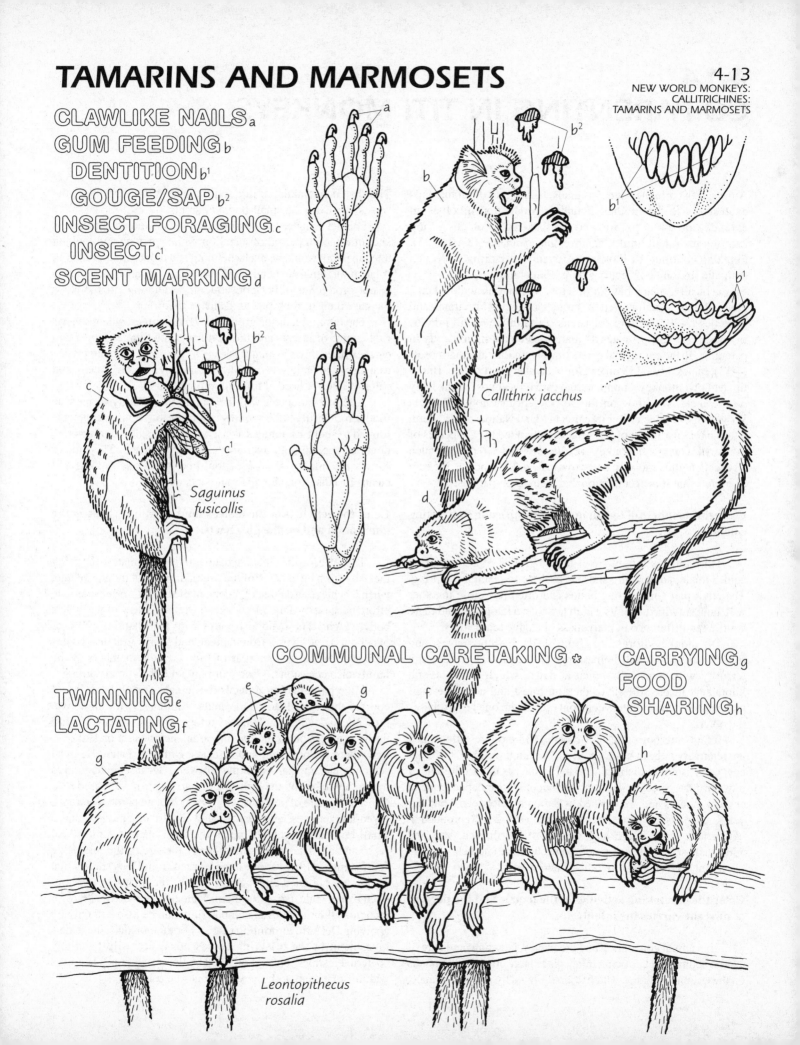

CLAWLIKE NAILS a
GUM FEEDING b
DENTITION b¹
GOUGE/SAP b²
INSECT FORAGING c
INSECT d
SCENT MARKING d

Saguinus fusicollis

Callithrix jacchus

COMMUNAL CARETAKING *

CARRYING g
FOOD
SHARING h

TWINNING e
LACTATING f

Leontopithecus rosalia

CO-PARENTING IN TITI MONKEYS

Among most primates and mammals, taking care of infants falls exclusively to the mother. Female reproduction involves an extended pregnancy, followed by suckling, protecting, and carrying the infant until it achieves independence (3-10, 3-25). Females continue to look after juvenile offspring and even maintain lifelong connections with adult children.

Typically, males have little close association with infants, although they usually tolerate, protect, or play with infants and juveniles (3-29). On rare occasions males injure or kill infants. In only a very few primates do males participate significantly in parenting. In the communal caretaking of tamarins and marmosets (4-13), males as well as other group members participate. But in titi and owl monkeys, nonmaternal care falls almost exclusively on the male. We draw on the work of primatologist Patricia Wright. She conducted her research in Manu National Park, Peru, a tropical moist forest of the Amazon inhabited by 13 species of monkeys. Dusky titi monkeys (*Callicebus moloch*) provide such an excellent illustration of extensive male involvement in the care of infants that it is accurate to label them as co-parents.

Color the members of the titi monkey group using contrasting colors.

Titi monkeys live in small family groups consisting of an adult female, adult male, and one to three sequential offspring. The adult pair form strong bonds and often rest close together with tails entwined. Adults weigh less than a kilogram, and there is little sex difference in body mass or canine tooth size.

Titi monkeys forage for fruit, seeds, insects, leaves, and flowers within a small home range (4–12 ha). They defend a territory with loud calls given at dawn, which carry several kilometers in the still air of the rain forest and advertise their presence. When neighbors confront each other, one group chases the other.

Infants are born after a 5-month (155 day) gestation; they are relatively large at birth, about 10% of adult weight. The infant coat color is not as distinct from the parents as it is for infants of other primate species. Titis achieve locomotor independence at about 4 months and are weaned by 8 months. Between 2 and 2.5 years, juveniles leave the group to find mates (3-28). Reproduction begins at 3 years of age, and females give birth each year. The adult male serves as a co-parent to each infant and helps ensure the infant's survival through his attentive care.

Color the caretaking activities of the female and the percent of time she carries the infant.

The annual conception and pregnancy, lactation, and care of a large neonate and growing infant place large energetic demands on these small females, which is ameliorated by male assistance.

The shared caretaking of infant titi monkeys thus distributes the "costs" between the small-bodied parents.

For the female, the combination of a 5-month pregnancy, and an 8-month period of lactation while carrying and looking after an infant would be overwhelming and reduce infant survival. A lactating female expends 50% more energy than a female who is not producing milk. Consequently, lactating titi monkeys increase their feeding rate and change their diet.

The female leads the group into feeding trees, where she has first choice of insects and the best fruit. She forages longer and catches three times as many insects as the adult male, and twice as many as juveniles. A diet of insects is high in fat, protein, and calories that are needed for milk production (4-1).

A female's contact with her infant is primarily to provide food. From birth until 8 months old, prior to weaning, contact is limited to about 15 minutes a day, when she feeds it during 4 to 5 bouts of suckling, an average of 3 minutes each. The mother carries the infant only 6% of the time; she alone grooms and cleans it. This is one job the male opts out of.

Color the activities of the male, subadult, and juvenile in the illustration and on the pie charts.

The male, on the other hand, does relieve his mate by carrying the baby from birth (92% of the time), until it is 4 months of age, when it achieves a degree of independence. This is a considerable effort, because by 3 months of age, the infant is 40% of the male's body weight! The male also plays with the offspring (72% of play bouts), retrieves it from danger, and shares fruit and insects each day during its first year of life. Juvenile members of the family also occasionally carry or play with their small sibling.

Male participation reduces the female's work load, but of course, shifts the load to the male. Burdened with an active, growing, and increasingly heavy infant, a male is usually the last in the progression to the feeding area and enters a picked over tree where the best fruit and insects are already eaten. He must search longer and harder for the leftovers. Because predation is a major threat, he and the little one he carries are at increased risk.

This system of parental care "works" for all parties—infants, juveniles, females, and males—and illustrates one way that a small-bodied anthropoid meets the high energy demands of reproduction. The male is most likely the sire of the infants he "co-parents." However, we have learned from DNA studies that even in pair bonded birds, about 30% of the offspring were not sired by the male caring for them. Male primates do not know or recognize their offspring, and paternity can be assessed only by applying DNA fingerprinting (2-12). For titi monkeys, the male's investment in the offspring comes not necessarily from any "paternal instinct" but is motivated by the strong bonds he forms with his mate and with the young ones he cares for.

TITI MONKEYS

FAMILY GROUP ✶
MALE a
FEMALE b
SUBADULT c

JUVENILE d
INFANT e

MALE CARETAKING ✶
CARRYING a¹
PLAYING a²

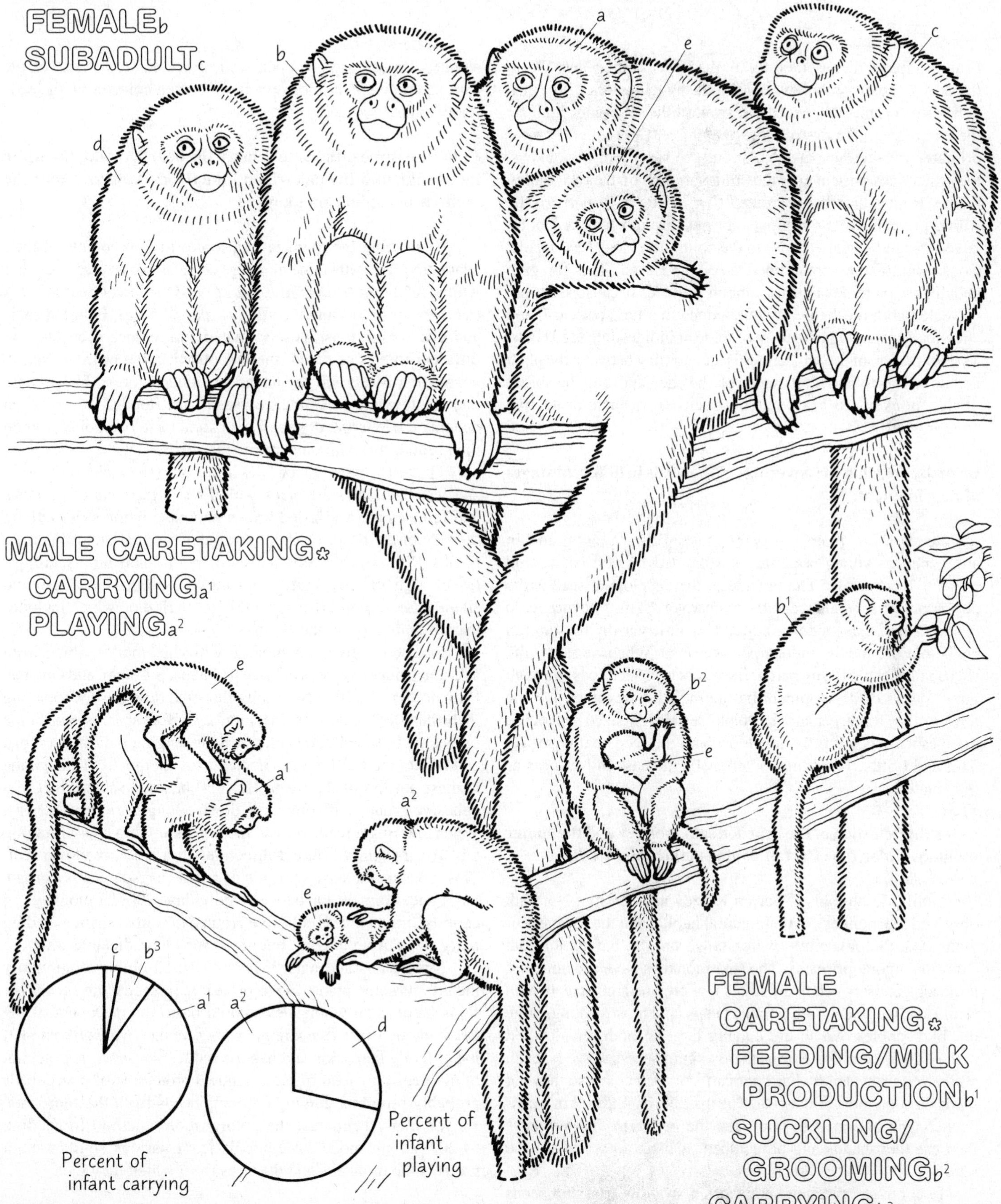

Percent of
infant carrying

Percent of
infant playing

FEMALE
CARETAKING ✶
FEEDING/MILK
PRODUCTION b¹
SUCKLING/
GROOMING b²
CARRYING b³

Fruit is a major dietary item for all the larger bodied New World monkeys. Usually monkeys eat the fleshy part of the fruit, then either drop or spit out the seeds, or swallow the seeds and eliminate them in feces, often far from the parent tree. Consequently, most primates are seed dispersers. Among the New World monkeys, the pitheciines present an interesting variation on the fruit-eating theme. Rather than being limited to the soft, juicy parts of the fruits, pitheciines are equipped to get through the hard outer coverings and so gain access to the softer nutritious seed inside. Consequently, they are dubbed "seed predators." This foraging and dietary pattern is unusual among primates because seeds are protected both mechanically (embedded in a hard pericarp) and chemically, usually in the form of toxic or indigestible seed coats. The adaptation of the pitheciines is an interplay between the plant and its efforts to protect its seeds on the one hand, and the ability of the monkeys to draw out the seeds from their protective covering.

Begin by coloring the coverings of the seeds in different stages of development.

Seeds are a plant's way of making new plants, and in angiosperms, young seeds are surrounded by nourishing and protective coverings. The outside of the developing seed is the pericarp with several layers: the exocarp or "skin," the mesocarp or flesh that has been enhanced in cultivation for human consumption, and the endocarp or seed coat. When we eat "fruit" we usually eat the fleshy part or the mesocarp. Seeds pass through many stages of development before the flesh develops and the seed is ready for dispersal. The "pink" seed is full-sized but young; the mesocarp is not fully developed and the seed coat is not yet hard and brittle. The fruits' outer shells increase in hardness as they mature.

Color the dentition of the bearded saki monkey and the spider monkey. Color the effect of canine action on a seed.

Until primatologists Warren Kinzey and Marilyn Norconk observed the monkeys in their natural habitat and the hardness of their food, the pitheciines were known only as having unusual dentition among primates. The saki monkeys have procumbent, projecting incisors, relatively small, low-crowned molar teeth with rounded rather than more pointed cusps, and most striking, large tusklike canines, which are equally large in both females and males! Their dentition equips them to gain access to seeds, even seeds well protected by hard pericarps or seed coats, so they eat seeds through most of the year. The tusklike canines act in a can-opener type of action to pop open the pericarp. The monkeys then use their hands and procumbent incisors to scoop out the seed.

In contrast, spider monkeys often swallow fruit and seeds with little preparation. Their incisors are not procumbent and their canines are not used to open well-protected fruit. Most of the fruit eaten by spider monkeys is soft, often colorful, with seeds ready to be dispersed.

Color the three pitheciine genera, the bearded saki, the white faced saki, and the uakari, and the flooded forest. Color the fruit-eating spider monkey

Comparing the monkeys illustrates the fine points of their adaptation. The pitheciine monkeys come in two sizes, the smaller white faced saki (*Pithecia*, 1.5–2 kg) and the larger bearded saki (*Chiropotes*, 3 kg) and uakari (*Cacajao*, 3.5 kg). Bearded sakis and uakaris are most closely related and replace each other in different forests of the northern neotropics; the bearded saki in terra firma forest and the uakari in flooded forest. Uakaris are one of a few large mammals to occupy the flooded forest. When waters recede in the dry season, uakaris have been observed on the ground, foraging on germinating seeds.

The term "white faced" describes only the male of this saki species. The males are black with a white face and black nose, and females are a grizzled brown and have white stripes along the side of the nose, another example of "sexual dichromatism" (3-30). White faced sakis live in pairs or small family groups, travel high in the canopy, and move extremely quickly and silently. Seeds comprise about 60% of their diet, which includes leaves, animal prey, and flowers.

Bearded sakis are sympatric with the smaller white faced saki and spider monkeys in French Guiana, Surinam, and Guyana. Primatologist Marilyn Norconk contrasted foraging and traveling in the bearded sakis and spider monkeys. Both species have home ranges that exceed 250 hectares; their ranging patterns contrast and reflect their differences in diet. Moving quickly through the highest portion of the trees, 15 to 30 bearded sakis travel in a cohesive group as if convoying down a long stretch of freeway. When entering a feeding area, they break up into small foraging units as if taking different directions in a freeway clover leaf. This is one method to move quickly between resources as a group, but reduce competition between individuals. Spider monkeys, in contrast, travel in less cohesive groups; they also change feeding party size during the day, but not in such a predictable way.

Since sakis and uakaris have "figured out" evolutionarily the secrets some plants use to protect their seeds, the success of sakis feeding on young seeds could be to the detriment of the tree if enough seeds were removed before they were dispersed. It is not likely that sakis and uakaris reduce the survival potential of the trees they feed from. Chemical protection of many seeds probably prohibits gorging on many seeds from the same tree. As for many primates, the smorgasbord method of feeding (4-20), taking moderate amounts from various sources, both protects the monkeys and the trees from which they feed.

PITHECIINES

SEED DEVELOPMENT*
PERICARP*
EXOCARP a
MESOCARP/
FRUIT b
ENDOCARP c
SEED d

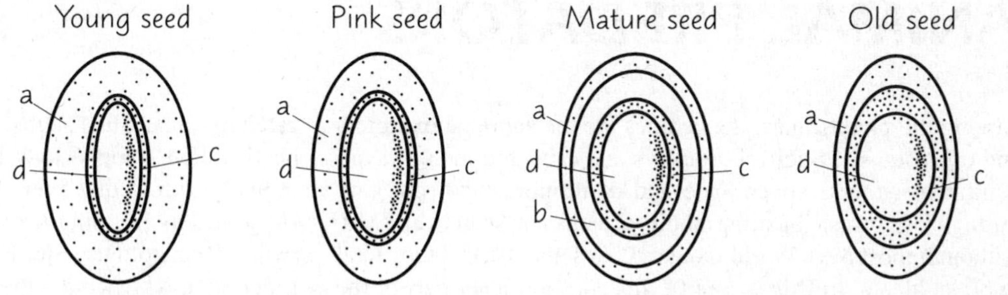
Young seed
Pink seed
Mature seed
Old seed
a
b
c
d

DENTITION*
INCISORS g, g^1
CANINES h, h^1
PREMOLARS i, i^1
MOLARS j, j^1

BEARDED SAKI e
SPIDER MONKEY f

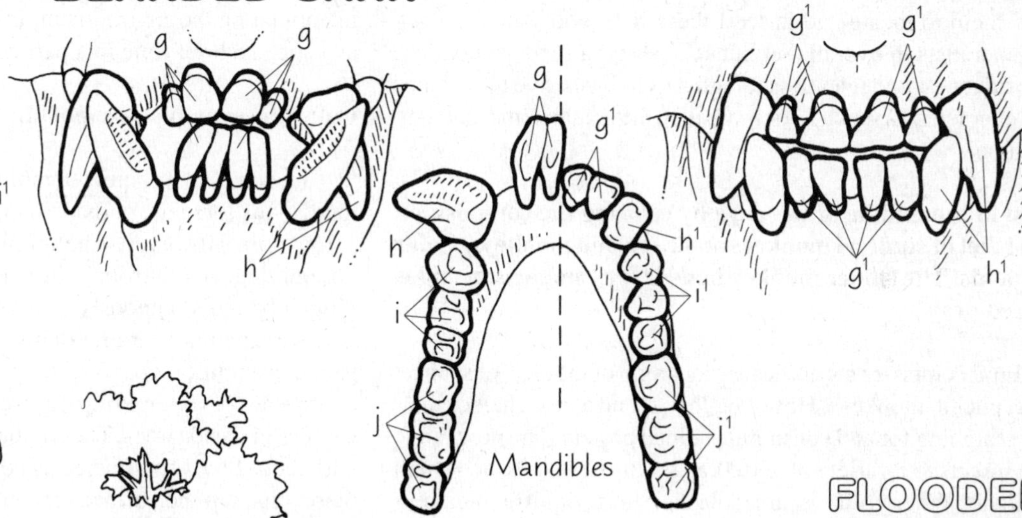
g
g^1
h
h^1
i
i^1
j
j^1
Mandibles

CANINE
ACTION h^2

FLOODED
FOREST k

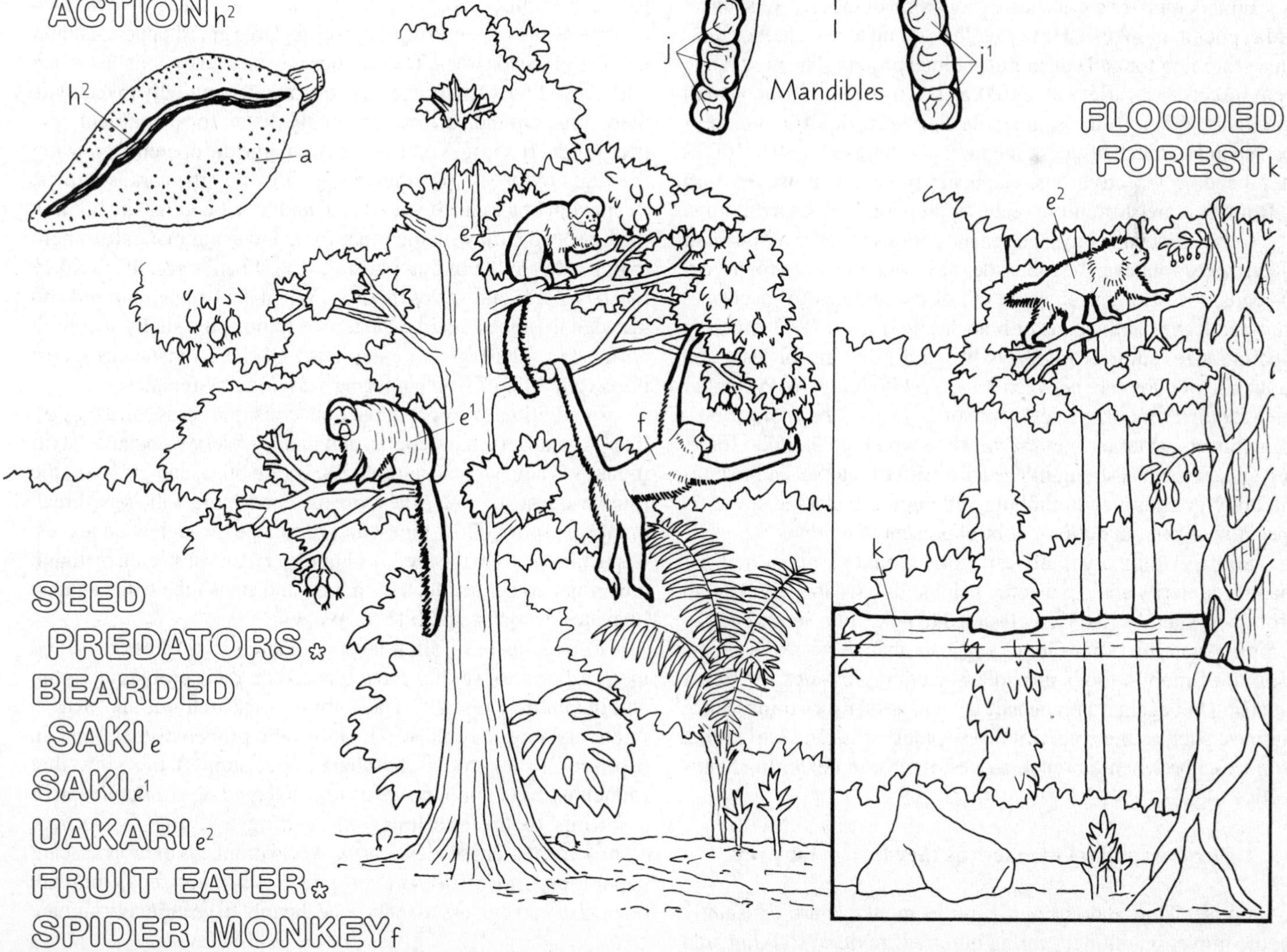
h^2
a
e
e^1
e^2
f
k

SEED
PREDATORS*
BEARDED
SAKI e
SAKI e^1
UAKARI e^2
FRUIT EATER*
SPIDER MONKEY f

4-16
CEBINES:
ANIMAL PREDATORS

Among the platyrrhines, the cebines are the supreme explorers and opportunists. Squirrel monkeys and capuchin monkeys are similar in general appearance and demeanor, busily moving through the forest, bustling about in constant search of food. Although most New World monkeys eat some insects, they tend to be incidental to fruit or seeds. Since a significant part of the diet consists of invertebrate and vertebrate prey, cebines qualify as "animal predators." Curiosity, endless energy, and active hands allow them to locate and harvest these rich food sources. They are generalists in overall diet but specialists in food acquisition. Inquisitiveness and relentless foraging techniques give the cebines their character, as much as or more than the actual items that they consume.

Begin in the middle of the page by coloring the composition of the diet of squirrel monkeys and capuchin monkeys. Color the hands. The spider monkey hand is for comparison and is colored gray.

Fruit comprises a significant proportion of the diets of squirrel and capuchin monkeys. However, they spend at least half of their time searching for and consuming animal protein. The prey range from insects to a variety of vertebrates—birds, snakes, and small mammals. When fruit is scarce, the diet shifts. Squirrel monkeys then spend so much of their time foraging for insects, 80 to 100%, they become insectivorous. Capuchin monkeys, however, turn to fruits that are difficult to reach or prepare, such as palm nuts.

Cebines lack the physical specializations of some of the other platyrrhine monkeys: the robust dentition of pitheciines for access to seeds; the strong prehensile tail of the atelines for access to fruit and leaves at the ends of branches (4-15, 4-17). Of small to medium size, squirrel monkeys weigh a kilogram or less, and capuchin monkeys are between 2 and 3.5 kilograms. With smaller teeth, squirrel monkeys seek out softer fruits. The more robust capuchins have larger molars, thicker enamel, greater bite force, and greater manual strength. The tail is well developed and secures the body in sitting and climbing, although it lacks the strength, specialized skin, and motor control present in atelines.

Squirrel monkeys and capuchin monkeys are noted for manual dexterity and precision. Their hands have long digits with prominent thumbs (3-11), well suited to poke, pry, seize, peel, or scrape. Anatomist Ted Grand suggests that these skills in the capture of mobile foods provided selection pressures for finger precision but against a prehensile tail and suspensory trunk. Since atelines, such as the spider monkey, pluck fruits and leaves that won't escape when a branch moves, their less dexterous hands suffice (4-17).

Color the squirrel monkeys as they forage for prey.

Enterprising and curious, squirrel monkeys are constantly on the move, searching, peering into tree crevices, stalking, and catching prey. Such items, mainly grasshoppers, cockroaches, beetles, and spiders, may be slow, immobile, or cryptic. The monkeys must discover them from beneath the surface of substrates by listening for rustles, unfurling leaves, or breaking twigs. Primatologist Sue Boinski describes a squirrel monkey group as a whirlwind—the animals spread across a wide area and flush insects from their hiding places, then pounce quickly on these fleeing and desirable morsels. Little time is spent manipulating the environment; instead they make a quick search and spend a brief time in a particular tree before they move off.

Color the example of capuchin foraging.

In contrast to squirrel monkeys, capuchins are diligent, meticulous foragers, perhaps spending as much as 20 minutes at 1 location. However, Capuchins, like squirrel monkeys are unremitting, active from before dawn to near dusk. They search diligently and strenuously, exerting great ingenuity and skill to discover and uncover prey. This ability is well illustrated by the frog consumption observed by primatologist Kosei Izawa. Two or 3 species of Hylidae frogs, as well as large grasshoppers, inhabit cavities in Guada trees. The cavities are marked by small, surface slits about 1 by 4 centimeters. The monkeys routinely investigate these slits, tap the surface repeatedly, listen for movement, and peer inside. If a frog is present, they enlarge the opening, gnawing the edges of the slit, peeling and ripping away the bark. At times, a capuchin braces itself with its tail and foot, bending and holding the loosened bark with the other foot, and using manual strength to pull away at the hiding place. As the slit enlarges, the monkey reaches inside and seizes the frog. When the frog is captured and killed, it is rubbed against the tree to remove the sticky secretion on its skin. The legs are eaten first. Of the 25 instances Izawa observed, 80% of frog capturing was done by females.

In addition to frogs, capuchins consume birds, birds' eggs, lizards, squirrels, bats, coatis, and in one observed instance, a titi monkey. They harvest caterpillars, spittle bugs, and grubs. In the routine quest for prey, they rip off dead bark, roll logs, break branches, split hollow vines, and rummage through dead leaves. Capuchins also eat the seeds or liquids of fruits protected by tough coverings: to get inside, they pound and smash the fruits against branches or rocks, and bite them open.

Capuchins have often been compared to chimpanzees, and many laboratory studies have focused on their problem-solving and manipulative skills. Their ability to search out and extract relatively inaccessible foods and their propensity, at least in captivity, to use tools and share food, support the view that capuchins and chimpanzees have converged on similar adaptive solutions to the challenge of making a living in tropical environments. These clever New World monkeys exhibit nascent capacities, more fully developed in chimpanzees, that are recognized precursors to traits once thought to be uniquely human.

CEBINES

SQUIRREL MONKEY FORAGING*
SEARCHINGa
PEERINGb   CAPTURINGd   CONSUMINGe
STALKINGc

DIET*
FRUITf
ANIMAL
PREYg

Percent of
foraging time

HANDSh,h1

Squirrel   Capuchin   Spider

CAPUCHIN FORAGING*
FROGi
TAPPING/   PEELING/   REACHING/   RUBBING/
LISTENINGj   BRACINGk   CAPTURINGl   CONSUMINGm

ATELINES AND PREHENSILE TAILS

The atelines are the largest of the neotropical monkeys, defined by the long, well-muscled tail, a fifth limb that helps suspend the animal below a branch to feed. Howler monkeys are quadrupedal and leaves are a major dietary item. The spider, woolly, and woolly spider monkeys are larger and more acrobatic, but have fewer species and more restricted ranges than howlers.

Atelines are 1 of 6 orders of mammals that have independently evolved prehensile tails. The orders include primates, marsupials, edentates, rodents, carnivores, and pangolins, representing some 16 genera. Five orders are found in South America. Ethologist Louise Emmons and botanist Alan Gentry attribute this disproportion to significant differences in the structure of the tropical forests. In South American forests, there are fewer lianas species compared to Africa, though more than in the Asian forests. Large palms are present in mature South American forests. Palms possess unusual features, including an adaptive mechanism for avoiding invasion by lianas, and are difficult to climb. Thus, the many palms and only a moderate number of lianas in the neotropics seem to provide a selective advantage for the prehensile tail, which is most advantageous to animals above 3 kilograms. Smaller animals do not deform branches and can jump between gaps with their higher strength to mass ratio.

Color the body suspension of the howler monkey, the bridging position of the spider monkey, and the anatomy associated with the prehensile tail.

The prehensile tail permits atelines to suspend themselves below branches without assistance from forelimbs or hindlimbs. The tail is also used to form bridges across gaps in the forest for the younger and smaller animals. Dependent infants use their tails to hold on to their mothers. Atelines feed securely as they pluck fruit and leaves, a pattern convergent with the gibbon's ability to suspend itself beneath the branch with one arm (4-26). Spider monkeys, as well as the woolly and woolly spider monkeys, have flexible shoulder joints, and are able to coordinate their forelimbs with the tail in suspension to hang beneath branches. Howler monkeys, however, have limited mobility in the shoulder joint.

The prehensile tail is part of the fabric of reorganization and engages other tissue and organ systems. The underside (ventrum) of the tail has naked skin equipped with dermal ridges identical to the loops and whorls of our fingerprints. The tail also carries sensory organs and sweat glands for a better grip (3-11). The tail comprises 6% of body mass, compared to less than 1% in other primates and has prominent representation in the sensory-motor cortex of the brain. Each hindlimb is 8% of body mass, not much heavier than the tail. Compared to the 24% hindlimbs of terrestrial macaques (3-9), the 16% hindlimb mass of the atelines indicates the reduced propulsive function.

Color the hands and the pie charts showing dietary composition and feeding postures of spider and howler monkeys.

Spider and howler monkeys represent two variants in foraging and feeding. Spider monkeys concentrate upon fruits, seeds, and flowers, but also consume leaves. Howler monkeys may prefer fruits, but appear to be "leaf adapted," selecting the young leaves with fewer tannins and less cellular fiber than mature leaves. Spider and howler monkeys do not eat mobile animal prey; also, fruit and leaves require little manipulation or preparation. Therefore, the selective pressure for finer hand dexterity to catch or prepare food items is quite reduced. With reduced selection pressure, spider monkeys have lost the thumb entirely. The peculiar split between the second and third digits of the howler monkey hand opens up the finger span for grasping but reduces the capacity for opposability between the thumb and fingers.

Although leaves constitute about half of their diet, howler monkeys do not have a specialized sacculated stomach for leaf digestion as do colobine monkeys (4-22). The ability to subsist on leaves when fruit is not available may give the howler monkeys more dietary flexibility than the other atelines or other neotropical monkeys. With the exception of capuchins, the howler monkeys have the widest geographical range across Central and South America, from Mexico to Argentina.

Feeding and foraging also differ. Primatologist David Bergeson observed that spider monkeys used their tails in below-branch suspension with and without the use of the feet almost half the time. In comparison, the quadrupedal howlers suspend one-fifth the time and sit over half the time.

Color the quadrupedal posture of the howler monkey and the anatomy of its howling apparatus.

Howler monkeys and ancestral atelines were quadrupedal and had already evolved prehensile tails for feeding and crossing gaps within the canopy. Howlers retained a quadrupedal carriage and evolved an elaborate vocal apparatus as part of their territorial display. The expanded hyoid bone and associated thyroid cartilage stabilize enlarged muscles attaching above (suprahyoid) and below (infrahyoid). This apparatus thus impinges upon and reduces the mobility of the shoulders. Because the remaining atelines never acquired a howling mechanism or an enlarged hyoid, they were able to expand the range of upper body mobility, forelimb suspension, and greater agility for below-the-branch locomotion, an option closed to the howler monkeys.

Howler monkeys live in relatively cohesive and stable groups that occupy a territory; each morning their roars carry for kilometers across the forest and signal the location of each troop, thereby helping to reduce troop contact and conflict. When male howler monkeys do fight, physical injury may be severe. The availability of leaves may reduce the tendency of howler troops to fission while they forage. In contrast, spider monkeys break into subgroups to search for fruit. Howlers are lethargic compared to spider monkeys and the lower quality diet may be a contributing factor.

ATELINES

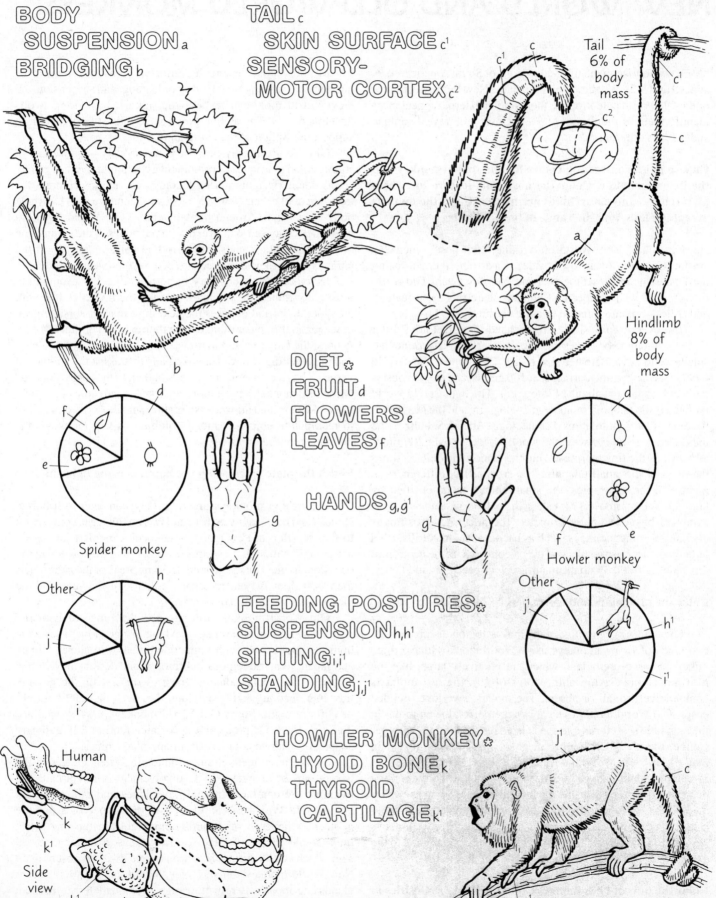

BODY
SUSPENSION a
BRIDGING b

TAIL c
SKIN SURFACE c¹
SENSORY-
MOTOR CORTEX c²

Tail
6% of
body
mass

Hindlimb
8% of
body
mass

DIET *
FRUIT d
FLOWERS e
LEAVES f

HANDS g, g¹

Spider monkey

Howler monkey

FEEDING POSTURES *
SUSPENSION h, h¹
SITTING i, i¹
STANDING j, j¹

Other

Other

HOWLER MONKEY *
HYOID BONE k
THYROID
CARTILAGE k¹

Human

Side
view

4-18
NEW WORLD AND OLD WORLD MONKEYS

Monkeys flourish in the tropical regions of South America, Asia, and Africa (3-2). Whether they inhabit the New World neotropics or the Old World paleotropics, their similar external appearances identify them as monkeys (2-13). A closer look reveals unique and distinct differences.

Choose light, contrasting colors for the spider monkey and the langur monkey. Color the noses, the feature for which platyrrhines and catarrhines are named. Color the animals except the tails, and the range of body weights.

Nostrils of New World platyrrhine ("flat nose") monkeys are far apart and open to the sides. Catarrhine ("down-facing nose") nostrils are closer together and open downward. Old World monkeys, as well as apes and humans share this nasal feature, and collectively are referred to as "catarrhines" (3-1).

The overall body shape, limbs, hands, and feet are similar (2-13). Although body sizes overlap, on average, platyrrhines are smaller, and have a greater size range. The lightest New World monkey is the pygmy marmoset at 100 grams, and the heaviest is the woolly spider at about 14 kilograms. The lightest Old World monkey is the talapoin monkey at 1 kilogram, and the heaviest is the mandrill at 35 kilograms. Primatologist Adolph Schultz stated the difference another way: the woolly spider is over 100 times as heavy as the tiny marmoset, but the mandrill is only 35 times the mass of the small talapoin. The sizes reflect differences in niches. In the neotropics, the small animal niche is filled by tamarins and marmosets (4-13); in the paleotropics this niche is occupied by nonmonkey primates, the nocturnal prosimians (4-5). Catarrhine monkeys, such as baboons and mandrills, fill a large-bodied terrestrial niche in the paleotropics. In the neotropics this niche is filled by nonprimates, such as peccaries and tapirs.

Color the premolars and ear region.

The number of premolars and the ear region distinguish the two kinds of living monkeys. New World monkeys have three rather than two premolars, which are relatively large, like the prosimians and Fayum anthropoids (4-10); the last molar is comparatively small or absent. The molars have low, rounded cusps. Old World monkeys have two premolars; the premolar in the mandible is sectorial and specialized for sharpening the upper canine, the so-called honing mechanism, which is absent in platyrrhines. Old World monkeys have sharply connected cusps in a bilophodont pattern (4-26). In platyrrhines, there is only a bony ring from the tympanic membrane to the external ear rather than a tube, a feature also like the Fayum primates. Like other catarrhines, tarsiers, and omomyids (4-3), Old World monkeys have a prominent bony tube from the tympanic membrane to the external ear that is visible on the outside of the skull.

Color the tails of both monkeys, and the ischial callosities in the Old World monkey.

Monkey posture and locomotion is a combination of quadrupedal running, scampering or leaping, and suspension. All New World monkeys, except the uakari, have long, well-developed tails. The ateline group have tails strong enough to support the weight of the entire animal (4-17).

Old World monkey tails vary enormously—reduced as in stump-tailed macaques or prominent as in langur monkeys. Tails act as counterweights during leaping and running through the trees, but unlike their New World cousins, none are used for whole body suspension. Around the tail region, Old World monkeys have thick calloused skin over the ischial bones of the innominate (4-25). These thick pads, called ischial callosities, support the animals while they sit in trees to feed, rest, or sleep.

Details of the hands vary in both groups. For example, in most platyrrhines, the orientation of the thumb lies in line with the other digits and opposes the next digit in a scissorslike grip; however, in the spider monkey, the thumb is lost entirely (4-17). Among the tamarins and marmosets, only the hallux has a nail, and the other digits have clawlike nails that assist the animals in vertical clinging on large tree trunks (4-13). In the cheek-pouched Old World monkeys, the thumbs are rotated and more opposable, more like ours, and allow considerable hand dexterity and ability to manipulate objects. Among colobine or leaf monkeys, the thumb is reduced or absent.

Finish the plate by coloring the habitats using light shades.

Platyrrhine monkeys are relatively confined to arboreal habitats and rely heavily on fruit and less on foliage in comparison to the catarrhines. Few platyrrhine species regularly travel on the ground, although those species occupying the lower canopy occasionally feed on the ground. In some areas of the neotropics, the forest floor is flooded for more than half the year, and the platyrrhines are confined to trees.

Old World monkeys tolerate a wider range of habitats: African and Asian rain forests, savanna fringe or open savanna, high mountain areas with temperate climates in Nepal, China, and Japan, semiarid regions in Ethiopia, and deserts in Namibia. Many species spend some or most of the day on the ground, traveling, feeding, and socializing; they seek the safety of trees or cliffs at night. Some Old World monkeys have specialized digestive tracts for processing low-value food (4-20), a dietary adaptation with no counterpart among platyrrhines.

Social, reproductive, and infant care systems differ in the two groups of monkeys. Male involvement in infant care and twinning are common among platyrrhines and rare or absent among Old World monkeys (4-14). Few species from the neotropics have social groups comparable to the one male, multifemale groups of Old World monkeys. Prominent sexual skin which swells during the estrous cycle (3-25) is absent in all New World monkey females. New World monkeys have scent glands and apparently rely more on scent to mark territories than do Old World species.

MORE THAN A MATTER OF NOSES

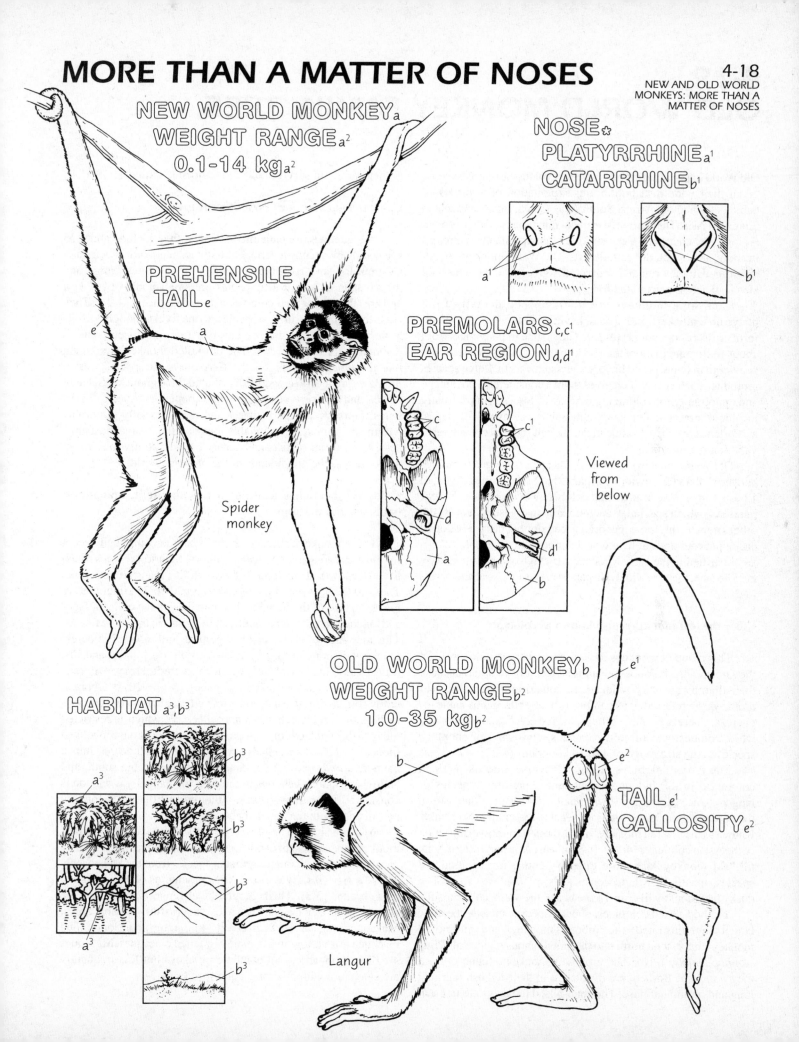

NEW WORLD MONKEY$_a$
WEIGHT RANGE$_{a^2}$
0.1-14 kg$_{a^2}$

NOSE*
PLATYRRHINE$_{a^1}$
CATARRHINE$_{b^1}$

PREHENSILE
TAIL$_e$

a^1

b^1

e

a

PREMOLARS$_{c,c^1}$
EAR REGION$_{d,d^1}$

Spider
monkey

c

c^1

Viewed
from
below

d

a

d^1

b

e^1

OLD WORLD MONKEY$_b$
WEIGHT RANGE$_{b^2}$
1.0-35 kg$_{b^2}$

e^2

HABITAT$_{a^3,b^3}$

b^3

a^3

b^3

b

TAIL$_{e^1}$
CALLOSITY$_{e^2}$

b^3

a^3

b^3

Langur

OLD WORLD MONKEY FAMILY TREE

Old World (catarrhine) monkeys are an evolutionary success story, given their wide distribution and exploitation of a variety of habitats throughout Africa, South Asia, China, Japan, and Island Southeast Asia. They thrive in tropical rain forests, high mountain regions, savannas, and even survive at environmental extremes in snow, and in hot, dry semideserts. Old World monkeys are all quadrupedal; they run and walk on the ground, in the trees, and also leap across gaps in the forests.

Catarrhine monkeys are distinguished dentally from platyrrhine monkeys and apes in having molar cusps that join to form crests (bilophodont) (4-26). They range in body mass from about 1 kilogram to more than 35 kilograms; males are generally heavier than females and have longer canine teeth. Some species reproduce each year, which gives them a considerable advantage and opportunity for colonizing new areas. Social groups usually include several adult females, young animals at several life stages, and often more than 1 adult male, though there is considerable variation in group size.

Old World monkeys (the cercopithecoids) diverged from apes between 20 and 25 mya (4-30), and the 2 subfamilies diverged 12 to 14 mya. One branch (the colobines) evolved into the leaf monkeys, which specialize anatomically in digesting leaves; the other branch, the more generalist cercopithecines, developed cheek pouches and eat fruit whenever possible (4-20). Monkeys are identified in the early Miocene African fossil record, and by the Pliocene, they are widely dispersed in Europe, Asia, and Africa (4-27).

Color the leaf monkeys, also known as colobines.

This group of monkeys derives its name from colobus, from the Greek word kolobos, meaning notched or maimed because their thumbs are very reduced. In equatorial Africa, the leaf monkeys are referred to as colobus (a[5]), after the genus name, or guereza. There are 3 main groups, the red colobus, the black and white colobus, and the olive colobus, consisting of about 10 species in the size range of 4 to 10 kilograms (4-22).

The Asian colobines are more diverse than the African colobines. In the Indian subcontinent, there are 4 species of langurs. One species, *Presbytis entellus* (a[1]), is distributed from the northern mountain regions in Nepal to the south in Sri Lanka. Known as the "sacred monkey," it has the easternmost distribution of the Asian colobines (4-23). In Southeast Asia and eastern Asia, the leaf monkeys are more diverse—consisting of about 17 species, mostly distributed on islands of Southeast Asia. The dusky leaf monkey lives in Thailand and the Malayan Peninsula.

The odd-nosed colobines, about 8 species, include the douc langurs (not illustrated), the proboscis monkeys, and snub-nosed monkeys that extend north into the mountainous regions of China (*Rhinopithecus*, 1-16). The proboscis monkeys, found only in the swamps of Borneo, are distinctive in their reddish hair and long and prominent nose. The snub-nosed monkeys are unusual

in their ability to survive cold and temperate climates.

Color the guenons, or *Cercopithecus* group.

The guenons are endemic to Africa; they include about 25 species. They occupy a variety of habitats in equatorial Africa—swamps; lowland, riverine, and gallery forests; forest fringe; and the savanna mosaic. Most species are small bodied (4–7 kg), and are striking for their colorful and marked faces (4-21). They are often sympatric, up to 6 species in one forest, though 3 to 4 is more common. The diet is mainly fruits and insects and is distinctive for each species. The red-tailed monkey is arboreal like the other guenons. Of the *Cercopithecus* species, vervet monkeys are the most widely distributed throughout subSaharan Africa and are very adaptable, with about 5 subspecies (3-5). Patas monkeys are the heaviest and most sexually dimorphic within the genus. They inhabit the woodland-savanna fringe across equatorial Africa and because of their ability to run fast, are known as the greyhounds of the monkey world.

Color the branches leading to the mandrill, mangabey, baboons, and macaque.

These monkeys share a 42 chromosome count, and except for most macaques, are African monkeys. Mandrills (*Mandrillus*) live in the lowland rain forests of western Africa and are terrestrial. They are the heaviest of the monkeys; males at 35 kilograms are twice the size of the females. The mandrills have colorful faces and hindquarters that serve as effective signals in the dense forests. The mangabeys consists of 2 genera and several species; *Cercocebus* is more closely related to the drill and mandrills, travels and feeds on the ground and understory, whereas *Lophocebus*, a gray-cheeked mangabey (3-6, 3-20) is arboreal, rarely comes to the ground, and is related to baboons. The baboons include the gelada baboon (*Theropithecus*), which is restricted today to the highlands of Ethiopa (3-5), although it once inhabited India (4-27). The "savanna" baboons (*Papio*) include the Guinea baboons in western Africa, chacma baboons in the south, and yellow and anubis baboons in the east; the hamadryas baboon is considered a separate species, although in Ethiopia it forms a hybrid zone with the anubis baboon.

Macaques are most closely related to the baboon group of monkeys and consist of about 15 species. Macaques are primarily Asian monkeys, although a remnant species from the Pleistocene, *Macaca sylvanus*, lives in the Atlas mountains of Morocco and on Gibraltar (3-2). Their geographical range extends into the mountains of Japan; some species successfully inhabit cities. Macaques range in size from about 3 kilograms in the long-tailed macaque to 15 kilograms in male pig-tailed macaques. Macaques are often sympatric with colobine monkeys but less frequently are sympatric with other macaque species (4-24).

OLD WORLD MONKEY FAMILY TREE

LEAF MONKEYS ✲
ASIAN ✲
LANGUR $_{a^1}$
DUSKY $_{a^2}$
PROBOSCIS $_{a^3}$
SNUB-NOSED $_{a^4}$
AFRICAN ✲
COLOBUS $_{a^5}$

CHEEK POUCH MONKEYS ✲
GUENONS $_b$
RED TAIL $_{b^1}$
VERVET $_{b^2}$
PATAS $_{b^3}$
MANDRILL $_c$
MANGABEY $_d$
BABOONS $_e$
GELADA $_{e^1}$
SAVANNA $_{e^2}$
HAMADRYAS $_{e^3}$
MACAQUE $_f$

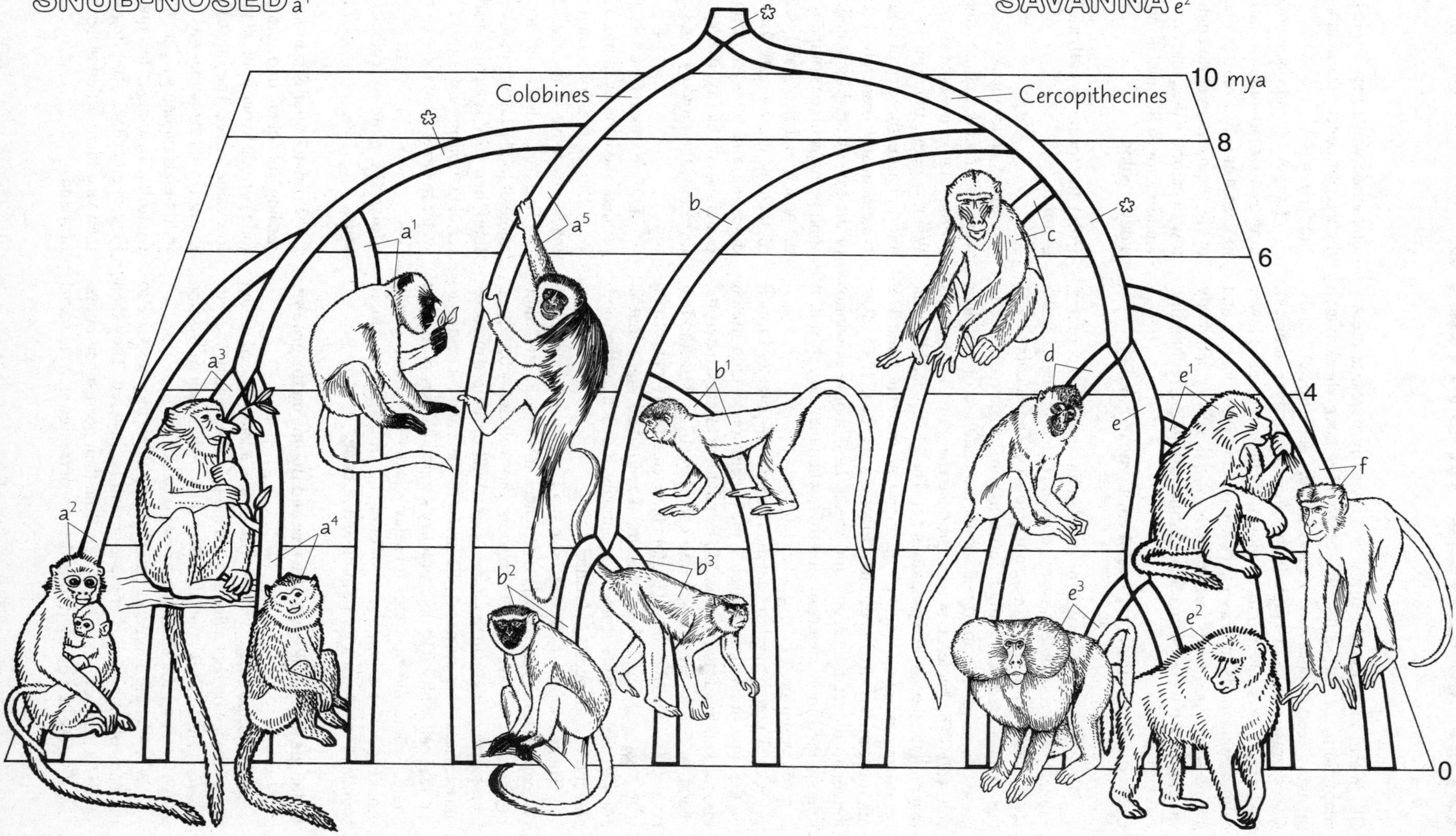
10 mya
8
6
4
0
Colobines
Cercopithecines
✲
a1
a2
a3
a4
a5
b
b1
b2
b3
c
d
e
e1
e2
e3
f

4-20
OLD WORLD MONKEYS

Old World monkeys illustrate two virtually opposite dietary adaptations. In one subfamily (cercopithecines), cheek pouch monkeys feed on an array of fruits, seeds, nuts, flowers, buds, leaves, grass, and animal prey. In the other subfamily (colobines), the leaf monkeys rely mainly on more difficult to digest and lower caloric value foods such as leaves and other foliage, lichens, and unripe fruit. Food type, feeding style, social activity, and body structure form webs of function, distinct within each subfamily.

Color the anatomical features of each type of monkey.

Leaf monkeys have enlarged, chambered sacculated stomachs that resemble those of cows and other ruminents, and a large intestinal tract for storing bulky foliage. The chambering of the stomach permits "foregut fermentation." Bacteria reside in these chemical vats and break down the cellulose of the plant cell walls. The bacteria, in turn, produce energy-rich fatty acids that are absorbed by the monkey's gut. Therefore, leaf fiber can be utilized for energy through the intervention of gut flora. The microorganisms also neutralize plant toxins. Leaf fiber takes longer to digest than fruits and seeds. Leaf monkeys cannot tolerate the simple sugars of ripe fruit; when they do eat fruit, it is green or unripe.

Cheek pouch monkeys get their name from pouches formed by the superficial facial muscles, the buccinators, which stretch into pockets inside the mouth. As an individual forages, the fruits, seeds, or leaves are stuffed into each pouch. This method of collection allows the animal to store food temporarily and permits it to "eat and run." When the monkey finds a place that is comfortable and safe from other animals, it dislodges the food, and chews and digests at leisure.

The two kinds of monkey have similar jaws and teeth. Close inspection, however, reveals differences in form and function. Leaf monkeys have smaller incisors, but well-defined, higher, and sharper cusps on their molars (4-22). Well-developed masseter muscles and sharp cusps act effectively to shear and cut (triturate) the leaf cell walls. The leaf monkey's mandible has prominent angles where the masseter muscles attach. The cheek pouch monkeys have larger incisors for biting into fruit (3-6), and more rounded molar cusps for pulping and grinding.

Color the leaf monkeys in the tree and the one on the ground.

While doing field work in Sri Lanka, anatomist Ted Grand filmed the feeding behavior of a leaf monkey, the langur (*Presbytis entellus*) and a cheek pouch monkey, the toque macaque (*Macaca sinica*) in order to contrast their two styles of feeding.

When langur monkeys enter feeding trees, they disperse to the ends of branches where leaf growth is clustered. They then space themselves 1.2 to 1.8 meters from their nearest neighbors. Usually they face outward from the core of the tree to avoid social interaction while they feed. The three-dimensional structure of the tree influences the number and arrangement of animals that can feed in it.

Langurs spend on average 5 to 20 minutes, sometimes as long as 40 to 50 minutes, sitting and feeding in one place. Each mouthful of leaves must be chewed and swallowed before another cycle begins. Leaves do contain protein, but they are bulky and low in caloric value, and enormous quantities must be ingested. Anthropologist Suzanne Ripley estimated they spend 3 to 6 hours a day feeding.

Color the foraging path and the cheek pouch monkey on the ground.

Cheek pouch monkeys collect food in a dramatically different way. The macaque climbs into a tree, scans for food, and checks for the relative position and social rank of other troop members. When it goes after fruit in particular, it stuffs one piece after another into the expanding cheek pouches. This continues systematically, branch by branch, until it has covered a quadrat of the tree or until its pouches are filled. Then it finds a shady spot, perhaps in the company of other monkeys, where it clears the pouch, and chews and swallows, piece by piece. This pattern of feeding disconnects food harvesting from processing and digesting and frees the monkeys to eat and socialize. Cheek pouches are handy if feeding on the ground when danger threatens; the monkey can beat a quick retreat with its meal in tow.

Differences in food selection of these two kinds of catarrhine primates become even more apparent during the cycle of a full year. During the dry season at Polonnaruwa, Sri Lanka, toque macaques move to parts of their large home range where they can find fruit, other foods, and water; they continue to eat a wide range of foods. Langur monkeys, on the other hand, progressively limit their food selection, especially with respect to dry leaves; fermentation provides them with both nutrition and sufficient water to carry them through the dry season.

Finish the plate by coloring the vignettes at the top of the page.

Primatologist Suzanne Ripley dubbed the two styles of feeding "banquet" and "smorgasbord." Leaf monkeys feed for long periods in one spot (at the table), filling their stomachs with low value leaves. They are too busy to do much interacting, which is limited in the same way as it is at the banquet table, to the individuals on one's right and left, the food consisting of small, controlled helpings. Macaques, like most cheek pouch monkeys, move a great deal, sampling the variety of what the forest offers, then take their "filled plates" to some safe spot in the company of friends.

BANQUET AND SMORGASBORD FEEDERS

LEAF MONKEY_a
SACCULATED STOMACH_{a1}

CHEEK POUCH MONKEY_b
CHEEK POUCH_{b1}

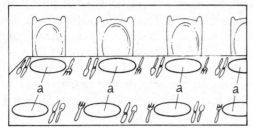

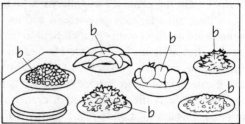

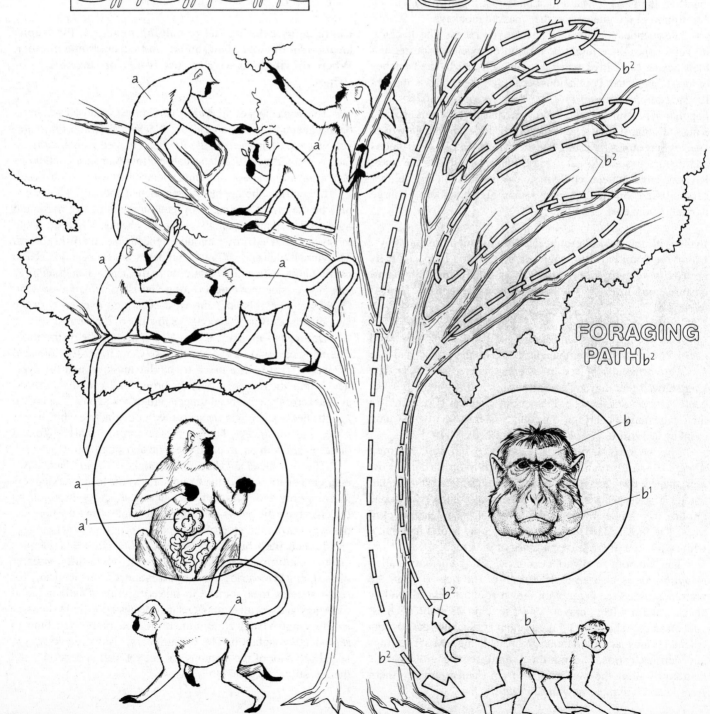

FORAGING PATH_{b2}

GUENONS: MASKED MONKEYS

Guenons live in the equatorial region of Africa. They consist of more than 25 species in the genus *Cercopithecus,* which means "monkey with a long tail." In body proportions and locomotor anatomy, guenons are so similar that Adolph Schultz remarked that under the skin they all look alike! On their bodies, the hair is usually a nondescript greenish gray, called "agouti," having a grizzled look because the colors are in bands along the hair shaft. However, each species has distinct and often dramatic facial marking, the basis for naturalist and artist Jonathan Kingdon's description of the guenons as the "masked monkeys."

The guenon radiation may be relatively recent. The diversity in facial appearance might be a result of speciation during the Pleistocene, 1 to 2 mya, when the climate fluctuated and patches of forest contracted. Populations became isolated and possibilities for speciation occurred (1-16). When forests expanded later, populations again became sympatric, but as different species. Kingdon suggests that guenons evolved along the changing river courses in central Africa, and like their close relatives the baboons and mangabeys, could get along on the ground or in the trees. Riverine environments could more easily support a low number of small-size resident monkeys than high numbers of large nomadic monkeys.

Begin with the swamp monkey, talapoin, and patas monkeys. Color the frame around each monkey with a light color, its approximate distribution on the map, and its body mass and chromosome number. You may color each monkey face as described.

The swamp monkey, talapoin, and patas monkey seemed distinct from all the other guenons based on their looks and size and were originally placed in different genera. Molecular data later showed that they are early branches and belong within the genus *Cercopithecus.* The diversity of guenons is reflected in their wide range of chromosome numbers, from 48 in the swamp monkey to 72 in *C. pogonius* (not illustrated).

The swamp monkey, *C. nigroviridis,* once named *Allenopithecus,* is found only in the Congo River Basin. It is the most ancient lineage and has 48 chromosomes, closest in number to the macaque-baboon group with 42 chromosomes. As its name implies, the monkeys swim in the swamp but spend their lives in trees. The face is dark with surrounding gray agouti hair and a white chin, one of the least patterned of the group.

The talapoin or dwarf guenon, *C. talapoin,* once called *Miopithecus,* is also an early branch of the tree. Its ears are prominent; the face is tan with brown agouti forehead, yellow cheeks, and a white "cravat" under its chin. It is the smallest guenon and the smallest Old World monkey. Socially, the talapoin resembles the macaque-baboon group in having sexual swellings and defined estrus, and multimale-multifemale groups. It is distributed along the western coast from Cameroon to northern Angola and is sympatric with *C. cephus.*

The patas monkey, *C. patas,* formerly *Erythrocebus,* is the largest of the guenons, with marked sexual dimorphism in body mass and canine size, but not color pattern. Patas monkeys are the most terrestrial, with long limbs, a large home range, and the ability to walk long distances and to run at high speeds. It is distributed across equatorial Africa. The face has a black mask across the eyes, a white nose, muzzle, and mustache, and reddish cheeks. The hair on the mid-forehead is reddish and tapers to sandy color on each side of the forehead.

Continue by coloring the remaining monkeys: the frame, location on the map, body mass, and chromosome number. Where distributions overlap, use two colors together or as stripes.

The diana monkey, *C. diana,* has the westernmost distribution of the guenons. It has an elegant black face with a thin pale-yellow band of hair across the forehead topped with agouti; the face is framed with dramatic pale-yellow hair in a continuous band from the temples to the chin, underscored with a white beard.

In contrast, the cephus or mustached monkey, *C. cephus,* may be the most amusing with its dramatic blue eye mask and nose, yellow "mutton chops" over the cheeks, V-shaped white mustache, grizzled brown agouti forehead, and small gray beard. The vibrant blue and yellow facial patches have been likened to traffic lights, which draw attention to the head when "flagging" in a side-to-side movement during courtship and appeasement. Cephus monkeys inhabit the west coast and overlap with the talapoin and deBrazza's monkeys in parts of their range.

DeBrazza's monkey, *C. neglectus,* has a wide distribution, extending east into Kenya and west to Cameroon. The forehead is layered, first with a black triangular mask around the eyes, then a dramatic rust color over the brows, and a solid black band arched across the forehead topped with black agouti. The brown agouti cheeks and jowls are set off with a distinctive white beard, nose, and mustache. The species combines marked sexual dimorphism with an arboreal lifestyle and small family group.

The owl-faced or Hamlyni's monkey, *C. hamlyni,* has a restricted distribution in the Congo. Its whole face is a relatively uniform gray agouti except for a tan band across the forehead directly above the brows and a dramatic white strip from between the eyes down to the top of its upper lip.

French field biologists Anne Gautier-Hion and Jacques Gautier confirm substantial overlap with subtle differences in diets among sympatric guenon species and a strong tendency for some species to associate in mixed groups. Distinct facial markings and vocalizations ensure species-specific systems of auditory and visual communication, and both contribute to reproductive isolation. The evolutionary history, ecology, and social behavior of the guenons are not yet well understood, and there is still a great deal to learn.

MASKED MONKEYS

CERCOPITHECUS SPECIES∗

SWAMP a   DIANA d   OWL-FACED g
TALAPOIN b   CEPHUS e
PATAS c   DE BRAZZA'S f

Africa

DISTRIBUTION a-g
BODY MASS a¹-g¹

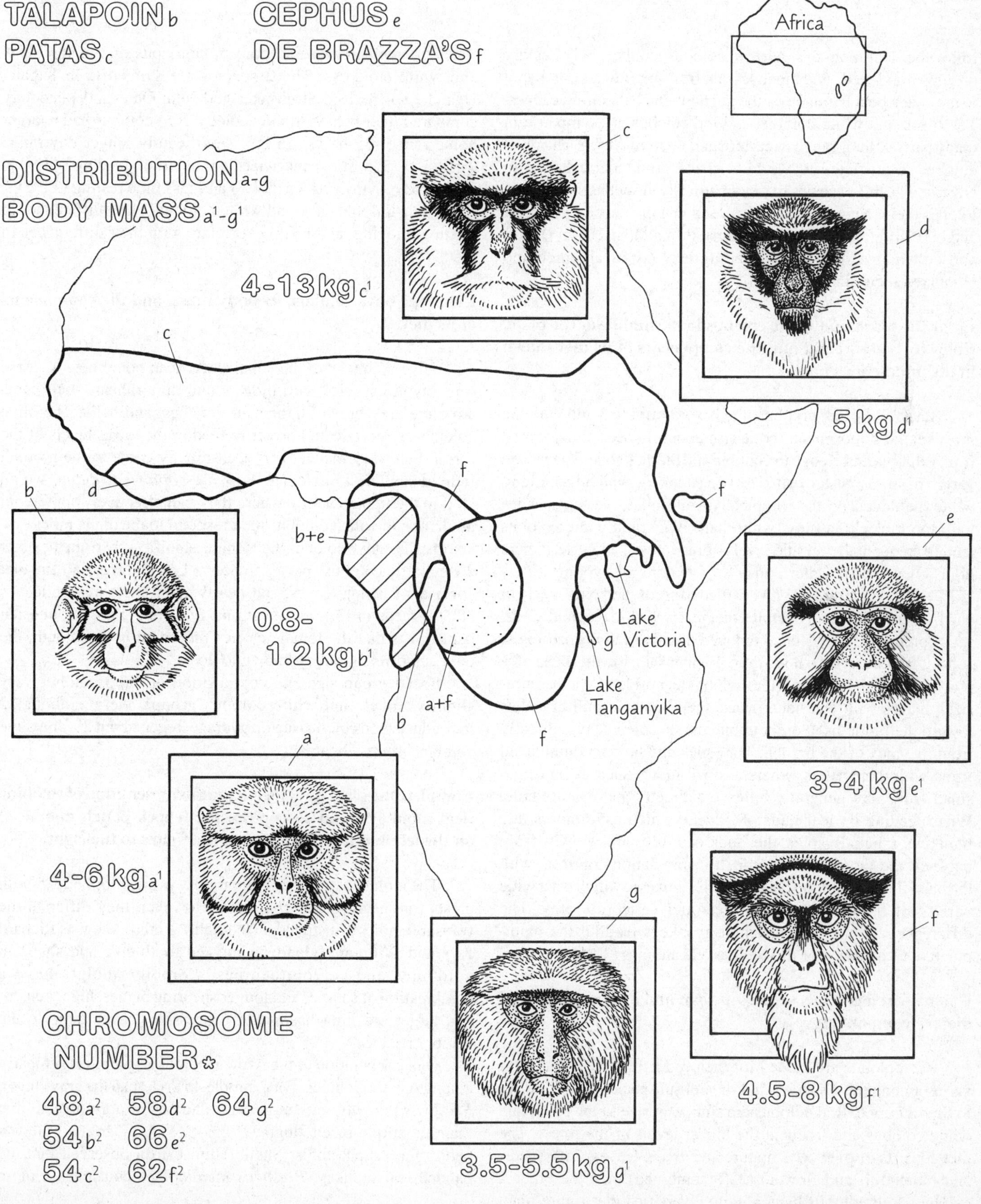

4-13 kg c¹

5 kg d¹

b+e

0.8-
1.2 kg b¹

a+f

Lake
Victoria

Lake
Tanganyika

3-4 kg e¹

4-6 kg a¹

4.5-8 kg f¹

CHROMOSOME
NUMBER∗

48 a²   58 d²   64 g²
54 b²   66 e²
54 c²   62 f²

3.5-5.5 kg g¹

AFRICAN COLOBUS MONKEYS

Like other leaf monkeys, African colobus monkeys rely heavily on leaves and seeds and much less on fruit and flowers compared to the cheek pouch monkeys, the guenons and baboon-macaques. The black and white colobus and red colobus are sympatric in many parts of their range in eastern and western Africa. The olive colobus is restricted to western Africa, from Sierra Leone to Nigeria. The three species live sympatrically in southeastern Sierra Leone; their ranges overlap in closed canopy secondary forest and in riverine and nonriverine forest. Primatologist Glyn Davies and colleagues studied the feeding ecology of all three and compared their dietary adaptations.

Color the black and white colobus in the middle of the plate. Color its body weight and the components of its diet shown in the middle pie chart.

Black and white colobus, the heaviest of the 3 and with the most sexual dimorphism, comprise about 5 species distributed from Ethiopia and Kenya to Gambia and Sierra Leone. The pelage varies from the eastern species (*C. guereza*), which has a long white shoulder cape and completely white tail, to western species with more black and less white hair. Black and white colobus tend to frequent the middle levels of the forests, about 18 meters high. Over half the diet consists of mature and young leaves (57%), with one-third (33%) devoted to seeds, and only 6% fruit and flowers combined, overall a diet that is 90% leaves and seeds.

Colobus monkeys have reduced thumbs, and primatologist John Oates describes how they compensate for the lack of a precision grip. Black and white colobus tear off large- or medium-sized leaves with one hand or use their hands to pull branches toward their mouths in order to bite the succulent leaves directly from the apex of the branch. They pick and hold medium-sized fruits with their hands, whereas small items, such as buds and small fruits, are generally bitten off directly and eaten whole. When feeding on leaf buds of *Acacia*, which have thorns, the monkeys manually pick the buds carefully and slowly from between the thorns. Their limited manipulation contrasts with the hand dexterity of the cheek pouch monkeys, which eat a wide variety of foods including insects and vertebrate prey. The differences among the catarrhine monkeys parallel the manipulative adaptations of the cebines and atelines (4-16).

Color the red colobus at the top right and its body mass and dietary components.

Red colobus are named for their red hair, though the color varies among the 4 species and several subspecies across Kenya to Sierra Leone. Red colobus are similar in size to the black and white colobus and frequent the higher levels of the forest. The diet consists of over 50% mature and young leaves, 25% seeds, and more fruit and flowers (22% combined) than the other 2 colobus. Red colobus have a more diversified diet (more plant species), compared to the more monotonous diet of the black and white monkeys. The 2 species are sympatric in Kibale, Uganda, where Tom Struhsaker and John Oates independently compared their behavior and ecology. Red colobus had a larger home range (35 ha vs. 15 ha), significantly longer day range (650 m vs. 535 m), spent twice as much time feeding (44% vs. 20%) and moving (9% vs. 5.4%) and less time resting (35% vs. 57%) than did the black and white colobus. Their differences in feeding, moving, and resting correlate with their differences in diet.

Color the olive colobus, its body mass, and the components of its diet.

Olive colobus are the smallest African colobines. A single (monotypic) species with little sexual dimorphism, their coats are olive gray-brown, lighter on the chest and belly. The olive colobus are cryptic and prefer to feed in the lower levels of the forest, below 15 meters, and occasionally come to the ground. Individuals like to associate with *Cercopithecus diana,* which feed in the upper canopy where they can effectively spot aerial predators; the olive colobus then respond to the diana monkeys' alarm calls. Olive colobus diet departs significantly from the other 2 sympatric colobus species in Sierra Leone. Over half the diet consists of young leaves, and nearly equal parts mature leaves (11%), seeds (14%), and fruit and flowers (11%). An unusual behavior is that the female carries the infant in her mouth, the only catarrhine monkey known to do so.

Social group size and composition of the 3 colobus vary slightly. Black and white colobus groups average about 12 individuals; red colobus are on average larger, about 20, and olive colobus groups about 8.

Complete the plate by coloring the molar dentition of colobine (leaf monkeys) and cercopithecine (cheek pouch monkeys) on the left and their location on the figure to the right.

The molars of all Old World monkeys are bilophodont, with crests for shearing and chopping. However, they differ in the two subfamilies (illustrated on the right). Anthropologists Richard Kay and William Hylander analyzed tooth size and shape in colobines and cercopithecines. Colobine molars have a combination of sharper and longer shearing blades, higher cusps, and larger crushing basins for processing leaves than do the cercopithecines.

Niche separation of the African colobines parallels sympatry among Asian colobines. For example, in Sri Lanka the gray langur, *Presbytis entellus,* eats more fruit and has a more diverse diet than the purple-faced langur, *Presbytis vetelus.* In the Malayan peninsula, primatologist Sheila Hunt Curtin observed that the banded leaf monkey, *Presbytis melalophus,* consumes a more

AFRICAN COLOBUS MONKEYS

BLACK AND WHITE a
RED b
OLIVE c

DIET *
  MATURE LEAVES d
  YOUNG LEAVES e
  SEEDS f
  FRUIT g
  FLOWERS h

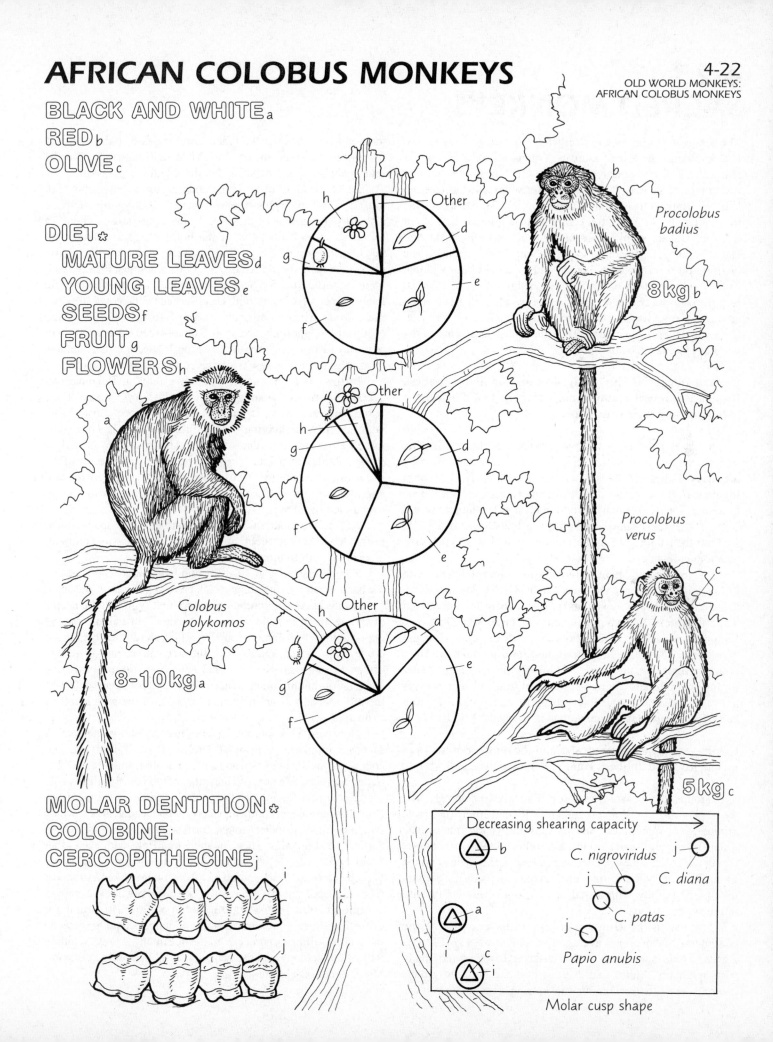

Procolobus
badius

8 kg b

Colobus
polykomos

8-10 kg a

Procolobus
verus

5 kg c

MOLAR DENTITION *
COLOBINE i
CERCOPITHECINE j

Decreasing shearing capacity →

b
i
C. nigroviridus
j
C. diana

a
i
j
C. patas

c
i
j
Papio anubis

Molar cusp shape

4-23
SACRED MONKEYS

The hanuman or gray langur, *Presbytis (Semnopithecus) entellus*, also known as the sacred monkey, is unusual for a number of reasons: it is the most terrestrial of the colobines; it thrives in a wide range of habitats; it has a long association with humans and features prominently in Indian mythology; it was the first colobine to be studied; and it is at the center of an ongoing debate about the evolutionary significance of male infant-killing behavior. Hanuman langurs constitute 1 species with 15 subspecies, and a distribution from Pakistan, Nepal, and Bangladesh through the Indian subcontinent to Sri Lanka. Although more than 20 populations have been observed, few studies have been continuous or of long duration, and most have focused on social behavior rather than ecology. This plate illustrates some of the variation in this adaptable species.

Color a sample of four study sites and habitats: Junbesi, Kanha, Polannaruwa, and Abu. Color the two illustrations of langurs and their body mass.

In the Himalayan foothills at 3000 meters, Junbesi langurs survive extreme temperature changes and occasional snow; they are heavy (20 kg) with thick coats. Kanha is situated in the central highlands, in moist and dry deciduous forests and meadows. Polonnaruwa in Sri Lanka is in extremely dry deciduous lowland forests; here the langurs are lightest in body size (10 kg). At Jodhpur the langurs live in the semidesert, and at Abu they live near and in towns.

Langurs occupy habitats ranging from forested areas with little human disturbance (Junbesi, Kanha, Orcha, Polonnuwara), to groves near temples, towns, and villages, where they are revered and offered food by local inhabitants (Jodhpur, Abu, Dharwar). Langur populations live in habitats with extreme seasonal variation in temperature, rainfall, and food production. Their ability to digest mature leaves and to go without drinking water for long periods helps them survive when fruit and young leaves are not available. Social interaction, for example in feeding behavior, is much less frequent than in macaques (4-20).

Color average mixed group size and the number of males in mixed groups at Junbesi, Kanha, Polannaruwa, and Abu.

Groups vary in size from a few to nearly 100 animals, in 3 social patterns: 1 male and several females and young (uni-male groups); 2 or more males and females and young (multi-male groups); lone or all-male groups. Like other Old World monkeys, langur males leave their natal group and join an all-male or mixed group. The rate of male turnover in mixed groups varies, and can take place rapidly with lethal aggression, or gradually with minimal aggression.

Junbesi in the Himalayas represents one end of the continuum. Social groups average 12 animals (range, 7–19) with 2 males; home range size is large (760 ha) and overlaps minimally with neighbors. Males within the group and between groups interact very little. During the mating season, one male temporarily drives out the other. Lone males or pairs of males have been observed in the area. Male replacement within the multimale group is gradual and without lethal aggression.

At Kanha in the central highlands, groups average about 20, most having 1 male plus 10 females and their offspring; there are also all-male groups in the area. Home range size is about 75 hectares, and 45% to 50% of the home range is shared with neighboring groups. Social groups interact with each other daily; males whoop, tussle, and chase each other. Zoologist Paul Newton made observations for 3 years and continued to monitor 350 langurs over a 10 year period. He observed the takeover in a one-male group when an all-male group of 16 invaded the mixed group and fought for 4 days; 3 of 6 infants died. Afterwards, one of the invaders settled in as the sole group male, the other 3 infants disappeared, and the new male stayed for almost 10 years.

In the southernmost population, groups at Polannaruwa averaged between 20 and 30 langurs with 2 or 3 males. Each home range size was 775 hectares and overlapped considerably with 1 or more neighboring groups. Unlike the Himalayan langurs, there was no clear breeding season, and males did not leave their groups. Males in neighboring groups displayed at each other, invading the territories of other groups, whooping and aggressively chasing. The lower ranking males in the group usually led the charge.

At Abu, Jodhpur, and Dharwar, one-male groups were the norm. Male replacement in one-male groups was frequent, associated with fighting and infant deaths.

The observations of volatility and lethal aggression became the basis for theorizing about its adaptive significance. Based on her studies at Abu, anthropologist Sarah Hrdy linked the deaths of infants to an intentional male "strategy" for gaining mating opportunities; by killing the nursing infant, she argues, the female comes into estrus, mates with the new male, and bears his offspring, an example of sexual selection. In an alternative explanation, anthropologist Thad Bartlett and colleagues interpret the infant deaths as an incidental outcome of the high levels of male aggression.

However, a broader view places langurs within the context of other monkeys. Zoologist Thelma Rowell analyzed and contrasted social interaction and communication among catarrhine males. Langurs, like guenons and other colobines, live in unstable social groups; males interact little with each other or with females. Rowell notes that, in contrast, baboon and macaque males, which live in permanent social groups, form coalitions, nurture young, and befriend females. They squabble and fight with each other but also reconcile, thereby minimizing group disruption and injury to each other and to other group members. Langur monkeys appear to be an ecologically adaptable species, but lack complex communication for mediating social relationships and for diffusing severe aggression. Studies on langurs tend to focus on the "infant killing hypothesis" to the detriment of understanding the overall ecology and the behavior of all age and sex classes. Much remains to be studied.

HANUMAN LANGURS

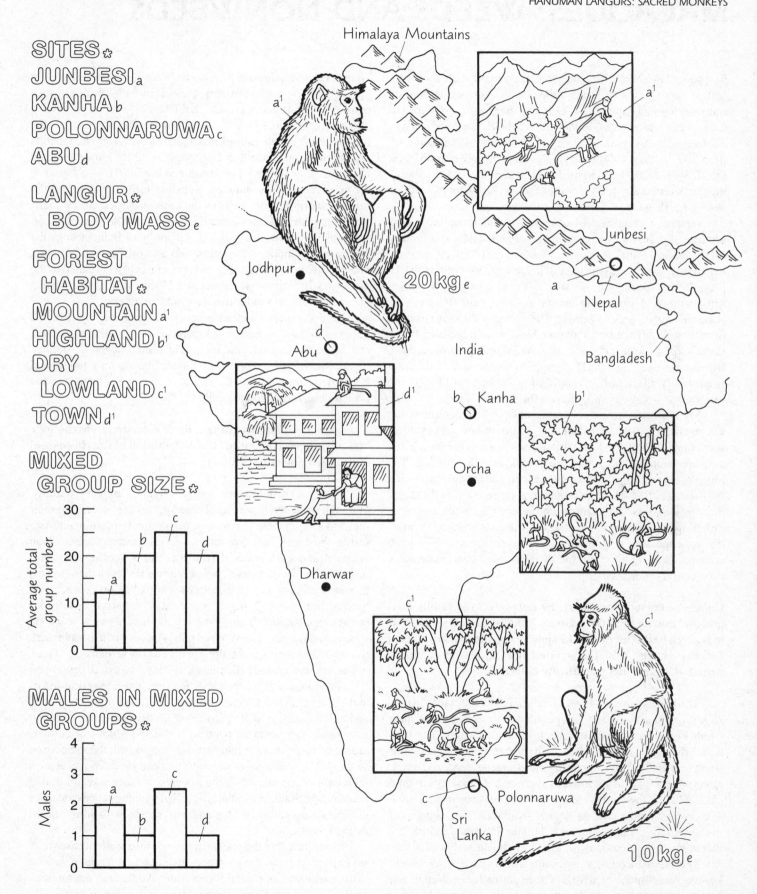

SITES *
JUNBESI a
KANHA b
POLONNARUWA c
ABU d

LANGUR *
  BODY MASS e

FOREST
  HABITAT *
MOUNTAIN a¹
HIGHLAND b¹
DRY
  LOWLAND c¹
TOWN d¹

MIXED
GROUP SIZE *

MALES IN MIXED
GROUPS *

Himalaya Mountains
Junbesi
Nepal
India
Bangladesh
Jodhpur
Abu
Kanha
Orcha
Dharwar
Polonnaruwa
Sri Lanka

20kg e
10kg e

4-24
MACAQUES: WEEDS AND NONWEEDS

Macaques have been observed extensively in the wild, semiwild, and in captivity. Long-term studies on macaques in Japan, on transplanted social groups in Texas and Oregon (*M. fuscata*), and on rhesus macaques (*M. mulatta*) from India released on Cayo Santiago, Puerto Rico, have revealed valuable information on their life history, infant survival, kinship, and reproduction (3-25, 3-27, 3-29). Used in medical research for decades, rhesus monkeys tested the polio vaccine, and the Rh factor in blood is named for them.

Despite a great deal of observation and research, a clear picture of macaque geographic expansion and evolutionary relationships remains elusive. There are 15 to 19 species, depending on the classificatory scheme applied. Four of the 15 present-day species are so successful in living near human settlements and exploiting human resources that they can be accurately described as "weeds." Their geographic range extends from western Afghanistan, Pakistan, India, and Sri Lanka to Japan, East China, Taiwan, and southeast Asia, including Sumatra, Java, Borneo, Sulawesi, and the Philippines. Their present distribution is probably the result of population movements following Pleistocene isolations and climatic fluctuation (4-27).

Macaque species are very much alike in their dentitions and in cranial and postcranial skeletons ("hard tissues"). They differ somewhat in body size and in soft tissues, such as the form of the tail; behaviorally, macaques show considerable variation. The morphological similarities suggest to anthropologist Nina Jablonski that the macaque radiation is recent, during the past 1 to 2 million years. Molecular relationships also indicate a recent radiation, about 2 million years for the divergence of most lineages, and more recently for closely related species. This plate conveys the complex evolutionary relationships and geographic distribution of *Macaca*.

Color the barbary macaque, its lineage on the family tree, and location on the African map. Proceed to each monkey as it is discussed. Ten of the 15 species are illustrated. Except for the rhesus and long-tailed macaques, geographic distributions are not specifically outlined.

The barbary macaque, *M. sylvanus,* is found in Morocco and Algeria, but may be a relict population from the once more widespread circum-Mediterranean fossil macaques. The lion-tailed macaque, *M silenus,* is restricted to a small enclave in southwest India. The sympatric bonnet macaque, *M. radiata,* is more widely distributed in India south of the Godavari river. A close relative, the toque macaque, *M. sinica,* lives in Sri Lanka. The successful rhesus, *M. mulatta,* is distributed from Afghanistan in the west to China in the east and into Thailand, Burma, and Indochina in the south, as indicated by the dashed border lines (d). The related assamese macaque, *M. assamensis,* is a little-known forest monkey distributed in north India, Nepal, and Vietnam. The stump-tailed or bear macaque, *M. arctoides,* and its relative the tibetan macaque, *M. thibetana,* are found from

Assam, eastward through Sichuan province in China, historically part of Tibet, and south on the Malay and Indochinese peninsulas—but not in present-day Tibet.

Similar to the wide distribution of the rhesus macaque, the long-tailed (or crab-eating) macaque, *M. fascicularis,* inhabits areas south on mainland Southeast Asia to Timor and the Philippines, as indicated by the dotted border (f). The Japanese *M. fuscata,* or snow monkey, lives the farthest north and the related, warm-weather version, the Formosan rock, *M. cyclopis*, is endemic to Taiwan (formerly Formosa). The pig-tailed *M. nemestrina* is widely dispersed from northeast India through the Malayan and Indochinese peninsulas and on Borneo, Sumatra, and the Mentawi Islands. Pig-tails are most closely related to the macaques on Sulawesi, the crested black (*M. nigra*), tonkean (*M. tonkeana*), and moor macaques (*M. maura*).

Note that seven macaque species live at the edges of the geographic range: barbary, Japanese, Formosan, pig-tailed, crested black, tonkean, and moor. The remaining eight (bonnet, toque, rhesus, assamese, stump-tailed, tibetan, long-tailed, and lion-tailed) are concentrated in the center in South Asia, what primatologist Jack Fooden calls the "heartland."

Complete the plate by using a dark color to circle the four "weed" species (j). Outline the distribution of the rhesus and long-tailed macaques with (j).

Macaques differ in their ability to tolerate human proximity, although some even prosper. These species are eclectic in their diet and so adaptable that niches are not finely partitioned. As a result, they may "eat out" other species. Primatologist Alison Richard and colleagues divide macaques ecologically into nonweed and weed species. Nonweed species reach their highest density in forests where they have minimal or no contact with human beings. Although "weed" has negative colloquial connotations, it does portray the relationship between macaque species and human culture. Weed plants thrive where people mark the land, and they spread along with human settlements. Weed macaques, particularly the rhesus and long-tailed, depend upon but also compete with people when they live alongside towns and villages. Weed species, such as the toque, bonnet, rhesus, and long-tailed, are all allopatric, that is, only one species is found in a particular habitat, a contrast with the guenons or colobus monkeys where three or more species may inhabit the same forest (4-21, 4-22). Examples of macaque sympatry are few and always include a weed and nonweed species: bonnet and lion-tailed macaques in Southeast India; long-tailed with pig-tailed macaques or with stump-tailed in Thailand; and rhesus with stump-tailed in southwest China.

Macaques, like the guenons, provide an excellent case study for exploring evolutionary processes, such as the role of genetic drift, variation, and natural selection. Additional anatomical, ecological, and molecular information is needed to more fully understand all dimensions of these fascinating monkeys.

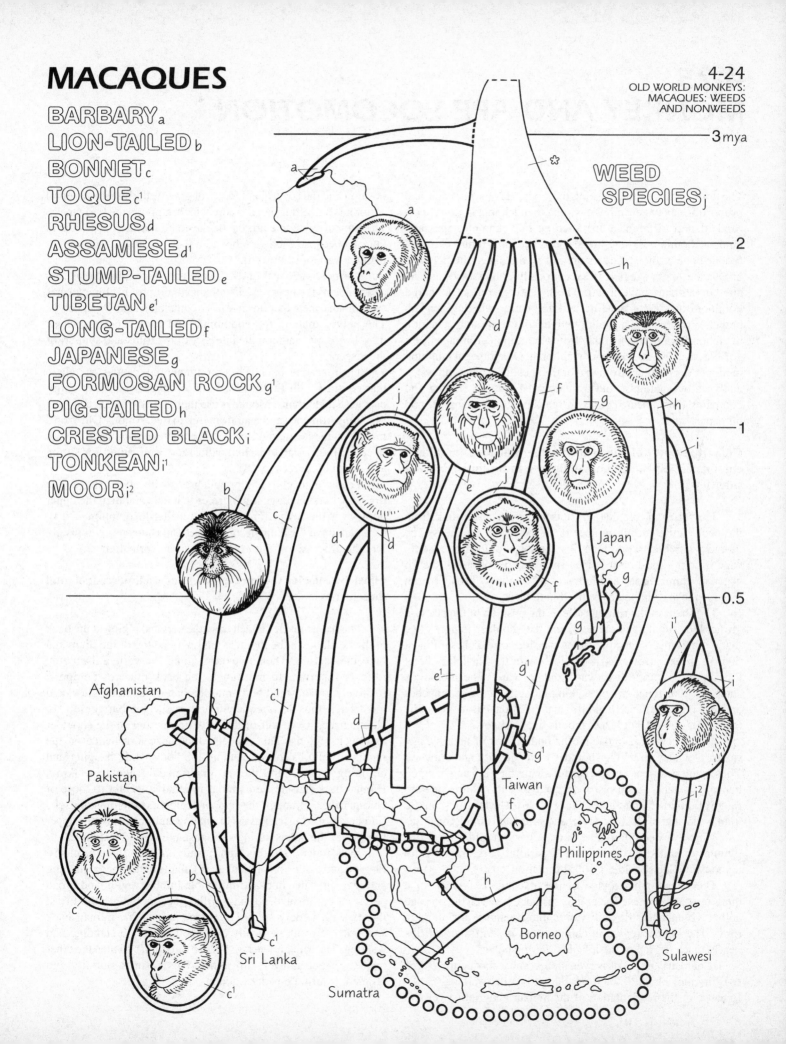

The trunk, the central mass of the body, differs in shape and proportions between monkeys, apes, and humans. It reflects fundamental differences in function. For example, apes and humans (hominoids) have broad chests and long, robust clavicles (collar bones); the shoulders are out to the sides; the pelvis is broad; the lumbar region is exceptionally compressed; and no apes or humans have a tail. These features reflect a shared hominoid history of hanging and acrobatic swinging beneath branch supports. It is a pattern with much variation; brachiation in gibbons differs considerably from locomotion in chimpanzees, gorillas, orangutans, and young children. Quadrupedal climbing in monkeys is distinct from that of the apes. This plates draws on analyses by anatomist and primatologist Adolph Schultz and compares the truncal regions in macaques, chimpanzees, and humans.

Color the parts of the trunk in the macaque (monkey), chimpanzee (ape), and human figures, in the top, front, and side views.

The vertebral column (3-7) runs the length of the trunk, from the neck to the coccyx in apes or to the tail in monkeys. The thoracic vertebrae support the ribs; the shape of the macaque rib cage is compressed on the sides and is deep, not broad; the rib cages of chimpanzees and humans are relatively broader from side to side and shallower from front to back.

The shape of the rib cage affects the position of the pectoral girdle, the scapula and clavicle, and the shoulder joint. Notice that the macaque's scapulae lie on the sides of the chest (almost doglike in its narrowness), and along with the clavicles, direct the shoulder joints downward and forward. The monkey's shoulder joint functions in walking along the tops of branches and in using its arms and hands for manipulation. It is more mobile than a dog's (3-9), but is less mobile than an ape's.

Chimpanzee's scapulae lie flat on the back of the rib cage; robust clavicles direct the shoulder joints upward and outward. These joint positions equip apes for swinging from and hanging beneath branches. Such suspensory movements require a greater range of motion than monkeys have (4-26). The human shoulder joint is like that of an ape's. Overhead straps and railings on buses and subways accommodate our apelike shoulder, and our gymnastic skills on the rings and parallel bars dramatically demonstrate the shoulder's 360° of rotation.

The long lumbar region of the macaque is typical for a quadrupedal mammal. The greater distance between the rib cage and pelvis enhances flexibility in running, leaping, and jumping (3-8). The lumbar region in chimpanzees is short; the last ribs nearly reach the top of the long and flaring pelvis.

In humans, the pelvis is even more compact but permits some twisting movement of the trunk during bipedal walking (5-14). Because of the reorientation of the human body into a vertical position and the consequent forces of gravity, the human vertebral column is a central, flexible core which supports the body mass. The lumbar vertebrae are the thickest and the sacrum widest in humans because each vertebra cumulatively takes more weight than the vertebrae above it.

The pelvis consists of two innominate bones plus the sacrum and connects the upper trunk with the hindlimbs. In chimpanzees and humans, the wider rib cage has a complementary wider pelvis. The pelvis anchors the abdominal and back muscles. These muscle groups maintain the integrity of the trunk and support of the viscera.

The macaque's pelvis has prominent tail (caudal) vertebrae that contrast with the tiny vestigial coccygeal bones in chimpanzees and humans. Monkeys use their tails for balance as they run along branches and leap from tree to tree. Among Old World monkeys, the ischium of the pelvis is flattened and padded with thickened skin, called ischial callosities, well suited for sitting and sleeping in trees (4-18).

The human pelvis is short and broad with a bowl shape. The ilium anchors the large hip muscles that help stabilize the upper body over the lower limbs during bipedal locomotion (5-14). Comparison of the ilium in chimpanzees and humans gives insight into the processes of our evolutionary transformation.

Finish by coloring the back muscles and their percent of total muscle mass.

The back muscles attach from the cervical region at the back of the head, down the thoracic region to the top of the ilium and onto the sacrum. Their thickness along the vertebral column reflects function. In macaques, the back muscles comprise relatively greater total body muscle than in the hominoids, and most back muscle is concentrated in the lumbar region. In chimpanzees, over half of the back muscle lies in the shoulder and neck regions. This reflects chimpanzees' reliance on the mobile forelimbs for suspending the body while hanging and climbing in trees and during quadrupedal knuckle walking. Human back muscles are similar in relative weight to those of chimpanzees, although the lumbar region has the most muscle. Lumbar region muscles assist in rotating and supporting the upper trunk over the pelvis during sitting, standing, and walking.

Back function differs significantly in these three primates. Flexion and extension in monkeys facilitate quadrupedal running and leaping. The short and inflexible lumbar region and broad pelvis in chimpanzees (and gorillas) accommodate the broad thorax with widely spaced shoulder joints. The human back supports the trunk vertically over the feet during standing and walking. The trunk rotates first in one direction and then the other over the right and left hip joints. This permits stability and efficiency during bipedal walking.

TRUNK PROPORTIONS

RIB CAGE_a

CLAVICLE_b VERTEBRAL COLUMN_d SACRUM_f

SCAPULA_c INNOMINATE_e CAUDAL/COCCYX_g

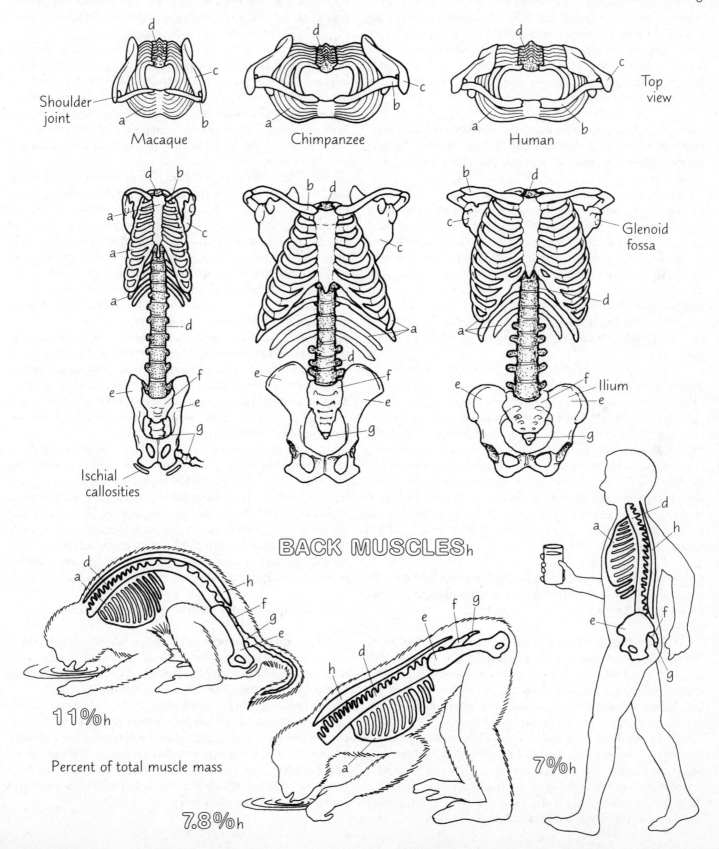

Shoulder joint

Macaque

Chimpanzee

Human

Top view

Glenoid fossa

Ilium

Ischial callosities

BACK MUSCLES_h

11%_h

Percent of total muscle mass

7.8%_h

7%_h

MONKEY AND APE FEEDING SPHERES

Old World monkeys and apes differ in body posture, locomotor behavior, musculoskeletal anatomy, and dentition. Diets are similar, but preferences are not. Nutritious "goodies" are concentrated at the ends of branches, and monkeys and apes gain access to these foods in dramatically different ways. This plate further illustrates limb structure and function that affects the feeding pattern of monkeys and apes.

Color the gibbon ape and macaque monkey and note their postures. Using light shades, color the two different feeding spheres allowed by monkey and ape shoulder joints.

Fruits, flowers, and tender leaves are desirable food items for many primates, rodents, edentates, and even some fruit-eating carnivores such as the kinkajou; these food items usually lie at the ends of branches. Various species have distinctive "techniques" for getting out to the food. Insects, birds, and bats fly in and perch or hover; squirrels and other small species can scamper out and back along the branch because their mass is insufficient to deform the terminal branch downward. However, when the animal weighs more than 2 or 3 kilograms, the branch may bend too much, making the support unstable, or causing it to break.

Anatomist Ted Grand compared the feeding postures of a gibbon and a macaque, with similar body mass, to contrast their foraging styles. Apes solve the problem of branch deformation by suspending themselves beneath the branch; they use the free arm and hand to reach for the food, which now, conveniently, hangs right in front of them! New World monkeys with prehensile tails converge in foraging style by suspending their bodies below the branch to "take advantage" of the downward bend of the branch; the free hand reaches the food (4-17). Above-the-branch feeders, such as the macaque, climb out as far as they can to retrieve fruit or young leaves before deforming the branch and retreating to a stable position.

Color the bones of the gibbon forelimb (on the left) and the macaque forelimb (right). Note the forelimb length relative to the trunk length.

The trunks of monkeys and apes differ in the orientation of the shoulder joint, the size of the clavicle, and the scapula's position on the rib cage (4-25). Apes have compressed lumbar regions and are without tails. Monkeys have moderately muscled, long lumbar regions for quadrupedal running and jumping along the tops of branches and on the ground (3-8).

Body proportions and the limb joints underlie the two different feeding spheres. The gibbon's elongated forelimbs and hands, particularly the digits, extend its reach when suspended below branches; the mobility of its shoulder, elbow, and wrist joints permit greater control of the space around it. The monkey has short forelimbs and less joint mobility.

Color the top view of each humerus, the disarticulated elbow joints, the side view of the ulnas, and the wrist joints.

The shoulder of the ape is directed to the side, a consequence of the broad chest and long clavicle. A monkey's shoulder joint is oriented narrowly and toward the front, like a dog. The monkey's shoulder permits fore-aft movement, but that of the apes permits a 360° range of motion—up, down, to the side, forward. This is because the head of the gibbon humerus is a lovely hemisphere, articulating with the complementary glenoid fossa of the scapula.

The elbow joint consists of three bones (shown here disarticulated). The ulna articulates with the humerus at the elbow joint in flexion/extension; the radial head of the radius rotates on the ulna at the radial notch. In monkeys, the ulna's prominent olecranon process prevents complete extension; in apes and humans, the olecranon is reduced and the elbow joint can be fully extended. The ape's elbow is also more mobile, rotating more than 180° from palm up (supination–carrying soup) to palm down (pronation). The monkeys achieve about 90° of rotation.

The wrist joint in monkeys has the stability essential for quadrupedal walking; both radius *and* ulna connect with the proximate row of the carpal bones. In the apes, the ulna has receded from this contact, and a cartilaginous insert has migrated in. This adjustment makes greater side-to-side movement possible, as shown by the arrow, and called adduction-abduction or ulnar-radial deviation. Although this is a less stable mechanism, when the apes are suspended, the animal's body can move while the hand remains secured to its branch support.

The flexibility of the shoulder, elbow, and wrist joints, full extension and rotation of the elbow joint, combined with long forelimbs and hands, give apes their stability during feeding, and maneuverability when moving through the trees. The apes exhibit variation on this theme; the gibbons and siamangs move like lightning through the trees in locomotion called brachiation. The larger bodied apes use their flexible limb joints to distribute their body weight among several supports when feeding and climbing in trees to maximize stability and minimize breaking branches.

Color the upper molar teeth of the monkey and ape.

Apes and Old World monkeys are also distinguished by their teeth. Ape molars have low crowns (bunodont) and simple rounded cusps. Monkey molars are high (hypsodont) and the four connected cusps form a bilophodont pattern (4-22).

Unfortunately, the identification of the early monkeys and apes in the fossil record has been biased by the more frequent preservation of teeth rather than limb bones. Evolutionary adaptations proceed in mosaic fashion, not at a single continuous rate. Therefore, unless we find limb bones associated with early teeth, we cannot really deduce the early relationships between locomotor and dental evolution (4-28).

LOCOMOTOR FEEDING ANATOMY

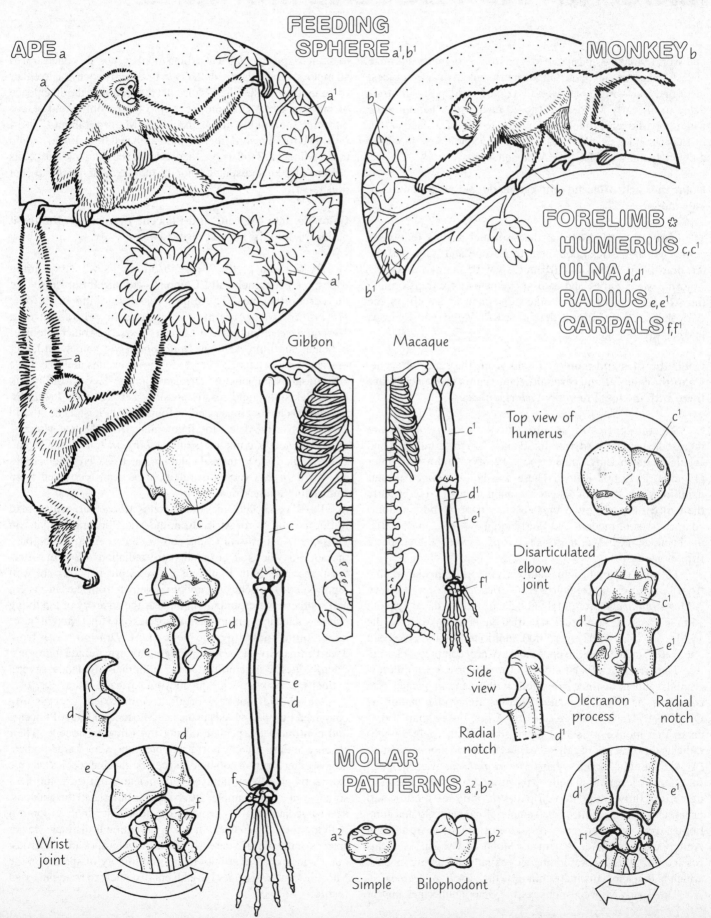

APE a

FEEDING SPHERE a¹,b¹

MONKEY b

FORELIMB ☀
HUMERUS c,c¹
ULNA d,d¹
RADIUS e,e¹
CARPALS f,f¹

Gibbon

Macaque

Top view of humerus

Disarticulated elbow joint

Side view

Radial notch

Olecranon process

Radial notch

Wrist joint

MOLAR PATTERNS a²,b²

a²   Simple

b²   Bilophodont

MIOCENE AND PLIOCENE MONKEYS

Old World Monkeys and apes diverged from a common catarrhine ancestor near the end of the Oligocene, about 25 mya. The oldest identified Old World monkey fossils come from deposits in Africa dated to the early Miocene, 17 to 20 mya. From then until the end of the Miocene, fossil monkeys are few in Africa and absent in Europe and Asia. But by Miocene-Pliocene times, monkeys are widely known in Europe, Asia, and Africa.

Color the early Miocene time range, the Tethys Sea, and the volcanos.

During the early Miocene, the warm and shallow Tethys Sea connected the African continent to Europe and Asia, and the Arabian peninsula was still merged with mainland Africa. Volcanos were active, and earth movements were transforming the African landscape. Tectonic movement and uplift of the African plate helped form the Great Rift Valley and Red Sea (1-18, 4-28).

Color the sites and monkey fossils from the early Miocene. Color the colobine and cercopithecine crania gray to compare them with the fossil monkey *Victoriapithecus*.

Several species of an early monkey *Prohylobates* are represented at North African fossil sites, Moghara in Egypt and Jebel Zelten in Libya dated about 19 mya, and a little later (17 mya) at Buluk, Kenya. These fossils are distinct in their dentition from those of Oligocene anthropoids (4-10) because their molar teeth show a crested cusp pattern (bilophodont) characteristic of modern Old World monkeys (4-22, 4-26). But, unlike modern Old World Monkeys, *Prohylobates* still retained a fifth molar cusp.

The majority of the remaining early Miocene monkeys come from the Lake Victoria region of East Africa. The most well known is *Victoriapithecus,* from Maboko Island, Kenya, dated at about 15 mya. Excavations were first carried out at Maboko during the 1930s, but since 1982 over 1000 additional fossils have been uncovered, including limb bones and a nearly complete cranium.

The craniofacial anatomy of *Victoriapithecus* with its low cranial vault is distinct from both living cercopithecines and colobines. Its cranial capacity (54 cc) is higher than that of the Oligocene *Aegyptopithecus* (30 cc) but lower than living catarrhine monkeys. Ischial tuberosities on the pelvic bones indicate the presence of callosities, an Old World monkey feature (4-18). The limb bones suggest *Victoriapithecus* was equipped for effective locomotion both on the ground and in the trees. The dentition shows well-developed bilophodont molars and prominent upper canines. The sample of canine teeth and limb bones from Maboko vary in size but not in morphology. Anthropologists Brenda Benefit and Monte McCrossin assess this fossil collection as representing one sexually dimorphic species, which belongs to a distinct subfamily, the victoriapithecines.

These early Miocene monkeys, the victoriapithecines, appear to be an "experimental" catarrhine monkey, possibly ancestral to all modern monkeys, but unlikely to be directly ancestral to either of the modern subfamilies. Molecular data estimate the divergence of modern Old World monkeys into the colobine and cercopithecine subfamilies during the middle Miocene, about 12 to 14 mya. The fossil record fits with this estimated time. In the middle to late Miocene, 8 to 10 mya, there is evidence from fossil deposits in Kenya for an undisputed colobine monkey, *Microcolobus* (not illustrated).

Color the late Miocene and Pliocene time range, the fossil monkeys, and the sites as discussed.

By the end of the Miocene, monkeys were becoming widespread geographically. Colobines colonized Eurasia before the cercopithecines. The oldest fossil colobine in Europe, *Mesopithecus*, occurs at several sites in central Europe. *Mesopithecus* resembles living langurs in size, and other colobines in dental and limb skeleton. *Dolichopithecus,* somewhat larger in size, appears later (2–4 mya) in Eurasian sites and may have affinities to Asian langurs. The late Miocene deposits of Siwalik Hills, Pakistan, yield fossils possibly belonging to *Presbytis*. *Rhinopithecus* (not illustrated) is found from Pleistocene sites in China (1-16). In Africa, fossil colobines from the late Miocene include a nearly complete skull of *Libypithecus* from Egypt. Large-bodied and terrestrial colobines such as *Cercopithecoides* and *Paracolobus* (not illustrated) have been recovered from Kenya and South Africa.

Fossil cercopithecines of the genus *Macaca* are widespread in Europe and North Africa from the Mio-Pliocene and later in Pleistocene deposits in China and Southeast Asia; the barbary macaque may be a relict from this early radiation (4-24). In Africa, fossil mangabeys and guenons are rare, but baboons are well represented. The genus *Parapapio* is known from sites in eastern and southern Africa and might lie near the ancestry of the living baboon-mangabey group. Several species of extinct baboons have been found including the near giant, *Dinopithecus* from Swartkrans cave (5-7). Although modern gelada baboons, *Theropithecus*, are confined to the Ethiopian highlands, several extinct species were widespread from Africa to India.

Old World monkeys originated in Africa, successfully colonized Europe and Asia in the late Miocene and early Pliocene, and continued to speciate during the Plio-Pleistocene. Their absence in Europe today is a relatively recent event. Large-bodied, almost giant forms of colobine and cercopithecine species became extinct by about a million years ago. Details of the evolution of some groups, for example, the Asian colobines, and the guenons, a recent radiation (4-21), remain to be fully understood. In contrast with the apes, the course of monkey evolution is distinct—fewer species of monkeys in the early Miocene when apes are numerous, but a widespread distribution and multiplicity of species in the Mio-Pliocene when apes have all but disappeared from the fossil record.

FOSSIL MONKEYS

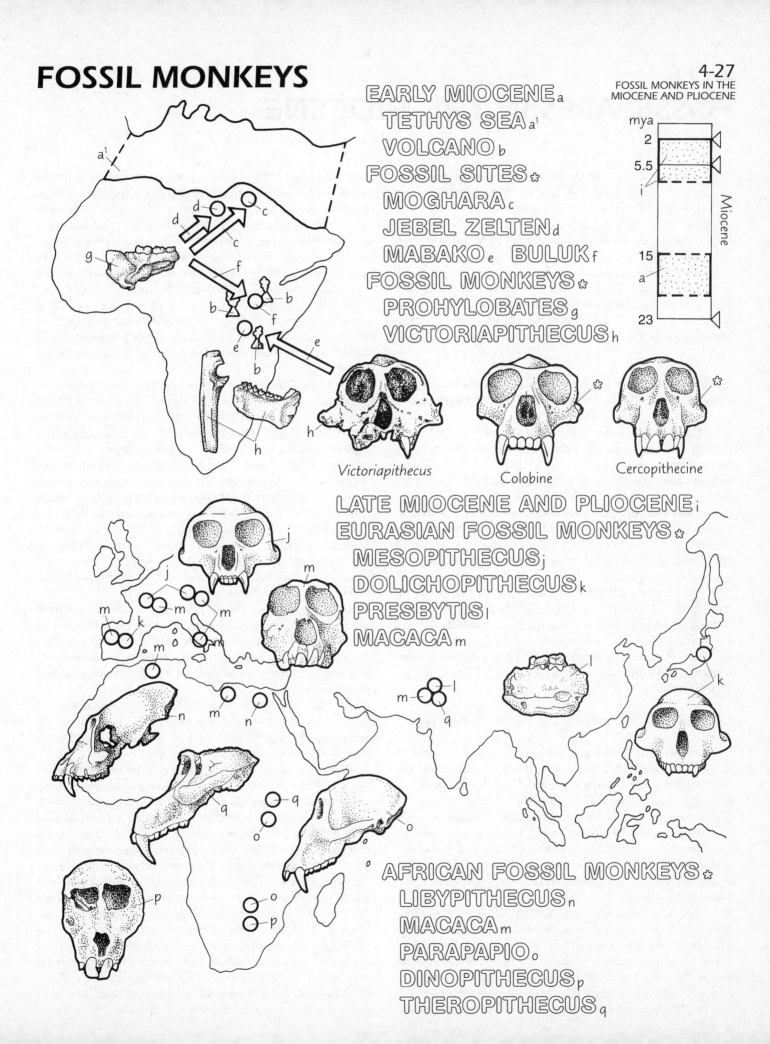

EARLY MIOCENE a
TETHYS SEA a¹
VOLCANO b
FOSSIL SITES *
MOGHARA c
JEBEL ZELTEN d
MABAKO e BULUK f
FOSSIL MONKEYS *
PROHYLOBATES g
VICTORIAPITHECUS h

Victoriapithecus   Colobine   Cercopithecine

LATE MIOCENE AND PLIOCENE i
EURASIAN FOSSIL MONKEYS *
MESOPITHECUS j
DOLICHOPITHECUS k
PRESBYTIS l
MACACA m

AFRICAN FOSSIL MONKEYS *
LIBYPITHECUS n
MACACA m
PARAPAPIO o
DINOPITHECUS p
THEROPITHECUS q

4-28
FOSSIL APES IN THE MIOCENE

The earliest fossil apes are known from Miocene sites about 17 to 20 mya. Dentally these early apes are distinct from monkeys and represent several genera and a number of species. The diversity of the early Miocene apes far exceeds the record of early monkeys. By the middle Miocene, the distribution of fossil apes extended beyond Africa to Europe and Asia, and the number of species notably expanded. By the end of the Miocene, fossil apes had virtually disappeared. The demise of fossil apes coincided with the expansion of fossil monkeys. Unlike the case with fossil monkeys in the Miocene and Pliocene, however, Miocene ape fossils cannot be linked directly to any of the living apes.

Color the time chart, the Tethys Sea, the ape fossils from the early Miocene, and the corresponding sites on the map.

In the early Miocene, Africa was separated from Europe and Asia by the Tethys Sea. The Great Rift Valley, the Red Sea, and the Arabian Peninsula had not yet developed; active volcanos created conditions for fossil preservation and left material for dating with potassium/argon techniques (5-4).

In this time period, localities in eastern Africa near now-extinct volcanos in Uganda (Moroto) and Kenya (Songhor and Rusinga) yield ape fossils. They are often referred to as "dental apes" because the dentition is similar to that of modern apes, whereas their limb bones resemble both monkeys and apes in joint size and shape. These dental apes ranged in size from the small-bodied *Dendropithecus* and *Proconsul* to larger bodied forms, such as *Afropithecus* (in Kenya) and related *Heliopithecus* (in Saudi Arabia) and *Morotopithecus* (in Uganda). Several species of *Proconsul* have been uncovered at a number of sites, including Koru, Moroto, Songhor, and Rusinga Island in Lake Victoria (4-29).

Color the Great Rift Valley and the middle Miocene apes.

Around 16 to 17 mya, continental uplift and faulting moved the African plate northward, forming the Great Rift Valley. The Arabian Peninsula became separated from the rest of Africa through the newly formed Red Sea. The colliding African and Eurasian continents encircled the waters that became the Mediterranean Sea. The recession of the Tethys Sea opened up land corridors and connections that facilitated the dispersal and exchange of animals between Africa and Eurasia. By the middle Miocene, fossil apes were numerous and widely distributed within and outside of Africa.

In Africa, fossil apes like *Kenyapithecus* are numerous between 12 and 15 mya. *Kenyapithecus* had dentition similar to *Proconsul*. The few available limb bones differ from those of living hominoids. *Otavipithecus*, named for the nearby town in central Namibia, was discovered at a fossil site dated about 12 mya and is difficult to place relative to other Miocene apes.

In Europe, a lower jaw of *Dryopithecus* ("oak" ape) was discovered about 1855 in France, prior to Darwin's book *On the Origin of Species*. In 1863 Thomas Henry Huxley recognized *Dryopithecus* as a link between apes and humans. The genus is known from Spain to Hungary between 8 and 13 mya. Limb bones have been few and rarely associated with cranial-dental remains. However, a partial skeleton uncovered from Spain, dated between 9 and 10 mya, preserves forelimb and hindlimb elements as well as a partial cranium. Paleontologists Salvador Moyà-Solà and Meike Köhler interpret the limbs as adaptations for suspension, similar to *Sivapithecus*. However, several critical joint surfaces that are diagnostic for locomotion are missing. Anthropologist David Pilbeam assesses the evidence as insufficient to connect it to modern apes.

Two other European fossils (not illustrated) come from this time range: *Pliopithecus* from France and Czechoslovakia, and *Oreopithecus* from Italy. Cranial, dental, and postcranial remains suggest *Pliopithecus* is not associated clearly to any particular group of Miocene apes or monkeys. *Oreopithecus* has unusual facial and dental anatomy, though its limb bones are apelike; its relationship to other Miocene apes or to living apes is uncertain.

A fossil cranium has been uncovered from northern Greece in the same time range (8–10 mya) and assigned to the genus *Ouranopithecus*. Its cranium is unique and differs from living apes and, especially in the absence of limb bones, is difficult to place. From central Turkey 9 to10 mya, a partial cranium and face have been assigned to *Ankarapithecus*, which shows affinities to *Dryopithecus* and *Ouranopithecus*.

Sivapithecus from the Siwalik Hills, Pakistan, and from Turkey and Hungary (*Griftopithecus*) is dated between 9 and 13 mya. At one time *Sivapithecus* was interpreted as an ancestral orangutan, but its cranial and dental remains do not resemble modern apes; its postcranial skeleton has both monkeylike and apelike elements.

In China *Lufengpithecus* about 8 to 9 mya is cranially and dentally distinct from modern apes, though it resembles orangutans. Without limb bones it is difficult to establish its connection to living orangutans.

The Miocene radiation of hominoids was widespread in Africa, Europe, and Asia, with numerous species and possibly several distinct lineages. However, Pilbeam notes that few, if any, can be directly linked to the origins and radiation of the African ape branch that gave rise to hominids. Critical evidence of the proper time frame (6–8 million years) and of the diagnostic limb bones (4-26) that could make those connections have yet to be discovered. Biologist Caro-Beth Stewart and anthropologist Todd Disotell take a different approach and suggest that the ancestors of modern African apes evolved in Asia, then migrated back into Africa after 10 mya. One of the intriguing aspects of this hypothesis is that it could explain the shared arboreal, suspensory adaptations of all apes, and the superimposed knuckle-walking adaptation of the African apes for a more terrestrial way of life. But at present, the evolution of the Miocene apes, and their relationship to living primates, remains a puzzle.

FOSSIL APES

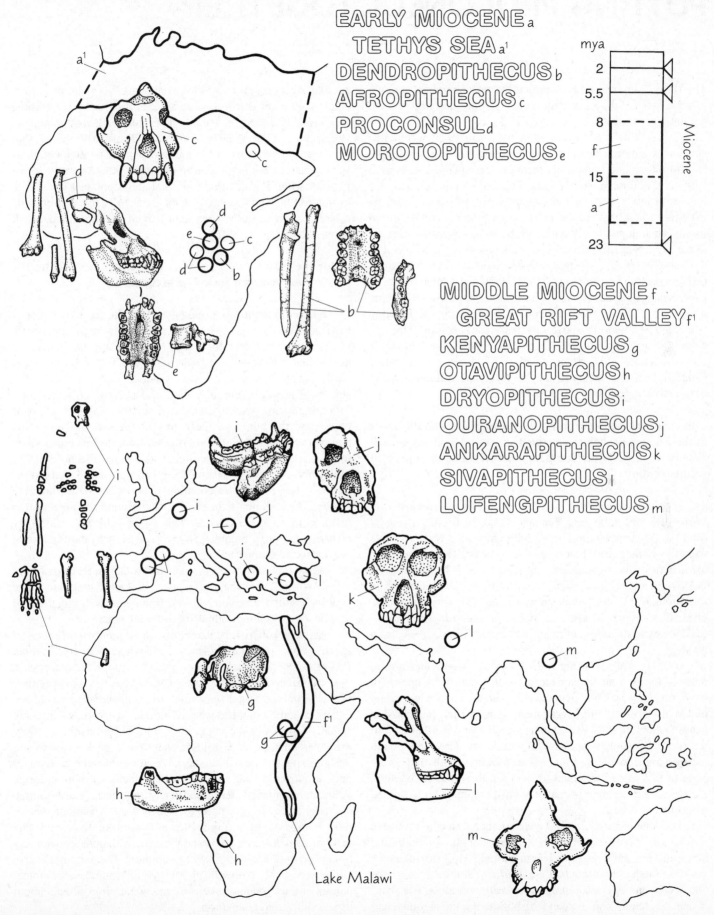

EARLY MIOCENE $_a$
TETHYS SEA $_{a^1}$
DENDROPITHECUS $_b$
AFROPITHECUS $_c$
PROCONSUL $_d$
MOROTOPITHECUS $_e$

MIDDLE MIOCENE $_f$
GREAT RIFT VALLEY $_{f^1}$
KENYAPITHECUS $_g$
OTAVIPITHECUS $_h$
DRYOPITHECUS $_i$
OURANOPITHECUS $_j$
ANKARAPITHECUS $_k$
SIVAPITHECUS $_l$
LUFENGPITHECUS $_m$

Lake Malawi

PUTTING PROCONSUL TOGETHER

The 18-million-year old *Proconsul* is the most completely known primate fossil of the early Miocene, but it took nearly 60 years to put the pieces together.

This scientific discovery story begins in 1927, when H.L. Gordon, a settler at Koru in western Kenya, found some fossils in a limestone quarry and sent them to paleontologist A. Tindall Hopwood at the British Museum, London. One fossil, that of a hominoid left upper jawbone, inspired Hopwood to go on an expedition to Kenya in 1931. There he found more hominoid fossils. He thought the jawbone was that of a new genus ancestral to the chimpanzee. Inspired by a chimpanzee called Consul at the Manchester Zoo who had entertained on the vaudeville stage riding a bicycle and smoking a pipe, Hopwood named his fossil *Proconsul africanus*. The next piece in the *Proconsul* story came in 1948 with a discovery made by Mary Leakey. On Rusinga Island in Lake Victoria, she discovered a nearly complete though slightly distorted skull of *Proconsul* (KNM-RU 7290) at site R 106, and later made more discoveries of a larger species named *Proconsul nyanzae*. Mary Leakey's *Proconsul* skull remains one of the most complete of these early apes.

Color the rock block (a) green, the Rusinga site, and the bones of the *Proconsul* skeleton as the pieces are described in each new discovery. The clear parts of the skeleton represent reconstruction.

The *Proconsul* story continues in 1951, when geologist Tom Whitworth was surveying Rusinga Island for fossils. There he found a green rock (site R 114) with embedded fossils visible from the surface (b). The green rock was circular and deep, and distinct from the surrounding sediments which had no fossils. Whitworth took a block of the green rock to the National Museum in Nairobi, Kenya, for further study. Among the fossils were pieces of skull, forelimb, hands, and foot of an individual *Proconsul* (b). However, the origin of this distinct green pipe of rock was a mystery.

In 1980, while working at the National Museum in Nairobi, paleontologist Alan Walker reexamined some of the bones (c) from the green rock and realized they belonged to the individual that Whitworth had discovered many years earlier. Interested in learning more, in 1984 Walker and paleontologist Martin Pickford returned to Rusinga Island to Whitworth's site. There they found the missing maxilla, half a clavicle, a canine tooth, and a foot bone of this same individual (d). Putting these pieces together, the *Proconsul* skeleton became the most complete large-bodied Miocene hominoid.

The remains of *Proconsul* were compared to both monkeys and apes in order to understand its locomotion. Its forelimbs and hindlimbs are about the same length, more like modern monkeys than like modern hominoids. *Proconsul's* wrist joint is more like Old World monkeys than like present-day hominoids. The ankle bones are slender and monkeylike, but the big toe is robust and

apelike. Analyzing the forelimb bones in 1951, anatomists John Napier and Peter Davis concluded that *Proconsul* was a leaping quadruped like today's Asian langurs. Studying more complete specimens, Alan Walker and Mark Teaford deduced that *Proconsul* was a slow-moving arboreal species with no obvious specializations for leaping, arm swinging, knuckle walking, or ground living. Walker, Pickford, and anthropologist Dean Falk estimated the cranial capacity to be about 167 cubic centimeters, a larger brain to body ratio than that of modern monkeys of comparable size.

Color the reconstructed events that led to unraveling the mystery of the green rock. Use green for (f).

Further excavations around the site of the green rock pipe at Rusinga Island ultimately revealed its origin through taphonomic analysis (taphos, Greek for burial) (5-12). A large tree had stood at this place 18 mya, alongside a stream. The water rose and partly buried the tree with silt and sand suspended in the moving stream. The tree eventually died and became hollowed out. Monitor lizards, pythons, bats, and small carnivores left their bones and the bones of their prey in the space. One of the carnivores probably dined on *Proconsul*; some of its bones show tooth marks. Over time, sediment also filled the hollow and ultimately solidified to become the green pipe of rock that proved so productive. During fossilization, the bark of the tree turned to calcite. The sediments that had settled around the ancient tree trunk contained no fossils. The green rock was dated by potassium/argon techniques (5-4) and indirectly by the other fossil species found in the rock.

While this work was going on, a new site on Rusinga Island was discovered near the original one Whitworth had found. The new site yielded thousands of bone fragments including those of several *Proconsul* individuals of different ages.

At present, there is no agreement on the number of *Proconsul* species. Some paleontologists think that there were at least three *Proconsul* species: the original specimen from Koru discovered by Gordon, another small species of Mary Leakey's type specimen of 1948, and the larger one which M. Leakey called "nyanze." Others conclude that the smaller individuals from Rusinga are actually females of the larger bodied *Proconsul nyanzae*. Body weight estimates give 37 kilograms for the larger specimens and 9.6 kilograms for the smaller ones, which would make the females only about one-fourth the mass of the males, a more extreme sexual dimorphism than is found in any living terrestrial mammal.

Like other Miocene hominoids, *Proconsul* is a unique species with a mosaic of monkeylike and apelike features. The combination does not suggest a particular relationship with any living cercopithecoid monkey or hominoid. Even though nearly all body parts have now been put together to make a complete picture of the *Proconsul* skeleton, many questions remain about its taxonomy and adaptation.

PROCONSUL

PROCONSUL FOSSILS *

GREEN ROCK BLOCK a

SURFACE, 1951 b

MUSEUM, 1980 c

RUSINGA SITE, 1984 d

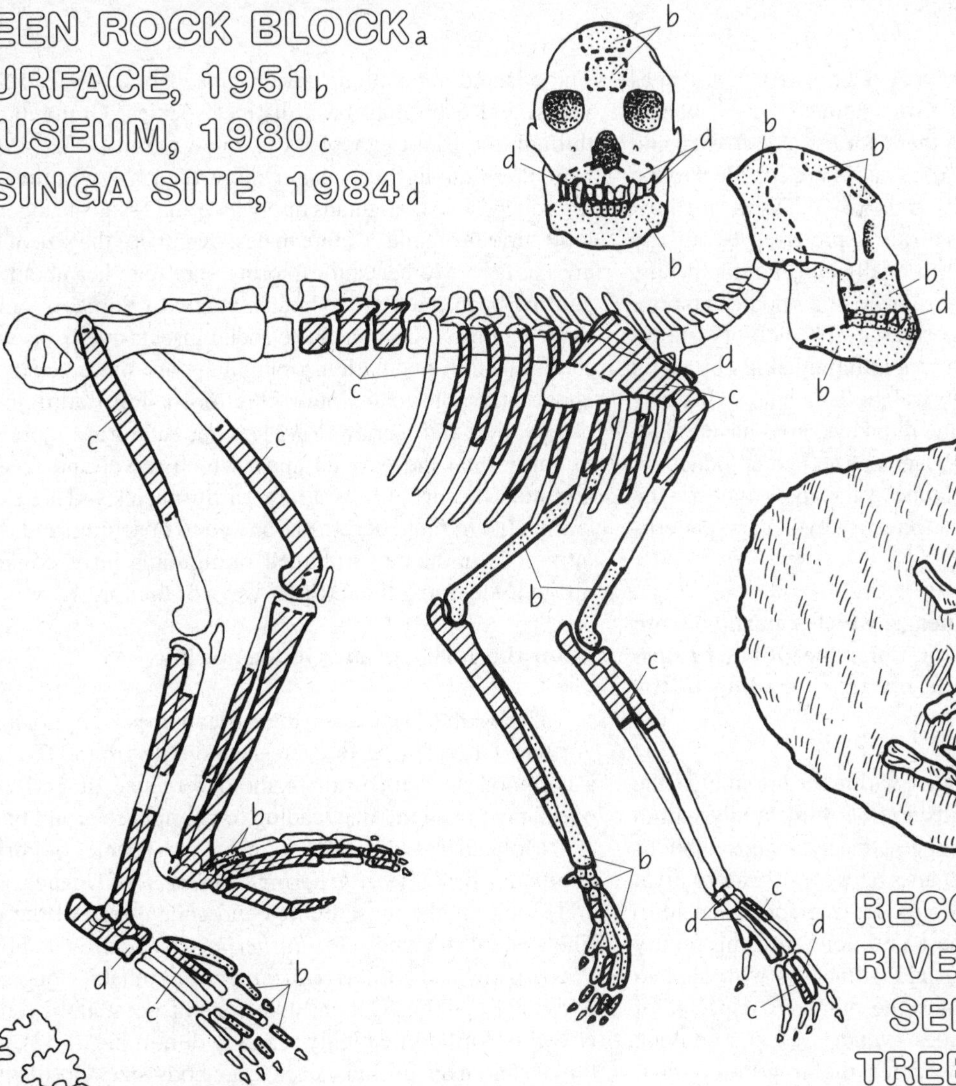

Rusinga
(In Lake
Victoria)

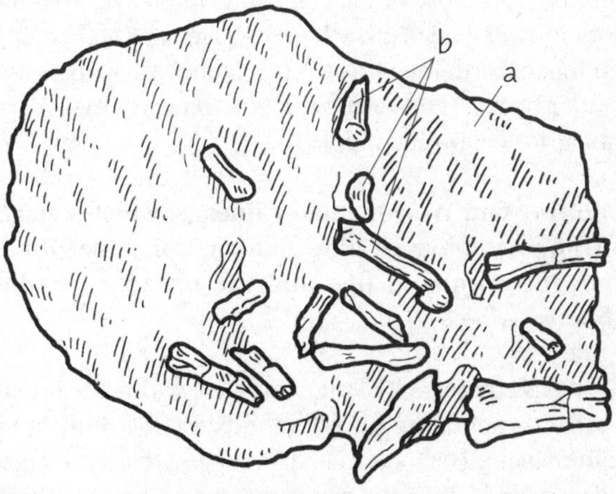

RECONSTRUCTION *
RIVER e
SEDIMENTS e¹
TREE f
SEDIMENTS f¹
BARK/CALCITE f²
CARNIVORE g
PREY/BONES h
TAPHONOMIST i

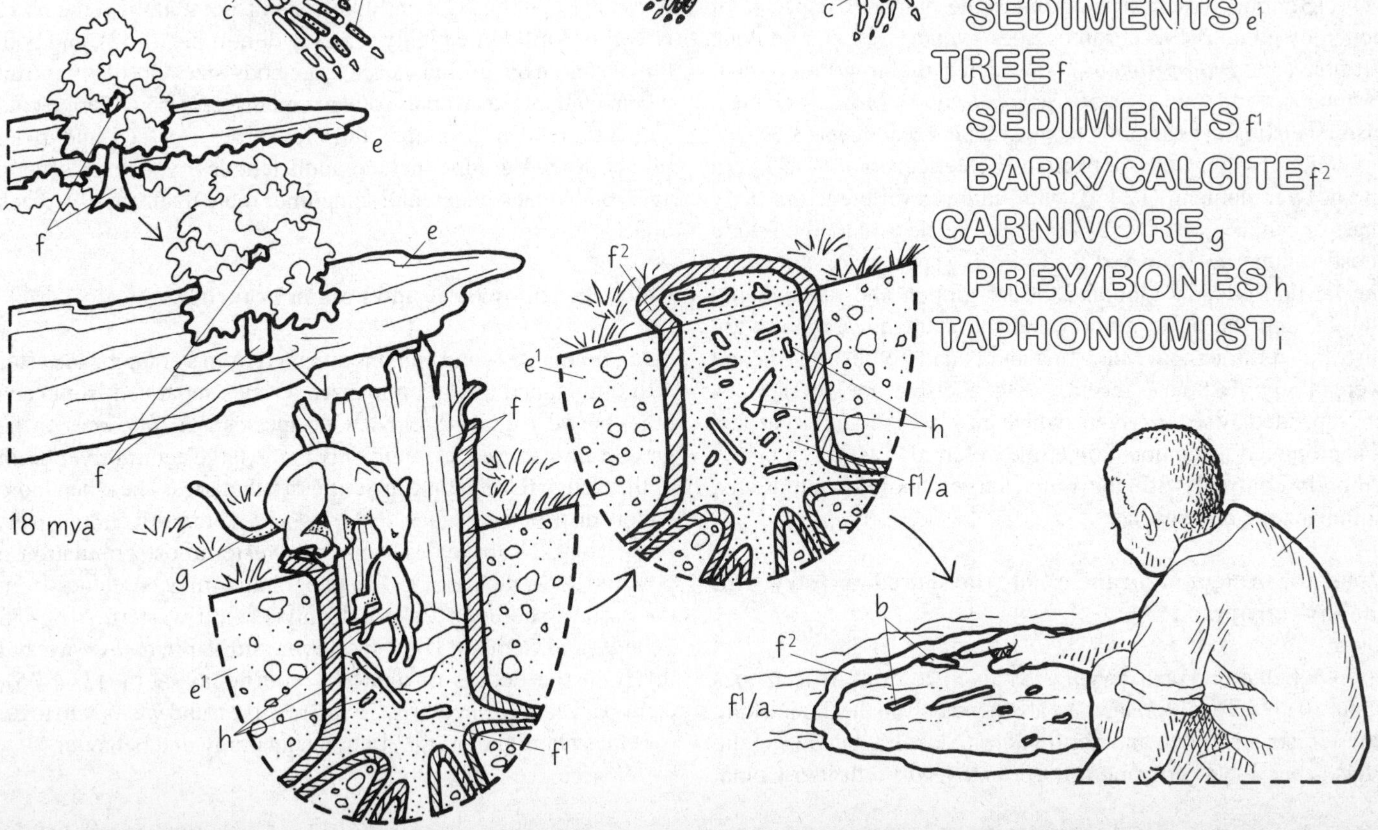

18 mya

4-30
APE FAMILY TREE

The origin of modern apes is somewhat of a mystery. Fossil apes are widely distributed, earliest in Africa about 18 mya, later in Europe and Asia. By about 8 mya there are few ape fossils, and none link to modern apes (4-28). Today apes are confined to the tropics of Africa and Southeast Asia (5-2). Apes are best understood as fruit eaters, that is, fruit is preferred by all ape species, although their diets vary seasonally and geographically.

Body size represents extremes from the small-bodied gibbons to the massive silverback male gorillas. Limb mobility allows apes to be large and yet maintain tree climbing skills by using several supports to distribute body weight. Life history features contrast with those of the catarrhine monkeys; apes have longer gestations, extended growth period, later age at first reproduction, and longer birth intervals (3-24). None of the apes, not even the small gibbons, reproduce each year or every two years, patterns typical for catarrhine monkeys.

Color the Old World monkey lineage, which separated from the hominoid lineage 20 to 25 mya. Color the gibbon branch from the hominoid line and the branches leading to the gibbons.

Apes comprise 2 of the 3 families within the hominoids, the hylobatids and pongids. (Hominids are the third family within Hominoidea). The molecular data suggest that hylobatids (gibbons and siamangs) diverged from other apes between 12 and 14 mya; there are no ancient fossils that are recognized and assigned to the hylobatid family. During the past 5 million years, this family diversified into 11 species falling into 4 lineages with distinct generic names based upon chromosome number: 3 species of concolor gibbons (52 chromosomes, *Nomascus*); the hoolock gibbon (38, *Bunopithecus*); 6 species of lar gibbons (44, *Hylobates*), and siamangs (50, *Symphalangus*). Most species can also be distinguished on the basis of their vocal duets (3-30).

Gibbons range in size from the lighter concolor (4–5 kg) to the heavier siamang (12 kg), with little sex difference in body mass or canine tooth size (3-30). The 6 species of lar gibbons are mostly allopatric. However, the following species are sympatric: the lar and pileatus gibbons, the lar gibbon and the siamang (4-31), and the agile gibbon and the siamang. Gibbons are distributed throughout Indochina and Island Southeast Asia and were in central China as recently as the Pleistocene. Most species are separated by seas or rivers, which may have served as barriers that promoted speciation. Sometimes referred to as "lesser apes," gibbons contrast with the much larger bodied orangutans, chimpanzees, and gorillas.

Color the orangutan branch; note the shared ancestry with the African apes.

Orangutans (*Pongo pygmaeus*) diverged from African apes about 10 mya. Today, orangutans are found only in the diminishing rain forests of Borneo and northwestern Sumatra, but during the Pleistocene their geographic range extended north into China.

The 2 island populations have been separated about 1.5 million years, and each may be a distinct species. Orangutans move through the forest canopy to search for fruit (4-32). Patches of fruit large enough to sustain more than a few animals occur infrequently, so orangutans rarely feed and associate together over long periods of time. Mature males, over twice the size of females, are solitary. Mother and offspring stay together about 6 years, and the birth interval is about 8 years. In Sumatra, orangutans make and use tools to acquire social insects and fruits with hard shells; in this population, orangutans are more social and are apparently able to maintain this tool-using tradition through observation and learning (3-34). Orangutans are more difficult to study than the African apes, which travel and feed on the ground. They are strictly a rain forest species and are extremely vulnerable to rapid deforestation and to poaching, and without a mother's guidance, orphaned orangutans have considerable difficulty learning the intricate ways of the forest.

Color the gorilla branch of the ape line.

Unlike the Asian apes, the African apes—chimpanzees and gorillas—travel, feed, or even sleep on the ground. They shared a common ancestor prior to the divergence of gorillas about 6 to 7 mya from the line leading to chimpanzees and humans.

Molecular studies now delineate two species of gorilla. The mountain gorilla (*Gorilla beringei beringei*) of Uganda, Rwanda, and Congo is the most studied and endangered of the gorillas. The eastern lowland (*Gorilla beringei grauri*) is a subspecies. Western lowland gorillas (*Gorilla gorilla*) inhabit Congo, Central African Republic, Gabon, and a small population remains in Nigeria. Gorillas are highly sexually dimorphic (4-33), and both female and male gorillas reach large body size. Gorillas eat fruit when available, as well as foliage and insects; they tolerate cold and wet, feed in swamps, and climb trees to feed and sleep (4-34). Social groups include adult females, young of several ages, black-back males, and sometimes more than one silverback male.

Color the chimpanzee and human branches.

Chimpanzees and humans diverged from a common ancestor 5 to 6 mya, and the 2 chimpanzee species separated from each other between 2 and 2.5 mya. One species, *Pan paniscus* or the gracile chimpanzee, is found only in the large central river basin of the Congo River, along its southern tributaries. The other, more widely distributed species, *Pan troglodytes* or robust chimpanzee, consists of 3 subspecies, with the westernmost population a possible separate species. The geographic range stretches from the eastern shores of Lake Tanganyika into western Africa in Senegal and Gambia. The 2 species are similar in many ways but differ in the details of anatomy and behavior (4-33, 4-35). Chimpanzees are our closest living relatives, and we look to them for clues about the origin of human anatomy and behavior.

APE FAMILY TREE

OLD WORLD MONKEYS $_a$

ASIAN APES*
GIBBONS $_b$
CONCOLOR b^1
LAR b^2
SIAMANG b^3
ORANGUTAN $_c$

AFRICAN APES*
GORILLA d^1
CHIMPANZEES*
GRACILE d^2
ROBUST d^3

HOMINIDS*
HUMAN $_e$

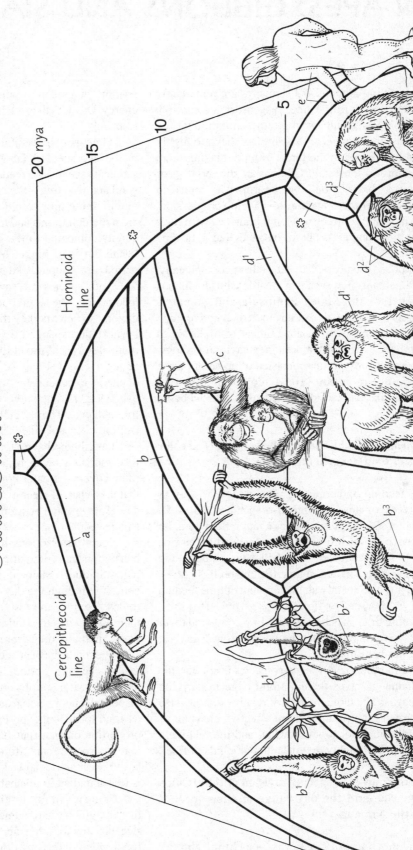

The 11 species of living gibbons and siamangs are remarkably alike in their adaptation to fruit eating, suspensory locomotion, territoriality, vocal duets, small social groups, and minimal sex differences in body and tooth size (3-4, 3-30). They are highly arboreal and rarely descend to the forest ground, making them vulnerable to loss of forest habitats. Gibbons are the aerialists of the forest; the term "brachiation" (brach=arm) was coined to describe their rapid under-the-branch, arm-swinging progression. They also walk bipedally in trees, grasping branches with their feet and holding their long arms out for balance, like tight-rope walkers (3-13).

Species of gibbons usually replace each other geographically. The large-bodied siamang, however, is sympatric with lar gibbons in forests in parts of the Malay Peninsula and Sumatra. Primatologist Jeremy Raemaekers carried out a comparative study on lar gibbons and siamangs in Kuala Lompat in Malaysia to highlight the similarities and differences in behavioral ecology. Each of Raemaeker's study groups consisted of an adult pair, a subadult male, and an infant. He discovered how two morphologically similar and closely related species avoid being major competitors.

Color the gibbon and siamang and their body mass. Next color the proportions of food items in their diets.

Comparing feeding and foraging patterns is one way to distinguish between or among sympatric species (3-5, 4-5). Although all gibbon species prefer fruit as a major food item, lar gibbons spend twice as much time as siamangs feeding on ripe fruit (28% vs. 14%). Raemakers found that lar gibbons and siamangs spend the same amount of time feeding on figs (22%), a dietary staple. They also spend a similar amount of time feeding on insects (13% vs. 15%) and on flowers (7% vs. 6%). However, siamangs focus more time on eating leaves, 43% compared to lar gibbons at 29%. Lar gibbons select the youngest and smallest leaves and eat fewer per minute.

Although the morphology of the two species is similar, the larger size of siamangs gives them a slight edge in deriving nutrition from leaves. The large molar size relative to body size and the molar crown both promote more effective chewing of leaves into smaller bits prior to swallowing, and the relatively longer hindgut more thoroughly digests larger amounts of fiber.

Color the activities and each species' division of time. Color the home range size and the day range of each species, beginning with the siamang.

Along with diet, activity patterns also highlight the differences between sympatric species. How each species spends its time gives some indication of an animal's expenditure of energy. Day length is 8.6 hours for lar gibbons and 10.3 hours for siamangs.

Time spent in feeding shows the most pronounced difference in the two species; lar gibbons spend 42% feeding, whereas siamangs spend 50% feeding. The siamangs' longer feeding time is related to eating a larger proportion of leaves and foliage that require more time to pluck, ingest, and process (4-20). Leaves are more ubiquitous and take less time to locate, but are of lower quality compared to the gibbon's fruit that takes more time to locate but is of higher quality. Siamangs also rest for longer periods, 28%, compared to 25.5% for lar gibbons.

Both species rely on brachiation for 60 to 75% of their locomotion. The lar gibbons, however, are more agile, frequently moving so quickly they throw themselves from one handhold to the next; they spend 32.5% of their day traveling. Siamangs move more slowly and travel only 22% of the time; because of their larger size, travel may be more costly. For the same proportion of energy expended, the smaller gibbons travel a greater distance over a larger home range of 57 hectares compared to 47 hectares for siamangs. The lar gibbons are therefore more likely to find fruiting trees and vines that are more widely dispersed.

Lar gibbons have a longer day range (1500 m) and visit more food sources a day than siamangs do. The lars' longer daily travel route covers a greater portion of their home range each day, so that they visit all areas every 2.5 days. Siamang travels less each day (850 m), and require an average of 6 days to cover their smaller home range.

Social interactions in both species are infrequent; social behavior is most dramatic and energetic when a female and male pair sing duets. Siamang groups show a high degree of spatial cohesion through the day as they travel together, taking similar routes, feeding, and resting. They are rarely separated by more than 30 meters. In contrast, lar gibbons forage across a broad front, and individuals spread out when traveling and feeding.

The foods they eat and the time spent feeding, traveling, and resting each day define the niche of each species. Lar gibbons have a greater emphasis on extensive travel to find small, dispersed, energy-rich fruit. The more sedentary siamangs travel less and spend longer periods feeding on young leaves for a large proportion of their diet. The siamang's larger body size means that this species can afford to eat relatively more leaves, which have fewer calories and take longer to digest than ripe fruit, which is less abundant in this habitat.

Comparison of closely related species that share a habitat like the gibbon and siamang illustrated here shows how body size, diet and foraging, and time spent in activities such as travel, feeding, and resting contribute to separating species and minimizing competition for resources.

GIBBONS AND SIAMANGS

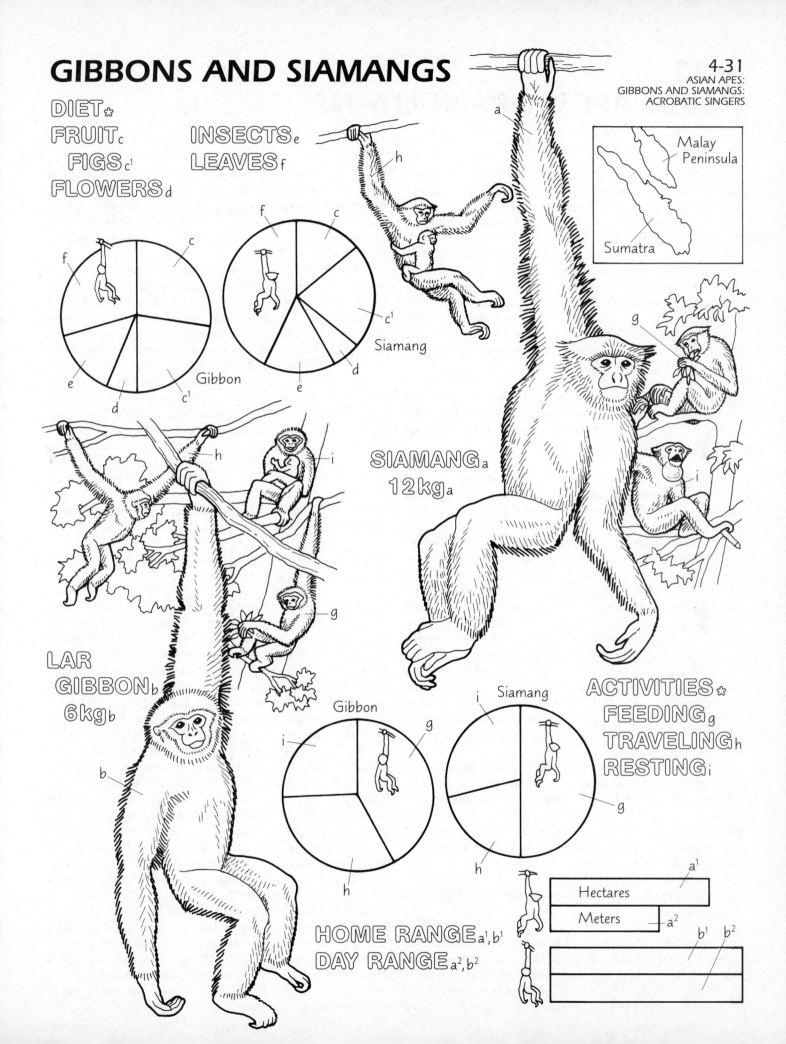

DIET *

FRUIT c   INSECTS e

FIGS c¹   LEAVES f

FLOWERS d

Malay Peninsula

Sumatra

Siamang

Gibbon

SIAMANG a
12 kg a

LAR
GIBBON b
6 kg b

Gibbon

Siamang

ACTIVITIES *
FEEDING g
TRAVELING h
RESTING i

HOME RANGE a¹, b¹
DAY RANGE a², b²

Hectares

Meters

ASIAN APES: ORANGUTANS

Orangutans, Indonesian for "people of the forest," are highly specialized for life in the tropical forests of Borneo and Sumatra, and have long arms, short legs, and large grasping feet. Their appearance is striking: long red hair over much of their body and a humanlike face. Field research of primatologist Birute Galdikas and others discovered that orangutans forage for fruit high in the forest canopy and travel with agility across arboreal pathways. To avoid competition for limited seasonal fruit, they sacrifice group membership and frequent social interaction. Travel on the ground is rare and extremely awkward. Orangutans contrast with the more terrestrial and more social African apes. Studies during the 1990s provide new insights into the adaptation of these highly endangered and unusual apes.

Color the orangutan as it reaches to bridge the gap in the trees. Using light colors, color the segments of the hindlimb. Color the femoral heads of the orangutan (*Pongo*) and chimpanzee (*Pan*).

Orangutans are by far the heaviest arboreal mammal (30–90 kg) and are remarkably adept at moving their large bodies through the forest. Their flexible limbs can reach in many directions. The long arms and strong hands anchor firmly to branches. The hindlimbs have greater range of motion than those of chimpanzees; the orangutan's femoral head forms a perfect sphere and is not restricted by the ligamentum teres. The knee and ankle joints also permit extensive rotation. The foot comprises one-third the length of the short hindlimb and has a powerful grip. Consequently, orangutans can distribute their body mass across two or three supports during feeding and traveling and so avoid falls if a supporting branch breaks. To bridge gaps in the forest canopy, their bodies act as pendulums which generate momentum and bring branches closer together. Their unconventional method of climbing has been referred to as "clambering." Primatologist Suzanne Chevalier-Skolnikoff interprets their locomotor skill as a reflection of highly developed cognitive and manipulative abilities.

The large body size is a trade-off; it requires more fuel and creates challenges in arboreal travel, but a larger body can store more fat without impeding movement. Often obese and diabetic in captivity, orangutans seem predisposed to add excess body mass. Is this a result of life in captivity or an important part of their adaptation? Field research with new methods is helping to answer the question.

Color the dietary composition, caloric intake, and presence of ketones.

Asian tropical forests are warm and wet with little seasonal change in temperature and rainfall, but fruit production can fluctuate dramatically, annually and superannually in what is called mast fruitings. Mast fruitings occur in 4- to 7-year cycles when a large proportion of the trees produce fruit at the same time. In a year-long study, primatologist Cheryl Knott documented what orangutans ate and calculated caloric intake of individuals at different seasons. She collected urine by spreading a large plastic sheet below individual orangutans—one of the many challenges of field work! Knott measured hormones and ketones in the urine.

When fruit is abundant, orangutans gorge themselves. During January, their diet was 100% fruit. Knott calculated a daily caloric intake for mature males to be about 8400 calories and for females to be about 7400. High calories translate into a weight gain of about .66 kilograms per day! The usually lone orangutans became social, fed together, and congregated in larger groups than at any other time. Estrogen levels were high, and matings occurred.

By May, when fruit consumption dropped to 21% of total food intake, bark increased to 37%. Caloric intake dropped to 3800 for males and 1800 for females. When fruit is in short supply, fat is broken down for energy, and ketones, the breakdown products of fat, appear in the urine. No ketones were present from October through March, but were present in April to September. In May more females than males tested positive for ketones. A lactating female carrying an infant with an accompanying juvenile was most stressed by the restricted diet, and a pregnant female was the next most affected by weight loss.

Color the three orangutans and their body mass. Color the secondary sexual characteristics.

Male reproduction and life history are unusual. All males produce viable sperm (primary sexual character) by about age seven, and all resemble subadults. Males then take one of two pathways. Some retain the appearance of subadults. Others go on to develop secondary sexual characteristics, such as higher body weight, fatty cheek pads or "flanges," fatty crown, throat and larynx development, long thick hair, and strong body odor. According to anthropologist Ann Maggioncalda and colleagues, these two male phenotypes indicate that fertility and secondary sexual trait development are decoupled, that is, they can develop at widely different times. Flanged males dominate all unflanged males and are more attractive to females; however, they are more aggressive, have higher mortality, and require more energy for maintenance and locomotion. Knott reports that flanged males maintain their prime condition for about three years. Unflanged males remain small, live longer, but in order to mate, they have to force the females while avoiding the short-tempered big males.

Cycles of ovulation, pregnancy, and lactation and a long birth interval suggest a high cost of reproduction for females too (3-26, 3-27). Thus orangutans have accommodated and adapted to dramatically fluctuating food resources, mitigated by weight gain and loss. Events such as mating and conception, and male sexual development coincide with mast fruitings. Confined to and dependent upon tropical forest habitats, orangutans are extremely vulnerable to habitat destruction and remain one of the most endangered primates.

ORANGUTANS

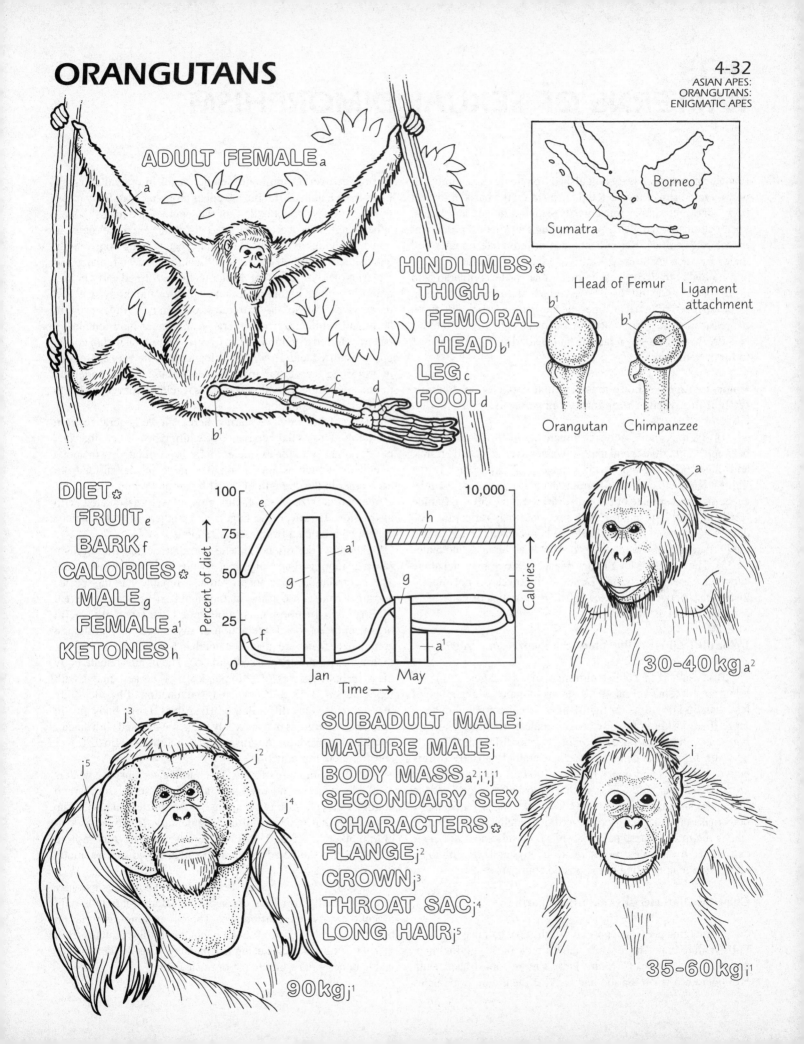

ADULT FEMALE a

Borneo

Sumatra

HINDLIMBS ✻
THIGH b
FEMORAL
HEAD b¹
LEG c
FOOT d

Head of Femur   Ligament
attachment

b¹   b¹

Orangutan   Chimpanzee

DIET ✻
FRUIT e
BARK f
CALORIES ✻
MALE g
FEMALE a¹
KETONES h

100   10,000

Percent of diet →

Calories →

Jan   May

Time →

30-40kg a²

SUBADULT MALE i
MATURE MALE j
BODY MASS a²,i¹,j¹
SECONDARY SEX
CHARACTERS ✻
FLANGE j²
CROWN j³
THROAT SAC j⁴
LONG HAIR j⁵

90kg j¹

35-60kg i¹

PATTERNS OF SEXUAL DIMORPHISM

Female primates can be distinguished from males in a number of ways. Field primatologists tell them apart on the basis of overall body size and shape, muscularity, hair color and markings, vocalizations, or females' sexual swellings and males' prominent or colored genitals. Researchers also differentiate females and males by such features as limb bone length., cranial capacity, and canine tooth size—measurements that can be compared with other species and with fossils. We compare females and males in three species of African apes because they represent three expressions of sex differences. African apes are also of interest because they are closely related to humans and are often compared to fossil hominids.

Color averages of body mass, cranial capacity, and canine teeth of the gracile chimpanzee, *Pan paniscus*.

Body mass of gracile chimpanzees differs moderately between adult females and males: females average 33 kilograms, and males 45 kilograms, with a range of 27 kilograms in the lightest female to over 60 kilograms in the heaviest male. Cranial capacities, an estimate of brain size, are similar (350 cc). Canine teeth are relatively small in both sexes and may reflect the low degree of aggression among males or between communities and the high degree of friendly behavior between females and males (4-35). The length of long bones of each sex overlaps and alone cannot be assigned to sex. Dental differences do not readily distinguish between the sexes, whereas extremes of body mass can distinguish them.

Color the features of the robust chimpanzee, *Pan troglodytes*.

Body mass of robust chimpanzees averages about 40 kilograms in females and 48 kilograms in males with a range of less than 30 kilograms for light-bodied females from Gombe to more than 60 kilograms for heavier males. In contrast to *Pan paniscus*, canine tooth size of *Pan troglodytes* differs significantly between females and males. Average cranial capacity differs between females and males (385 vs. 400 cc); the humerus and femur are shorter in females. Although most dimensions overlap in females and males, the extreme ends of the ranges, for example, body mass, cranial capacity, and limb bone lengths, do not. Canine size is the most consistent marker of sex in this species. Larger canine teeth in males might relate to higher levels of male aggression than is found in the gracile chimpanzees.

Color the characteristics of lowland gorillas.

Adult female lowland gorillas weigh about half that of males. Fully mature males have white hair on their backs, giving them the name "silverbacks." Males have a more robust head, with prominent crests on the top and back of the cranium. Females

and males overlap minimally or not at all in cranial capacity. Long bone lengths differ but are not as pronounced as body mass; females' bones are about 85% of the length of the males' bones. When lengths do overlap, the shaft and joints are more robust in males. Although body mass, cranial capacity, long bone length, and canine size usually differ significantly between females and males, molar size does not. Molar teeth are formed early in life, are fully erupted before males reach their mature body size, and therefore do not express extreme sex difference. Males grow in body and canine size for several years longer than females, a pattern referred to as bimaturism (3-30). Aggression within gorilla groups is infrequent. However, resident males are very aggressive in protecting their group from outside threats, such as nongroup males or predators, and bloody injuries resulting from canine tooth bites are not uncommon.

Using what we have learned here, can we generalize from morphology to social behavior? Sex differences in canine size, but not body size, for example, might be correlated with social interactions, such as aggression. The three species differ from each other in the strength of social bonds and social interaction. Large canine size is the factor most closely associated with aggression. However, the targets and triggers of this behavior cannot be predicted from tooth size alone.

Attempts are often made to correlate sexual dimorphism (di=two; morph=shape) in primates with their social organization. These correlations have not proved to be reliable in living species and are of limited use in speculating about extinct species. Sexual dimorphism in body mass does not correlate with social organization or social interaction in any simple way. Although chimpanzee males are much heavier than females in both species, their behavior differs markedly (4-35). The lighter female body mass in both species of chimpanzee may be associated with reproduction (3-25, 3-26), whereas the function of heavier body mass in males may differ in the two species. Large body size in both sexes of gorillas may have advantages associated with dietary adaptation, predator defense, and for females, pose fewer constraints in reproduction.

When trying to sex fossils, paleontologists must use what is available, which is mostly bones and teeth. Soft tissue, which comprises about 85% of an animal, is not preserved (5-3). The few bones that exist are often fragmentary. Imagine the two chimpanzees as fossil species, represented by incomplete skeletons. It would be difficult to distinguish two species, much less two sexes.

Let's review the lessons. Females and males are not simply larger or smaller versions of each other. Body mass tells only part of the story of sex differences. There is no simple correlation between morphology and social behavior. Telling females from males in extinct species using fragmentary parts of skeletons or whole bones can be unreliable or misleading.

AFRICAN APES

BODY MASS$_{a,a^1}$
CRANIAL CAPACITY$_{b,b^1}$
CANINE TEETH$_{c,c^1}$

FEMALES✳

MALES✳

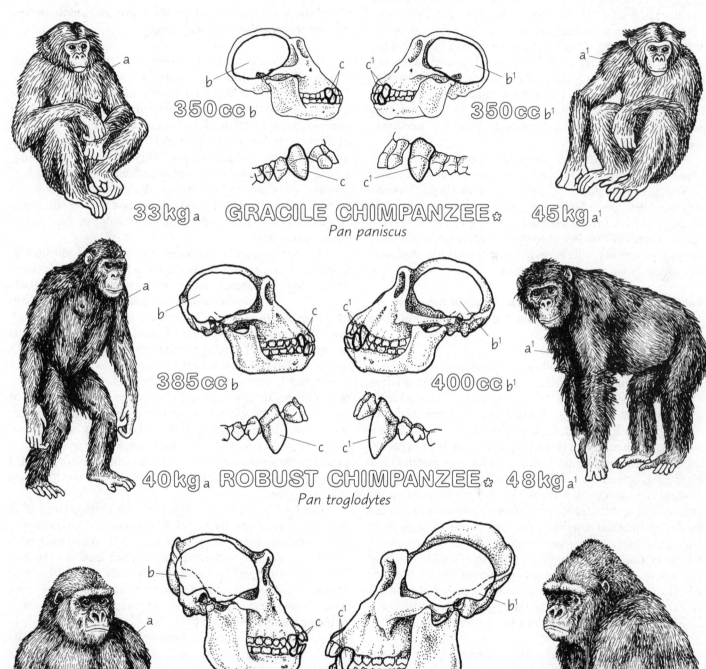

350cc$_b$

350cc$_{b^1}$

33kg$_a$ GRACILE CHIMPANZEE✳ 45kg$_{a^1}$
Pan paniscus

385cc$_b$

400cc$_{b^1}$

40kg$_a$ ROBUST CHIMPANZEE✳ 48kg$_{a^1}$
Pan troglodytes

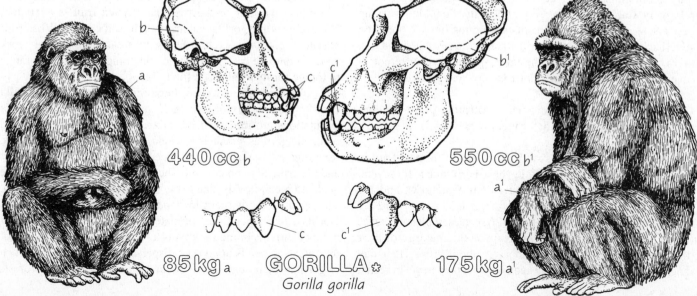

440cc$_b$

550cc$_{b^1}$

85kg$_a$ GORILLA✳ 175kg$_{a^1}$
Gorilla gorilla

4-34
GORILLAS: GENTLE GIANTS

Gorillas, first "discovered" by Western explorers in the mid 19th century, have captured the imagination of scientists, film makers, and the lay public. The largest of the great apes, they were misrepresented to several generations of movie-goers in the image of the gigantic King Kong climbing the Empire State Building with Fay Wray in hand. In the 19th century, anatomist Thomas Henry Huxley first suggested a close kinship between gorillas and humans, based on their anatomical resemblances. Zoologist George Schaller's pioneering field study in 1960 on mountain gorillas in the Virunga volcanos began to dispel the "murderous ape" misconception.

For over a decade free-ranging gorillas were known from Dian Fossey's long-term studies on mountain gorillas at Karisoke in Rwanda. Primatologists generalized to all gorillas and concluded they were of low energy, relied almost exclusively on foliage, and lived in large cohesive stable groups with short day ranges. Later field studies of lowland gorillas revealed a more complex picture of gorilla behavior—variation in locomotion, in diet, and in group size and composition.

Color the mountain gorilla, its altitude on the mountain, the number of plant species it consumes, the percent composition of its diet, and its day range.

Mountain gorillas in the Virunga volcanos are the most robust species. They tolerate cold and wet environments at high altitudes. Their diet consists of foods from 41 species of plants. Leaves (25%) and pith and bark (38%) make up half of their diet. Fruit consumption is less than 12%, as very few fruits are available at these high altitudes. The herbaceous plants are high in protein and low in tannins (chemicals that make foods more difficult to digest), but are mechanically protected with spines, thorns, and thistles. The gorillas are particularly adept at manipulating and gaining access to the edible plant parts by removing thorns and thistles, peeling and stripping away outer coverings to get at the pith. Mountain gorillas have short day ranges. They live in relatively stable groups averaging 9 individuals but varying between 2 and 34. One-third of the groups have 2 breeding silverback males. Mountain gorillas are the most studied and best known population, but are the most specialized, different in several ways from the more numerous lowland gorillas.

Color the eastern lowland gorilla, altitude, plant species, dietary composition, and day range.

Eastern lowland gorillas at Kahuzi-Biega National Park in northeastern Congo (formerly Zaire) have been studied for several years by Japanese primatologist Juichi Yamagiwa and his colleagues. This population inhabits forests at 500 meters to 2400 meters altitude. The gorillas rely on 126 species of plants. Leaves (40%) and pith and bark (35%) comprise the majority of their diet, and fruit consumption comprises about 20%. Their day ranges are variable and depend upon whether they travel in search of fruit. The average group size is from 11 to 16 individuals.

Color the western lowland gorillas, altitude, plant species, dietary composition, and day range.

Western lowland gorillas have the widest distribution from Congo, Central African Republic, Cameroon, Gabon, and Equatorial Guinea, to Nigeria and are the most genetically diverse of gorilla populations. The western and eastern lowland populations are as distinct from each other as are the two species of chimpanzee. Western lowland gorillas are shy and have proved much more difficult to habituate for study than the eastern groups. During the past two decades, dedicated field workers, such as primatologist Caroline Tutin and colleagues at Lopé, Gabon, and primatologist Melissa Remis and colleagues at Bai Hokou, Central African Republic, have added to our knowledge of these dense-forest inhabitants.

At Lopé, the gorillas eat about 165 plant species that include epiphytes, ferns, grasses, lichens, and mushrooms, and plant parts such as flowers, fronds, roots, and rotten wood. Leaves and fruits can be chemically protected, and the gorillas must be selective to avoid items with high tannins. Leaves (25%) and pith and bark (16%) comprise about 40% of the diet, and on average, fruits comprise about half the diet. Gorillas prefer fruit, and climb trees to feed. At Bai Hokou, during the wet season, as much as 75% of gorilla diet is fruit. When fruit is abundant, the gorillas cover nearly 5 times the day range of the mountain gorillas. At times of plentiful fruit, the social group is less cohesive and individuals fan out to forage. Remis describes the gorillas as "seasonal frugivores." During the dry season when little or no fruit is available, the gorillas switch to the more continuously distributed foliage, leaves, and herbs; day ranges are shorter, and the group more cohesive.

Lowland gorillas are sympatric with chimpanzees (*Pan troglodytes*) at several study sites. When Tutin and her colleagues began their long-term study at Lopé, they discovered considerable overlap in the diet of the two apes. When fruit is available, chimpanzees and gorillas eat many of the same foods. When fruit is scarce, gorillas switch to herbs, whereas chimpanzees work hard to continue eating fruit by maintaining a huge home range to forage for their fall-back food, figs.

At a time when we are beginning to understand gorilla ecology and behavior, we face the fact that all the gorilla populations are in danger of extinction. Only several hundred mountain gorillas remain in Rwanda, Uganda, and the Democratic Republic of Congo; they are located in areas of political conflict and are critically endangered. The eastern lowland gorillas have declined precipitously, due to the war and conflict in this region. The threat to the western lowland comes from human hunting. Gorillas, like other forest primates, are hunted for meat; their numbers are declining rapidly as a result. Since the integrity of the forests depends upon seed dispersal by its inhabitants, such as gorillas, their demise also threatens the viability of the forests (4-1).

GORILLAS

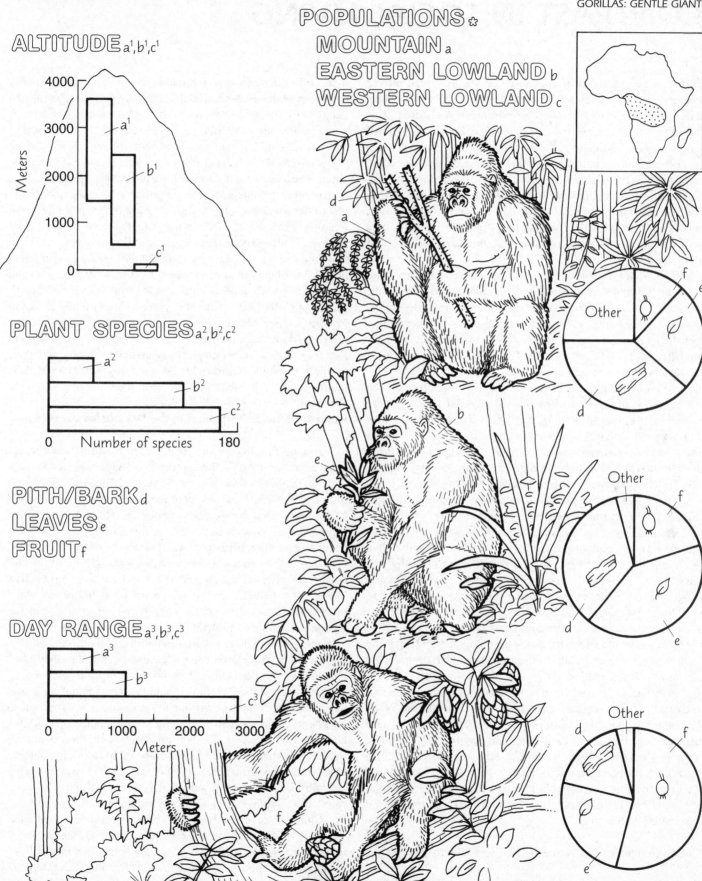

ALTITUDE a^1, b^1, c^1

4000
3000
2000
1000
Meters
a^1
b^1
c^1

POPULATIONS *
MOUNTAIN a
EASTERN LOWLAND b
WESTERN LOWLAND c

PLANT SPECIES a^2, b^2, c^2

a^2
b^2
c^2
0   Number of species   180

PITH/BARK d
LEAVES e
FRUIT f

DAY RANGE a^3, b^3, c^3

a^3
b^3
c^3
0   1000   2000   3000
Meters

Other

CONTRAST IN SOCIAL LIVING

Chimpanzees fascinate us because we see a rippled-mirror reflection of ourselves in their anatomy and behavior. Their scientific namesake, *Pan,* was the mischievous Greek god of forests. One species, *Pan troglodytes,* was known to western scholars by the 19th century, but the other species, *Pan paniscus,* was not recognized until 1933 when Harold Coolidge described some of its distinctive features. In the early 1970s, primatologist Takayoshi Kano and his colleagues began field research on *Pan paniscus* at Wamba in the Congo Basin. Kano's observations, and those of researchers at another site, Lomako, revealed many surprises about this gracile species and altered our ideas about chimpanzees.

If we look for evolutionary links between chimpanzees and humans, we find that *Pan paniscus* resembles early hominids, particularly AL 288, dubbed "Lucy," more so than the robust *Pan troglodytes* does in the following respects: smaller canine teeth, narrower and slighter chests, shorter forelimbs, and longer hind limbs (5-17). Furthermore, *Pan paniscus* has more of a propensity than its sister species to stand and walk on two legs, and we know from fossil bones that AL 288 was bipedal. The convergence of several lines of evidence led me and three colleagues to propose in 1978 that, of all living primates, *Pan paniscus* was most like the common ancestor of apes and humans and could help generate models on how a quadrupedal ape made the transition into a bipedal hominid. When we made this proposal, very little was known about the behavior of *Pan paniscus* in the wild. Since then, discoveries about their behavior have contributed further to speculations about human origins (5-13).

Chimpanzee social organization is the most flexible among the apes. The 2 chimpanzee species are similar in that they live in communities or unit groups of about 50 mixed females and males; these individuals share a home range, in which smaller subgroups associate, come together, or separate according to social and ecological circumstances; adolescent females leave and take up residence in other communities, and males remain in the community into which they were born. Mothers and offspring have strong bonds, and adult interactions are mediated by complex modes of communication.

However, in the specific expression of community interaction and of adult social relationships, the two species contrast. When *Pan paniscus* individuals from different communities come into contact, they may greet each other and groom, play, or mate; tension is relatively low. In contrast, *Pan troglodytes* establish boundaries, territorial markers actively patrolled by alert males, who may display aggressively or attack individuals from other communities. Females entering from another community are particularly vulnerable.

Color the females and males in the *Pan paniscus* group.

Adult social relationships in *Pan paniscus* individuals are more affiliative and tolerant than in *Pan troglodytes*. Female-male bonds are strong; they are frequent grooming partners, and males often share food with females. Temporary parties usually have both adult females and adult males traveling together; sexual behavior is frequent even when the female is not in estrus. A mating pair maintains eye contact, nonexistent in *Pan troglodytes*, and have 3 kinds of call associated with mating. Bonds among *Pan paniscus* females are also strong. When an adolescent female enters a new community, she forms a bond with an older female, which helps her integrate into the group where she spends the rest of her life. Grooming and sharing are frequent among adult females. Females eat meat and apparently hunt. Primatologist Barbara Fruth and colleagues working at Lomako report that in 7 instances of eating duikers (small antelopes), females had possession of the carcass and shared food with other females and occasionally with males. Females share fruit with each other 15 times more often than meat; both patterns are virtually absent in *Pan troglodytes*. Males associate with each other much less often than they do with females, and there is no single alpha male as in *Pan troglodytes*. Male *Pan paniscus* associate closely with their mothers throughout life, whereas *Pan troglodytes* shift their interactions to other males during adolescence.

Color the females and males in the *Pan troglodytes* group.

Among *Pan troglodytes*, bonds established between males are the strongest within the community, and there is an obvious alpha male. Males band together to patrol boundaries, hunt, and form complex coalitions in supporting or deposing the alpha male. Males more often than females are observed hunting; they share meat from a kill with each other and with females. The most frequent grooming partners of adult males are other adult males. Grooming thus reduces tensions between competitors and facilitates reconciliation and reassurance after aggressive interactions. Females and males groom most frequently when the female is in estrus, and sexual activity is confined to the female's estrus state. Adult females interact less frequently, ignore new females, and do not share food with other adult females.

Because chimpanzees are occasionally bipedal, they offer clues about the development of hominid bipedal locomotion. Primatologist Akio Mori studied both *Pan* species and compared their behavior. Bipedal behavior in *Pan paniscus* is frequent in all age-sex classes, and is often a starting point of complex behaviors when one individual approaches another to initiate social interaction, such as to groom or beg for food. In contrast, bipedal behavior in male *Pan troglodytes* occurs most often during charging displays or running and is accompanied with conspicuous erection of the hair on the shoulders and body.

Chimpanzees exhibit considerable variation in the expression of social relationships and the pattern of social bonds. Social interactions of *Pan paniscus* expand the behavioral possibilities for speculating about early hominids and offer alternatives beyond the limitations of aggressive males and less bonded females of *Pan troglodytes*.

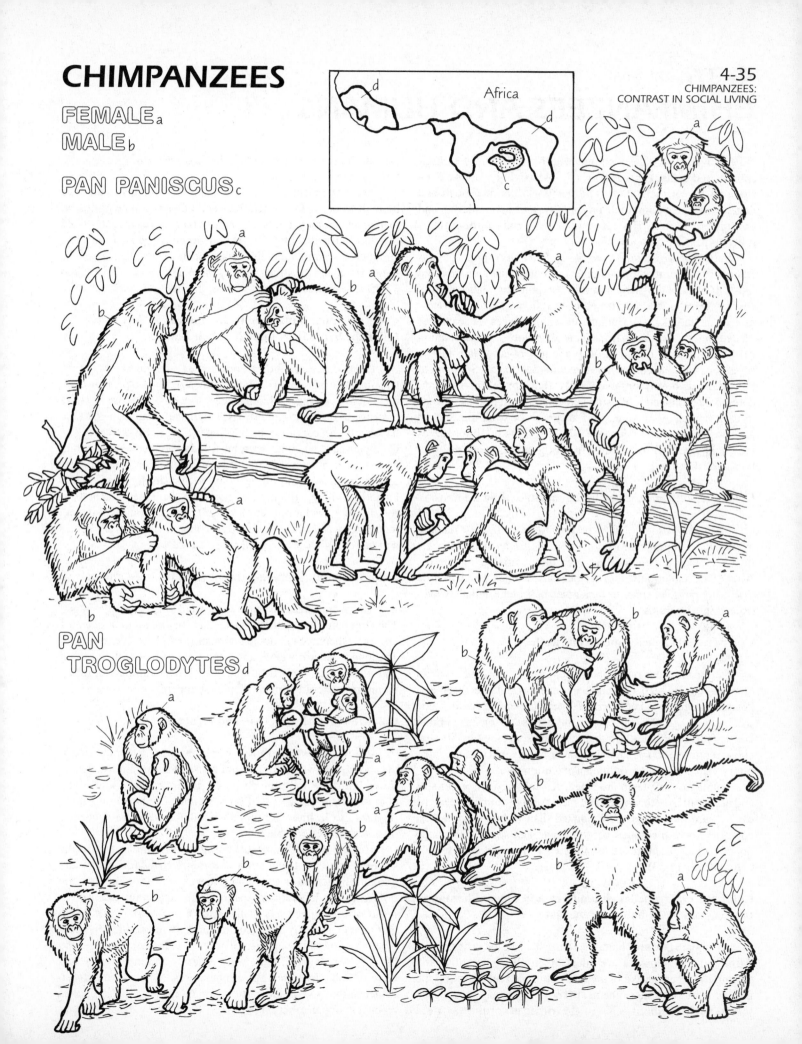

CHIMPANZEES

FEMALE a
MALE b

PAN PANISCUS c

Africa

PAN
TROGLODYTES d

4-36
CHIMPANZEES AND HUMANS

No one would mistake a chimpanzee for a human, yet chimpanzees and humans are each others' closest living relatives. They share 98.5% of their DNA, and many aspects of growth and development, anatomy and physiology, and manipulative and communication skills. But their external appearances (phenotypes) are quite distinct.

In his 1863 *Evidence as to Man's Place in Nature*, Thomas Henry Huxley argued on anatomical grounds that humans were most similar to the African apes, a hypothesis elaborated by Charles Darwin, and confirmed over 100 years later with new molecular studies (2-7). Humans and chimpanzees are so closely related that by estimates from molecular clocks, the separation of the 2 lineages occurred only about 5 mya, a date that is congruent with the current fossil record (Section 5). So much of chimpanzee behavior, especially their problem-solving, communication, and tool-using skills, are familiar to us. We see in their actions and expressions an image of what our ancient ancestors might have been like. The 2 species of chimpanzees are equally related to humans. In this comparison we use *Pan paniscus*, the gracile chimpanzee.

Color the body mass range for chimpanzees and humans.

Chimpanzees range in body mass from the lightest females at about 25 kilograms to well over 60 kilograms in the heaviest males. Human populations are even more variable; among the !Kung San, hunter-gatherers in Botswana, women weigh as little as 40 kilograms, whereas the larger members of the human species exceed 90 kilograms.

Color cranial capacity and canine teeth.

Chimpanzee and human heads contrast in the size of the brain case and canine teeth. The human head has a dome shape and houses a large brain between 1000 and 2000 cubic centimeters, with an average of 1400 cubic centimeters. Chimpanzee brain size is only about one-third that of humans, averaging 350–400 cubic centimeters. The large human brain expanded in the later, rather than early stages of human evolution (5-1, 5-21).

Human canine teeth are small, resembling incisors in size and are small in both women and men. Among chimpanzees, the canines are larger and more pointed than in humans, and the enlarged lower premolars accommodate and sharpen the large upper canines. Canines are usually larger in male than in female chimpanzees (4-33).

Color the quadrupedal chimpanzee and bipedal human in the diagram at the bottom of the plate.

Chimpanzees and humans contrast in body proportions. Although chimpanzees are adept at climbing, feeding, and sleeping in trees, unlike orangutans, chimpanzees travel on the ground from one tree to the next. They walk quadrupedally on their knuckles about 85% of the time, according to field primatologist Diane Doran, and in this sense chimpanzees can be considered "terrestrial."

The differences in muscles, bones, and the distribution of body mass between chimpanzees and humans can be attributed to their locomotor patterns. The human body has been reorganized for habitual upright posture and bipedal locomotion. The circulatory system, including heart function, the integrity of the pelvic floor, and the stress-bearing lumbar region and lower limb joints accommodate to the forces of gravity.

Color the upper limbs, hands, and thumbs in the two species. Color the bones first, then the whole limb.

Chimpanzee and human arm bones—the humerus, radius, and ulna—are similar in overall length, size, and shape. However, relative to body mass, chimpanzee upper limbs are almost twice as heavy as those of humans. The length and relative mass of the hands and the curvature of the finger bones also differ (5-23). Chimpanzee hand bones are robust, and the finger bones are long and curved; their hands function in locomotion—in hanging, climbing, and in supporting body weight during quadrupedal knuckle walking. Even so, chimpanzee hands are capable of relatively fine manipulation (3-33). Human hands have no locomotor weight-bearing function; consequently they are lighter and more flexible with a well-muscled thumb.

Color the trunk, including the clavicle, rib cage, and pelvis.

The overall size and shape of the trunks are generally similar. The chimpanzee scapula, clavicle, and shoulder joint are angled upward, whereas the human shoulder joint is directed outward. The long and narrow chimpanzee pelvis contrasts with the broad and wide bowl-shaped human pelvis. The lumbar region is therefore longer in humans than in chimpanzees

Color the lower limbs, foot, and great toe.

Chimpanzees have short lower limbs relative to their trunks; the upper and lower limbs are similar in length. In contrast, human lower limbs are long, much longer than the upper limbs, and comprise more than 32% of body weight. The human great toe (hallux) lies in line with the others compared to chimpanzee's divergent and opposable hallux.

Huxley pointed out that the numerous similarities in the skeleton, muscles, teeth, brain, and embryos of African apes and humans indicated a common ancestry. He thought that the differences in locomotion, canine teeth, and brain size were a result of divergent ways of life. He, and later Darwin, argued that human anatomy changed dramatically in adopting habitual bipedal locomotion and use of tools. At the time Huxley and Darwin were writing, there were no early hominid fossils, and therefore no way to test these hypotheses. Now we have fossil evidence that shows the earliest hominids can be described as bipedal chimpanzees (5-17).

COMPARATIVE ANATOMY

BODY MASS $_a$
CRANIAL CAPACITY $_b$
CANINE TEETH $_c$
UPPER LIMB $_d$
HAND $_{d^1}$
THUMB $_{d^2}$

TRUNK $_e$
CLAVICLE $_{e^1}$
RIB CAGE $_{e^2}$
PELVIS $_{e^3}$

LOWER LIMB $_f$
FOOT $_{f^1}$
GREAT TOE $_{f^2}$

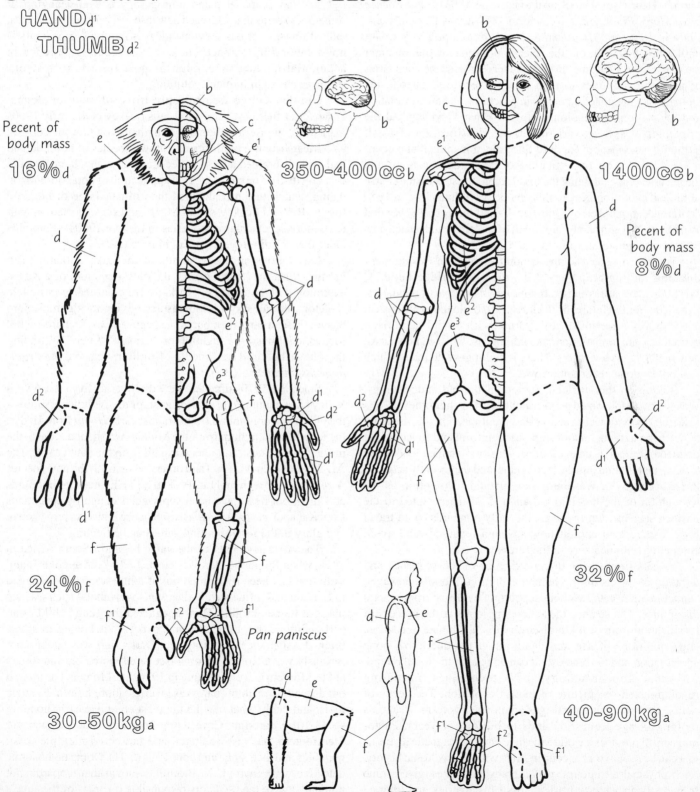

Pecent of body mass
16% $_d$

350-400cc $_b$

1400cc $_b$

Pecent of body mass
8% $_d$

24% $_f$

32% $_f$

Pan paniscus

30-50kg $_a$

40-90kg $_a$

SECTION 5
HUMAN EVOLUTION

In his 1859 book, *On the Origin of Species,* Darwin laid the foundation for the scientific study of human evolution. His friend Thomas Henry Huxley took up the task in his 1863 book, *Evidence as to Man's Place in Nature*; and in 1871 it was Darwin's turn again in *Descent of Man and Selection in Relation to Sex.* Not until 1950, however, did the science of human evolution enter the modern era, when the "bridge builders" crossed the boundaries of narrow disciplines to map a larger territory. Theodosius Dobzhansky integrated advances in genetics with human variation and adaptation. Population biologist, Ernst Mayr applied the principles of species variation to the classification of fossil hominids; and George Gaylord Simpson, a mammalian paleontologist, pointed out the limitations of comparative anatomy and the necessity for examining the fossil record to establish the course of human evolution. Key to this "modern synthesis" was a 1950 conference, organized by Dobzhansky and the young Sherwood Washburn, "Origin and Evolution of Man," that emphasized new themes of population, variation, and adaptation.

Washburn served as the conduit of modern evolutionary thinking into anthropology. Like the other bridge builders, Washburn saw issues and problems, not disciplinary boundaries. In a vision for the future, he declared: "To build the new physical anthropology we must collaborate with social scientists, geneticists, anatomists, and paleontologists; we need new ideas, new methods, new workers. There is nothing we do today which will not be done better tomorrow."

Taking on the artificial barriers of the old anthropology, Washburn emphasized experiments to test hypotheses. His research on the lower jaw revealed the impact of soft tissue on bone shape and the relationship between form and function. He pointed out the mosaic evolutionary history retained by our ape thorax, our hominid bipedal locomotion, and our recently acquired large brain (5-1). Washburn saw bipedal locomotion as the foundation of the hominid radiation (5-2) that adapted to the African savanna. On two legs, the early hominids could travel long distances to exploit new savanna resources and avoid competing with denizens of the forests.

Fossils provide the direct evidence of the sequence and duration of events during human evolution. Fossils, however, cannot be interpreted without supporting evidence from several disciplines. The science of taphonomy looks at the process of fossilization from death to discovery (5-3). Climate, predation, and conditions of life and death affect the quality of bone preservation and to some extent can be read in the fossil record.

From geochronology, new techniques in dating revolutionized our picture of human evolution. The decay of radioactive potassium to the gas argon dates volcanic materials ranging in age from thousands to billions of years. Paleomagnetism provides a worldwide time chart of magnetic reversals that can be read like a bar code in strata without a volcanic history. Such physical techniques, yielding absolute dates, give a time framework in which to orient fossil discoveries and liberate geologists and paleontologists from the uncertainties of relying exclusively on "faunal dating" (biostratigraphy).

The landscape of paleoanthropology is ever-changing. It sometimes seems that with each new discovery from African sites, radical revision of our previous ideas is required (5-5). Ours is not a laboratory science but one that requires patience in accumulating evidence, such as new fossils, to test our reconstructions of human evolution.

Olduvai Gorge is a treasure-trove of such evidence. Discoveries there by Mary and Louis Leakey in the early 1960s mark the modern era in the study of human evolution and confirm an African origin. Fossils document two species of hominid and that a small-brained ancestor preceded one with a larger cranial capacity (5-6). The site is the first application of potassium/argon dating, which instantly doubled the estimated age of hominid fossils. Richard Leakey, son of Mary and Louis, carried on with even more spectacular discoveries in the late 1960s—hominids older than 2 million years at Koobi Fora (5-7).

Excavations on the west side of the Lake Turkana basin brought forth the "black skull," the oldest cranium of a robust australopithecine and the "Turkana Boy," a nearly complete skeleton, the rarest of fossil treasures, giving us a glimpse into the youth of an early member of the genus *Homo*. Richard's wife, Meave, continued the tradition of "Leakey's Luck" by finding the oldest hominid yet known, 4-million-year-old *Australopithecus anamensis* (5-8).

Since the 1970s dramatic new discoveries from the Awash Valley have continued to provide grist for the evolutionary mill— the oldest ape or hominid from Aramis; early *Homo* from Hadar; the large Bodo cranium from the Middle Awash; and Konso, the most complete australopithecine skull from the south (5-9). The AL-288 skeleton ("Lucy") and others assigned to the new species *A. afarensis* were thought in 1978 to be THE ancestral hominids at 3 mya, but now have been superseded in age by specimens from Kanapoi and by *A. anamensis*. Science is always provisional, and glory in the fossil-hunting game can be fleeting.

The African chapter of the game began in South Africa in 1924, when Raymond Dart was electrified by the apelike Taung skull that had been dynamited out of a limestone cave. Trained in London and influenced by Darwin's view that Africa was the place of human origins, Dart recognized the Taung child as an early hominid, but the European "experts," believing in a big-brained Asian ancestor, disagreed. Dart's find was taken more seriously when Robert Broom discovered more hominid fossils at Sterkfontein Cave beginning in 1936. Sterkfontein has poured out a steady stream of major discoveries: more hominids, stone tools, and lately what may be the most complete early hominid yet (5-10). Swartkrans Cave, a limestone cave that is adjacent to Sterkfontein, has also sheltered and preserved multiple fossil hominids and their stone and bone tools (5-11). Doing taphonomic detective work there, C.K. Brain has shown that leopards, not hominids, were the predators responsible for most of the cave's accumulation of bones, including some hominid ones (5-12).

How did the behavior of our early ancestors differ from that of apes? From several lines of evidence—molecular, comparative anatomy and behavior, the fossil record, and ecology—we infer that our early ancestors were adapting to life on the savanna, not as hunters and meat eaters as is so often emphasized, but as opportunistic omnivores dependent on tool-using skills for collecting food (5-13). We know that hominids walked differently, on two legs rather than four based on direct evidence of bipedalism from the lower limb anatomy (5-14). The changes are documented in the fossil record too—for instance, in the Kanapoi tibia (5-15), fossil footprints and foot bones (5-16), and "Lucy's" body size and limb proportions (5-17). Hominids then were already accomplished bipeds, but with skeletal equipment significantly different from our own.

They also had distinct skulls, faces, and teeth (5-18, 5-19). Australopithecine brains were bigger than those of apes, and big teeth and heavily muscled jaws signal heavy chewing and grinding. There were "gracile" and "robust" australopithecines, the latter more specialized and surviving later, until 1.2 mya (5-20). Although bipedal walking was established by 4 mya, brain expansion did not begin in earnest until 2 mya (5-21).

As Washburn foresaw, new techniques give new insights into the fossil record—literally, in the case of CT scanning, which can reveal hidden inventories inside the bone. Locked inside the tooth is the daily growth of the enamel, which records the individual's exact age (5-22). With new techniques, old fossils can speak to scientists in new ways.

Unlike other primates, we no longer use our hands in locomotion for bearing weight or swinging through the trees. Consequently, our hands are smaller, with straighter phalanges. Fossil hand bones 2 to 3 million years old reveal this shift in specialization of the hand from locomotion to manipulation. The early hominid hand bones retain some apelike curvature but have enough modern features to suggest a long evolutionary period of tool use (5-23). Modified stone tools left by early human ancestors provide further evidence of the hominids' increasing manual skills.

The genus *Homo* appears on the evolutionary stage at about 2.5 mya, in the form of fragmentary jaws and teeth accompanied by these first stone tools (5-24). Larger brains and further postcranial and bipedal modifications distinguish this new genus. Less than 1 million years later, *Homo erectus* migrated into tropical Southeast Asia and mid-latitude Eurasia. Why was this species so successful? We don't know, but possible factors are its larger body size and longer legs for improved locomotion; bigger brain, capable of more complex social and cognitive behavior; better tools and mastery of fire, denoting greater skill; and more effective foraging and an expanded diet with more elaborate food preparation.

By the Middle Pleistocene (800,000–200,000 years ago) *Homo* was widespread in Africa, Europe, and Asia, but how many species there were is a contested issue. Was *Homo erectus* ubiquitous (5-25)? This period of human evolution was once referred to as "the muddle in the middle" because of the few fossils, their confusing morphology, and the poor dates. There was no overall framework for choosing among competing hypotheses. Now, DNA comparisons among living human groups point to *Homo sapiens* origin in Africa about 150,000 years ago, and DNA from two Neanderthal fossils clocks a 600,000 year old separation between the lineages leading to Neanderthals and *Homo sapiens*. Early Middle Pleistocene fossils in Africa and Europe have now been assigned to *Homo heidelbergensis*, the presumed common ancestor of these two lineages.

Who were the Neanderthals? This question preoccupied anthropologists for more than a century (5-26). Widespread in Eurasia, well adapted to the cold with their robust compact bodies, and distinct from *Homo sapiens* in skull shape and pelvis, Neanderthals survived in Europe until about 27,000 years ago. This time was long after *Homo sapiens* had occupied other areas of the world. Once-popular theories that Neanderthals were ancestral to *Homo sapiens* or interbred with them are ruled out by Neanderthal DNA. The DNA shows them to have been a separate species, four times as different from us as we are from each other, with no molecular evidence of interbreeding.

Fascinated with the earlier stages of human evolution 1 to 4 mya, paleoanthropologists focused less on the origin of *Homo sapiens* until recently. There was a general notion that humans arose in Europe with Cro-Magnon 40,000 years ago. By the 1980s, there were two competing scenarios. The "multiregional hypothesis" maintained that modern humans evolved in parallel during the past half million years in different parts of the world. The "recent replacement" hypothesis, on the contrary, proposed that *Homo sapiens* evolved in a single location, most likely sub-Saharan Africa, and subsequently dispersed and replaced earlier hominid species in the rest of the world.

Molecular studies of living populations have confirmed the recent African origin of our species and ruled out the multiregional picture. This new framework, together with new fossils and new dating techniques (thermoluminescence), explains the appearance of *H. sapiens* in the Levant, the path out of Africa, about 100,000 years ago (5-28), and the subsequent spread of the species to South Asia and Australia, Europe, and the Americas (5-29). About 40,000 years ago a flowering of art and artifacts commenced wherever our species lived and has continued in a crescendo until this day.

Neurological research reveals that the two halves of the modern human brain have specialized, so that we effectively have two brains in one head, the left side being linguistic and logical, the right side artistic and global (5-30). Perhaps the layout of this book is a mirror reflection of those two extraordinary human skills, the artist on one side, the linear thinker on the other, both contributing equally to our growing understanding of the evolution of our species.

5-1
SHERWOOD WASHBURN

Sherwood Washburn altered our approach to the study of human evolution. He tested ideas by experiments and integrated primate research with modern mammalian biology. Prior to his work in the 1940s, descriptions of anatomical structures and measurements of isolated traits such as head shape, bone lengths, and stature defined physical anthropology. This approach gave little indication of a trait's function or evolutionary history.

Washburn rejected these methods as static and nonadaptive and developed a way to analyze morphological change. He argued that because the human lineage has evolved, physical traits must contribute to survival, and therefore be subject to natural selection. Fossil fragments represent individuals who had lived and survived. Measurements must have biological meaning, he argued. Isolated traits must be integrated into a functional whole, so that the trait's adaptive significance becomes apparent.

During the 1940s Washburn's research demonstrated that living bones are far from the rigid structures we see in the anatomy laboratory. He showed that bones are shaped by the mechanical force of muscles and other tissues that attach to them. Washburn focused on the lower jaw, the basis of the feeding apparatus essential to life, and a body part that most frequently survives as a fossil.

Color the parts of the human jaw that illustrate three functional regions.

Muscle action shapes the jaw. For example, if the temporal muscle is weak or absent, the coronoid process fails to develop. The masseter muscle, which attaches on the outside of the angle, and the pterygoid muscle, which attaches on the inside, exert forces that produce bony ridges and influence the shape of the angle. The size and shape of tooth crowns and roots rely on bony support. The body of the mandible reflects the compressive forces from jaw action. This type of analysis goes beyond traditional measurements of the size and shape of the jaw and teeth. Washburn presented fossils in a new light based on his awareness of the forces on living bone.

Color the parts of the mandible in the female, immature male, and adult male baboon. Note that the proportions of the braincase and face differ in the adult female and male.

The mandible changes in size and shape during its growth and development. Adult male and female baboon mandibles differ due to the male's large canine teeth and the robust supporting bone and muscle. Adult female and immature male mandibles are similar because the young male's canine teeth are not yet fully erupted. As the male's canines continue to grow, the mandibular shapes become markedly different (3-30).

Using this approach, Washburn argued that during human evolution, relatively small genetic changes affecting growth could result in large differences in bodily appearance. He concluded that only a small number of genes would have to be altered to account for differences between early australopithecines and later hominids. In the 1980s new molecular data supported his deduction. Molecular genetic comparisons demonstrated only a 1.5% difference between humans and chimpanzees and less than 0.1% difference among various human populations from Africa, Europe, and Asia (5-27).

The shape of the human mandible is the consequence of 1) the eruption and function of the teeth and the roots embedded in the bone; 2) the action of the masseter and pterygoids at the angle of the mandible; 3) the temporalis muscle and its attachment on the coronoid. Washburn later tied the anatomy of the mandible to baboon female/male social dynamics and male aggression and so extended the understanding of mandibular function to include the social processes of the group.

Color the human skeleton separated into three functional complexes based on the order in which they evolved.

Washburn applied the idea of functional regions to the entire body. He pointed out that during the recent evolutionary history of hominids, three regions evolved somewhat independently, that is, the body evolved in a mosaic fashion.

Reflecting an ape ancestry, human arms and thorax represent the bone-muscle-joint mechanism that was basic to brachiation in apes, the way of life that involved hanging and swinging under tree branches. This anatomical complex includes mobile shoulder joints, long arms, and a short lumbar region (4-26). Humans share these features with the great apes and gibbons.

Bipedal locomotion is a defining feature of hominids. Washburn delineated the anatomical features associated with bipedal function. The short, broad shape of the ilium and the altered attachment points for gluteal muscles appeared in the australopithecines and confirmed their pattern of bipedal locomotion (5-15). With hands freed from any locomotor function, early hominids systematically made and used tools (5-23). The feet changed shape in response to being the body's only support during locomotion (5-16).

The large brain and reduction in tooth size came later in human evolution. Our large braincase and small face, fitted with small teeth, was refined within the last 200,000 years. The uniquely human brain correlates with complex tool traditions, language, symbolic and abstract thinking, and art and ritual (5-29).

With his Darwinian perspective, Washburn emphasized that bipedal locomotion, not simply a large brain, first defined hominid life. He transcended earlier traditions in anthropology based on isolated measurements and classification of bones and teeth and taught anthropologists to think in terms of process and natural selection.

NEW PHYSICAL ANTHROPOLOGY

REGIONS OF THE
MANDIBLE⁎
CORONOID PROCESS a
ANGLE a¹
DENTITION b/CANINE b¹
CONDYLE/BODY c

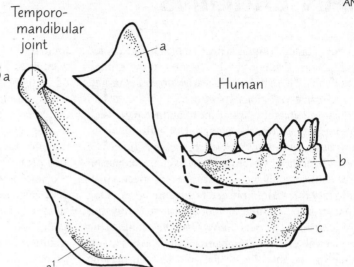

Temporo-mandibular joint

Human

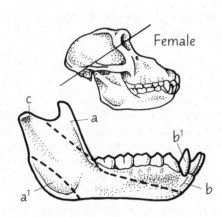

Female

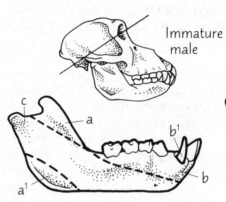

Immature male

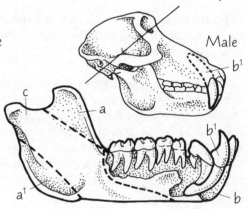

Male

REGIONS OF THE
HUMAN BODY⁎

THORAX/
SHOULDER d

HAND e
PELVIS/
LOWER LIMBS e

HEAD/
BRAINCASE f

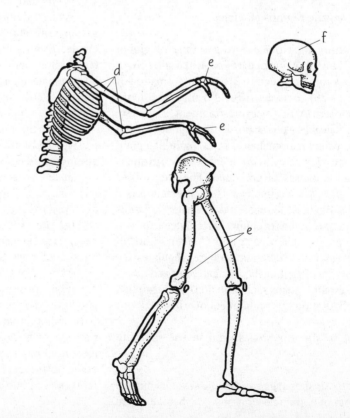

5-2
HUMAN ORIGINS

A popular scenario of human origins states that the climate cooled and forests disappeared, driving tree-living apes to the ground and to open grasslands. There these apes learned to walk upright. Such scenarios recognize a relationship between environment and evolution, but do not adequately explain the relationship between them. In biological evolution, the potential of individuals to survive and reproduce determines species change over time. The environment provides a stage, which biologist Evelyn Hutchinson describes as "the ecological theater," in which actor species play out their evolutionary roles. Hominid actors are defined by being bipedal. This mode of locomotion did not appear suddenly, but more probably emerged in two acts. In Act One, they came to the ground as knuckle-walkers, like chimpanzees and gorillas today. In Act Two, they moved into the savanna mosaic and became habitually bipedal.

Color the ecological Mediterranean zones in northern Africa and in southern Africa at the Cape. Color the desert and semidesert areas.

Mediterranean regions have a mild climate and seasonal rainfall with lush vegetation and scrub. In contrast, the Sahara Desert in the north and the Namib Desert in the southwest receive less than 30 centimeters of rainfall per year. Monkeys, but not apes, inhabit dry regions in Africa. Monkeys live on the ground and are quadrupedal and therefore illustrate that neither ground living nor savanna dwelling is a sufficient explanation for the origin of bipedality.

Color the savanna mosaic regions of Africa.

Hominoid evolution took place during a time of global tectonic movements. The formation of the Great Rift Valley broke up the once continuous forest and contributed to the formation of the savanna mosaic (4-28). Between 10 and 5 mya, the dense tropical forests in eastern Africa became fragmented, and by 5 mya the savanna mosaic was well established throughout eastern and southern Africa. Many mammalian species, including giant baboons, expanded into this new environment (4-27). Savannas are not simply broad expanses of grassland. They are mixed ecologically, as the term mosaic implies. Their vegetation is a patchy network of tall grass, shrubs, and a variety of trees distributed in discontinuous stands or clumps. The savanna mosaic falls within the tropics of Capricorn and Cancer. Rainfall (100–150 cm per year), rather than temperature, regulates the long dry season. Plants are often drought resistant; roots and tubers store nutrients underground; plants such as melons bear fruit that is protected from dehydration by tough outer coverings.

Color the hominid fossils and sites found in the savanna mosaic.

The location of fossil sites suggests that the savanna mosaic was the earliest theater of hominid operations. Ape habitats were limited to forests and woodlands, but early hominid fossil sites were widely distributed in the Great Rift Valley, in the high veldt of southern Africa, and in the savanna regions of north central Africa. Hominid sites usually occur near ancient margins of lakes or rivers, sources of water for hominids, as well as places of danger. Water movement deposited sediments to cover mortal remains. Cave sites provided protection from the weather and also preserved hominid bones (5-10, 5-11). Each environment presented its inhabitants with particular advantages and disadvantages. The savanna mosaic offers a bounty of plant foods and potential prey for opportunistic omnivorous primates, such as the hominids and monkeys. However, periodic droughts and resulting food shortages pose difficulties, and open spaces turn primates into meal opportunities for big cats and other predators (5-12).

Color the distribution of living African apes in the equatorial rain forest and the woodlands.

Our closest relatives, chimpanzees and gorillas, inhabit equatorial regions that include forests and woodlands. They climb into trees to feed, rest, and build sleeping nests. They also feed and rest on the ground and travel exclusively there. They forage in three dimensions, up and down, between trees and ground, in contrast with the largely two-dimensional geometry of the savanna mosaic. Gorillas typically cover less than 1 kilometer each day, although when attracted by seasonal fruits, they travel over 2.5 kilometers in a day (4-34). Chimpanzees generally move 2 to 3 kilometers daily and occasionally more than 5 kilometers.

Ancestral hominids foraging for dispersed resources in the savanna mosaic probably had larger home ranges and covered greater distances each day than modern apes, perhaps on average 6 to 7 kilometers. Chimpanzees in dry open habitats have larger home ranges than forest-dwelling chimpanzees. Savanna-living baboons also have larger home ranges than forest-living baboons and travel farther each day.

Given the many genetic correspondences between chimpanzees and humans, it is likely that in Act One, the common ape-hominid ancestor was a quadrupedal knuckle-walker, dominated by its hindlimbs. In Act Two, hominids came to rely on resources that required long-distance travel. The shoulder joints of chimpanzees and gorillas are not well suited to weight bearing, and the necessity for hominids to traverse a greater area would have placed even more stress on this anatomical region. Sparing the shoulder was a particular advantage of bipedal locomotion.

Thus, about 5 mya ecological and evolutionary events set the stage for hominid origins: climatic change as a result of geological forces and expansion of the savanna mosaic; and an African hominoid in central Africa already equipped for ground travel, but who now had to travel longer distances each day. By 4 mya, hominids were habitually bipedal, and their way of life as nomadic foragers persisted with numerous variations for the remainder of human prehistory.

THE SAVANNA MOSAIC

MEDITERRANEAN SCRUB a

DESERT AND SEMIDESERT b

SAVANNA MOSAIC c

EARLY HOMINIDS c^1

EQUATORIAL FOREST d

GRACILE CHIMPANZEES d^1

ROBUST CHIMPANZEES d^2

GORILLAS d^3

WOODLANDS e

ROBUST CHIMPANZEES d^2

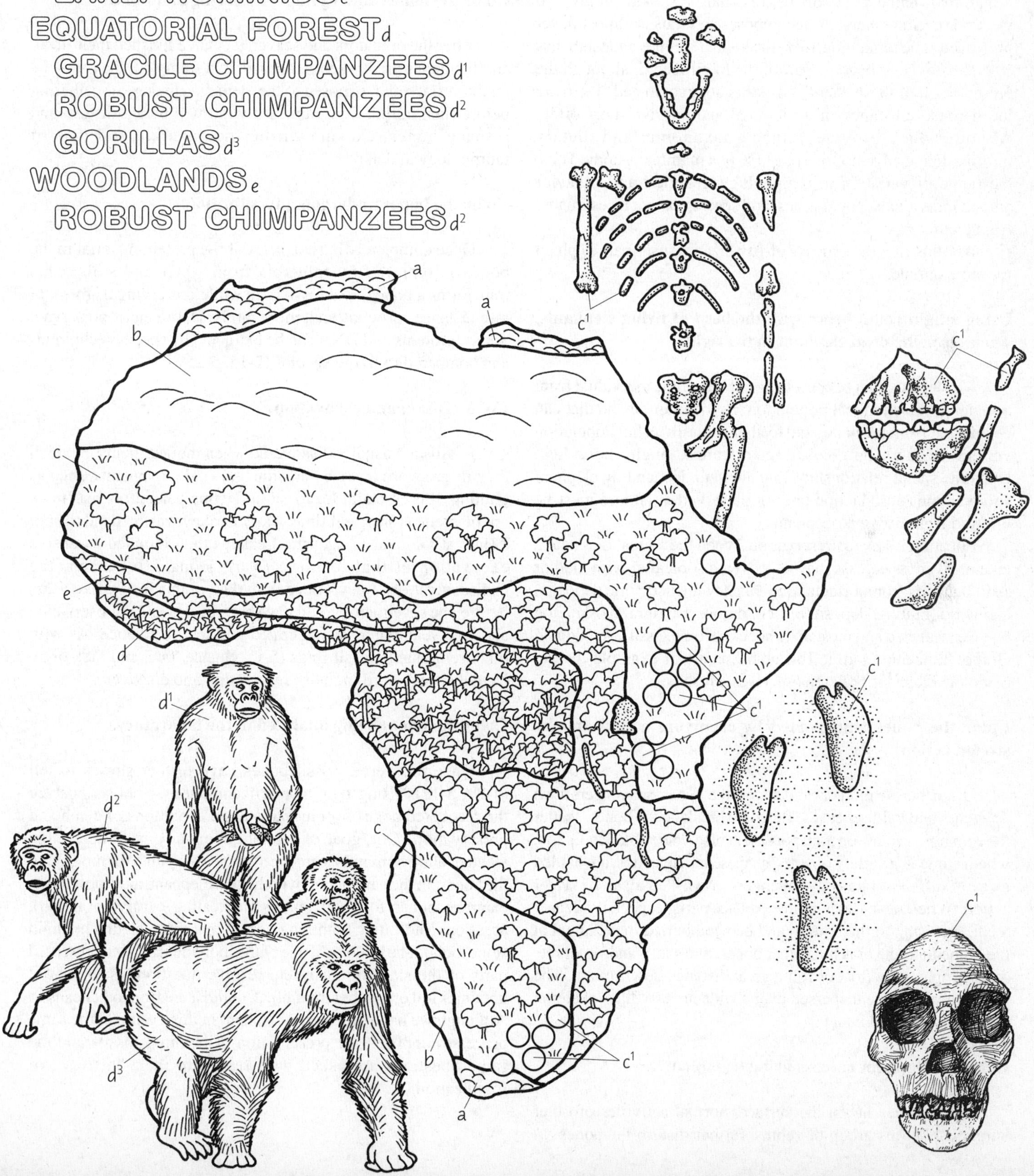

5-3
FOSSILS IN THE MAKING

The making of a fossil—from the death of an organism to its final discovery in geological deposits—is a story that reveals the incomplete nature of the fossil record. After death, about 85% of a mammal, namely its soft tissues (muscles, skin, brain, and viscera), is either eaten or decomposes and thus is almost never preserved. The remaining 15%, the animal's bones and teeth, has a better chance to become part of the fossil record, although the preservation of these "hard" tissues is not guaranteed. Teeth are the hardest substance in a mammal and survive most often. Although they provide valuable taxonomic and dietary information, teeth comprise only 1% of a mammal's body. Thus, the range of variation in morphology, genetics, and behavior among individuals, populations, and species cannot be estimated from teeth.

We illustrate the process of fossilization using an elephant for our example.

Using a light color, begin with the herd of living elephants. Then color the dead elephant to the right.

An elephant that becomes a fossil is a single individual from a social group and local population. Its locomotion and diet can be inferred from the bones and teeth that fossilize, but population variation cannot be reconstructed from a single individual. Dynamic social relationships that aid in understanding elephant survival and reproduction are not preserved at all and must be inferred from living descendants.

Location is key to preservation. When the animal dies near a lake or river, its carcass may be covered soon after with mud or sand deposits from a fluctuating lake level (lucustrine deposits) and wind (alluvial deposits). If conditions are right, its skeleton may be protected and most of its bones become fossils. At Olduvai Gorge, Tanzania, and at Torralba, Spain, for example, nearly complete elephant skeletons survive as fossils.

Color the bones transported by carnivore action and by stream action.

Often, before mud or sand covers the bones, scavengers such as hyenas and vultures eat the flesh and break up the bones, scatter the remaining ones, or transport them elsewhere. Skeletal parts, which come in a variety of sizes, shapes, and densities, are hauled away at different rates by scavengers or washed away by water action. When near water, some skeletal parts, especially denser teeth, may sink to the bottom and become buried in sediment at the immediate site of death. Other bones, like skulls and vertebrae, for example, may float or roll a great distance downstream. The bones then become dispersed over a wide area so that a skeleton is rarely preserved intact.

Color the elephant carcass being trampled.

When bones lie on the surface, normal activities of other animals, like this group of zebras, further disturb the bones. In the course of their movements, animals trample and abrade the bones, which become further damaged and disarticulated.

Color the bones undergoing weathering and burial.

After the predators and scavengers have finished their meal, and the bones are broken, scattered, and trampled, they may lie on the surface and, exposed to the elements, undergo weathering before final burial. Sun, rain, and wind will break, distort, and reshape bones, causing further degradation and loss of morphological detail.

Color the bones undergoing fossilization.

Once completely buried, most of the protein material in the bones is replaced by minerals from water and soils. This transforms a bone into a fossil rock while preserving its form. In rare instances proteins and, more rarely, DNA can be preserved. Today, proteins and DNA can be extracted by special techniques and compared to living species (2-15, 5-25).

Color erosion and excavation.

Fossils are usually discovered when the sediments in which they lie are worn away by erosion and land movements, such as faulting. It is essential for fossil-collecting paleontologists to be on the scene at the right time. Mary Leakey was on hand to spot "Zinj" at Olduvai Gorge; the Leakeys then initiated extensive excavation at that location (5-6). Donald Johanson, the codiscoverer of "Lucy," once remarked of this fossil: five years before, the specimens would have been buried and unobservable, and five years later, disintegrated and lost to science. As with other remarkable fossil finds (5-8), chance, fate, and luck often have the final word in their preservation and discovery.

Color the bones being analyzed in the laboratory.

Once recovered, fossil bones have further stories to tell (4-29, 5-12). Using taphonomic techniques, scientists analyze the recovered bones for clues about the conditions of death and preservation. One goal of taphonomic study is to determine whether early hominids were the agents responsible for modifying the bones. In the case of our hypothetical elephant, anthropologists examine bones for tooth marks (indicating carnivore action), abrasions (indicating trampling), or cut marks (indicating hominid stone tools). The biological age of the individual and the preserved parts of the skeleton also help resolve questions, such as did hominids kill or butcher the animal, or did it die from other causes. Although we have utilized an elephant in this example, the same processes apply in the preservation of hominid fossils and the same questions are asked with regard to their "history" of fossilization.

FROM DEATH TO DISCOVERY

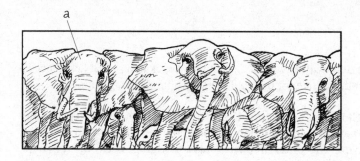

HERD_a

DEATH AND
DECOMPOSITION_b

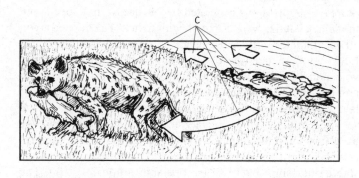

TRANSPORT_c

TRAMPLING_d

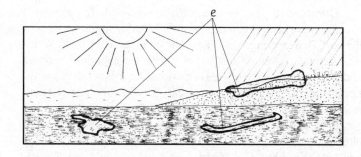

WEATHERING AND BURIAL_e

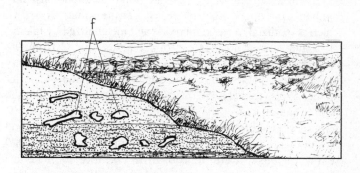

FOSSILIZATION_f

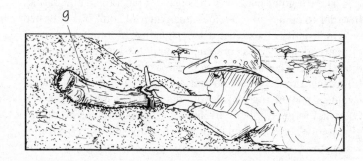

EROSION AND EXCAVATION_g

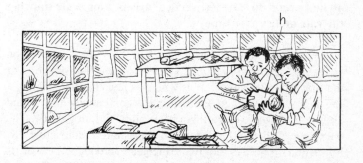

LABORATORY ANALYSIS_h

5-4
MEASURING TIME

The geological record of rocks and fossils preserve *what* happened through time, but not *when* events happened. Deeper deposits are generally older than those above, but deposition rates are variable and the depth and thickness of geological strata are unreliable indicators of age. Nevertheless, until a few decades ago, geologists and paleontologists had to rely on such rough time estimates. Just as the molecular clock has revolutionized the study of biological evolution, radioactive and paleomagnetic clocks have revolutionized the earth sciences.

Radioactivity was discovered by Henri Becquerel in 1896, when he developed some film that he had stored in a drawer with a piece of uranium ore. The images were clouded by some mysterious radiation. Unstable uranium atoms had given off particles that exposed the film. All elements, from hydrogen to uranium, have different forms called isotopes. Isotopes have different weights but behave like each other in chemical reactions. Most common isotopes are stable and do not change with time; but some, such as uranium, are radioactive: they give off particles as they decay and change into other isotopes at constant clocklike rates, called half-lives. The rate is unaffected by temperature, acidity, moisture, or other conditions that affect rocks and fossils.

Carbon 14 (^{14}C) was the first radioactive clock used to date archaeological sites from organic materials such as charcoal or wood. Three isotopes of carbon are found, ^{12}C and ^{13}C, which are stable and ^{14}C, which is radioactive and decays to nitrogen 14 (^{14}N) with a half-life of 5730 years. Solar radiation constantly bombards the upper atmosphere, converting some ^{14}N to ^{14}C, which is oxidized to carbon dioxide and metabolized by plants.

When a tree dies, it no longer takes up ^{14}C from the atmosphere. After 5730 years, its preserved wood will have only half as much ^{14}C, but the same amount of ^{12}C and ^{13}C. After another 5730 years (11,460 years total), there will be half of the half, or one-quarter of the original ^{14}C. The ratio of ^{14}C to ^{12}C in fossil wood correlates well with its actual age. This method does not work well, however, for dates older than about 50,000 years, because there is too little ^{14}C left to measure accurately. Human origins go back about 5 million years, so we need a slower clock than ^{14}C for the earlier time periods.

Color the diagram at the top that illustrates the half-life of potassium 40 and its decay into daughter isotopes, calcium 40 and argon 40. The left vertical axis is a log scale showing the rate of loss over time.

Potassium 40 (^{40}K) has a very long half-life, 1250 million years, and can be used to date events as old as the formation of the first rocks 3800 mya, or as young as lava that flowed only a few thousand years ago. Potassium is a common element found almost everywhere on earth, in lava and in all living tissue. One out of every ten thousand atoms of potassium is radioactive ^{40}K. Potassium 40 decays into two daughter byproducts: 11% of its atoms decay to argon 40 (^{40}Ar), 89% to calcium 40 (^{40}Ca). Because calcium 40 is widely distributed in rock and soil, its presence is not accurate for dating due to possible contamination.

Color the potassium 40 and argon 40 in the molten lava, and the tuffs and sediments that hold the fossil bones and artifacts. Note the older deposits have a higher ratio of argon to potassium.

When lava is molten, argon gas diffuses off into the atmosphere, so that little or none is left. After the lava solidifies, however, argon atoms generated by ^{40}K decay are trapped, and the "clock" of the ^{40}Ar/^{40}K ratio begins to tick. The trapped argon 40 accumulates in the solid lava, and the ratio rises with time. Luckily for science, the Great Rift Valley in Africa has been volcanically active for a very long time, so that many fossil hominid sites can be dated by measuring the ^{40}Ar/^{40}K ratio in the lava layers above or below where they are found (5-7).

Recently, the potassium/argon method has been improved by a new method called argon/argon dating. Lava samples are irradiated in a nuclear reactor, which converts some of the stable potassium 39 (^{39}K) isotope into argon 39 (^{39}A). The ^{40}Ar/^{39}Ar ratio can be derived from one sample and gives more accurate dates than does the ^{40}Ar/^{40}K ratio.

Color the pattern of alternating magnetic polarities.

During earth history, the north-south magnetic poles have reversed many times at irregular intervals, due to movements of the earth's iron core, which generates its magnetic field. When iron-rich lava cools, or iron particles settle to the bottom of rivers and oceans, the iron particles are oriented north-south or south-north like tiny magnetic compasses. The direction and strength of the magnetic field is permanently "frozen" in the rocks and can be measured with a magnetometer. The irregular pattern of alternating normal and reversed magnetism in the rocks is like a bar code that identifies specific time periods in earth history. Normal is defined by the present-day orientation north; reversed is to the south. The recent normal period is called Brunhes-Normal; the long, mostly reversed polarity is the Matuyama, between 1 and 2.4 mya.

The irregular pattern is the basis for paleomagnetic dating. In order to be useful as a clock, the pattern had to be calibrated with radioactive clocks. The paleomagnetism (normal or reversed) of many rock layers is correlated with potassium/argon dates of those layers. The Jaramillo Event was a period of normal polarity following a reversed period and dated at 0.9 mya. The Olduvai Event is named for rock layers dated at 1.9 million years at Olduvai Gorge. Similar correlations from other sites produce a global time scale that can be used to date fossils, even from sites where there was no volcanic activity for deriving potassium/argon dates. Where applied, however, enough of the pattern or "bar code" must be present in order to locate the time of the site within the paleomagnetic scale.

NUCLEAR AND PALEOMAGNETIC CLOCKS

HALF-LIFE OF POTASSIUM 40 (K)✴

$^{40}K_a$ $^{40}Ar_b$

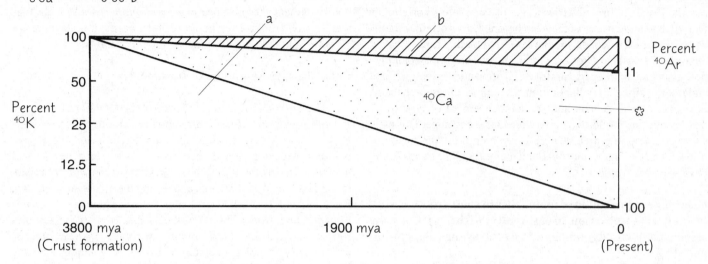

a

b

100

50

25

12.5

0

Percent
^{40}K

^{40}Ca

Percent
^{40}Ar

0

11

✩

100

3800 mya
(Crust formation)

1900 mya

0
(Present)

MOLTEN LAVA$_c$ TUFF$_{c^1}$ SEDIMENTS$_d$

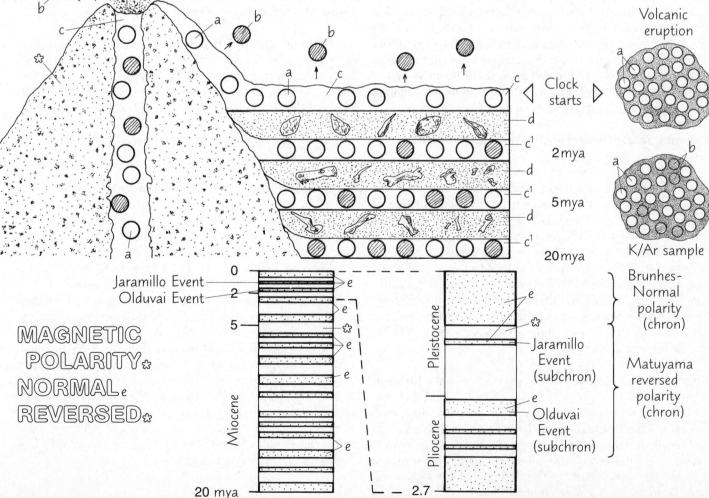

Volcanic
eruption

Clock
starts

2 mya

5 mya

20 mya

K/Ar sample

MAGNETIC
POLARITY✴
NORMAL$_e$
REVERSED✴

Jaramillo Event
Olduvai Event

Miocene

20 mya

2.7

Pleistocene

Pliocene

Brunhes-
Normal
polarity
(chron)

Jaramillo
Event
(subchron)

Matuyama
reversed
polarity
(chron)

Olduvai
Event
(subchron)

5-5
HOMINID SITES

In 1925 Raymond Dart, a young Australian neuroanatomist at the University of Witwatersrand, Johannesburg, identified the fossil skull of a child as a human ancestor. He became convinced that the fossil confirmed Africa as the place of human origins, as Darwin had argued almost 50 years before. Dart's original claims were supported when, during the 1960s, Mary and Louis Leakey uncovered fossils at Olduvai Gorge. A new era in paleoanthropology began, marked by careful excavation and by international and interdisciplinary collaborations. A number of research teams now excavate in Africa, and the announcement of new fossil discoveries rarely fails to receive wide media coverage. This plate surveys a few key areas where early hominids, the australopithecines, bone and stone tools, and members of the genus *Homo* have been recovered.

Color time ranges of three major sites in southern Africa (d), (e), and (f) as well as one in east central Africa (g). Color the associated hominids and tools. Use contrasting colors for (a) and (b).

Cave sites, such as Sterkfontein, Swartkrans, Makapansgat, and Drimolen (not illustrated) and other sites in South Africa have produced a rich record of hominid fossils and stone tools. The absence of clearly stratified sediments and volcanic deposits posed problems with dating when the first discoveries were made during the 1930s and 1940s. However, later excavations revealed distinct depositional layers, and analysis of associated fauna established relative ages of the cave deposits that range from about 3.3 mya to about 1 mya. These sites contain hominids belonging to the genus *Australopithecus* and to the genus *Homo*, as well as stone tools (5-10, 5-11). Urahu site in Malawi is about 2.4 million years old and has the mandible of an early *Homo*.

Color the Tanzanian sites of Olduvai Gorge and Laetoli.

The fossils uncovered at Olduvai Gorge by the Leakeys, along with abundant animal bones and stone tools spanned a time range of a little less than 2 million years containing species belonging to *Australopithecus* and *Homo* (5-6). The Laetoli deposits are part of the Olduvai sediment pattern and lie about 50 kilometers to the south of Olduvai. Laetoli yielded adult and juvenile mandibles, a collection of isolated teeth, and the famous footprints dated about 3.7 million years belonging to *Australopithecus* (5-16). Laetoli was first explored during the 1930s by German paleontologists who recovered part of a mandible, but not until Mary Leakey's fossil footprints discovery in 1978 did the site become well known.

Color the Omo River sites in Ethiopia north of Lake Turkana.

Excavations began in the early 1960s along the Omo River, part of the Lake Turkana drainage basin, by an international team of French, American, and Kenyan researchers. The Omo's Shungura Formation yields a well-dated stratigraphic sequence with excellent potassium/argon dates from deposits with a time span from about 3.5 mya to about 1 mya. The excellent stratigraphic and faunal records make it possible to correlate the dates of sites in eastern Africa with each other (5-7). The older Omo deposits yield mainly isolated hominid teeth and a few jaws that document the presence of *Australopithecus* and *Homo,* as well as stone tools. The younger Kibish Formation, dated about 120,000 years old yields evidence of *Homo sapiens* (5-27).

Color the sites around Lake Turkana, Kenya.

The Turkana Basin, an extension of the Omo River drainage system, is rich with fossil hominid sites. Through the efforts of Richard and Meave Leakey, their colleagues, and the Kenya National Museum, fossils have been recovered from several localities. During the 1970s, the Leakeys excavated at Koobi Fora, in the 1980s at West Turkana, and during the 1990s, at Allia Bay, Kanapoi, and Turkwel. These sites yield evidence of *Australopithecus* and *Homo.* West Turkana sites from the Nachukui formation yield the oldest cranium of robust *Australopithecus* and a nearly complete skeleton of *Homo.* At Kanapoi we have well-established evidence of hominids at about 4 mya. Stone tools have been recovered from several localities at Koobi Fora and West Turkana (5-7, 5-8).

Color the time range for sites from the Afar Triangle, Ethiopia, the northeasternmost reaches of early hominids.

Since the early 1970s, hominid and vertebrate fossils have been recovered from several areas along the Awash River, belonging to sediments generally called the Awash Group, which span a time range of over 4 mya to about 500,000 years ago. Sites from Hadar, well known for the australopithecine skeleton AL-288, dubbed "Lucy" (5-17) and from the Middle Awash yield a range of fossils assigned to *Australopithecus* and *Homo,* and stone tools about 2.5 million years old (5-9).

Color the site from Chad which lies in north central Africa.

In 1959, French paleontologist Yves Coppens and colleagues reported on the discovery of fragmentary early hominid fossils near Koro Toro, Chad. Excavations at Bahr el Ghazal, Chad, in the 1990s by French paleontologist M. Brunet and colleagues uncovered an australopithecine mandible, estimated from associated animal fossils to be about 3 million years old. No stone tools have been recovered. This site extends the known geographic distribution of early australopithecines.

All together, these fossil sites preserve a record of hominids over a 4-million-year time frame. A few other sites have fragmentary and as yet unspecified fossils that may be earlier hominids but the record is too incomplete at this time to be certain (e.g. Tabarin at Lake Baringo, and Lothagam in the Turkana Basin, Kenya, and Aramis, Ethiopia). It is important to keep in mind that in this rapidly changing field, no one can predict what new fossils may be discovered tomorrow.

SITE DISTRIBUTION

FOSSILS *

AUSTRALOPITHECUS a

HOMO b

TOOLS c

SITES *

STERKFONTEIN d

SWARTKRANS e

MAKAPANSGAT f

MALAWI g

OLDUVAI GORGE h

LAETOLI h1

OMO RIVER BASIN i

KIBISH i1

LAKE TURKANA j

KOOBI FORA j1

NACHUKUI j2

KANAPOI j3

AFAR TRIANGLE/
AWASH GROUP k

CHAD l

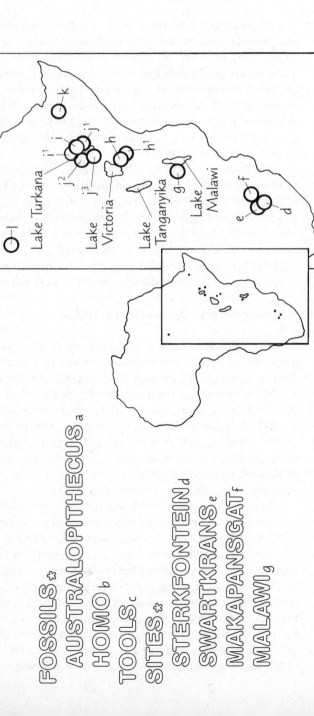

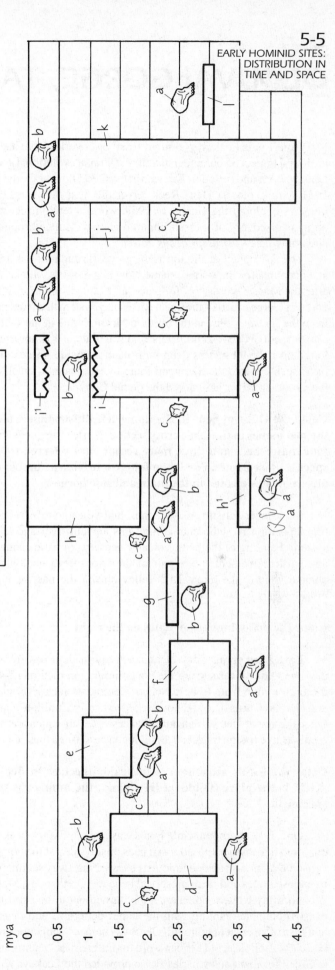

mya
0
0.5
1
1.5
2
2.5
3
3.5
4
4.5

Mary and Louis Leakey's hominid fossil discoveries have had a profound impact on our understanding of human evolution. Louis Leakey, born and raised in Kenya, first visited Olduvai Gorge in 1931 with geologist Hans Reck. Over the next 30 years, the Leakeys explored the Gorge. In 1959, world attention focused on their discovery of a fossil hominid named "Zinjanthropus," now known as *Australopithecus boisei*.

The sisal plant at the top right grows throughout the area and accounts for the gorge's name, "the place of the wild sisal" after the Maasai words "ol" for place, and "dupai" for wild sisal. Olduvai Gorge is part of the Great Rift Valley system that stretches from the Jordan Valley in the north to Mozambique in the south, a distance of over 6400 kilometers. Olduvai is about 40 kilometers long and over 90 meters deep with main and side gorges that have been cut into the Serengeti Plain by river action, much as the Colorado River has carved the Grand Canyon.

Color the Olduvai beds in the upper left illustration. Color the bed names in the large cross section. Notice the gorge has four major beds and three more recent ones referred to by specific place names. Fossil hominids come from a number of different sites located in the main and side gorges.

Rock layers of silts, clays, sands, and volcanic tuffs reflect the deposition of sediments around this ancient river and lake system. Faulting of the beds, volcanic activity, climatic change, and earth movements were part of the widespread geological changes within the Great Rift Valley during the past several million years.

Color the potassium/argon dates on the right.

Lava from prehistoric volcanic activity made it possible to date the Olduvai tuffs using the potassium/argon method (5-4), the first hominid site to be so dated. Geologists Jack Evernden and Garniss Curtis dated the lowest bed to nearly 2 million years, twice the age of then known human ancestors. Subsequent dating methods like fission track and argon/argon confirmed these dates.

Color the fossils attributed to australopithecines in Bed I. "OH" is the place (O)lduvai (H)ominid, the number is the specimen.

On a July afternoon while Louis was in camp, Mary Leakey explored the newly exposed fossil beds on the sides of the gorge. Seasonal rains assist paleontologists by washing away sediments to expose bones and teeth preserved beneath. On that day, Mary spotted shiny white tooth enamel that turned out to be part of a nearly complete cranium with the upper dentition, brain case, and face of an ancient hominid. OH 5 was named "Zinjanthropus boisei." "Zinj" is an old Persian word for East Africa; "anthropus" is Greek for man; and Charles Boise provided the Leakeys with financial support for their research.

When anatomist Phillip Tobias prepared the scientific description, he renamed "Zinj" *Australopithecus boisei*, recognizing its resemblance to South African hominids called *Australopithecus robustus*. The robust face of OH 5 and its small brain case (about 500 cc) resembled no other hominid known at the time. Its enormous teeth earned it the nickname "nutcracker man," the Leakeys referred to it affectionately as "dear boy." The femoral fragment OH 20 may also belong to this species.

Color the *Homo* fossils in Bed 1, II, IV, Masek, and Ndutu.

Excavations began where "Zinj" was discovered, and within two years the Leakeys recovered a number of fossils that differed significantly from OH 5 but were of the same geological age. These newer discoveries had smaller teeth, a larger brain case, and smaller limb bones, all together, the basis for a new species, *Homo habilis* (handy man). A nearly complete foot (5-16), tibia and fibula, hand bones, and cranial (675 cc) and dental parts were attributed to this new species (OH 7, 8, 35), as well as a reconstructed cranium OH 24 (600 cc).

The fragmentary OH 13 (675 cc) in Bed II was also classified as *Homo habilis*. The partial cranium OH 9 (1000 cc) at the top of Bed II and those above it are considered *Homo erectus*. Femoral and innominate fragments (OH 28) suggest a larger body size. In 1987, after Mary Leakey retired from leading Olduvai excavations, Donald Johanson recovered a new specimen (OH 62) consisting of cranial and dental fragments, upper limb bones, and partial femur which he attributed to *Homo habilis*.

Complete the plate by coloring the tools.

Olduvai was the first hominid site where stone tools were associated in undisturbed sediments with animal bones. Mary Leakey systematically excavated the sites and set a new standard for field techniques. Artifacts uncovered in Bed 1 included simple pebble choppers, cores, and small flakes, which became the basis for the "Oldowan" tradition, subsequently uncovered at other sites (5-10). Bifaces, such as handaxes and cleavers, from Bed II showed skilled workmanship; material is removed from both sides of the tool, producing sharp edges and a distinct point, features that define the Acheulian tool tradition (5-23).

Between 1913 and 1987, 62 hominid specimens were discovered at Olduvai, 15 of which were found between 1959 and 1963. More than 20 sites with stone tools and many species of extinct animal bones were recovered. Olduvai Gorge is significant because its layered beds with sequences of fossils and tools cover a long time range that could be accurately dated using new techniques. The discoveries documented the coexistence of two distinct hominid species living between 1.5 and 2 mya. The Leakeys' work at Olduvai Gorge launched a new era in studies of human evolution, and incidentally founded a family dynasty of hominid fossil hunters, now in its third generation.

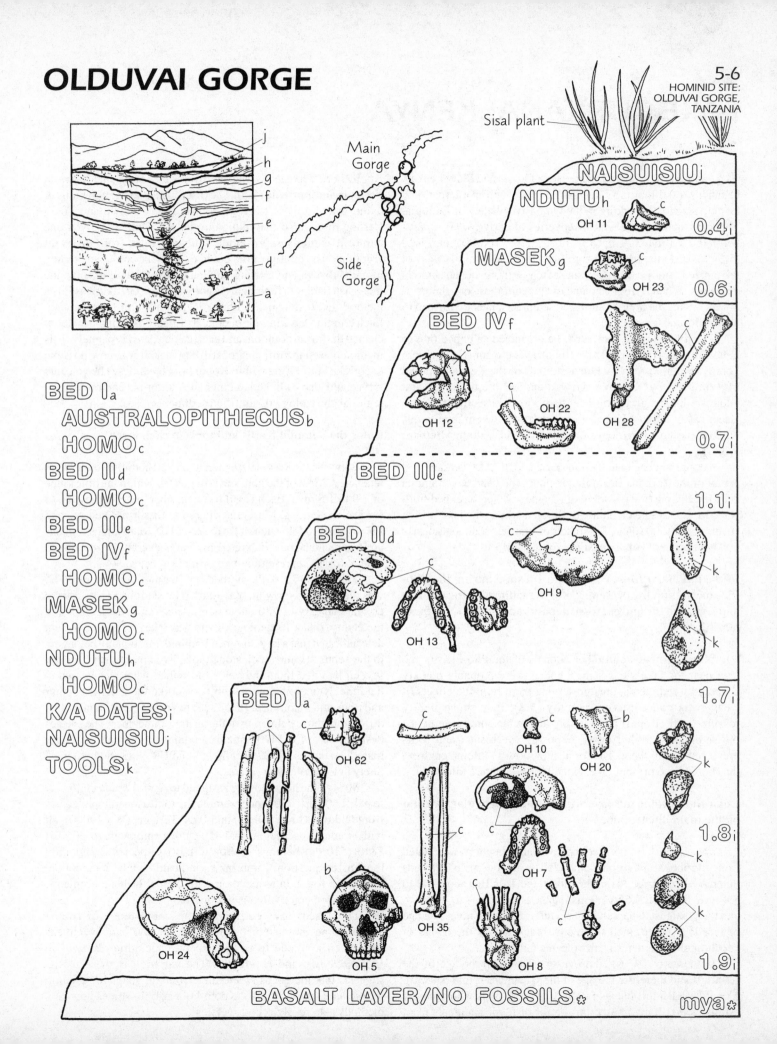

OLDUVAI GORGE

Sisal plant

Main Gorge

Side Gorge

NAISUISIU j

NDUTU h   OH 11   c   0.4 i

MASEK g   c   OH 23   0.6 i

BED IV f   c   c   OH 22   OH 28   0.7 i
OH 12

BED III e   1.1 i

BED II d   c   OH 9   k
OH 13   c   k

BED I a   c   c   OH 62   c   OH 10   b   OH 20   k   1.7 i
b   c   OH 7   k   1.8 i
OH 24   c   b   OH 35   c   OH 8   c   k   1.9 i

BASALT LAYER/NO FOSSILS *

mya *

BED I a
  AUSTRALOPITHECUS b
  HOMO c
BED II d
  HOMO c
BED III e
BED IV f
  HOMO c
MASEK g
  HOMO c
NDUTU h
  HOMO c
K/A DATES i
NAISUISIU j
TOOLS k

5-7
LAKE TURKANA, KENYA

As a young man, Richard Leakey, son of Louis and Mary Leakey, began his fossil-hunting career in the 1960s with an international team of scientists working in the Omo River Valley of Ethiopia. There he made spectacular discoveries of early *Homo sapiens* from the Kibish Formation more than 120,000 years old (5-5, 5-27). At the time, the significance of these fossils was not recognized, and Leakey went in search of more ancient human ancestors. When flying his plane over the northeastern shores of Lake Turkana, he noticed stratified sediments, later confirmed to be of Plio-Pleistocene age.

The following year in 1968, he organized an expedition to Lake Turkana (formerly Lake Rudolf). The team of the Koobi Fora Research Project included the staff of the Kenya National Museum led by Kamoya Kimeu, and an international and interdisciplinary group of scientists with archaeologist Glynn Isaac, paleontologist Kay Behrensmeyer, for whom the famous KBS tuff is named, geologist Carl Vondra, and anatomist Bernard Wood.

Koobi Fora is situated on the east side of Lake Turkana and is part of the Turkana Basin that includes the Omo River and its delta in Ethiopia (5-8). Koobi Fora (home base for the expedition) is the local Dassenetch name for the area around the lake, which covers about 1500 square kilometers of stratified sediments nearly 600 meters deep with extensive exposed surfaces.

In the top illustration, color Lake Turkana during the Plio-Pleistocene and the present. Color the sediments, the volcano and lava, and the ancient fossil deposits and present-day fossil localities.

When hominids and other animals of the Plio-Pleistocene died near the lake's edge, their bodies were probably quickly covered by sediments, thus preserving them from the effects of weathering and carnivore activity (5-3); they subsequently fossilized. After uplift and faulting due to tectonic movements, the sediments eroded away, exposing the fossils and tools preserved within them. The fossil sites, now 13 kilometers from the shore of the present lake, extend for 800 square kilometers.

Color the volcanic tuff layers in the upper right diagram and on the main illustration.

Layers of ash from the periodic volcanic eruptions were dated using the potassium/argon method. There are four main lava beds that have been dated, from the oldest, the Tulu Bor about 3.2 to 3.4 mya, the KBS 1.6 to 1.9 mya, the Okote tuff 1.4 to 1.5 mya, and the youngest, Chari and Karari tuffs, 1.2 to 1.3 mya. The age of fossils is determined indirectly, bracketed by the layers of geochronological dates from volcanic material.

In the early 1970s, controversy surrounded the age of the KBS tuff and therefore the age of the specimens found below it. The older KBS tuff dates of 2.4 mya were at odds with younger estimates of 1.8 mya based on species of fossil mammals from Koobi Fora deposits as well as from other well-dated sites in Ethiopia and Tanzania (5-5). The discrepancy in the two kinds of dating was resolved when geologists Frank Brown and Thure Cerling discovered that, although the KBS tuff was given one name, it actually represented volcanic tuffs from different eruptions. The multiple tuffs could explain the confusing variety of ages. Brown and Cerling applied a new method to solve the inconsistent dates. Tephrachronology (tephra, Greek for ash) is a method that distinguishes one volcanic eruption from another. Each eruption has a unique chemical "fingerprint" of the material ejected during an eruption, and each can be dated separately. This method placed the tuff at almost 1.9 mya so it was now possible to correlate tuff layers within Koobi Fora localities. The volcanic tuffs could also be linked to other sites to form a comprehensive regional chronology of stratified sediments (5-5).

Color the hominid fossils and tools in each layer.

Between 1968 and 1979, more than 230 hominid fossils were recovered. Most of the hominid remains fall within the time range of 1.9 to 1.5 mya. Each fossil has a number, preceded by KNM for Kenya National Museum, where the fossils are housed, and ER for East Rudolf, such as KMN-ER 1470. Many of the remains are fragmentary but illustrated here are several well-preserved cranial fossils representing two or more species.

The ER 1470 skull, sighted by Bernard Ngeneo in 1972, was discovered below the KBS tuff. The skull had an estimated cranial capacity of 780 cubic centimeters and was assigned to the genus *Homo*. Its geological age was a key issue. An ancient date indicated that a large-brained hominid, presumably belonging to the genus "Homo" with stone tools, lived more than 1.9 mya, several hundred thousand years older than what was known at the time. Numerous lower limb bones, like the ER 1481 femur and tibia, and innominate (ER 3228) have also been found which differ from those belonging to the australopithecines. The species designation of ER 1470 remains a point of disagreement. Other material, such as ER 3733 (850 cc) and ER 3883 (804 cc) most likely belong to *Homo erectus*.

Most of the hominids are assigned to *Australopithecus boisei* (e.g. ER 406, ER 732) and resemble the robust australopithecines from Olduvai Gorge (OH 5) and West Turkana (WT 17000), all with cranial capacities around 450 cubic centimeters (5-20). ER 1813 (510 cc) belongs to *Homo*, but its species designation remains in question. Limb bones indicate bipedal locomotion, but unless found in association with cranial or dental remains, species designation often is not possible.

The discoveries confirmed the coexistence of robust australopithecines and members of the genus *Homo*. Specimens have been assigned to several species including *H. habilis*, *H. rudolfensis*, and *H. erectus*. The variation in these fossils suggests that the genus *Homo* underwent an adaptive radiation into several species (5-24). Koobi Fora also illustrates how new methods help resolve controversies.

KOOBI FORA, LAKE TURKANA

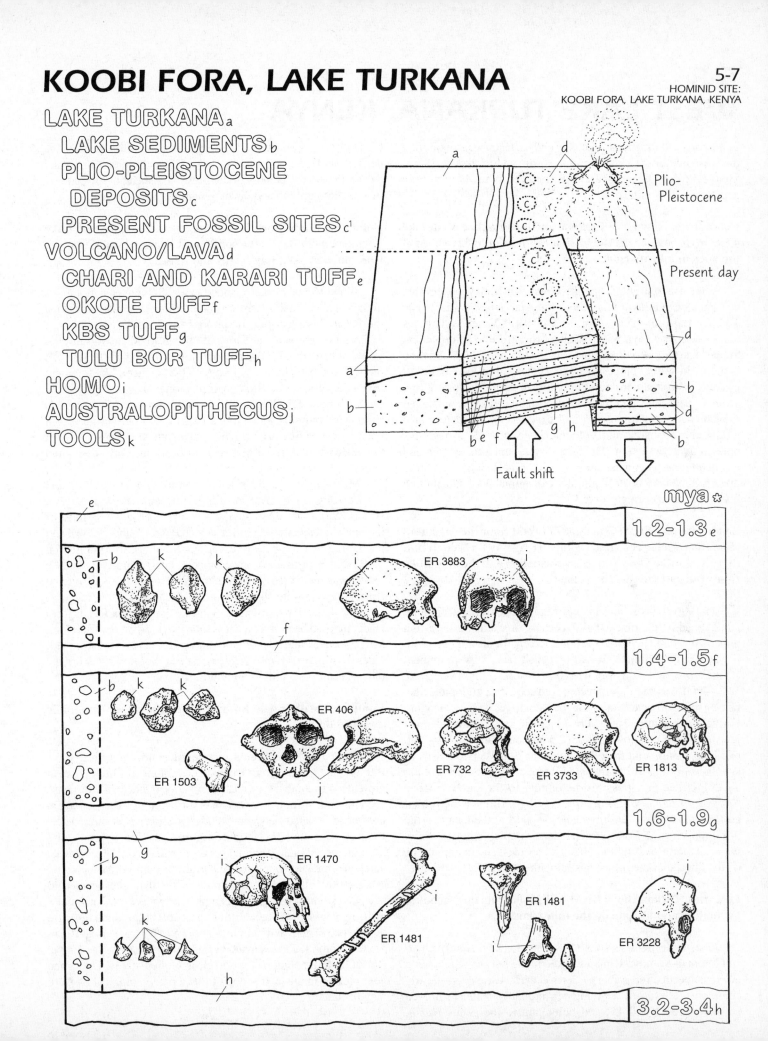

LAKE TURKANA a
  LAKE SEDIMENTS b
  PLIO-PLEISTOCENE
    DEPOSITS c
  PRESENT FOSSIL SITES c1
VOLCANO/LAVA d
  CHARI AND KARARI TUFF e
  OKOTE TUFF f
  KBS TUFF g
  TULU BOR TUFF h
HOMO i
AUSTRALOPITHECUS j
TOOLS k

Plio-Pleistocene

Present day

Fault shift

mya *

1.2-1.3 e

ER 3883

1.4-1.5 f

ER 1503

ER 406

ER 732

ER 3733

ER 1813

1.6-1.9 g

ER 1470

ER 1481

ER 1481

ER 3228

3.2-3.4 h

5-8
WEST LAKE TURKANA, KENYA

In the early 1980s, Richard Leakey and his team began exploring the west side of the Lake Turkana Basin, and in the late 1980s, Meave Leakey began searching for even older hominids in deposits to the southwest.

Color present day Lake Turkana and the shoreline of the lake 4 to 5 mya. Notice that the fossil localities would have been at the ancient lake margin.

Lake Turkana is part of the Great Rift Valley system that also includes Olduvai Gorge and the Afar Triangle (5-5). The Turkana Basin in the heart of the Great Rift Valley system lies mainly within Kenya but extends northward into Ethiopia and Sudan. The Omo River originates in the Ethiopian highlands and is the main water source for Lake Turkana. The lake and river systems deposited considerable sediment during the past 2 to 4 million years. The area has numerous faults and volcanos; land movements promote erosion and exposure of fossil treasures within the deposits, and volcanic lavas provide a basis for potassium/argon dating. The lake levels, which have risen and receded numerous times, are recorded in the sediments. Within these sedimentary layers a multitude of animal fossils, including hominids, have been preserved.

Begin with the W(est) T(urkana) site and color the Nachukui formation. Color the "black skull" (KNM-WT 17000) found there. Color the Omo Shungura formation and the mandible. Color the dates on the time chart.

In 1986, Leakey and his colleagues discovered a cranium and dubbed it "the black skull," because of the manganese-rich mineral that darkly colored the bone. Except for the missing teeth, it was nearly complete; it had a rugged face, very prominent sagittal crest, and a tiny brain (410 cc). At 2.5 million years old, WT 17000 was the oldest recognized robust australopithecine. During the 1960s, excavations in the Omo River Valley (Shungura Formation) had turned up a very robust and very weathered lower jaw (OMO 125); it too was about 2.5 million years old. Although one is a cranium and the other a mandible, these two fossils of similar age and robustness indicate that both are robust australopithecines, possibly belonging to the same species, *Australopithecus aethiopicus*. Having evidence of robust australopithecines at 2.5 mya lends support to the idea that the 3-million-year-old fossils from Hadar, Ethiopia, called *Australopithecus afarensis* might include two species, and one might be on the lineage of the robust australopithecines (5-21).

Color the "Turkana boy" KNM-WT 15000 from the Nachukui Formation and its date on the time chart.

Over three field seasons (1984–86) Leakey, Alan Walker, and foreman Kamoya Kimeu worked in the hot sun to recover a precious specimen spread in pieces over the landscape—the nearly complete skeleton of a youngster, probably male, estimated between age 11 and 15, and belonging to the genus *Homo*.

Geologist Frank Brown and colleagues radiometrically dated the deposits and the specimen to 1.6 mya. The individual's immature age and the completeness of the preserved skeleton offered rare insights into growth and development in early hominids.

Color the Koobi Fora formation on the east side of Lake Turkana, Allia Bay to the south, and Kanapoi site. Color the Kanapoi and Allia Bay fossils and dates.

When Meave Leakey decided to search for ancient hominids in the Turkana Basin, there was no hominid evidence older than the 3.7-million-year-old footprints from Laetoli. She chose to explore the sediments at Kanapoi known to be about 4 million years old. In the 1960s, paleontologist Bryan Patterson had recovered a distal humerus (KNM-KP 271) there. The fragment revealed very little. Isolated limb bones are inadequate for establishing species identity, especially the humerus, which is similar in hominids and chimpanzees (4-36). Furthermore, arm bones provide no evidence for bipedal locomotion. Thus, the fossil humerus was described and shelved to await more fossils and later diagnosis.

Meave Leakey and her team went to work at Kanapoi, and before long uncovered an upper jaw and most of a tibia (KP 29285). Later they found a second upper jaw with most of the teeth and a complete lower jaw (KP 29281 and 29283), and the ear region of a skull. Excavations expanded to Allia Bay on the east side of the lake in sediments dated at 4 mya, where a radius was recovered. A wrist bone (not shown) was recovered from Turkwel, a site about 3.5 million years old.

The collection of fossils was unlike the younger fossils from Hadar that had been assigned to *A. afarensis* (5-5, 5-9). Therefore, Meave Leakey and Alan Walker named these newly discovered, older fossils *Australopithecus anamensis*. For now, they are the oldest securely identified hominids.

Complete the plate with Lothagam and the piece of mandible and its date.

Older fossil fragments recovered from Tabarin at Lake Baringo and Lothagam in Kenya, and Aramis in Ethiopia are at present too fragmentary to classify and must remain in a suspense account until sufficient evidence is forthcoming. The Lothagam jaw piece is dated between 5 and 7 million years old. Meave Leakey searched this site for hominids for 5 years; she accumulated abundant animal fossils of rhinoceros, pigs, giraffe, antelope, three horse species, and multiple carnivores, including sabre-tooth cats. But no hominids. After that, she decided to excavate slightly younger sites with sediments between 4 and 5 million years old. Recall that the molecular data indicate divergence of apes and hominids about 5 to 6 mya. Perhaps there are few hominids to excavate at this earlier time of 5 to 7 mya. But in hominid studies, the search is unpredictable. Under the next rock or in the next scoop of dirt a paleontological treasure may be hidden!

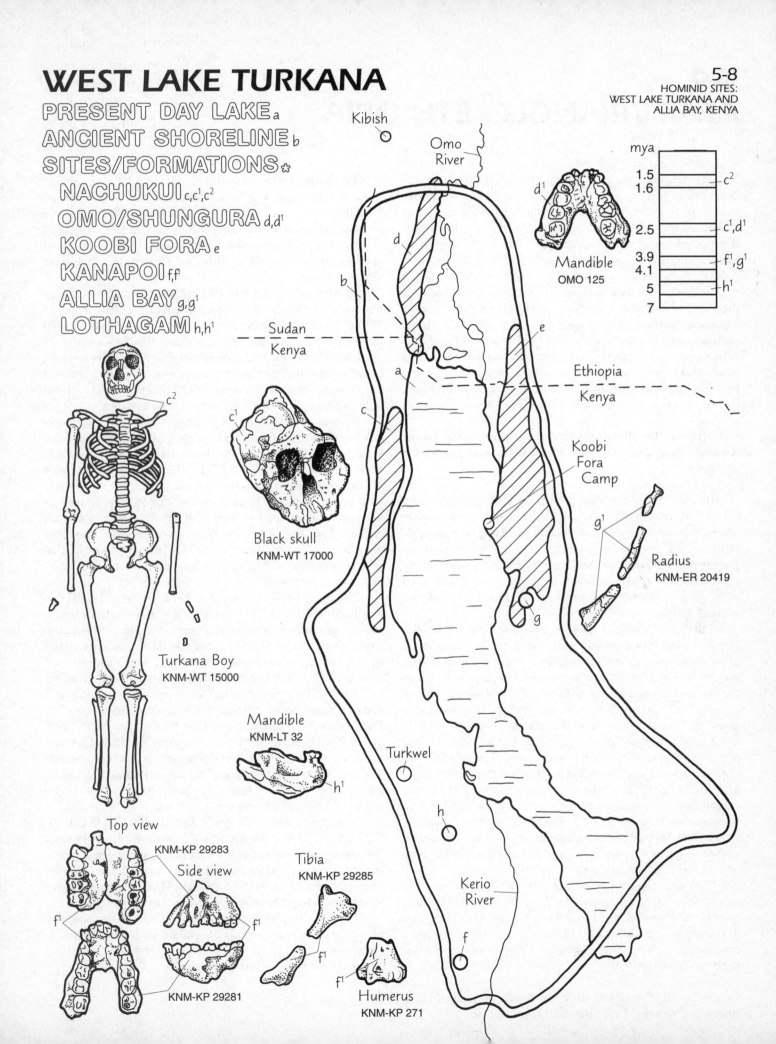

WEST LAKE TURKANA

PRESENT DAY LAKE a
ANCIENT SHORELINE b
SITES/FORMATIONS ✱
NACHUKUI c,c¹,c²
OMO/SHUNGURA d,d¹
KOOBI FORA e
KANAPOI f,f
ALLIA BAY g,g¹
LOTHAGAM h,h¹

Kibish

Omo River

Mandible
OMO 125

mya	
1.5	c²
1.6	
2.5	c¹,d¹
3.9	f¹,g¹
4.1	
5	h¹
7	

Sudan
Kenya

Ethiopia
Kenya

Black skull
KNM-WT 17000

Koobi Fora Camp

Radius
KNM-ER 20419

Turkana Boy
KNM-WT 15000

Mandible
KNM-LT 32

Turkwel

Kerio River

Top view
KNM-KP 29283
Side view

Tibia
KNM-KP 29285

KNM-KP 29281

Humerus
KNM-KP 271

5-9
AFAR TRIANGLE, ETHIOPIA

The Afar Triangle, also known as the Danakil, is trisected by the East African Rift, the Red Sea Rift, and the Gulf of Aden Rift. Currently a desert, the landscape during the Pliocene was dominated by lakes where the present-day Awash River flows. Riverine grasslands later developed along the Awash River Valley. Although the Afar was explored earlier by Italian geologists, major fossil vertebrate deposits were first discovered in 1970 by French geologist Maurice Taieb at Hadar in the Lower Awash; in 1974 the AL-288 skeleton ("Lucy") was discovered by Donald Johanson. During the mid to late 1970s, geologist Jon Kalb and his team mapped extensive hominid-bearing sites in the Middle Awash, and discovered the Bodo cranium and the Aramis site where fossils were later discovered by Tim White. Over 300 hominid fossils and tens of thousands of stone tools have been recovered from a number of Plio-Pleistocene sites in this region.

Color the Awash River and Hadar localities in the Lower Awash. Color a few of the Hadar fossils from the (A)far (L)ocality.

Hadar is one of the more prolific of the Afar sites; its soil deposits are relatively uniform and horizontal. The deposits are layered between volcanic tuffs readily dated by argon methods (5-4), and are predominately of Pliocene age. Three formations include Sidi Hakoma (SH) Member dated at 3.4 mya and of the same volcanic ash layer as Tulu Bor (5-7), the Denen Dora (DD) Member dated at about 3.2 mya, and Kada Hadar (KH) Member, at about 3 mya.

The famous Hadar treasure AL-288 "Lucy" consists of 40% of a skeleton with limbs sufficiently intact to give researchers a glimpse of body size and proportions in early hominids (5-17). AL-288 was nicknamed after the popular Beatles song "Lucy in the Sky with Diamonds." Later classified as an *Australopithecus afarensis*, AL-288 dates to 3.18 mya and probably lived in a lakeshore environment with mixed open landscape.

Excavation at the AL-333 site, dated at 3.2 mya, yielded hominid remains of about 15 individuals. The AL-333-105 cranium depicted here is a composite reconstruction from multiple individuals. In 1992, a relatively intact cranium (AL-444-2) classified as *A. afarensis* was recovered from the KH Member by anatomist Yoel Rak and dated to about 3.0 mya. It displays robust features in the brows and cheeks, a jutting snout, a single-cusped first premolar, protruding canines, and a cranial capacity around 500 cubic centimeters.

Evidence of an early *Homo*, a partial maxilla AL-666-1 was recovered by Afar fossil hunters Ali Yesuf and Maumin Alahandu from the KH Member dated to about 2.33 mya. Associated with grassland fauna, this early *Homo* lived in drier, savanna conditions. AL-666-1 was associated with very early Oldowan flakes and chopper tools.

The Bodo cranium described by Glenn Conroy is dated to about 600,000 years; with its large braincase, super-robust brows, and thick cranial bones, it is similar to the Broken Hill cranium and may belong to *H. heidelbergensis* (5-24). In 1990, a piece of an upper arm at the elbow was found, modern in shape, but small in size. Late surviving Oldowan tools, and Acheulean tools were also found here.

At Maka the upper part of a subadult femur with a long femoral neck (MAK-VP-1/1) was discovered by Tim White in 1981 (VP=vertebrate paleontology). New surface finds in 1990 included cranial and postcranial remains dated at 3.4 mya. A mandible (MAK-VP 1/12) reassembled from 109 fragments is thick-boned with large canines, large cheek teeth, and a bicuspid third molar. The ancient climate was similar to the DD Member of Hadar, that of a mixed open and wooded environment.

Aramis has yielded multiple fragmentary and carnivore-processed fossils dated around 4.4 mya. The dental fragments suggest larger canines and smaller molars than *A. afarensis*. A deciduous molar tooth (ARA-VP-1/12) most resembles *Pan paniscus* in overall size and narrow shape, and the canine/molar ratio matches that of *P. paniscus*. Associated fauna, such as colobus monkeys, and fossilized plant remains suggest a wooded ecology. The specimens could be recent ape fossils. They have been classified as "Ardipithecus ramidus," but until more detailed descriptions are available, their place in human evolution remains in a suspense account.

The Bouri fossils recovered in 1997 consist of cranial and maxillary fossils (BOU-VP-12/130), shafts of several long bones, and a foot phalanx, similar to remains of *A. afarensis* in size, length, and curvature. A femoral shaft (BOU 12/1) was recovered from the surface in 1996. Other cranial and postcranial fragments were also discovered littered throughout the landscape, all dating to 2.5 mya. The partial cranium has a small braincase (around 450 cc), robust bones, prognathism, and some sagittal cresting. The molars are massive, larger than "nutcracker man" OH 5 (5-6, 5-20). The Bouri fossils have been designated a new species, *Australopithecus garhi* by their discoverers, paleoanthropologist Berhane Asfaw and colleagues, and interpreted as a candidate for the ancestor of early *Homo*. The Bouri fossils might also be interpreted as australopithecine.

A complete skull of a robust australopithecine (KGA-10-525) dated at 1.4 mya was recovered from Konso-Gardula about 200 kilometers northeast of the Turkana Basin. Japanese paleoanthropologist Gen Suwa and colleagues attribute it to *A. boisei*; it shares similarities with OH 5 at Olduvai Gorge, having massive molar teeth, a larger braincase, and a less prominent sagittal crest.

The Afar Triangle has been uplifted and eroded away to reveal one of the best documented hominid geographies in Africa. Future research may very well uncover new fossils that will add insights to the study of human evolution.

Color the Middle Awash sites and fossils of Bodo, Maka, Bouri, and Aramis. Color the skull from Konso.

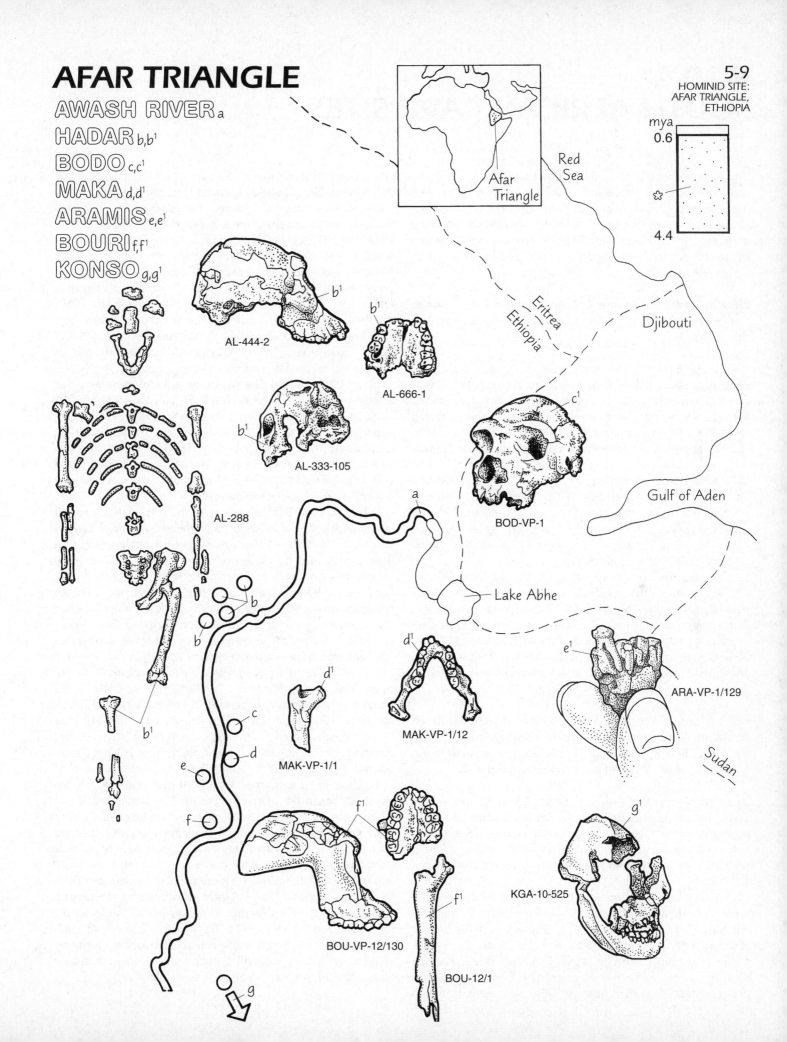

AFAR TRIANGLE

AWASH RIVER a
HADAR b,b¹
BODO c,c¹
MAKA d,d¹
ARAMIS e,e¹
BOURI f,f¹
KONSO g,g¹

Red Sea

Eritrea
Ethiopia

Djibouti

Gulf of Aden

Lake Abhe

Sudan

Afar Triangle

mya
0.6

4.4

AL-444-2

AL-666-1

AL-333-105

AL-288

BOD-VP-1

a

MAK-VP-1/1

MAK-VP-1/12

ARA-VP-1/129

BOU-VP-12/130

BOU-12/1

KGA-10-525

When Raymond Dart held the unusual skull from Taung, he recognized its significance in human evolution (5-5). The immature skull was distinct from fossil monkeys; it looked like an ape, but apes were not known to live so far south. Dart regarded the Taung child as a "missing link" between our ape ancestors and the lineage leading to modern humans, an idea not accepted for several decades.

Color the dentition of Taung and a three-year-old chimpanzee. Notice the features of the face and cranium in the front and side views.

The Taung child preserved the face, endocast, and complete dentition, and an attached mandible. Its stage of dental development and erupting first permanent molars, M1, suggested to Dart a chronological age comparable to a six-year-old human child. The most striking feature was Taung's small canine teeth, in contrast with those of a young chimpanzee, whose canines and incisors are larger and molar teeth relatively smaller. The large molars are now known to be characteristic of the australopithecines (5-20). Dart estimated that a higher forehead contained a larger brain than that of chimpanzees, confirmed by the preserved endocast. Currently, the Taung child age is estimated between age 3 and 3.5 years and would have had an adult cranial capacity of 440 cubic centimeters.

The scientific community was skeptical about Dart's missing link. Earlier fossil discoveries in Java and later ones in China persuaded many that Asia was the homeland of the human lineage. Dart's controversial opinions could only be confirmed by discovering adult specimens of Taung's species. Robert Broom, a Scottish physician and fossil hunter, believed Dart was right, and in 1936 he set out to prove it by exploring a cave site in the Transvaal, at Sterkfontein ("strong fountain").

Color Members 1 through 6 in the schematic section through Sterkfontein cave deposits. Use contrasting light colors. Color the dates where indicated and the fossils and stone tools found within Members 4, 5, and most recently, Member 2.

Sterkfontein cave is within dolomitic limestone, extensively carved out and eroded by water. Accumulated debris and bones became cemented together in a mass called breccia. Bone-bearing breccias had been discovered there when the site was quarried for limestone, but Broom was the first to search for hominid fossils.

Geologist Tim Partridge and colleagues established the relative stratigraphic sequence of the deposits within the cave and identified Members 1 though 6. Broom's early discoveries came from Member 4, now dated between 2.6 and 2.8 mya. A complete cranium lacking dentition (Sts 5) had a face and cranial vault unlike apes, and a cranial capacity of 485 cubic centimeters, one-third that of modern humans. Other specimens had even smaller brains (Sts 60, 428 cc; Sts 71, 428 cc). Cranial and dental morphology (Sts 36, Sts 71) revealed large and well-worn molar teeth, small canines and incisors, and a rugged face. A partial skeleton with a nearly complete pelvis (Sts 14) and other limb bones (Sts 34) provided clear evidence that these hominids were bipedal, again linking them with humans rather than with apes. No stone tools were recovered from Member 4. When Broom published his results in 1950, the scientific community began to take notice. John Robinson worked with Broom during the 1950s and they uncovered 100 specimens. Another 550 specimens came to light during later excavations organized by anatomist Phillip Tobias and supervised by Alun Hughes. Most came from Member 4 and were assigned to *Australopithecus africanus*.

The 1990s yielded new and exciting discoveries, including a large-brained *A. africanus* (Sts 505) with a capacity of 515 cubic centimeters, and a partial skeleton Sts 431, that had longer upper limbs and shorter lower limbs than modern humans, according to paleoanthropologists Henry McHenry and Lee Berger. Partial skeletons from the Afar (AL-288) (5-9, 5-17) and from Olduvai (OH 62) also have limb proportions that indicate a gradation between apes and ourselves.

The younger Member 5, about 1.5 to 2 mya, yielded a partial cranium (StW 53) of a nonaustralopithecine, designated *Homo habilis*, and a variety of animal bones. Fossil antelope suggest a drier climate at that time period. Thousands of stone artifacts have been recovered from this remarkable trove since the 1960s. During the 1990s, paleoanthropologist Ron Clarke increased the collection to over 9000 artifacts. Archaeologist Kathleen Kuman distinguishes several Stone Age industries including the Oldowan (choppers, cores, and flakes) and an early Acheulian with bifaces and handaxes. A few bone tools appear to be digging implements.

Ron Clarke, a true paleodetective, made a stunning discovery in the lowest level, Member 2, in the Silberberg Grotto dated about 3.3 mya. The story begins in 1994 when Clarke and Tobias described 4 foot bones (StW 573) discovered in fossil-bearing breccia blocks stored from earlier excavations. After further sleuthing, uncovering more bones from the foot and leg, Clarke became convinced that the remainder of the skeleton had to be somewhere in the dark cave. With hand-held lamps, he and his assistants began the search for the fossil skeleton, much like looking for a needle in a haystack at night. Miraculously, they were able to match the foot bones with the tibia exposed on the rock face deep in the cave. This skeleton (StW 573) is the most complete early fossil individual ever found: skull, torso, limb, and hand bones all in close association and unquestionably from the same individual. The enlarged illustration of the breccia containing hand bones shows the preservation of all 5 metacarpals, as well as wrist bones, and a fragmentary radius and ulna. Extracting this skeleton from the concretelike rock is a daunting task, but when completed will provide another important chapter in the study of this early stage of human evolution.

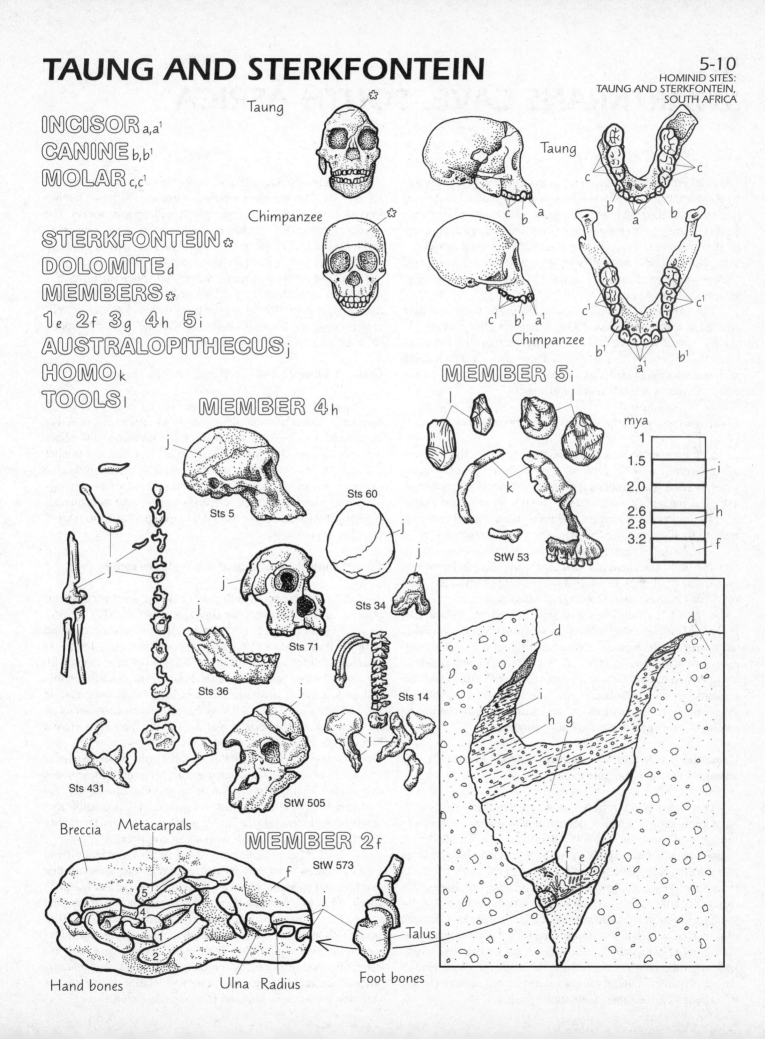

TAUNG AND STERKFONTEIN

INCISOR a,a¹
CANINE b,b¹
MOLAR c,c¹

STERKFONTEIN ✱
DOLOMITE d
MEMBERS ✱
1e 2f 3g 4h 5i
AUSTRALOPITHECUS j
HOMO k
TOOLS l

Taung

Chimpanzee

Taung

Chimpanzee

c c

b a

c¹ b¹ a¹

b¹ a b¹

b¹

c¹ c¹

a¹ b¹

MEMBER 5 i

l l

k

StW 53

mya
1
1.5
2.0
2.6
2.8
3.2

i

h

f

MEMBER 4 h

j

Sts 5

Sts 60

j

j

Sts 34

j

j

Sts 71

j

Sts 36

j

Sts 14

j

j

Sts 431

StW 505

Breccia   Metacarpals

MEMBER 2 f

StW 573

f

5

4

j

3

1

2

Talus

Hand bones

Ulna Radius

Foot bones

d

d

i

h g

f e

The deep multilayered cavern at Swartkrans was first excavated by Robert Broom and John Robinson in 1948 and 1949. During the estimated 800,000 years of deposits, there have been multiple eroded openings and closings of access to the underground cavern (5-12). Irregular filling, variation in sediment-trapping entryways, as well as erosion and mining all contribute to Swartkrans' complex geology. The cave was not a living site, but a hollowed subterranean area.

Paleontologist and taphonomist C.K. Brain and others have worked at Swartkrans since 1951, deciphering the geology and chronology of the cave and excavating the rich fossil remains from the cave's walls and floors. Three distinct depositional periods are recognized, designated Members 1, 2, and 3 (the more recent Members 4 and 5 are not illustrated).

Color the geology of the cave using contrasting colors.

Dolomite, or compact limestone, encapsulates the structure of the cavern. Travertine, resulting from mineral deposits in spring water, borders the member deposits of the cave. Each member is a distinct stage of deposition. Fossils and tools are embedded in the cavern breccia, which has the property of natural concrete, making fossil recovery difficult and time consuming (5-10).

Surface debris that fell into the cave included the remains of animals and other material (5-12). Swartkrans sheltered and preserved the bones of early hominids, approximately 333 specimens from at least 132 individuals. Robust australopithecines account for 275 of the fragments from at least 117 individuals, the most numerous robust australopithecine remains (*Australopithecus robustus* and also referred to as *Paranthropus*) recovered at any one site. Over 875 stone tools, including pebble choppers, cores, and flakes have been recovered. About 68 bone implements have been uncovered, a majority from Member 3. Fossil baboons, carnivores, horses, suids, bovids (including antelope), and large rodents are also found here.

Color the fossils and tools recovered from Member 1, the oldest level. Color the time range.

Fragments of 100 robust australopithecine individuals have been recovered from this deposit and 4 *Homo* individuals represented here by SK 847 (SwartKrans). SK 48 has a characteristic robust sagittal crest, high cheekbones, and large molar teeth (5-20). The partial cranium and mandible of SK 23 retains the prognathic lower face, robust zygomatic bones, and expanded attachment surface on the mandible for powerful grinding muscles. The endocast (SK 1585), estimated at 476 cubic centimeters, has prominent impressions for the occipital/marginal sinus (5-21). SKW 5 (W=Witwatersrand University, which sponsored the later excavations) is the mandible of a subadult whose permanent molars were not fully erupted, though even at this young age, the robust features are present.

Innominate (SK 50) and limb bones indicate bipedal locomotion. The innominate bone is somewhat distorted but has a broad "beaked" ilium and relatively small hip joint socket. The proximal femur (SK 82) has a small femoral head, long neck, and robust shaft, similar to other hominid femora (OH 20).

Member 1 also contains stone and bone tools. SKX 8692 has a bulb of percussion on the lower end which identifies this chert flake tool (about 10 cm long and 5.5 cm wide) as struck from a larger core. Bone and horn tools such as SK 5011, a well-preserved bovine (blesbok) horncore with the tip worn smooth, show microscopic evidence of digging and rubbing.

Color Member 2 fossils, artifacts, and time range.

Numerous fossils have been recovered from Member 2, especially robust australopithecines from at least 17 different individuals. Two individuals that are clearly not australopithecines have been assigned to *Homo erectus* (SK 15), which has smaller molar teeth and a less robust mandible. The australopithecine lower jaw fragment (SKX 4446) preserves the robust morphology of a young individual whose permanent molars were still erupting. Additional bone and stone tools demonstrate a varied tool kit of foraging implements.

Color Member 3 fossils, artifacts, and time range.

All hominid remains in Member 3 belong to robust australopithecines. An example is the right upper canine (SKX 25296). Its diminished crown height and length demonstrate hominid affinities that contrast with chimpanzees or baboons (4-33, 5-1) and suggest it formed part of the grinding adaptation along with the large molars and premolars. Implements include pebble choppers made of quartzite (SKX 26168), bone tools, and an unusual horse jaw (SKX 29388), broken and smooth. Study of the wear patterns indicate it was used to dig, probably while a hominid clutched it tightly around the tooth row.

An unusual feature from this Member is the presence of over 250 pieces of charred bone remains. Brain interprets these bones as evidence for the exploitation of naturally occurring fire (for example, from lightning storms) for campfires. It is possible that newly opened areas into the cavern may have provided temporary shelters where the hominids used such campfires.

Robust australopithecines dominated Swartkrans from 1.8 to 1 million years ago. Evidence from the site indicates that two hominid species, robust australopithecines and at least one species of *Homo* (perhaps *Homo erectus*) overlapped in time and space. The abundance and diversity of bone and stone tools strongly support the conclusion that the robust australopithecines were tool makers and users. Their impressive array of tools for extracting food from the environment and a specialized anatomy adapted for eating gritty and tough vegetation illustrate one variation on the early hominid foraging adaptation.

SWARTKRANS

DOLOMITE a
TRAVERTINE b
MEMBERS *
1 c 2 d 3 e
AUSTRALOPITHECUS f
HOMO g
BONE TOOL h
STONE TOOL h¹

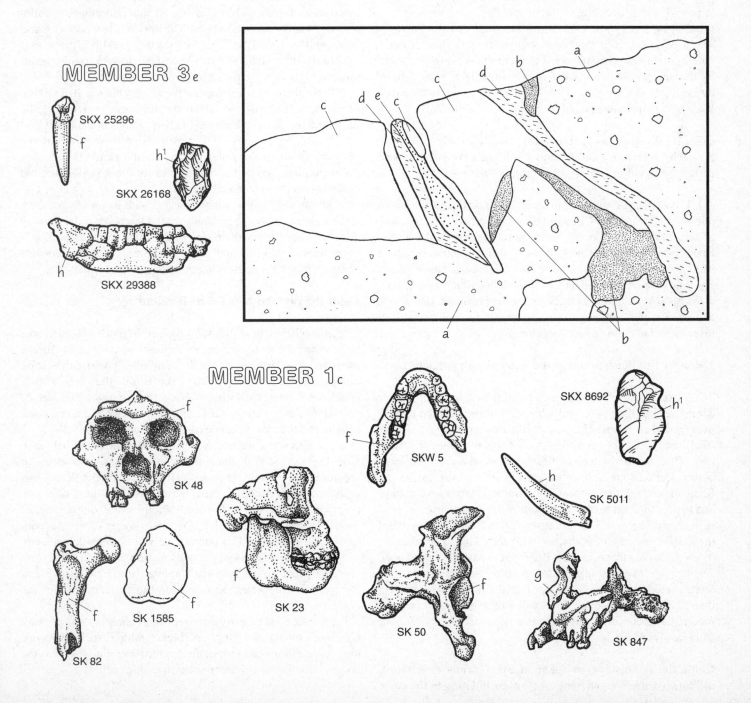

MEMBER 2 d

SKX 1650 — h¹

g — SK 15

f — SKX 4446

h — SKX 10158

e — 1 mya
d — 1.5 mya
c — 1.8 mya

MEMBER 3 e

SKX 25296 — f

h¹ — SKX 26168

h — SKX 29388

a · b · d · c · c · d · e · c

a · b

MEMBER 1 c

f — SK 48

f — SKW 5

SKX 8692 — h¹

h — SK 5011

f — SK 82

f — SK 1585

f — SK 23

f — SK 50

g — SK 847

5-12
BONES IN SOUTH AFRICAN CAVES

Raymond Dart had a plausible explanation for the mix of fossil hominid and animal bones discovered together in Makapansgat Cave, South Africa. He argued that the animal bones were the leftovers of early hominid meals, and that the antelope jawbones, horns, and limb bones served as the hominids' weapons. Therefore Dart concluded that the bone use constituted a culture. He gave it a jaw-breaking name—osteodontokeratic culture (osteo=bone, donto=tooth, kerat=horn). Robert Ardrey's *African Genesis* popularized Dart's idea of early man as a "killer ape" who hunted to provide meat for his mate and offspring.

During the 1960s, C.K. Brain surmised that the bones in South African caves might not be due to activities of early hominids. Instead, he suspected that carnivores might account for the bone accumulations. Brain set about testing his hypothesis by exploring the questions: How did the bones get into the cave? What agents were responsible?

Color the illustration of present day Swartkrans Cave showing a nearby tree and cave filling. Near the cave's damp and protected opening, young trees readily take root.

Using a taphonomic approach, Brain analyzed the fossil remains of Swartkrans Cave and described the species, the parts of the skeleton, and breaks, wear, and markings on the bones. Bones of antelopes and rock hyraxes were abundant, but there were also insectivores, rodents, baboons, leopards, and hyenas. Hyraxes were represented only by their skulls, which were broken at the base. Antelope bones included mainly jawbones, horn cores, and limb bones and large bone fragments. Small rodent and insectivore bones were found in clumps.

Color the two illustrations of the leopard with antelope prey.

Next, Brain observed how modern leopards and other carnivores kill their prey, and what parts of the skeleton are left over from their meals. The prey of leopards typically consists of small antelopes, baboons, and hyraxes. Leopards eat the soft parts, ribs, vertebrae, and hands and feet, leaving the jaws and large bones; hyraxes are consumed entirely except for the heads. Leopards often drag their prey into a tree to eat over several days and to prevent theft by the more powerful lions and hyenas. Owl pellets could account for the clumps of small animal bones, and the telltale gnawing of porcupines is detected on some bones.

To rule out human activity, Brain analyzed thousands of bone fragments from caves inhabited by people living during the Late Stone Age. Brain found that over half the fragments were less than five centimeters long. The small size of bones from human food remains contrasts with the much larger fragments left over from carnivore meals.

Color the reconstructed scene of Swartkrans cave site a million years ago when bones were accumulating in the cave.

Putting the pieces together, Brain envisioned what might have happened a million years ago. He reasoned that leopards used the safety of the trees near cave openings to eat their prey; bones from remains of their meals fell into the cave or nearby and were washed into the cave along with other debris.

Color the hominid skull and leopard jaw illustration.

The "smoking gun" pointing to leopards came from the discovery of a cranial bone from an australopithecine child, recovered at Swartkrans in 1950. The bone has two perfect round holes, and the bone flaps from the puncture are still in place, as if the child's injury had no time to begin healing. A fossil leopard jaw found in the cave fits exactly into the pair of holes.

Brain then collected another piece of evidence. In a sample of modern leopard jaws from the museum collections, he measured the distance between the two canines of the lower jaw. The "smoking canines" fell within the narrow range of the distance between the holes on the child's skull. It is highly probable that a leopard is responsible for the juvenile hominid death in this Pleistocene killing.

All lines of evidence are consistent with Brain's hypothesis, that carnivore action, specifically that of leopards, is the primary agent responsible for the bones in the cave. Contrary to Dart's hypothesis of early hominids as hunters, Brain concluded leopards were the hunters and the hominids a main dish!

Color the eagle with its Taung hominid prey.

In another taphonomic analysis, Lee Berger and Ron Clarke hypothesized that large predatory eagles were responsible for the particular fossil assemblage at the hominid site where the Taung hominid child was recovered. Like Brain, they based their conclusions on several observations: the condition and size of animal species represented at Taung, the behavior of modern black eagles, and the marks they leave on the bones of their prey.

In contrast to Swartkrans where 50% of the bones belong to large animals, 85% of the animals from Taung were small- or medium-sized—hares, moles, small birds, and complete skulls of baboons. And, unlike other South African sites, only one hominid, a child, was recovered. Like the other Taung prey, its mandible was still attached. Rather than having carnivore tooth marks, the Taung hominid bones have V-shaped marks on them. Modern African eagles leave characteristic V nicks on bone, from carrying small- to medium-sized animals into tree nests. When the meal is complete, the mandible remains attached to the cranium.

Predators were clearly a danger to early hominids, especially the more vulnerable youngsters. Early hominid social behavior may have minimized threats from predation, but we have the corpus delicti to prove that predation took its toll.

PREDATORS AND PREY

SWARTKRANS
CAVE SITE*
  TREE a
  CAVE b
  CAVE FILL/
    FOSSILS c
    BONES c¹
  LEOPARD/
    MANDIBLE d
  PREY*
    ANTELOPE e
    HOMINID e¹

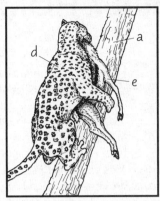

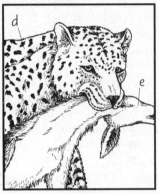

Present Day

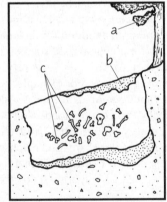

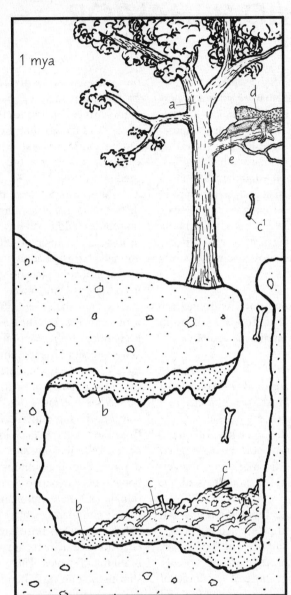

1 mya

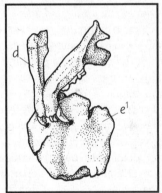

TAUNG CAVE
  SITE*
  EAGLE f
  TAUNG
    HOMINID e²

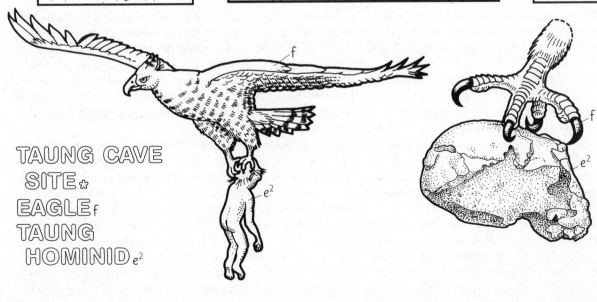

5-13
EARLY HOMINID BEHAVIOR

What change in behavior might account for the separate pathway of early hominids? Raymond Dart thought that the hominids' new direction was hunting and meat-eating, and his notion of humans as killer apes, compared to the "peaceable vegetarian apes," gained notoriety. Variation on the themes of hunting (man-the-hunter) and scavenging continue to absorb many anthropologists. Such scenarios extend into sexual behavior and the assumption that social life centered around a bonded pair and their offspring, where males provisioned females (food exchanged for sex). Females are presented as dependent on males for food, protection, and survival. When we speculate about the past, as we inevitably do, we must use all the evidence and take into account both sexes and all ages.

Color each line of evidence: molecular data, comparative anatomy of chimpanzee, human, and fossil hominids, comparative behavior, and the savanna mosaic ecology.

Molecular studies establish evolutionary history: chimpanzees (*Pan*) are the nearest living relatives to humans, and the 2 diverged about 5 mya. Comparative anatomy and behavior point up a fundamental difference: chimpanzees are quadrupedal, climb into trees to feed and sleep, but travel on the ground about 3 kilometers each day. Human bodies are redesigned by natural selection for walking long distances over uneven terrain; an average distance for foraging people is about 12 kilometers.

The hominid fossil record is consistent with molecular and comparative anatomical evidence. Fossil pelvic and leg bones, body proportions, and footprints all read "biped." The fossil bones are not identical to modern humans, but were likely functionally equivalent and a marked departure from those of quadrupedal chimpanzees. Fossil dentition is distinctive: large molar and premolar teeth, considerably larger than chimpanzee and human teeth, though with smaller canines on the human scale. Hominid brains were smaller than ours, but larger than those of chimpanzees.

Fossil hand bones show greater potential for tool using. No tools are preserved from this early stage of human evolution, but we can infer their existence. Though stone tools are not recognizable in an archaeological context until 2 to 2.5 million years ago, the level of workmanship suggests a long period of prior tool making. Furthermore, chimpanzees in the wild and in captivity make and use tools. Early hominids would have been at least this innovative, using tools mainly of organic, perishable materials and unmodified stones.

The earliest hominid fossils are found in Africa at 4-million-year-old sites in the savanna mosaic, an ecological zone formed as a result of faulting and uplift. The once continuous lowland rain forest was transformed into a seasonally dry habitat. Baboons are well adapted to this environment and exploit 250 species of plants there, along with insects and various animal prey. Like baboons and chimpanzees, early hominids were opportunistic omnivores, but departed from baboons by habitually using tools as they moved into this new adaptive zone. The ancestral chimpanzees and gorillas flourished in the forests and woodlands. Hazards of the savanna are recorded in the fossil hominid bones. Taphonomic analysis shows their bones were chewed by carnivores, and that they were a prey item for leopards and predatory birds.

Let's consider what the hominids were doing out there on the savanna, if not hunting and eating meat. Being bipedal, the hominids could cover a wide area at the periphery of woodlands or into the savanna mosaic to collect many available plants and animals. Large grinding teeth suggest foods that were tough and gritty, probably plant foods. Initially, the hominids must have used tools as chimpanzees do, to give them access to new foods, such as hard-shelled nuts, fruits with thick casings, or underground roots and tubers. Tool using necessitates learned traditions, transmitted by mothers to offspring, and probably maintained across generations by females. Increased reliance on tools may have been a factor in the emergence of childhood—a period for extended learning of skills.

When we move into the realm of social behavior—food sharing, mating patterns, and child care—we are far removed from the fossil evidence for locomotion, dentition for diet, hand bones for tool using, and ecology for potential food sources and danger. Social behavior does not fossilize, so we rely on behavioral comparisons with other primates. For example, both female and male chimpanzees capture animals for meat. Adult female chimpanzees share both plant and animal foods with their offspring, with unrelated females and infants, and even occasionally share meat with males. Males share food much less often than females. There is little basis for concluding that food sharing among early hominids was a one-way transaction from males to females.

Although most depictions of early hominids propose a pair bond or nuclear family with the male provisioning females and young, very few primates or mammals actually live in pair-bonded family groups. Furthermore, studies of monkeys and apes show that females exercise choice among males and that male mating success is highly influenced by female choice. There is no logical reason why these primate trends would be suddenly reversed in early hominids.

The popular focus on male hunting, scavenging, and meat-eating seems much too narrow a basis for explaining hominid origins and behavior. It would seem more logical, given the weight of the evidence and the role of females, that early hominids were walking bipedally over long distances, relying on consistent use of tools to collect, carry, and share a wide range of plant and animal foods obtained on the savanna. Sophisticated spears and hafted tools for hunting appear much later in human evolution, about 300,000 years ago. The behavioral innovation of gathering a variety of plant and animal foods rather than hunting led our ancestors into a different technical and conceptual world from that of their ape forebears.

LINES OF EVIDENCE

CHIMPANZEE a
HUMAN b
HOMINID c
MOLECULAR DATA d
COMPARATIVE ANATOMY e
COMPARATIVE BEHAVIOR f
SAVANNA MOSAIC g

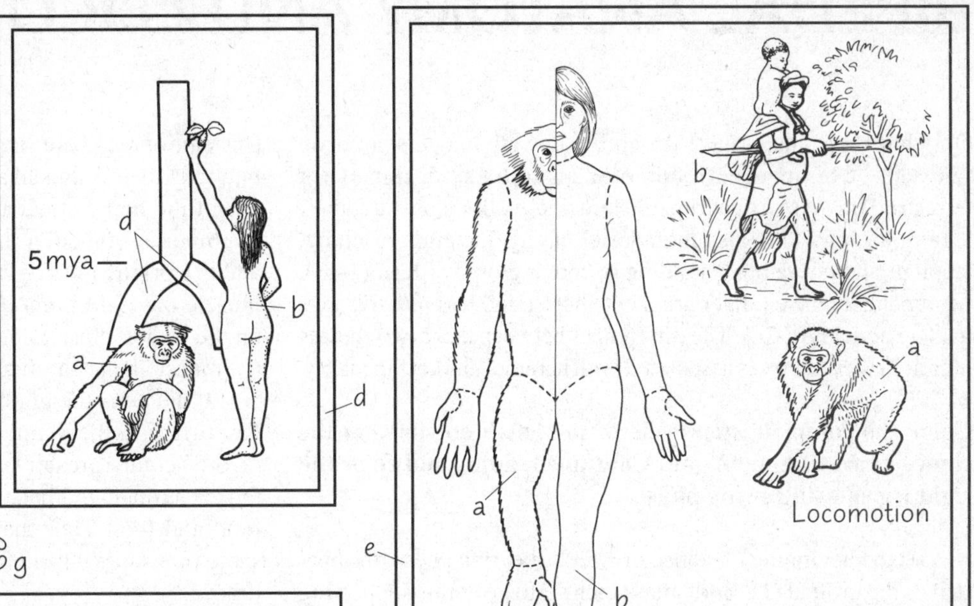

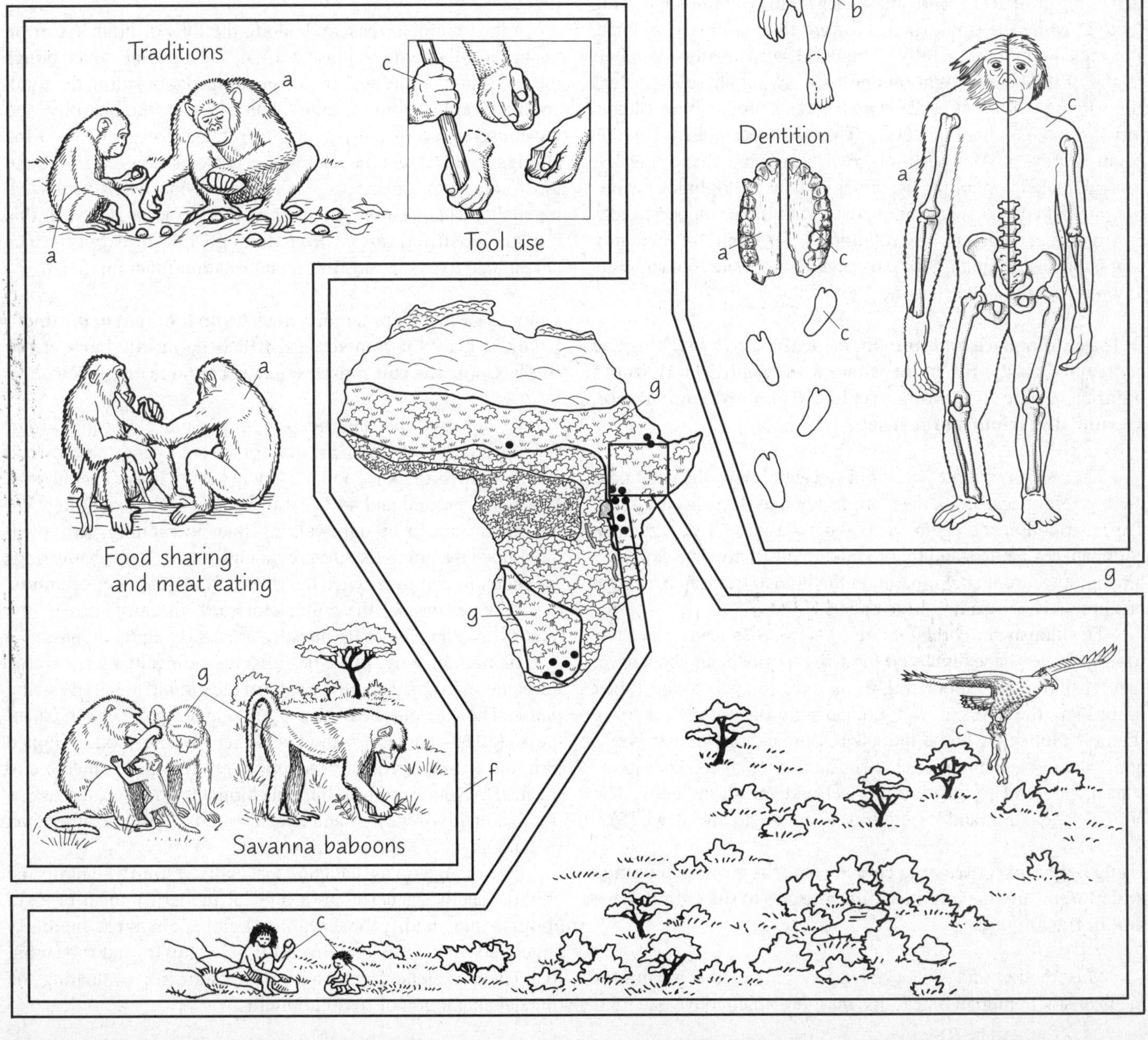

5 mya
d
a
b
d
b
a
Locomotion
a
e
b

Traditions
a
a
c
Tool use
Dentition
a
c
c
a
c
Food sharing
and meat eating
a
g
g
g
g
c
g
f
Savanna baboons
c

BIPEDAL ANATOMY AND LOCOMOTION

Only human primates have the ability to walk long distances on two legs. Chimpanzee locomotor anatomy is designed for terrestrial travel in a quadrupedal knuckle-walking posture; their locomotor repertoire also includes climbing, hanging, reaching, leaping, and occasional standing or moving on two legs (3-13). Chimpanzees have longer arms but shorter and less massive legs than do humans (4-36). The differences between these two species highlight the structures associated with habitual human bipedality.

Color the complete step cycle of the left limb showing the stance phase of human gait. Continue reading and color the right leg showing swing phase.

At the beginning of stance or weight-bearing phase, the heel strikes the ground (1). Body mass then shifts over this supporting foot (2) while the trunk rotates toward the midline. Hip, knee, and ankle joints become fully extended (3, 4, 5) in order to support all the of the body weight on one foot. Swing phase (right leg) begins with toeing off (1, 2), which gives a propulsive push and forward momentum to the body. The hip, knee, and ankle joints begin to flex (3, 4). The trunk rotates over the supporting left foot which helps stabilize the upper body as the right leg swings forward. The arms swing in opposition to the unsupported legs in order to counteract body rotation (5, 6). While the swinging foot is off the ground (3, 4, 5, 6), and the opposite foot supports all body weight, balance is most precarious.

In the chimpanzee and human, color the circle marking the center of gravity, the point where a suspended body would balance. Color the lumbar region. Color the innominate, sacrum, and femur in the insets.

The human center of gravity is located low in the body near the hip joint because the legs are heavy and the arms are light. This distribution of body mass gives humans greater stability than chimpanzees while standing or walking bipedally. The extended hip and knee joints help maintain the human trunk in a vertical posture while expending little energy.

The human vertebral column forms an S-shaped curve. The robust wedge-shaped intervertebral discs form the lumbar curve; they cushion and support the trunk over the pelvis and lower limbs. The flexibility of the lumbar region is critical for trunk rotation. Notice the broad human sacrum and innominate bones and the narrower chimpanzee's. The human femur and knee joints cant inward and so position the feet underneath the body. The chimpanzee femur and knee joints do not angle inward (5-15).

Using light and contrasting colors, color the gluteus maximus and gluteus medius and minimus muscles in the chimpanzee and in the human.

Muscle size and shape are a key part of the locomotor mechanism. In human bipedality, muscles which move one joint (instead of two) are large. Gluteus maximus gives the human buttocks their unmistakable rounded shape and comprises over 6% of the body's total amount of muscle. Its large size reflects its important function: it straightens and supports the hip joint, and is working much of the time in walking. In chimpanzees the muscle has a different shape and position; it attaches far down on the femur, close to the knee joint. The low and heavy part of the muscle lies near the hamstring muscles.

In humans the gluteus medius and minimus muscles cover the surface of the ilium, cross the hip joint, and attach on the top of the femur (greater trochanter). During stance phase, these muscles rotate and balance the trunk over the single supporting limb and foot. Thus they move the body forward while at the same time keep it from falling toward the unsupported swinging limb.

When chimpanzees walk along the tops of branches or on the ground, their gluteal muscles rotate the hip joint, which brings the foot into the midline. In this quadrupedal position, the trunk and ilium are in front of, rather than on top of the hip joint, and the muscles are in the position to rotate. However, when the chimpanzee stands bipedally, these muscles now lie above the hip joint, so chimpanzees sway side to side when they walk bipedally. The rotation potential of the hip joint is lost in this upright position, suggesting that the hominid pelvis was redesigned to ensure this important rotation function (5-15).

Color the quadriceps femoris muscles on the front of the thigh. Color in gray the hamstrings, which lie on the back of the thigh. Color the calf muscles, gastrocnemius and soleus.

In humans, the quadriceps femoris muscles (quad=four, ceps=head) are over twice the mass of the hamstrings; they extend and straighten the knee joint. They act as a "brake" as the heel strikes the ground and so assist in balance. The hamstrings are less important in human walking than in running. In typical quadrupedal animals like the greyhound dog (3-9), the hamstrings are much larger, over twice the mass of the quadriceps femoris, because they propel the animal forward. In chimpanzees, the quadriceps and hamstring muscles are nearly equal in mass.

In human gait, the calf muscles contract and provide momentum in pushing the toe against the ground to initiate swing phase. The calf muscles insert by a long strap of tendon called the Achilles—named for the Greek hero whose mother dipped him into a magic protective solution, but left him vulnerable in the heel by which she held him. In chimpanzees, the calf muscles run the length of the calf and attach by muscle fibers rather than by tendon.

The changes in musculature that evolved from a quadrupedal chimpanzeelike ancestor to a bipedal modern human brought about some readily observable skeletal changes: medially angulated femur, enlarged lateral tibial condyle, and robust big toe. These skeletal features are also useful for evaluating the bipedal adaptation of fossil hominids.

CHIMPANZEES AND HUMANS

STEP CYCLE ✿
STANCE a
SWING b

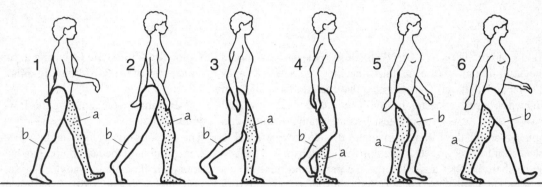

1 2 3 4 5 6

INNOMINATE e
SACRUM f
FEMUR g

CENTER OF GRAVITY c
LUMBAR REGION d, d¹

LOWER LIMB MUSCLES ✿
GLUTEUS MAXIMUS h
GLUTEUS MEDIUS
 AND MINIMUS i
QUADRICEPS
 FEMORIS j
HAMSTRINGS k ✿
CALF l

Pelvis from above
Human

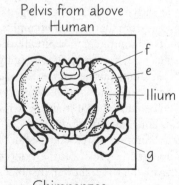

f
e
Ilium
g

Chimpanzee

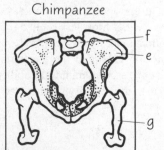

f
e
g

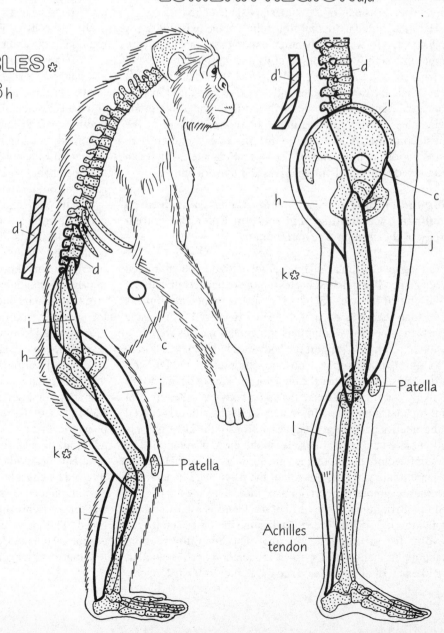

Patella
Achilles
tendon
Patella

Walking habitually on two legs distinguishes the early members of the hominid family (the australopithecines) from African apes (5-1). When Raymond Dart claimed that the child's skull from Taung was a human ancestor, he boldly pronounced that it walked on two legs. His was a lucky guess because cranial features and the placement of the foramen magnum do not provide reliable indicators of locomotion. Dart's claim for bipedalism was proved correct when the first australopithecine pelvis and thigh bones were found in South Africa in the 1940s: two adolescent ilia from Makapansgat and a nearly complete pelvis from Sterkfontein (5-10). Since then, limb and pelvic bones have been found at several sites in southern and eastern Africa. In 1974, Donald Johanson recovered a knee joint at Hadar, and in 1975, a nearly complete pelvis as part of a fragmentary skeleton (5-17).

Habitual bipedal locomotion relies upon two limbs for propulsion and forward momentum; braking to dampen forward momentum; stabilizing and rotating the upright trunk; and balancing on one foot during walking (5-14). African apes and humans share the same muscles and bones but they differ in size, shape, and orientation. Fossil pelvic and limb bones and joints provide clues for interpreting the locomotor adaptation of the earliest hominids. The australopithecine fossils shown here possess various components of the bipedal complex which can be compared to those of chimpanzees and modern humans.

Color the chimpanzee, *Australopithecus*, and human innominate, acetabulum, and sacrum. Color the gluteal muscles of the chimpanzee and human.

A diagnostic feature of bipedal locomotion is a shortened and broadened ilium that indicates a more extensive attachment for the gluteal muscles (5-14). The australopithecine ilium is shorter than that of apes, and it is slightly curved. This shape suggests that the gluteus minimus and gluteus medius were in a position to rotate and support the body during bipedal walking.

In chimpanzee bipedal posture, the gluteus medius and minimus muscles lie above the hip joint and are not positioned to effectively stabilize and rotate the upper body over the hip joint during bipedal locomotion. In contrast, the human ilium is curved and the anterior part of the ilium lies in front of the hip joint; this position places the gluteal muscles in the plane of rotation. The australopithecines are more like humans than apes in this regard. The sacrum increases the breadth of the pelvis, and in australopithecines resembles modern humans more than apes.

In modern humans, the head of the femur is robust and the acetabulum (hip socket) is deep, indicating increased stability at this joint for greater load bearing. The australopithecine acetabulum is shallow and smaller, the femoral head is smaller, more like that of chimpanzees, and the femoral neck is longer.

Color the femur, the tibia, the articular surfaces of the knee joint, and the weight-bearing axis.

In humans, the femur angles inward from the hip to the knee joint, so that the lower limbs stand close to the body's midline. The line of gravity and weight are carried on the outside of the knee joint, and the lateral condyle has a relatively larger surface area than the medial condyle. The surface of the tibia is slightly concave, scooped out like a shallow dish, for a relatively tight fit at the knee joint. In contrast, the chimpanzee femur articulates at the hip, then continues in a straight line downward to the knee joint. The femur lacks any twisting, and as a result, the line of force goes on the inside of the knee joint, on the medial condyle, corresponding to a larger medial condyle. The surface of the tibia is slightly convex, like a small hill, which accommodates more rotation in the chimpanzee knee joint than exists in humans.

The morphology of the australopithecine femur is distinct and suggests a slightly different function for the hip and knee joints. The femoral shaft is angled more than that of a chimpanzee and indicates that the knees and feet were well planted under the body; the lateral condyle on the femur suggests a weight-bearing axis more like that of modern humans. The joint surface of the tibia from Kanapoi (5-8) apparently is concave, which suggests this specimen had a somewhat more stable knee joint with less rotation, similar to humans and unlike chimpanzees.

In modern humans, the lower limbs bear all the body weight and perform all locomotor functions; consequently, the hip, knee, and ankle joints are all large with less mobility than their counterparts in chimpanzees. In the australopithecines, the joints (sacroiliac, hip, knee, and ankle joints) remain relatively small; in part, this might be due to smaller body size. The smaller joint size may also be due to a unique early hominid form of bipedal locomotion that differed somewhat from that of later hominids.

Hominid locomotion, with its commitment to habitual two-legged movement, has antecedents in African apes. The emerging hominids were moving into the savanna mosaic habitat beyond the forests and woodlands of the ape ancestors (5-2). Monkeys and apes employ an upright stance and bipedal movement for looking around, reaching, carrying, and displaying (3-13), behaviors that no doubt the early hominids also found useful. In addition, bipedal locomotion apparently proved to be a more efficient means of distance travel than the shorter distances traveled by knuckle-walking African ape ancestors. Although the australopithecines had shorter legs, wider hips, less rotated ilia, and longer ischia than modern humans, they were some type of biped. This new form of locomotion extended the terrestrial adaptation of knuckle walking and gave early hominids the ability to forage over longer distances than their forest-living ancestors.

PELVIS AND LOWER LIMB

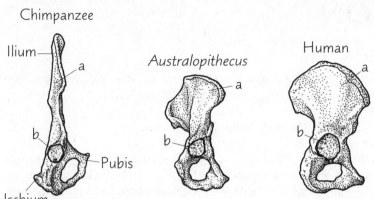

Chimpanzee

Ilium
a
b
Pubis
Ischium

Australopithecus
a
b

Human
a
b

INNOMINATE a
ACETABULUM b
SACRUM c
GLUTEAL MUSCLES d
FEMUR e
TIBIA f
WEIGHT-BEARING AXIS g

CHIMPANZEE ✿   AUSTRALOPITHECUS ✿   HUMAN ✿

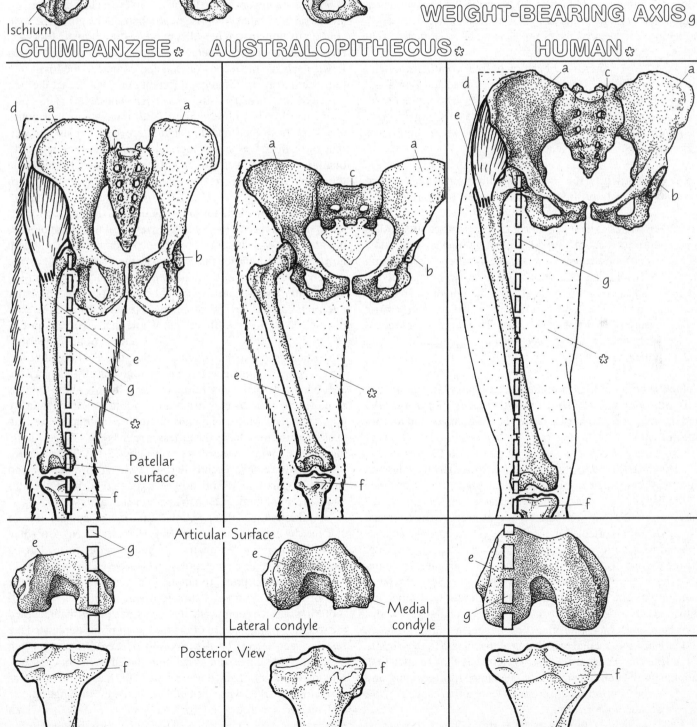

Patellar surface

Articular Surface

Lateral condyle   Medial condyle

Posterior View

5-16
HOMINID LOCOMOTION

One day long, long ago three early australopithecines living in what is now Tanzania walked on ground softened by a recent rain shower and left footprints as they moved cross the plain. An erupting volcano had scattered ash over the landscape. A light rain fell, mixed with and hardened the ash, and preserved the footprints. As luck would have it, Mary Leakey uncovered the prints 3.7 million years later in 1978 during her excavations at Laetoli. The hominid prints alongside those of monkeys, gazelles, and guinea fowl record the comings and goings in that ancient world.

Fossil foot bones have been recovered from Sterkfontein, Swartkrans, Olduvai Gorge, and Hadar. A tibia and fibula and 12 foot bones belonging to one individual, and a terminal great toe bone come from Bed 1, Olduvai Gorge (5-6). Comparison of the footprints and fossil foot and ankle bones with chimpanzees and humans illustrate the features of each.

Color the footprints, the soles of the chimpanzee and human left feet, and each outlined area around the foot bones.

When walking, the heel part of the chimpanzee foot strikes first. Their prints record a broad flat foot without an arch, and a great toe that is divergent from the others; the weight-bearing hands leave small knuckle prints. Human footprints preserve a uniquely robust and convergent great toe, longitudinal arch, and well-defined heel. The Laetoli feet are less well delineated because of the soft surface on which they walked. Their impressions record a deep heel position, a convergent hallux, a longitudinal arch, and a distinct lateral border.

Color the bones of the human and chimpanzee feet in the top and side views. Note the relative lengths of the tarsals, metatarsals, and phalanges. Color the chimpanzee and human infant feet.

Human tarsal bones are more robust, especially the talus and calcaneus, compared to those of chimpanzees; the metatarsals are longer and straighter; and the phalanges are shorter. Notice the human foot's long arch formed by the tarsals and metatarsals. The ankle joint is oriented in the flexion-extension plane and has reduced rotation (eversion-inversion). During bipedal walking, the big toe and heel are in line; the ankle joint extends, "pushing off" the big toe. This movement gives the body forward momentum. The chimpanzee foot has a less robust talus and calcaneus, less robust first metatarsal and phalanges, and a divergent and opposable great toe typical of other primates (3-12). The more medial orientation of the talus, and the slightly curved metatarsals, indicate the ankle joint has more rotation than in humans. The chimpanzee foot is equipped for grasping and for weight bearing during quadrupedal locomotion on the ground, its primary locomotor activity.

The two species differ in the proportions of their foot bones. Human tarsals comprise half the length of the foot; the phalanges are short. Chimpanzee tarsals, metatarsals, and phalanges each comprise about a third of the total foot length.

Color the early hominid foot bones.

The Olduvai foot bones are adapted for bipedal weight bearing in having a relatively robust first toe, short metatarsals, and tarsal bones that comprise nearly half the length of the foot, similar to humans. When discovered, the Olduvai foot was reconstructed with a convergent hallux. When anatomist Owen Lewis analyzed the reconstruction and compared the fossil foot to modern apes, he offered a different conclusion: that the first toe was divergent and possibly somewhat opposable. Later studies confirmed Lewis's observations. Additional fossil foot bones recovered from Sterkfontein dated 3.3 mya (5-10) also showed that the hallux was not completely convergent among early hominids. The Olduvai talus and tibia also suggest that the ankle joint was capable of greater rotation than in that of modern humans.

The function of the fossil foot bones and the implication for locomotion has been a focus of controversy. Some anthropologists maintain that early hominids were bipeds comparable to modern humans. Others argue that, because the foot phalanges are somewhat curved and the hallux is divergent, early hominid locomotion had a significant climbing component. The latter interpretation has several problems. First, foot bones are only one unit in a structural-functional whole that involves most of the body (4-36, 5-1). The leg and pelvic bones and limb proportions support the conclusion that the australopithecines were bipeds, even though they were morphologically distinct from apes and modern humans. Furthermore, climbing ability of apes is powered by muscular arms and shoulders rather than by opposable toes. Modern humans climb trees with less ease than apes because they have much less upper body strength, long, heavy legs, and a lower center of gravity (5-14). The australopithecines were only recently derived from an ape ancestor, and fossils of this age would not be expected to have the full complement of modern human anatomical features.

Anthropologist Peter Schmid contributed another line of evidence by carrying out experiments. His research on the original Laetoli footprints demonstrated their bipedal form, but he wondered about the deep impression clearly visible on the lateral border of the foot print. To pursue this question, he studied the gait of human children with a foot size similar to the fossil footprints. The children walked across force plates that recorded the weight-bearing pattern of the foot; their prints duplicated the fossils' deep lateral border. Schmid observed that when the children walked, they did so without the adult rhythm of trunk rotation and a coordinated arm swing. This lack of rotation was particularly marked when the children were carrying large objects that interfered with arm and trunk movements. Schmid's research reemphasizes the importance of studying parts relative to the whole and of conducting experiments.

FOOTPRINTS AND FOOT BONES

TALUS a
CALCANEUS a¹
OTHER TARSALS a²

METATARSALS b
PHALANGES c

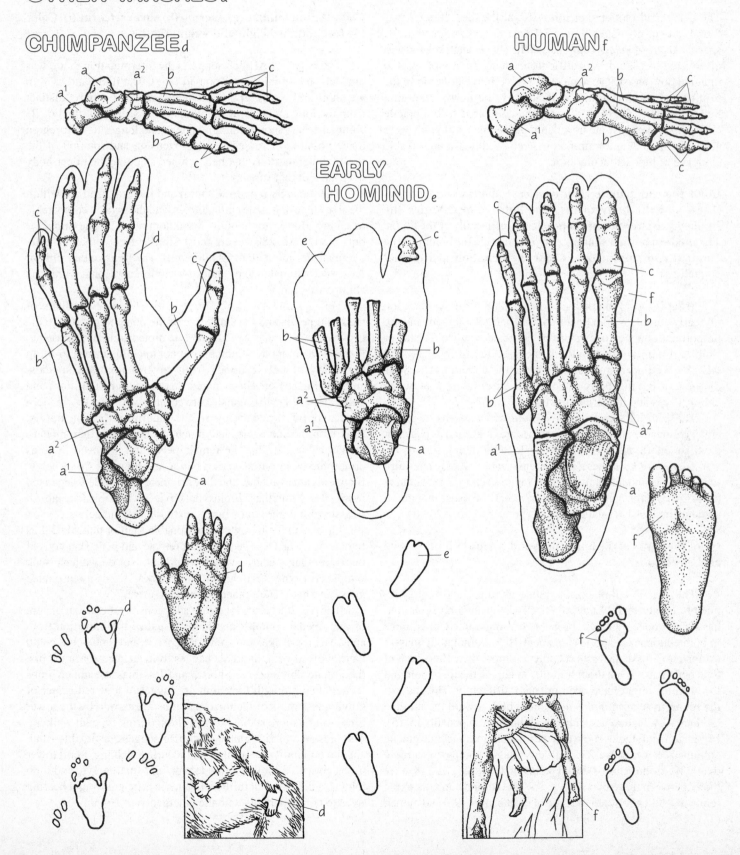

CHIMPANZEE d

EARLY HOMINID e

HUMAN f

5-17
HOMINID LOCOMOTION

The celebrated partial skeleton (AL-288), called "Lucy," was found in deposits dated almost 3.2 mya; it was assigned to the species *Australopithecus afarensis*. When the Hadar skeleton was discovered in 1975, it was difficult for many anthropologists to imagine how an African ape could evolve into a hominid in the 5-million-year time frame indicated by the newly emerging molecular data. The AL-288 skeleton compared with a gracile chimpanzee demonstrate how "chimpanzeelike" hominids were at 3 mya in size and morphology, yet exhibited unmistakable evidence of bipedal locomotion.

Color the chimpanzee (*Pan paniscus*) and *Australopithecus* titles, and the body forms. Use light colors. Notice the similarity in size and the shape of each, especially of the limbs. The modern human shadow provides a scale for height in the hominid and chimpanzee. Color the dentition and cranial capacities.

What is most remarkable about AL-288 is the preservation of nearly complete limb bones so that their total length, and the proportions of upper to lower limbs can be determined. The lower limbs are similar in length in the gracile chimpanzee and AL-288, the upper limbs are shorter in the hominid. AL-288 is distinct in having body proportions intermediate between chimpanzees and modern humans.

The teeth and supporting jaws of *Australopithecus* are unlike either chimpanzee or human; its canines are small, and its posterior teeth are enormous with a well-developed grinding surface (5-20). *Australopithecus* has a small cranial capacity, only one-third the volume of modern humans'; the range of chimpanzee cranial capacities overlaps slightly with these early fossils, though on average the fossil cranial capacity is greater (5-18).

Color the bones of the upper limb and the lower limb, as well as their lengths.

The gracile chimpanzee's humerus, ulna, and radius are notably longer than "Lucy's." AL-288's upper limb is shorter, has slender bones, and was probably less muscular. Upper limbs in both chimpanzee species are about 16% of total body mass. I estimate the fossil as less, probably not more than 10 to 12% of total body mass. Even though similar in length, the fossil hominid lower limbs might have been oriented differently. The shaft of the femur in *Australopithecus* is brought in toward the midline (adducted), a feature associated with hominid bipedality (5-15). My anatomical studies show that the lower limbs of female gracile chimpanzees comprise 24% of body mass, (compared to more than 32% in humans, 4-36). The lower limbs of AL-288 were likely between these two values. The ratio of the humerus to the femur at 84, lies between the ratio of chimpanzee (98) and human (75).

Color the innominate (g), sacrum (h), and vertebrae (i). Color the feet and the height and weight figures.

The pelvis of AL-288 supports the interpretation that it was bipedal—a hominid, not a pongid (ape). The ilium and sacrum are short and broad, giving the pelvis more of a flare, distinct from the long and narrow innominate and sacrum of the gracile chimpanzee. A shorter hominid pelvis and longer lumbar region make possible increased flexion-extension and rotation of the lower spine, motions that help a biped stabilize the upper body over the feet that support it.

The AL-288 femur (280 mm) and femoral head are within the size range of gracile chimpanzees, and the two are comparable in stature. Body weight of the fossil hominid is a "guesstimate," but overall AL-288 seems most similar to a female gracile chimpanzee, about 30 to 32 kilograms. The fragmentary tibia of AL-288 is estimated to be about 240 millimeters long, within the chimpanzee range.

Do we know that "Lucy" is actually a female? The shape of the fossil pelvis and the small size of the bones suggested to the discoverers a female skeleton. Pelvic dimensions can be used to identify sex in modern humans but not in chimpanzees (6-8). In her study of pelvic bones from several hominid species, anthropologist Lori Hager noted that features of the ilium and pubic bone that distinguish between the sexes in the modern human pelvis are lacking in the australopithecine pelvis. Australopithecine babies had much smaller heads than modern human babies, so that the female pelvis did not need to be as dimorphic as in our species. Only a few hominid fossil pelvic fragments are available, and they originate from widely separated fossil sites. From these limited data, it is not possible to establish sexually dimorphic traits in the australopithecine pelvis.

On size alone it might be reasonable to infer that AL-288 is female, if we had a large sample of female and male skeletons of that particular species—which we do not. Nor do we have such samples for other early hominids. "Lucy's" sex is a reasonable guess and has a 50% chance of being correct.

The AL-288 "Lucy" skeleton adds considerably to our picture of the bipedal complex and helps visualize the transition from apes. The fossil skeleton shows that pelvic and limb bones could have evolved with minimal changes from an ancestor much like the gracile chimpanzee. Shorter and less massive upper limbs reduce their strength for climbing, suggest a lowered center of gravity, less mass of the torso that must be carried by the lower limbs, and a more stable body position during bipedal walking. The presence of six lumbar vertebrae suggests a flexible trunk and the possibility for trunk rotation during walking. Short lower limbs go with a limited stride length; and small pelvic and limb joint size indicate that further changes in efficient weight bearing were to come, perhaps with the emergence of *Homo*.

WHAT DOES LUCY TELL US?

CRANIAL CAPACITY c
HUMERUS d
RADIUS e
ULNA f
PELVIS *
INNOMINATE g
SACRUM h
VERTEBRAE i
FEMUR j
TIBIA k
FIBULA l
FOOT m
HEIGHT/ WEIGHT n

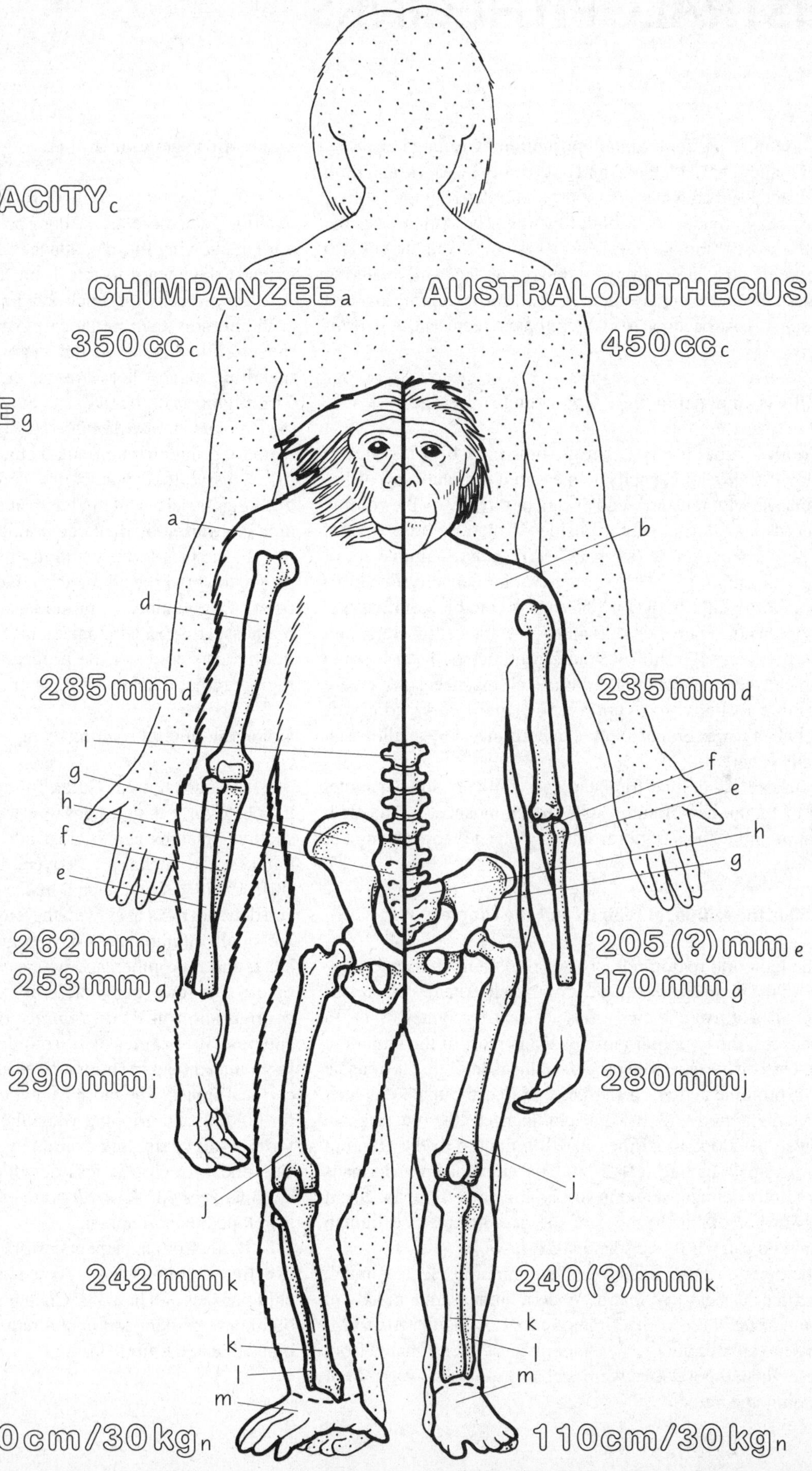
CHIMPANZEE a
AUSTRALOPITHECUS b
350cc c
450cc c
a
b
d
285mm d
235mm d
i
g
h
f
e
f
e
h
g
262mm e
253mm g
205(?)mm e
170mm g
290mm j
280mm j
j
j
242mm k
240(?)mm k
k
l
k
l
m
m
110cm/30kg n
110cm/30kg n

DENTITION *

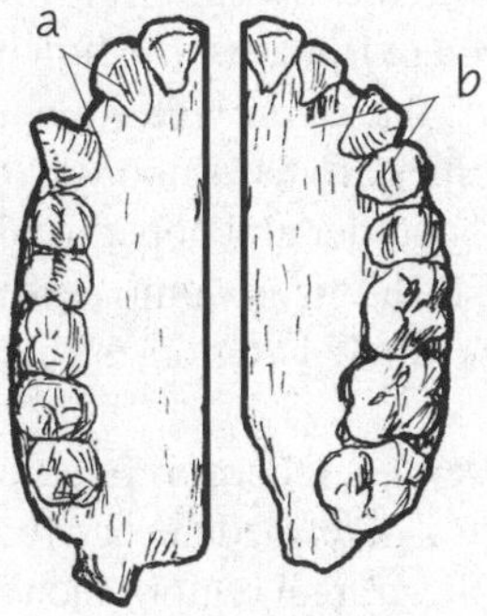
a
b

5-18
AUSTRALOPITHECINES

Fossil hominids are represented most often by isolated teeth, by parts of mandibles and crania, and only rarely by pelvic and limb bones. Dental and cranial traits are useful for determining species, and they also provide clues about function. The skull houses the brain, the senses, and the masticatory system. In this first of two plates, we identify major bony landmarks on the skull related to these systems and compare them in *Pan*, *Australopithecus,* and *Homo sapiens.* A specimen from Sterkfontein represents *Australopithecus.*

Color the cranial capacities. Color the brow ridges.

Cranial capacity is a rough index of brain volume. Traditionally, cranial capacity is measured indirectly by filling the braincase with mustard seed or shot or directly by the volume of a mold or endocast of the inside of the cranium. Recent noninvasive techniques (such as CAT scans) achieve more accurate measures (5-22). Average cranial capacity of chimpanzees (*Pan*) falls between 350 and 400 cubic centimeters, australopithecines between 400 and 500 cubic centimeters, and humans between 1200 and 1600 cubic centimeters. There is some overlap between the early hominids and chimpanzees, which are comparable in body size. On average these early hominids probably had larger brains relative to body size, but smaller than originally reported.

Compare the domed forehead and relatively smaller facial region of the human cranium with the chimpanzee's, and with the australopithecine's flatter frontal region and more prominent brow ridges.

Next color the temporal regions and the canines.

The temporal region reflects two important characteristics: the size of the brain and the quantity of muscle. The forces exerted by the masticatory (chewing) muscles scar the bones (5-1). In chimpanzees, the temporal muscle covers most of the braincase and attaches on the coronoid process of the mandible. The muscle leaves a prominent line on the bone, called the temporal line, noted by the dotted line. In some chimpanzees the muscles can be so well developed that they meet on the top of the cranium and form a small sagittal crest (5-20). The temporal area in humans is only faintly delineated and in size is similar to chimpanzees; it appears to be smaller because of the greatly enlarged human cranium and can hardly be seen in the top view.

The mass of the chimpanzee's temporal muscle is as much as four times as heavy as that of modern humans, due mostly to the chimpanzee's use of its larger canines. Although *Australopithecus* has small canines, the temporal muscles, estimated from the preserved temporal line, were probably quite heavy as part of its grinding apparatus.

Color the zygomatic arches.

The zygomatic arch is formed by the zygomatic bone anteriorly and the temporal bone posteriorly. The masseter muscle, a main chewing muscle, attaches along the zygomatic arch and extends downward to attach on the angle of the mandible. In *Australopithecus* the thick zygomatic arch flares out from the cranium more than in the chimpanzee. The marks made by the muscle attachment on the zygomatic arch and angle of the mandible suggest heavy masseter muscles in *Australopithecus.* The migration of the masseter attachment more directly over the back molars in *Australopithecus* gave more power to the posterior teeth for grinding tough, small objects. Modern humans, because of extensive food preparation and cooking, do not have large chewing muscles and big teeth, and the rather gracile zygomatic arch is dwarfed by the large braincase.

In the profile view and in the view from above, notice the prognathism of the chimpanzee face, that is, its projection far in front of the braincase. In humans, the face is tucked under the braincase. In the australopithecines the face projects, but less than in chimpanzees, and the prognathism begins below the nasal region, rather than above it, as in chimpanzees.

Color the nuchal regions using a light color.

The nuchal area (Greek for neck) provides attachment for the posterior trunk muscles (e.g. trapezius) and for neck muscles such as splenius capitis, that attach on the cervical spines. In humans, the nuchal area covers a large and relatively smooth surface with a slight nuchal line, except in very muscular males, and does not meet at all with the temporal line. The cervical spines are small. Chimpanzees have a more prominent nuchal line or crest, and a protuberance where the temporal and nuchal lines meet; the long cervical spines are well developed. The configuration in *Australopithecus* differs from the other two species. Its braincase is rounder and the nuchal line less pronounced than in chimpanzees, and there is no information on cervical spines. The muscles in the nuchal area provide strength for holding and gripping when the canines are used in biting or for motions of strength exerted by the shoulder and upper trunk. The nuchal region is less developed in humans compared to chimpanzees; in *Australopithecus* the nuchal region is more developed than in humans.

Skulls from ancient ancestors preserve a record of function in extinct hominids that in some respects is intermediate between chimpanzees and humans. Changes to the cranial region, such as brain enlargement and dental reduction, occurred later than the bipedal adaptation (5-1).

CRANIAL AND FACIAL COMPARISONS

CRANIAL CAPACITY a TEMPORAL REGION c ZYGOMATIC ARCH e
BROW RIDGE b   CANINE d   NUCHAL REGION f

CHIMPANZEE *   AUSTRALOPITHECUS *   HUMAN *
400 cc a   450 cc a   1400 cc a

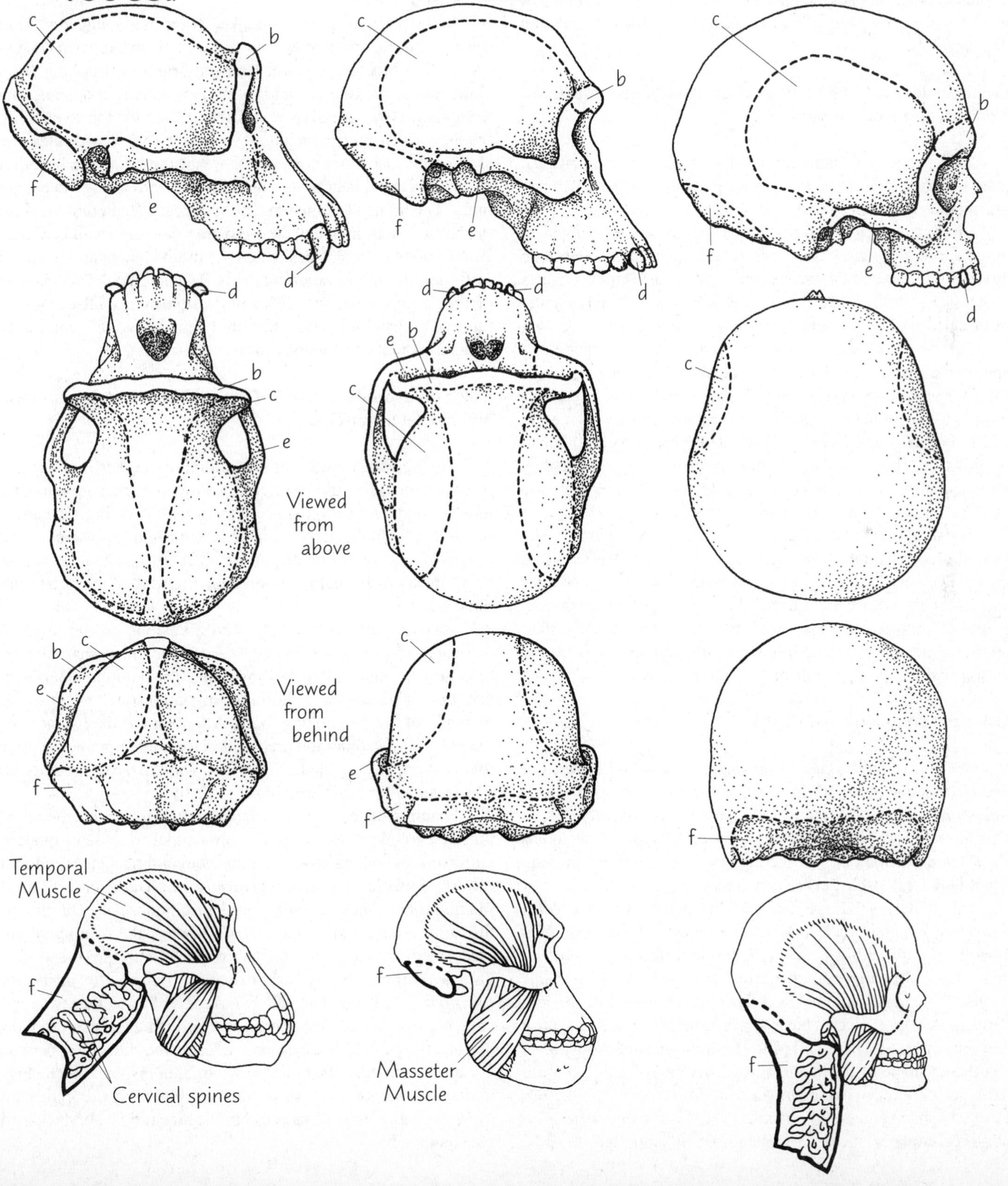

Viewed
from
above

Viewed
from
behind

Temporal
Muscle

Cervical spines

Masseter
Muscle

Bony landmarks on the cranium and mandible reflect the size and shape of the teeth and the corresponding chewing muscles. Dental remains of *Australopithecus* help identify the species, and comparison with humans and chimpanzees aid in interpretation of dietary adaptations. The cranial, facial, and dental features of *Australopithecus* suggest that fibrous and hard foods were main dietary items.

Color the incisors and canines of the chimpanzee, *Australopithecus*, and modern human.

Chimpanzee and human incisors are more prominent than those of *Australopithecus*. Incisors are particularly well developed in fruit-eating monkeys and apes.

Chimpanzee canine sizes vary from small and pointed to moderate in size, and overall are notably more prominent than those of humans. Male great apes usually have larger canines than females (4-33). Male canines probably serve a social function in threat displays, in fighting with other males, or in dealing forcefully with predators. Even so, both female and male great apes have broad upper canines and distinctly shaped lower premolars to accommodate the larger upper canines. The canines of the australopithecine species vary, but tend to be reduced to nearly human size, a change that has both dietary and social significance. The small australopithecine canines suggest that they were using nondental means, probably tools, to prepare food items, to interact aggressively, and to ward off predators.

The diastema between the chimpanzee's upper canines and second incisors allows space for interlocking and sharpening of the lower canines. This feature is absent in the australopithecines and humans, whose canines occlude rather than interlock. Hominid canines are described as "incisiform," that is, they resemble incisors in size and line up with them in the tooth row as opposed to being prominent as in chimpanzees.

Color the premolars and the molars.

The chimpanzee's first lower single-cusp sectorial (cutting) premolars differ in shape and orientation from that of *Australopithecus* and humans. The premolars of *Australopithecus* have an extended grinding surface; some early hominid specimens show the development of a second cusp. Human premolars are small with two cusps and are called bicuspids.

The molars are large and thickly enameled in *Australopithecus* compared to chimpanzee and human. Thick enamel is associated with eating dry, tough, and hard foods. In contrast, apes like chimpanzees (primarily fruit-eaters) and gorillas (vegetation-eaters/folivores) have thin tooth enamel, as do modern humans. All three species have the same dental formula because they are catarrhines (2:1:2:3) (4-9). Note the differences in palate length and shape of the dental arcade. In chimpanzees the tooth rows are parallel, whereas in *Australopithecus* the tooth rows form a U-shape and the third molars (M3) curve in toward each other. In humans, the arch is parabolic in shape and may be

functionally correlated with the disappearance of the locking canine complex and reduction in canine size.

Color the zygomatic arch and the foramen magnum.

In the previous plate, we looked at the zygomatic arch from top and side views. Here we view the arch from below and assess its relationship to the palate and the cranium. Looking from chimpanzee to early hominid to modern human, it appears that the palate is progressively "tucked in" under the expanding cranium. The foramen magnum, where the spinal cord enters the skull, progresses forward as the back of the braincase becomes more rounded; it is largest in humans and correlates with a large brain. The human foramen magnum appears "centered" because the brain case is large and the teeth are relatively small in adults. But in infant chimpanzees, when the brain is large and teeth are just erupting, the foramen magnum is "centered." The position of the foramen magnum is an indication of cranial expansion relative to facial reduction, age, and dental development, rather than an indication of locomotion.

Color the ascending ramus of the mandible and the temporal and masseter muscles.

The vertical ramus of the mandible is higher in *Australopithecus*, providing more surface area for attachment of masseter muscles and a longer lever arm for forceful chewing. The angle of the jaw is more perpendicular in both hominids than in the chimpanzee, reflecting the more efficient placement of the grinding teeth beneath, rather than in front of, the chewing muscles.

Analysis of wear patterns and abrasions on the teeth of *Australopithecus* suggest heavy wear early in life, perhaps related to a diet of tough and gritty food items that required significant grinding. This period of hominid evolution occurred prior to evidence of fire for cooking foods. Although it is likely that tools may have assisted in food preparation (cutting or pounding prior to ingestion) and enabled a diet with a wide range of foods, teeth were needed for most grinding.

Features of the skull of *Australopithecus* are a product of mosaic evolution. Some features are similar to those of modern chimpanzees; others show definite human tendencies; and still others, especially the big grinding teeth and craniofacial modifications that went with them, are unique. The evolution of the human skull and its pattern of growth—the neurocranium, face, jaw joint, mandible, and dentition—exemplifies the mosaic nature of the evolutionary process, that is, the parts are functionally independent (5-1, 6-4). The big teeth, jaws, and chewing muscles of early hominids were an adaptation to their diet and life on the African savanna. Later, the chewing apparatus became smaller and the brain grew larger in response to changes in diet and way of life. The overall trend from australopithecine to *Homo* was a marked increase in the size ratio of braincase to face and teeth.

DENTAL COMPARISONS

INCISOR a
CANINE b
PREMOLAR c
MOLAR d

ZYGOMATIC ARCH e
FORAMEN MAGNUM f
ASCENDING RAMUS g

TEMPORAL MUSCLE h
MASSETER MUSCLE i

CHIMPANZEE *   AUSTRALOPITHECUS *   HUMAN *

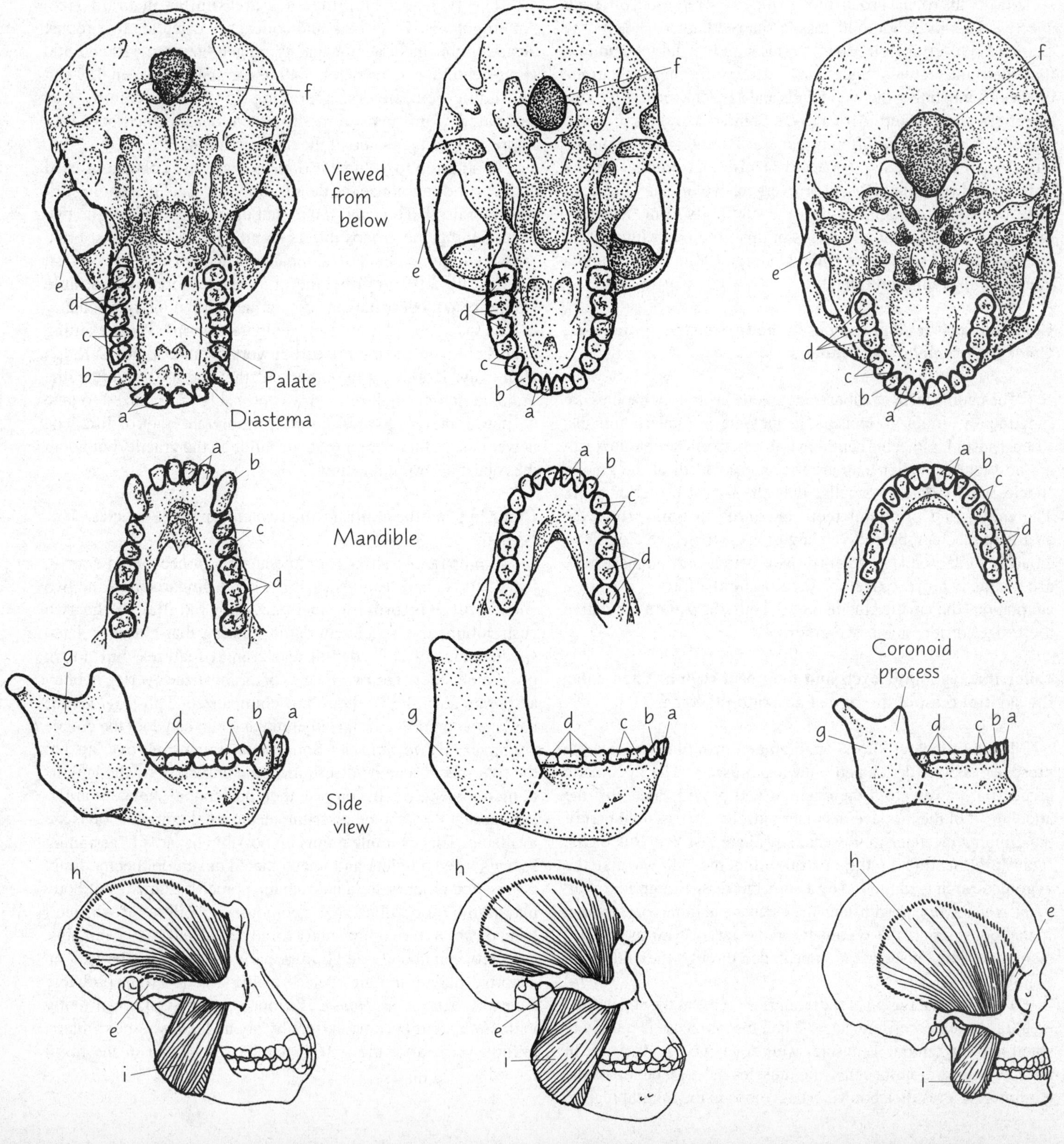

Viewed
from
below

Palate

Diastema

Mandible

Coronoid
process

Side
view

5-20
AUSTRALOPITHECINE ADAPTATION

Studying the fossil hominids recovered in the 1950s from Sterkfontein and Swartkrans, anthropologist John Robinson recognized two groups, "gracile" and "robust." The gracile group included the hominids from Taung, Sterkfontein, and Makapansgat, and the robust group referred to specimens from Swartkrans and nearby Kromdraai. Subsequent fossil discoveries from Olduvai Gorge, Omo, Koobi Fora, and West Turkana were sorted with the robust group, though they may represent different species. The early hominid fossils share enlarged and thickly enameled posterior teeth, small brains, and bipedal locomotion; these defining features suggest an "australopithecine adaptation" of species inhabiting the woodlands and savanna mosaic regions of eastern and southern Africa (5-2). Some researchers prefer to place each group in a different genus, "Paranthropus" (robust) and "Australopithecus" (gracile) in order to emphasize the differences in morphology and in divergent evolutionary lineages. Here we use *Australopithecus* or the subfamily term "australopithecine" to represent all species of this group. For illustration we use a robust skull from Olduvai Gorge ("Zinj" OH 5) and a gracile skull from Sterkfontein.

Color the incisors and canines in the two australopithecines. Color the premolars and molars.

The canine teeth of robust and gracile australopithecines are functionally similar to incisors, as they are in modern humans. Robust australopithecine dentition is distinctive. The anterior teeth are absolutely smaller than are the anterior teeth of the gracile species, and markedly smaller than the robust posterior teeth. The molar and premolar teeth are large in both groups of australopithecines, but they are largest in the robust species. Their enlarged molars and premolars provide a greater grinding surface area, and a more extreme development of the "grinding adaptation" than in the gracile group. Thus, the pattern of relative tooth sizes differs in the two groups.

Color the zygomatic arch and temporal region. Then color the sagittal crest of the robust australopithecine.

The morphology of the cranium and mandible indicate the presence of well-developed chewing muscles. The zygomatic arches flare away from the cranium and provide areas for the attachment of the massive masseter muscles, an essential part of the grinding mechanism. Research by anatomist Yoel Rak on the facial architecture of the australopithecines shows that the zygomatic arch is supported by a bony buttress, an anterior pillar, in the facial region to withstand the mechanical forces of chewing. In the robust group, the zygomatic arch is far forward and creates a characteristic "dish-faced" appearance through the mid-facial region.

The temporal region of the braincase serves as the attachment area for the temporalis muscles. When the braincase is relatively small and the temporal muscles well developed, as they are in the robust australopithecines, the muscles meet at the top of the cranium. As a result, a bony crest develops in the sagittal region,

hence "sagittal crest." The crest gives added bony surface for the attachment of muscle and supporting connective tissue. The gracile australopithecine braincase is smoother and without a crest, suggesting relatively less massive temporal muscles.

Color the cranial capacities.

The two australopithecines are similar in brain size. Anthropologist Dean Falk and colleagues calculate that robust australopithecine cranial capacity ranged between 410 and 500 cubic centimeters, averaging 449, the graciles between 425 and 515 cubic centimeters, averaging 451. Brain volume was estimated from measurements of endocasts that record an impression of the inside of the neurocranium.

In addition to volume estimates, Falk and colleagues used endocasts to reproduce the details of the external morphology of the brain itself. The team found that the morphology of the two australopithecine groups differs significantly! The robust brain is very similar in detail to chimpanzees and gorillas. In contrast, the gracile australopithecine endocasts show considerable similarity to modern humans in external morphology, particularly in having expanded frontal and temporal regions. These exciting results build on and modify earlier work of anthropologist Ralph Holloway. Holloway hypothesized that the australopithecine brain, although small in size, was probably reorganized to take on new functions associated with a hominid way of life. The newer data point to brain reorganization in the gracile, but not in the robust australopithecine.

Color in gray the skulls of the two chimpanzee species.

Chimpanzees differ from the australopithecines in cranial, facial, and dental features (5-18, 5-19). Comparison of the two species of *Pan* provide an interesting parallel to the two australopithecine species in demonstrating that closely related species can differ in dental and cranial features, but not in postcranial ones. The two species of chimpanzee overlap in body and brain size (4-33); the robust chimpanzee (*Pan troglodytes*) has larger canine teeth and larger molar teeth than does the gracile chimpanzee, *Pan paniscus*. Some facial dimensions overlap, but the two species can be discriminated completely by the lengths of their lower jaws. In contrast, their postcranial skeletons are so similar that they can be discriminated only if complete ones are available. This example points up possible hazards in assigning species to incomplete and unassociated australopithecine limb, pelvic, and other postcranial remains; precise estimates of body mass, limb proportions, and locomotor capabilities are difficult to reconstruct from fragmentary fossil dental and cranial remains.

Between about 4 and 2 mya, early hominids underwent an adaptive radiation. One species of the gracile group probably gave rise to the genus *Homo*. The robust group lived concurrently with *Homo* and became extinct by about 1.2 mya, more than a million years after the first appearance of *Homo* in the fossil record.

GRACILE AND ROBUST SPECIES

GRACILE✴
450 CCh

*Australopithecus
africanus*

ROBUST✴
450 CCh

*Australopithecus
robustus*

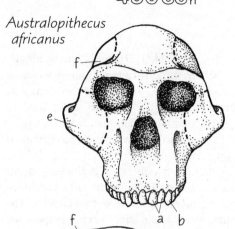

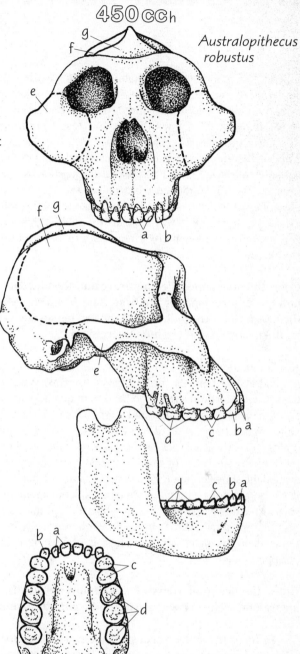

INCISORa
CANINEb
PREMOLARc
MOLARd

ZYGOMATIC
ARCHe
TEMPORAL
REGIONf
SAGITTAL
CRESTg
CRANIAL
CAPACITYh

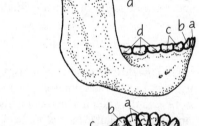

Upper
jaw

Viewed
from
below

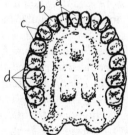

GRACILE CHIMPANZEE✴

ROBUST CHIMPANZEE✴

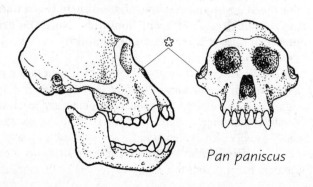

Pan paniscus

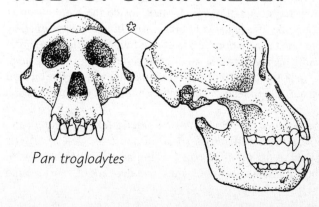

Pan troglodytes

5-21
THE GREAT BRAIN DRAIN

Bipedal locomotion became established in the earliest stages of the hominid lineage, about 4 million years ago, whereas brain expansion came later (5-1). Early hominids had brains slightly larger than those of apes (5-18), but fossil hominids with significantly increased cranial capacities did not appear until about 2 mya. What might account for this later and rapid expansion of hominid brain size? Dean Falk tackled the question by integrating several lines of evidence from paleontology, anatomy and physiology, and medicine. In her view, a necessary factor for brain expansion in hominids was a means for cooling this vital heat-generating organ—namely a new pattern of cerebral blood circulation.

Color the quadrupedal chimpanzee and the bipedal human, noting the placement of the head (and brain) in relation to the heart. Color the pathways of the venous sinuses as shown on the inside view of the human cranium.

Gravitational forces on blood draining from the brain differ in quadrupedal animals versus bipedal humans. When humans lie down, blood drains from the head as in quadrupeds and goes through the jugular foramina and through the major interior neck veins. When humans stand bipedally, most blood alternatively drains into veins at the back of the neck, called the vertebral plexus (not shown), a network of small veins that form a complex system around the spinal column. This network is so fine that it does not leave impressions within the cranium as do some larger routes, such as the transverse/sigmoid and superior sagittal sinuses. The occipital/marginal (O/M) sinus (shown here for orientation) is reduced or absent in adult humans; it is present at birth but disappears soon after.

Color the occipital views of the venous sinuses in robust australopithecine, gracile australopithecine, and human.

In fossil hominids, venous sinuses can be detected on the occipital bone or on endocasts which retain impressions of the venous routes that formed on the outside of the brain.

All robust and Hadar australopithecines for which we have preserved occipital bones (15 specimens) show a deep, enlarged channel, the occipital/marginal sinus inside the cranium on at least one side (it is not always bilateral). This channel, formed by a large stream of blood during the individual's life, can either drain into the jugular veins, or into the vertebral plexus. The large O/M sinus indicates that the blood passageway in the bipedal robust australopithecines was achieved through one major blood pipe.

In contrast, the South Africa gracile (except Taung) and Laetoli australopithecines (6 specimens) as well as fossils attributed to the genus *Homo*, are similar to modern humans in having a transverse/sigmoid sinus, and network of veins around the vertebral plexus; the occipital/marginal sinus is usually absent.

Falk wondered whether these different cranial vascular patterns had functional significance, which might explain why one pattern persisted and the other did not. Falk had a flash of insight when she had her car repaired, and the mechanic explained that an engine cannot function efficiently unless the radiator is big enough to cool it properly.

It occurred to Falk that the two different drainage patterns might reflect two systems of cooling brains in early hominids. Active brains and bodies generate a lot of metabolic heat. The brain is a hot organ, but must maintain a fairly rigid temperature range to keep it functioning properly and to prevent permanent damage. Although the cranial network system of the venous plexus in humans serves to drain blood from the brain, other researchers had shown that the cranial veins *also* serve as a cooling mechanism when humans are overheating (hyperthermic). It works like this: heads/foreheads sweat, which serves to cool the outer cranial layers. During intense exercise, the blood flow of cranial veins actually *reverses* course; the newly cooled blood flows into the innermost parts of the brain—a natural radiator. Savanna-dwelling hominids with this network of veins had a way to cool a bigger brain, allowing the "engine" to expand, contributing to hominid flexibility in moving into new habitats and in being active under a wide range of climatic conditions

Color Falk's cactus.

Falk's observations on the differences in the sinus pattern in the two species of australopithecine had other implications and led her to two conclusions regarding hominid evolution: the robust australopithecines, including the Hadar australopithecines, are specialized in having a well-developed occipital/marginal sinus, that is, a pattern that represents a departure from the ape or human pattern, and therefore could not be ancestral to *Homo*. On the other hand, according to her data, gracile australopithecines, including Laetoli hominids, could serve as an ancestor to *Homo*. Although these observations are not the final word, they are suggestive and must be considered in any analysis of hominid phylogeny.

Color the diagram showing the relationship between time and cranial capacity of different hominids. Note the cranial capacity of apes relative to that of hominids.

Brain size remains near 450 cubic centimeters for robust australopithecines until almost 1.5 mya. At this same time, fossils assigned to *Homo* exceed 500 cubic centimeters and reach almost 900 cubic centimeters. Falk's hypothesis, called "the radiator theory" provides an explanation for the evolutionary sequence: bipedalism first, followed by an increase in brain size that ultimately became four times as great as that of the apes (5-21).

BRAIN EVOLUTION

FORCE OF GRAVITY a
BRAIN a¹
HEART a²

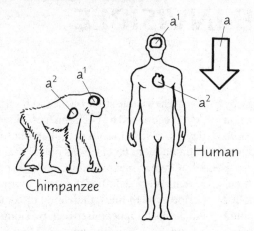

Chimpanzee

Human

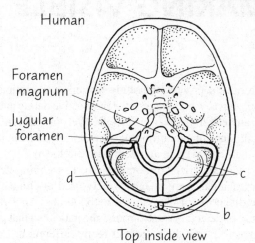

Human

Foramen magnum

Jugular foramen

Top inside view

VENOUS SINUSES *
SUPERIOR SAGITTAL b
OCCIPITAL/MARGINAL c

TRANSVERSE/SIGMOID d

HOMO SAPIENS g¹

A. ROBUSTUS e

Foramen magnum

Jugular foramen

A. AFRICANUS f

CACTUS e,f

BRAIN SIZE *
CHIMPANZEE h
HOMO SPECIES g

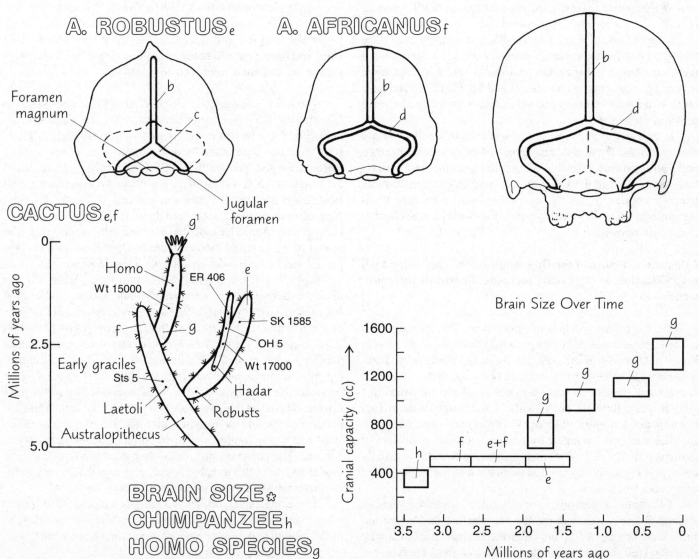

Brain Size Over Time

We have seen how the study of human evolution advances by applying new techniques, like radioactive dating and the detection of ancient molecules in fossils. We now review two research techniques that anthropology has borrowed from the disciplines of medical imaging and dental research.

Computerized tomographic (CT) scanning generates three-dimensional x-ray images widely used in clinical medicine for the diagnosis of many disease conditions. An x-ray source and array of detectors rotate around the patient so that the x-ray beam passes through the patient at many different angles. Data from the detectors are processed by a computer to display a "map" of the patient's tissue densities: bones, the densest tissue, are shown in white, lungs, the least dense, nearly black, with muscle, nerves, and fat in shades of gray. These images can be viewed on film or on a computer screen either as two-dimensional slices or as a three-dimensional see-through human being.

When applied to fossils, the great advantage of CT scanning is that it is noninvasive, does not damage the fossil, and can visualize and quantify such morphological features as surface area, thickness, and volume not easily measured by conventional methods. Anthropologist Glenn Conroy and his team have scanned partial crania such as Sts 71 and Sts 505 (5-10) and have obtained accurate cranial capacities that have altered or confirmed previous estimates.

In an early application of CT scanning to fossils, Conroy reexamined the Taung child and found that its stage of tooth crown and root formation, within the bone and not otherwise visible, were more rapid in the fossil than in modern humans. In more precise studies of tooth formation, markings that form incrementally and very quickly within the enamel can be counted using light microscopy.

Color the structure of the first molar tooth. Then color each magnification as it reveals more detail within the tooth structure.

Teeth are dense packets of information. The forming tooth is a reliable yardstick of human growth and development, closely linked with growth of the skeleton, brain, and whole body. Teeth also have the hardest structure in the body and therefore are the commonest element to survive in the fossil record. Anatomist Alan Boyde calls teeth "born fossils." Once formed, a tooth does not remodel during the individual's life as bone does, nor is the internal structure changed by fossilization but is preserved permanently. Tooth enamel and dentine are formed on a daily basis, and formation of the first permanent molar begins about two weeks before birth.

Two sets of periodic growth lines in enamel enable anthropologists to establish age at death. The first, the long-period lines, called striae of Retzius (after the German anatomist who first observed them in 1836), are laid down about every seven days. The visible striae on the tooth surface are called perikymata. Age is estimated by counting these lines and multiplying by seven days. If a fossil tooth is broken, these long-period lines can be counted more precisely, as not all of them appear on the surface.

Greater magnification under a polarized light microscope reveals more detail of the same tooth structure. Now the short-period growth lines, indicating the daily secretion of enamel by ameloblasts, appear. Between two long-period lines, seven short-period lines can be counted. Thus it is possible to obtain an accurate age for the individual. It is even possible to distinguish the neonatal line, a disruption of the regular pattern marking the day the individual was born.

Anatomist Christopher Dean and his colleagues studied australopithecine teeth and deduced that these early hominids had a fast pattern of dental growth more like chimpanzees than like modern humans. They also analyzed the first permanent molar in a young Neanderthal from Devil's Tower, Gibraltar.

Color the erupted and unerupted teeth of the Neanderthal child and the 5-year-old modern human. Color the skull pieces preserved and their mirrored components.

The Devil's Tower child, discovered in 1926, consisted of a fused frontal, left parietal, right temporal, right maxilla, and partial mandible. Some who examined these fragments thought that they were from two different individuals, because the temporal bone suggested a younger age (about 3) than did the stage of dental development. Dean's study of the enamel growth lines in the teeth established an age of 3, and showed that the teeth of young Neanderthals matured faster than those of modern humans. The faster-than-expected Neanderthal dental development was similar to that of a 5-year-old modern human. They concluded that the cranial pieces were probably all from a single 3-year-old.

Applying CT scanning, anthropologists were able to distinguish fossil bone from matrix filling, and the endocranial and other cavities by their different densities; the crown and roots of the forming teeth became visible. Anthropologist Christoph Zollikofer and his team from Zurich did a CT reconstruction of the Devil's Tower skull. First, the available pieces were scanned, then mirror images were created to fill in the missing parts on the opposite side. Finally the pieces were assembled on a computer screen and contact points established between the frontal and left parietal bones, and the mandible and maxilla. The reconstituted skull was nearly complete, with an estimated cranial capacity of 1400 cc. The computer image was then converted into a plastic model by stereolithography, which employs lasers and resin. Further analysis can be carried out on this model.

These techniques, one from research on tooth formation, the other from medical imaging, have created a new understanding of the growth and development of our extinct human relatives.

NEW TECHNIQUES

MOLAR TOOTH ✶
CROWN a
ENAMEL b ROOT d
DENTINE c BONE e

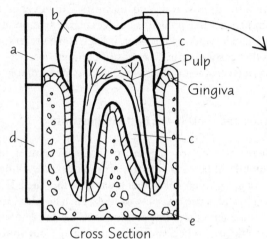

Pulp

Gingiva

Cross Section

GROWTH LINES ✶
LONG PERIOD f
SHORT PERIOD g

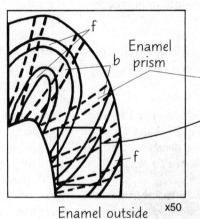

Enamel prism

Enamel outside surface

x50

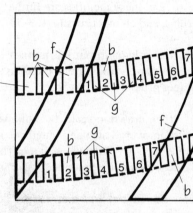

x500

DENTAL DEVELOPMENT ✶
ERUPTED h UNERUPTED i

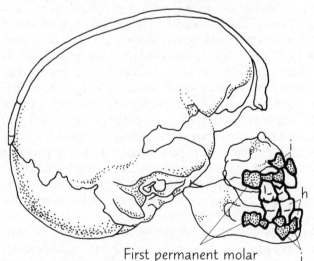

First permanent molar

H. sapiens
5-year-old

First permanent molar

SKULL FRAGMENTS ✶
ORIGINAL j
MIRRORED COMPONENTS k
CONTACT POINTS l

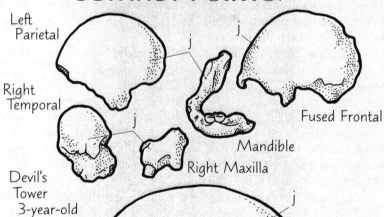

Left Parietal

Right Temporal

Devil's Tower 3-year-old

Fused Frontal

Mandible

Right Maxilla

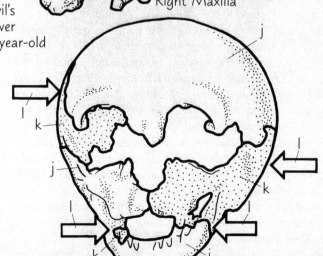

5-23
HANDS AND TOOLS

The human hand is a key component in the hominid way of life, opening up new possibilities for enhancing tool-making and tool-using skills. Manual dexterity is not unique to hominids. Capuchin monkeys use their hands in feeding and manipulating objects (4-16), and these facilities are further developed in orangutans, gorillas, and chimpanzees (4-1, 3-33).

Color the titles chimpanzee, human, and early hominid. Color the chimpanzee and human hands at the top of the plate. Color the feet gray.

When drawn to scale, the chimpanzee's hand and foot are similar in overall size and length, reflecting the hand's use for bearing weight in knuckle walking. The human hand, which has no direct locomotor function, is shorter than the foot.

Color the carpal and metacarpal bones in the chimpanzee, human, and then in the early hominid. Color the finger bones in the side view and in the hands. Color the terminal thumb phalanx, flexor tendon, and trapezium in all three species. Notice the finger and thumb proportions in relation to overall hand size.

A look "inside" each hand reveals variation in size and proportions in the three species. Chimpanzees have a narrow palm with tightly packed carpals, long metacarpals, and long and adducted finger bones. The side view shows the curvature of the finger bones and the pronounced bony ridges from the strong ligaments that keep the flexor tendons from "popping out" or bow stringing. The chimpanzee thumb is relatively short. The long thumb flexor tendon is slim (or absent) and attaches on the terminal phalanx. The human hand has a broad mobile palm with easy tip-to-tip contact among the fingers. The metacarpals are straight and slender; the phalanges are short, smooth, and uncurved. The thumb is relatively long and well muscled. The flexor pollicis longus muscle tendon is broad and attaches to the base of the terminal thumb phalanx, which accounts for its robust appearance compared to the chimpanzee's thumb.

Fossil hand bones have been found at several early hominid sites: Olduvai, Hadar, Swartkrans, Sterkfontein, and Turkwel. The hand depicted here is a composite reconstruction based on the juvenile hand from Olduvai Gorge (OH 7), presumed to be *Homo habilis*, possibly from the same individual as the OH 8 foot. Taken as a group, hominid hand bones are distinct but share features with both humans and chimpanzees.

When anatomist John Napier described the OH 7 hand, he noted the curved finger bones with marked ridges and a relatively well developed terminal phalanx. Later, anthropologists Randall Susman and Normal Creel analyzed the trapezium, a carpal bone that articulates with the thumb metacarpal. Its expanded articular surface suggests increased thumb rotation, which would provide improved mobility in opposing the other fingers. The thumb's broad terminal phalanx also suggests a sturdy flexor tendon and perhaps a distinct flexor pollicis longus muscle belly. Studying the Hadar hand bones, anthropologist Mary Marzke deduced that the capitate, a central carpal bone, renders the palm more mobile compared to chimpanzees.

The larger thumb of early hominids seems to testify to increased strength, opposition, and mobility. However, the retention of chimpanzeelike phalangeal ridges can be interpreted as denoting a knuckle-walking ancestor, though some prefer the interpretation that early hominids were still climbing trees. The morphology is consistent with either view, lacking more complete information.

Color the hands and tools in the bottom illustration.

Chimpanzee hands are a compromise. They must be relatively immobile in bearing weight during knuckle walking, but dexterous for using tools. Like other great apes, they are adept manipulators. They also use a variety of tools, such as sticks for termiting and stone hammers for pounding nuts (3-33). Human hands are capable of power and precisions grips but more importantly, are uniquely suited for fine manipulation and coordination, exemplified here in playing a stringed instrument.

Stone tools have been found at several sites dated 2 to 2.5 mya (5-24). As old as these stone artifacts are, the tradition of making and using tools almost certainly goes back much earlier to a period of utilizing unmodified stones and organic tools of wood or leaves that would not be preserved in the fossil record. Stone tools were first recognized as artifacts in 1790 by Englishman John Frere, Mary Leakey's great-great-great-grandfather, who found handaxes associated with extinct animal bones "fabricated and used by people who had not the use of metals." These tools with flakes removed on both sides are called bifaces and include handaxes and cleavers. First described from St. Acheul, France (hence Acheulian), they are abundant in Europe, although they first appeared in Africa and Eurasia about 1.6 mya, associated with *Homo erectus*. Simpler tools—pebble choppers, flakes, and cores—comprise the Oldowan tradition, the earliest yet recognized (5-24).

How can we tell a hominid-made artifact from a stone generated by natural processes? First, the manufacturing process of hitting one stone with another to form a sharp cutting edge leaves a characteristic mark where the flake has been removed. Second, under a microscope the edges of the tool show wear patterns that provide clues about usage. Third, the raw material for the tools often comes from some distance away and indicates transport to the site by hominids.

Modification of rocks into predetermined shapes was a technological breakthrough. Possession of such tools opened up new possibilities in foraging—for example, the ability to crack open long bones and get at the marrow, to dig, and to sharpen or shape wooden implements. Even before the fossil record of tools between 2 and 2.5 mya, australopithecine brains were larger than chimpanzee brains, suggesting increased motor skills and problem solving. All lines of evidence point to the importance of skilled making and using of tools in hominid evolution.

HANDS AND TOOLS

CARPAL d
TRAPEZIUM d¹
METACARPAL e

FINGER PHALANX f
THUMB PHALANX g
FLEXOR TENDON g¹

TOOL h

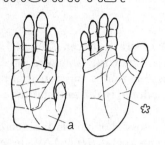

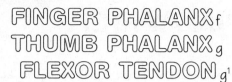

Side view

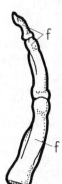
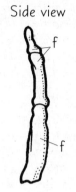
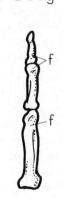

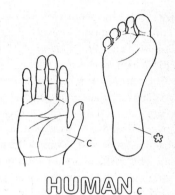

CHIMPANZEE a

EARLY HOMINID b

HUMAN c

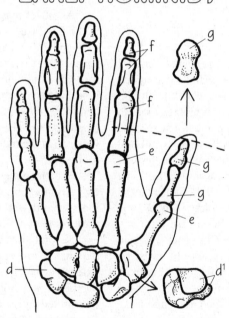
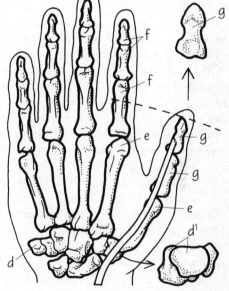

Articular surface

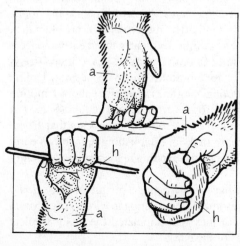
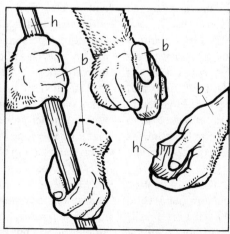
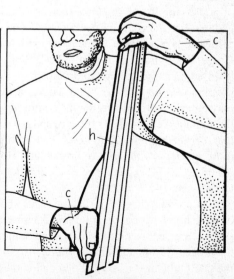

5-24
EARLY HOMO IN AFRICA

The origin of the genus *Homo* is one of the least understood topics in human evolution. Unresolved questions abound. Which earlier hominid is ancestral to *Homo*? How many species of *Homo* are there? Which species first left Africa? Was it biology or technology that accounted for hominid dispersion beyond the African homeland? The australopithecines, widely distributed in Africa, spanned a time range from 4 mya to late survivors at 1.2 mya. Between 2 and 2.5 mya, hominids distinct from the australopithecines appeared, along with the earliest evidence of stone tools. The artifacts document a hominid presence and mark the beginning of the archaeological record. In this plate we review the evidence for early *Homo* and stone tools in Africa, and key fossils and sites that document the earliest wave, perhaps the first of several waves of hominids out of Africa.

Color the sites for early *Homo*, stone tools, and the time chart 2.5 to 2 mya. Color the fossils in Africa for the later period between 2 and 1.5 mya.

Members of the genus *Homo* differ from the australopithecines in several key features: larger brain size with an expanded cranial vault, smaller and straighter face, less massive mandible, rounded dental arcade with smaller-crowned, narrower cheek teeth and reduced third molar, and postcranial skeleton similar to modern humans. The earliest *Homo* fossils are few in number. The maxilla from Hadar (AL-666), well dated at 2.3 million years old and associated with stone tools, has a rounded dental arcade with small and narrow cheek teeth. The cranium from Koobi Fora, Lake Turkana (ER 1470), a mandible (ER 1802), and other material (not illustrated) found below the KBS tuff are older than 1.9 mya and share with *Homo* a flatter face, larger brain case (750 cc), and smaller teeth. The mandible from the Chiwonda Beds in Malawi (UR 501) estimated at 2.4 million years old based on biostratigraphy, closely resembles the ER 1802 mandible from Koobi Fora. Simple stone tools characteristic of the Oldowan culture come from sites in Ethiopia (Hadar and Gona) and Lake Turkana.

The sample size of *Homo* increases between 2 and 1.5 mya, and stone artifacts become abundant. Cranial remains attributed to the genus *Homo* have come from South African caves, Olduvai Gorge, Koobi Fora, and West Lake Turkana. The OH 7 hominid inspired Leakey, Tobias, and Napier in 1964 to name a new species, *Homo habilis*. The Turkana boy (WT 15000) is particularly valuable, with its complete skull (900 cc) and postcranial skeleton. Tall (160 cm) and possessed of a larger body than earlier hominids, the youth had limb proportions close to those of *Homo sapiens*. Anthropologist Holly Smith estimates dental age as 11, skeletal age as 13, and stature more appropriate to a 15-year-old.

At present, there is little consensus about the classification of these hominids between 1.5 and 2.5 mya, and how many valid species are represented. Malawi and some Koobi Fora fossils have been designated *Homo rudolfensis*; *Homo habilis* might include Olduvai (OH 7, OH 13) and some Koobi Fora fossils.

The Turkana skeleton has been assigned to *Homo ergaster* and to *Homo erectus*.

Color the four non-African sites between 2.0 and 1.5 mya, the fossils, and time range. Color the later sites, fossils, and time range. Color the possible routes and note that the sites out of Africa are on approximately the same latitude.

Eugene Dubois found a fossil hominid in Java more than a century ago, in 1891, when he went to tropical Asia in search of the missing link. The skullcap from Trinil had a small brain (940cc), low forehead, and robust brow ridges. Other specimens were found from Sangiran, 60 kilometers west of Trinil, also with small cranial capacities (800–900 cc). These are all assigned *Homo erectus*. Geologist Carl Swisher and his team resolved long-standing disputes about their age, dating them to 1.8 mya for the earliest site (Mojokerto) using the argon method.

Another breakthrough came from Dmanisi, a site in Georgia in the Caucasus with a well-preserved mandible and two crania (650 and 750 cc) and over 1000 stone artifacts—chopping tools, scapers, and flakes. Georgian paleontologist Leo Gabunia and his team note that in facial and dental morphology the Dmanisi hominids are most similar to the Turkana skeleton (WT 15000) and to ER 3733 (Koobi Fora). The site is well dated to 1.7 mya by paleomagnetism. Archaeologist Ofer Bar-Josef comments that Dmanisi is the oldest known site in Eurasia with Oldowan stone tools.

Sketchy material from other sites in tropical Eurasia suggest an early hominid presence, for instance, simple core and flake tools from Riwat, Pakistan, and a lower jaw fragment and stone artifacts from Longgupo, China.

Several sites between 1.5 and 1 mya also hint at *Homo*'s expansion out of Africa. Ubeidiya in the Jordan Valley has extensive mammalian fauna and stone artifacts comparable to the fauna and Acheulian bifaces in Bed II in Olduvai Gorge, interpreted by paleontologist Eitan Tchernov as indicating the presence of *Homo erectus*. In North Africa at Tighenif, Algeria, three mandibles are similar to those from Zhoukoudian in China and are classified as *Homo erectus*. At Orce, Spain, stone tools, and bones identified as hominid by molecular tests are older than 1 mya by paleomagnetic dating. Evidently these early pioneers did not survive; not until 200,000 or more years after Orce is there further evidence for hominids in Spain at Gran Dolina (5-25). The Lantian (Gongwangling) fossils are about 1 million years old, older than the fossils from Zhoukoudian (5-25) but with a smaller cranial capacity (800 cc). It appears that *Homo erectus* had a long tenure in Asia, establishing habitations early in Java and later in China, and persisting in the region as recently as 50,000 years ago.

The evidence we have so far paints a picture of early *Homo* as a curious, adventuresome lot, emigrating in waves out of Africa into new territory, until they had populated the major tropical and temperate regions of the earth.

HOMINIDS LEAVE AFRICA

2.0-1.5 mya $_d$
JAVA $_{d^1}$
DMANISI $_{d^2}$
PAKISTAN $_{d^3}$
LONGGUPO $_{d^4}$

1.5-1 mya $_e$
UBEIDIYA $_{e^1}$
TIGHENIF $_{e^2}$
ORCE $_{e^3}$
LANTIAN $_{e^4}$

POSSIBLE
ROUTES $_f$

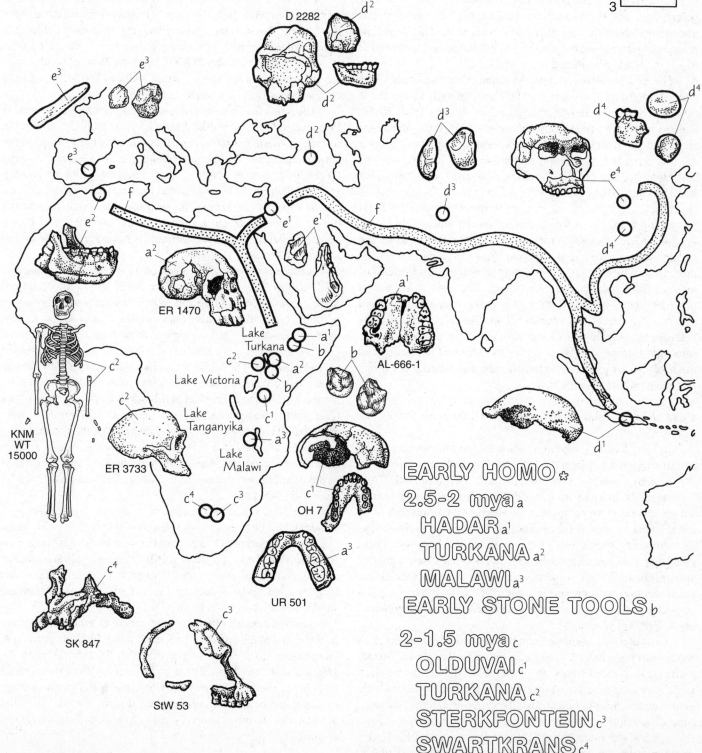

EARLY HOMO ✱
2.5-2 mya $_a$
HADAR $_{a^1}$
TURKANA $_{a^2}$
MALAWI $_{a^3}$
EARLY STONE TOOLS $_b$

2-1.5 mya $_c$
OLDUVAI $_{c^1}$
TURKANA $_{c^2}$
STERKFONTEIN $_{c^3}$
SWARTKRANS $_{c^4}$

5-25
EXPANSION INTO EUROPE

Hominids traveled out of Africa in several waves; the earliest record of more than 1.5 mya is from Southeast Asia (5-24). Hominid remains in Europe prior to 800,000 years ago are rare, but along with stone tools become more numerous thereafter. The Middle Pleistocene between 800,000 and 150,000 years follows the origin of *Homo erectus* but precedes the appearance of Neanderthals and modern *Homo sapiens*. This period has been referred to as "the muddle in the middle" because of the uncertainty about the fate of *Homo erectus* in the Old World. In Europe, a sparse fossil record, few reliable dates, and the absence of a framework contributed to the "muddle."

The well-preserved, isolated Mauer mandible was discovered near Heidelberg, Germany in 1907 and thought to be about 500,000 years old. It was recognized as distinct from *Homo sapiens* in having a thick body, robust ascending rami, and larger teeth, and was named *Homo heidelbergenesis*, the type specimen for the species. Subsequent finds, such as Steinheim, Swanscombe, and Petralona in Europe and Broken Hill in Africa were distinct from *Homo erectus* in having larger cranial capacities, higher forehead, discontinuous brow ridges and less protruding face. These fossils did not clearly fall within *Homo erectus* or *Homo sapiens*; for a time they were set apart by the rather unsatisfactory term "archaic *Homo sapiens*." With the discovery of more fossils, new dating techniques, and studies of ancient DNA, the picture improved. The new information provided a basis for paleoanthropologist Christopher Stringer and others to resurrect the species, *Homo heidelbergensis*. This heterogeneous group of fossils may represent the people who inhabited Europe and Africa during the Middle Pleistocene and the species that gave rise to the Neanderthal lineage in Europe and modern humans in Africa.

Color the molecular family tree. Use a light color for (c).

In 1997 Svante Pääbo and his team from Munich succeeded in extracting mitochondrial DNA (mtDNA) from an arm bone of the original Feldhofer Cave Neanderthal. The fossil mtDNA is four times as different from that of living humans as the human subgroups are from each other. Furthermore, the mtDNA is no more similar to that of Europeans than it is to New Guineans, as a continuous regional evolution in Europe would suggest. These results provide genetic evidence that Neanderthals were a distinct species from *Homo sapiens*, that there was no significant interbreeding between species, and that the two species had a common African ancestor, presumably *Homo heidelbergensis*, about 600,000 years ago.

The 600,000 year time frame is calculated from studies of modern human mtDNA. *Homo sapiens* originated about 150,000 years ago. Neanderthals are 4 times as distant as modern populations are from each other; 4 times 150,000 equals 600,000 years ago for the common ancestral population and the estimated time of speciation. Thus, the molecular family tree provides a framework for interpreting Middle Pleistocene fossils. By organizing the fossils geographically, as anthropologist Phillip

Rightmire has done, we can highlight the questions.

Color the speciation event below. Color the *Homo erectus* fossils. Use two colors for *H. heidelbergensis*, one for Africa and one for Europe. Color the tools.

By 1 mya, fossils assigned to *Homo erectus* are abundant in Africa and in Asia. *Homo erectus* remains are found throughout the Middle Pleistocene in Asia, suggesting a long habitation. Stone artifacts such as handaxes are abundant in Africa. In Asia, stone tools well dated at 800,000 years from Bose in South China are the oldest known large cutting tools in East Asia and are compatible with Acheulian technologies in Africa.

The Asian fossils raise a number of questions. Dali in Shaanxi Province in China is unlike *Homo erectus*; its higher braincase resembles *Homo heidelbergensis*, but its affinity to groups in the West is uncertain. On the other hand, the Solo material in Java (Ngandong) is now dated to about 50,000 years ago, much younger than might be interpreted from the robust cranium and cranial capacity (1000 cc). The Solo specimens may represent a different species, *Homo soloensis*, or the persistence of *Homo erectus* at a time when Neanderthals were in Europe and *Homo sapiens* in Africa.

Another long-standing question is whether *Homo erectus* made it into Europe. A hominid presence at Orce in southern Spain represented by Oldowan tools and fragmentary (possibly hominid) bones that are more than a million years old may belong to *Homo erectus*. A fairly complete thick-boned braincase from Ceprano in Italy is about 800,000 years old and might be attributed to *Homo erectus*. The remains of 4 individuals from Gran Dolina have a paleomagnetic date of 780,000 years old. Unfortunately, the most complete individual at this site is a child, which makes it difficult to assign species. These Gran Dolina hominids may represent the ancestral *Homo heidelbergensis*, though they also have been assigned to a new species, *H. antecessor*. At a much later site, Sima de Los Huesos, Neanderthal features are evident in the cranium and mandible of 3 adult skulls dated at 250,000 years old (5-26).

In Africa, several specimens resemble each other. Bodo in Ethiopia, the best dated specimen at 600,000 years old, has a large cranial capacity (1250 cc) as does the Broken Hill cranium from Zambia. Bodo and Broken Hill also resemble each other in cranial and facial shape, and Broken Hill closely resembles Petralona and Arago. Saldanha (Elandsfontein) and Florisbad are similar to each other and to Omo II (5-27).

This framework elucidates the course of *Homo* speciation. In the initial stages of divergence, at about 500,000 years ago, morphology does not clearly distinguish the two lineages. By 150,000 years ago Neanderthal and *Homo sapiens* fossils can be recognized morphologically. As additional fossil and molecular evidence and better dates accumulate, this once-muddled period in human evolution is sure to yield fascinating stories about our origins.

HOMO HEIDELBERGENSIS

MOLECULAR DATA ✱
  H. NEANDERTHALENSIS a
  H. SAPIENS b
  SPECIATION c
FOSSIL RECORD ✱
  H. ERECTUS d
  H. HEIDELBERGENSIS ✱
    AFRICA e   TOOLS g
    EUROPE f

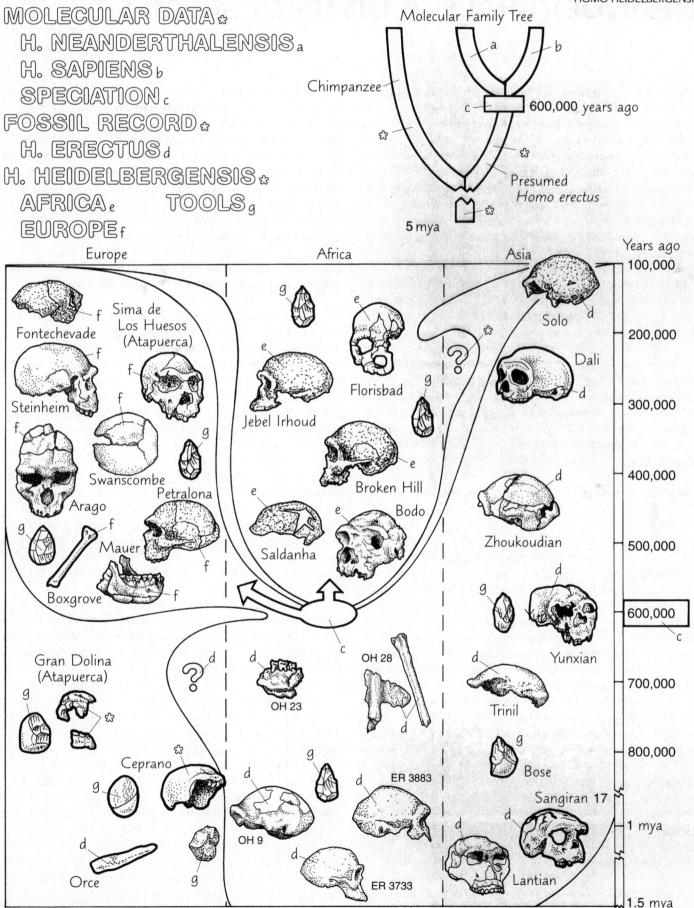

5-26
NEANDERTHALS: A DISTINCT SPECIES

In 1856 a strange skeleton was blasted out of Feldhofer Cave in the Neander Valley (thal=valley) near Dusseldorf, Germany. The skull cap was as large as that of a present-day human but very different in shape; the vault was low, brow ridges were large, and the occipital bone prominent. Ribs and leg bones were heavier and stronger than those of a contemporary human.

Initially this skeleton was interpreted as that of a congenital idiot, a man suffering from rickets (bone malformations due to vitamin D deficiency), or a Cossack fleeing from Napoleon's army who had crawled into the cave and died. Subsequently, numerous Neanderthal remains were found in Belgium, Croatia, France, Spain, Italy, Israel, and Central Asia.

Anthropologists debated for 100 years whether Neanderthals were a distinct species or an ancestor of *Homo sapiens*. In 1997, mitochondrial DNA from the Feldhofer Cave specimen showed decisively that Neanderthals were a distinct lineage. These conclusions were further confirmed when a Russian team led by I.V. Ovchinnikov analyzed mtDNA from a Neanderthal found at Mezmaiskaya Cave in the northern Caucasus, one of the easternmost Neanderthal populations. The mtDNA is very similar to that of the Feldhofer specimen. These data imply that Neanderthals and *Homo sapiens* were separate lineages with a common ancestor, *Homo heidelbergensis*, about 600,000 years ago (5-25).

Color the sample of Neanderthal fossils, the sites, and the time range.

The distribution of the Neanderthals extended from Uzbekistan in the east to the Iberian peninsula in the west, from the margins of the Ice Age glaciers in the north to the shores of the Mediterranean in the south. They lived from about 250,000 Sima to 30,000 years ago in Eurasia. The earlier ones, like Sima de Los Huesos (5-25), were more generalized; the later ones, illustrated here, are the more specialized, "classic" Neanderthals. The last Neanderthals lived in southwest France, Portugal, and Spain as recently as 27,000 years ago. No Neanderthal remains have been discovered in Africa.

The Forbes Quarry, Gibraltar, female cranium was discovered in 1848, eight years before the Feldhofer find, but its distinctive features were not recognized at that time. The Dordogne region of France is among the richest in Neanderthal cave shelters with La Chapelle aux Saints, La Ferrassie, and St. Cesaire, which is one of the younger sites at 36,000. Neanderthals are found across Europe from Krapina in Croatia, Saccopastore in Italy, and Shanidar in Iraq. The 9-year-old youngster from Teshik-Tash, Uzbekistan, lies at the most easterly known part of their range.

Color the Mousterian tools.

Many stone artifacts come from open air or rock-shelter sites and are termed Mousterian (named for Le Moustier Cave, France).

These Middle Paleolithic tools include fine points, sharp knives, scrapers, and points made to haft onto wooden spears. Each of more than 60 such tools had a specialized use. Neanderthals used fire and probably constructed shelters to cover their dwellings in the cold climate. Plant food would have been seasonal and unavailable during the long harsh winters of the glacial environment. They hunted woolly mammoth, woolly rhinoceros, cave bear, ibex, and other game. They doubtless made use of warm animal skins for clothing, blankets, and shelters, although their tool kits lacked items like sewing needles.

Color the Neanderthal and *Homo sapiens* titles, the body outlines, and anatomical features of the skull and limbs.

The Neanderthal braincase has a low forehead, and prominent brow ridges and occipital bone. Cranial capacities overlap and even exceed the average for *Homo sapiens*. The robust face with a broad nasal region projects out from the braincase. The mandible has a high coronoid process and a retromolar space behind the lower third molar. Note that in contrast, the face of modern *Homo sapiens* is tucked under the brain box, the forehead is high, the occipital region rounded, and the chin prominent.

The barrel-shaped chest, and short legs and arms are characteristic of a body type that conserves heat, like modern-day native Alaskans. Neanderthals were strong, rugged, and built for cold weather. Large elbow, hip, and knee joints and robust bones suggest great muscularity. The pelvis had a longer and thinner pubic bone than modern humans. All adult skeletons exhibit some kind of disease or injury. Healed fractures and severe arthritis show that they had a hard life, and individuals rarely lived past 40 years.

Unlike earlier hominids who lived near lakes and rivers, Neanderthals dwelt in cave shelters and buried their dead. Both of these favored fossilization. Also unlike earlier hominids, except for a few rare finds like AL-288, "Lucy" (5-9), the Turkana boy (WT 15000), and the Sterkfontein skeleton (StW 573), the Neanderthals are represented by many complete or nearly complete skeletons. Neanderthals provide the best hominid fossil record of the Plio-Pleistocene, with remains from 500 individuals. About half the skeletons were children, for instance, the 3-year-old child from Devil's Tower, Gibraltar (5-22), the Amud 10-month-old infant (5-28), and Teshik-Tash. Typical cranial and dental features are present in the young individuals, indicating that the Neanderthal features were inherited, not acquired. The rate of dental development was accelerated compared to *Homo sapiens* (5-22).

Despite their abundant fossil record, many questions remain about the lives of this mysterious ice-age species which inhabited Eurasia for at least 200,000 years, until they were replaced by their closest human relatives, our ancestors.

NEANDERTHALS

FOSSIL RECORD ✱
FORBES QUARRY a
FELDHOFER CAVE b
LA CHAPELLE c
LA FERRASSIE d
ST. CESAIRE e

KRAPINA f
SACCOPASTORE g
SHANIDAR h
TESHIK-TASH i
MOUSTERIAN TOOLS j

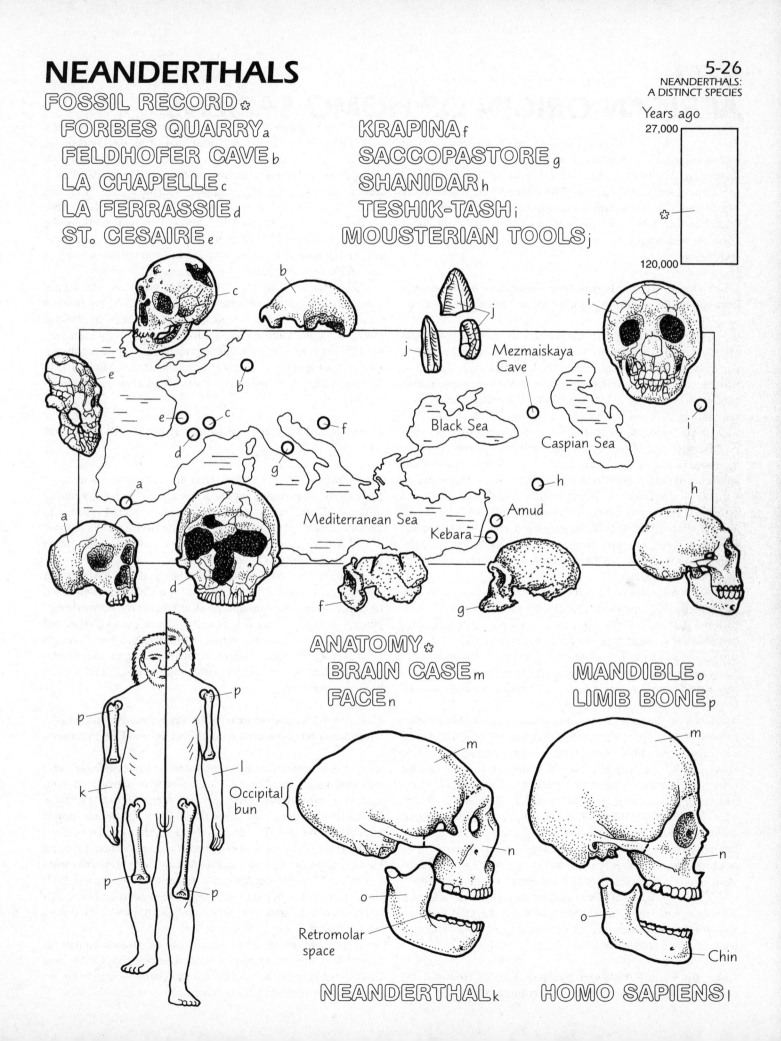

Years ago
27,000

✱

120,000

b

j

i

Mezmaiskaya
Cave

Black Sea

Caspian Sea

e

c
e
d

b

f

h

a

Mediterranean Sea

Amud
Kebara

h

a

d

f

g

g

ANATOMY ✱
BRAIN CASE m
FACE n

MANDIBLE o
LIMB BONE p

p
p
p

l

k

Occipital
bun

m

n

o

Retromolar
space

m

n

o

Chin

p
p

NEANDERTHAL k

HOMO SAPIENS l

AFRICAN ORIGIN OF HOMO SAPIENS

The time and place of *Homo sapiens* origin has preoccupied anthropologists for more than a century. Modern *Homo sapiens* (called Cro-Magnon for its site of discovery in France) appeared in Europe about 35,000 years ago. But where did they come from? Many assumed their origin was in western Asia. In 1987, new mitochondrial DNA data pointed to an African origin about 150,000 years ago. Several lines of evidence support this conclusion.

Color the molecular family tree illustrating relationships between modern human populations in Africa and Eurasia.

Anthropologist Rebecca Cann and colleagues compared the mitochondrial DNA (mtDNA) of Africans, Asians, Caucasians, Australians, and New Guineans. The findings were striking in two respects. First, the variability observed within each population was greatest by far in Africans, which implied the African population was oldest and thus ancestral to the Asians and Caucasians. Second, there was very little variability between populations—only one-tenth as much as between geographically separated populations of chimpanzees—which indicated that our species originated quite recently. The human within-species variability was only one twenty-fifth as much as the average difference between human and chimpanzee mtDNA. The human and chimpanzee lineages diverged about 5 mya, based on much molecular data (2-8). One twenty-fifth of 5 million is 200,000. Cann therefore concluded that *Homo sapiens* originated in Africa about 200,000 years ago.

MtDNA resides in the cell cytoplasm and is passed on only by mothers, since sperm have essentially no cytoplasm (2-11). It follows that all 6 billion human beings on earth today are descended from an African woman who lived about 200,000 years ago. This doesn't mean that only one woman was alive then, more likely there were several thousand, but the mtDNA of the others was lost during intervening generations due to some women having no children or having only sons.

DNA on the male Y chromosomes is passed only through sons (6-7). Analysis of Y chromosomes confirms the mtDNA data: very little variability compared to other species, greatest variability among Africans, and the estimated time of descent (this time from an African male) about 200,000 years. Much additional molecular data involving nuclear DNA and mini- and microsatellites (used in DNA fingerprinting, 2-12) further support a recent African origin of *Homo sapiens*, now estimated to be around 150,000 years ago. The "multiregional hypothesis" of an origin on several different continents between 500,000 to 1 million years ago is not consistent with the molecular genetic evidence.

The fossil record of *Homo sapiens* was difficult to interpret. Although some resembled modern humans, the total evidence was slim and inconclusive. Four sites did suggest modern humans were in Africa at an early date.

Color the Omo Kibish and Ngaloba (Laetoli Hominid 18) crania and sites. Color the time chart gray.

In 1967 Richard Leakey and his team uncovered *in situ* a partial hominid skeleton (Omo I, not illustrated) from the Omo site in Ethiopia, on the banks of the Kibish River. The skull had a high round dome and prominent chin, and the skeleton indicated a tall light frame—features characteristic of Cro-Magnon. A cranial vault (Omo II) had a cranial capacity of over 1400 cubic centimeters. Yet uranium-series dating of shells from the same level gave a date of 130,000 years. Though the Leakeys had found much older hominid species in Africa, this was the first to suggest that *Homo sapiens* too may have had an African origin.

The nearly complete LH 18 skull was found in Upper Ngaloba Beds, dated at about 120,000 years old based on a correlation with the lower unit of the Ndutu Beds at Olduvai Gorge. Like the Omo Kibish skulls, its morphology is largely modern yet it retains some archaic features such as prominent brow ridges and a receding forehead. Anatomist Michael Day described LH 18 as being most similar to Omo I and *Homo sapiens*.

Color the Border Cave and Klasies River Mouth fossils and sites.

Border Cave, near Swaziland, yielded remains of 4 individuals—a partial cranium, 2 lower jaws, and a tiny buried infant. Although fragmentary, the fossils appeared modern to anatomist Hertha de Villiers. The associated tools, similar to those from Klasies River, indicated to archaeologist Peter Beaumont an age of at least 90,000 years.

Klasies River Mouth, located at the tip of South Africa, is a site occupied on and off from 120,000 to 60,000 years ago based on oxygen isotopes, uranium, and electron-spin resonance dating. Human fossils here are fragmentary—cranial, mandibular, and postcranial pieces. Like the remains at Border Cave, human fossils at Klasies River appear modern, especially a fragmentary frontal bone that lacks a brow ridge. Chin and tooth size also have a modern aspect.

Color the Klasies River hearth, food remains, and stone tools. The human remains come from the SASU and LBS members.

The site contains 20 meters of deposits with occupation layers and sand layers interspersed, consistent with nomadic coming and going rather than a permanent settlement. Abundant remains of shellfish gathered off the rocks suggested to archaeologist Hilary Deacon that the site may be the oldest-known seafood "restaurant." The people also hunted eland and buffalo, favoring the very young or very old, and smaller antelope prey. They used red ochre pigment, imported raw material for tools, and built fires. Burnt layers of plants surrounded their hearths. Thousands of flakes, blades, and cores were used and thrown away during the many successive occupations of this site.

The fossil and archaeological finds of modern humans at these 4 African sites, which confused anthropologists for decades, finally make sense in light of the molecular evidence for an African origin about 150,000 years ago.

ORIGIN OF HOMO SAPIENS

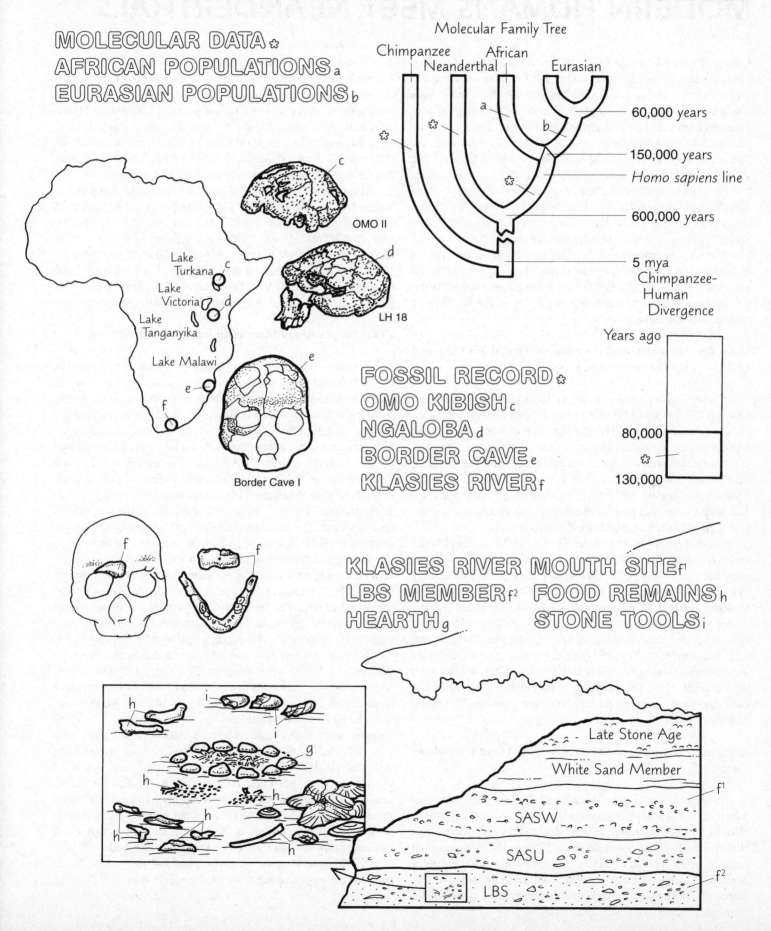

MOLECULAR DATA ✱
AFRICAN POPULATIONS a
EURASIAN POPULATIONS b

Molecular Family Tree

Chimpanzee   Neanderthal   African   Eurasian

60,000 years

150,000 years
Homo sapiens line

600,000 years

5 mya
Chimpanzee-
Human
Divergence

OMO II

LH 18

Lake Turkana
Lake Victoria
Lake Tanganyika
Lake Malawi

Border Cave I

FOSSIL RECORD ✱
OMO KIBISH c
NGALOBA d
BORDER CAVE e
KLASIES RIVER f

Years ago

80,000

130,000

KLASIES RIVER MOUTH SITE f¹
LBS MEMBER f² FOOD REMAINS h
HEARTH g   STONE TOOLS i

Late Stone Age

White Sand Member

f¹

SASW

SASU

LBS

f²

MODERN HUMANS MEET NEANDERTHALS

During the 1930s, excavations led by archaeologist Dorothy Garrod at Mount Carmel Caves, Skhul and Tabun, just yards apart, yielded over a dozen fossil skeletons. About the same time a French team worked at Qafzeh, a cave near Nazareth and uncovered several skeletons, remarkably modern. The individuals appeared to be deliberately buried. Stone tools belonged to a tradition called Levelloiso-Mousterian, so called because the variety of flakes were produced by a prepared core technique. No dating technique known then gave reliable dates for the bones and stones. How were the fossils and tools to be interpreted? Did these sites document the linear evolution of Neanderthal into *Homo sapiens*? Were populations of *Homo sapiens* and Neanderthals interbreeding? Or were there two distinct species living sympatrically in the Jordan Valley? These questions began to be answered during the 1990s. New excavations and new dating techniques revealed a surprising turnabout in the meeting of hominids in the Levant.

Color the time range and the remains from Skhul Cave and Qafzeh Cave. The time range is based on TL dating.

Remains of ten individuals including two infants were recovered from Skhul, a cave hollowed into a steep limestone escarpment southeast of Haifa. Skhul V is the preserved skull, with an estimated cranial capacity of over 1500 cubic centimeters; worn teeth and bones suggest abscess cavities and gum disease. The flint implements recovered belonged to the Levelloiso-Mousterian industry. Wild ox, deer, rhinoceros, hippopotamus, and hyena were also present. Based on tools and fauna, the site was then estimated at 30,000 to 40,000 years old.

Early excavations plus those carried out by anthropologist Bernard Vandermeerch at Qafzeh between 1965 and 1980 uncovered a total of 21 skeletons that were apparently intentionally buried in the cave. Qafzeh IX, the most complete skeleton, is a female about age 20 age; beside her flexed legs lay a very young child. More stone tools of Levalloiso-Mousterian type were also recovered, along with faunal remains of horse, deer, rhinoceros, wild ox, and gazelle. Even though the skeletons were modern looking, Vandermeerch suspected they must be older than 50,000 years. On the basis of the artifacts, archaeologist Ofer Bar-Yosef estimated an even older age, between 70,000 and 100,000 years.

Color the time range and the remains from Amud and Kebara Caves.

From a cave site on the Wadi Amud (Hebrew for pillar) near Tiberius, a Tokyo University team directed by paleontologist Hisashi Suzuki uncovered 4 individuals in 1961. Amud 1 is a skeleton badly crushed, a male about 25 years old, with a cranial capacity over 1700 cubic centimeters, more than any known fossil hominid. Associated Levalloiso-Mousterian tools and fossils of mammals, birds, and reptiles were then estimated to be 30,000 years old.

During 1992, anatomist Yoel Rak carried out further excavations; he had been inspired by a visit to the site as a teenager. Rak's team unearthed the remains of a 10-month-old child (Amud 7). Its elongated, oval foramen magnum, lack of a chin, and mandibular tubercle are unique Neanderthal traits, and their presence in an infant indicates they are genetically determined—strong evidence that Neanderthals were a separate and distinct species, not merely a branch of *Homo sapiens*.

Excavations in 1983 at Kebara Cave revealed a skeleton that lacked the cranium and lower limbs, but preserved an important bone, the most complete Neanderthal pelvis known (Kebara 2). The cave, inhabited over a long time, yielded more than 25,000 tools of the Levallois industry, as well as hearths used to roast vegetables and gazelle and deer. Dumps of animal bones and stone tool waste were found at the rear of the cave. Burnt flint from the hearths turned out to be crucial in dating the cave.

Color the process of thermoluminescence (TL) dating.

Thermoluminescence, a new dating method, confirmed that the Qafzeh and Skhul sites with modern humans *predated* those of the Neanderthals by about 30,000 years. Prehistorian Helene Valladas and colleagues used flint tools to measure the cumulative effects of radioactivity on flint tools. Radioactive decay of elements such as potassium, thorium, and uranium cause electrons to be trapped in the crystal structures of stones and calcified tissues. When a scientist heats a sample of ancient stone or tooth, the trapped electrons are released and emit light—known as thermoluminescence—from which the age of the sample can be calculated. The more intense the light given off, the longer the time elapsed since those flints were burnt in a hearth.

Recall that the potassium/argon clock (5-4) is at zero while lava flows and argon gas escapes into the atmosphere. In a similar fashion, the flint artifacts were set to zero when hominids heated them in a hearth. The heat drove out any electrons that were already trapped. Electrons began to accumulate again when the burnt flint cooled off, just as argon gets trapped when lava cools.

Neanderthal remains and artifacts in the Israeli caves of Kebara and Amud were dated by TL to about 60,000 years. Modern-looking skeletons from the nearby caves of Qafzeh and Skhul, dated in the same way, turned out to be about 90,000 years old. The Neanderthals could not have been ancestral to modern humans, since *Homo sapiens* arrived 30,000 years earlier than they did. The 90,000 year date for *Homo sapiens* in Israel fits well with an "Out of Africa" hypothesis, for western Asia is on the direct path between Africa and Asia. Furthermore, anatomically modern humans from eastern and southern Africa dated even earlier, about 120,000 years old, whereas Neanderthals have not been found south of the Levant. Thus, several lines of evidence converge—mtDNA, the morphology of the fossils, and modern dating techniques—to support an African origin for *Homo sapiens*, a lineage distinct from the Neanderthals.

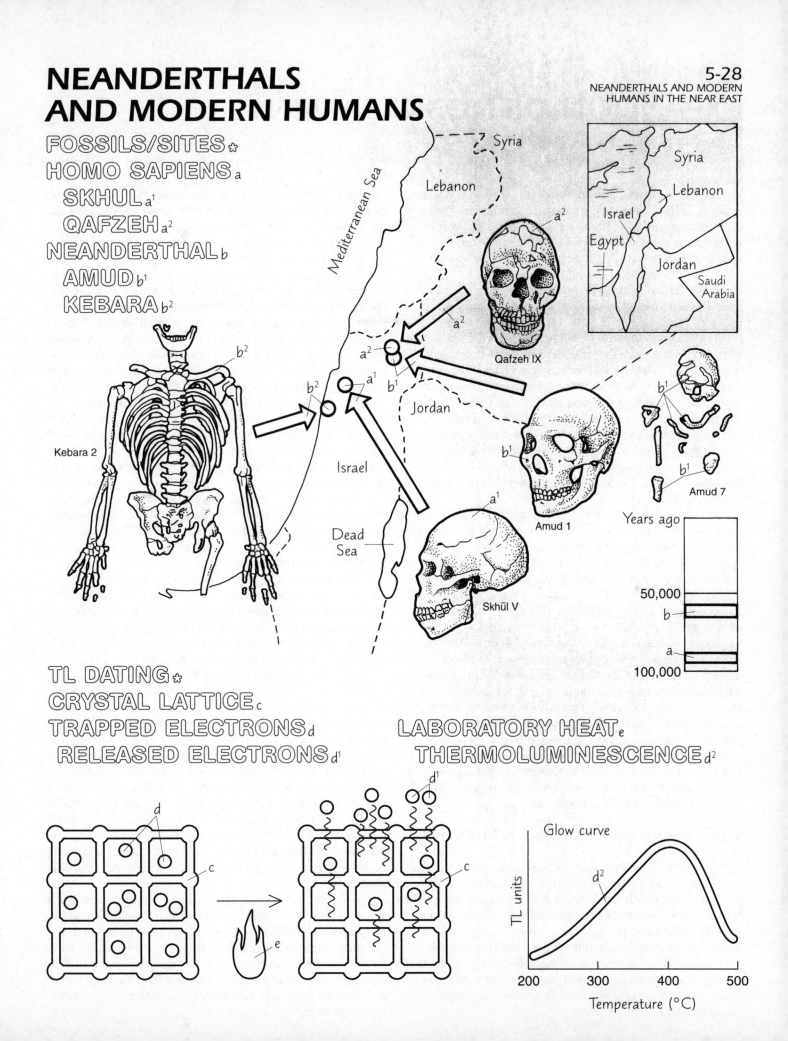

NEANDERTHALS AND MODERN HUMANS

FOSSILS/SITES ✷
HOMO SAPIENS a
  SKHUL a¹
  QAFZEH a²
NEANDERTHAL b
  AMUD b¹
  KEBARA b²

Mediterranean Sea

Syria

Lebanon

a²

a²

a²

b¹

Qafzeh IX

b²

Kebara 2

b²

a¹

Jordan

Israel

Dead
Sea

b¹

Amud 1

b¹

b¹

Amud 7

a¹

Skhūl V

Syria

Lebanon

Israel

Egypt

Jordan

Saudi
Arabia

Years ago

50,000

b

a

100,000

TL DATING ✷
CRYSTAL LATTICE c
TRAPPED ELECTRONS d   LABORATORY HEAT e
  RELEASED ELECTRONS d¹   THERMOLUMINESCENCE d²

d¹

d

c

c

e

Glow curve

d²

TL units

Temperature (°C)

200   300   400   500

5-29
EXPANSION OF HOMO SAPIENS

We turn now from the physical features of our ancestors to their material culture. Their sophisticated artifacts and art challenge us to comprehend the minds and emotions thus expressed. What made our ancestors so successful? How can their created works and symbols help us understand the sources of that success?

Color the arrows on the map and the time chart showing the approximate times of expansion. Use light colors.

Homo sapiens evidently left Africa by way of the Near East some 90,000 years ago. They may have avoided the Neanderthals, flourishing in Europe at this time, by taking the warmer, more southerly pathway into South and Southeast Asia, reaching Australia between 50,000 and 60,000 years ago. Some migrants expanded into central and northern Asia and still later to North and South America via the Beringian land bridge from Siberia about 15,000 years ago. A site at Monte Verde in Chile may be twice that age, and its inhabitants may have arrived by boat along the western coasts. The peopling of the New World is a subject of ongoing debate.

For many decades Western Europe was considered the center for modern human evolution, but we now know that this area was one of the later to be occupied, rather than the earliest. Anatomically modern fossils of Cro-Magnon associated with spectacular cave paintings and mobile art led many to assume that art originated here. But looking more globally, we find artistic expression to be a universal human feature, perhaps independent of language.

Artistic creativity takes innumerable forms: carvings on objects and walls, paintings, and engravings. They depict scenes of people and animals, abstract notations, and designs. Items that have endured to the present time display only one component of the ancient artistry that almost certainly included body adornment and perishable baskets, mats, bags, and cloth. Red ochre pigment preserved at Klasies River Cave and Blombos Cave in South Africa may have been used as body decoration around 100,000 years ago, and 70,000-year-old decorated ostrich eggshells at Diepkloof Cave near Cape Town, South Africa, are perhaps the oldest known examples of deliberate art.

Color examples of artistic expression as each is discussed.

In Africa, engravings and paintings of people and animals are preserved in numerous rock faces and shelters not well protected from the elements, and it is likely that far more have been lost due to weathering and erosion. Some are dated to more than 20,000 years, though many others cannot be dated. Renderings of giraffe and springbok prey, and of people at work, such as the San women with weighted digging sticks and collecting bags at KwaZulu Natal, men returning from the hunt, or the musician playing his pipe, all illustrate the imagination, creativity, and skill of the artists.

Rock paintings and engravings in Australia may be more than 35,000 years old; many cannot be dated. In Arnhem Land the Tasmanian wolf, there extinct more than 3000 years, is depicted, and engravings of animal footprints, perhaps of emu, and abstract rayed circles are pecked into rock faces.

In Europe, spectacular multichromed images of mammoths, rhinoceros, big cats, bears, and bison have been well preserved, protected deep within caves. The pigments of the Chauvet Cave paintings in southeastern France are dated at 32,000 years by carbon 14. Altamira in Spain and Lascaux Cave in the Dordogne region of France, dated at 17,000 years old depict dynamic action paintings of horses, bison, and deer. We see carved bone with elaborate designs and a series of "Venus figures" of well-endowed females; the oldest is the Dolni Vestonice at 26,000 years. The "spotted horse" of mammoth ivory from Russia, almost 30,000 years old may have decorated a garment and then been buried with its owner. Wildlife from Patagonia is depicted in cave art from Monte Verde, along with the stenciled human hand, one of the most ancient and frequently rendered objects at many sites.

Circles and crescents gouged into bone dated at 32,000 years may have been the first known astronomical notation according to archaeologist Alexander Marshack. Personal decoration flourished in the form of necklaces made from shells, lions' and bears' teeth, and colored stones.

This outburst of artistic creativity did not spring full-blown from the *Homo sapiens* brain. Foreshadowing of artistic ability can be seen in elaborately made stone and bone tools for over a million years. Nevertheless the rather sudden explosion of paintings and carvings depicting figures of humans and animals suggests a new level of human awareness and technical skill.

Brain research shows that spatial skills such as drawing, building, and navigating are located in the right hemisphere, whereas language and analytical thinking are in the left. The key brain area for painting, according to neurologist Bruce Miller, is the right posterior parietal lobe. If this area is injured, the individual cannot draw. Miller has observed a condition known as "frontotemporal dementia" in which individuals deteriorate mentally and become unable to speak or take care of themselves; yet several of these patients suddenly developed remarkable artistic ability. Nuclear scans demonstrate the die-off of brain cells in the right anterior temporal region. Miller hypothesizes that this region normally inhibits a center for art creation in the posterior parietal region, and when damaged, it releases the artistic module.

Whatever the neurological basis for artistic creativity, it seems to be as distinctive a characteristic of modern humans as language, and indeed it is another form of expression and communication highly valued by all human societies. We don't know how long our *Homo sapiens* ancestors were able to exchange thoughts and ideas by talking with each other, but we do know they were extraordinarily sophisticated artists for thousands of generations.

EXPANSION OF HOMO SAPIENS

AFRICA a   SOUTH ASIA c   CENTRAL/NORTH EUROPE f

WESTERN ASIA b   AUSTRALIA d   ASIA e   NORTH AMERICA/

SOUTH AMERICA g

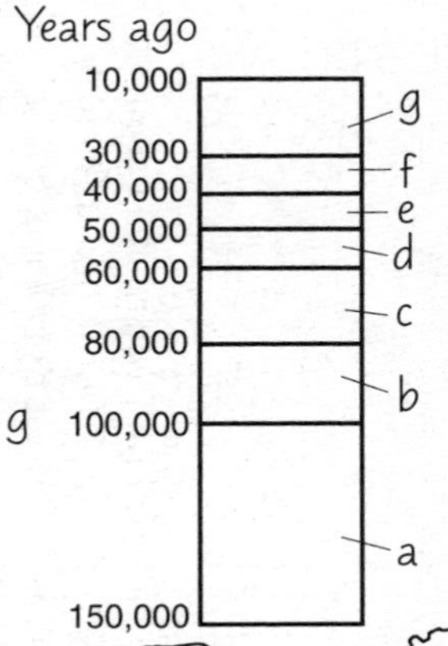

Years ago

10,000
30,000
40,000
50,000
60,000
80,000
100,000

150,000

g
f
e
d
c
b

a

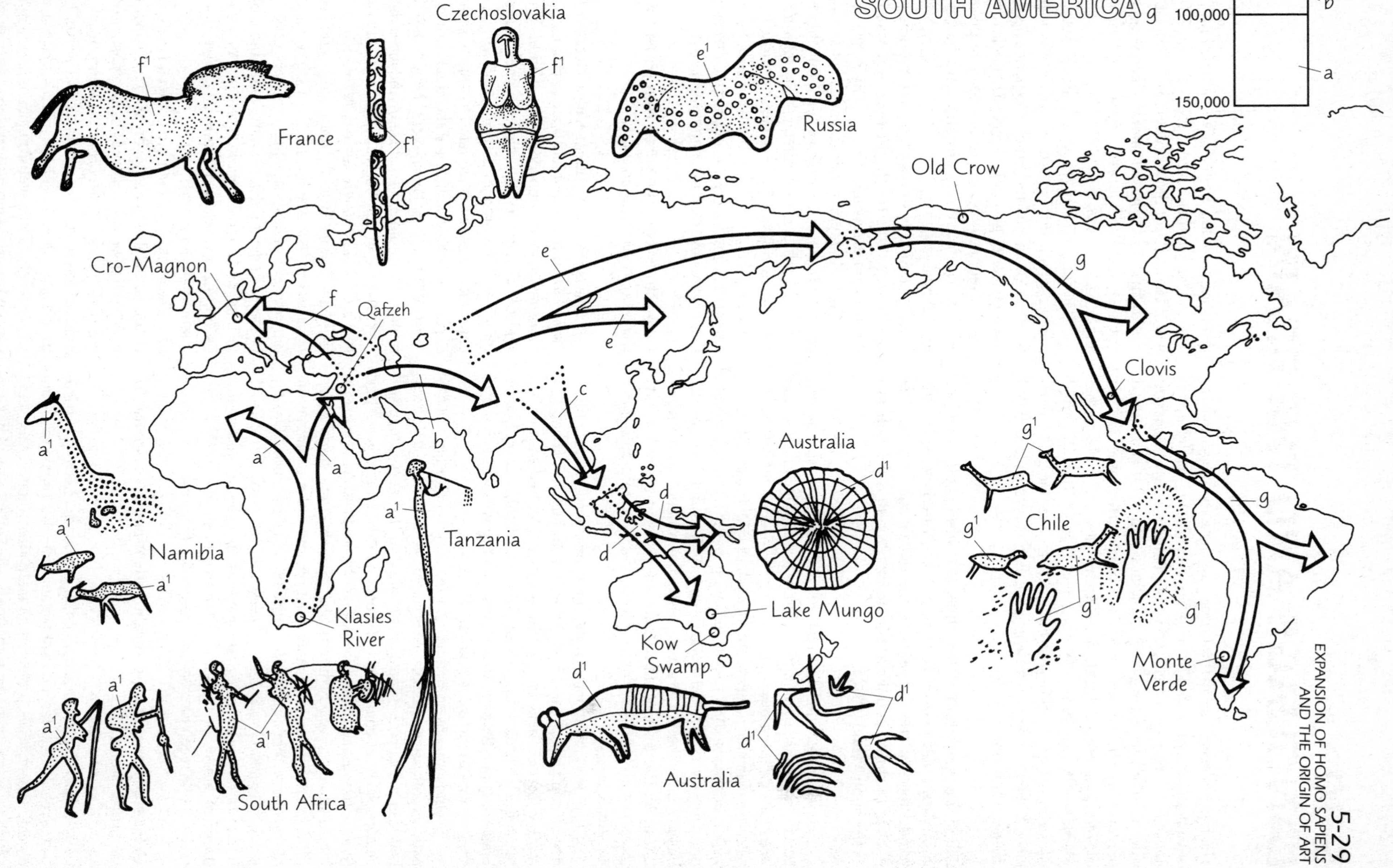

Clovis

Monte
Verde

Chile

Old Crow

Russia

Czechoslovakia

France

Cro-Magnon

Qafzeh

Australia

Lake Mungo

Kow Swamp

Australia

Tanzania

Klasies
River

South Africa

Namibia

5-30
LANGUAGE AND THE BRAIN

The two halves of the cerebral cortex appear to be mirror images of each other, but each half becomes specialized. The left brain houses the language centers and verbal abilities, whereas the right side is suited for such tasks as facial recognition and spatial perception. The corpus callosum connects the two cerebral cortices and transmits their perceptions back and forth, so that we have the subjective experience of a single integrated consciousness. Studies of split-brain patients over the last 40 years have shown the degree to which the two halves have evolved different functions.

Color the upper half of the plate. It is important to choose contrasting light colors for (b) and (c). Note how the right-hand image, a tree, appears in the left visual cortex at the back of the brain and the left-hand image, a squirrel, appears at the right visual cortex.

Sensations affecting the right side of the body—vision, touch, hearing—are projected onto the left brain, as in the image of the tree. This crossing over explains why damage to the left brain, where the language centers are located, usually causes difficulty with speech as well as loss of sensation on the right side. Right-brain injury causes left-sided sensory loss but less speech impairment. The left brain processes information in a verbal, linear, logical manner. The right, nonspeaking brain responds more emotionally and more globally—we might say, more artistically.

The two hemispheres of the brain are connected by a thick neural cable called the corpus callosum. In humans, about 250 million nerve fibers pass through this cable, and billions of messages go back and forth all the time. In chimpanzees, with brains only one-third the size of ours, the corpus callosum is much smaller, and in monkeys it is smaller still.

Neurosurgeons sometimes cut the corpus callosum to help patients with severe epilepsy. This surgery cuts off communication between the right and left hemispheres, so that nerve impulses causing seizures cannot spread from one side to the other. After this operation, each half of the brain becomes unaware of sensory information received by the other half. Patients show surprisingly little overt change in mental function, but close examination reveals some remarkable alterations in thought patterns. During the 1960s, neurologist Roger Sperry and his associates carried out tests on these split-brain patients that demonstrated the different modes of thinking in the two hemispheres. For this research, he received a Nobel Prize.

Color study one, the split-brain patient and his response to the word "horse."

Michael Gazzaniga and his colleague, Joseph LeDoux carried out psychological tests on split-brain patients. The name of an object, "horse," was projected on the patient's left visual field, which is connected to the right brain. The patient denied having seen anything. Without an intact corpus callosum, the speechless

right brain couldn't tell the verbal left brain what it had seen. The patient was then asked to try to draw a picture of the "unseen" word. He couldn't draw it with his dominant right hand, but he could draw it with his left hand, which is controlled by the right brain. He drew a picture of a horse—and still denied having seen anything.

These responses show how art can retrieve sensations and images which the individual cannot access through language. Since so many of the crucial experiences in our life—birth, nursing, learning to walk—preceded our acquisition of language, we can see why conscious memories of these formative events are hard to retrieve, and why art often achieves insights that elude logical analysis.

Gazzaniga believes that there are not just two but many modules within the brain that process sensory input and information independently. It's only when all the modules have sent in their reports that the conscious mind tries to make a coherent narrative. The story is put together by what Gazzaniga calls "the left brain interpreter." The interpreter does the best it can, but it doesn't have access to most of the modules that determine behavior, only the ones with verbal labels. Lacking complete knowledge, the interpreter makes up an explanation that bridges over the missing information.

Color study two, the split-brain patient who is correlating the images and responses.

One split-brain patient had a picture of a chicken's foot projected on his verbal left brain and at the same time a picture of a snowman surrounded by snow on his right brain. Asked to select from a group of pictures the ones he associated with these images, he simultaneously pointed with his right hand to a chicken, and with his left hand to a snow shovel. When asked to explain his choices, he cited the chicken foot but not the snow. "Why did you pick the shovel?" he was asked. He thought for a minute and replied, "To clean up the mess the chicken makes."

One job of our "logical" left brain is to explain things, even if the explanations are just-so stories like Kipling's "How the Elephant Got its Trunk." (A crocodile grabbed and stretched its nose!) There is a fine line between science and story-telling. But our mastery of language and numbers gave us the explanatory power to understand and control much more of the world we live in than our remote ancestors could. As we saw in 3-35, even chimpanzees can use symbols to overcome some of their instinctual limitations.

The evolution of our big brain and the specialized functions of the hemispheres has given us two distinct minds in the same head. What we call reality is being constantly negotiated across the fiber optics of the corpus callosum. Just as the left and right brain chat constantly, scientists and artists have a lot to learn from each other. Two hemispheres make a whole brain and a whole world. To be well-rounded individuals and members of a well-balanced community, we need both science and art.

LEFT BRAIN INTERPRETER

INTACT CORPUS CALLOSUM a

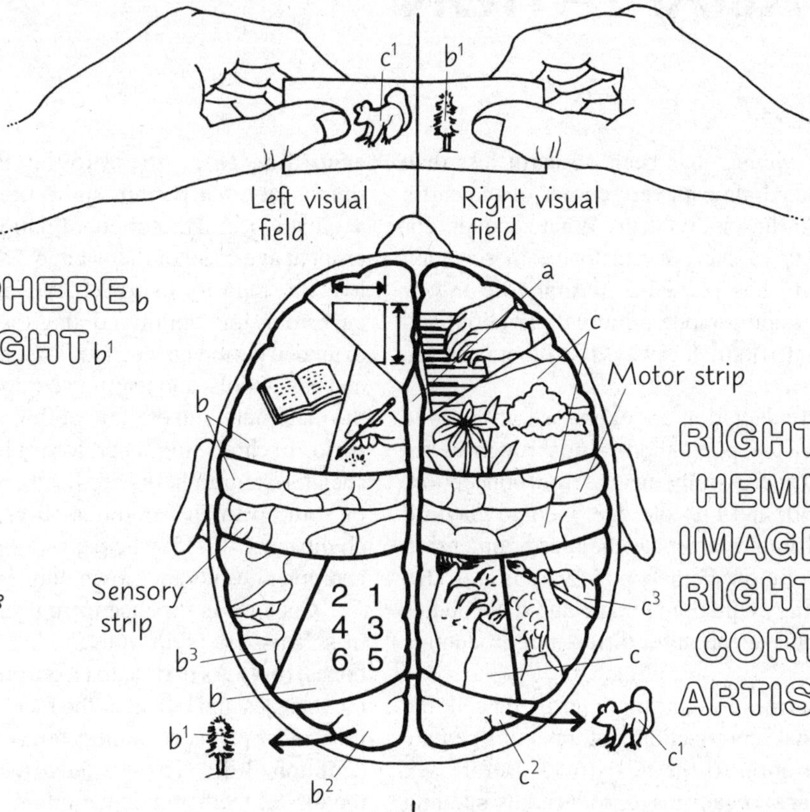
c1
b1
Left visual field
Right visual field
a
c
Motor strip
b
Sensory strip
2 1
4 3
6 5
b3
b
b1
b2
c3
c
c1
c2

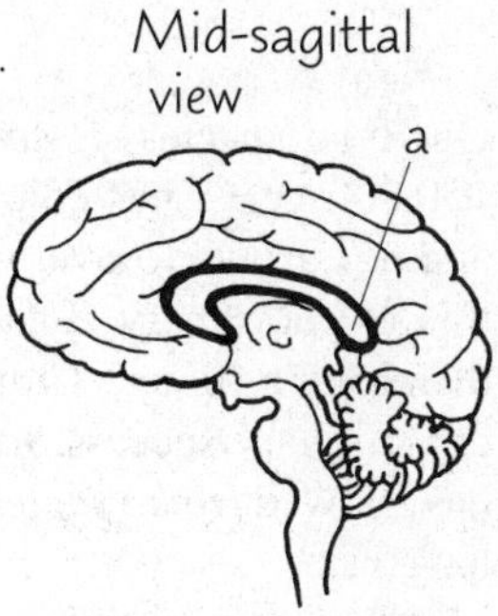
Mid-sagittal view
a

LEFT HEMISPHERE b
IMAGE ON RIGHT b1
LEFT VISUAL CORTEX b2
VERBAL b3

RIGHT HEMISPHERE c
IMAGE ON LEFT c1
RIGHT VISUAL CORTEX c2
ARTISTIC c3

SPLIT BRAIN*

STUDY 1*
VISUAL STIMULUS c
RIGHT HEMISPHERE c
LEFT HEMISPHERE b

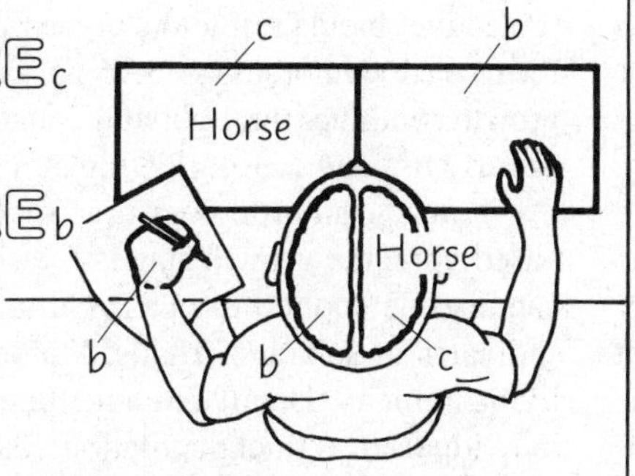
c
b
Horse
Horse
b
b
c

VERBAL RESPONSE*
LEFT HEMISPHERE b

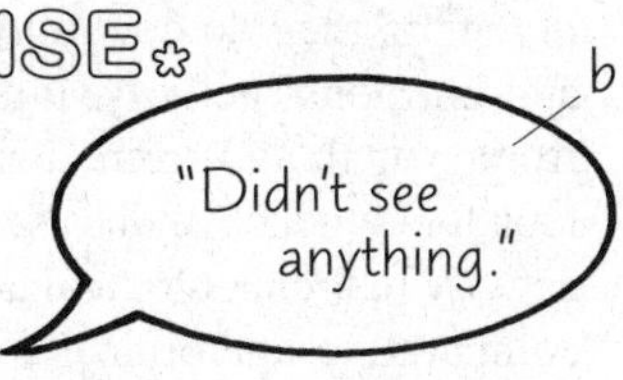
b
"Didn't see anything."

ARTISTIC RESPONSE*
RIGHT HEMISPHERE c

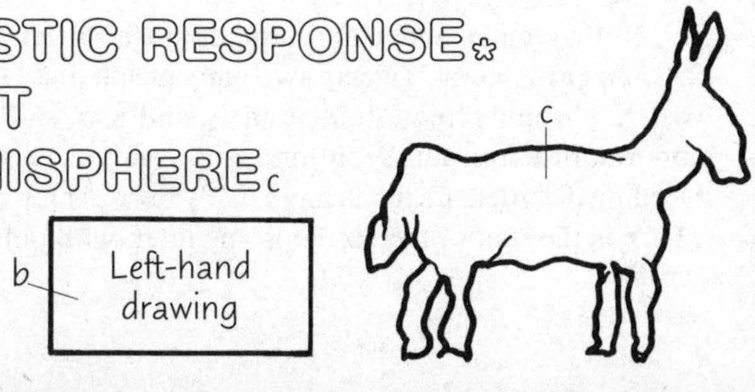
b
Left-hand drawing
c

STUDY 2*
VISUAL STIMULUS c,b

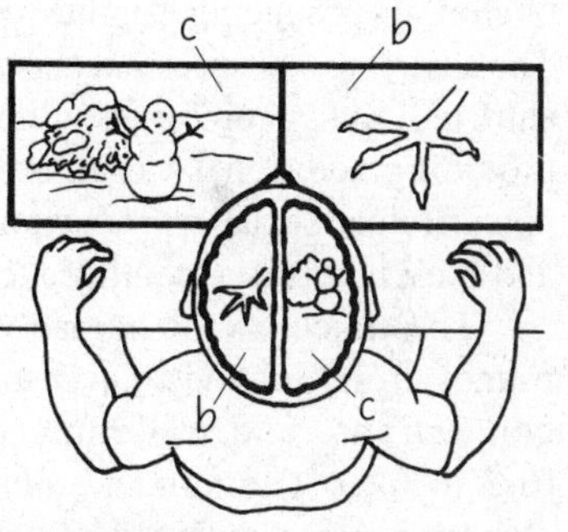
c
b
b
c

VISUAL RESPONSE*

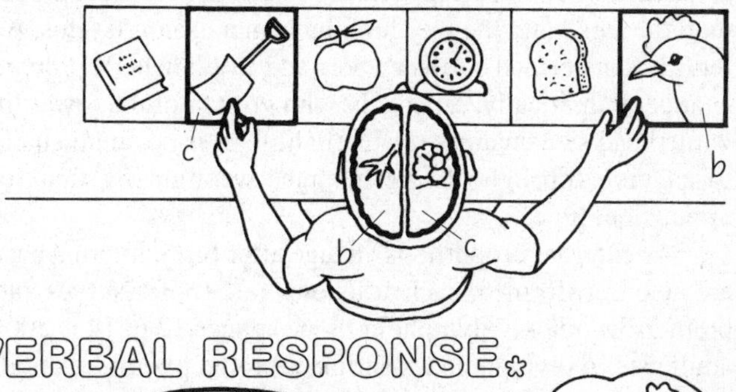
c
b
b
c

VERBAL RESPONSE*

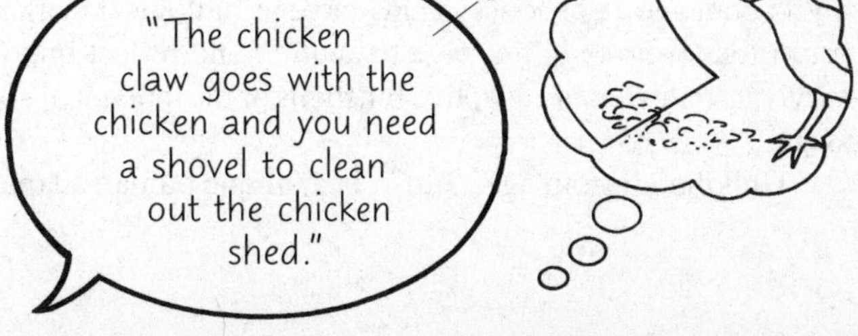
b
"The chicken claw goes with the chicken and you need a shovel to clean out the chicken shed."

SECTION 6
HUMAN ADAPTATION

Our own species, *Homo sapiens,* has been on earth less than 150,000 years, has colonized almost every corner of the earth, and has grown to over 6 billion individuals. What accounts for this extraordinary capacity to survive and thrive in so many different milieus? Culture has played a pivotal role in our evolutionary success, in shaping modern human variation, and has allowed *Homo sapiens* to flourish in ways that other primates have not.

Human variation and adaptation are expressed at multiple levels—genetic, individual, and population—and through all life stages. An individual must successfully survive from conception, through growth, adulthood, and into old age. George Gaylord Simpson referred to this "time" element as the fourth dimension in the study of human evolution. Female/male variation is also factored into the evolutionary equation; female and male bodies have been shaped by natural selection for different reproductive functions.

A human individual grows from a single fertilized cell, the zygote—a product of sexual reproduction that transmits genetic variation from one generation to the next (6-1). Before sex originated a billion years ago, organisms reproduced by budding or cloning, producing daughter cells identical to the single parent. The advantage of sex is that genes from two parents are constantly shuffled and recombined within a breeding population, thus providing additional variation for natural selection to operate upon. Human sexual reproduction, like that of Old World monkeys and apes, involves a monthly cycle of egg production and release.

The trajectory of human development plays out in time frames, from cell division, gestation, life stages, parent to child, generations, and millennia of adaptation and migration (6-2 to 6-5). The human embryo follows an ancient genetic blueprint for a segmented body (6-2), encountered in our earlier discussion of homeobox genes (2-14). The head is more prominent than the torso and the tiny limb buds in a 2-month fetus. As the fetus is transformed into a newborn and an adult, body proportions change dramatically, especially with growth of the lower limbs, while head size changes relatively little. It is no small challenge to survive through all the changes wrought by that fourth dimension, time.

As external proportions change after birth, internal systems are also transformed, each at its own rate (6-3). Nerves and the brain grow quickly; lymphoid tissue at ages 12 to 14 is 200% of adult size. As lymph nodes shrink, reproductive tissues undergo their growth spurt. Bones, teeth, and body mass continue to grow until about age 18. These systems serve as biological markers of transitions from one life stage to another and reflect important survival strategies and adaptive functions of the individual at each stage.

Childhood, from ages 3 to 7, is a unique human adaptation according to anthropologist Barry Bogin—an extended immaturity that permits more time for brain growth, language acquisition, and motor coordination. Our first permanent molars erupt at age 6 rather than at age 3 as in chimpanzees, and it takes twice as long for us to achieve 90% of adult brain size. In our ancestors, this childhood stage would have been vital for the extended period needed to master social communication, making and using tools, and learning complex foraging techniques. From the maternal point of view, childhood involves a more prolonged period of caretaking. Therefore, it is essential to have a supportive social system to help care for the young, a phenomenon we see in some primate societies (lion tamarins, 4-13, and gracile chimpanzees, 4-35) where group members share food with infants and juveniles not their own, thus freeing mothers to breed again.

Changes in the face from birth to old age reflect alterations in soft tissues (skin, muscle, hair) and hard tissues (teeth and bones) (6-4). As permanent teeth erupt and the child chews harder, the muscles and bones of the face are transformed. In contrast to most other primates, human females and males have very similar dentition (3-30). The use and disuse of masticatory muscles, and the loss of teeth and concomitant resorption of bone modify the shape of an individual's head and face with advancing age. These complex considerations must be applied in interpreting the fragmentary fossil remains of teeth, jaws, and skulls.

The skeleton is the scaffold on which our body is built, a protective shield for internal organs, and, conjoined with muscles, forms the locomotor system (6-5). Unlike reptiles, whose skeletal growth continues throughout life, mammalian bones grow rapidly in early life and cease growing at maturity.

Forensic anthropologists can assign age in years to skeletons based upon the growth stage of various bones. Such evaluation can also be applied to our fossil ancestors to assess rough age estimates of subadult fossils. Mathematical estimates based on living humans also give us a method to reconstruct the stature of individuals in extinct populations. Although bones cease to grow in length, they do continue to remodel in response to muscular and hormonal activity, injury, aging, and disease. Using clues from growth and formation of cortical and trabecular bone, we look for evidence of disease and occupational markers of physical activity in archaeological and fossil skeletal remains. Using this comparative anatomical perspective, anthropologists interpret diet, health, and environmental insults that affected our ancient relatives (6-6).

Both female and male humans have 46 chromosomes, 23 from each parent. Twenty-two pairs match, but females have two X chromosomes, males an X and a Y (6-7). Genetic abnormalities on an X chromosome such as hemophilia, a bleeding disorder, are much more likely to be expressed in males. The Y is the runt of the chromosome litter, with only 20 genes, compared to 3000 genes on other chromosomes. Its main function is to switch the growing embryo from default female to male. Most of the Y chromosome does not recombine and so is passed virtually unchanged from father to son, tagging male lineages, the way mitochondrial DNA tags female lineages (2-11). For instance, analysis of Y chromosomes of European men showed that 80% of them were descended from a common male ancestor who lived about 40,000 years ago.

Females and males differ primarily in their reproductive apparatus but secondarily in body shape and tissue composition (6-8). Adult women on average are shorter than men in the same population, have broader pelvises, narrower shoulders, and more body fat, especially in the breasts and thighs. This extra fat may have been an adaptation to the energy demands of walking long distances while carrying and nursing infants. Abundant food and the sedentary lifestyle of modern urban people turns this evolutionary advantage into a problem, as obesity with its attendant diseases, such as diabetes, is becoming epidemic in both women and men.

All women have the same basic biology, but cultural practices produce profoundly different patterns of reproduction in foragers, farmers, and industrialized urban dwellers (6-9). In all cultures, women have the main responsibility for raising the children. Among the !Kung San foragers of Botswana, a woman walks on average 12 kilometers a day, much of that time carrying a child and 11 kilograms of food. Infants suckle vigorously until they are 3 to 4 years old, thus suppressing ovulation in women and delaying their next pregnancy. !Kung women average 5 offspring. In agricultural communities, women breast-feed less, have children at shorter intervals, and a greater lifetime total of 8 to 10 children. The average modern urban woman delays her first pregnancy and has few (2 or 3) children.

Skin, the largest organ of the human body, was essential for the survival of our ancestors on the African savannas. Rather than consisting of a single trait, skin forms a functional complex that cools and protects the brain and body in a sunny tropical environment (6-10). Eccrine sweat glands cool the skin by evaporation, and dark pigmentation protects the body from the damaging effects of ultraviolet light. Ultraviolet light also stimulates the manufacture of vitamin D, essential for normal bone growth. Skin color varies within and between populations. The light-colored skin of higher latitudes such as Scandinavia, where the sun is less intense, permits better absorption of ultraviolet rays.

Milk is the main food of newborn mammals, its digestion is made possible by the enzyme lactase in the small intestine (6-11). In most of the world's human populations, lactase decreases rapidly with age, so that after age 4, drinking milk produces indigestion and diarrhea. A few populations in northern Europe and Africa, who have kept dairy cattle for thousands of years, maintain high lactase levels and drink milk throughout life.

Millions of people live at high altitudes where oxygen is scarce (6-12). Low oxygen affects the whole body, especially the muscles and brain, and increases infant mortality. The body adapts in the short term by breathing more rapidly and deeply and by increasing cardiac output. Longer range adaptations involve increased numbers of red cells and increased lung volume. People who have been living at high altitudes for longer periods of time, like the Tibetans, are physiologically better adapted than Andeans, who in turn are better adapted than North American groups who have lived in the high Rockies for only a few generations.

Genetic traits, such as the ABO blood groups, vary in frequency among populations around the world (6-13). Traits that defend against disease can be favored by natural selection, even if these traits themselves cause harm to the individual. Sickle cells are red cells of abnormal shape due to a variant hemoglobin (6-14). Heterozygotes, with both normal and sickle hemoglobin, are resistant to malaria, the biggest killer in the tropical world. Homozygotes have sickle cell anemia, a painful, life-shortening genetic disorder. Cultural practices such as slash-and-burn agriculture favored the mosquitoes that cause malaria, and the sickle trait is common in these areas (6-15).

Migrating populations take their genes and their languages with them, and both genes and language evolve with time (6-16). Geneticist L.L. Cavalli-Sforza has found remarkable correspondences in modern human populations between their genetic and linguistic family trees. Human tongues are not inborn but must be taught and learned by each new generation. Nevertheless, the capacity for language is written in our genome and manifested in the structures of our brain. These two kinds of languages are intimately intertwined in reflecting our evolutionary history. With usual prescience, Charles Darwin wrote in *On Origin of Species,* "If we possessed a perfect pedigree of mankind, a genealogical arrangement of the races of man would afford the best classification of the various languages now spoken throughout the world."

Cultural responses to the environment, mediated through features such as language and technology, give the human species the ability to go beyond biology to tap into the knowledge and tools of previous generations. These expanded possibilities can be used in innovative ways in the present and in the future to respond to ecological, social, and biological challenges. Our ability to adapt with nongenetic, traditional, and cultural means is a major evolutionary breakthrough and has increased the survival and reproduction of humans to an unprecedented degree.

6-1
SEXUAL REPRODUCTION

Eukaryotes, organisms with nucleated cells, appeared about a billion years ago, according to the fossil record. Eukaryotes reproduce sexually, combining genetic material from two parents to form two new individuals. In contrast, prokaryotes, cells without a nucleus, divide asexually to form two new organisms identical to the original. The mixture of genetic material from two parents, rather than one, increases the genetic diversity and variation within a species. Sexual reproduction through recombination of genes, along with mutation, is a source of variation within populations. Genetic variation is essential for evolutionary change through natural selection (1-17).

Fertilization is the first of several steps involved in sexual reproduction. Fertilization is internal in mammals, rather than external as it is in most invertebrates and fishes. In most mammals, females ovulate only during an annual or biannual breeding season. In humans, apes, and Old World monkeys, mating is not seasonal, but can occur monthly. Fertilization is synchronized with an ovarian cycle, when the uterine lining, called the endometrium, thickens in preparation for implantation of a newly fertilized egg and is sloughed off if fertilization does not occur.

Begin with the diagram below and color the components of the ovarian and menstrual cycles. Choose a light color for (d).

A woman's two ovaries at birth contain her lifetime supply of eggs, approximately 400,000 oocytes arrested in the first stage of meiosis (1-14). When she reaches sexual maturity, her ovarian cycles begin and continue until menopause. Each cycle passes through three phases—the follicular, ovulatory, and luteal. A follicle is a sac that surrounds the developing oocyte. One follicle matures each month, under the influence of follicle-stimulating hormone (FSH) from the pituitary gland in the brain, and on or about day 14, the mature oocyte bursts through the ovarian wall, a process called ovulation. The now-empty follicle collapses and forms the corpus luteum ("yellow body") under the influence of the pituitary's luteinizing hormone (LH).

The corpus luteum secretes the female hormones progesterone and estrogen, which stimulate the endometrium to grow and prepare for pregnancy. At ovulation, the endometrium is thick and velvety. If the egg is fertilized, the corpus luteum produces more progesterone, which enhances the endrometrium's ability to sustain the embryo. If fertilization and implantation fail, the corpus luteum degenerates and the endometrium is shed, producing menstrual bleeding. Then a new ovarian cycle begins.

On the diagram in the center right, color the arrow representing sperm, and the vagina, cervix, and uterus.

During mating, sperm enter the vagina, then pass through the cervix into the uterus, and swim toward the egg that has been released into the fallopian tube.

Color the follicle as it matures in the ovary in the large central diagram. Color the oogonium, oocyte, and the corpus luteum there. Now color the events associated with fertilization. First color the structures on the small right hand diagram, then on the large one, starting with the ovary and the released oocyte. Four enlarged drawings illustrate the steps leading to fusion of the female and male gametes to form the zygote. As you read, color your way to the left and around to the right, through events leading to the implantation of the blastocyst in the uterine wall.

When the oocyte is released from the ovary, it finishes the first meiotic division, and a secondary oocyte and the first polar body are produced (1-14). The secondary oocyte, now the ovum (left enlargement), is drawn into the horn-shaped opening of the fallopian tube. Normally, several sperm reach the ovum simultaneously, but only one is able to digest its way through the cell wall. This entry of the sperm into the ovum, the act of fertilization, stimulates the second meiotic division, which produces a second polar body without cytoplasm.

The ovum carries cytoplasm containing the mitochondrial DNA (2-11). The female and male pronuclei each carry a haploid set of 23 chromosomes. These two sets unite to form the zygote and make up a full complement of 46 chromosomes, the genetic material of the new offspring. Within 20 hours the zygote divides by mitosis into two cells called blastomeres, each half the size of the ovum. (Here the metaphase of mitosis is illustrated.)

The polar bodies disintegrate and disappear. After 4 mitotic divisions, the zygote consists of 16 cells and is called a morula (Latin for mulberry). The zygote hollows out, as shown in the cross section. Now called the blastocyst, it implants in the endometrium, where a new human being begins to grow.

Women's reproductive cycles are very variable. Athletes and dancers with low body fat, or women who have anorexia and lose a lot of weight, tend to have low fertility and may even become amenorrheic, with no menstrual cycles. Western women have their menarche (beginning of menstruation) at an average age of 12.5 years and give birth to an average of 2 or 3 children. (6-9). After two or three 9-month pregnancies and less than 6 months of breast feeding each time, women today spend about 35 years in monthly ovarian cycles, unlike women in foraging societies, women in prehistory, and female apes and monkeys that spend most of their reproductive years pregnant or lactating.

FERTILIZATION

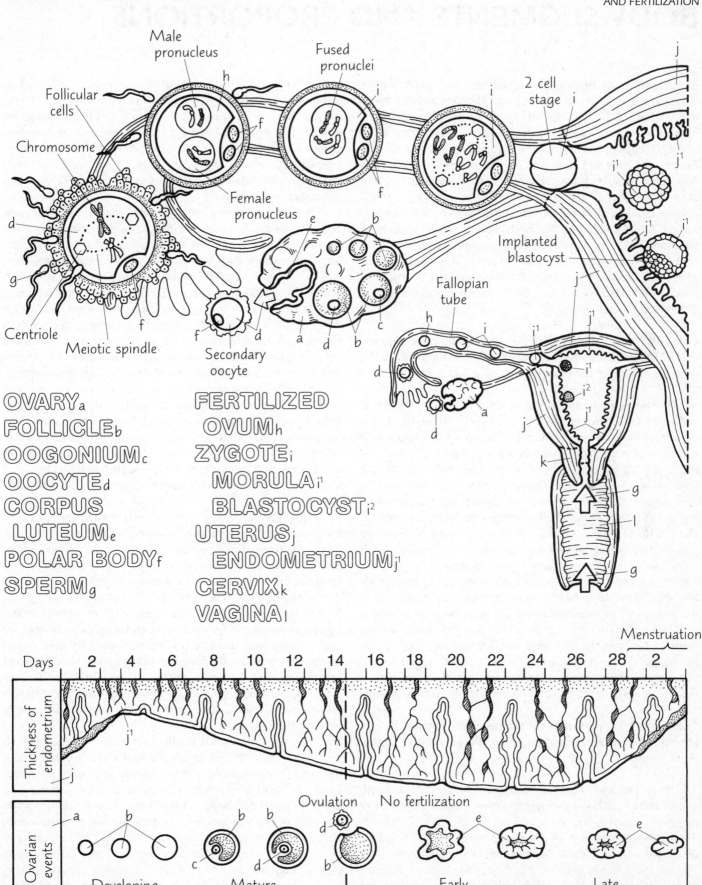

Male pronucleus

Fused pronuclei

2 cell stage

Follicular cells

Chromosome

Female pronucleus

Implanted blastocyst

Fallopian tube

Centriole

Meiotic spindle

Secondary oocyte

OVARY a
FOLLICLE b
OOGONIUM c
OOCYTE d
CORPUS
  LUTEUM e
POLAR BODY f
SPERM g

FERTILIZED
OVUM h
ZYGOTE i
MORULA i¹
BLASTOCYST i²
UTERUS j
ENDOMETRIUM j¹
CERVIX k
VAGINA l

Menstruation

Days   2   4   6   8   10   12   14   16   18   20   22   24   26   28   2

Thickness of endometrium

Ovarian events

Ovulation   No fertilization

Developing follicle   Mature follicle   Early corpus luteum   Late corpus luteum

6-2
BODY SEGMENTS AND PROPORTIONS

The human body undergoes radical transformation from a fertilized egg and early fetus to an adult. The early embryo shows segmentation (2-14) but does not begin to resemble the adult until limbs, hands, and feet take shape. At about 30 days, paddlelike limb buds appear, and by about 60 days, the digits are separated. Because the head and neck dominate the embryo, development of the upper limb buds precedes those of the lower limb by a day or so. In the seventh embryonic week, the upper and lower limbs rotate in opposite directions so the future elbows point backwards and the future knees point forwards. Formation and rotation of the limbs and development of body proportions from fetus to adult illustrate the transformation process that characterizes growth. As we also observed in 1-3, a comparative approach to growth provides insights into the evolution of morphological differences in related species.

Color the cervical and thoracic segments in the early embryos that illustrate three stages of upper limb development. In the adult figure, color the dermatomes by spinal region.

The upper limb buds develop opposite the lower cervical and upper thoracic segments of the embryo (C_3–T_1) and the lower limb buds (not shown) form opposite the lumbar and sacral segments (L_2–S_2). Spinal nerves are distributed in segmental bands (e.g. C_3, L_2, etc), and each supplies sensation to a specific area of the skin's surface. Dermatomes (Greek, derma=skin, tome=slice) refer to the area of skin supplied by a single spinal nerve. As the limbs elongate, the cutaneous nerve supply migrates along with them. In the first 30 days dermatomes show the primitive segmental arrangement; by about 35 days, as upper limb buds take shape, the primitive segmental pattern, but not the sequence, has disappeared. As the limbs elongate and rotate, they no longer show the parallel pattern. Dermatomes illustrate how the process of growth transforms the basic body plan from a formless embryo into a human adult. This embryonic history explains, for example, why heart attack victims may feel pain on the inside of their upper arms, (because the T_2 spinal nerves innervate both the heart and inner arms) and why arthritis and a pinched nerve in the C_7 vertebra causes tingling in the fingertips.

Color each body part in all the figures on the bottom. Height is held constant and other stages are shown relative to this adult height.

By two months of age, the fetal limbs and digits are formed, and the large head houses the rapidly growing brain. During early pregnancy, neurons can grow at a rate of 250,000 per minute. The forebrain, the center of planning, personality, and language (3-24) grows more rapidly than the midbrain or hindbrain (1-4). The sense of touch is well developed, probably because the fetus must avoid becoming entangled in the umbilical cord. By the fifth embryonic month, the fetal proportions reflect a relatively reduced head and elongated torso and limbs.

At birth, the newborn's head is large relative to the adult, and its legs are relatively short. The brain grows rapidly during the first and second years of life, when it acts like a sponge for learning and imitation. Brain growth correlates with language acquisition at about age two. The big head diminishes in relative size with age, and the limbs grow longer. Compare the newborn and 6-year-old. Adult brain size is reached by age 12, although internal changes continue.

The locomotor system undergoes major transformation during postnatal development. The disproportionate size of the infant head and thorax raises the center of gravity. Compare the fetus and newborn with two-year-old body proportions. Two-year-olds are normally walking alone, although are less stable than adults when walking and standing. They spread their feet apart and stretch out their arms for balance, thus compensating for their short legs and underdeveloped lumbar curve. As their legs lengthen, children take longer steps and rotate their thorax and pelvis rhythmically as they walk. The locomotor system approaches the adult pattern around 6 years of age and continues to mature to around age 8 to 9. Adult body composition and metabolism are reached during late adolescence, so that during locomotion the body consumes relatively less oxygen. The locomotor system continues to change throughout life. During aging, loss of muscle tone and skeletal flexibility restrict movements at all joints, so the stride is shorter and feet are placed wider apart to maintain stability, rather like a child when it begins to walk.

Comparing growth between closely related species (1-3), for example, between humans and our cousins the chimpanzees, we see the fine-tuning of genes that regulate the morphology of limb growth. In humans, arms and legs are roughly equal in length at birth. By the end of infancy, human legs are longer than arms; in adolescents and adults arm length is only about 72% of leg length. Chimpanzees, too, are born with arms and legs about the same length, but by the end of infancy, chimpanzee upper limbs are longer than lower limbs. By adulthood, chimpanzee arms are 6% longer than legs; when hands and feet are factored in, upper limb length becomes even more pronounced. Slight genetically determined modifications in growth rates produce these marked morphological differences between the two species (4-36).

Anthropologists study the human species at the individual, population, and species level. We learn how the individual functions, is transformed, and survives through each life stage. In the broader evolutionary picture, similar genetic and developmental processes make it possible to compare the ontogeny of our own species with close kin like chimpanzees or with very distant relatives like insects. The comparative study of growth and development illustrates how species reflect common evolutionary history and how altered growth patterns during development produce differences in morphology and function, even in closely related species.

BODY PROPORTIONS

DERMATOMES ❋

CERVICAL c
THORACIC T
LUMBAR l
SACRAL s
CAUDAL Ca

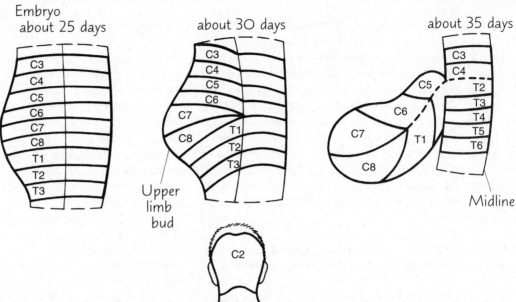

Embryo about 25 days

about 30 days

about 35 days

Upper limb bud

Midline

ADULT ❋

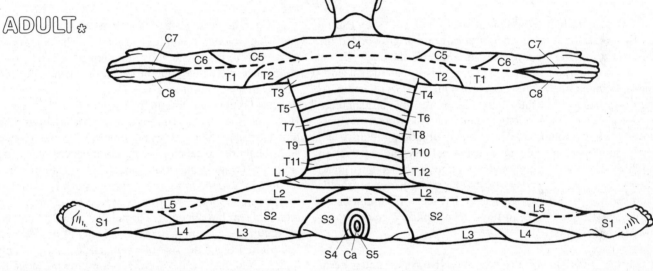

GROWTH CHANGES ❋

HEAD a
BRAIN b
TORSO c
UPPER LIMBS d
LOWER LIMBS e

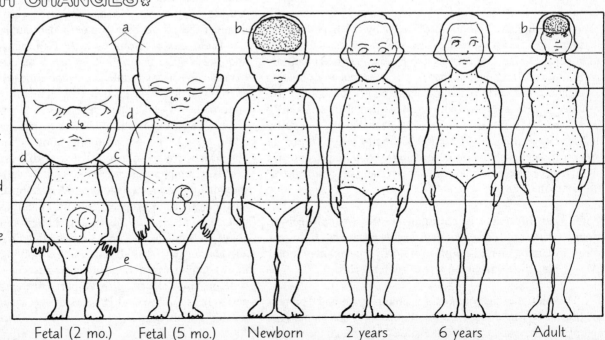

Fetal (2 mo.)   Fetal (5 mo.)   Newborn   2 years   6 years   Adult

6-3
BODY SYSTEMS AND LIFE STAGES

Between birth and the adult stage of life, the human body changes externally in size and shape. Internally, tissues and organs grow and change at different rates, a pattern first observed by anatomist R.E. Scammons in his classic study of human growth. Growth patterns correspond to transition in life stages, for example, the onset of reproductive growth marks the beginning of the adolescent stage. The pattern of growth and length of each stage varies from one species to the next (3-24). The human species has long life stages with extended immaturity, late eruption of permanent dentition, and a large brain. Comparisons between chimpanzees and modern humans constrain speculation as to when during human evolution fossil hominids express an extended immaturity.

Color the growth lines for the brain (neural tissue) and immune system (lymphoid tissue) from birth to adult.

At birth the human brain is about 25% of adult size. During its first year, the infant's energy goes to brain growth and the curve is steep. The brain reaches its adult size about age 12.

Lymphoid tissues—lymph nodes, tonsils, and the spleen—make antibodies and defend the individual against infection. At birth an infant has little immunity of its own. It relies on antibodies from its mother's milk; a long lactation provides protection in its early years. Lymphoid tissue grows rapidly during infancy and early childhood, reaches an apex in puberty and declines in adulthood. Certain lymphocytes mature in the thymus gland (hence the name "T" cells). The thymus gland in infants extends from the neck to just above the heart. It reaches maximum size at about age 12 in girls, 14 in boys, then rapidly regresses to its small size in adults.

Color the growth lines for the reproductive system and general growth.

During infancy, hormones excreted by the hypothalamus stimulate the ovaries to release estrogens or the testes to release androgens. During late infancy the hypothalamus temporarily stops its gonadal stimulation, then reactivates at puberty, initiating differential growth in the female and male bodies and reproductive systems (6-8). General growth includes dental (6-4), skeletal (6-5), and body mass growth (6-8), each having a specific developmental trajectory. Eruption of the first permanent molar (M1) correlates with the brain reaching 90 to 95% of adult size in catarrhine primates, according to observations of anthropologist Holly Smith (3-28).

Color each life stage in chimpanzees, australopithecines, *Homo erectus*, and *Homo sapiens* as it is discussed. Color the arrow indicating dental eruption of the first permanent molar (M1). Color the adult brain size of each species.

The fetal stage lasts 8 months in chimpanzees and 9 months in humans. During infancy, young chimpanzees and humans are completely dependent and require close contact with the mother for transportation and food (3-10, 3-27). Chimpanzee infants are weaned gradually between ages 3 to 4 years, and if orphaned prior to weaning, do not survive. When fully weaned, juveniles travel under their own power, learn what to eat, forage independently, but remain socially connected to their mothers, who give birth after a 4 to 5 year interval (3-28). Human infants nurse for 3 to 4 years; although weaned, they remain dependent upon the mother and other adults for food until about age 7. This prolonged immaturity and dependency of human young constitutes a new life stage, childhood, proposed by anthropologist Barry Bogin. During this stage (from about age 3 to 7 years), while learning physical, social, and cognitive skills, children require extensive care from others in addition to their mothers. A childhood stage, then, developed along with a social system that contributed to the survival of children and made it possible for foraging women to keep the birth interval between 4 and 5 years (6-9).

When might this stage have appeared in human evolution and what function might it have served? The length of infancy of australopithecines may have been similar to that of chimpanzees. The eruption of M1 in the australopithecines has been estimated from tooth root development and dental growth lines as comparable to chimpanzees at 3 to 3.5 years of age. However, in contrast to chimpanzees, the australopithecines were bipedal, had a larger average brain size (5-21) and likely required additional time to develop locomotor independence and acquire skills for foraging and tool using. This transition period from infancy to juvenile in australopithecines can be described as an incipient childhood. Australopithecine youngsters, while not increasing the birth interval of the mother, relied upon food shared by adults while learning the foraging way of life. *Homo erectus* had a brain twice the size of chimpanzees and probably had a longer childhood, which allowed brain growth, social learning, and development of complex tool using skills. Its estimated M1 eruption between age 5 and 6 years occurred later than in chimpanzees, but earlier than in modern humans.

Field observations on wild chimpanzees describe an adolescent stage between about age 8 to 11, a distinct period between juvenile and adult. During this time males produce viable sperm without the physical and social maturity to compete with adult males (6-8). Females develop sexual swellings, copulate, and have a period of sterility before conceiving their first infant about age 12. This extended time allows chimpanzees to learn and practice elaborate tool using with hammers and anvils (3-33). Chimpanzees, however, lack a well-defined skeletal growth spurt characteristic of modern human adolescents. The australopithecines probably followed a chimpanzee adolescent pattern. In *H. erectus,* this adolescent period might have begun about age 9 but lasted to age 14, providing time for brain growth and learning social skills and problem solving required in their more complex way of life. Human adolescence incorporates, and is defined by, a skeletal growth spurt and weight gain (6-8). This period lasts until around 18 years of age, when all body tissues reach the adult stage.

BODY SYSTEMS

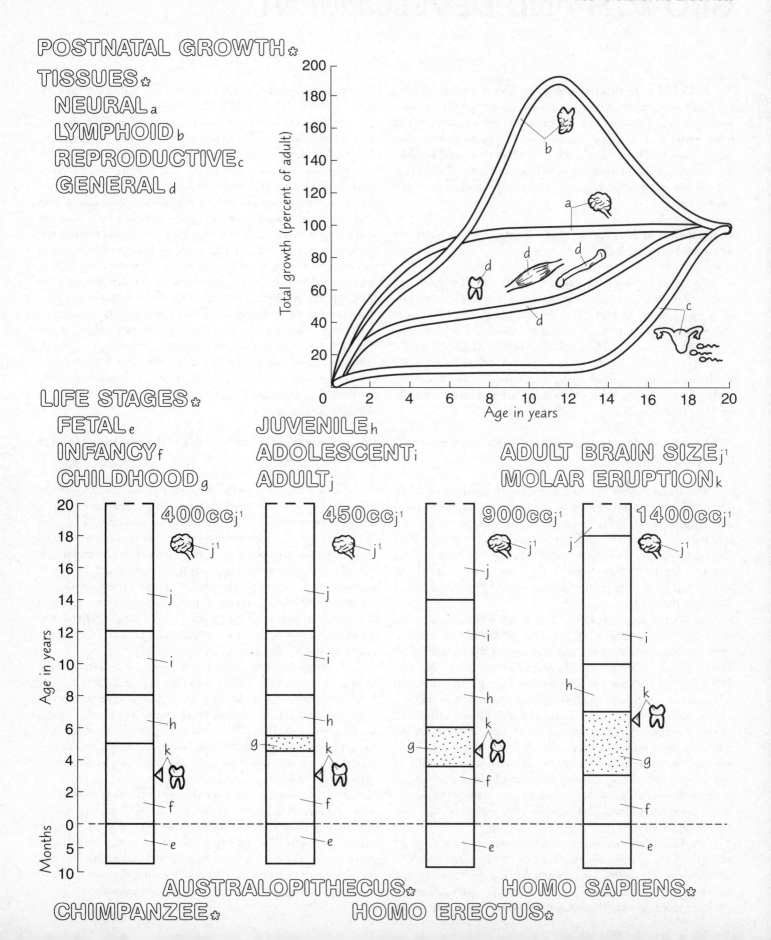

POSTNATAL GROWTH.*
TISSUES.*
  NEURAL.a
  LYMPHOID.b
  REPRODUCTIVE.c
  GENERAL.d

LIFE STAGES.*
  FETAL.e   JUVENILE.h
  INFANCY.f   ADOLESCENT.i   ADULT BRAIN SIZE.j¹
  CHILDHOOD.g   ADULT.j   MOLAR ERUPTION.k

400cc.j¹   450cc.j¹   900cc.j¹   1400cc.j¹

AUSTRALOPITHECUS.*

CHIMPANZEE.*   HOMO ERECTUS.*

HOMO SAPIENS.*

GROWTH AND DEVELOPMENT

The head has three functional regions. The braincase (neuro-cranium) protects the brain, the control center for the nervous system. The facial bones form the eye orbits and nasal cavity and house visual and olfactory structures of the sensory system. The jaws encase the developing tooth crown and roots, and provide the anchor for the masticatory (chewing) muscles. These three regions are interrelated but grow and change at different rates during life.

Color the small illustration of the heads of a newborn, an adult, and an aged individual.

The head includes hard tissue (skull) and overlying soft tissue: skin, scalp and facial hair, facial and masticatory muscles, eyes, nasal tissue, and lips. The newborn usually has little hair, and no teeth or functioning masticatory muscles. The adult face is fully formed with the full complement of teeth and the braincase is relatively smaller per body mass than that of the infant. With tooth loss or extreme wear, masticatory muscles fall into disuse, and the face shortens from nose to chin, characteristic features of an older individual.

Color the bones of the cranium and face in the newborn, adult, and aged individual.

The large human head of a newborn must be malleable enough to squeeze through the birth canal. The frontal, parietal, and temporal bones of the newborn's skull are not fused. Instead, a fontanelle connects the bony plates by membranes and skin. During birth, this "soft spot" allows the infant's head to fold inward in order to pass through the bony birth canal of the mother's pelvis. At birth, the braincase and eye orbits seem to dominate the head.

Newborns suckle with the help of strong cheek muscles (buccinator), at a time when the teeth are unerupted, and the chewing muscles (masseter and temporalis) are undeveloped. Thus, the shape of the newborn head reveals important functions. The teeth and jaws are less important and comparatively small, whereas the sensory centers housed in the neocortex—auditory, visual, olfactory—are highly developed at birth and efficiently prepared for perceiving, storing, and processing information. As a future culture-bearing human, the infant requires a large brain of synaptic networks for learning social and language skills in order to survive. The high energy demands of this newborn brain for growth and the delayed dental development make the human infant completely dependent on others for nutrition, well into childhood (6-3).

The head (the cranial bones and brain within) grows rapidly and gains over 20 centimeters of circumference from infancy to adulthood as soft and hard tissues expand. The individual cranial bones grow and meet at the sutures, which are well defined in younger people but may become obliterated with age. The suture patterns provide a means for forensic scientists to estimate the age of an individual at death.

The eyes and nose lie in the center of the face. The orbits of the eyes are influenced by the frontal, maxillary, and nasal bones. The nasal passage, an airway and organ of smell, is shaped by a series of nasal and maxillary bones. The maxillary and dentary bones support the teeth. The left and right halves of the newborn's mandible are separate but fuse by adulthood, a trait shared with other anthropoids. The masticatory muscles attach to the zygomatic arches and temporal bones. As the bones forming the braincase expand around the growing brain, erupting teeth stimulate the formation of surrounding bone in the jaws. If teeth are removed before they erupt, the jaws never form properly. In the adult, the completed growth of the face corresponds to the full eruption of the permanent teeth, making the lower jaw prominent. With age, the maxillary and dentary bones resorb. The process accelerates considerably if the tooth roots are removed from the bone, due to disease or old age. Loss of blood flow to the area causes the bone resorption and new bone does not form. The absence of teeth and supporting bone changes the shape of the face again.

Color the x-rays of the milk teeth and the permanent teeth at three stages of life.

In this x-ray view of the 6-month old, we see the forming tooth buds, and the beginning of tooth eruption. Tooth calcification sequences are fairly regular and provide a good indictor of age. The lower incisors erupt first, at about six months of age. The two incisors, canine, and first and second molars are the only types of milk or deciduous (Latin for "to fall off") teeth humans have. Between ages 5 and 6, the dental arches are completely developed and all of the milk or deciduous dentition are in and have good biting function due to the development of the masticatory muscles (1-6). The distinct pattern of tooth wear characteristic of each species has already begun.

The first permanent molars start coming in at about 6 years of age—2 to 4 months later in boys than in girls. At this age, the brain has completed about 90% of its growth. The permanent incisors follow and are in place by age 8. By age 12, the canines are fully developed, and the second of 3 molars have erupted in each quadrant of the mouth. The last molar erupts (if the bud forms into a tooth) by 16 years of age, but full crown and root maturity is not achieved until about age 21.

Dental eruption is a strong indicator of chronological age of an individual, and helpful to forensic anthropologists, paleo-anthropologists, and archaeologists in assigning ages to sub-adult skeletal remains. The interrelations of tooth size and shape, muscles, and underlying bone help us understand the different facial forms in closely related species, like the two kinds of australopithecines (5-20) or *Homo neanderthalensis* and *Homo sapiens* (5-26).

HEAD AND DENTITION

FONTANELLEd
BONES *
FRONTALe   ZYGOMATICh
PARIETALf   MAXILLARYi
TEMPORALg   NASALj
                  DENTARY (MANDIBLE)k

NEWBORNa   ADULTb   AGEDc

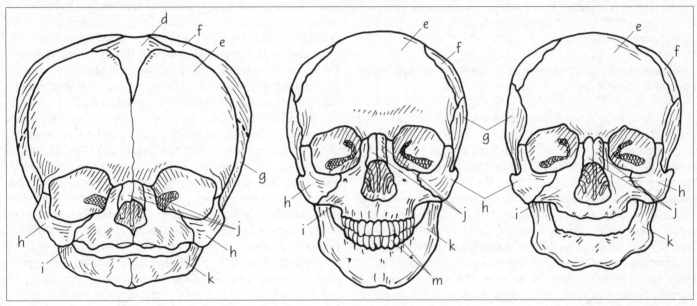

DENTITION *

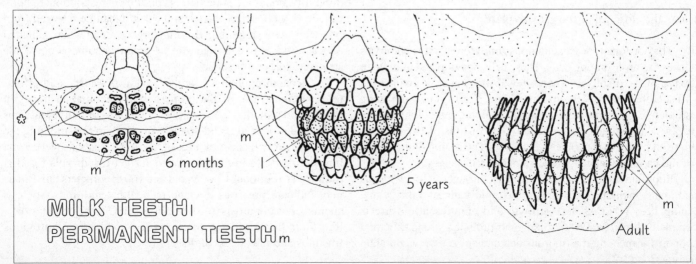

6 months

5 years

Adult

MILK TEETHl
PERMANENT TEETHm

6-5
GROWTH AND DEVELOPMENT

The skeleton acts as the architectural foundation for soft tissue that enables an organism to get around in its environment, supports and protects internal organs, and serves the adult in successful reproduction. In a vertebrate embryo, the "skeletal system" is not yet bone, but is a solid cartilaginous skeletal precursor. During fetal life, primary ossification centers transform from cartilage to bone (ossify). During growth and development, cartilage ossification continues in primary centers and at secondary centers at the joints of long bones. In adult life, the skeletal system ceases to increase in length, but bones cells are continually produced and resorbed, which allows remodeling of the skeleton in response to the body's needs.

Color bone growth in the long bone (humerus). Use contrasting colors for (h) and (i).

Cortical or compact bone is a thick layer of calcified bone material that forms the outer layer of the long bone shaft. Trabecular or spongy bone lies toward the ends of the shaft and is durable due to its matrixlike structure. This property allows the bone more flexibility and torque during locomotion. Deep inside the cavity of the bone lies the bone marrow, which is the center of red blood cell production. A nutrient channel, which enters through the nutrient foramen, supplies the bone with a steady supply of blood and minerals needed during its growth.

Immature long bones have two main parts. The diaphysis, or bone shaft, is the main body of the bone. The epiphysis, located on either end of the long bone shaft, fuses with the diaphysis when growth is completed and the bone no longer can increase in length. During skeletal growth, the area between the epiphysis and the diaphysis, the growth plate, is a cartilaginous zone where bone formation takes place. Cartilage is a connective tissue that is flexible and slightly elastic, but moderately firm. Bone is a more rigid connective tissue than cartilage, owing its additional strength largely to the deposition of inorganic calcium salts. A relationship exists between low levels of milk in a youngster's diet and stunted growth, a probable function of the low levels of calcium available to growing bones.

Color the close-up of the growth plate.

The portion of the cartilaginous zone closest to the epiphysis houses the proliferating cells. These cells develop and migrate to the top of the diaphysis where they absorb minerals and harden and attach themselves onto the bone shaft. When the zone completely converts from cartilage to bone, the epiphysis and diaphysis meet and begin to fuse. When this fusion is complete, the adult length of that bone is achieved. The timing of the fusion for the various skeletal parts differs in each species.

Reptilian skeletal growth continues throughout life, whereas mammals, including primates, grow rapidly during infancy and young life. When skeletal growth and epiphyseal closure is complete, the skeletal system and joints provide a strong structural support for meeting the rigorous demands of active mammalian locomotion (3-7).

Color the humerus of the newborn and adult, and the stages of growth in between. Color the innominate bones in the newborn and adult.

At birth the shaft of the humerus is calcified and a small epiphysis indicates that the proximal (shoulder) joint is beginning to ossify. By age 5, distal epiphyses of the elbow joint are present and further ossified by age 10. The shoulder joint fuses between 17 and 20 years and the elbow joint is completely fused by 16 years. Bone fusion is influenced by hormones released during sexual development (6-8). Human females tend to mature skeletally earlier than boys; on average girls' bones fuse 1 to 2 years earlier. However, the quality of the social and ecological environment, coupled with genetics, can quicken or prolong skeletal development. The cranium and clavicle develop differently than the bones described in this plate.

The newborn innominate bone has an ossification center in each of the 3 bones: the ilium, ischium, and pubis. In reptiles these 3 bones remain distinct and do not fuse (3-7). In humans, the 3 bones fuse at the acetabulum (hip joint) between 11 and 15 years old. Mammalian locomotion, and especially bipedal locomotion in humans, requires a solid pelvic anchor. The human pelvis provides a highly durable weight-bearing, structurally strong support for torso rotation and lower limb swing-step (5-14). It continues growth well after puberty and is not fully mature until about 19 years. During childbirth, the human pelvis plays another major role. Females who try to reproduce early risk having too narrow a pelvic inlet through which to pass an infant, as well as compromising the calcium stores in their own bones during a 9-month pregnancy and long period of lactation (6-9).

Color the healed fracture on the humerus.

Although they do not grow in length after fusion, bones continue to remodel in a dynamic process of bone resorption and new bone cell production. The humerus you have today is not the same bone you had six years ago! Hard tissue in terms of durability, bones are nonetheless "plastic" in responding to body functions. Cells are replaced, and calcium can be released from bone cells when required. Bone undergoes repair when damaged or fractured; this calcified site of repair becomes one of the strongest parts of the bone.

Paleoanthropologists, forensic anthropologists, and primatologists make use of the properties of mammalian bones in growth and remodeling to decipher conditions of individual lives and population health and disease. Bones help in estimating the stature or growth stage of a fossil, as in the case of the Turkana boy (5-8), whose limb bones were not yet fused. This fossil is estimated to be about 13 years old and 160 centimeters tall. Bones may indicate previous damage or health conditions, such as anemia or osteoporosis (6-6). The bones of Gombe chimpanzees, like their human counterparts, reveal evidence of previous fractures and the effects of disease (3-31).

BONES AND THE SKELETON

BONE GROWTH *
  CARTILAGE a
  TRABECULAR BONE b
  CORTICAL BONE c
  MARROW CAVITY d
  NUTRIENT ARTERY e
  OSSIFICATION CENTER f
  GROWTH PLATE *
    GROWING CELLS g
    CALCIFYING CELLS g1
  EPIPHYSIS h
  DIAPHYSIS i

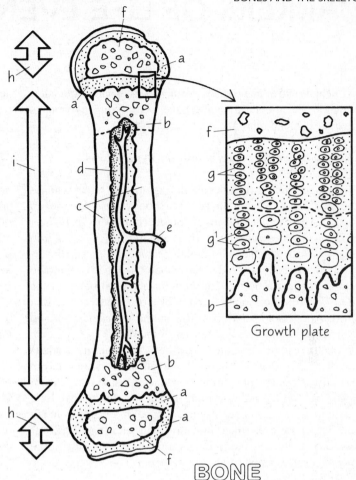

Growth plate

SKELETON *
CALCIFIED HUMERUS i1
INNOMINATE i2

BONE REMODELING j

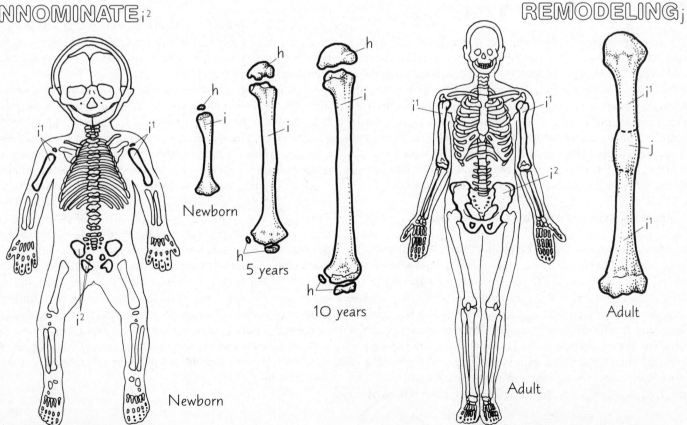

Newborn

5 years

10 years

Newborn

Adult

Adult

MARKERS OF LIFE EVENTS

As hard and solid as it appears in death, bone is dynamic, remodels during life, and after death retains traces of the living individual's activities, diet and reproductive history.

Color the upper eye orbits exhibiting hyperostosis.

Rapid cranial growth occurs during infancy. Cranial bones have an inner and outer layer with spongy bone (diploe) in between, where red blood cells are produced. Hyperostosis (over formation of bone) can occur during early life, due to lack of iron in the blood or anemia. The diploe becomes enlarged (hypertrophic) due to increased red blood cell production in response to anemia; its growth pushes out the thinner cranial bones of the eye orbits (cribra orbitalis) or parts of the cranial vault (cribra cranii). Anthropologist Debra Martin and colleagues studied skeletons of the cliff dwelling Anasazi from Black Mesa, Arizona; 88% of all age groups exhibit hyperostosis. The majority of adults show healed, remodeled bone. Although the condition is not necessarily fatal, anemia during the vulnerable first two years of life can be, and the infants younger than two did not live long enough for healing to occur. Anemia has multiple causes, such as poor diet, chronic diarrhea, infection, and parasites. Whatever the cause, hyperostosis signifies poor health or nutritional deficiencies in a population.

Color the incisor teeth exhibiting hypoplasia.

In normal growth, tooth enamel is deposited in a regular pattern and thickness. Enamel (unlike bone) does not remodel and, once formed, is permanent. If this process is interrupted due to nutritional stress or disease, enamel will be thinner, leaving bands or holes permanently "imprinted" on the teeth. This condition, enamel hypoplasia (under grown) marks the anterior surface of incisors and canines with horizontal lines observable to the naked eye. The frequency of enamel hypoplasia in one individual, and its relative frequency within a population, reflect the overall health and severity of environmental insults.

Color the activities of grinding and throwing.

In an analysis of over 60 skeletons from a Neolithic site in Abu Hureya, Syria, British anthropologist Theya Molleson observed anomalies in the females' bones, not observed in the males. The deltoid crest of the humerus and radial notch showed bone remodeling such as is seen in those in modern women who spend much time grinding grain. As Neolithic women prepared flour for baking, they probably leaned over a quern (a long flat grinding stone), their toes anchored for support, the weight of the whole body giving strength to the grinding action. The mechanical stress from the muscles which powered shoulder action (deltoid) and elbow flexion and rotation (biceps brachii) was so great on the humerus and radius, that their attachment points left bony scars. The females' big toes, vertebrae, and knees also showed signs of severe arthritis with "lipping" and erosion of joint surfaces.

In a study of 16 skeletons from a hunting-gathering population in Niger dating from 3000 to 4000 years ago, French anthropologist O. Dutour observed a bony pad on the lower edge of the medial epicondyle of the right, but not the left, humerus in a mature adult male. The lesion indicates hyperactivity of the pronator teres, flexor carpi ulnaris, and superficial flexor muscles, a condition that generally affects javelin throwers. The action of frequent spear-throwing stresses the attachment point of the muscles, so that remodeling produces a characteristic notch.

Color the dowager's hump and the thoracic vertebra.

Bones change during life, and life events may be recorded in the bones. As women and men age, individuals lose stature. Shrinking stature in old age is due in part to loss of intervertebral cartilage and compression of the vertebral bodies. In addition, older women may suffer severe loss of calcium and bone mass, a condition call osteoporosis. The vertebrae become wedge shaped from top to bottom and the upper spinal region bows out into a "dowager's hump." Men, too, may suffer from "old age" osteoporosis, but women are much more vulnerable. Women's bones are less dense than are those of men to begin with, partly because of having less muscle mass and less mechanical stress on the bones. Calcium and bone mass are lost more rapidly after menopause.

Anthropologist Alison Galloway takes a life history approach in evaluating bone loss in women. When a woman lactates, her body provides the essential nutrients to build the infant's body systems (6-3). Calcium concentration in mother's milk remains constant, even if her diet is low in calcium. The infant takes what it needs from its mother's calcium warehouse, her skeleton. A change in female hormones during lactation (6-9) triggers the resorption of bone, which releases calcium into the maternal blood stream and thus to the newborn in breast milk. After weaning and resumption of the menstrual cycle (6-1), hormones trigger the rebuilding of calcium supplies and bone density. If a female has another infant too quickly (6-9) or has a chronic lack of calcium in her diet, her calcium stores are depleted and her chances of post-menopausal osteoporosis increase. Hormone production again changes during menopause, mimicking changes as during lactation, and calcium is resorbed from bone. As vertebrae lose mass, osteoporotic fractures may occur. In prehistory, most women did not live long enough to experience post-menopausal osteoporosis.

HARD TISSUE MARKERS

EARLY YEARS*
HYPEROSTOSIS a
SPONGY BONE a1

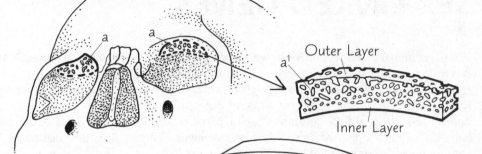

Outer Layer

a1

Inner Layer

Normal

HYPOPLASIA b

Upper
Incisors

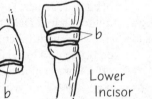

b

Lower
Incisor

b   b

Normal

ADULT ACTIVITY*
BONE
REMODELING c

GRINDING*

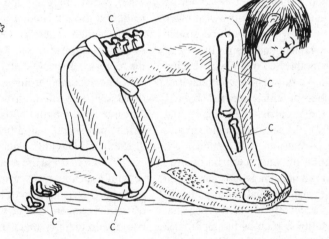

c

c

c

c   c

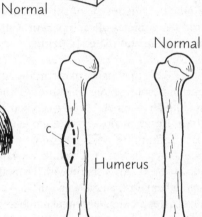

c   Humerus

Normal

c

Radius

THROWING*

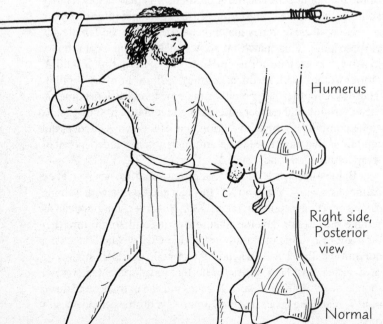

Humerus

c

Right side,
Posterior
view

Normal

AGED*
DOWAGER'S   OSTEOPOROTIC
HUMP d   VERTEBRA d1

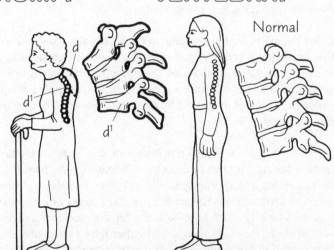

d

d1

d1

Normal

6-7
SEX CHROMOSOMES AND SEX-LINKED GENES

Like all mammals, females and males are variations on a species theme, that is, they have much in common but are distinguished by one pair of chromosomes. The biological variation between females and males is due to the influence of that pair. In each human cell, there are 46 chromosomes in 23 pairs: 22 are homologous and one pair, the X and Y, are nonhomologous. These chromosomes determine an individual's sex. Females have two X chromsomes, and males have one X and one Y chromosome.

Color the phenotype of the parents, their sex chromosomes, and the gametes of each parent. Color the representations of the female and male offspring.

Like other pairs of homologous chromosomes, the sex chromosomes segregate into different gametes during the first meiotic division (1-11, 1-14). When gametes are formed during the process of meiosis, or gametogenesis, females always produce ova containing an X chromosome. Males produce sperm containing an X or Y. The father's gamete determines the sex of the offspring. An X sperm with the mother's X ovum will develop into a baby girl, and a Y sperm, into a boy. These combinations result in approximately equal numbers of female and male babies.

The X chromosome, unlike the Y, carries many genes that affect normal development aside from the sex-determining genes. Females have two X chromosomes, males one X. A female might carry an abnormal recessive gene on one X chromosome. However, it will not be expressed if a normal gene is carried on the other X. In contrast, a male with an abnormal gene on his one and only X chromosome will be adversely affected when that gene is expressed. Some abnormalities, such as hemophilia, a bleeding disorder in humans, and white eyes in fruit flies (1-15), are X-linked and much more common in males because they have only one X chromosome. In females, the additional X chromosome is likely to be normal. Over 100 X-linked traits have been identified in human males, including hemophilia, Duchenne's muscular distrophy (a degenerative disease of the skeletal muscles), and red-green color blindness.

Color the genes for hemophilia on the X chromosomes. Notice the female has a heterozygous genotype; one chromosome has the normal clotting gene and the other has the hemophilia gene. The male has one normal gene, so he has normal clotting. Color the gametes produced by these individuals. Then color the offspring.

Hemophilia was common in European royalty during the last century because frequent marriages between cousins increased the possibility of acquiring a deleterious gene. Females were the "carriers," but were not "bleeders," whereas a number of the royal sons had fatal hemorrhages. When a female carrier married a normal male, their offspring could either have two normal Xs (a normal female), a normal X and a hemophiliac X (a female carrier), a normal X and normal Y (normal male), or hemophiliac X and normal Y (hemophiliac male). Therefore, on average, the offspring had about one out of four chances of being a hemophiliac male.

Of our 46 chromosomes, the Y is unique in several respects. It is the smallest by far. It is passed down virtually unchanged from father to son, while the other 22 chromosome pairs "recombine" and mix the genes of each pair, like shuffling 2 decks of cards together. The Y chromosome tags male lineages the way mitochondrial DNA tags female lineages (2-11).

The main function of the Y is to differentiate the growing embryo into a male. It does this by creating testes, which then set off a hormonal and physical chain reaction that creates a baby boy. It took 30 years of intensive searching before the testis-determining gene was finally located on the Y chromosome in 1990. What this gene does on the biochemical level to trigger testicular growth is not a straightforward process like turning on a light switch. There is a repressor gene that prevents the light switch from turning on. The testis-determining gene represses the repressor, thereby switching on the process of testis formation.

The average chromosome contains about 3000 genes, each of which has a role in growth, development, or function. The Y chromosome, the runt of the litter, has the fewest genes. After an exhaustive search using the latest techniques, geneticists Bruce T. Lahn and David C. Page were able to identify only 20 genes.

Eleven of these are related to testicular function and fertility; several contribute to sperm production. Deletions or mutations of these genes can lead to low sperm counts, no sperm at all, or testicular cancer. The new knowledge of testis-specific genes could help identify males predisposed to infertility or testicular tumors and make possible early diagnosis and treatment. Study of the matching genes on the X chromosome may help to clarify some of the frequent mysterious cases of female infertility.

Nine of the Y genes match genes on the X, the female sex chromosome. This match-up shows that back in evolutionary history, several hundred million years ago, the X and Y chromosomes were identical, as they still are in many reptiles. These XX reptiles can be either male or female, depending on the environmental temperature during incubation of the eggs. At some point in vertebrate evolution, one of the two Xs underwent mutations that gave it testis-determining potency independent of temperature, and it became a Y.

Babies need at least one X chromosome to survive. They cannot live with a Y and no X. They can and do live with a single X and no Y, a genotype called XO. However, they appear as female but do not develop mature ovaries and so are infertile; they are also short in stature with widened "webbed" necks, a condition called Turner's syndrome. A male needs a single dose of X genes plus the Y genes for normal development. A normal female needs a single dose of X genes plus an extra dose of those nine Y- matching genes that the Turner's syndrome person doesn't have.

SEX CHROMOSOMES AND SEX-LINKED GENES

SEX CHROMOSOMES AND
SEX-LINKED GENES

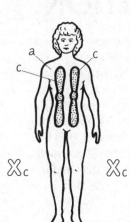
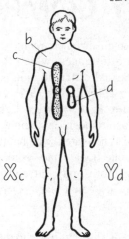

PHENOTYPES ✳
FEMALE $_a$
MALE $_b$
SEX CHROMOSOMES ✳
X_c
Y_d

X_c X_c X_c Y_d

GAMETES ✳   Gametogenesis

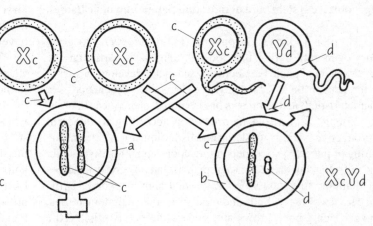

Recombination of genes during fertilization

OFFSPRING ✳ X_cX_c X_cY_d

TRANSMISSION OF HEMOPHILIA ✳
GENES ✳
CLOTTING A_e
HEMOPHILIA a_f

A_e a_f A_e

GAMETES ✳   Gametogenesis

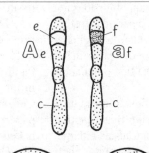
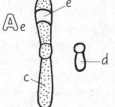

A_e a_f A_e

Recombination of genes during fertilization

OFFSPRING ✳
NORMAL FEMALE $_a$ $A_e A_e$
CARRIER FEMALE $_{a^1}$ $A_e a_f$
NORMAL MALE $_b$ A_e
HEMOPHILIAC MALE $_{b^1}$ a_f

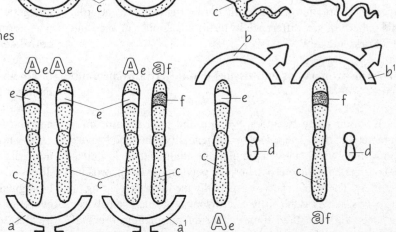

6-8
BODY COMPOSITION

Women and men have characteristic body shape and tissue composition differences, which they acquire during sexual maturation. Sexual differentiation begins with the presence or absence of a Y chromosome (6-7). From birth onward, females and males differ in their external genitalia, the main basis for identifying a newborn as female or male. At puberty the hypothalamus is activated, which initiates differential growth in female and male bodies and reproductive systems. As adults, women have more body fat and less muscle than men. A comparative and evolutionary perspective helps explain these differences.

Color the areas that change during development, shape the reproductive system, and define adult female and male bodies.

Hormonal changes at puberty (Latin *pubescere*, to grow hairy) generate noticeable bodily changes, in particular the development of pubic hair. Females and males develop "primary" differences in their reproductive systems and "secondary" sex characteristics such as breasts in girls and deeper voices in boys.

Young women and men develop according to different reproductive patterns, as described by biologist R.V. Short. The timing of puberty varies, depending upon family history, health, and nutrition, but the sequence remains relatively constant across populations. In young women, the first sign of puberty is the appearance of breast buds and pubic hair; then height increases, and the pubic bone grows and widens the pelvis prior to the menarche, the first menstrual bleeding. Ovulation often does not take place during the first few menstrual cycles, a period therefore referred to as adolescent sterility. Regular ovulation begins at about 15 or 16 years of age. Weight gain continues, with fat deposited in breasts, hips, and thighs prior to the first pregnancy, a characteristic unique to human females.

In contrast, young men begin their sexual development with the production of viable sperm before any significant genital development has occurred. Then, the penis and testes enlarge, followed by pubic hair. Males grow rapidly in height; their shoulders broaden through clavicular growth; and they gain weight and muscle mass. What is remarkable and often not appreciated is that adolescent boys, despite their less mature appearance, are on average fertile earlier than adolescent girls. This pattern of sex difference in fertility is similar in apes and Old World monkeys.

Color the proportions and tissues that differ in women and men.

By their early twenties, women and men acquire their characteristic body shapes. Men are generally taller and heavier than women within a given population, although there is a great deal of overlap. Women have broader pelvises, and men, broader shoulders. The female pelvis, especially the inner pelvic ring or true pelvis, serves as the birth canal. Women's backs and pelvises are more flexible than men's. During pregnancy, prenatal hormones relax the ligaments of the sacroiliac, pubic, and lumbosacral joints and allow the pelvic opening to expand for giving birth. The pelvis is the most reliable of all bones for assigning sex: the female pelvic opening is round, the male rather triangular. Thus, bioarchaeologists can determine sex ratios from skeletal remains and learn about events that affected past societies.

The shapes of women's and men's bodies also depend on their soft tissues, which differ to a greater degree than do the skeletons. On average, muscle comprises about 36% of body mass in young adult women, and about 43% in young adult men, who, partly for this reason, have denser bones. Young women's bodies are about 25% fat, men's about 17%. Proportions of muscle and fat change with age and lifestyle—for example, athletes have less body fat, middle-aged adults more. Elite athletes have the least body fat. Female Olympic swimmers, divers, track and field athletes, and gymnasts have 11 to 16% body fat; male athletes have even less, but rarely less than 8%.

The distribution of soft tissue contributes further to body shape. The greater amount of body fat in women is stored mostly in the torso, in the breasts, and in the hips and thighs. The latter fat deposits are close to the center of mass near the hip joints, where body fat is not likely to interfere with locomotion. Men store their fat in the abdomen. Women have less muscle mass in the shoulders, arms, and hands than men do, but about the same amount in hips and thighs, which maintains an effective bipedal locomotor system. With more muscle in upper limbs, men have broader shoulders and greater upper body strength. Male shoulder breadth and female pelvic breadth have both skeletal and soft tissue components.

The human species is unique among primates in having relatively much more body fat and in having pronounced difference in body fat between the sexes. All mammals deposit fat around the tail, thighs, and pectoral region, and, in primates, in the abdomen, according to the research of British biologist Caroline Pond. Humans retain this mammalian and primate pattern in fat storage, but because of a vertical orientation and naked skin, appear significantly different from other primates.

During human evolution, our ancestors walked long distances to collect their food. Hominid women carried and nursed infants which had large brains at birth and required long periods of care. This extended investment in offspring placed a considerable energetic burden on hominid women to a greater degree than it does for many species of monkeys and apes. Increased body fat correlates with successful pregnancy and lactation in other primates (3-27). These factors might account for the sex difference in amount of body fat and for the human female's ability to mobilize the depots from the thigh during lactation.

In modern industrial urban cultures, abundant food intake and a sedentary lifestyle cause men and women to accumulate excess body fat to a degree that had few counterparts in past nomadic or agrarian societies (6-9). Obesity and associated diseases, such as diabetes, are major health problems. Thus a biological pattern of body composition is broadly determined by evolutionary history, but its individual expression is influenced by diet, activity, and culture.

SEX DIFFERENCES

DEVELOPMENTAL CHANGES*
  FEMALE a
    BREAST BUD a¹
    GROWTH SPURT a²
    MENARCHE a³
    OVULATION b
    WEIGHT GAIN a⁴
  MALE c
    SPERMATOGENISIS d
    GENITAL
      DEVELOPMENT
      BEGINS c¹
    GROWTH SPURT c²
    ADULT GENITALIA c³

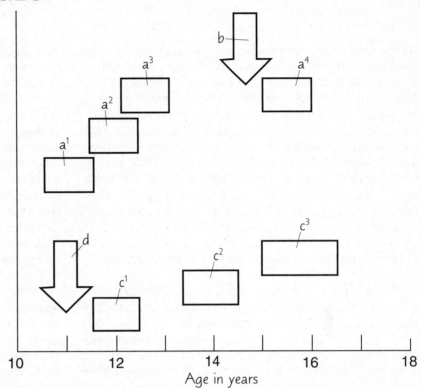

ADULT DIFFERENCES*
BODY PROPORTIONS*
  SHOULDERS e
  PELVIS e¹
TISSUE COMPOSITION*
  MUSCLE f
  FAT g

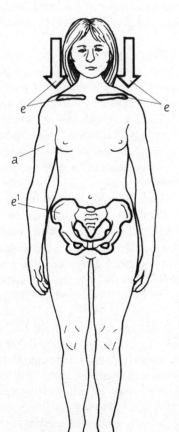

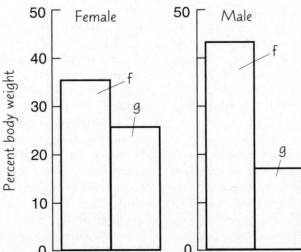

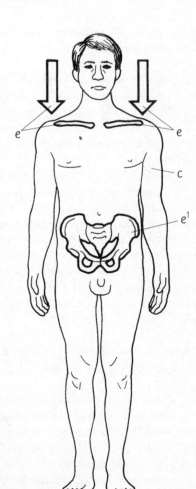

6-9
REPRODUCTION AND CULTURE

All women have the same basic biology, but different life styles influence the patterns of reproduction. Making a living, getting enough food for herself and her children, and cultural practices surrounding lactation, contraception, and the treatment of women all play a part. Our female and male ancestors lived as foragers, collecting and hunting for food and walking long distances while carrying heavy loads (5-13). When people began to cultivate plants, women no longer walked as much. They lived in settlements, had more children, and local populations grew larger. In this plate we contrast patterns of fertility and reproduction in three societies: foragers, farmers, and industrialized urban dwellers.

Color the examples of women working in three cultures.

Women's activities have changed historically and differ cross-culturally. Foragers go out and collect food; agriculturalists plant and gather crops; women in urban industrial economies work in offices and factories. In all cultures, however, women have the main responsibility for raising the children. No matter how much other work they do, they have child care as a "second shift," in sociologist Arlie Hochschild's terminology.

Color points for menarche, marriage, and events leading to first pregnancy.

The !Kung San in Botswana, studied by anthropologists Nancy Howell and Richard Lee, are nomadic people who collect their food by walking long distances. Young women on average have a late menarche at age 16, marry near that age, and after a period of adolescent sterility, conceive and give birth around age 19.

In agricultural societies that lack contraception, similar to early 20th century America, the average age at menarche is 14. Adolescent sterility and later marriage ("cultural sterility") at age 20 postpone the average first pregnancy to age 22.

Better nutrition has improved health in modern Western urban societies and reduced the mean age at menarche to 12.5 years. Adolescent sterility lasts about 2 years. Though sexual activity may commence in the late teens prior to marriage, widespread use of contraception often delays the first pregnancy to the early 20s.

Color the pregnancies, birth interval, lactation, and menopause for each society.

In the !Kung economy, woman's work, gathering wild vegetable foods, provides over half of all the food consumed. On each workday, a woman walks on average 12 kilometers round trip, and on the return leg carries about 11 kilograms of food. In addition, a woman carries a child 4 years old or younger in a special baby carrier on her back. Richard Lee estimates that over the 4-year period of dependency, a child is carried for about 10,000 kilometers.

Infants suckle frequently and vigorously until they are 3 or 4 years old. Nipple stimulation suppresses progesterone production and delays the next pregnancy. Women's work effort and long period of lactation widen the average birth interval to 4 years. The !Kung say, "A woman who gives birth like an animal to one offspring after another has a permanent backache." The young are not completely weaned until the mother becomes pregnant again. A woman forager has on average 5 offspring and only 4 years of menstrual cycles in her lifetime. Her last infant is born in her mid 30s, and she reaches menopause at about 40. Lee comments that the long birth spacing provides opportunity for a high parental investment in each child, so that their emotional as well as nutritional needs are met.

In the world's many rural agricultural societies, women work continuously in the fields and around the home before, during, and after pregnancy. They breast-feed their infants for about 6 months, therefore ovulation is suppressed only briefly. Women cycle and conceive again, and births are spaced about 2 years apart. The means of food production (cultivation and animal husbandry), reduced mobility, and not carrying a child all the time make different demands on rural women compared to foraging women. It is not uncommon for women in agricultural societies or in early rural America to have 10 children. Usually the last child is born when a woman is in her 40s, and she reaches menopause at about 45.

In modern urban society, contraception may delay the first pregnancy until the early 20s, or even much later, and allow families to space children as they wish. Because most women have jobs outside the home, lactation is usually intermittent, lasts only 2 to 4 months, and is not effective in suppressing ovulation and conception. Families are typically small with 2 or 3 children who are likely to survive with good medical care. Women experience menstrual cycles through most of their fertile years and have a late menopause about age 50.

Where and how families live, the nutrition and health of women, and social, cultural, and religious traditions all affect fertility. In American society the transition from rural to modern urban life dramatically reduced family size within a generation. Anthropologist Patricia Draper witnessed a parallel shift when traditional !Kung foragers adopted a settled way of life, keeping animals and cultivating crops. Birth intervals began to shorten and family size to increase.

Taking the longer historical view, we can see how the gradual change from foraging to farming, beginning some 10,000 to 15,000 years ago, boosted human populations. Women didn't have to carry their children long distances, nutrition improved, and infants could be weaned earlier. Though infant mortality rates remained high, increased fertility still led to population growth. Families are smaller in urban industrial societies around the world, but population continues to expand due to markedly decreased infant mortality and increased longevity.

HUMAN REPRODUCTION

MENARCH d
MENSTRUAL CYCLE e
MARRIAGE f
  SEXUAL
  ACTIVITY f1

PREGNANCY/INFANT g
LACTATION h
BIRTH INTERVAL i
CONTRACEPTION j
MENOPAUSE k

FORAGERS a

Age in years

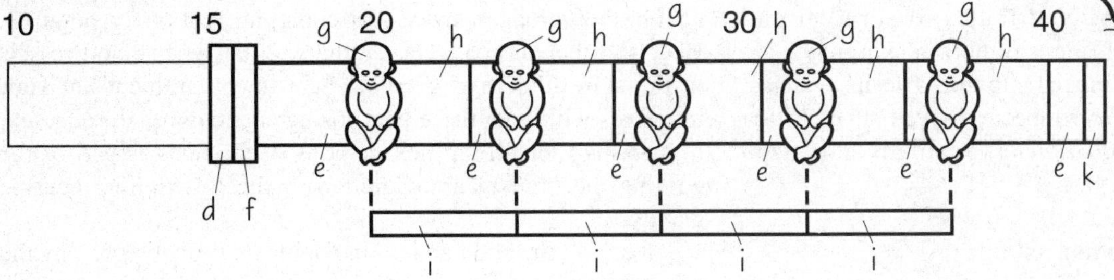

PREMODERN/ RURAL b

Age in years

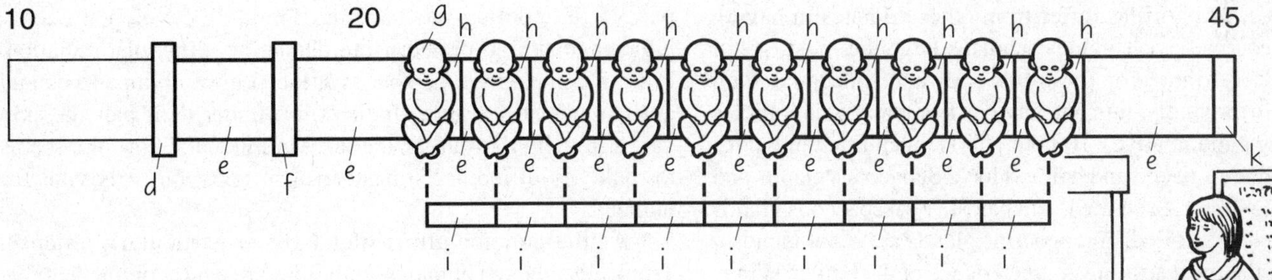

MODERN/ URBAN c

Age in years

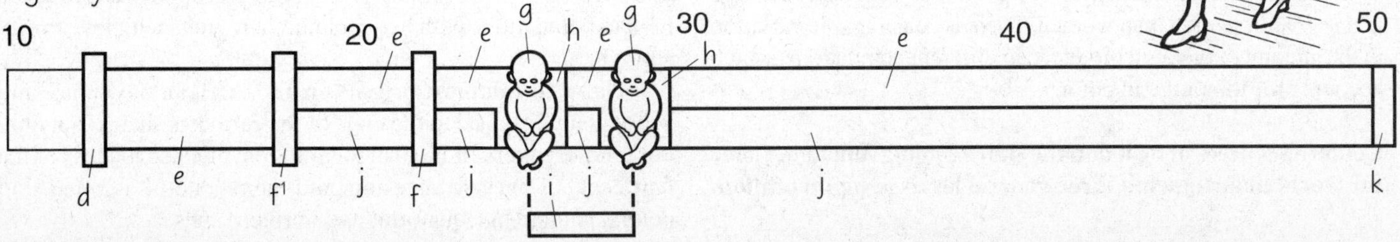

6-10
THE PROTECTIVE SHIELD

Skin is the largest organ of the human body. It is a protective envelope for the sensitive internal structures and a shield against attack by physical and biological agents. A network of nerves and blood vessels, glands, hair shafts, and melanocytes, the skin regulates body temperature, protects from ultraviolet damage, acts as a touch sensor, and affects appearance and sexual attraction through hair, color, and odors. Human skin is similar in many ways to the skin of other primates, as documented in the pioneering studies on primate skin by biologist William Montagna. The characters of human skin can best be appreciated through comparative functional anatomy and by looking at skin as an adaptive complex that contributes to survival and reproduction. The distinctive features of human skin may have evolved when early hominids moved into the African savannas, with continued change when *Homo* species moved out of Africa (5-24) and later, when *Homo sapiens* eventually colonized northern Europe and Asia (5-29).

Color the structure of the human skin.

The skin has two main parts, the epidermis, the thin outer surface, and the deeper dermis. The epidermis has two layers: the thick and fibrous horny layer made of tough, flattened, dead cells, and the living, growing layer. During embryological development, epidermal cells differentiate into hair follicles, sebaceous (oil) glands, and two types of sweat glands, eccrine and apocrine.

All primates have eccrine glands on the palms and soles to keep the skin soft and pliable for grasping (3-11). Humans, chimpanzees, and gorillas differ from other primates in having additional eccrine sweat glands; humans have the most, about two million, distributed on the whole body and concentrated on the trunk. Surprisingly, humans have just as many hair follicles as our shaggy ape relatives. But our hair is much finer and gives the human body a naked and hairless look. Sebaceous glands and apocrine glands are associated with hair shafts; sebaceous glands keep the hair shaft oiled, and apocrine glands are scent glands.

One of the most striking characteristics of the human skin is its variation in color within and between populations, which ranges from blue-back, espresso, chocolate, and dark brown, to bronze, café au lait, honey, tan, beige, ivory, ruddy, and pink. Melanocytes in the epidermis produce melanin, the pigment which gives the skin its color. All people have the same number of melanocytes, but the amount of melanin produced is under genetic control. Ultraviolet light stimulates the activity of the melanocytes to produce melanin, so both genetics and environment play a role. Skin pigmentation generally increases with sun exposure and age and is greater in men than women. There is considerable variation in the amount of melanin produced in different populations, which accounts for the range in color.

Color the sources of heat and the skin's cooling function. Color the world map showing three general levels of pigmentation.

The African savanna mosaic habitat, where hominids originated, has less continuous shade than the forest, and equatorial regions are hot during the day, particularly during the dry season. Tropical savanna mammals have developed physiological mechanisms to prevent overheating, such as panting, sweating, and resting in the hottest part of the day. People today, like our hominid ancestors, are exposed to high levels of solar heat. Through muscular activity associated with work effort, they generate a great deal of heat in foraging for and collecting food (5-2). Eccrine glands respond to external heat, from solar or other sources and to internal body heat, generated by muscle action; they produce sweat that cools the skin by evaporation. Heat is further dissipated by a radiator effect when blood vessels in the skin dilate and give off heat to the ambient air. Hair interferes with both these heat-losing adaptations, so reduction in hair shaft length on most regions of the body is part of the cooling mechanism associated with the functioning eccrine glands.

Keeping the body and brain cool from heat absorbed by the sun and generated by muscular action was essential for survival. Mammalian brains are sensitive to temperature, and an increase of a few degrees in body temperature disturbs function. According to Dean Falk, the cranial blood drainage system in *Homo* is in part designed to cool the brain under conditions of hyperthermia (5-21). Active eccrine sweat glands throughout the body combined with reduction of hair shafts may have evolved as part of this cooling system.

Thick hair helps protect the skin of other primates from the damaging effects of ultraviolet light. With hair protection lost as part of the cooling mechanism, hominids developed deeply pigmented skin to protect from damaging ultraviolet radiation. From a comparative perspective, the skin of chimpanzees and gorillas has no uniform single color; under their hair the skin varies from light to dark in the same individual. Skin color seems to make no difference for survival in apes, but it is vital for humans.

At the equator ultraviolet light is particularly intense. Tropically adapted human populations are darkly pigmented; the populations with the most pigment are found in Africa, where our species first originated (5-27). Increased melanin in the epidermis blocks the ultraviolet rays and minimizes damage to tissue and to the DNA. Ultraviolet rays can be beneficial too; they stimulate the dermis to manufacture vitamin D, essential for calcium absorption from the intestines and normal bone growth and development. Dark skin lets fewer ultraviolet rays through the epidermis than the light-colored skin of higher latitudes such as Scandinavia. Natural selection has produced human populations with less melanin in regions with less annual sunlight.

Our evolutionary origins in the African savannas and subsequent dispersal to the ends of the earth has shaped not only our unique pattern of bipedal locomotion, but also the loss of the hair coats of our ape ancestors and the palette of assorted skin colors, painted by equatorial and northern suns.

HUMAN SKIN

STRUCTURE*
  EPIDERMIS a
    HORNY LAYER b
    LIVING LAYER c
  DERMIS d
    ECCRINE GLAND e
    HAIR FOLLICLE/
      SHAFT f
    SEBACEOUS
      GLAND g
    APOCRINE GLAND h
  MELANOCYTE i

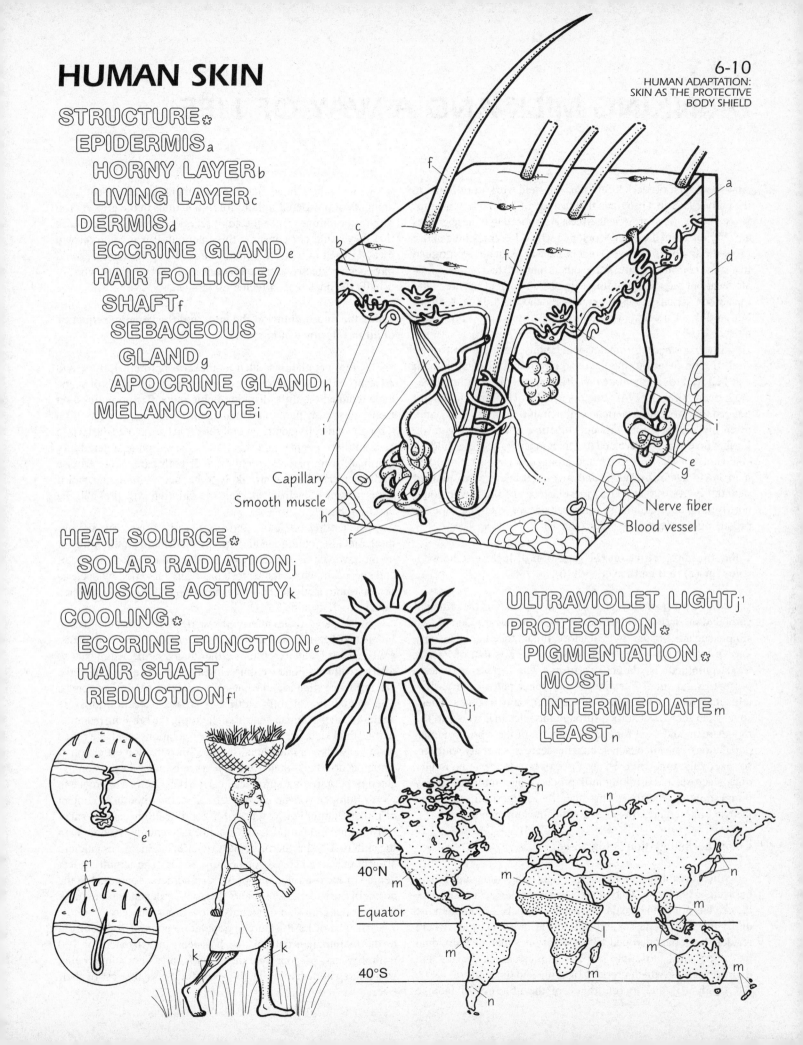

Capillary
Smooth muscle
Nerve fiber
Blood vessel

HEAT SOURCE*
  SOLAR RADIATION j
  MUSCLE ACTIVITY k
COOLING*
  ECCRINE FUNCTION e
  HAIR SHAFT
    REDUCTION f¹

ULTRAVIOLET LIGHT j¹
PROTECTION*
  PIGMENTATION*
  MOST i
  INTERMEDIATE m
  LEAST n

40°N
Equator
40°S

DRINKING MILK AND A WAY OF LIFE

Anthropologist Frederick Simoons did field work in Ethiopia in the early 1950s in a province that included Christians, Moslems, Jews, and a variety of African tribes. He noticed that these groups ate very different diets and wondered why different people chose to eat certain foods and avoid others. He was particularly intrigued that some consumed milk, while others that also had herd animals ate meat but did not drink milk. He made a map of the area, and then all of Africa, showing the milking and nonmilking regions, but he did not understand the meaning of this map until much later.

Since northern European populations were the first to be studied with regard to medical and physiological conditions, it was believed for a long time that drinking milk in adulthood was the human norm. In 1965, doctors at Johns Hopkins University noticed that African-American children in Baltimore, Maryland, often had indigestion, gas, and bloating after drinking milk. Further investigation revealed that three-quarters of these children could not digest lactose, the main carbohydrate of milk. Simoons' map of African milk drinkers and nonmilk drinkers corresponded with those groups that could digest lactose and those who could not! It turns out that lactose tolerance occurs when the gene for producing the lactase enzyme is present.

Color the top picture on the digestion of lactose. Choose a color for (a) that contrasts with (b).

Milk is the main food of newborn mammals, and the principal carbohydrate in milk is lactose, a compound sugar made of two simple sugars, glucose and galactose, linked together. (The only known mammalian milk with no lactose in it is that of Pacific Coast pinnipeds: seals and walruses.) The lactase enzyme is present in the small intestine, in the upper part of the gastro-intestinal tract; its function is to unlink these two sugars. These sugars can then be absorbed through the intestinal wall into the bloodstream and used for energy. In most of the world's human populations, intestinal lactase enzyme decreases rapidly with age, so that by the time children are three or four they can no longer digest lactose, and drinking milk produces uncomfortable gassy indigestion and diarrhea. This inability to digest milk is called lactose "intolerance" in spite of being the human norm.

Color the "indigestion" of lactose.

Microorganisms are the cause of the indigestion suffered by the lactose intolerant. Due to the absence of the lactase enzyme, lactose has not been broken down and cannot be absorbed in the upper intestine. It passes into the lower, large intestine, where resident bacteria, equipped with the enzymes that the individual lacks, ferment lactose into lactic acid, plus carbon dioxide and hydrogen gases, which produce bloating and discomfort.

Ironically, due to ignorance of the ubiquity of lactose intolerance, the United States government has often sent large amounts of powdered milk to foreign nations in the grip of crop failures or famine. Since the adult recipients quickly discovered that they could not consume this material, it was often thrown away or used to white-wash buildings, though in fact, it would have been perfectly suitable for consumption by infants, who are usually the ones most affected by famine.

Color the populations on the map and the genetic frequency of adult tolerance of lactose.

A few populations, such as those in northern Europe and African herders who have kept dairy cattle for thousands of years, have retained the milk-drinking habit and suffer no indigestion from it because their intestinal lactase enzyme remains high throughout life. Evidently natural selection has favored the lactase gene in these people, and this trait is passed on as a hereditary dominant from parents to children. If both parents are lactose intolerant, the children are likely to be lactose intolerant; but if either parent is lactose tolerant, the children will probably be lactose tolerant.

Most other Africans and almost all Asians are lactose intolerant after childhood and thus avoid drinking milk. Many of them, however, do eat fermented milk products, such as yogurt and cheese, in which the lactose has been converted by bacteria or yeasts into lactic acid prior to ingestion and is readily digested in the small intestine.

Subsequent studies all over the world showed that the African Fulani and Tussi, as well as the Swiss, Swedes, Finns, and others, are lactose-tolerant exceptions rather than the rule. Adult lactose tolerance illustrates how culture, in this case the keeping of cattle, can influence what is and what is not adaptive for human beings. The availability of milk cattle has created selection pressure operating on the human gene pool, favoring the life-long retention of intestinal lactase enzyme in a few populations that have relied on milk as a major nutritional source. Since the domestication of cattle occurred less than 10,000 years ago, natural selection has acted rather rapidly to produce nearly 100% lactose tolerance in North Europeans, who also benefit from the vitamin D content of milk. Vitamin D is essential for good health because weaker sunshine at high latitudes may not produce enough vitamin D in the skin (6-10). Furthermore, lactase enzyme increases calcium absorption, also needed for healthy bones. The slightly lesser degree of lactose tolerance in African herders, compared to the northern Europeans, is probably due to their dependence on milk for a shorter period of time, only a few thousand years.

The rest of Earth's human population continues to conform to the mammalian pattern that has been in existence for 100 million years—drinking mother's milk for a short time, being weaned, and consuming lactose-free foods for the rest of their lives.

MILK AND CULTURE

TOLERANT
 POPULATION a
INTOLERANT
 POPULATION b
INTESTINAL WALL c
LACTOSE SUGAR d, d[1]
LACTASE ENZYME e
BLOOD VESSEL f
BACTERIA g
CARBON DIOXIDE h
LACTIC ACID i

PERCENT TOLERANCE *

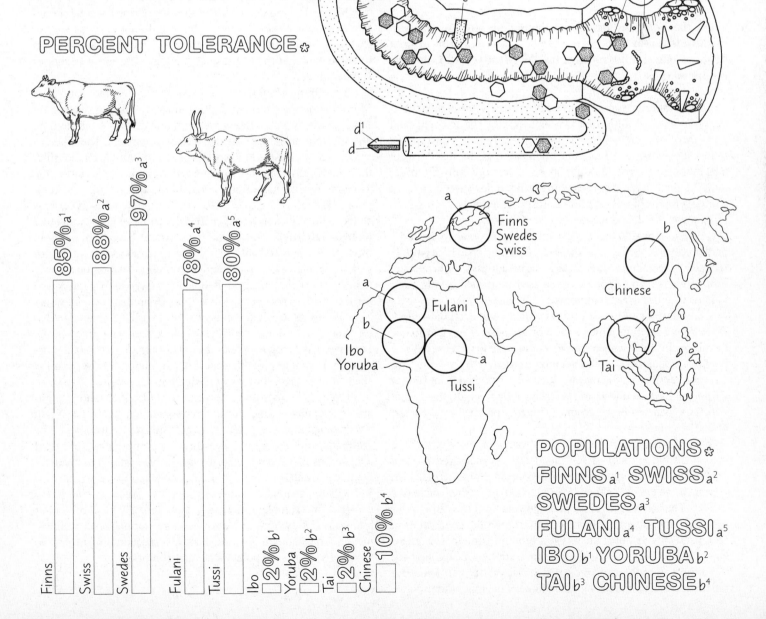

DIGESTION a

Small intestine

Large intestine

INDIGESTION b

POPULATIONS *
FINNS a[1] SWISS a[2]
SWEDES a[3]
FULANI a[4] TUSSI a[5]
IBO b[1] YORUBA b[2]
TAI b[3] CHINESE b[4]

85% a[1]
88% a[2]
97% a[3]
78% a[4]
80% a[5]

Finns
Swiss
Swedes
Fulani
Tussi
Ibo 20% b[1]
Yoruba 20% b[2]
Tai 20% b[3]
Chinese 10% b[4]

Finns
Swedes
Swiss

Chinese

Fulani

Ibo
Yoruba

Tussi

Tai

6-12
HIGH ALTITUDE ADAPTATIONS

The human body has three adaptive responses to environmental stress: behavioral, physiological, and genetic. Behavioral adaptations, such as wearing warm clothes in cold weather, provide the most flexibility, whereas physiological adaptations are less flexible and genetic adaptations, the least. In this plate, we discuss the range of human adaptations to high-altitude, low-oxygen environments.

Today nearly 40 million people reside at elevations above 2500 meters and 25 million live at altitudes above 3000 meters in the Himalayas, the Andes, and the Rocky Mountains. These populations have inhabited thin-air, low-oxygen environments for very different lengths of time and thus provide an opportunity to study whether each community's success is due to cultural factors (behavioral), short-term acclimatization (physiological), or long-term (genetic) adaptations.

Color the high-altitude population regions and the diagram of altitude versus inspired oxygen pressure. Available oxygen drops as one climbs from sea level to Mt. Everest. Color the red blood cells.

High altitude stresses the body primarily through oxygen deprivation, a condition known as hypoxia. The lower partial pressure of oxygen in the air at 3000 meters is only 70% as much as it is at sea level. All 3 mountain populations exhibit behavioral adaptations: wearing multiple layers of warm woolly clothing; building thick-walled houses with small windows to retain heat; and developing herds of altitude-resistant animals from which milk, meat, wool, and leather can be obtained.

Physiologically, low oxygen affects every organ in the body, particularly the muscles and the brain. On going up to high altitude from sea level, adults often experience breathlessness, headache, loss of energy and appetite, decreased motor skills, impaired judgment, and nausea. Symptoms usually abate within a few hours to a few days or weeks, a process called adult acclimatization. Body tissues at high altitude do not get normal oxygen loads, therefore physiological changes occur in order to increase oxygen intake. The quickest way to get more oxygen into the body is to increase ventilation, the rate at which air is breathed in and out of the lungs. The second is to increase cardiac output, the rate at which oxygenated blood from the lungs is pumped by the heart to body tissues.

Longer-range adaptations over weeks or months involve increasing the number of red blood cells as measured when a tube full of blood is spun in a centrifuge to determine hermatocrit. Normal hermatocrit is about 45% red blood cells, which increases to 54%. The increase means that blood volume carries 20% more oxygen. Other adaptations include increasing the concentration of muscle myoglobin, an oxygen-binding protein related to hemoglobin (2-6); increasing the concentration of capillaries in the lungs, which improves diffusion of oxygen into the bloodstream; and increasing the volume of the lungs themselves.

Color the figures of the sea level and high-altitude males and the associated graphs. Males at sea level achieve taller stature than do high-altitude males, but the situation reverses with chest circumference.

People native to high altitudes can adapt during the early stages of life, a process called developmental acclimatization. Anthropologist Roberto Frisancho compared the development outcomes of Peruvian Nuñoa males between 11 and 19 years of age who live at altitudes between 4000 and 5500 meters to those of Peruvian males raised at sea level.

In addition to an increased ratio of red blood cell volume to plasma volume (adult acclimatization), the high-altitude Nuñoa have increased chest, lung, and heart size. Hypoxia has profound effects on fetal development, mainly a reduction in birth weight. The higher the altitude, the lower the average birth weight. Small babies grow into small adults; children do not grow as well in low oxygen environments, and growth of the chest and lungs is to some extent at the expense of the legs. The result is shorter stature adults.

Low birth weight is also a risk factor in infant mortality. Many mothers-to-be adapt behaviorally by visiting relatives at lower altitudes where they give birth and delay a return to high altitude until the infant is as much as two years old. The Tibetans are an exception to the low birth weight/ high altitude relationship; their newborns tend to be of normal weight. Furthermore, the Tibetans mostly have normal red blood cell counts and their pulmonary artery pressure is like that of sea level natives. This suggests that Tibetans have genetic adaptations unique from other mountain dwellers. North American groups have been living in the high Rockies for only 150 years, much too short a time for genetic change to take place and their present adaptation appears to be due to acclimatization. People have lived in the high Andes for less than 10,000 years, since modern humans arrived in the New World relatively recently, 13,000 to 15,000 years ago. No one knows how long the Tibetans' ancestors have lived in the Himalayas, but *Homo sapiens* arrived in China about 50,000 years ago, so it is quite possible that this population has lived in the shadow of Everest for tens of millennia.

Anthropologist Lorna Moore concludes that human high-altitude populations include all three adaptation levels. The North American mountaineers represent acclimatized newcomers. The Andeans and Tibetans have developmental physiological adaptations that include improved birth weights, high levels of ventilation, enlarged lung volumes, and better exercise capacity. The Tibetan adaptation exceeds that of the Andeans' and likely provides an example of genetic adaptation. They exhibit better brain-blood flow during exercise, more normal birth weights, more normal hemoglobin levels, and less susceptibility to chronic mountain sickness, a potentially fatal condition.

HIGH ALTITUDE ADAPTATIONS

HUMAN POPULATIONS *
SEA LEVEL a   ROCKIES c   HIMALAYAS e
HIGH ALTITUDE b   ANDES d

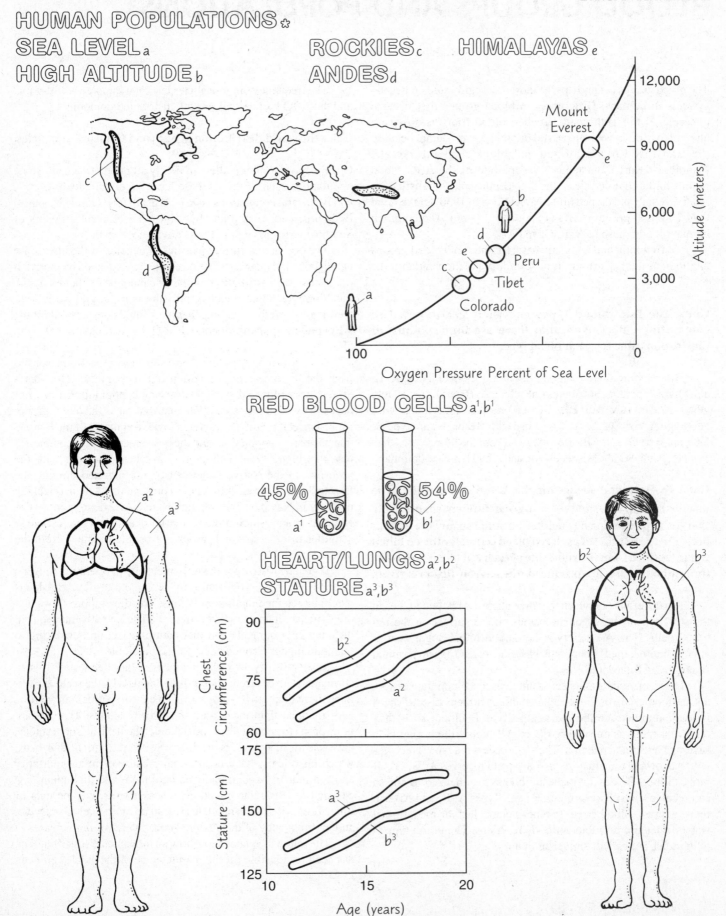

Mount Everest e

12,000
9,000
6,000
3,000

Altitude (meters)

b

d
e
Peru
c
Tibet
Colorado

a

100   0
Oxygen Pressure Percent of Sea Level

RED BLOOD CELLS a¹,b¹

45%   54%
a¹   b¹

HEART/LUNGS a²,b²
STATURE a³,b³

a²
a³

b²
b³

90

75

60

Chest Circumference (cm)

b²
a²

175

150

125

Stature (cm)

a³
b³

10   15   20
Age (years)

The blood groups are perhaps the most thoroughly studied genetic systems in humans. Differences in blood groups first became apparent in the 19th century, when blood transfusions were attempted. Some were successful but others were lethal because the transfused blood clotted and blocked blood vessels. Pathologist Karl Landsteiner's recognition of the ABO blood groups in the first decade of the 20th century made transfusions relatively safe and earned him a Nobel Prize in 1930. Of the more than 20 blood groups, ABO is the major system. The common human blood types are A, B, O, and AB.

We first look at the genetic basis for the ABO blood groups and then at their distribution in several populations around the world.

Color the four blood types and their genotypes. Use contrasting colors. Note that there are four columns of illustrations, one for each blood type.

Three major alleles can be present at the ABO locus: A, B, and O. Each parent contributes one allele, A, B, or O, so possible genotypes are AA, AO, BB, BO, OO, or AB. Individuals with genotype AA or AO are type A; those with BB or BO are type B; OOs are type O; and ABs are type AB. From the blood types, it is evident that the O allele is recessive, and A and B are co-dominant.

Color the terminal sugars for the A and B molecules. The terminal sugars, (a^1) and (b^1) are given different shapes. Note that the O phenotype has neither terminal sugar; the AB has both. On the left side of each red blood cell, color the terminal sugar (antigen). On the right side of each red blood cell, color the antibodies that are produced when a transfusion is given.

The difference between the three alleles, A, B, and O, lies in the structure of the sugar molecules on the surface of the red blood cells. The A phenotype has the terminal sugar acetyl-galactosamine; the B phenotype has galactose; O has no terminal sugar; and AB has both.

These terminal sugars act as antigens in a blood transfusion, and antibodies are produced against those antigens (2-8). Type A individuals make antibodies against type B blood, so if they receive a transfusion of types B or AB blood, there may be a severe or even fatal reaction. The same occurs if a type B receives a type A or AB transfusion, or if a type O receives A, B, or AB blood. Type AB does not make antibodies to either A or B and so can receive transfusions of either type. Types A, B, and AB can receive type O blood, because type O blood, lacking the terminal sugars, does not promote antibody reactions. Therefore, type O individuals are called "universal donors."

The frequency of these alleles has been sampled world-wide, and the ABO blood types are not distributed randomly.

Color the world distribution of A, B, and O allele frequencies.

O is the most common allele in nearly all populations, but some populations such as the Chinese have large amounts of both A and B. Several populations have no B at all, for example Navahos, Bedouins, and Australian aborigines. The Xavante Indians of South America have only the O allele, no A or B.

The population differences in frequencies of the alleles are not random and their distribution cannot be explained by mutation rate. When the distribution of alleles cannot be explained by the mutation rate, some selective pressure is usually at work. Two well-known evolutionary mechanisms could help account for the ABO polymorphisms: genetic drift (1-16) and natural selection (1-17).

Genetic drift may occur when a small group becomes isolated from the larger parent population due to migration (founder's effect) or a physical barrier. The small population does not necessarily have the same allele distribution as the larger group; for instance, it might have a much lower frequency of the B allele than the parent population, and the descendants might completely lose this blood type. This could have been the case with the ancestors of the Native Americans, who migrated through the Bering Straits from eastern Asia. At present, the B allele is lacking not only in Navahos, but in many Native American groups. The Xavante Indians (in South America) probably lost the A allele in a similar fashion, as small groups of people migrated from the north.

If genetic drift were the only mechanism operating on gene frequencies, it is likely that only one allele at the ABO locus would be retained in all populations. The illustration shows that this is not so. It appears that different alleles are advantageous in different environments and that natural selection is working to maintain higher frequencies of these favorable alleles.

Susceptibility to certain diseases has been statistically correlated with different alleles. Individuals with the A allele seem to be more likely to develop stomach cancer, pernicious anemia, and smallpox than those with the B or O alleles. Type Os are more prone to peptic ulcers and bubonic plague. But, some studies have shown that type Os are more resistant to infant diarrheas, which historically have been a major cause of infant mortality and continue to be so in many parts of the world. In populations exposed to particular infectious diseases over long periods of time, those with resistant alleles would be more likely to survive, and the frequency of the advantageous allele would increase.

The following plates show how an infectious disease, malaria, has been responsible for the maintenance of the sickle cell gene in Africa.

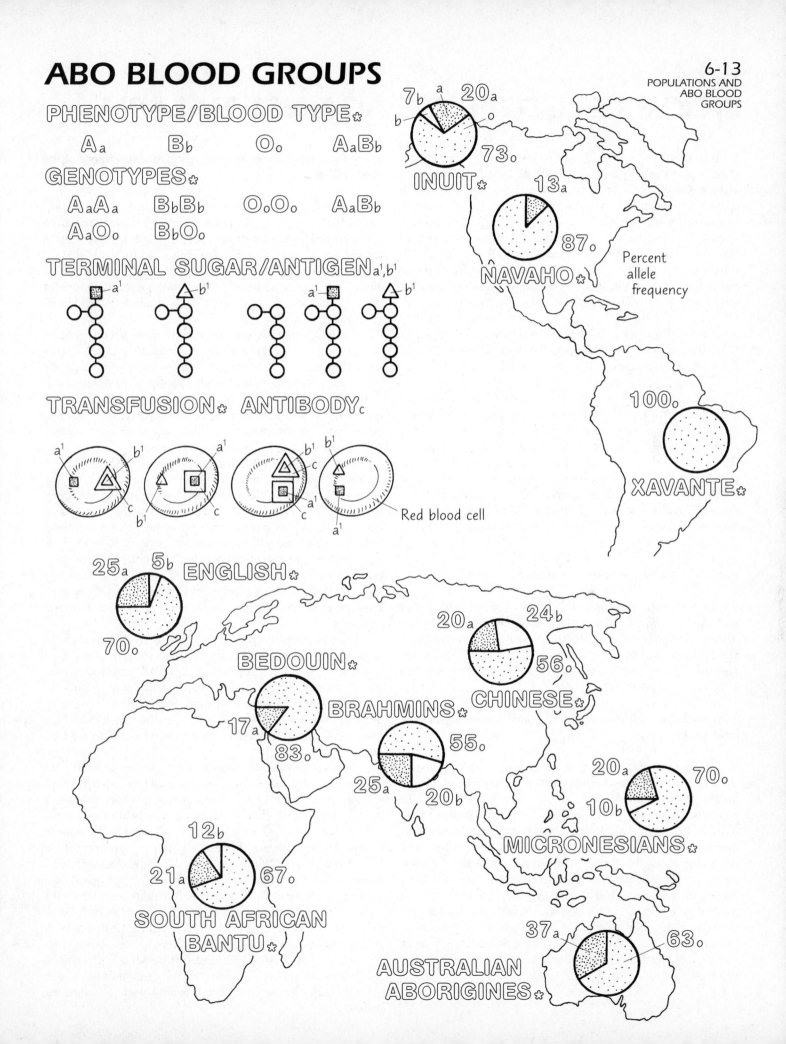

ABO BLOOD GROUPS

PHENOTYPE/BLOOD TYPE*

A$_a$ B$_b$ O$_o$ A$_a$B$_b$

GENOTYPES*

A$_a$A$_a$ B$_b$B$_b$ O$_o$O$_o$ A$_a$B$_b$

A$_a$O$_o$ B$_b$O$_o$

TERMINAL SUGAR/ANTIGEN$_{a^1,b^1}$

TRANSFUSION*   ANTIBODY$_c$

Red blood cell

INUIT*
7$_b$ 20$_a$
73$_o$

NAVAHO*
13$_a$
87$_o$

Percent allele
frequency

XAVANTE*
100$_o$

ENGLISH*
25$_a$ 5$_b$
70$_o$

BEDOUIN*
17$_a$
83$_o$

BRAHMINS*
25$_a$ 20$_b$
55$_o$

CHINESE*
20$_a$ 24$_b$
56$_o$

MICRONESIANS*
20$_a$ 70$_o$
10$_b$

**SOUTH AFRICAN
BANTU***
12$_b$
21$_a$ 67$_o$

**AUSTRALIAN
ABORIGINES***
37$_a$ 63$_o$

6-14
SICKLE CELL DEFENSE AGAINST MALARIA

In 1904, Dr. James Herrick of Chicago saw a young black student from Grenada, in the Caribbean, who complained of palpitations and weakness. Dr. Herrick found that the patient had severe anemia, and when he examined the blood under a microscope, he saw some peculiar red cells that were elongated and sickle-shaped. This was the first recognition that the shape of red blood cells was connected with a disease. Now we know that sickle cell anemia is a serious genetic disease, common among Africans and African-Americans. Until the advent of modern medicine, sickle cell disease was usually fatal before the age of twenty.

At the top of the plate, color the normal red blood cells and those from a person with sickle cell disease. Use contrasting colors. Color the hemoglobin types as well.

Some of the red blood cells of individuals afflicted with sickle cell disease have a crescent or sickle shape rather than the normal disc shape. On the molecular level, the "sickling" can be traced to the presence of a variant hemoglobin called hemoglobin S (HbS). In 1949, chemist Linus Pauling and colleagues showed that hemoglobin S is structurally different from normal hemoglobin, HbA, and thus identified the first "molecular disease." (As we saw in 2-9, Pauling was also a codiscoverer of the "molecular clock," based on further observations on hemoglobin.)

Next color the amino acids at positions 5, 6, and 7.

In 1956, Vernon Ingram at Cambridge, in research suggested by Francis Crick of DNA fame, sequenced the two hemoglobin proteins and pinpointed the difference between HbS and HbA. He demonstrated that the amino acid valine (2-5) replaces glutamic acid in the HbS, the sickle hemoglobin. This research won Ingram a Nobel Prize.

Now color the nucleotide bases on the mRNA codons and the DNA strands.

A point mutation resulting in a single nucleotide base change causes this amino acid substitution. When uracil replaces adenine on the messenger RNA codon, valine rather than glutamic acid gets coded for in the protein of HbS. This codon is the genetic basis of the sickle cell hemoglobin. Thus, a single mutation dramatically changes the shape of red blood cells. When HbS molecules release their oxygen in the capillaries, they stack up in long rigid chains called polymers. Individuals with sickle cell disease suffer from problems caused by blocked capillaries and reduced circulation to various organs of the body. They experience intermittent bouts of severe pain, serious anemia, and injury to tissues resulting in joint and brain damage, kidney and heart failure, and abnormal growth. Normal hemoglobin does not form polymers.

Color the bottom illustration showing the inheritance of the sickle cell gene.

Individuals with two normal hemoglobin alleles (AA) will have normal red blood cells. Heterozygous (AS) individuals have the sickle cell trait; some of their hemoglobin is normal, some is the sickle type, therefore some of their cells are sickle shaped. Except in extreme conditions, such as physical exertion at high altitudes, persons with sickle cell trait do not suffer symptoms of disease. Homozygous (SS) individuals suffer from sickle cell disease.

Sickle cell disease, which is fatal to many in childhood, is so pervasive throughout tropical Africa that investigators wondered how such a serious defect could survive in the population without being eliminated by natural selection. Geneticist Anthony Allison in the 1950s suspected that the sickle cell allele persisted generation after generation because it provided protection against the world's most important infectious disease, the greatest killer of the tropical world: malaria.

Malaria is transmitted from the blood of one individual to the next by mosquito bites, which introduce a disease-causing parasite. The parasite, *Plasmodium falciparum*, reproduces during part of its life cycle in human red blood cells. The *Plasmodium* parasite infects HbS and HbA red cells equally. However, HbS red cells sickle faster when infected; rapid sickling somehow kills the parasite and therefore it cannot complete its 48-hour reproductive cycle. Mutant hemoglobin is not completely protective but does lessen the severity of the infestation, helping the diseased individual to survive long enough to build up natural immunity.

In malarial areas, a person with an AA genotype has little or no protection against the disease. A person with an SS genotype has sickle cell disease. A person with an AS genotype has the sickle cell trait, which confers some resistance to malaria. In particular, young children without the sickle cell trait are twice as likely to die from heavy malarial infections, which cause high fever and severe tissue damage, than those who do carry the HbS gene.

From studies of DNA, it appears that sickle hemoglobin arose independently by different mutations at least four different times: twice in West Africa, once in Bantu Africa, and once in India or Arabia. These distinctive genes make it possible to track the source of the sickle cell gene in North Africa and Mediterranean Europe. The northern gene is not a new one but came from central West Africa, probably via the caravan trade that exchanged horses, cattle, salt, and manufactured goods for ivory, gold, and slaves. These genes were used by geneticist Ronald Nagel to trace the origin of African-Americans living in Baltimore, Maryland. About 18% of their ancestors came from Bantu Africa, 15% from West Africa's Atlantic coast, and 62% from central West Africa.

Sickle cells illustrate the trade-off between a trait that is deleterious in terms of a primary function (transporting oxygen to the tissues), but beneficial for a secondary function (combating malaria).

SICKLE CELL TRAIT

RED BLOOD CELLS*
  NORMAL n
  SICKLE CELL s
HEMOGLOBIN TYPE n[1], s[1]

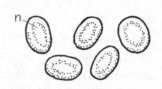

HbA n[1]

HbS s[1]

AMINO ACIDS*
PROLINE pro
GLUTAMIC ACID glu
VALINE val

Hemoglobin beta-chain positions

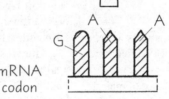

pro   glu   glu

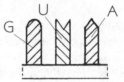

pro   val   glu

NUCLEOTIDE BASES*
GUANINE G
ADENINE A
URACIL U
THYMINE T
CYTOSINE C

mRNA codon

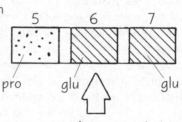

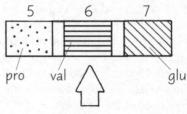

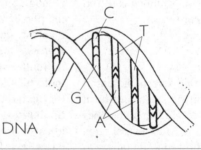

DNA

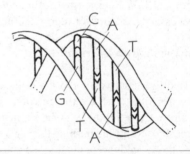

RED BLOOD CELLS AND MALARIA*

GENOTYPE*
ALLELES n[2], s[2]

$A_{n^2} A_{n^2}$

$A_{n^2} S_{s^2}$

$S_{s^2} S_{s^2}$

PHENOTYPE*   NORMAL*

SICKLE CELL TRAIT*

SICKLE CELL DISEASE*

RED BLOOD CELLS n, s

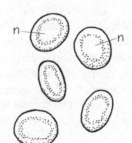

MALARIA ENVIRONMENT*   NO PROTECTION*   SOME RESISTANCE*   SICKLE CELL DISEASE*

SICKLE CELL: ENVIRONMENT AND CULTURE

As a killer of millions in the tropics for at least thousands of years, malaria has been a powerful selective agent on human populations. Until near the end of the 18th century, it was believed that the disease was contracted by breathing "bad air" (Italian= mala aria), especially the moist night air. Ronald Ross, a British medical officer working in India, suspected that malaria was transmitted by mosquitoes. He did experiments on birds, which also suffer from malaria, and proved that infected red cells are passed from one bird to another by a particular species of mosquito. The same mode of transmission takes place in humans. For this work, carried out alone with no official support, Ross received one of the first Nobel prizes in 1901.

Color the map at the top of the plate, which shows where malaria is year-round, seasonal, and sporadic in Africa.

The endemic areas that suffer the highest incidence of malaria are tropical rain forests where *Anopheles* mosquitoes can find the necessary moisture for reproduction year-round.

Color the map on the right.

Two thousand years ago the tropical rain forests of central Africa were altered by the introduction of slash-and-burn agriculture from Southeast Asia. Farmers cleared small patches of forest by cutting and burning the vegetation. After several years of use, these fields were abandoned and allowed to lie fallow to replenish soil nutrients. Water gathered on the fields in open sunlit pools, an ideal breeding ground for mosquitoes. Agriculture had a profound effect on human populations. Peoples of Africa had been primarily gatherers and hunters, living in small nomadic social groups. With the introduction of agriculture, human groups became more sedentary, had more food at hand, and population density increased. With more people living in stable groups in a small area, transmission of the malarial parasite from one person to another was unavoidable.

Notice that the endemic malarial area surrounds and includes the entire range of slash-and-burn agricultural practice. This practice promoted malaria into a major health hazard in central Africa.

Now color the lower map, using contrasting colors.

In areas of slash-and-burn, individuals with the sickle cell trait are less susceptible to malarial infection and so have a selective advantage over those with only normal hemoglobin (6-16). Therefore, the incidence of sickle cell trait is highest (10-16%) in populations where slash-and-burn agriculture is more pervasive and where there is a year-round risk of malaria.

Persistence of the sickle cell gene in more than 10% of Africans is an evolutionary trade-off between the adverse effects of the gene on red cells and the beneficial effects in combating malaria. But what is an advantage to Africans in their malarial environment has become a disadvantage to their descendants in the temperate United States, where the risk of malaria is very slight. During the four hundred or so years that descendants of Africans have lived in North America, the incidence of the sickle cell trait has decreased from about 10% to about 5%, probably due to the combined effects of natural selection now favoring HbA rather than HbS, and genetic mixing with non-Africans.

Humans in malarial regions have evolved many defenses against the parasite other than HbS. Hemoglobin C (HbC) is common in West Africa, Hemoglobin E in Southeast Asia. These hemoglobins are less effective against malaria than HbS, but, on the plus side, produce milder diseases in homozygous carriers than the sickle gene does. The thalassemias (from the Greek *thalassa*, meaning sea) are found around the Mediterranean and in Southeast Asia; these are anemias in which the hemoglobin molecules are synthesized at abnormally low rates, thus depriving the malaria parasite of its intracellular nest for replication. Similarly, widespread deficiencies of the red blood cell enzyme glucose 6 phosphate dehydrogenase (G6PD) also discourage parasite infestation, as does another shape disorder called elliptocytosis, in which the red blood cells are oval rather than round.

Several hundred abnormalities of hemoglobin and other red blood cell factors have been identified, but only a few of these provide some protection against malaria. In thalassemia, the genes are sufficiently different in different regions to indicate that this protection against malaria has arisen at least six times in New Guinea alone, according to biologist Jared Diamond. Occasionally some of these antimalarial genes are found in isolated European families, but as they have no selective advantage in nonmalarial environments, they do not spread through the population.

The sickle cell story weaves together the themes of Mendelian genetics, Darwinian evolution, molecular biology, and the interplay of biology and culture. Despite the development of new antimalarial drugs, malaria still kills nearly three million people per year and so acts as a powerful force for selecting those individuals whose genes provide some protection against the contagion. The saga of the red crescent that spares many lives by sacrificing others is far from ended.

SICKLE CELL: ENVIRONMENT AND CULTURE

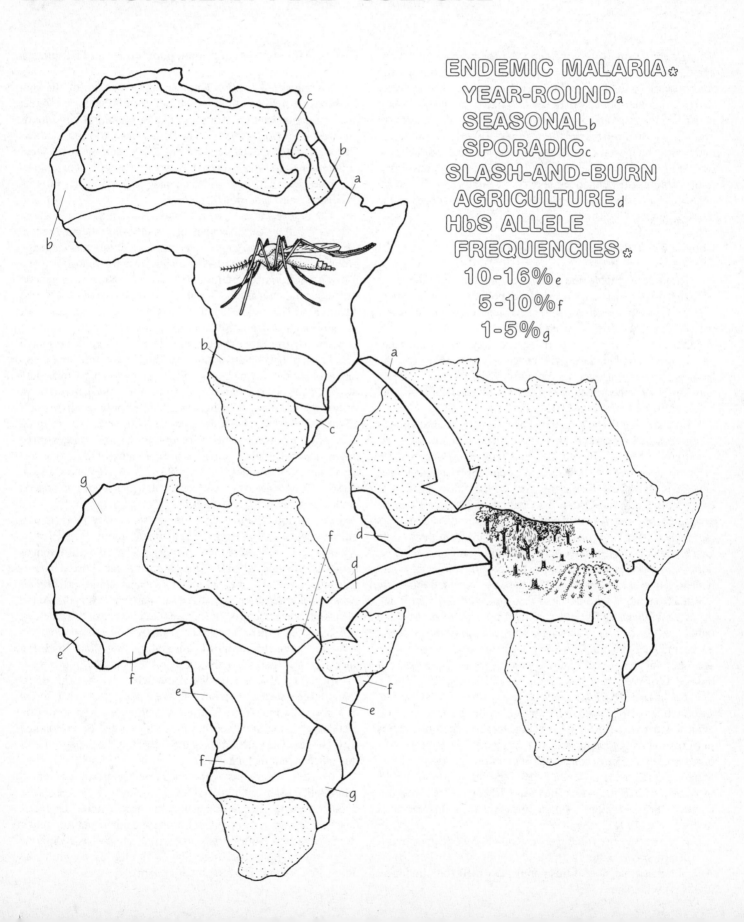

ENDEMIC MALARIA*
YEAR-ROUND a
SEASONAL b
SPORADIC c
SLASH-AND-BURN
AGRICULTURE d
HbS ALLELE
FREQUENCIES *
10-16% e
5-10% f
1-5% g

6-16
HUMAN MIGRATIONS

When populations migrate, they take their genes and their languages with them, and so both genetic studies and linguistic studies can shed light on past human migrations and history. After two populations split apart, the genes of each group continue to undergo mutations, and the longer the separation, the greater the number of differences in their genes. Likewise, language undergoes changes in words, sounds, and structure that increase with separation time. Geneticist L.L. Cavalli-Sforza has found remarkable correspondences between a family tree based on genetic relationships and another based on the languages of the world's peoples.

Color the distribution of Rh negative genes.

The Basque people, their language, and the high frequency of Rh negative genes suggest a model of how Europe was settled. The Rh factor is a well-known genetic marker, a human blood antigen that is either positive or negative. When a mother is Rh negative and her fetus Rh positive, she may make antibodies against the fetus, who may suffer neonatal jaundice. Worldwide, Rh negative genes are common in Europe, uncommon in Africa and West Asia, and virtually absent in East Asia and the aboriginal populations of America and Australia.

Basques live in the mountains between northern Spain and southwestern France and have the highest incidence of Rh-negativity (25%) in the world. Their language is profoundly different from that of surrounding groups. Both language and genetics suggest that the Basques may be the oldest inhabitants of Europe. The present-day distribution of Rh genes can be accounted for by the spread of agriculture. Cavalli-Sforza suggests that early Neolithic farmers moving westward from the Middle East brought their Rh positive genes and Indo-European languages with them. Farther west, the admixture of migrant genes would be less, as we see on the map. The Basques remained relatively isolated from migrant influence by their greater distance, by living in the mountains, and by their cultural practice of pastoralism rather than farming. Thus, they have retained more of their original genes and language than have any other European people.

Human genetic affiliations can be traced back tens of thousands of years based on comparing DNA. Linguistic family trees can be traced back at most 5000 years to the origin of writing. Linguistic anthropologist Joseph Greenberg has presented evidence that virtually all known languages have commonalities in words referring to body parts like finger and low numbers like one, two, three. For instance, the number one is "tek" in Nilo-Saharan, "tak" in Afro-Asiatic, "deik" in Indo-European, "tik" in Amerind, Eskimo-Aleut and Sino-Tibetan, "dik" in Indo-Pacific. Our word "digit" obviously derives from this universal root.

A genetic tree of evolutionary origins of 42 world populations shows a high correlation with the clustering of their languages. An abbreviated version of this combined genetic and linguistic tree is presented here.

Color the family trees of human populations and languages.

Among the Africans, Khoisan, the language of the San Bushmen, is believed to be possibly the world's oldest tongue, just as the San seem to represent one of the oldest continuous populations of *Homo sapiens*. The Bantus of central and southern Africa migrated extensively within Africa, starting about three millenniums ago. According to Greenberg, the 400 Bantu tongues are all descended from a single language spoken by early farmers in Nigeria and Cameroon.

The Indo-European group includes most of the Iranian, East Indian, and all the European languages, including Italian, French, German, Spanish, and English, the most widely spoken language group on earth. Along with Altaic and Amerind, Indo-European forms a Nostratic superfamily of languages. Numerous genetic studies have shown close relationships between Asians and Native Americans. The Altaic language groups include the cluster of Mongol, Japanese, and Siberian.

One of the most controversial areas of gene-language correlation is that of Native Americans and New World languages. Independent studies of genes and languages suggest that there were several discrete migrations from Asia into the Americas. Although the Americas have been inhabited only within the past 15,000 years or so, Native American groups speak 100 or more different languages, which Greenberg classifies under three linguistic superfamilies: Amerind includes most of the languages; Na-Dene and Eskimo-Aleut are spoken in Alaska and Canada. The three language groups correlate well with genetic distinctions among geographical subgroups.

The various dialects of Chinese, spoken by more than a billion people, belong to the Sino-Tibetan family. Genetically, Asians can be subdivided into two groups based on differences in their mitochondrial DNA. One group of Asians lacks a 9 base-pair sequence that is present in other Asians and in virtually all Africans and Europeans. Migration patterns from the Asian mainland can be traced by the presence or absence of this deletion, which acts as a genetic marker. Nearly 100% of Polynesian islanders have this deletion, indicating that their founding ancestors also had the deletion. Melanesians and many other Pacific Islanders lack the deletion, which shows that their founding ancestors came from a different population in a different migration. People from Southeast Asia entered Australia by 50,000 years ago, much earlier than they settled Polynesia and New Guinea. The uniqueness of the Australian languages reflects this independent history.

Correspondence between genetic and linguistic clusters is remarkably high but not perfect. Language can be replaced without genetic change and genes replaced without language change. Latin spread to western Europe and other countries under Roman rule. The United States in the past century has undergone considerable genetic change due to immigration, while the dominant language has remained the same.

GENES AND LANGUAGE

FREQUENCY OF Rh NEGATIVE FACTOR ✷

25%/BASQUE a

9-24% b

4-9% c

1-4% d

0-1% e

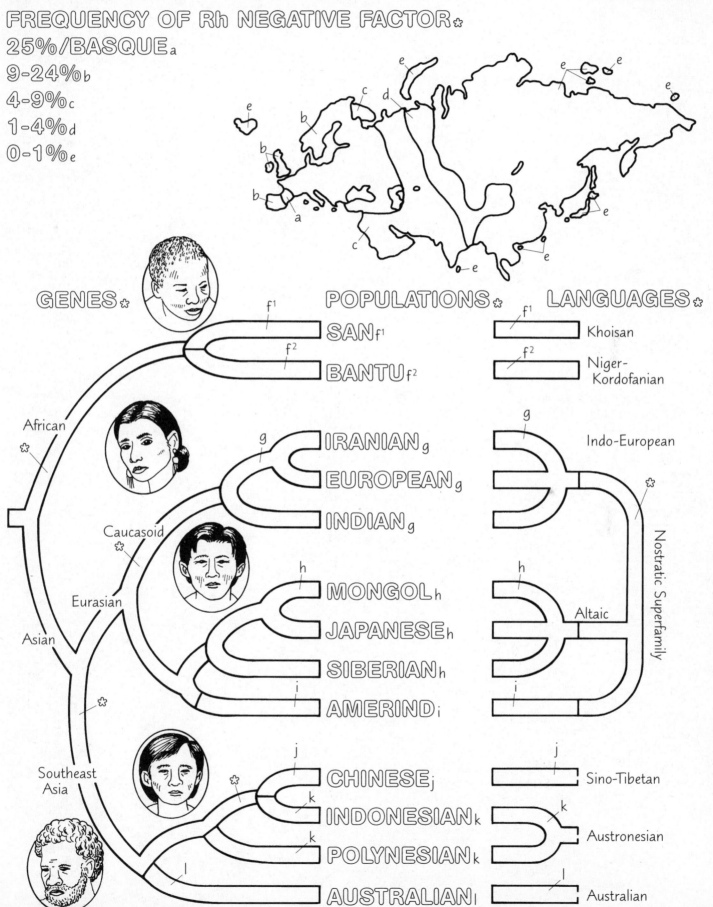

GENES ✷

POPULATIONS ✷

LANGUAGES ✷

African ✷

Caucasoid ✷

Eurasian

Asian

Southeast Asia

SAN f¹	f¹	Khoisan
BANTU f²	f²	Niger-Kordofanian
IRANIAN g	g	Indo-European
EUROPEAN g		
INDIAN g		
MONGOL h	h	Altaic
JAPANESE h		
SIBERIAN h		
AMERIND i	i	
CHINESE j	j	Sino-Tibetan
INDONESIAN k	k	Austronesian
POLYNESIAN k		
AUSTRALIAN l	l	Australian

Nostratic Superfamily

GETTING THE MOST OUT OF COLOR

This book involves coloring. Lots of it. You will be using color to identify a structure and link it to its name (title). Color will be used to differentiate one structure from another, and to show relationships among structures. You will give an aesthetic quality to the plates you have colored. What you have colored you will remember for years based partly on the colors you selected. This brief introduction on the use and character of color will give real support to your coloring goals by providing you with a basic understanding of colors and color matching. It will also provide you with the ability to extend a basic collection of twelve hues to thirty-six or more colors.

What color will you choose? On what basis will you choose it? How many values of a color do you need and how many do you *have*? How can you extend your coloring pen/pencil set to make far more colors than you have? Finally, how can you plan the coloring of each plate to get a really pleasing result? Read on.

PRINCIPLES OF COLOR

Sunlight is white light. White light contains all of the colors in the visible spectrum. Visible light represents a very small band in an immensely large band of radiant energy, most of which is not visible to the human eye. If one places a prism in sunlight, an array or spectrum of colors emerge. Light is the essence of color, yet in itself, it is not a color. Without light, there is no color. Night is the absence of light and therefore the absence of color.

Color vision is based on reflectance. White light, as we have mentioned, is composed of all colors. When light strikes an object such as a lemon, most of the spectrum colors in the light are absorbed by the lemon. A small amount is reflected off of the surface of the lemon—the reflected light. This is the color we perceive. It is the color of the object. In the case of the lemon, the reflected color is yellow.

A good example of a spectrum or sequence of color bands can be seen in a rainbow. Rainbows appear when the sun is shining and it is raining. When the white light of the sun passes through raindrops, the light is bent or refracted. When white light is refracted (as by a prism or by raindrops), the colors of the spectrum separate and become visible. Each color of the spectrum has a different wavelength or characteristic. Simply stated, the rainbow spectrum begins with violet and moves to red, then orange, yellow, green, blue, and back to violet. If we bend the rainbow into a circle and join the violets, we have a color wheel.

To appreciate these color changes, color the rainbow below using the colors indicated. Then color the wheel below the rainbow in the same sequence as the rainbow, starting at the notch with violet.

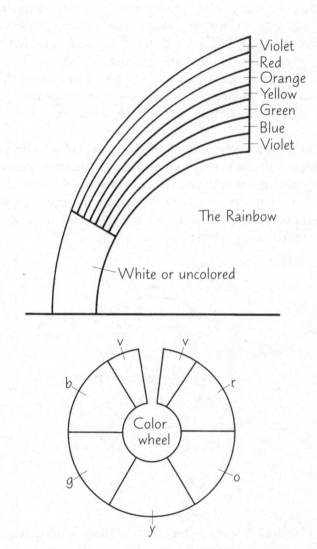

The Rainbow

There are three **primary** colors in the spectrum:

Primary colors cannot be created by mixing other colors. They can be combined (mixed) to make other colors.

By mixing two primary colors you create what is called a **secondary** color:

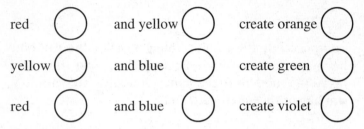

red ( ) and yellow ( ) create orange ( )

yellow ( ) and blue ( ) create green ( )

red ( ) and blue ( ) create violet ( )

This processing can be continued by mixing a primary and a secondary color, creating what is known as a **tertiary** color. Tertiary colors have simple names based on the colors combined. Thus mixing red and orange creates the tertiary color red orange. There are six tertiary colors.

Below we have another color wheel made up of three concentric circles. The color wheel is divided into six wedges, each marked with a primary or secondary color.

Color each wedge completely with the color indicated. Begin with the primary colors. For the secondary colors, try mixing the primaries instead of using the secondary colors that you may have. This may not turn out well with coloring pens, in which case you may have to use the secondary colors.

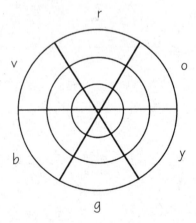

Color is known as **hue**. A pure color means maximum **intensity** or **saturation** of color.

Every pure hue (color) has another set of characteristics known as **value**. Value is the lightness or darkness of a color. Each color has a range of value that extends from very light (near white) to very dark (near black). When we lighten a color, we **tint** it. When we darken a color, we **shade** it. For example, red is a saturated color of maximum intensity. Pink is a tint of red; burgundy is a shade of red.

On your color wheel, color over all of the colors in the outer band or circle with white (or the closest to white that you have). Again, pencils work better than pens in this exercise. Now color all of the colors in the inner band or circle with black, but not enough to obscure the color.

You have now tinted and shaded the primary and secondary colors. There are now three colors for each hue on the wheel. *You can use a color many times by changing its value.* This fact has importance to you as you select various tints and shades of a single color for relating similar structures or related processes in the plates you are working.

Pure or intense colors have different value. Look at the pure colors on your color wheel; notice that blue has a darker value than yellow. Each color has its own value.

Below is a black/white value scale consisting of 11 boxes arranged in a horizontal line (identified as number 1). It is called a gray scale. Starting with white (w) at far left, we have added 10% of black to each square progressively until we have pure, 100% black (b) at far right.

Below this scale, numbered 2, there is another 11-box scale that is blank. Set aside your six primary and secondary colors. One at a time, place the point of one of the pencils/pens over the gray scale and move it across until you find a gray that has the same value (darkness). Fill the box in under that gray with the matching color. In the event that more than one color has the same value, color the space under that square.

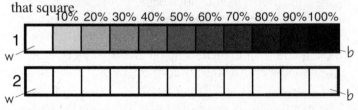

In the series of boxes identified as 3, 4, and 5, you can make your own value scale from three colors. Leave the boxes at far LEFT uncolored (white, w), and fill in the box at far RIGHT with black (b). Locate one pure (intense) hue from scale 2 and color the same box on scale 3. To the left of the hue, progressively tint the boxes until you reach the white box. To the right, progressively shade the color until you reach black. Repeat the process with two different colors in boxes 4 and 5.

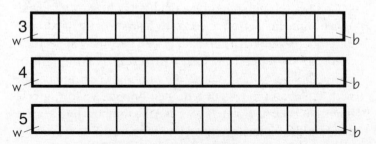

HOW TO USE COLORS

Our next step is to understand how to use color. Colors do many things visually and psychologically. One can create a sense of quiet relaxation, emotional stress, or intellectual excitement. Through color combinations the artist can make one color look like another color, or make a color look brighter than it actually is.

We associate colors with physical phenomena. Colors that are associated with the sun and fire are called "warm colors." Warm colors, such as red, yellow, and orange, visually **advance** or come forward in a scene or painting. "Cool colors" are associated with ice and water; they are blue and green, and they visually **recede**. We cool the far distance in a painting to create **atmospheric** perspective.

Combinations of colors can have many effects. When we use colors that are next to each other on the color wheel, they create a sense of harmony and are called harmonious or **analogous colors**. Analogous colors have a restful nature. An example of harmonious colors on your color wheel would be red, violet, and blue. Place a patch of these colors on the page next to this paragraph to see the harmony. Pick two more harmonious color schemes and place them on the margin.

Color combinations that use colors located far from each other are contrasting in their nature. Contrasting colors create a greater sense of emotion than harmonious colors do. If we use contrasting colors that are an equal distance apart we have a **triad**. Primary colors are triadic. Red, yellow, and blue will create strong contrast. Secondary colors are also triadic.

Colors directly across the color wheel from each other are **complementary colors**. On the color wheel, red and green are complementary colors. Yellow-violet, and blue-orange are also complementary. When complementary colors are placed next to each other, they intensify the color of each; red is a brighter red and green is a brighter green. This is known as simultaneous contrast.

In the boxes below, color the primary colors on the top bar and their complementary secondary color on the lower bar.

If the colors you used are pure hues, you should be able to observe the effects of simultaneous contrast. Artists like Vincent Van Gogh, Paul Gauguin, Toulouse-Lautrec were masters of color contrast. Black and white also create simultaneous contrast.

It is interesting to note that while placing complementary colors next to each other, they brighten the color of each. When we mix complementary colors, they dull or neutralize each other.

With the above insights, you can extend your enjoyment and your skill in coloring the plates in this book. Happy Coloring!

-Jay and Christine Golik
Napa Valley College, California

APPENDIX

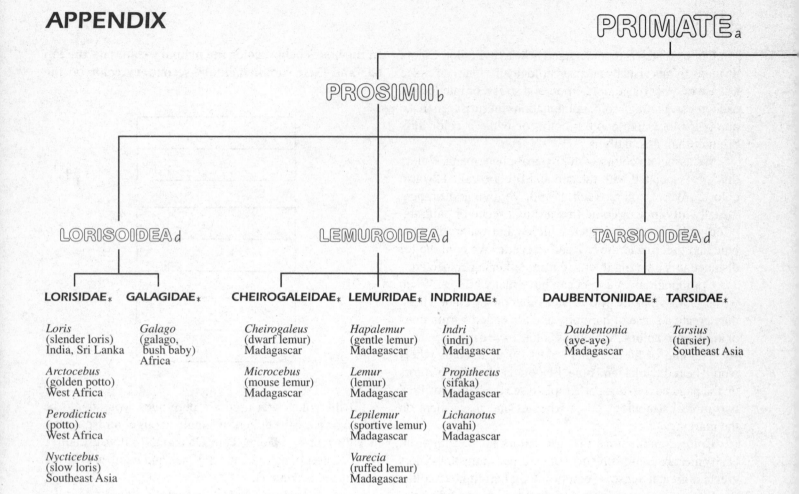

PRIMATE a

PROSIMII b

LORISOIDEA d   **LEMUROIDEA** d   **TARSIOIDEA** d

LORISIDAE *   **GALAGIDAE** *   **CHEIROGALEIDAE** *   **LEMURIDAE** *   **INDRIIDAE** *   **DAUBENTONIIDAE** *   **TARSIDAE** *

Loris
(slender loris)
India, Sri Lanka

Arctocebus
(golden potto)
West Africa

Perodicticus
(potto)
West Africa

Nycticebus
(slow loris)
Southeast Asia

Galago
(galago,
 bush baby)
Africa

Cheirogaleus
(dwarf lemur)
Madagascar

Microcebus
(mouse lemur)
Madagascar

Hapalemur
(gentle lemur)
Madagascar

Lemur
(lemur)
Madagascar

Lepilemur
(sportive lemur)
Madagascar

Varecia
(ruffed lemur)
Madagascar

Indri
(indri)
Madagascar

Propithecus
(sifaka)
Madagascar

Lichanotus
(avahi)
Madagascar

Daubentonia
(aye-aye)
Madagascar

Tarsius
(tarsier)
Southeast Asia

LEGEND

ORDER... a
SUBORDER... b
INFRAORDER... c
SUPERFAMILY... d
FAMILY... *
SUBFAMILY... **
GENUS... *italicized*

ANTHROPOIDEA *b*

PLATYRRHINE *c*
(New World Monkeys)

CEBOIDEA *d*

CALLITHRICIDAE*
(tamarins and marmosets)

Callithricinae**

Callithrix
(marmoset)
Tropical South
America

Cebuella
(pygmy
marmoset)
South America

Saguinus
(tamarin)
Tropical South
America

Leontopithecus
(golden lion
tamarin)
Tropical South
America

Callimico
(Goeldi's
monkey)
Amazon Basin

CEBIDAE*

Cebinae**

Cebus
(capuchin)
Central and
South America

Saimiri
(squirrel
monkey)
Central and
South America

Atelinae**

Ateles
(spider monkey)
Mexico to
Amazon Basin

Brachyteles
(woolly spider
monkey)
Brazil

Lagothrix
(woolly
monkey)
South America

Alouatta
(howler
monkey)
Mexico to
Tropical South
America

Pithecinae**

Callicebus
(titi monkey)
Tropical South
America

Pithecia
(white faced saki)
Amazon Basin

Cacajao
(uakari)
South America

Chiropotes
(bearded saki)
South America

Aotinae**

Aotus
(owl monkey)
Tropical
South America

CATARRHINE *c*
(Old World Monkeys, Apes, and Humans)

CERCOPITHECOIDEA *d*
(Old World Monkeys)

COLOBIDAE*
(leaf monkeys)

Colobus
(colobus)
Africa

Presbytis
(leaf monkey)
Southeast Asia

Pygathrix
(douc langur)
Vietnam

Nasalis
(probiscus)
Borneo

Rhinopithecus
(snub-nosed
monkeys)
Vietnam, China

CERCOPITHECIDAE*
(cheek pouch monkeys)

Cercopithecus
(guenon, vervet,
patas)
Africa

Cercocebus
(sooty mangabey)
West, Central,
and East Africa

Lophocebus
(gray-cheeked
mangabey)
West, Central,
and East Africa

Papio
(baboon, gelada,
hamadryas)
Sub-saharan
Africa

Mandrillus
(drill, mandrill)
West and
Central Africa

Macaca
(macaque, rhesus
monkey)
Europe, North
Africa, Asia

HOMINOIDEA *d*
(Apes and Humans)

HYLOBATIDAE*

Hylobates
(gibbon)
Southeast
Asia

PONGIDAE*

Pongo
(orangutan)
Borneo,
Sumatra

Pan
(gracile and
robust
chimpanzees)
Equatorial
Africa

Gorilla
(gorilla)
Equatorial
Africa

HOMINIDAE*

Australopithecus
(extinct hominid
ancestor)
Africa

Homo
(living and
extinct)
Worldwide

BIBLIOGRAPHY

Section 1

Bowman, RI. 1961. Evolutionary Patterns in Darwin's Finches. *California Academy of Sciences*, Occasional Papers, 44:107-140.

Browne, Janet 1995. *Charles Darwin. Voyaging.* Princeton University Press: Princeton, New Jersey.

Colbert, EH. 1966. *Evolution of the Vertebrates.* 2nd edition, John Wiley and Sons: New York.

Darwin, C. 1839. *Journal of Researches into the Natural History and Geology of the Countries Visited During the Voyage of H.M.S. Beagle.* London. Reprinted by D. Appleton and Company: New York, 1897.

Darwin, C. 1859. *On The Origin of Species.* John Murray: London. Reprinted by The Modern Library: New York.

Darwin, C. 1868. *The Variation of Animals and Plants Under Domestication, Volumes 1 and 2.* John Murray: London. Reprinted by D. Appleton and Company: New York, 1896.

Darwin, C. 1872. *The Descent of Man and Selection in Relation to Sex.* London. Reprinted by The Modern Library: New York.

Ghiselin, MT. 1969. *The Triumph of the Darwinian Method.* University of California Press: Berkeley.

Glen, W. 1982. *The Road to Jaramillo: Critical Years of the Revolution in Earth Science.* Stanford University Press: Stanford.

Grant, P. 1986. *Ecology and Evolution of Darwin's Finches.* Princeton University Press: New Jersey.

Grant, P. 1991. Natural selection and Darwin's finches. *Scientific American.* October: 82-87.

Hildebrand, M. 1995. *Analysis of Vertebrate Structure.* John Wiley and Sons: New York.

Hoagland, M and Dodson, B. 1995. *The Way Life Works.* Times Books, Random House: New York.

Jablonski, Nina 1998. *The Natural History of the Doucs and Snub-Nosed Monkeys.* World Scientific: Singapore.

Kurten, B. 1969. Continental Drift and Evolution. *Scientific American.* March: 1-11.

Lowenstein, JM & Zihlman, Adrienne L. 1998. The Pulse of Life. In *A Brief History of Science.* Gribbin, J. (ed.) Barnes and Noble Inc: New York. 181-214.

Lyell, C. 1830-1833. *Principles of Geology vol 1-3.* London. Reprinted with an introduction by Martin Rudwick. University of Chicago Press: Chicago.

Margulis, Lynn 1970. *Origin of Eukaryotic Cells.* Yale University Press: New Haven.

Mayr, E. 1978. Evolution. *Scientific American.* 239(3):46-55.

Mayr, E. 1997. *This is Biology: the Science of the Living World.* Harvard University Press: Cambridge.

Mayr, E & Provine, W. 1980 *The Evolutionary Synthesis: Perspectives on the Unification of Biology.* Harvard University Press: Cambridge, Massachusetts.

Medawar, PB. 1979. *Advice to a Young Scientist.* Harper and Row: New York.

Moore, J. 1993. *Science as a Way of Knowing: The Foundation of Modern Biology.* Harvard University Press: Cambridge, Massachusetts.

Moore, Ruth 1963. *Man, Time, and Fossils. The Story of Evolution.* 2nd ed. Knopf: New York.

Moore, Ruth 1964. *Evolution.* Time-Life Books: New York.

Romer, AS. 1959. *The Vertebrate Story.* University of Chicago Press: Chicago.

Schopf, JW. 1999. *Cradle of Life: The Discovery of Earth's Earliest Fossils.* Princeton University Press, Princeton: New Jersey.

Sibley, CG & Ahlquist, J. 1981. The phylogeny and relationship of the Ratite birds as indicated by DNA-DNA hybridization. In GCE. Scudder and J.L. Reveal, eds. *Evolution Today.* Hunt Inst. Botanical Document: Pittsburgh, PA. 301-335.

Simpson, GG. 1949. *The Meaning of Evolution: A Study of the History of Life and its Significance for Man.* Yale University Press: New Haven.

Simpson, GG. 1964. *This View of Life.* Harcourt Brace: New York.

Thompson, DW. 1917. *On Growth and Form.* Abridged edition, J.T. Bonner (ed.) Cambridge University Press: Cambridge, 1977.

Van Tuinen, M, et al. 1998. Phylogeny and biogeography of Ratite birds inferred from DNA sequences of the mitochondrial ribosomal genes. *Molecular Biology and Evolution* 15(4):370-376.

Weiner, J. 1994. *Beak of the Finch: Evolution in Real Time.* Random House Publishing: New York.

Young, D. 1992. *The Discovery of Evolution.* Cambridge University Press: UK.

Section 2

Allegre, C & Schneider, S. 1994. The evolution of the earth. *Scientific American.* 271(4): 66-75.

Avise, J. 1994. *Molecular Markers, Natural History, and Evolution.* Chapman and Hall: New York.

Berard, JD, et al. 1993. Male rank, reproductive behavior and reproductive success in free ranging rhesus macaques. *Primates.* 34(4):481-489.

Bercovitch, F. 1997. Reproductive strategies of rhesus macaques. *Primates.* 38(3): 247-263.

Charles-Dominique, P & Martin, RD. 1970. Evolution of lorises and lemurs. *Nature.* 227:257-260.

DeRuiter, JR, et al. 1993. Male dominance rank and reproductive success in primate groups. *Primates.* 34(4): 513-523.

Dixson, AF, et al. 1993. Male dominance and genetically determined reproductive success in the mandrill (*Mandrillus sphinx*). *Primates.* 34(4): 525-532.

Doolittle, WF & Sapienza, C. 1980. Selfish genes, the phenotype paradigm and genome evolution. *Nature*. 284:601-603.

Gagneux, P, et al. 1997. Furtive mating in female chimpanzees. *Nature*. 387(6631):358-359.

Gehring, W. 1998. *Master Control Genes in Development and Evolution: The Homeobox Story*. Yale University Press: New Haven.

Gerloff, U, et al. 1999. Intercommunity relationships, dispersal pattern and paternity success in a wild living community of Bonobos (*Pan paniscus*) determined from DNA analysis of faecal samples. *Proceedings of the Royal Society of London, B*(266):1189-1195.

Goodman, M. 1962. Immunochemistry of the primates and primate evolution. Yearbook of Physical Anthropology. 10:83-98.

Hashimoto, Chie, et al. 1996. Matrilineal kin relationship and social behavior of wild bonobos (*Pan paniscus*): sequencing the D-loop region of mitochondrial DNA. *Primates*. 37(3):305-318.

Higuchi, RG, et al. 1984. DNA sequence from the quagga, an extinct member of the horse family. *Nature*. 312:282-284.

Inoue, M, et al. 1993. Male dominance rank and reproductive success in an enclosed group of Japanese macaques: with special reference to post-conception mating. *Primates*. 34(4): 503-511.

Kimura, M. 1979. The neutral theory of molecular evolution. *Scientific American*. 241(5):98-126

King, Mary-Claire & Wilson, AC. 1975. Evolution at two levels in humans and chimpanzees. *Science*. 188:107-116.

Lewin, R. 1997. *Patterns in Evolution: the New Molecular View*. Scientific American Library: New York.

Lowenstein, JM & Ryder, OA. 1985. Immunological systematics of the extinct quagga (Equidae). *Experientia*. 41:1192-1193.

Lowenstein, JM & Scheuenstuhl, G. 1991. Immunological methods in molecular paleontology. *Philosophical Transactions of the Royal Society of London*. B333:375-380.

Lowenstein, JM, et al. 1981. Albumin systematics of the extinct mammoth and Tasmanian wolf. *Nature*. 291:409-411.

McGinnis, W & Kuziora, M. 1994. The molecular architects of body design. *Scientific American*. 270(2):58-66.

Melnick, D & Hoelzer, G. 1991. Differences in male and female macaque dispersal lead to contrasting distributions of nuclear and mitochondrial DNA variation. *International Journal of Primatology*. 13(4) 379-393.

Moore, Ruth 1961. *The Coil of Life: The Story of Great Discoveries in the Life Sciences*. Alfred Knopf: New York.

Nagai, K, et al. 1988. Evolution and hemoglobin studied by protein engineering. *BioEssays*. 8(2) 79-82.

Nuttall, G. 1904. *Blood Immunity and Blood Relationship*. Cambridge University Press: Cambridge.

Paul, A, et al. 1993. The association between rank, mating effort, and reproductive success in male Barbary macaques (*Macaca sylvanus*). *Primates*. 34(4):491-502.

Robertis, E, et al. 1990. Homeobox genes and the vertebrate body plan. *Scientific American*. 263(1):46-52.

Sarich, VM & Wilson, AC. 1967. Immunological time scale for hominid evolution. *Science*. 154:1563-1566.

Sibley, CG & Ahlquist, JE. 1984. The phylogeny of the hominoid primates, as indicated by DNA-DNA hybridization. *Journal of Molecular Evolution*. 26:99-121.

Watson, JD. 1968. *The Double Helix*. Athenaeum: New York.

Wilson, AC, et al. 1977. Biochemical evolution. *Annual Review of Biochemistry*. 46:573-639.

Wilson, EO & Eisner, T. (eds.) 1975. *Life on Earth*. Sinauer Associates Inc: Sunderland, Massachusetts.

Wooding, GL & Doolittle, RF. 1972. Primate fibropeptides: evolutionary significance. *Journal of Human Evolution*. 1(6):553-563.

Zihlman, Adrienne & Lowenstein J. 1979. False start of the human parade. *Natural History*. 88(7):86-91.

Zuckerkandl, E & Pauling, L. 1965. Evolutionary divergence and convergence in proteins. In *Evolving genes and proteins*. Bryson, V. and Vogel, HJ (eds.) Academic Press: New York. 97-166.

Section 3

Altmann, Jeanne 1980. *Baboon Mothers and Infants*. Harvard University Press: Cambridge, Massachusetts.

Altmann, Jeanne, et al. 1993. Body size and fatness of free-living baboons reflect food availability an activity levels. *American Journal of Primatology*. 30:149-161

Altmann, S. 1998. *Foraging for Survival: Yearling Baboons in Africa*. Cambridge University Press: Chicago, Illinois.

Bateman, G. ed. 1984. *Primates: All The Worlds Animals*. Torstar Books Inc: New York.

Biegert, J. 1963. The evaluation of characteristics of the skull, hands, and feet for primate taxonomy. In *Classification and Human Evolution*. Washburn, SL. (ed.) Aldine de Gruyter: New York. 116-145.

Boesch, C. 1991. Teaching in wild chimpanzees. *Animal Behavior*. 41:530-533.

Boesch, C & Boesch, Hedwidge. 1983. Optimization of nut cracking with natural hammers by wild chimpanzees. *Behaviour*. 3(4):265-286.

Boesch, C & Boesch, Hedwidge. 1984. Possible Causes of Sex Differences in the Use of Natural Hammers by Wild Chimpanzees. *Journal of Human Evolution*. 13: 414-440.

Boesch, C & Boesch, Hedwidge. 1990. Tool use and tool making in wild chimpanzees. *Folia Primatologica*. 54:86-99.

Boesch, C & Tomasello, M. 1998. Chimpanzee and human culture. *Current Anthropology*. 39(5): 591-614.

Bourlière, F. 1985. Primate communities: their structure and role in tropical ecosystems. *International Journal of Primatology*. 6(1):1-26.

Boysen, Sarah T. 1996. "More is less": The elicitation of rule-governed resource distribution in chimpanzees. In *Reaching Into Thought: The Minds of the Great Apes*. Russon, Anne E, et al. (eds.) Cambridge University Press: Cambridge. 177-189.

Byrne, R & Whiten, A. 1987. The thinking primate's guide to deception. *New Scientist.* December:54-57. Thanks to David Bygott for his original art, which inspired the top illustration on 3-32.

Cheney, Dorothy L & Seyfarth, R. 1990. *How Monkeys See the World.* University of Chicago Press: Chicago Illinois.

Cheney, Dorothy L, et al. 1988. Reproductive success in vervet monkeys. In *Reproductive Success.* Clutton-Brock, TH. (ed.) University of Chicago Press: Chicago.

Chism, Janice, et al. 1984. Life history patterns of female patas monkeys. In *Female Primates: Studies by Women Primatologists.* Small, Meredith E. (ed.) Alan R. Liss: New York.

Clutton-Brock, TH, ed. 1977. *Primate Ecology: Studies of Feeding and Ranging Behavior in Lemurs, Monkeys and Apes.* Academic Press: London.

Darwin, C. 1872. *The Expression of the Emotions of Man in Animals.* Reprinted with an introduction by Paul Ekman in 1998, Oxford University Press, New York.

Deitz, JM & Baker, AJ. 1993. Polygyny and female reproductive success in golden lion tamarins, *Leontopithecus rosalia. Animal Behavior.* 46:1067-1078.

Dunbar, RIM & Dunbar, EP. 1974. Ecological relations and niche separation between sympatric terrestrial primates in Ethiopia. *Folia Primatologica.* 21:36-60.

Eisenberg, JF. 1973. Mammalian social systems: are primate social systems unique? *Symposium of the IVth International Congress of Primatologists, vol 1: Precultural Primate Behavior.* 232-249.

Fagan, R. 1993. Primate juveniles and primate play. In *Juvenile Primates: Life History, Development, and Behavior.* Pereira, M and Fairbanks, Lynn. (eds.) Oxford University Press, New York. 182-196.

Falk, Dean 2000. *Primate Diversity.* W.W. Norton and Company, New York.

Fedigan, Linda Marie, et al. 1986. Lifetime reproductive success in female Japanese macaques. *Folia Primatologica.* 47: 143-157.

Fedigan, Linda Marie 1992. *Primate Paradigms: Sex Roles and Social Bonds.* University of Chicago Press: Chicago.

Goodall, Jane 1986. *The Chimpanzees of Gombe: Patterns of Behavior.* The Belknap Press of Harvard University Press Cambridge, Massachusetts. Thanks to J. Goodall, B. Gray, H. van Lawick for original photographs of individuals inspiring illustrations on 3-31.

Grand, TI. 1977a. Body weight: its relation to tissue composition, segment distribution, and motor function. *American Journal of Physical Anthropology.* 47(2): 211-239.

Grand, TI. 1977b. Body weight: its relation to tissue composition, segment distribution, and motor function. *American Journal of Physical Anthropology.* 47(2): 241-248.

Greenfield, Susan 1996. *The Human Mind Explained: An Owner's Guide to the Mysteries of the Mind.* Henry Holt and Company: New York.

Haimoff, EH. 1984. Acoustic and organizational features of gibbon songs. In *The Lesser Apes: Evolutionary and Behavioral Biology.* Preuschoft, H, et al. (eds.) Edinburgh University Press, Edinburgh. 333-353.

Harding, RSO & Olson, D. 1986. Patterns of mating among male patas monkeys (*Erythrocebus patas*) in Kenya. *American Journal of Primatology.* 11:343-358.

Hausfater, G. 1975. *Dominance and reproduction in baboons: a qualitative analysis.* S. Karger: Basel.

Huffman, MA. 1992. Influences of female partner preference on potential reproductive outcome in Japanese macaques. *Folia Primatologica.* 59(2):77-88.

Huffman, M. 1993. Tool-assisted predation on a squirrel by a female chimpanzee in the Mahale Mountains, Tanzania. *Primates.* 34(1) 93-98.

Jenkins, FA. 1974. Tree shrew locomotion and primate arborealism. In *Primate Locomotion.* Jenkins, FA. (ed.) Academic Press: New York. 85-115.

Lee, Phyllis C. 1983. Play as a means for developing relationships. In *Primate Social Relationships.* Hinde, R. (ed.) Simauer Assoc: Sunderland, Massachusetts. 82-89.

Lee, Phyllis C. 1987. Nutrition, fertility and maternal investment in primates. *Journal of Zoology, London.* 213:409-422.

Lee, Phyllis C, et al. 1991. Growth, weaning, and maternal investment from a comparative perspective. *Journal of Zoology, London.* 225:99-114.

Leigh, SR & Terranova, CJ. 1998, Comparative perspectives on bimaturism, ontogeny, and dimorphism in lemurid primates. *International Journal of Primatology.* 19(4):723-749.

Lowenstein, JM. 1995. The Selfish Chimp. *Pacific Discovery,* Spring.

Matsuzawa, T. 1989. Spontaneous pattern construction in a chimpanzee. In *Understanding Chimpanzees.* Heltne, PG and Marquardt, Linda A. (eds.) Harvard University Press: Cambridge.

McFarland, Robin 1992. *Body Composition and Reproduction in Female Pigtail Macaques.* Ph.D. Dissertation, University of Washington, Seattle.

McFarland, Robin 1997. Female primates: fat or fit? In *The Evolving Female: A Life History Perspective.* Edited by Morbeck, Galloway, and Zihlman. Princeton University Press: Princeton, New Jersey.

McGrew, WC. 1992. *Chimpanzee Material Culture: Implications for Human Evolution.* Cambridge University Press: Cambridge, England.

McGrew, W, et al. 1996. *Great Ape Societies.* Cambridge University Press: Cambridge, UK.

McLean, P. 1985. Brain evolution relating to family, play, and the separation call. *Archives of General Psychiatry*. 42, 405-417.

Milton, Katherine 1993. Diet and primate evolution. *Scientific American*. 269(2):86-93.

Nishida, T. 1987. Local traditions and cultural transmission. In *Primate Societies*. Smutts, Barbara, et al. (eds.) University of Chicago Press: Chicago. 462-474.

Parker, S. 1994. *How the Body Works*. Readers Digest: New York.

Pavelka, Mary 1993. *Monkeys of the Mesquite*. Kendall Hunt Publishing Company: Iowa.

Pavelka, Mary & Fedigan, Linda Marie 1991. Menopause: a comparative life history perspective. *Yearbook of Physical Anthropology*. 34:13-38.

Pereira, M & Fairbanks, Lynn 1993. *Juvenile Primates: Life History, Development, and Behavior*. Oxford University Press: New York.

Price, EC & Feistner, Anna TC. 1993. Food sharing in lion tamarins: tests of three hypotheses. *American Journal of Primatology*. 31:211-221.

Rowe, N. 1996. *The Pictorial Guide to the Living Primates*. Pogonias Press: East Hampton, New York.

Schultz, AH. 1969. *The Life of Primates*. Weidenfeld and Nicolson: London.

Seyfarth, RM, et al. 1980. Monkey responses to three different alarm calls: evidence of predator classification and semantic communication. *Science*. 210(4471):801-803.

Smith, Kathleen K. 1992. The evolution of the mammalian pharynx. *Zoological Journal of the Linnean Society*. 104:313-349.

Smuts, Barbara B. 1985. *Sex and Friendship in Baboons*. Aldine de Gruyter: New York.

Smuts, Barbara B, et al. 1987. *Primate Societies*. University of Chicago Press: Chicago.

Steklis, HD. 1999. The primate brain and the origin of intelligence. In *The New Physical Anthropology: Science, Humanism, and Critical Reflection*. Strum, Shirley, et al. (eds.) Prentice Hall: Upper Saddle River, New Jersey.

Struhsaker, TT. 1967. *Behavior of vervet monkeys (Cercopithecus aethiops)*. University of California Press: Berkeley.

Strum, Shirley C. 1987. *Almost human: a journey into the world of baboons*. Random House: New York.

Strum, Shirley C. 1991. Weight and age in wild Olive Baboons. *American Journal of Primatology*. 25: 219-237.

Strum, Shirley C. 1994. Reconciling aggression and social manipulation as means of competition: 1, life-history perspective. *International Journal of Primatology*. 15(5):739-765.

Sugiyama, Y. 1997. Social tradition and use of tool-composites by wild chimpanzees. *Evolutionary Anthropology*. 23-27.

Sussman, R. 1979. *Primate Ecology: Problem-Oriented Field Studies*. John Wiley and Sons: New York.

Tanner, Joanne & Byrne, R. 1993. Concealing facial evidence of mood: perspective taking in a captive gorilla. *Primates*. 34(4): 451-457.

Tanner, Joanne & Byrne, R. 1999. The development of spontaneous gestural communication in a group of zoo-living lowland gorillas. In *The Mentalities of Gorillas and Orangutans: Comparative Perspectives*. Parker, Sue, et al. (eds.) Cambridge University Press, Cambridge. 211-239.

Teleki, GP. 1974. Chimpanzee subsistence technology: materials and skills. *Journal of Human Evolution*. 3:575-594.

Teleki, GP. 1975. Primate subsistence patterns: collector-predators and gatherer-hunters. *Journal of Human Evolution*. 4(2):125-184.

de Waal, FBM. 1982. *Chimpanzee Politics: Power and Sex Among Apes*. Harper & Row: New York.

Watanabe, K, et al. 1992. Characteristic features of the reproduction of Koshima monkeys, *Macaca fuscata fuscata*: a summary of thirty-four years of observation. *Primates*. 33:1-32.

Waser, PM. 1985. What does "whoop-gobble" mean? In *Primates: All The Worlds Animals*. Torstar Books Inc: New York. 94-95

Whiten, A, et al. 1999. Cultures in chimpanzees. *Nature*. 399:682-685.

Wrangham, R, et al. 1994. *Chimpanzee Cultures*. Chicago Academy of Science: Chicago, Illinois.

Yamakoshi, G. 1998. Dietary responses to fruit scarcity of wild chimpanzees at Bossou, Guinea: possible implications for ecological importance of tool use. *American Journal of Physical Anthropology*. 106:283-295.

Zihlman, Adrienne, et al. 1990. Skeletal biology and individual life history of Gombe chimpanzees. *Journal of Zoology, London*. 221:37-61.

Zuckerman, S.1932. *The Social Life of Monkeys and Apes*. Kegan Paul Trench Trubner: London.

Section 4

Bartlett, TQ, et al. 1993. Infant killing in primates: a review of observed cases with specific reference to the sexual selection hypothesis. *American Anthropologist*. 94:958-990.

Begun, DR, et al. 1997. *Function, Phylogeny, and Fossils : Miocene Hominoid Evolution and Adaptations*. Plenum Press: New York.

Benefit, Brenda R. 1999. *Victoriapithecus*: the key to Old World monkey and Catarrhine origins. *Evolutionary Anthropology*. 7(5)155-174.

Benefit, Brenda R & McCrossin, ML. 1997. Earliest known Old World monkey skull. *Nature*. 388(6640):368-371.

Bennett, Elizabeth L & Davies, AG. 1994. The ecology of Asian colobines. In *Colobine Monkeys: Their Ecology, Behavior, And Evolution*. Davies, AG & Oates, JF. (eds.) Cambridge University Press: Cambridge. 129-171.

Bergeson, DJ. 1998. Patterns of suspensory feeding in *Alouatta palliata*, *Ateles geoffroyi*, and *Cebus capucinus*. In *Primate Locomotion: Recent Advances*. Strasser, Elizabeth, et al. (eds.) Plenum Press: New York. 45-60.

Bishop, Naomi H. 1979. Himalayan langurs: temperate colobines. *Journal of Human Evolution*. 8:251-281.

Boggess, Jane E. 1979. Troop male membership changes and infant killing in langurs (*Presbytis entellus*). *Folia Primatologica*. 32:65-107.

Boggess, Jane E. 1984. Infant killing and male reproductive strategies in langurs (*Presbytis entellus*). In *Infanticide. Comparative and Evolutionary Perspectives*. Hausfater, G & Hrdy Sarah B. (eds.) Aldine de Gruyter: New York. 283-319.

Boinski, Sue 1987. Habitat use by squirrel monkeys (*Saimiri oerstedi*) in Costa Rica. *Folia primatologica*. 49(3-4):151-167.

Boinski, Sue & Fragaszy, DM. 1989. The ontogeny of foraging in squirrel monkeys, *Saimiri oerstedi*. *Animal Behavior*. 37:415-428.

Carr, A. 1964. *The Land and Wildlife of Africa*. Time Life Books: New York.

Chapman, C. 1995. Primate seed dispersal: coevolution and conservation implications. *Evolutionary Anthropology*. 4(3):74-83.

Charles-Dominique, P. 1977. *Ecology and Behavior of Nocturnal Primates*. Columbia University Press: New York.

Chevalier-Skolnikoff, Suzanne 1982. The adaptive significance of higher intelligence in wild orangutans: a preliminary report. *Journal of Human Evolution*. 11:639-652.

Ciochon, RL & Chiarelli, AB. (eds.) 1979. *Evolutionary Biology of the New World Monkeys and Continental Drift*. Plenum Press: New York.

Clutton-Brock, TH. 1977. *Primate Ecology: Studies of Feeding and Ranging Behavior in Lemurs, Monkeys, and Apes*. Academic Press: New York.

Conroy, GC. 1990. *Primate Evolution*. WW Norton & Company: New York.

Coolidge, HJ. 1933. *Pan paniscus*. Pygmy chimpanzee from south of the Congo River. *American Journal of Physical Anthropology*. 18(1):1-59.

Cronin, JE, et al. 1980. Molecular evolution and systematics of the genus *Macacca*. In *The Macaques: Studies in Behavior and Evolution*. Lindburg, DG. (ed.) Van Nostrand Reinhold Company: New York. 31-51.

Curtin, RA & Dolhinow, P. 1978. Primate social behavior in a changing world. *American Scientist*. 66:468-475.

Curtin, Sheila H. 1976. Niche separation in sympatric Malaysian leaf-monkeys (*Presbytis obscura* and *Presbytis melalophos*). *Yearbook of Physical Anthropology*. 421-439.

Davies, AG & Oates, JF. (eds.) 1994. *Colobine Monkeys*. Cambridge University Press: Cambridge.

Davies, AG, et al. 1999. Patterns of frugivory in three West African colobine monkeys. *International Journal of Primatology*. 20(3):127-357.

de Waal, F & Lanting, F. 1997. *Bonobo: the Forgotten Ape*. University of California Press: Berkeley.

Dolhinow, Phyllis 1978. A behavior repertoire for the Indian langur monkey (*Presbytis entellus*). *Primates*. 19:449-472

Dolhinow, Phyllis & Fuentes, A. 1999. *The Nonhuman Primates*. Mayfield Publishing Company: Mountain View, CA.

Doran, Diane M. 1993. Comparative locomotor behavior of chimpanzees and bonobos: the influence of morphology on locomotion. *American Journal of Physical Anthropology*. 91(1):83-98.

Eimerl, S & DeVore I. (eds.) 1974. *The Primates*. Time Life Books: New York.

Emmons, Louise H & Gentry, AH. 1983. Tropical forest structure and the distribution of gliding and prehensile-tailed vertebrates. *The American Naturalist*. 121(4):513-524.

Fa, JE & Lindburg DG. (eds.) 1996. *Evolution and Ecology of Macaque Societies*. Cambridge University Press: Cambridge.

Falk, Dean 1983. Reconsideration of the endocast of *Proconsul africanus*: implications for primate brain evolution. In *New Interpretations of Ape and Human Ancestry*. Ciochon, R and Corruccini, R. (eds.) Plenum Press: New York. 239-248.

Fedigan, Linda M. 1990. Vertebrate predation in *Cebus capucinus*: meat eating in a neotropical monkey. *Folia Primatologica*.. 54:196-205.

Fedigan, Linda M, et al. 1996. Critical issues in cebine evolution and behavior. In *Adaptive Radiations of Neotropical Primates*. Norconk, Marilyn A, et al. (eds.) Plenum Press: New York. 219-228.

Fleagle, JG. 1999. *Primate adaptation and evolution*, 2nd ed. Academic Press: San Diego.

Fooden, J. 1980. Classification and distribution of living macques (*Macaca lacépède*, 1799). In *Macaques*. Lindburgh, DG. (ed.) Van Nostrand Reinhold: New York. 1-9.

Fooden, J. 1982. Ecogeographic segregation of macaque species. *Primates*. 23(4):574-579.

Fossey, Dian 1983. *Gorillas in the Mist*. Houghton Mifflin: Boston, Mass.

Fox, Elizabeth A. 1998. *The Function of Female Mate Choice in the Sumatran Orangutan (Pongo pygmaeus abelii)*. Ph.D. Dissertation, Duke University.

Fox, Elizabeth A, et al. 1999. Intelligent tool use in wild Sumatran orangutans. In *The Mentalities of Gorillas and Orangutans. Comparative Perspectives*. Parker, Sue Taylor, et al. (eds.) Cambridge University Press: Cambridge.

Fruth, Barbara 1998. Comment on "The social behavior of chimpanzees and bonobos." *Current Anthropology*. 39(4):408-409.

Gagneux, P, et al. 1999. Mitochondrial sequences show diverse evolutionary histories of African hominoids. *Proceedings of the National Academy of Science*. vol 96: 5077-5082.

Galdikas, Birute MF. 1988. Orangutan diet, range, and activity at Tanjung Putting, Central Borneo. *International Journal of Primatology*. 9(1):1-35.

Garber, Paul 1980. Locomotor behavior and feeding ecology of the Panamanian tamarin, *Saguinus oedipus geoffroyi*, Callitrichidae primates. *International Journal of Primatology*. 1(2):185-201.

Garber, Paul 1997. One for all and breeding for one: cooperation and competition as a tamarin reproductive strategy. *Evolutionary Anthropology*. 5:187-199.

Gautier-Hion, Annie, et al. 1988. *A Primate Radiation: Evolutionary Biology of the African Guenons*. Cambridge University Press: New York.

Goodall, Jane 1964. Tool-using and aimed throwing in a community of free-living chimpanzees. *Nature*. 201:1264-1266.

Grand, TI. 1968. Functional anatomy of the upper limb [of the howler monkey]. *Bibliotheca Primatologica*. 7:104-125.

Grand, TI. 1972. A mechanical interpretation of terminal branch feeding. *Journal of Mammology*. 53:198-201.

Grand, TI. 1978. Adaptations of tissue and limb segments to facilitate moving and feeding in arboreal folivores. *Ecology of Arboreal Folivores*. Montgomery, GG. (ed.) Smithsonian Institution Press: Washington. 231-241.

Gursky, Sharon L. 1997. *Modeling Maternal Time Budgets: The Impact of Lactation and Infant Transport on the Behavior of the Spectral Tarsier*. Ph.D. Dissertation, SUNY- Stoneybrook.

Gursky, Sharon L. 1999. The effect of moonlight on the behavior of spectral tarsiers. *American Journal of Physical Anthropology*, Supplement 28:142.

Hladik, CM. 1975. Ecology, diet, and social patterning in Old and New World primates. In *Socioecology and Psychology of Primates*. Tuttle, RH. (ed.) Mouton: The Hague. 3-35.

Hoelzer, GA & Melnick, DJ. 1996. Evolutionary relationships of the macaques. In *Evolution and Ecology of Macaque Societies*. Fa, JE & Lindburgh, DG. (eds.) Cambridge University Press: Cambridge. 3-19.

Hohmann, G & Fruth, Barbara 1993. Field observations on meat sharing among bonobos (*Pan paniscus*). *Folia Primatologica*. 60:225-229.

Hohmann, G & Fruth, Barbara 1996. Food sharing and status in unprovisioned bonobos. In *Food and the Status Quest*. Weissner, P and Schiefenhoevel, W. (eds.) Berghahn Books: Providence, UK. 47-67.

Hrdy, Sarah 1977. Infanticide as a primate reproductive strategy. *American Scientist*. 65:40-49.

Hrdy, Sarah 1977. *The Langurs of Abu: Female and Male Strategies of Reproduction*. Harvard University Press: Cambridge, Mass.

Izawa, K. 1978. Frog-eating behavior of wild black-capped capuchin (*Cebus apella*). *Primates*. 20:503-512.

Izawa, K & Mizuno, A. 1977. Palm-fruit cracking behavior of wild black-capped capuchin (*Cebus apella*). *Primates*. 18(4):773-792.

James, W. 1960. *The Jaws and Teeth of Primates*. Pitman Medical Publishing Co: London.

Jay, Phyllis C. (ed.) 1968. *Primates: Studies in Adaptation and Variability*. Holt, Rinehart, and Winston: New York.

Jay, Phyllis C. 1965. The common langur of north India. In *Primate Behavior: Field studies of Monkeys and Apes*. DeVore, I. (ed.) Holt, Rinehart and Winston: New York. 114-123.

Jolly, Alison 1966. *Lemur Behavior: A Madagascar Field Study*. Chicago University Press: Chicago.

Jacobs, M. 1981. *The Tropical Rain Forest: A First Encounter*. Kruk, R, et al. (ed.) Springer-Verlag: Heidelberg.

Kano, T. 1987. Social organization of the pygmy chimpanzee and the common chimpanzee: similarities and differences. In *Evolution and Coadaptation in Biotic Communities*. Kawano, S, et al. (eds.) University of Tokyo Press: Tokyo. 53-64.

Kano, T. 1992. *The Last Ape: Pygmy Chimpanzee Behavior and Ecology*. Stanford University Press: Stanford.

Kay, RF & Hylander, WL. 1978. The dental structure of mammalian folivores with special reference to primates and phalangeroids (Marsupialia). *Ecology of Arboreal Folivores*. 173-191.

Kay, RF, et al. 1998. A new Pitheciin primate from the middle Miocene of Argentina. *American Journal of Primatology*. 45(4):317-336.

Kingdon, J. 1988. What are face patterns and what do they contribute to reproductive isolation in guenons? In *A Primate Radiation: Evolutionary Biology of the African Guenons*. Gautier-Hion, Annie, et al. (eds.) Cambridge University Press: Cambridge. 227-245.

Kingdon, J. 1989. *Island Africa*. Princeton University Press: New Jersey.

Kinzey, WG & Norconk, Marilyn A. 1990. Hardness as a basis of fruit choice in two sympatric primates. *American Journal of Physical Anthropology*. 81(1):5-15.

Knott, Cheryl 1998. Changes in orangutan caloric intake, energy balance, and ketones in response to fluctuating fruit availability. *International Journal of Primatology*. 19(6):1061-1079.

Knott, Cheryl 2000. Testosterone and behavioral differences in fully developed and undeveloped wild Bornean orangutans (*Pongo pygmaeus pygmaeus*). *American Journal of Physical Anthropology*, Supplement 30:198.

Kress, WJ, et al. 1994. Pollination of *Ravenala madagascariensis* (Strelitziaceae) by lemurs in Madagascar: evidence for an archaic coevolutionary system? *American Journal of Botany*. 81(5):542-551.

Kuroda, S. 1984. Interaction over food among pygmy chimpanzees. In *The Pygmy Chimpanzee*. Sussman, RL. (ed.) Plenum Press: New York. 301-325.

LeGros Clark, WE. 1959. *The Antecedents of Man*. Harper & Row: New York.

Lucas, PW & Teaford, MF. 1994. Functional morphology of colobine teeth. In *Colobine Monkeys*. Davies AG and Oates JF. (eds.) Cambridge University Press: Cambridge. 173-204.

Maggioncalda, Anne N, et al. 1999. Reproductive hormone profiles in captive male orangutans: implications for understanding developmental arrest. *American Journal of Physical Anthropology*. 109:19-32.

Mittermeier, R, et al. 1994. *Lemurs of Madagascar*. Conservation International: Washington, DC.

Morbeck, Mary Ellen & Zihlman, Adrienne 1989. Body size and proportions in chimpanzees with special reference to *Pan troglodytes schweinfurthii* from Gombe National Park, Tanzania. *Primates*. 30(3):369-382.

Mori, A. 1984. Ethological study of pygmy chimpanzees in Wamba, Zaïre: a comparison with chimpanzees. *Primates*. 25(3):255-278.

Moya-Sola, S. & Kohler, M. 1996. A *Dryopithecus* skeleton and the origins of great-ape locomotion. *Nature*. 379(6561):156-159.

Napier, JR & Davis, PR. 1959. The forelimb skeleton and associated remains of *Proconsul africanus*. *Fossil Mammals of Africa*, 16. British Museum of Natural History: London.

Napier, JR & Napier PH. 1967. *A Handbook of Living Primates*. Academic Press: New York.

Napier, JR & Napier PH. 1994. *The Natural History of the Primates*. The MIT Press: Cambridge, Massachusetts.

Newman, A. 1990. *Tropical Rainforest: A World Survey of our most Valuable and Endangered Habitat with a Blueprint for its Survival*. Facts on File: New York.

Newton, P. 1987. The social organization of forest Hanuman langurs (*Presbytis entellus*). *International Journal of Primatology*. 8(3):199-232.

Newton, P. 1992. Feeding and ranging patterns of forest Hanuman langurs (*Presbytis entellus*). *International Journal of Primatology*. 13(3):245-285.

Nishida, T. (ed.) 1990. *The Chimpanzees of the Mahale Mountains: Sexual and Life History Strategies*. University of Tokyo Press: Tokyo.

Norconk, Marilyn A & Kinzey, WG. 1994. Challenge of neotropical frugivory: travel patterns of spider monkeys and bearded sakis. *American Journal of Primatology*. 34(2):171-183.

Norconk, Marilyn A. 1996. Seasonal variation in the diets of White-Faced and Bearded sakis (*Pithecia pithecia* and *Chiropotes satanas*) in Guri Lake, Venezuela. In *Adaptive Radiations of Neotropical Primates*. Norconk, Marilyn, et al. (eds.) Plenum Press: New York. 403-423.

Oates, JF. 1977. The guereza and its food. In *Primate Ecology: Studies of Feeding and Ranging Behavior in Lemurs, Monkeys and Apes*. Clutton-Brock, TH. (ed.) Academic Press: London. 276-321.

Parker, Sue Taylor & Gibson, Kathleen Rita 1990. *"Language" and Intelligence in Monkeys and Apes. Comparative Developmental Perspectives*. Cambridge University Press: Cambridge.

Petter, JJ & Petter, Arlette 1967. The Aye-aye of Madagascar. In *Social Communication Among Primates*. Altmann, S. (ed.) University of Chicago Press: Chicago. 195-205.

Petter, JJ. 1965. The lemurs of Madagascar. In *Primate Behavior: Field Studies of Monkeys and Apes*. DeVore, I. (ed.) Holt, Rinehart, and Winston: New York. 292-319.

Pilbeam, D. 1996. Genetic and morphological records of the Hominoidea and hominid origins: a synthesis. *Molecular Phylogenetics and Evolution*. 5(1):155-168.

Preuschoft, H, et al. (eds.) 1984. *The Lesser Apes: Evolutionary and Behavioral Biology*. Edinburgh University Press: Edinburgh.

Raemaekers, JJ. 1979. Ecology of sympatric gibbons. *Folia Primatologica*. 31(3):227-245.

Remis, Melissa J. 1997. Western lowland gorillas as seasonal frugivores: use of variable resources. *American Journal of Primatology*. 87-109.

Richard, Alison F. 1985. *Primates in Nature*. Freeman Press: New York.

Richard, Alison F. 1987. Malagasy prosimians: female dominance. In *Primate Societies*. Smuts, Barbara, et al. (eds.) University of Chicago Press: Chicago. 25-33.

Richard, Alison F, et al. 1989. Weed macaques: the evolutionary implications of macaque feeding ecology. *International Journal of Primatology*. 10(6):569-594.

Ripley, Suzanne 1967. Intertroop encounters among Ceylon gray langurs (Presbytis entellus). In *Social Communication Among Primates*. Altmann, SA. (ed.) University of Chicago Press: Chicago. 237-253.

Ripley, Suzanne 1970. Leaves and leaf monkeys: the social organization of foraging in gray langurs *Presbyits entellus*. In *Old World Monkeys: Evolution, Systematics, and Behavior*. Napier, JR and Napier, PH (eds.) Academic Press: New York. 481-509.

Rowe, Noel 1996. *The Pictorial Guide to the Living Primates*. Pogonias Press: East Hampton, New York.

Rowell, Thelma 1988. The social system of guenons, compared with baboons, macaques, and mangabeys. In *A Primate Radiation: Evolutionary Biology of the African Guenons*. Gautier-Hion, Annie, et al. (eds.) Cambridge University Press: Cambridge. 439-451.

Rowell, Thelma 1988. What do male monkeys do besides competing? In *Evolution of Social Behavior and Integrative Levels*. Greenberg, G & Tobach E. (eds.) Lawrence Erlbaum Assoc: Hillsdale, NJ. 205-212.

Sarich, VM & Cronin, JE. 1976. Molecular systematics of the primates. In *Molecular Anthropology*. Goodman, M and Tashian, RE. (eds.) Plenum Press: New York. 141-170.

Sauther, Michelle L, et al. 1999. The socioecology of the ringtailed lemur: thirty-five years of research. *Evolutionary Anthropology*. 8(4):120-132.

Schaller, GB. 1976. *The Mountain Gorilla: Ecology and Behavior*. University of Chicago Press: Chicago.

Schultz, AH. 1970. The comparative uniformity of the Cercopithecoidea. In *Old World Monkeys: Evolution, Systematics, and Behavior*. Napier, JR and Napier PH (eds.) Academic Press: New York. 39-52.

Simons, EL & Rasmussen, D. 1996. Skull of *Catopithecus browni*, an early Tertiary catarrhine. *American Journal of Physical Anthropology*. 100(2):261-292.

Smith, Holly 1989. Dental development as a measure of life history in primates. *Evolution*. 43(3): 683-688.

Stewart, Caro-Beth & Disotell, TR. 1998. Primate evolution—in and out of Africa. *Current Biology*. 8(16): R582-R588.

Strier, Karen B. 1992. *Faces in the Forest: The Endangered Muriqui Monkeys of Brazil*. Oxford University Press: New York.

Strier, Karen B. 2000. *Primate Behavioral Ecology*. Allyn and Bacon: Boston.

Sterling, Eleanor J. 1993. Patterns of range use and social organization in Aye-ayes (*Daubentonia madagascariensis*) on Nosy Mangabe. In *Lemur Social Systems and Their Ecological Basis*. Kappeler, PM & Ganzhorn, JU. (eds.) Plenum Press: New York. 1-10.

Struhsaker, T & Oates, J. 1979. Comparison of the behavior and Ecology of Red Colobus and Black-and-White Colobus monkeys in Uganda: a summary. In *Primate Ecology: Problem Oriented Field Studies*. Sussman, R (ed.) John Wiley & Sons: New York. 165-183.

Sussman, RW. 1995. How primates invented the rainforest and vice versa. In *Creatures of the Dark: the Nocturnal Prosimians*. Alterman, L, et al. (eds.) Plenum Press: New York. 1-10.

Sussman, RW. 1999. *Primate Ecology and Social Structure, Volume 1: Lorises, Lemurs and Tarsiers*. Pearson Custom Publishing: Massachusetts.

Sussman, RW. 1999. *Primate Ecology and Social Structure, Volume 2: New World Monkeys*. Pearson Custom Publishing: Massachusetts.

Sussman, RW & Kinzey, WG. 1984. Ecological role of the Callitrichidae: a review. *American Journal of Physical Anthropology*. 64(4):419-449.

Sussman, RW & Raven, PH. 1977. Pollination by lemurs and marsupials: an archaic coevolutionary system. *Science*. 200:731-736.

Swindler, DR. 1976. *Dentition of Living Primates*. Academic Press: New York.

Szalay, FS & Delson, E. 1979. *Evolutionary History of the Primates*. Academic Press: New York.

Tan, Chia 1999. Group composition, home range size, and diet of three sympatric bamboo lemur species (Genus *Hapalemur*) in Ranomafana National Park, Madagascar. *International Journal of Primatology*. 20(4):547-566.

Tattersall, I & Sussman, RW. 1998. 'Little brown lemurs' of northern Madagascar: phylogeny and ecological role in resource partitioning. *Folia Primatologica*. 69(1):379-388.

Terborgh, J. 1983. *Five New World Primates: A Study in Comparative Ecology*. Princeton University Press: Princeton, NJ.

Terborgh, J. 1992. *Diversity and the Tropical Rain Forest*. Scientific American Library: New York.

Tutin, Caroline 1991. Foraging profiles of sympatric lowland gorillas and chimpanzees in the Lope Reserve, Gabon. *Philosophical Transactions of the Royal Society of London*, B:1334.

Uchida, Akiko 1996. What we don't know about great ape variation. *Trends in Research in Ecology and Evolution*. 11(4):163-168.

Walker, A & Teaford, M. 1989. The hunt for *Proconsul*. *Scientific American*. 260:76-82.

Watts, DP. 1996. Comparative socio-ecology of gorillas. In *Great Ape Societies*. McGrew, W, et al. (eds.) Cambridge University Press: UK. 16-28.

Whitworth, T. 1953. A contribution to the geology of Russinga Island, Kenya. *Quarterly Journal of the Geological Society of London*. 109:75-96.

Woolsey, CN. 1960. Some observations on brain fissuration in relation to cortical localization of function. In *Structure and Function of the Cerebral Cortex*. Tower, DB and Schade, JP. (eds.) Elsevier Publishing Company: Amsterdam. 64-68.

Wright, Patricia C. 1984. Biparental care in *Aotes trivigatus* and *Callicebus moloch*. In *Female primates: Studies by Women Primatologists*. Small, Meredith. (ed.) Alan R. Liss: New York. 59-75.

Wright, Patricia C. 1999. Lemur traits and Madagascar ecology: coping with an island environment. *Yearbook of Physical Anthropology*. 42:31-72.

Wolfheim, Jaclyn H. 1983. *Primates of the World: Distribution, Abundance, and Conservation*. University of Washington Press: Seattle.

Yamagiwa, J, et al. 1996. Dietary and ranging overlap in sympatric gorillas and chimpanzees in Kahuzi-Biega National Park, Zaire. In *Great Ape Societies*. McGrew, W, et al. (eds.) Cambridge University Press: Cambridge. 82-98.

Yoder, Anne D, et al. 1996. Ancient single origin for Malagasy primates. *Proceedings of the National Academy of Science*. 93:5122-5126.

Zihlman, Adrienne 1996. Reconstructions reconsidered: chimpanzee models and human evolution. In *Great Ape Societies*. McGrew, W, et al. (eds.) Cambridge University Press: Cambridge. 293-304.

Zihlman, Adrienne 1997. Natural history of apes: life-history features in females and males. In *The Evolving Female: a Life History Perspective*. Morbeck, Mary Ellen, et al. (eds.) Princeton University Press: Princeton. 86-103.

Section 5

Aiello, Leslie & Dean, C. 1990. *An Introduction to Human Evolutionary Anatomy*. Academic Press: London.

Akazawa, T, et al. (eds.) 1998. *Neandertals and Modern Humans in Western Asia*. Plenum Press: New York.

Arsuaga, JL, et al. 1993. Three new human skulls from the Sima de los Huesos Middle Pleistocene site in Sierra de Atapuerca, Spain. *Nature*. 362:534-537.

Asfaw, B, et al. 1999. *Australopithecus garhi*: a new species of early hominid from Ethiopia. *Science*. 284(5414):629-634.

Behrensmeyer, AK & Hill, AP, et al. (eds.) 1980. *Fossils in the Making: Vertebrate Taphonomy and Paleoecology*. University of Chicago Press: Chicago.

Berger, LR & Clarke, RJ. 1995. Eagle involvement in accumulation of the Taung child fauna. *Journal of Human Evolution*. 29:275-299.

Beynon, AD & Dean, MC. 1988. Distinct dental development patterns in early fossil hominids. *Nature*. 335:509-514.

Bowler, PJ. 1986. *Theories of Human Evolution*. Johns Hopkins University Press: Baltimore.

Brain, CK. 1981. *The Hunters or the Hunted: An Introduction to African Cave Taphonomy*. University of Chicago Press: Chicago.

Brain, CK. 1993. *Swartkrans: A Cave's Chronicle of Early Man*. Transval Museum: Pretoria.

Bromage, TG, et al. 1995. Paleoanthropology of the Malawi Rift: an early hominid mandible from the Chiwondo Beds, northern Malawi. *Journal of Human Evolution*. 28:71-108.

Broom, R, et al. 1950. *Sterkfontein Ape-Man Plesianthropus*. Transval Museum: Pretoria.

Brown, FH. 1992. Methods of dating. In *The Cambridge Encyclopedia of Human Evolution*. Jones, S, et al. (eds.) Cambridge University Press: Cambridge. 179-186.

Brown, FH, et al. 1985. An integrated Plio-Pleistocene Chronology for the Turkana Basin. In *Ancestors: the Hard Evidence*. Delson, E. (ed.) Alan R. Liss: New York. 82-90.

Brunet, M, et al. 1995. The first australopithecine 1,500 kilometres west of the Rift Valley (Chad). *Nature*. 378:273-274.

Burenhult, G. (ed.) 1993. *The First Humans: Human Origins and History to 10,000 BC*. Harper Collins: San Francisco.

Butzer, KW & Isaac, GL. 1975. *After the Australopithecines*. Mouton, The Hague: Paris.

Cann, Rebecca L, et al. 1987. Mitochondrial DNA and human evolution. *Nature*. 325:31-36.

Carbonell, E, et al. 1995. Lower Pleistocene hominids and artifacts from Atapuerca-TD6 (Spain). *Science*. 269:826-829.

Chauvet, JM, et al. 1996. *Dawn of Art: the Chauvet Cave*. Harry N. Abrams, Inc: London.

Clarke, RJ. 1998. First ever discovery of a well-preserved skull and associated skeleton of an *Australopithecus*. *South African Journal of Science*. 94(10).

Clarke, RJ & Tobias, PV. 1995. Sterkfontein Member 2 foot bones of the oldest South African hominid. *Science*. 269:521-524.

Cold Springs Harbor Symposia on Quantitative Biology, vol XV. 1950. *Origin and Evolution of Man*. The Biological Laboratory: New York.

Cole, Sonia 1975. *Leakey's Luck: the Life of Louis Seymour Bazett Leakey 1903-1972*. Harcort Brace Jovanovich: New York.

Conroy, GC. 1997. *Reconstructing Human Origins: A Modern Synthesis*. WW Norton & Co: New York.

Conroy, GC, et al. 1998. Endocranial capacity in an early hominid cranium from Sterkfontein, South Africa. *Science* 280:1730-1731.

Conroy, GC, et al. 2000. Endocranial capacity in Sts 71 (*Australopithecus africanus*) by three-dimensional computed tomography. *The Anatomical Record*. 258:391-396.

Dahlberg, Frances (ed.) 1981. *Woman the Gatherer*. Yale University Press: New Haven.

Day, MH. 1986. *Guide to Fossil Man, Fourth Edition*. University of Chicago Press: Chicago.

Deacon, HL & Deacon, Janette. 1999. *Human Beginnings in South Africa: Uncovering the Secrets of the Stone Age*. David Phillip Publishers: Cape Town.

Dean, MC. 1989. The developing dentition and tooth structure in hominoids. *Folia Primatologica*. 53:160-176.

Dean, MC, et al. 1986. Age at death of the Neanderthal child from Devil's Tower, Gibraltar and the implications for studies of general growth and development in Neanderthals. *American Journal of Physical Anthropology*. 70:301-309.

Dillehay, TD. The late Pleistocene cultures of South America. *Evolutionary Anthropology*. 7(6)206-216.

Edgar, B. 1999. The symbol and the spear. *California Wild*. 52(3):22-25.

Falk, Dean 1990. Brain evolution in *Homo*: the 'radiator' theory. *Behavioral and Brain Sciences*. 13:333-381.

Falk, Dean, et al. 2000. Early hominid brain evolution: a new look at old endocasts. *Journal of Human Evolution*. 38:695-717.

Gabunis, L, et al. 2000. Earliest Pleistocene hominid cranial remains from Dmanisi, Republic of Georgia: taxonomy, geological setting, and age. *Science*. 288:1019-1026.

Gamble, C. 1994. *Timewalkers: the Prehistory of Global Colonialization*. Harvard University Press: Cambridge.

Gazzaniga, MS. 1985. *The Social Brain: Discovering the Networks of the Mind*. Basic Books, Inc.: New York.

Gazzaniga, MS & LeDoux, JE. 1978. *The Integrated Mind*. Plenum Press: New York.

Gowlett, JAJ. 1993. *Ascent to Civilization: the Archaeology of Early Humans*, 2nd ed. McGraw-Hill, Inc: New York.

Hager, Lori D. 1991. The evidence for sex differences in the hominid fossil record. In *The Archaeology of Gender*. Walde, D & Willows, N. (eds.) Archaeological Association, University of Calgary: Calgary. 46-49.

Hager, Lori D. (ed.) 1997. *Women in Evolution*. Routledge: New York.

Howells, W. 1962. *Ideas on Human Evolution*. Harvard University Press: Cambridge.

Hutchinson, GE. 1965. *The Ecological Theater and the Evolutionary Play*. Yale University Press: New Haven, CT.

Johanson, D & Edey, M. 1981. *Lucy : the Beginnings of Humankind*. Simon & Schuster: New York.

Johanson, D & Edgar, B. 1996. *From Lucy to Language*. Simon and Schuster: New York.

Jones, S, et al. (eds.) 1992. *The Cambridge Encyclopedia of Human Evolution*. Cambridge University Press: Cambridge.

Kalb, JE. 1993. Refined stratigraphy of the homonid-bearing Awash group, Middle Awash Valley, Afar Depression, Ethiopia. *Newsletter of Stratigraphy, Berlin*. 29(1):21-62.

Klein, RG. 1989. *The Human Career: Human Biological and Cultural Origins*. University of Chicago Press: Chicago.

Kuman, Kathleen. 1994. The archaeology of Sterkfontein – past and present. *Journal of Human Evolution*. 27:471-495.

Kuman, Kathleen & Clarke, RJ. 2000. Stratigraphy, artifact industries and hominid associations for Sterkfontein, Member 5. *Journal of Human Evolution* 38:827-847.

Kunzig, R. 1997. The face of the ancestral child. *Discover*. December: 88-101.

Krings, M, et al. 1997. Neandertal DNA Sequences and the Origin of Modern Humans. *Cell*. 90:19-30.

Laporte, L. 2000. *George Gaylord Simpson: Paleontologist and Evolutionist*. Columbia University Press: New York.

Laporte, L & Zihlman, Adrienne L. 1983. Plates, Climates, and Hominoid Evolution. *South African Journal of Science*. 79:96-110.

Larick, R & Ciochon, RL. 1996. The African emergence and early Asian dispersals of the genus *Homo*. *American Scientist*. 84:538-551.

Leakey, Mary D. 1984. *Disclosing the Past*. Doubleday: Garden City, NY.

Leakey, Meave & Walker, A. 1997. Early hominid fossils from Africa. *Scientific American*. 276(6):74-79.

Leakey, RE & Lewin, R. 1977. *Origins*. EP Dutton: New York.

Lewin, R. 1988. *In the Age of Mankind*. Smithsonian Institution: Washington D.C.

Lewin, R. 1993. *The Origin of Modern Humans*. Scientific American Library: New York.

Lewis, OJ. 1989. *Functional Morphology of the Evolving Hand and Foot*. Clarendon Press: Oxford.

Lowenstein, JM. 1999. The other people: first Neandertal tells all. *California Wild*. 52(3):34-36.

Marshack, A. 1989. Evolution of the human capacity: the symbolic evidence. *Yearbook of Physical Anthropology*. 32:1-34.

Marzke, MW. 1983. Joint functions and grips of the *Australopithecus afarensis* hand, with special reference to the region of the capitate. *Journal of Human Evolution*. 12:197-211.

Marzke, MW. 1986. Tool use and the evolution of hominid hands and bipedality. In *Primate Evolution, Vol. 1*. Else, JG & Lee, Phyllis C. (eds.) Cambridge University Press: UK. 203-209.

McHenry, HM & Berger, LR. 1998. Body Proportions in *Australopithecus afarensis* and *A. africanus* and the origin of the genus *Homo*. *Journal of Human Evolution*. 35:1-22.

Meikle, WE & Parker, Sue Taylor 1994. *Naming Our Ancestors: An Anthology of Hominid Taxonomy*. Waveland Press: Prospect Heights, Illinois.

Miller, B, et al. 1998. Emergence of artistic talent in frontotemporal dementia. *Neurology*. 51(4):978-982.

Morris, AG & Tobias, PV. 1997. South Africa. In *History of Physical Anthropology, Volume 2, M-Z*. Spencer, F. (ed.) Garland Publishing, Inc: New York. 968-976.

Ovchinnikov, IV, et al. 2000. Molecular analysis of Neandertal DNA from the northern Caucasus. *Nature*. 404:490-493.

Pares, JM & Perez-Gonzalez, A. 1995. Paleomagnetic age for hominid fossils at Atapuerca archaeological site, Spain. *Science*. 269:830-832.

Rak, Y. 1983. *The Australopithecine Face*. Academic Press: New York.

Rak, Y, et al. 1994. A Neandertal infant from Amud Cave, Israel. *Journal of Human Evolution*. 26:313-324.

Rightmire, GP. 1998. Human evolution in the Middle Pleistocene: the role of *Homo heidelbergensis*. *Evolutionary Anthropology*. 6(6):218-227.

Schmid, P. 2000. Functional interpretation of the Laetoli footprints. *American Journal of Physical Anthropology*. Suppl 30:271.

Smith, Holly 1992. Life history and the evolution of human maturation. *Evolutionary Anthropology*. 1(4):134-142.

Smith, Holly 1993. The physiological age of KNM-WT 15000. In *The Nariokotome Homo erectus Skeleton*. Walker, A and Leakey, R. (eds.) Harvard University Press: Cambridge. 195-220.

Stringer, CB. 1995. The evolution and distribution of later Pleistocene human populations. In *Paleoclimate and Evolution, with Emphasis on Human Origins*. Vrba, S, et al. (eds.) Yale University Press: New Haven. 524-531.

Stringer, C & Gamble, C. 1993. *In Search of the Neanderthals*. Thames and Hudson Ltd: New York.

Stringer, C, et al. 1989. ESR dates for the hominid burial site of Es Skhul in Israel. *Nature*. 338:756-758.

Strum, Shirley C, et al. *The New Physical Anthropology*. Prentice Hall: Upper Saddle River, New Jersey.

Susman, RL. 1994. Fossil evidence for early hominid tool use. *Science*. 265:1570-573.

Susman, RL & Creel, N. 1979. Functional and morphological affinities of the subadult hand (O.H. 7) from Olduvai Gorge. *American Journal of Physical Anthropology*. 51:311-332.

Suwa, G, et al. 1997. The first skull of *Australopithecus boisei*. *Nature*. 389:489-492.

Tattersall, I. 1999. *The Last Neanderthal: the Rise, Success, and Mysterious Extinction of our Closest Human Relatives*. Nevraumont Publishing Company: New York.

Tobias, PV. (ed.) 1985. *Hominid Evolution: Past, Present, and Future*. Alan R. Liss: New York.

Tobias, PV. 1997. Sterkfontein. In *History of Physical Anthropology, Volume 2, A-L.* Spencer, F. (ed.) Garland Publishing, Inc: New York. 996-999.

Tobias, PV. 1997. Taung. In *History of Physical Anthropology, Volume 2, M-Z.* Spencer, F. (ed.) Garland Publishing, Inc: New York. 1022-1025.

Valladas, Helene, et al. 1991. Thermoluminescence dating of Neandertal and early modern humans in the Near East. *Endeavour.* 15(3): 115.

Walker, A & Leakey, R. 1993. *The Nariokotome Homo erectus Skeleton.* Harvard University Press: Cambridge.

Walker, A & Shipman, Pat 1996. *The Wisdom of the Bones: in Search of Human Origins.* Knopf, Random House: New York.

Wanpo, H, et al. 1995. Early *Homo* and associated artifacts from Asia. *Nature.* 378:275-278.

Ward, R & Stringer, C. 1997. A molecular handle on the Neanderthals. *Nature* 388:225-226.

Washburn, SL. 1951. The analysis of primate evolution with particular reference to the origin of man. In *Cold Springs Harbor Symposia on Quantitative Biology*, Origin and Evolution of Man. 15:67-58.

Washburn, SL. 1951. The new physical anthropology. In *Transactions of the New York Academy of Sciences*, Series II. 13:298-304.

Washburn, SL & Moore, Ruth 1979. *Ape Into Human.* 2nd ed. Little Brown and Co: Boston.

White, TD. 1997. Afar Triangle. In *History of Physical Anthropology, Volume 1, A-L.* Spencer, F. (ed.) Garland Publishing, Inc: New York. 12-17.

White, TD. 1997. Omo. In *History of Physical Anthropology, Volume 2, M-Z.* Spencer, F. (ed.) Garland Publishing, Inc: New York. 777-779.

White, TD, et al. 1994. *Australopithecus ramidus*, a new species of early hominid from Aramis, Ethiopia. *Nature.* 371:306-312.

Wood, B. 1997. Koobi Fora. In *History of Physical Anthropology, Volume 1, A-L.* Spencer, F. (ed.) Garland Publishing, Inc: New York. 580-583.

Wood, B & Collard, M. 1999. The changing face of the genus *Homo. Evolutionary Anthropology.* 7:195-207.

Zihlman, Adrienne, et al. 1978. Pygmy chimpanzee as a possible prototype for the common ancestor of humans, chimpanzees and gorillas. *Nature.* 275:744-746.

Zihlman, Adrienne 1981. Woman as shapers of the human adaptation. In *Woman the Gatherer.* Dahlberg, F. (ed.) Yale University Press: New Haven, CT. 75-120.

Zihlman, Adrienne L. 1990. Knuckling under: controversy over hominid origins. *From Apes to Angels: Essays in Anthropology in Honor of Philip V. Tobias.* 185-196.

Zihlman, Adrienne L & Lowenstein, JM. 1999. From eternity to here. *California Wild.* 52(3):16-21.

Zihlman, Adrienne & Tanner, Nancy 1978. Gathering and the hominid adaptation. In *Female Hierarchies.* Tiger, L and Fowler, HT. (eds.) Beresford Book Service: Chicago. 163-194.

Zollikofer, CPE, et al. 1998. Computer-Assisted Paleoanthropology. *Evolutionary Anthropology.* 6(2):41-54.

Section 6

Bentley, Gillian R. 1999. Aping our ancestors: comparative aspects of reproductive ecology. *Evolutionary Anthropology.* 7(5):153-190.

Blackburn, MW & Calloway, DH. 1979. Energy expenditure and consumption of mature, pregnant, and lactating women. *Journal of the American Dietary Association.* 69:29-37.

Bogin, B. 1999. *Patterns of Human Growth, Second Edition.* Cambridge University Press: Cambridge.

Brues, Alice M. 1977. *People and Races.* Waveland Press: Prospect Heights.

Capasso, L, et al. 1999. *Atlas of Occupational Markers on Human Remains.* Edigrafital SpA: Teramo, Italy

Cavalli-Sforza, LL. 1991. Genes, peoples, and languages. *Scientific American.* 265(5):104-110.

Cavalli-Sforza, LL. 2000. *Genes, Peoples, and Languages.* North Point Press: New York.

Clarys, JP, et al. 1999. Human body composition: a review of adult dissection data. *American Journal of Physical Anthropology.* 11:167-174.

De Rousseau, C. Jean (ed.) 1990. *Primate Life History and Evolution.* Wiley-Liss Inc: New York.

Diamond, JM. 1989. Blood, genes, and malaria. *Natural History.* 2:8-12.

Draper, Patricia 1975. !Kung women: contrasts in sexual egalitarianism in foraging and sedentary contexts. In *Toward an Anthropology of Women.* Reiter, RR. (ed.) Monthly Review Press. 77-109

Dukelow, WR & Erwin, J. 1986. *Comparative Primate Biology, Volume 3: Reproduction and Development.* Alan R. Liss: New York.

Dutour, O. 1986. Enthesopathies (lesions of muscular insertions) as indicators of the activities of Neolithic Saharan populations. *American Journal of Physical Anthropology.* 71:221-224.

Forbes, GB. 1987. Human Body Composition: Growth , Aging, Nutrition and Activity. Springer-Verlag: New York.

Frisancho, AR. 1969. Human growth and pulmonary function of a high-altitude Peruvian Quecha population. *Human Biology.* 41:365-379.

Frisancho, AR. 1993. *Human Adaptation and Accommodation.* University of Michigan Press: Ann Arbor.

Galloway, Alison 1997. The cost of reproduction and the evolution of postmenopausal osteoporosis. In *The Evolving Female: A*

Life History Perspective. Morbeck, Mary Ellen, et al. (eds.) Princeton University Press: Princeton, NJ. 132-146.

Hochschild, A. 1989. *The Second Shift*. Avon Books: New York.

Howell, Nancy. 1979. *Demography of the Dobe !Kung*. Academic Press: New York.

deKleer, VS. 1982. Development of bone. In *Bone in Clinical Orthopaedics. A Study in Comparative Osteology*. Sumner-Smith, G. (ed.) WB Saunders: Philadelphia. 1-80.

Kretchmer, N. 1972. Lactose and lactase. *Scientific American*. 227(4):71-78.

Landsteiner, Karl 1931. Individual differences in human blood. *Science*. 73:403-409.

Larsen, CS. 1997. *Bioarchaeology. Interpreting Behavior from the Human Skeleton*. Cambridge University Press: Cambridge.

Lahn, BT & Page, DC. 1997. Functional coherence of the human Y-chromosome. *Science*. 278:675-680.

Lee, RB. 1972. The !Kung Bushmen of Botswana. In *Hunters and Gatherers Today*. Bicchieri, MG. (ed.) Holt, Rinehart & Winston. 326-368.

Lee, RB. 1979. *The !Kung San: Men Women and Work in a Foraging Society*. Cambridge University Press: Cambridge. Special thanks for the photograph, which inspired the illustration on 6-9.

Lee, RB & DeVore, I. (eds.) 1976. *Kalahari Hunter Gatherers: Studies of the !Kung San and Their Neighbors*. Harvard University Press: Cambridge.

Marshall, Lorna 1976. *The !Kung of Nyae Nyae*. Harvard University Press: Cambridge.

Martin, Debra L. 1991. *Black Mesa Anasazi Health: Reconstructing Life From Patterns of Death and Disease*. Southern Illinois University at Carbondale.

Molleson, Theya 1994. The Eloquent Bones of Abu Hureya. *Scientific American*. 271(2): 70-75.

Molnar, S. 1998. *Human Variation: Races, Types, and Ethnic Groups, Fourth Edition*. Prentice Hall:New Jersey.

Montagna, W. 1967. The skin. *Scientific American*. February: 56-67.

Montagna, W. 1972. The skin of nonhuman primates. *American Zoologist*. 12:109-124.

Moore, KL. 1988. *The Developing Human: Clinically Oriented Embryology, Fourth Edition*. WB Saunders Company: Philadelphia.

Moore, Lorna Grindlay & Regensteiner, Judith G. 1983. Adaptation to high altitude. *Annual Review of Anthropology*. 12:285-304.

Morbeck, Mary Ellen, et al. (eds.) 1997. *The Evolving Female: a Life-History Perspective*. Princeton University Press: Princeton.

Ortner, DJ & Putschar, WGJ. 1981. *Identification of Pathological Conditions in Human Skeletal Remains*. Smithsonian Institution Press: Washington.

Panter-Brick, Catherine (ed.) 1998. *Biosocial Perspectives on Children*. Cambridge University Press: Cambridge.

Patten, BM. 1953. *Human Embryology, Second Edition*. McGraw-Hill Book Company: New York.

Peacock, Nadine R. 1991. Rethinking the sexual division of labor: reproduction and women's work among the Efe. In *Gender at the Crossroads of Knowledge: Feminist Anthropology in the Post Modern Era*. di Leonardo, Micaela. (ed.) University of California Press: Berkeley.

Pond, Caroline M. 1997. The biological origins of adipose tissue in humans. In *The Evolving Female: A Life History Perspective*. Morbeck, Mary Ellen, et al. (eds.) Princeton University Press: Princeton, NJ. 147-162.

Pusey, Anne E. 1978. The physical and social development of wild adolescent chimpanzees (*Pan troglodytes schweinfurthii*). Ph.D. Dissertation. Stanford University.

Pusey, Anne E. 1990. Behavioral changes at adolescence in chimpanzees. *Behavior*. 115:203-246.

Scammon, RE. 1930. The measurement of the body in childhood. In *The Measurement of Man*. Harris, JA, et al. (eds.) University of Minnesota Press: Minneapolis. 173-215.

Scheuer, Louise & Black, Sue 2000. *Developmental Juvenile Osteology*. Academic Press: San Diego.

Short, RV. 1976. The evolution of human reproduction. *Proceedings of the Royal Society of London*. 195:3-24.

Shostak, Marjorie 1981. *Nisa. The Life and Words of a !Kung Woman*. Harvard University Press: Cambridge.

Smith, Holly & Tompkins RL. 1995. Toward a life history of the hominidae. *Annual Review of Anthropology*. 24:257-279.

Sussman, RW. 1981. Preagricultural mobility—a factor limiting growth in human populations. *The Perception of Evolution: Essays Honoring Joseph B. Birdsell. Anthropology UCLA*. 7:199-212.

Ulijaszek, SJ, et al. 1998. *The Cambridge Encyclopedia of Human Growth and Development*. Cambridge University Press: Cambridge.

Wannenburgh, A. 1979. *The Bushmen*. Mayflower Books: New York.

Weisenfeld, SL. 1969. Sickle-cell trait in human biological and cultural evolution. In *Environment and Cultural Behavior*. Vayda, AP (ed.) Natural History Press (AMNH): Garden City, New York.

White, T. 1991. *Human Osteology*. Academic Press: San Diego.

Zihlman, Adrienne L & Cohn, BA. 1988. The response of human skin to the savanna. *Human Evolution*. 3(5):397-409.

INDEX